Microsoft®
Outlook®
Version 2002
INSIDE OUT

The CD that helps you put your software to work!

Dig in—for the work-ready tools and resources that help you go way beyond just using Outlook. You'll conquer it! Just like the INSIDE OUT book, we've designed your INSIDE OUT CD to be both comprehensive and supremely easy to use. All the tools, utilities, and add-ins have been tested against final Outlook Version 2002 code—not beta. The sample chapters from other INSIDE OUT books help take your Office XP learning experience even deeper. You get essential links to online software updates, product support, and more—direct from the Microsoft Office team. And with the CD's intuitive HTML interface, you'll always know exactly where you are and what else you can do!

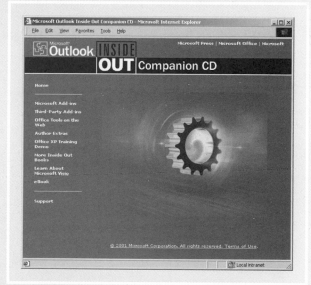

Your Inside Out CD features:

- Microsoft and Third-Party Add-Ins—must-have tools, utilities, demos, and trial software

- Office Tools on the Web—complete descriptions and links to official Microsoft Office resources on line

- Author Extras—sample code to help build your own applications using Microsoft Visual Basic® for Applications (VBA)

- More INSIDE OUT Books—sample chapters from other INSIDE OUT Office XP books

- Complete Microsoft Press® eBook—the entire MICROSOFT OUTLOOK VERSION 2002 INSIDE OUT book in easy-search electronic format

- Step by Step Interactive Tutorials—trial version of official Microsoft interactive training for Office XP

Want to learn more? Read on for full details, including System Requirements (last page of this section).

Microsoft Add-Ins

Get Microsoft add-ins and tools for Outlook—straight from the source.

Includes:

- **Microsoft Outlook Mobile Manager**—install this cutting-edge add-in on your desktop PC and receive e-mail, calendar, and reminders on a whole range of mobile devices—so you get the information you need no matter where you go!

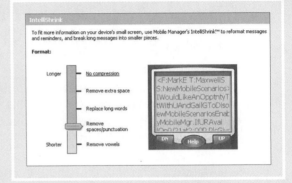

- **Microsoft Office Internet Free/Busy Service**—publish the blocks of time when you are free and busy to a shared Internet location, so people who don't normally have access to your Outlook calendar can check your schedule on the Web

- **Microsoft Visual Keyboard**—type in multiple languages on the same computer by using an on-screen keyboard for other languages

- **Microsoft Visio® Auto-Demos**—use these customizable auto-demos to see how to put Visio diagramming software to work on your next project

- **Step by Step Interactive Tutorials**—try official Microsoft interactive training for Office XP, and teach yourself common tasks and key features and functions

Microsoft®
Outlook®
Version 2002

INSIDE OUT

Third-Party Utilities, Demos, and Trials

All the third-party add-ins on this CD have been tested for use with Outlook Version 2002. In this section, you'll find all the details you need about each tool—including a full description, application size, system requirements, and installation instructions.

Includes:

- **Nereosoft ProWrite™**—use existing information from the contact manager to create new e-mail and letter merges, faxes, memos, labels, and envelopes in a flash

- **Caelo Software Nelson Email Organizer**—with full send/receive capability, this tool automatically organizes your e-mail into easy-to-access views by correspondent, date, mailing list, attachments, and more

- **MileHi Software TimeCards for Outlook**—streamline the creation and management of linked Outlook items, including journal entries, tasks, appointments, and notes

- **Micro Eye ZipOut**—automatically compresses attachments to outgoing messages and items stored in your mailbox or personal folders, speeding message transfer and freeing disk space

- **Mark Wilson Classify for Outlook™**—easily add a classification label to e-mail containing sensitive or classified information to help ensure proper security handling

Office Tools on the Web

Here you'll find ready links to the most helpful and informative online resources for Office XP, direct from Microsoft. Find out exactly how each site can help you get your work done—then click and go!

Office Assistance Center

Get help using Office products with articles, tips, and monthly spotlights. Learn more about working with documents, data, and graphics; using e-mail and collaboration features; creating presentations and Web pages; and using everyday time-savers.

Office eServices

Use these Web services to get the most from Office. Learn how to store and share files on the Web; build and host Web sites; find communication services, language translation, learning and reference, and online postage resources; tune up your computer; and much more!

Office Product Updates

Obtain recommended and critical updates to enhance your Office XP experience.

Office Download Center

Download updates, add-ins, viewers, and more from the Office Download Center. Use the online search tool to find the utilities to help you work faster and smarter.

Design Gallery Live

Pick out clip art or photos for your Office project from this huge royalty-free selection. New items are constantly added to meet your needs. The advanced search facility makes finding the right artwork quick and easy.

Microsoft Office Template Gallery

Instead of starting from scratch, download a template from Template Gallery. From calendars to business cards, marketing material, and legal documents, Template Gallery offers hundreds of professionally authored and formatted documents for Microsoft Office.

Online Troubleshooters

Microsoft has developed Office XP online troubleshooters to help you solve problems on the fly. Access them using the links on the CD—and get the diagnostic and problem-solving information you need.

Author Extras

Here's where your INSIDE OUT author went the extra mile—great sample code for you to take apart and study! In this section of the CD, you'll find the code used to create the VBA applications in Chapter 42, "Using VBA in Outlook," and Chapter 43, "Integrating Outlook and Other Applications with VBA." Make the examples from inside the book come to life—and use the code to develop your own applications faster.

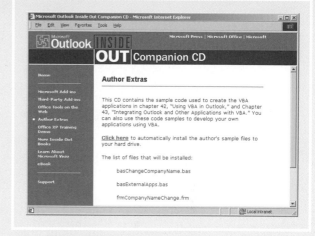

More Inside Out Books

The INSIDE OUT series from Microsoft Press delivers comprehensive reference on the Office XP suite of applications. On this CD, you'll find sample chapters from the companion titles listed below, along with details about the entire line of books:

- Microsoft FrontPage® Version 2002 Inside Out
- Microsoft Office XP Inside Out
- Microsoft Excel Version 2002 Inside Out
- Microsoft Word Version 2002 Inside Out
- Microsoft Visio Version 2002 Inside Out

Complete Microsoft Press eBook

You get the entire MICROSOFT OUTLOOK VERSION 2002 INSIDE OUT book on CD—along with sample chapters from other INSIDE OUT books—as searchable electronic books. These Microsoft Press eBooks install quickly and easily on your computer (see System Requirements for details) and enable rapid full-text search.

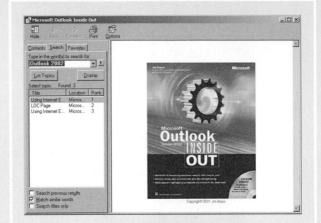

Features:

- Super-fast HTML full-text search
- Full-size graphics and screen shots
- Copy, paste, and *print* functions
- Bookmarking capabilities
- A saved history of every file viewed during a session

CD Minimum System Requirements

- Microsoft Windows® 95 or higher operating system (including Windows 98, Windows Millennium Edition, Windows NT® 4.0 with Service Pack 3, Windows 2000, or Windows XP)
- 266-MHz or higher Pentium-compatible CPU
- 64 megabytes (MB) RAM
- 8X CD-ROM drive or faster
- 46 MB of free hard disk space (to install the eBook and interactive tutorials)
- 800 x 600 with high color (16-bit) display settings
- Microsoft Windows–compatible sound card and speakers
- Microsoft Internet Explorer 4.01 or higher
- Microsoft Mouse or compatible pointing device

NOTE

System Requirements may be higher for the add-ins available on the CD. Individual add-in system requirements are specified on the CD. An Internet connection is necessary to access the hyperlinks in the Office Tools on the Web section. Connect time charges may apply.

Jim Boyce
*Expert author and former contributing editor
to Windows Magazine*

Microsoft

Microsoft®
Outlook®
Version 2002

INSIDE
OUT

- **Hundreds of timesaving solutions—easy to find, easy to use!**

- **Get tips, tricks, and workarounds, plus the straight scoop**

- **Work smarter—and take your Outlook experience to the next level**

PUBLISHED BY
Microsoft Press
A Division of Microsoft Corporation
One Microsoft Way
Redmond, Washington 98052-6399

Library of Congress Cataloging-in-Publication Data
Boyce, Jim, 1958-
     Microsoft Outlook Version 2002 Inside Out / Jim Boyce.
         p. cm.
     Includes index.
     ISBN 0-7356-1282-X
     1. Microsoft Outlook--Handbooks, manuals, etc. 2. Business--Computer
programs--Handbooks, manuals, etc. I. Title.

     HF5548.4.M5255 B69 2001
     005.369--dc21

                                                                    2001030207

Printed and bound in the United States of America.

2 3 4 5 6 7 8 9   QWT   6 5 4 3

Distributed in Canada by H.B. Fenn and Company Ltd.

A CIP catalogue record for this book is available from the British Library.

Microsoft Press books are available through booksellers and distributors worldwide. For further information about international editions, contact your local Microsoft Corporation office or contact Microsoft
Press International directly at fax (425) 936-7329. Visit our Web site at mspress.microsoft.com. Send
comments to *mspinput@microsoft.com*.

Acquisitions Editor: Kong Cheung
Series Editor: Sandra Haynes
Project Editor: Sandra Haynes

Body Part No. X08-05013

To David, a perfect little grandson

Contents At A Glance

Table of Contents

newfeature!

Chapter 8
Filtering, Organizing, and Using Automatic Responses

225

Chapter 9

Sending and Receiving Faxes   261

Chapter 10

Integrating Outlook Express and Outlook   281

Chapter 11
Using Outlook Express for Public and Private Newsgroups

297

Chapter 12
Securing Your System, Messages, and Identity

329

Chapter 13
Processing Messages Selectively

365

newfeature!

Chapter 16
Making Notes   **439**

Chapter 17
Keeping a Journal   **449**

Part 4
Scheduling
477

Chapter 21
Integrating Microsoft Outlook and Microsoft Project   573

Chapter 25
Automating Common Tasks   653

Part 6
Managing Outlook   663

Chapter 26
Integrating Outlook with Other Office Applications   665

Chapter 27
Delegating Responsibilities to an Assistant   679

Chapter 30
Backing Up, Exporting, and Importing Information

Part 7
Using and Administering Outlook with Exchange Server

Chapter 31
Exchange Server Overview and Setup

Chapter 32
Configuring the Exchange Server Client

Chapter 33

Messaging with Exchange Server   789

Chapter 34

Sharing Information with Others   809

Chapter 35
Working Offline and Remotely 849

Chapter 36
Accessing Messages Through a Web Browser 871

Chapter 37
Network, Platform, and Deployment Considerations   901

Chapter 38
Supporting Outlook Under Exchange Server   917

newfeature!

Chapter 41

Programming Forms with VBScript   1013

Chapter 42

Using VBA in Outlook   1031

Integrating Outlook and Other Applications with VBA — 1063

Appendixes — 1089

Appendix A
Installing and Updating Outlook — 1091

Appendix B
Office XP Resource Kit — 1099

Appendix C
Update and Troubleshooting Resources — 1103

Appendix D
Outlook Files and Registry Keys — 1107

Appendix E
Outlook Add-Ins — 1113

Appendix F
Outlook Symbols — 1121

Appendix G
Outlook Shortcuts — 1127

Appendix H
Outlook Fields and Properties — 1141

Acknowledgments

I've authored and coauthored over 45 books, and each project has been much the same in terms of compressed schedules and tight deadlines. This book was no different in that respect, but what made it one of the most enjoyable writing experiences of my career and eased the deadline woes was the phenomenal dedication to the project shown by all of the Microsoft Press staff.

I offer sincerest thanks to Sandra Haynes, who served as project editor and helped mold the content and kept the project and people all moving forward as a team, and to Mary Renaud, who served as lead copy editor and did an outstanding job guiding the editing efforts. Both Sandra and Mary spent countless long hours editing and refining the material to give it a quality it would have lacked without their efforts. I also offer thanks to Norreen Holmes, Nancy Albright, and ProImage project manager Jimmie Young, who also worked long and hard to polish the book and get it ready for publication.

My sincere thanks also go to Kong Cheung, acquisitions editor, for the opportunity to do the project and for his graciousness. David Fugate, my agent at Waterside Productions, gets a well-deserved thanks for not only bringing me this opportunity but also being my sounding board and keeping me focused.

Thanks also go to Michelle Roudebush, Julie Xiao, and Allan Wyatt, who had the difficult task of not only verifying the accuracy of a wide range of information but also trying to do that with a moving target during the beta process. The technical editors did an outstanding job and took on some additional tasks to get the book out on time, and the book is all the better for it.

I thank Susan Pink and Rebecca McKay, who served as copy editors and along with Mary and Sandra did an incredible job tightening up and clarifying the manuscript. Many authors don't fully appreciate what editors can do to improve the quality of their work, but I am one. My appreciation to desktop publisher Barb Levy, for putting together a layout that is as attractive as it is functional. I also thank Bill Teel for his efforts in cleaning up and processing the screen shots and other artwork. Thanks also to Patricia Masserman, copy editor, for checking everyone's work and catching those errors that always seem to sneak by somehow.

Many thanks go to the other authors who contributed to this book: Blair Rampling, Rob Tidrow, Deanna Maio, Tyler and Rima Regas, Dan Newland, John Durant, Matthew Nunn, and KC Lemson. All of them poured heart and soul into their contributions. I offer an extra bit of thanks to Blair and Rob for making time in their schedules to take on some extra material and help us make our deadlines.

I offer my appreciation and admiration to the Outlook development team for their efforts in making a great program even better!

Last, but not least, my deepest love and appreciation to my wife, Julie, for tolerance of my obsessive work habits and understanding of my myriad other annoying character traits and bad habits.

We'd Like to Hear from You!

Our goal at Microsoft Press is to create books that help you find the information you need to get the most out of your software.

The INSIDE OUT series was created with you in mind. As part of an effort to ensure that we're creating the best, most useful books we can, we talked to our customers and asked them to tell us what they need from a Microsoft Press series. Help us continue to help you. Let us know what you like about this book and what we can do to make it better. When you write, please include the title and author of this book in your e-mail, as well as your name and contact information. We look forward to hearing from you.

How to Reach Us

E-mail: nsideout@microsoft.com
Mail: Inside Out Series Editor
            Microsoft Press
            One Microsoft Way
            Redmond, WA 98052

Note: Unfortunately, we can't provide support for any software problems you might experience. Please go to http://support.microsoft.com *for help with any software issues.*

Introduction

Ten years ago the average computer user spent most of his or her time using a productivity application such as Microsoft Word or Microsoft Excel. In the ensuing decade, users have become more sophisticated, network implementations have become the rule rather than the exception, and collaboration has become a key facet of a successful business strategy. Perhaps the most significant change of all has been the explosive growth of the Internet. All these factors have led to a subtle but significant shift in the way people work. Today most users of Microsoft Office spend a majority of their time in Microsoft Outlook. That change alone signifies a shift toward information management as an increasingly important everyday task. Getting a handle on daily information management can be critical to your productivity, success, and sanity.

Outlook is an extremely versatile program. Most of the other applications in the Office suite have a fairly specific purpose. Outlook, however, serves as personal information manager (PIM), e-mail application, fax machine, task manager, and much more. With so much power and flexibility at your fingertips, you need to have a good understanding of Outlook's features. Understanding the ins and outs will not only help you get the most from this program but will also have a positive impact on your workday.

Who This Book Is For

Understanding all of Outlook's features and putting them to work is the focus of *Microsoft Outlook Version 2002 Inside Out*. Most Outlook books act mainly as how-to guides for users who want to learn about the software. This approach leaves out workgroup managers and administrators when it comes to deployment, collaboration, server-side issues, and administration. *Microsoft Outlook Version 2002 Inside Out* offers a comprehensive look at the features most people will use in Outlook and serves as an excellent reference for users who need to understand how to accomplish what they need to do. In addition, this book goes a step or two further, providing useful information to advanced users and IT professionals who need to understand the bigger picture. Whether you want to learn Outlook for your own use, need to support Outlook on a peer-to-peer network, or are in charge of supporting Outlook under Microsoft Exchange Server, you'll find the information and answers you need between the covers of *Microsoft Outlook Version 2002 Inside Out*.

This book makes some assumptions about the reader. You should be familiar with your client operating system, whether it's Microsoft Windows 9*x*, Windows Me, Windows NT, or Windows 2000. You should be comfortable working with a computer and have a good understanding of how to work with menus, dialog boxes, and other aspects of the user interface. In short, *Microsoft Outlook Version 2002 Inside Out* assumes you're an experienced computer user who might or might not have an understanding of Outlook and what it can do. The purpose of this book is to give you a comprehensive look at what Outlook can do, how to put Outlook to work, and how to manage Outlook at the user, workgroup, and server levels.

How This Book Is Organized

Microsoft Outlook Version 2002 Inside Out offers a structured, logical approach to all aspects of using and managing Outlook. Each of the nine parts of the book focuses on a specific aspect of Outlook use or management.

Part 1—Working with Outlook

Part 1 starts with the basics. Chapter 1 takes a look at Outlook's architecture, setup, and startup options to help you understand how Outlook stores its data. In Chapter 2 you'll learn how to perform advanced setup and configuration tasks such as setting up e-mail accounts, using profiles, making Outlook work with other e-mail services, configuring receipt and delivery options, and using add-ins that extend Outlook's functionality. Chapter 3 gets you up to speed using Outlook to send and receive messages, manage your workday, locate information on the Internet, and perform other common tasks. Chapter 4 rounds out Part 1 with a detailed look at how you can use categories and types to organize your data in Outlook.

Part 2—Messaging

Part 2 delves deeper into Outlook's e-mail and fax messaging components and features. In Chapter 5 you'll learn how to manage address books and distribution lists. Chapter 6 explains how to send and receive Internet-based messages through Outlook. Chapter 7 will make you comfortable with the range of features Outlook has for creating messages both simple and complex. In Chapter 8 you'll learn how to organize your messages, apply filters and rules to process messages automatically, exclude junk and spam e-mail senders, and generate automatic responses to incoming messages. Chapter 9 gives you a detailed look at Outlook's capabilities for sending and receiving faxes. Because Outlook isn't the only option available for messaging, in Chapter 10 you'll also learn how to integrate Outlook with Outlook Express and move messages, accounts, and addresses between the two applications.

Outlook relies on Outlook Express as its default newsgroup reader, so you'll learn in Chapter 11 how to send, receive, and manage newsgroup messages with Outlook Express. Because security is an increasingly important topic, Chapter 12 will help you secure your system and your data, send messages securely, and prevent others from impersonating you to send messages. Chapter 13 offers a comprehensive look at how Outlook's Remote Mail features can be indispensable for managing your mail online and offline.

Part 3—Contact Management

Part 3 explores Outlook's features for managing your contacts. Chapter 14 starts with a look at how to manage contact information, including addresses, phone numbers, e-mail addresses, fax numbers, and a wealth of other information. You'll also learn how to sort, filter, and categorize your contacts, as well as share contact data with others. Chapter 15 provides a look at Lightweight Directory Access Protocol (LDAP) directory services. You'll learn how to use Outlook to query an LDAP service to obtain addresses and other information about contacts and other objects in the directory.

Chapter 16 takes a look at Notes, a useful feature in Outlook that will help you get rid of those little slips of paper cluttering your desk and the sticky notes taking over your monitor. You'll learn how to create notes, assign categories to them, change their color, move them to other applications, put them on your desktop, and much more. Chapter 17 completes Part 3 with a look at journaling, an important feature in Outlook that allows you to keep track of time spent on projects and documents and to track contacts and other items of interest.

Part 4—Scheduling

Part 4 covers scheduling, one of the most widely used features in Outlook. Chapter 18 provides an in-depth look at Outlook's appointment-scheduling capabilities. You'll learn how scheduling works, and how to schedule appointments, create recurring appointments, use color effectively to manage your schedule, allow others to access your schedule, and publish your schedule to the Web. Chapter 19 takes a look at scheduling meetings and resources using Outlook and explains the subtle differences between scheduling appointments and scheduling meetings. Chapter 20 examines all aspects of managing tasks with Outlook. You can use the Outlook Tasks folder to keep track of your own tasks as well as assign tasks to others. Integrating your tasks in Outlook can help you ensure that your tasks get done on time and are allocated to the appropriate person to complete them. Chapter 21 rounds out the coverage of scheduling with a look at integrating Outlook with another scheduling and time-management application from Microsoft called Microsoft Project. You should turn to Microsoft Project when you need advanced project scheduling features. Understanding how to integrate Outlook with Project will help you provide a seamless transition between the two.

Part 5—Customizing Outlook

Customizing an application or the user interface for your operating system isn't just a matter of picking and choosing your personal preferences. Your ability to customize the way an application functions or appears can have a profound impact on its usefulness to you and to others. In short, the ability to customize an application allows you to make that application do what you want it to do in the way that makes the most sense to you. Chapter 22 starts the coverage of customization with a look at templates and how they can simplify the creation of e-mail messages, appointments, events, and other Outlook objects. You'll learn not only how to create and edit templates, but also how to share those templates with others.

Chapter 23 provides the detailed information you need to customize the Outlook Bar, the toolbar that appears by default to the left of the Outlook window and gives you quick access to Outlook's components. Chapter 24 will help you customize the other aspects of the Outlook interface including command bars, the Outlook Today view, folders, and print styles for organizing and displaying your Outlook data. Chapter 25 gives you a look at a host of ways you can automate tasks in Outlook.

Part 6—Managing Outlook

Part 6 begins the transition from user-focused topics to more advanced topics of interest to administrators and IT professionals. In Chapter 26 you'll learn how to integrate Outlook with other Office applications, such as performing a mail merge in Microsoft Word based on contacts stored in Outlook or moving contact data between Outlook and Microsoft Access. Chapter 27 will help you simplify your life by teaching you how to delegate many of your responsibilities—including managing your schedule—to an assistant. In Chapter 28 you'll learn how Outlook uses folders to store your data and how to manage those folders. Chapter 28 also offers in-depth coverage of how to organize and archive your important data. Chapter 29 extends the look at data management with an examination of how to find and organize data in Outlook. Chapter 30 concludes the discussion of management topics with a look at some important issues: backing up your data, exporting data, and importing data from other sources into Outlook.

Part 7—Using and Administering Outlook with Exchange Server

Outlook can be an effective information management tool by all by itself, whether you use it on a standalone computer or on a network in collaboration with other users. Where Outlook really shines, however, is in its integration with and as a client for Microsoft Exchange Server. Part 7 steps up to a more advanced level to explain a broad range of Outlook/Exchange integration topics. Chapter 31 begins the coverage with an overview of Exchange Server and how to set it up. Chapter 32 turns the focus to the client, explaining how to configure Outlook as an Exchange Server client. Chapter 33 explores the wealth of features in Outlook specifically geared toward messaging with Exchange Server, such as the ability to recall sent messages before they are read, prioritize messages, and much more. This chapter also contains a detailed look at voting, an interesting feature in Outlook. You can use Outlook as a tool to solicit input from others on any issue or topic, receiving and tallying their votes quite easily. Chapter 33 explains how voting works and covers all the topics you'll need to implement voting effectively.

Life isn't just about working in the confines of your office, and Part 7 takes that into account. Chapter 34 takes a detailed look at features in Outlook and Exchange Server that allow you to share data with others, including how to set up and use public folders, share personal folders, set up a message board, manage public folders, and even use the Network News Transfer Protocol (NNTP) service included with Windows 2000 Server to set up a newsgroup server for intranet or Internet users. Chapter 35 helps you continue working when you're away from the office or when your server is offline, covering how to use remote features to access and manage your Outlook data. Chapter 36 takes remote access one step further, explaining how to configure Exchange Server to allow users to access their data through a Web browser and offers tips on security, site considerations, and other important issues. Chapter 37 offers information and support for network, platform, and deployment considerations. Chapter 38 is targeted to anyone who needs to support Outlook clients under Exchange Server, including coverage of client options, mailbox management, configuring alternate recipients, message forwarding, and message journaling (archival). This chapter also includes topics that will help you to support collaboration and group scheduling. Chapter 39 completes the discussion of Exchange Server with an examination of backup strategies and virus protection. The chapter not only covers the importance of a sound backup and recovery strategy but will also help you develop and implement your own strategy that takes into account the unique requirements of Outlook and Exchange Server. For example, you learn how to structure an Exchange 2000 Server into multiple message stores for fault tolerance and quicker backup and restore. Chapter 39 also includes a detailed analysis of the importance of virus protection and how to guard against virus infections and outbreaks. You'll read about both client-side and server-side solutions, covering a range of platforms in addition to Exchange Server 5.5 and 2000. And since up-to-date virus definitions are the key to successful prevention, Chapter 39 also takes a close look at developing a virus definition update strategy. You'll also find a detailed discussion of how to configure attachment blocking at the server as well as in Outlook itself.

Part 8—Developing Custom Forms and Applications

The Microsoft Office suite offers an impressive ability to customize and integrate applications, and Outlook is no exception. Whether you need to create a few custom forms or develop full-blown interactive applications with Outlook and other Office applications, Part 8 provides the solutions you need.

Chapter 40 begins the discussion with a look at creating and using custom forms for a variety of tasks. In Chapter 41 you'll begin to delve into Outlook programming with a look at programming forms using Visual Basic Scripting (VBS). Chapter 42 continues the coverage of programming and development with a look at using Visual Basic for Applications (VBA) to develop Outlook applications. Chapter 43 completes the discussion with a detailed look at integrating Outlook and other applications through VBA.

Part 9—Appendixes

Microsoft Outlook Version 2002 Inside Out includes eight appendixes. The topics covered range from installing and updating Outlook to other sources of information, such as the Office XP Resource Kit and the Outlook Deployment Kit. You'll also find background data such as registry keys, add-ins, symbols, and shortcuts.

> See the section "Conventions and Features Used in This Book" (page li) for a list of some of the features you will find used throughout the book.

What's New in Outlook 2002

The first step to getting a handle on Outlook is to understand what it can do. Chances are you're familiar with Outlook or with similar programs. Throughout *Microsoft Outlook Version 2002 Inside Out* you'll find information on Outlook's features. Whether or not you're experienced with a previous version of Outlook, the following section will bring you up to speed on the new features in Outlook 2002.

Core Product Enhancements

Outlook 2002 provides several key enhancements to the core Outlook components to improve ease-of-use, offline and remote use, synchronization, and more. These core enhancements include:

- **E-Mail Accounts Wizard.** In previous versions of Outlook, adding e-mail accounts wasn't an intuitive process and could be difficult for inexperienced users. Outlook 2002 provides a new E-Mail Accounts Wizard to simplify the process of setting up accounts, adding information stores and address books, and configuring account options. The wizard has a feature that allows you to test an account as you're creating it to ensure that the settings are correct.

- **Unified Reminders Window.** In previous versions of Outlook you had to process reminders one at a time. If you'd been out of the office for a while, you could have dozens of reminders to deal with upon your return. Outlook 2002 provides a unified reminders window that presents all reminders in a single interface, making it much easier to dismiss or snooze groups of reminders.

- **Improved preview pane.** The preview pane lets you preview messages and appointments without opening them. In Outlook 2002 the preview pane adds new functionality. You can double-click addresses in the preview pane header to view address properties. The InfoBar is now available in the preview pane, and the pane offers a new area for displaying attachments. You can also accept or decline meeting requests through the preview pane without opening them.

- **Smart tags.** One of the new features in the Office XP suite is smart tags, which offer quick access to item-specific features right where the data appears. Paste some text from the Clipboard, for example, and a smart tag appears beside the text. Click the tag and select different paste formats and other options that change the pasted content. AutoCorrect entries are another example of where smart tags shine. If you type some text referenced by an AutoCorrect entry, Office changes the text automatically but adds a smart tag beside the modified text so that you can select other changes or undo the correction.

Messaging

Messaging is a big part of Outlook's functionality, and Microsoft has improved messaging in several significant ways. These changes and new features include the following:

- **Outlook Unified Mode.** Outlook no longer uses Internet Mail Only (IMO) and Corporate Workgroup (C/W) modes for e-mail. All modes are merged into a single Unified Mode that allows you to access Exchange Server, POP3, IMAP, and Hotmail/HTML accounts without switching profiles. This is a significant improvement in usability.

- **Word as the default e-mail editor.** Word is now the default e-mail editor, which allows you to take advantage of the editing and rich text features in Word when you create e-mail. As in previous versions, you can make Outlook the default e-mail editor if you prefer. Outlook also offers improvements for creating and editing messages and provides a consistent interface for message creation regardless of which e-mail editor you choose.

- **HTML as the default protocol.** Outlook uses HTML as the default protocol for message content, extending the capabilities for creating rich content in messages. If you prefer, you can configure Outlook to use text-only as the default protocol for compatibility.

- **Hotmail support.** Through integrated support for Hotmail, Outlook 2002 allows you to send and receive e-mail messages through your Hotmail account and work with them offline.

- **Autocomplete for addresses.** With either Outlook or Word as your e-mail editor, Outlook 2002 automatically completes addresses as you type them in the To, Cc, and Bcc fields.

- **Virus detection and prevention.** Outlook 2002 includes security features that prevent you from opening or sending attachments that contain viruses. Outlook also prevents external scripts from gathering e-mail addresses from your system or silently sending e-mail, thereby helping to control and prevent viruses and worms from spreading through your e-mail system.

Calendar

The Calendar is an important component in Outlook, and Microsoft has implemented two main changes to the Calendar to improve usability and functionality:

- **Calendar coloring.** You can label individual and recurring appointments with one of 10 predefined colors, each of which has a corresponding label (Personal, Business, Urgent, and so on). You can modify these labels to suit your needs. Each appointment can have only one label, but you can use exceptions to apply a color to individual appointments in a series that is different from the default color of the series. Outlook also allows you to use rules to automatically color appointments that meet the same criteria. For example, you might apply a specific color to all meeting requests from a particular person.

- **Meeting planner enhancements.** You can now propose a new time for a meeting at the same time that you tentatively accept or decline a meeting request. The person who proposes the meeting can view all counterproposals in the scheduler and decide which counterproposal to use. Group scheduling allows you to view the schedules of multiple people in a single calendar that contains a graph of when each user is free or busy. The unified calendar also displays details about the users' appointments (unless they have been marked as private). Another usability improvement is that when you hover the pointer over an appointment, a pop-up window displays the appointment details. If you hover the pointer over a selection of time slots, Outlook displays a list of all appointments for the selected group member during that time period.

Contacts

Microsoft has also improved the Contacts component of Outlook. The Contacts list now supports instant messaging addresses. The default Contacts form also includes a new Display As address field for each contact item, allowing you to control how the contact's name appears in the Contacts list. For example, to differentiate between contacts with the same name but different e-mail addresses, you might use the Display As field to display the contact's e-mail address after the name. Or you might change the display name for contacts who have the same name to distinguish them from one another.

Offline/Online Enhancements

Outlook 2002 offers several improvements in online and offline use, including improved synchronization. One improvement is particularly worth noting: Outlook gives you the ability to automatically change send/receive behavior when the offline/online state changes, including such options as server polling frequency or whether a particular send/receive group is included when polling all groups.

New Synchronization Architecture

Outlook 2002 implements a new synchronization architecture to improve folder synchronization, improve usability, and enhance performance. This new synchronization architecture offers the following advantages:

- **Integrated synchronization.** Sending, receiving, and offline synchronization have been integrated into the same feature, simplifying message processing and synchronization.

- **Flexibility between scheduled and background send/receive.** You can configure scheduled and background message send/receive to behave differently according to the offline/online state. In addition, you can have Outlook perform predetermined send/receive tasks independently of other background send/receive tasks.

- **Selective send/receive.** Outlook makes it easy to perform a send/receive of only the selected folder depending on the account type.

- **Control send/receive behavior.** You can turn on or off all background send/receive tasks without changing Outlook's offline state.

- **Improved remote mail capability.** Outlook 2002 allows you to configure most account types to download message headers only.

- **Multiple account support.** Outlook simplifies managing multiple accounts, making it easy to send and receive through multiple accounts at one time. This is a significant usability improvement. In addition, each account can use different Dial-Up Networking settings, allowing you to easily control which dial-up connection a given account uses and ensure that the correct one is used when processing messages for that account.

- **Downloaded message behavior.** Downloaded messages automatically change their offline/online states based on the detected availability of the server.

- **Better progress notification.** Outlook 2002 now offers more detailed information regarding in-progress message processing.

Directory Enhancements

Outlook 2002 provides several improvements in the way it stores and presents information in address books and other directory services. These improvements include the following:

- **Better control over address book display.** Outlook now provides resizable address book columns and gives you more control over the address book display to let you view contacts in a way that best suits your needs.

- **Active Directory recovery.** If an Active Directory General Catalog (GC) loss occurs, Exchange Server transparently redirects Outlook to a new GC in the domain.

- **Better offline address book support.** You can download your address book, allowing you to easily use addresses from the address book while working offline to create messages, meeting requests, appointments, and so on.

Improved International Support

Outlook offers improvements for users who work in an international environment, including the following:

- **Conditional formatting.** Outlook provides conditional formatting rules that work independently of the selected user interface language.

- **Automatic decoding detection.** Outlook automatically selects the appropriate encoding for Internet mail based on the content of the message. This feature relies on Microsoft Internet Explorer 5.5.

- **Improved alternate calendar support.** Outlook provides support for a lunar calendar, enabling you to create recurring meetings based on lunar months.

Conventions and Features Used in This Book

This book uses special text and design conventions to make it easier for you to find the information you need.

Text Conventions

Convention	Meaning
Abbreviated menu commands	For your convenience, this book uses abbreviated menu commands. For example, "Choose Tools, Track Changes, Highlight Changes" means that you should click the Tools menu, point to Track Changes, and select the Highlight Changes command.
Boldface type	**Boldface** type is used to indicate text that you enter or type.
Initial Capital Letters	The first letters of the names of menus, dialog boxes, dialog box elements, and commands are capitalized. Example: the Save As dialog box.
Italicized type	*Italicized* type is used to indicate new terms.
Plus sign (+) in text	Keyboard shortcuts are indicated by a plus sign (+) separating two key names. For example, Ctrl+Alt+Delete means that you press the Ctrl, Alt, and Delete keys at the same time.

Design Conventions

newfeature!

This text identifies a new or significantly updated feature in this version of the software.

InsideOut

These are the book's signature tips. In these tips, you'll get the straight scoop on what's going on with the software—inside information on why a feature works the way it does. You'll also find handy workarounds to different software problems.

tip Tips provide helpful hints, timesaving tricks, or alternative procedures related to the task being discussed.

Troubleshooting

Look for these sidebars to find solutions to common problems you might encounter. Troubleshooting sidebars appear next to related information in the chapters. You can also use the Troubleshooting Topics index at the back of the book to look up problems by topic.

Cross-references point you to other locations in the book that offer additional information on the topic being discussed.

This icon indicates sample files or text found on the companion CD.

caution Cautions identify potential problems that you should look out for when you're completing a task or problems that you must address before you can complete a task.

note Notes offer additional information related to the task being discussed.

Sidebar

The sidebars sprinkled throughout these chapters provide ancillary information on the topic being discussed. Go to sidebars to learn more about the technology or a feature.

Part 1

Working with Outlook

Chapter 1

Outlook Architecture, Setup, and Startup

This chapter provides an overview of Microsoft Outlook's architecture to help you learn not only how Outlook works but also how it stores data. Having that knowledge, particularly if you're charged with administering or supporting Outlook for other users, will help you use the application more effectively and address issues related to data storage and security, archiving, working offline, and moving data between installations.

This chapter also explains the different options you have for connecting to e-mail servers through Outlook and the protocols (POP3 and IMAP, for example) that support those connections. In addition to learning about client support and the various platforms on which you can use Outlook, you'll also learn about the options that are available for starting and using the program.

If you're anxious to get started using Outlook, you could skip this chapter and move straight to Chapter 2, "Advanced Setup Tasks," to learn how to configure your e-mail accounts and begin working with Outlook. However, this chapter provides the foundation on which many subsequent chapters are based, and reading it will help you gain a deeper understanding of what Outlook can do so that you can use it effectively and efficiently.

Overview of Outlook

In many respects, Outlook is a personal information manager (PIM). A traditional PIM lets you maintain information about your contacts, such as your customers, coworkers, and clients. Traditional PIMs also let you keep track of your daily schedule, tasks to complete, and other personal or work-related

3

information. Outlook does all that, but it goes well beyond the features of most PIMs to provide e-mail and fax support, group scheduling capability, and task management.

Outlook provides a broad range of capabilities to help you manage your entire work day. In fact, a growing number of Microsoft Office users work in Outlook more than 60 percent of the time. An understanding of Outlook's capabilities and features is important not only to using Office effectively but also to managing your time and projects. The following sections will help you learn to use the features in Outlook to simplify your work day and enhance your productivity.

Messaging

One of the key features Outlook offers is messaging. You can use Outlook as a client to send and receive e-mail through a variety of services. Outlook offers integrated support for the following e-mail services:

> **note** A *client application* is one that uses a service provided by another computer, typically a server.

Exchange Server Outlook provides full support for Microsoft Exchange Server, which means you can take advantage of workgroup scheduling, collaboration, instant messaging, and other features offered through Exchange Server that aren't available with other clients. For example, you can use any POP3 e-mail client, such as Outlook Express, to connect to an Exchange Server (assuming the Exchange Server is running an Internet Mail Connector), but you're limited to e-mail only. Advanced workgroup and other special features—being able to recall a message before it is read, use public folders, and vote, for example—require Outlook.

Internet e-mail Outlook provides full support for Internet e-mail servers, which means you can use Outlook to send and receive e-mail through mail servers that support Internet-based standards, such as POP3 and IMAP. What's more, you can integrate Internet mail accounts with other accounts, such as an Exchange Server account, to send and receive messages through multiple servers. For example, you might maintain an account on your Exchange Server for interoffice correspondence and use a local Internet service provider (ISP), CompuServe, Bigfoot, or other Internet-based e-mail service for messages outside your network. Or perhaps you want to monitor your personal e-mail along with your work-related e-mail. In that situation, you would simply add your personal e-mail account to your Outlook profile and work with both simultaneously. You can use rules and custom folders to help separate your messages.

> For more information about messaging protocols such as POP3 and IMAP, see "Understanding Messaging Protocols," page 18.

Chapter 1: Outlook Architecture, Setup, and Startup

newfeature!

HTTP-based e-mail   Outlook 2002 supports HTTP-based e-mail services, such as Microsoft Hotmail. HTTP (Hypertext Transfer Protocol) is the protocol used to request and transmit Web pages. This means you can use Outlook to send and receive e-mail through Hotmail and other HTTP-based mail servers that would otherwise require you to use a Web browser to access your e-mail (see Figure 1-1). In addition, you can download your messages to your local inbox and process them offline, rather than re-maining connected to your ISP while you process messages. Another advantage is that you can keep your messages as long as you want—most HTTP-based messaging services, including Hotmail, purge read messages after a given period of time. Plus, HTTP support in Outlook lets you keep all your e-mail in a single application. Currently, Outlook 2002 directly supports Hotmail. Check with your e-mail service to determine whether your mail server is Outlook-compatible.

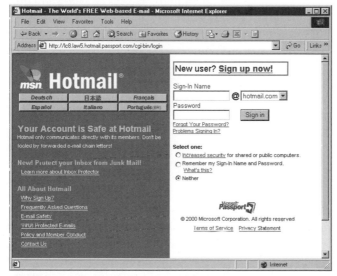

Figure 1-1.   HTTP-based mail servers such as Hotmail have traditionally required access through a Web browser.

Fax send and receive   Outlook 2002 includes a Fax Mail Transport provider, which allows you to send and receive faxes using a fax modem. The Fax Mail Transport included with Outlook provides Messaging Application Programming Interface (MAPI) support so that incoming fax messages can be routed through your Outlook Inbox, with the MAPI-aware fax application handling the actual fax processing (send, receive, view, and so on). Most Microsoft platforms provide built-in fax capability, but actual support varies from one platform to another. In addition, third-party developers can provide MAPI integration with their fax applications, allowing you to use Outlook as the front end for those applications to send

5

Chapter 1

and receive faxes. Symantec's WinFax is a good example of such an application. The fax service in Microsoft Windows 2000 also supports MAPI and Inbox integration with Outlook and is the only Microsoft-supplied fax service supported by Microsoft for Outlook.

Windows 2000 fax service is now the only fax support offered for Windows. Windows 9x users will need to purchase a third-party fax application such as WinFax.

For a detailed explanation of how to use Outlook to send and receive faxes (complete with cover pages and other details), see Chapter 9, "Sending and Receiving Faxes."

Extensible e-mail support   Outlook's design allows developers to support third-party e-mail services in Outlook, such as cc:Mail and Lotus Notes. This support doesn't guarantee the availability of these third-party tools, however. For example, although earlier versions of Outlook included support for cc:Mail, Microsoft no longer offers its own service provider for support of cc:Mail.

InsideOut

Outlook 2002 does not include the Microsoft Mail service provider. Microsoft no longer supports this product and customers who used this service will need to find another service provider.

Whatever your e-mail server type, Outlook provides a comprehensive set of tools for composing, receiving, and replying to messages. Outlook provides support for rich-text and HTML formatting, which allows you to create and receive messages that contain much more than just text (see Figure 1-2). For example, you can send a Web page as a mail message or integrate sound, video, and graphics in mail messages. Outlook's support for multiple address books, multiple e-mail accounts, and even multiple e-mail services makes it an excellent messaging client, even if you forgo the application's many other features and capabilities.

Scheduling

Scheduling is another important feature in Outlook. You can use Outlook to track both personal and work-related meetings and appointments (see Figure 1-3), whether at home or in the office, a useful feature even on a stand-alone computer.

Chapter 1: Outlook Architecture, Setup, and Startup

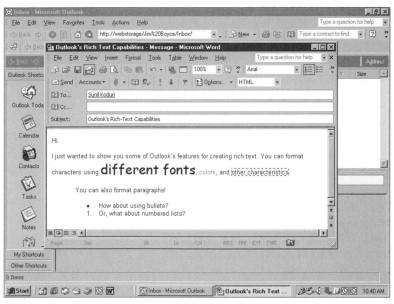

Figure 1-2. Use Outlook to create rich-text and multimedia messages.

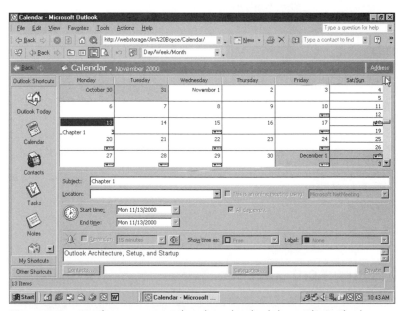

Figure 1-3. Track your personal and work schedules with Outlook.

Where Outlook's scheduling capabilities really shine, however, is in group scheduling. When you use Outlook to set up meetings and appointments with others, you can view the schedules of your invitees, which makes it easy to find a time when everyone can attend. You can schedule both one-time and recurring appointments. All appointments and meetings can include a reminder with a lead time that you specify, and

Outlook will notify you of the event at the specified time. A new feature in Outlook 2002 lets you process multiple reminders at one time, a useful feature if you've been out of the office for a while.

newfeature!

Organizing your schedule is also one of Outlook's strong suits. You can use categories and types to categorize appointments, events, and meetings; to control the way they appear in Outlook; and to perform automatic processing. Color labels allow you to identify quickly and visually different types of events on your calendar.

In addition to managing your own schedule, you can delegate control of the schedule to someone else, such as your assistant. The assistant can modify your schedule, request meetings, respond to meeting invitations, and otherwise act on your behalf regarding your calendar. Not only can others view your schedule to plan meetings and appointments (with the exception of items marked personal), but you can also publish your schedule to the Web to allow others to view it over an intranet or the Internet (see Figure 1-4).

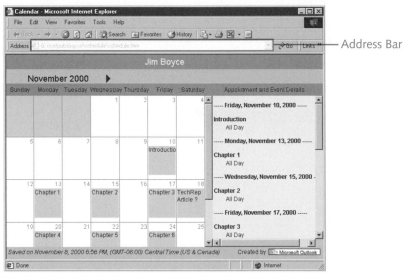

Figure 1-4. You can easily publish your schedule to the Web.

Contact Management

Being able to manage contact information—names, addresses, and phone numbers—is critical to other aspects of Outlook, such as scheduling and messaging. Outlook makes it easy to manage contacts and offers flexibility in the type of information you maintain. In addition to basic information, you can also store a contact's fax number, cell phone number, pager number, Web page URL, and more (see Figure 1-5).

Chapter 1: Outlook Architecture, Setup, and Startup

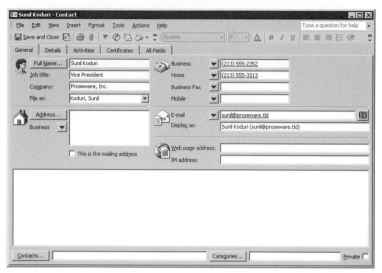

Figure 1-5. You can manage a wealth of information about each contact.

Besides using contact information to address e-mail messages, you can initiate phone calls using the contacts list, track calls to contacts in the journal, add notes for each contact, use the contacts list to create mail merge documents, and perform other tasks. The Contacts folder also provides a means for storing a contact's digital certificate, which you can use to exchange encrypted messages for security. Adding a contact's certificate is easy—just receive a digitally signed message from the contact and Outlook will add the certificate to the contact's entry. You can also import a certificate from a file provided by the contact.

> For details about digital signatures and encryption, see "Encrypting Messages," page 354. For additional information on the Journal, see "Tracking with Outlook's Journal," page 10. For complete details on how to use the journal, see Chapter 17, "Keeping a Journal."

Task Management

Managing your work day usually includes keeping track of the tasks you need to perform and assigning tasks to others. Outlook makes it easy to manage your task list. You assign a due date, start date, priority, category, and other properties to each task, which makes it easier for you to manage those tasks (see Figure 1-6). As with meetings and appointments, Outlook keeps you informed and on track by issuing reminders for each task. You control whether the reminder is used and the time and date it's generated, along with an optional, audible notification. You can designate a task as personal, preventing others from viewing the task in your schedule—just as you can with meetings and appointments. Tasks can be one-time or recurring.

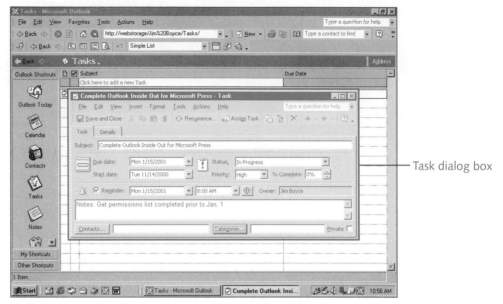

Task dialog box

Figure 1-6. Use Outlook to manage tasks.

If you manage others, Outlook makes it easy to assign tasks to other Outlook users. When you create a task, you simply click Assign Task, and Outlook prompts you for the assignee's e-mail address. You can choose to keep a copy of the updated task in your own task list and receive a status report when the task is complete.

Tracking with Outlook's Journal

Keeping track of events is an important part of managing your work day, and Outlook's journal makes it simple. The Journal folder allows you to keep track of the contacts you make (phone calls, e-mails, and so on), meeting actions, task requests and responses, and other actions for selected contacts (see Figure 1-7). You can also use the journal to track your work in other Microsoft Office applications, giving you a way to track the time you spend on various documents and their associated projects. You can have Outlook journal items automatically based on settings that you specify, and you can also add items manually to your journal.

Chapter 1: Outlook Architecture, Setup, and Startup

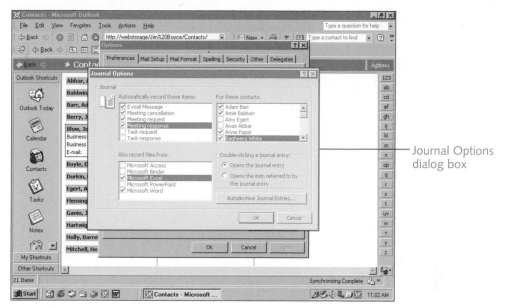

Journal Options dialog box

Figure 1-7. Configure your journal using Outlook's options.

When you view the journal, you can double-click a journal entry to either open the entry or open the items referred to by the entry, depending on how you have configured the journal. You can also configure the journal to automatically archive items to the default archive folder or a folder you choose, or you can have Outlook regularly delete items from the journal, cleaning out items that are older than a specified length of time. Outlook can use group policies to control the retention of journal entries, allowing a system administrator to manage journaling and data retention consistently throughout an organization.

Organizing Your Thoughts with Notes

With Outlook, you can keep track of your thoughts and tasks by using the Notes folder. Each note can function as a stand-alone window, allowing you to view notes on your desktop outside Outlook (see Figure 1-8). Notes exist as individual message files, so you can copy or move them to other folders, including your desktop, or easily share them with others through network sharing or e-mail. You can also incorporate the contents of notes into other applications or other Outlook folders by using the clipboard. For example, you might copy a note regarding a contact to that person's contact entry. As you can with other Outlook items, you can assign categories to notes to help you organize and view them.

Chapter 1

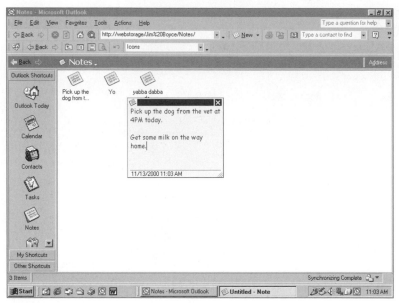

Figure 1-8. Use notes to keep track of miscellaneous information.

How Outlook Stores Data

If you work with Outlook primarily as a user, understanding how the program stores data will help you use it effectively to organize and manage your data on a daily basis, including storing and archiving Outlook items as needed. If you're charged with supporting other Outlook users, understanding how Outlook stores data will allow you to help others create and manage their folders and ensure the security and integrity of their data. And finally, because data storage is the foundation of all Outlook's features, understanding where and how the program stores data is critical if you're creating Outlook-based applications—for example, a data entry form that uses Outlook as the mechanism for posting the data to a public folder.

> For information on building Outlook-based applications, see Chapters 40 through 43, which cover programming Outlook using Visual Basic and VBScript to create custom forms and applications.

You're probably familiar with folders (directories) in the file system. You use these folders to organize applications and documents. For example, the Program Files folder in the Microsoft Windows operating system is the default location for most applications that you install on the system, and the My Documents folder serves as the default location for document files. You create these types of folders in Windows Explorer.

Chapter 1: Outlook Architecture, Setup, and Startup

Outlook also uses folders to organize data, but these folders are different from your file system folders. Rather than existing individually on your system's hard disk, these folders exist within Outlook's file structure. You view and manage these folders within Outlook's interface, not in Windows Explorer. Think of Outlook's folders as windows into your Outlook data rather than as individual elements that exist on disk. By default, Outlook includes several folders, as shown in Figure 1-9.

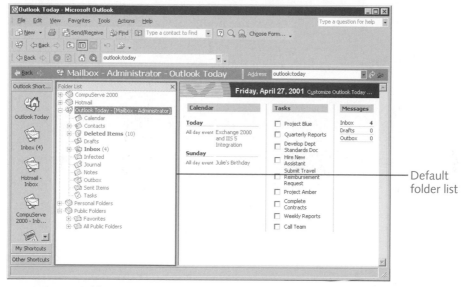

Figure 1-9. Folders organize your data in Outlook.

Personal Folders—PST Files

If your Outlook folders aren't stored as individual folders on your system's hard disk, where are they? The answer to that question depends on how you configure Outlook. As in earlier versions of Outlook, you can use a personal folders file to store your Outlook data. Outlook uses the PST file extension for a personal folders file, but you specify the file's name when you configure Outlook. For example, you might use your name as the file name to help you easily identify the file. The default PST file contains your Contacts, Calendar, Tasks, and other folders.

You can use multiple PST files, adding additional personal folders to your Outlook configuration (see Figure 1-10 on the next page). For example, you might want to create another set of folders to separate your personal information from work-related data. As you'll learn in Chapter 2, you can add personal folders to your Outlook configuration simply by adding another PST file to your profile.

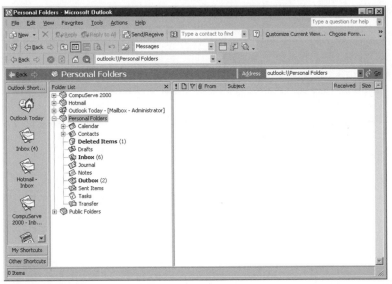

Figure 1-10. You can add multiple sets of folders to your Outlook configuration.

> **note** If you use Outlook as an Exchange Server client, you probably store your data in the Exchange Server mailbox rather than in a local PST file. If that's the case, you need to use an offline folder (OST) file in order to work offline. OST files are covered in the following section.

OST Files

If you use Outlook as an Exchange Server client and do not use PST files to store your data (instead storing your data on the Exchange Server), OST files will allow you to work offline. The OST file acts essentially as an offline copy of your data store on the Exchange Server. When you're working offline, changes you make to contacts, messages, and other Outlook items and folders occur in the offline store. When you go online again, Outlook synchronizes the changes between the offline store and your Exchange Server store. For example, if you've deleted messages from your offline store, Outlook deletes those same messages from your online store when you synchronize the folders. Any new messages in your Inbox on the server are added to your offline store. Synchronization is a two-way process, providing the most up-to-date copy of your data in both locations, ensuring that changes made in each are reflected in the other.

> For detailed information on important offline and remote access topics, see Chapter 35, "Working Offline and Remotely." For a discussion of the differences between remote mail and offline use, see Chapter 13, "Processing Messages Selectively."

Where Storage Files Are Located

When you create an Outlook storage file, Outlook defaults to a specific location for the file that varies according to your operating system:

- **Windows 9x.** The default location is \Windows\Local Settings \Application Data\Microsoft\Outlook. On systems running Windows 9*x* that are configured to maintain unique user profiles (useful where multiple users share a single Windows 9*x* computer), the user profiles are stored in the \Profiles folder. On these systems, Outlook places the storage files by default in \Profiles\<*user*>\Local Settings\Application Data\ Microsoft\Outlook.

> **tip**   To maintain unique user profiles in Windows 98, configure Windows through the Users icon in Control Panel.

- **Windows NT.** The default location for systems running Windows NT is \%systemroot%\Profiles\<*user*>\Local Settings\Application Data\ Microsoft\Outlook, where %systemroot% by default is \Winnt.

- **Windows 2000.** The default location is \Documents And Settings\<*user*> \Local Settings\Application Data\Microsoft\Outlook. On systems running Windows 2000 that were upgraded from Windows NT, the user profiles still reside in the \Winnt\Profiles folder. On these systems, therefore, Outlook places the storage files by default in \%systemroot%\Profiles\ <*user*>\Local Settings\Application Data\Microsoft\Outlook. As with Windows NT, %systemroot% defaults to \Winnt.

> **tip**   **Find your data store**
>
> If you're having trouble locating your existing storage files, choose File, Data File Management. In the Outlook Data Files dialog box (see Figure 1-11 on the next page), select the file you want to locate and then determine the file location from the File-name column. If you can't see the entire path, drag the column border to expand the column. Alternatively, to go straight to the folder containing the file, select the file and click Open Folder. In the folder window, choose Tools, Folder Options. From the View tab of the Folder Options dialog box, select Display The Full Path In The Title Bar to view the absolute, full path to the file. You can also use your operating system's Find/Search command to search for all files with a PST or OST file extension.

Part 1: Working with Outlook

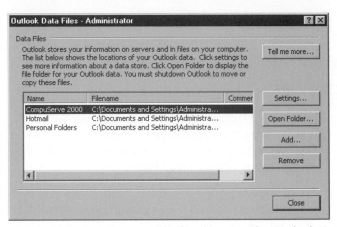

Figure 1-11. Locate your data files by using the Outlook Data Files dialog box.

If you use the same computer all the time, it's generally best to store your Outlook files on your system's local hard disk. In some situations, however, you will probably want to store them on a network share. For example, you might connect from different computers on the network and use a roaming profile to provide a consistent desktop and user interface regardless of your logon location. (A *roaming profile* allows your desktop configuration, documents, and other elements of your desktop environment to be duplicated wherever you log on.) In this situation, you (or the network administrator) would configure your profile to place your home folder on a network server that is available to you from all logon locations. Your Outlook files would then be stored on that network share, making them available to you on whichever computer you use to log on to the network. Placing your Outlook files on a server gives you the added potential benefit of incorporating your Outlook data files in the server's backup strategy.

For a detailed discussion of using roaming profiles to provide seamless access to Outlook, see Chapter 37, "Network, Platform, and Deployment Considerations." To learn how to move your Outlook files from one location to another (such as from a local drive to a network share), see "Changing Your Data Storage Location," page 54.

Troubleshooting

You use a roaming profile and logon time is increasing.

If you use Outlook as a client for Exchange Server, your best option is to use your Exchange Server mailbox as the store location for your data rather than using a PST file. However, if you use a roaming profile for consistent logon from multiple locations on the local area network (LAN), consider including the OST file in the roaming profile so that you'll always have access to it. If the Exchange Server is unavailable, you'll still be able to work with your Outlook data through the OST file; and placing the OST file in your roaming profile allows you to use it regardless of your logon location.

Keep in mind, however, that the OST file can become quite large if you have a lot of data in your Exchange Server mailbox. The size of the profile affects logon time, and a large profile can cause an excessive amount of network traffic as the files are copied from the server to your workstation. Use aggressive archiving and other housecleaning methods to keep your Outlook data to a minimum, and monitor your roaming profile size as often as possible.

Sharing Storage Files

Outlook provides excellent functionality for sharing information with others. Toward that end, you can share your data using a couple of different methods. You can configure permissions for individual folders to allow specific users to connect to those folders and view the data contained in them. You can also configure delegate access to your folders to allow an assistant to manage items for you in the folders. For example, you might have your assistant manage your schedule but not your tasks. In that case, you would configure delegate access for the Calendar folder but not for the Tasks folder.

For a detailed discussion of delegation, see Chapter 27, "Delegating Responsibilities to an Assistant." To learn how to configure sharing permissions for individual folders and additional methods for sharing data, see Chapter 34, "Sharing Information with Others."

Understanding Messaging Protocols

A *messaging protocol* is a mechanism that messaging servers and applications use to transfer messages. Being able to use a specific e-mail service requires that your application support the same protocols the server uses. In order to configure Outlook as a messaging client, you need to understand the various protocols supported by Outlook and the types of servers that employ each type. The following sections provide an overview of these protocols.

SMTP/POP3

Simple Mail Transport Protocol (SMTP) is a standards-based protocol used for transferring messages and is the primary mechanism that Internet-based and intranet-based e-mail servers use to transfer messages. It's also the mechanism that Outlook uses to connect to a mail server to send messages for an Internet account. Therefore, SMTP is the protocol used by an Internet mail account for outgoing messages.

SMTP operates by default on TCP port 25. When you configure an Internet-based e-mail account, the outgoing mail server setting is determined by the port on which the server is listening for SMTP. Unless your e-mail server uses a different port (unlikely), you can use the default port value of 25.

Post Office Protocol 3 (POP3) is a standards-based protocol that clients can use to access messages from any mail server that supports POP3. This is the protocol that Outlook uses when retrieving messages from an Internet-based or intranet-based mail server that supports POP3 mailboxes. ISP-based mail servers invariably use POP3, as do other mail servers. For example, CompuServe Classic provides POP3 support, allowing you to retrieve your CompuServe mail through Outlook. Exchange Server also supports the use of POP3 for retrieving mail.

POP3 operates on TCP port 110 by default. Unless your server uses a nonstandard port configuration, you can leave the port setting as is when defining a POP3 mail account. Figure 1-12 shows the Internet E-Mail Settings dialog box, which you use to configure the incoming and outgoing mail server settings for an Internet mail account. Click the More Settings button if you need to change port settings for the account.

To learn how to set up an Internet e-mail account for an SMTP/POP3 server, see "Using Internet POP3 E-Mail Accounts," page 154. To learn how to add the account and configure advanced properties, such as SMTP or POP3 port assignments, see "Configuring Advanced Settings for Internet Accounts," page 159.

Chapter 1: Outlook Architecture, Setup, and Startup

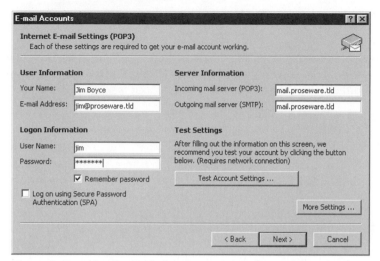

Figure 1-12. Use the E-Mail Accounts Wizard's Internet E-Mail Settings page to configure the incoming and outgoing mail server settings.

IMAP

Like POP3, Internet Mail Access Protocol (IMAP) is a standards-based protocol that enables message transfer. However, IMAP offers some significant differences from POP3. For example, POP3 is primarily designed as an offline protocol, which means you retrieve your messages from a server and download them to your local message store (such as your local Outlook folders). IMAP is designed primarily as an online protocol, which allows a remote user to manipulate messages and message folders on the server without having to download them. This is particularly helpful for users who need to access the same remote mailbox from multiple locations, such as from home and work, using different computers. Because the messages remain on the server, IMAP eliminates the need for message synchronization.

> **tip** **Keep messages on the server**
>
> You can configure a POP3 account in Outlook to leave a copy of messages on the server, allowing you to retrieve those messages later from another computer. To learn how to configure a POP3 account, see "Using Internet POP3 E-Mail Accounts," page 154.

IMAP offers other advantages over POP3. For example, with IMAP, you can search for messages on the server using a variety of message attributes, such as sender, message size, or message header. IMAP also offers better support for attachments, because it can separate attachments from the header and text portion of a message. This is particularly useful with multipart MIME messages, allowing you to read a message without downloading the attachments so that you can decide which attachments you want to retrieve. With POP3, the entire message must be downloaded.

Security is another advantage of IMAP, because IMAP uses a challenge-response mechanism to authenticate the user for mailbox access. This prevents the user's password from being transmitted as clear text across the network, as it is with POP3.

IMAP support in Outlook allows you to use Outlook as a client to an IMAP-compliant e-mail server. Although IMAP provides for server-side storage and the ability to create additional mail folders on the server, it does not offer some of the same features as Exchange Server or even POP3. For example, you can't store nonmail folders on the server. Also, special folders such as Sent Items, Drafts, and Deleted Items can't be stored on the IMAP server. Even with these limitations, however, IMAP serves as a flexible protocol and surpasses POP3 in capability. Unless a competing standard appears in the future, it is likely that IMAP will replace POP3.

> For information about other advantages and disadvantages of IMAP and how they affect Outlook, see "Using IMAP Accounts," page 161.

> **note** For additional technical information on IMAP, point your browser to *http://www.ima.com/whitepaper/index.html* or *http://www.cyrusoft.com/imap/imapInfo.html*, or refer to RFC 2060, which you can find at *http://www.ietf.org/rfc/rfc2060.txt.*

MAPI

Messaging Application Programming Interface (MAPI) is a Microsoft-developed application programming interface (API) that facilitates communication between mail-enabled applications. MAPI support makes it possible for other applications to send and receive messages using Outlook. For example, third-party fax applications, such as Symantec's WinFax, can place incoming faxes in your Inbox through MAPI. As another example, a third-party MAPI-aware application could read and write to your Outlook Address Book through MAPI calls. MAPI is not a message protocol, but understanding its function in Outlook will help you install, configure, and use MAPI-aware applications to integrate Outlook.

LDAP

Lightweight Directory Access Protocol (LDAP) was designed to serve with less overhead and fewer resource requirements than its precursor, the Directory Access Protocol, which was developed for X.500. LDAP is a standards-based protocol that allows clients to query data in a directory service over a TCP connection. For example, Windows 2000 uses LDAP as the primary means for querying the Active Directory (AD). Exchange Server supports LDAP queries, allowing clients to look up address information for subscribers on the server. Other directory services on the Internet, such as Bigfoot, InfoSpace, Yahoo!, and others, employ LDAP to implement searches of their databases.

Like Outlook Express, Outlook 2002 allows you to add directory service accounts that use LDAP as their protocol to query directory services for e-mail addresses, phone numbers, and other information regarding subscribers.

> To learn how to add and configure an LDAP directory service in Outlook, see "Configuring a Directory Service Account in Outlook," page 425.

> **note** For additional information regarding LDAP, refer to "MS Strategy for Lightweight Directory Access Protocol (LDAP)," available in the NT Server Technical Notes section of Microsoft TechNet or on the Web at *http://www.microsoft.com/TechNet/winnt/Winntas/technote/ldapcmr.asp*.

NNTP

Network News Transport Protocol (NNTP) is the standards-based protocol for server-to-server and client-to-server transfer of news messages, or the underlying protocol that makes possible public and private newsgroups. Outlook does not directly support the creation of accounts to access newsgroup servers, but instead relies on Outlook Express as its default newsreader (see Figure 1-13).

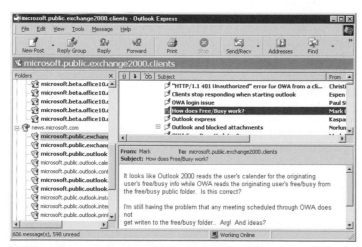

Figure 1-13. Outlook relies on Outlook Express for reading and posting to public and private newsgroups.

> **note** Microsoft Windows 2000 Server includes an NNTP service that lets a network admin-
> istrator set up a news server to host newsgroups that can be accessed by local intranet
> or remote Internet users. Exchange Server allows the NNTP service to interface with
> other public or private news servers to pull newsgroups and messages via news feeds.
> Therefore, Windows 2000 Server by itself lets you set up your own newsgroup server
> to host your own newsgroups, and Exchange Server lets you host public Internet
> newsgroups.

Using Outlook Express, you can download newsgroups, read messages, post messages, and perform other news-related tasks. Other third-party news applications,
such as Forte's Agent, offer extended capabilities. Forte's Web site is located at
http://www.forteinc.com.

> For a detailed explanation of setting up Outlook Express as a news reader, see Chapter 11,
> "Using Outlook Express for Public and Private Newsgroups."

HTML

Hypertext Markup Language (HTML) is the protocol used most commonly to define
and transmit Web pages. Several e-mail services, including Hotmail and Yahoo!, provide access to client mailboxes via Web pages and therefore make use of HTML as their
message transfer protocol. You connect to the Web site and use the features and commands found there to view messages, send messages, and download attachments.

Outlook provides enhanced HTML support, which means you can configure Outlook as
a client for HTML-based mail services. As mentioned earlier in the chapter, Outlook includes built-in support for Hotmail. HTML support is purely a server-side issue, so
HTML-based mail services other than Hotmail will have to provide Outlook support
on their own sites. Hotmail accomplishes this support programmatically by means of
Active Server Pages (ASP).

> **tip** **Find Hotmail's Outlook-based access**
>
> The URL for Hotmail's Outlook-based access is *http://services.msn.com/svcs/hotmail/*
> *httpmail.asp.* Outlook configures the URL automatically when you set up a Hotmail
> account in Outlook (see Figure 1-14). You can't browse to this URL through your
> Web browser to retrieve your e-mail, however.

Chapter 1: Outlook Architecture, Setup, and Startup

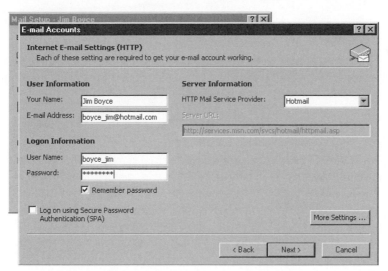

Figure 1-14. Outlook configures the URL automatically for Hotmail, but you must enter the URL manually for other HTTP-based e-mail services.

MIME

Multipurpose Internet Mail Extensions (MIME) is a standard specification for defining file formats used to exchange e-mail, files, and other documents across the Internet or an intranet. Each of the many MIME types defines the content type of the data contained in the attachment. MIME maps the content to a specific file type and extension, allowing the e-mail client to pass the MIME attachment to an external application for processing. For example, if you receive a message containing a WAV file attachment, Outlook passes the file to the default WAV file player on your system.

S/MIME

Secure Multipurpose Internet Mail Extensions (S/MIME) is a standard that allows e-mail applications to send digitally signed and encrypted messages. S/MIME is therefore a mechanism through which Outlook permits you to include digital signatures with messages to ensure their authenticity and to encrypt messages to prevent unauthorized access to them.

> For a detailed discussion of using Outlook to send digitally signed and encrypted messages, as well as other security-related issues such as virus protection and security zones, see Chapter 12, "Securing Your System, Messages, and Identity."

MHTML

MIME HTML (MHTML) represents MIME encapsulation of HTML documents. MHTML allows you to send and receive Web pages and other HTML-based documents and to embed images directly in the body of a message rather than attaching them to the message. See the preceding sections for an explanation of MIME.

iCalendar, vCalendar, and vCard

iCalendar, vCalendar, and vCard are Internet-based standards that provide a means for people to share calendar free/busy information and contact information across the Internet. The iCalendar standard allows calendar/scheduling applications to share free/busy information with other applications that support iCalendar. The vCalendar standard provides a mechanism for vCalendar-compliant applications to exchange meeting requests across the Internet. The vCard standard allows applications to share contact information as Internet vCards (electronic business cards). Outlook supports these standards in order to share information and interact with other messaging and scheduling applications across the Internet.

Security Provisions in Outlook

Outlook 2002 provides several features for ensuring the security of your data, messages, and identity. This section of the chapter presents a brief overview of security features in Outlook to give you a basic understanding of the issues involved, with references to other locations in the book that offer more detailed information on these topics.

Support for Security Zones

Like Microsoft Internet Explorer, Outlook supports the use of security zones. In Internet Explorer, security zones allow you to specify the types of actions that scripts can take on your system, based on the zone from which they were accessed. This prevents a malicious script from surreptitiously gathering information from your system and sending it to a Web site or doing local damage such as deleting files. In Internet Explorer, you can configure four zones, each with different security settings that define the tasks scripts can perform. For example, you can disable download of signed and unsigned ActiveX controls, specify how cookies are stored on your system, or disable scripting of Java applets.

Because Outlook can receive HTML-based messages, your computer is exposed to the same security risks posed by Internet browsing with Internet Explorer. The risk is actually worse with e-mail, considering that you generally make a conscious effort to visit a Web page—e-mail messages, in contrast, come at you unbidden, therefore making your system subject to a more active form of attack. By supporting Internet Explorer's security zones, Outlook allows you to specify the zone from which e-mail messages should be considered to have originated, letting you guard against HTML-based security risks.

To learn how to apply security zones to protect your system, see "Using Security Zones," page 330.

newfeature!

Attachment and Virus Security

You probably are aware that a *virus* is an application that infects your system and typically causes some type of damage. The action caused by a virus can be as innocuous as displaying a message or as damaging as deleting data from your hard disk. One especially insidious form of virus, called a *worm*, spreads itself automatically, usually by mailing itself to every contact in the infected system's address book. Guarding against such viruses, then, is a critical issue.

Outlook offers two levels of attachment security to guard against virus and worm infections, Level 1 and Level 2. Outlook automatically blocks Level 1 attachments, a category that includes almost 40 file types with the potential to allow a virus to cause damage to your system—for example, EXE and VBS files. If you receive a Level 1 attachment, Outlook displays a paper clip icon beside the message but does not allow you to open or save the attachment. When you send a Level 1 attachment, Outlook displays a reminder that other Outlook users might not be able to receive the attachment, giving you the option of converting it to a different file type (such as a ZIP file) before sending it. If you receive a Level 2 attachment, Outlook allows you to save the attachment to disk but not open it directly. You can then process the file with your virus checker before opening it.

> **tip** **Update your virus definitions often**
>
> Your virus scanner is only as good as its definition file. New viruses crop up every day, so it's critical that you have an up-to-date virus definition file and put in place a strategy to ensure that your virus definitions are always current.

If you use Exchange Server to host your mailbox, the Exchange Server administrator can configure Level 1 and Level 2 attachments, adding or removing attachment types for each level. In addition, Outlook allows all users to control the security-level assignments for attachments.

For a detailed discussion of Outlook's virus protection, see "Protecting Against Viruses in Attachments," page 360.

Macro Viruses

Although viruses were once found almost exclusively in executable files, viruses embedded in document macros have become very common, and Office documents are as subject to them as any. However, Outlook and other Office applications provide a means for you to guard against macro viruses. In Outlook, you can select one of three macro security levels, as shown in Figure 1-15 on the next page. These security levels let you configure Outlook to run only signed macros from trusted sources (High), prompt you to choose whether to let the macro execute (Medium), or allow all macros to execute (Low). You can also specify which sources are trusted.

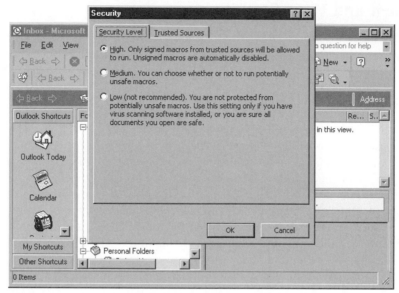

Figure 1-15. Use macro security to prevent macro-borne viruses from affecting your system.

To learn how to configure and use macro virus protection, see "Protecting Against Office Macro Viruses," page 364.

Digital Signatures

Outlook allows you to add a certificate-based digital signature to a message to validate your identity to the message recipient. Because the signature is derived from a certificate that is issued to you and that you share with the recipient, the recipient can be guaranteed that the message originated with you, rather than with someone trying to impersonate your identity.

For information about how to obtain a certificate and use it to digitally sign your outgoing messages, see "Protecting Messages with Digital Signatures," page 332.

In addition to signing your outgoing messages, you can also use secure message receipts that notify you that your message has been verified by the recipient's system. The lack of a return receipt indicates that the recipient's system did not validate your identity. In such a case, you can contact the recipient to make sure that he or she has a copy of your digital signature.

> **note** Although you can configure Outlook to send a digital signature to a recipient, there is no guarantee that the recipient will add the digital signature to his or her contacts list. Until the recipient adds the signature, digitally signed messages will not be validated, nor will the recipient be able to read encrypted messages from you.

Message Encryption

Where the possibility of interception exists (whether someone intercepts your message before it reaches the intended recipient or someone else at the recipient's end tries to read the message), Outlook message encryption can help you keep prying eyes away from sensitive messages. This feature also relies on your digital signature to encrypt the message and to allow the recipient to decrypt and read the message. Someone who receives the message without first having the public key portion of your certificate installed on his or her system will see a garbled message.

> To learn how to obtain a certificate and use it to encrypt your outgoing messages, as well as how to read encrypted messages you receive from others, see "Encrypting Messages," page 354.

newfeature!
Security Labels

The security labels feature in this version of Outlook relies on security policies in Windows 2000 (and is therefore supported only on clients running Windows 2000). Security labels let you add additional security information, such as message sensitivity, to a message header. You can also use security labels to restrict which recipients can open, forward, or send a specific message. Security labels therefore provide a quick indicator of a message's sensitivity and control over the actions that others can take with a message.

newfeature!
Understanding Outlook Service Options

If you've been using an earlier version of Outlook, you're probably familiar with Outlook's service options. Earlier versions of Outlook supported three service options: No Mail, Internet Mail Only (IMO), and Corporate/Workgroup (C/W). Outlook 2002 changes that with a new *unified mode*. Outlook unified mode refers to the integration of mail services in Outlook, which allows you to configure and use multiple services in a single profile. This means that you can use Exchange Server, POP3, IMAP, and Hotmail accounts all in one profile and at the same time.

> To learn how to work with profiles and add multiple accounts to a profile, see "Understanding User Profiles," page 44.

Part 1: Working with Outlook

Although Outlook makes a great e-mail client for a wide range of mail services, you might prefer to use only its contact management, scheduling, and other nonmessaging features and to use a different application (such as Outlook Express) for your messaging needs. There is no downside to using Outlook in this configuration, although you should keep in mind that certain features, such as integrated scheduling, rely on Outlook's messaging features. If you need to take advantage of these features, you should switch to using Outlook as your primary messaging application.

Options for Starting Outlook

Office offers several options to control startup, either through command-line switches or other methods. You can choose to have Outlook open forms, turn off the preview pane, select a profile, and perform other tasks automatically when the program starts. The following sections describe some of the options you can specify.

Normal Startup

When you install Outlook, Setup places a Microsoft Outlook icon on the desktop. You can start Outlook normally by double-clicking the icon. You also can start Outlook by using the Start menu (choose Start, Programs, Microsoft Outlook).

When Outlook starts normally and without command-line switches, it prompts you for the profile to use (see Figure 1-16) if more than one exists. The profile contains your account settings and configures Outlook for your e-mail servers, directory services, data files, and other Outlook settings.

Figure 1-16. Outlook prompts you to choose a profile at startup.

You can use multiple profiles to maintain multiple identities in Outlook. For example, you might use one profile for your work-related items and a second one for your personal items. To use an existing profile, simply choose it from the drop-down list in the Choose Profile dialog box and click OK. Click New to create a new profile (covered in Chapter 2, "Advanced Setup Tasks"). Click Options to expand the Choose Profile dialog box to include the following options (as shown in Figure 1-16):

- **Set As Default Profile.** Select this option to specify the selected profile as the default profile, which will appear in the drop-down list by default in subsequent Outlook sessions. For example, if you maintain separate personal and work profiles, and your personal profile always appears in the drop-down list, select your work profile and choose this option to make the work profile the default.

- **Show All Logon Screens.** Select this option to have Outlook prompt you for all startup options, including which address book to use; how to display names in the address book; the display name, file name, and password for your local data store; options for individual services such as Exchange Server or the Fax Mail Provider; and personal folders options.

> For an in-depth discussion of creating and configuring profiles, see "Understanding User Profiles," page 44. The details of configuring service providers (such as for Exchange Server) are covered in various chapters where appropriate—for example, Chapter 6, "Using Internet Mail," explains how to configure POP3 and IMAP accounts; and Chapter 32, "Configuring the Exchange Server Client," explains how to configure Exchange Server accounts.

newfeature!
Safe Mode Startup

Safe mode is a new startup mode available in Outlook 2002 and the other Microsoft Office XP applications. Safe mode makes it possible for Office applications to automatically recover from specific errors during startup, such as a problem with an add-in or a corrupt registry. Safe mode allows Outlook to detect the problem and either correct it or bypass it by isolating the source.

When Outlook starts automatically in safe mode, you see a dialog box that displays the source of the problem and asks whether you want to continue to open the program, bypassing the problem source, or try to restart the program again. If you direct Outlook to continue starting, the problem items are disabled, and you can view them in the Disabled Items dialog box (see Figure 1-17 on the next page). To open this dialog box, choose Help, About Microsoft Outlook, and click Disabled Items. To enable a disabled item, select the item and click Enable.

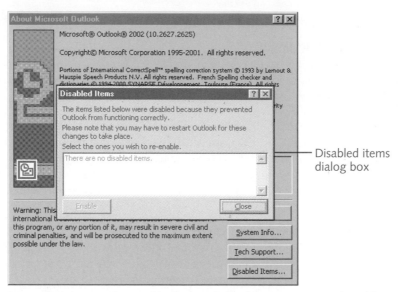

Disabled items
dialog box

Figure 1-17. Use the Disabled Items dialog box to review and enable items.

In certain situations, you might want to force Outlook into safe mode when it would otherwise start normally—for example, if you want to prevent add-ins from loading or prevent customized toolbars or command bars from loading. To start Outlook (or any other Office application) in safe mode, hold down the Ctrl key and start the program. Outlook detects the Ctrl key and asks whether you want to start Outlook in safe mode. Click Yes to start in safe mode or No to start normally.

If you start an application in safe mode, you will not be able to perform certain actions in the application. The following is a summary (not all of which apply to Outlook):

- Templates can't be saved.

- The last used Web page is not loaded (FrontPage).

- Customized toolbars and command bars are not opened. Customizations that you make in safe mode can't be changed.

- The AutoCorrect list isn't loaded, nor can changes you make to AutoCorrect in safe mode be saved.

- Recovered documents are not opened automatically.

- No smart tags are loaded, and new smart tags can't be saved.

- Command-line options other than /a and /n are ignored.

- You can't save files to the Alternate Startup Directory.

Chapter 1: Outlook Architecture, Setup, and Startup

- You can't save preferences.
- Additional features and programs (such as add-ins) do not load automatically.

To start Outlook normally, simply shut down the program and start it again without pressing the Ctrl key.

Starting Outlook Automatically

If you're like most Office users, you work in Outlook a majority of the time. Because Outlook is such an important aspect of your work day, you probably want it to start automatically when you log on to your computer, saving you the trouble of starting it later. Although you have a few options for starting Outlook automatically, the best solution is to place a shortcut to Outlook in your Startup folder.

Follow these steps to start Outlook automatically in Windows 98 and Windows 2000:

1 Close or minimize all windows on the desktop.

2 Locate the Microsoft Outlook icon on the desktop, and drag it to the Start button. Don't release the mouse button.

3 Hold the pointer over the Start menu until it opens; then, while continuing to hold down the mouse button, open the Programs menu and then the Startup menu.

4 Place the cursor on the Startup menu and release the mouse button. Windows informs you that you can't move the item and asks whether you want to create a shortcut. Click Yes.

---

tip **Create a new Outlook shortcut**

If you don't have a Microsoft Outlook icon on the desktop, you can use the Outlook executable to create a shortcut. Open Windows Explorer and browse to the folder \Program Files\Microsoft Office\Office10. Create a shortcut to the executable Outlook.exe. Note that the default syntax for the standard Microsoft Outlook shortcut is "C:\Program Files\Microsoft Office\Office10\Outlook.exe" /recycle. For an explanation of the /recycle switch and other Outlook startup options, see "Startup Switches," page 35.

You can use the following procedure to accomplish the same task in Windows 95 and Windows NT:

1 Right-click an empty area of the taskbar, and choose Properties.

2 Click the Advanced tab, and then click Advanced.

Chapter 1

3 In the resulting Windows Explorer window, open the Startup folder.

4 Using the right mouse button, drag the Microsoft Outlook icon from the desktop to the Startup folder, release it, and choose Create Shortcut(s) Here.

5 Close the Windows Explorer window and the taskbar dialog box.

---

tip **Change Outlook's shortcut properties**

If you want to change the way Outlook starts from the shortcut in your Startup folder (for example, you might want to add command switches), you need only change the shortcut's properties. For details, see "Changing the Outlook Shortcut," below.

Adding Outlook to the Quick Launch Bar

The Quick Launch bar appears by default on the taskbar just to the right of the Start menu. Quick Launch, as its name implies, gives you a way to easily and quickly start applications—just click the application's icon. By default, the Quick Launch bar includes the Show Desktop icon, as well as the Internet Explorer and Outlook Express icons (if Outlook Express is installed). Quick Launch offers easier application launching because you don't have to navigate the Start menu to start an application.

Adding a shortcut to the Quick Launch bar is easy:

1 Minimize all windows so that you can see the desktop.

2 Using the right mouse button, drag the Microsoft Outlook icon to the Quick Launch area of the taskbar and then release it.

3 Choose Create Shortcut(s) Here.

---

note You can also left-drag the Microsoft Outlook icon to the Quick Launch bar. Windows will inform you that you can't copy or move the item to that location and will ask whether you want to create a shortcut instead. Click Yes to create the shortcut or No to cancel.

Changing the Outlook Shortcut

Let's assume that you've created a shortcut to Outlook on your Quick Launch bar or in another location so that you can start Outlook quickly. Why change the shortcut? By adding switches to the command that starts Outlook, you can customize the way the application starts and functions for the current session. You can also control Outlook's startup window state (normal, minimized, maximized) through the shortcut's properties. For example, you might want Outlook to start automatically when you log on, but you want it to start minimized. In this situation, you would create a shortcut to Outlook in your Startup folder and then modify the shortcut so that Outlook starts minimized.

Chapter 1: Outlook Architecture, Setup, and Startup

To change the properties for a shortcut, first locate the shortcut, right-click its icon, and choose Properties. You should see a dialog box similar to the one shown in Figure 1-18.

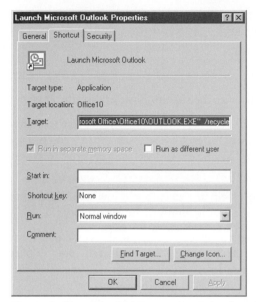

Figure 1-18. A typical Properties dialog box for an Outlook shortcut.

The following list summarizes the options on the Shortcut tab of the Properties dialog box (some of which do not appear in Windows 9*x*):

● **Target Type.** This read-only property specifies the type for the shortcut's target, which in the example shown in Figure 1-18 is Application.

● **Target Location.** This read-only property specifies the directory location of the target executable.

● **Target.** This property specifies the command to execute when the short-cut is executed. The default Outlook command is "C:\Program Files\Microsoft Office\Office10\Outlook.exe" /recycle. The path could vary if you have installed Office in a different folder. The path to the exe-cutable must be enclosed in quotes, and any additional switches must be added to the right, outside the quotes. See "Startup Switches," page 35, to learn about additional switches you can use to start Outlook.

● **Run In Separate Memory Space.** This option is selected by default and can't be changed for Outlook. All 32-bit applications run in a separate memory space. This provides crash protection for other applications and for the operating system.

● **Run As Different User.** Select this option to run Outlook in a different user context, which lets you start Outlook with a different user account from the one you used to log on to the computer. Windows will prompt you for the user name and password when you execute the shortcut.

 tip You also can use the RUNAS command from a command console (Windows NT and Windows 2000) to start an application in a different user context. For additional information, see the following section, "Use RUNAS to Change User Context."

- **Start In.** This property specifies the startup directory for the application.

- **Shortcut Key.** Use this property to assign a shortcut key to the shortcut, which will allow you to start Outlook by pressing the key combination. Simply click in the Shortcut Key box and press the keystroke to assign it to the shortcut.

- **Run.** Use this property to specify the startup window state for Outlook. You can choose Normal Window, Minimized, or Maximized.

- **Comment.** Use this property to specify an optional comment. The comment appears in the shortcut's ToolTip when you rest the pointer over the shortcut's icon. For example, if you use the Run As Different User option, you might include mention of that in the Comment box to help you distinguish this shortcut from another that launches Outlook in the default context.

- **Find Target.** Click this button to open the folder containing the Outlook.exe executable file.

- **Change Icon.** Click this button to change the icon assigned to the shortcut. By default, the icon comes from the Outlook.exe executable, which contains other icons you can assign to the shortcut. You also can use other ICO, EXE, and DLL files to assign icons. You'll find several additional icons in Moricons.dll and Shell32.dll, both located either in the Windows folder or in the %systemroot%\System32 folder (Windows NT and Windows 2000).

When you're satisfied with the shortcut's properties, click OK to close the dialog box.

Use RUNAS to Change User Context

As explained in the preceding section, you can use the option Run As Different User in a shortcut's Properties dialog box to run the target application in a different user context from the one you used to log on to the system. This option is applicable on systems running Windows NT and Windows 2000 but not on those running Windows 9x or Windows Me.

Chapter 1: Outlook Architecture, Setup, and Startup

You can also use the RUNAS command from a command console in Windows NT and Windows 2000 to run a command—including Outlook—in a different user context. The syntax for RUNAS is

```
RUNAS [/profile] [/env] [/netonly] /user:<UserName> program
```

The parameters for RUNAS can be summarized as follows:

- **/profile** Use this parameter to indicate the profile for the specified user if that profile needs to be loaded.

- **/env** Use the current user environment instead of the one specified by the user's profile.

- **/netonly** Use this parameter if the specified user credentials are for remote access only.

- **/user:<UserName>** Use this parameter to specify the user account under which you want the application to be run.

- **Program** This parameter specifies the application to execute.

Following is an example of the RUNAS command used to start Outlook in the Administrator context of the domain ADMIN. (Note that the command should be on one line on your screen.):

```
RUNAS /profile /user:admin\administrator
""C:\Program Files\Microsoft Office
\Office10\Outlook.exe" /recycle"
```

It might seem like a lot of trouble to type all that at the command prompt, and that's usually the case. Although you can use RUNAS from the command console to run Outlook in a specific user context, it's generally more useful to use RUNAS in a batch file to start Outlook in a given, predetermined user context. For example, you might create a batch file containing the sample RUNAS syntax just noted and then create a shortcut to that batch file so that you can execute it easily without having to type the command each time.

Startup Switches

Microsoft Outlook supports a number of command-line switches that modify the way the program starts and functions. Although you can issue the Outlook.exe command with switches from a command prompt, it's generally more useful to specify switches through a shortcut, particularly if you want to use the same set of switches more than once. Table 1-1 on the next page lists the startup switches you can use to modify the way Outlook starts and functions.

For an explanation of how to modify a shortcut to add command-line switches, see "Changing the Outlook Shortcut," page 32.

Table 1-1. Startup switches and their purposes

Switch	Purpose
/a *<filename>*	Open a message form with the attachment specified by *<filename>*
/c ipm.activity	Open the journal entry form by itself
/c ipm.appointment	Open the appointment form by itself
/c ipm.contact	Open the contact form by itself
/c ipm.note	Open the message form by itself
/c ipm.post	Open the discussion form by itself
/c ipm.stickynote	Open the note form by itself
/c ipm.task	Open the task form by itself
/c *<class>*	Create an item using the message class specified by *<class>*
/CheckClient	Perform a check to see whether Outlook is the default application for e-mail, news, and contacts
/CleanFreeBusy	Regenerate free/busy schedule data
/CleanReminders	Regenerate reminders
/CleanSchedPlus	Delete Schedule+ data from the server and enable free/busy data from the Outlook calendar to be used by Schedule+ users
/CleanViews	Restore the default Outlook views
/Folder	Hide the Outlook Bar and folder list if displayed in the previous session
/NoPreview	Hide the preview pane and remove Preview Pane from the View menu
/Profiles	Display the Choose Profile dialog box even if Always Use This Profile is selected in profile options
/Profile *<name>*	Automatically use the profile specified by *<name>*
/Recycle	Start Outlook using an existing Outlook window if one exists
/ResetFolders	Restore missing folders in the default message store
/ResetOutlookBar	Rebuild the Outlook Bar
/select *<folder>*	Display the folder specified by *<folder>*

Choosing a Startup View

When you start Outlook, it defaults to using Outlook Today view (see Figure 1-19), but you might prefer to use a different view or folder as the initial view. For example, if you use Outlook primarily as an e-mail client, you'll probably want Outlook to start in the Inbox. If you use Outlook mainly to manage contacts, you'll probably want it to start in the Contacts folder.

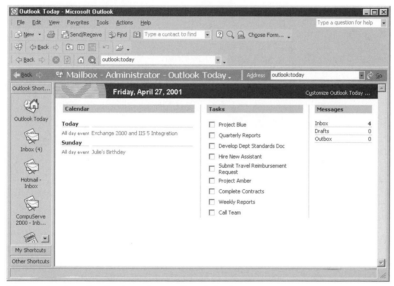

Figure 1-19. Outlook Today is the default view.

To specify the view that should appear when Outlook first starts, follow these steps:

1. Open Outlook and choose Tools, Options.

2. Click the Other tab and then click Advanced Options (see Figure 1-20).

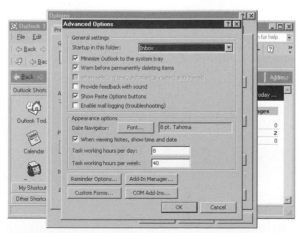

Figure 1-20. Use the Advanced Options dialog box to specify the startup view.

3 From the Startup In This Folder drop-down list, choose the folder you want Outlook to open at startup.

4 Click OK and then close the dialog box.

If you switch Outlook to a different default folder and then want to restore Outlook Today as your default view, you can follow the previous steps to restore Outlook Today as the default.

Simply select Outlook Today from the drop-down list or follow these steps with the Outlook Today window open:

1 Open Outlook and open Outlook Today view.

2 Click Customize Outlook Today at the top of the Outlook Today window.

3 On the resulting page, select When Starting Go Directly To Outlook Today and then click Save Changes.

Advanced Setup Tasks

Because Microsoft Outlook has so many features, configuring the program—particularly for first-time or inexperienced users—can be a real challenge. However, after you master the basic concepts and experiment with the configuration process, it quickly becomes second nature.

This chapter examines Outlook setup issues, including what you see the first time you start Outlook and how to use the E-Mail Accounts Wizard to create, modify, and test e-mail accounts. You'll also learn about user profiles, including how to create and modify them, how to use multiple profiles for different identities, how to copy profiles, and how to configure profile properties.

After you have a solid understanding of profiles, you're ready to tackle configuring the many e-mail and data file services Outlook offers. This chapter discusses configuring both online and offline storage and will help you add, modify, and remove personal message stores (personal folders) for a profile.

In addition, the chapter explains how to configure Outlook to maintain an offline copy of your Microsoft Exchange Server mailbox and folders so that you can work with your account while disconnected from the network. You'll also learn how to change the storage location for your data and how to set options to control mail delivery.

Starting Outlook for the First Time

The first time you run Outlook after a fresh installation (as opposed to an upgrade of an earlier version of Outlook), Outlook runs the Outlook 2002 Startup Wizard. The wizard steps you through the process of setting up e-mail accounts and *data stores* (the files used to store your Outlook data). When you've completed all the steps, Outlook opens, as shown in Figure 2-1. Note that Outlook 2002 doesn't add a welcome message to your Inbox, as it did in previous versions. Outlook configures the Outlook Bar based on the selections you made in the wizard.

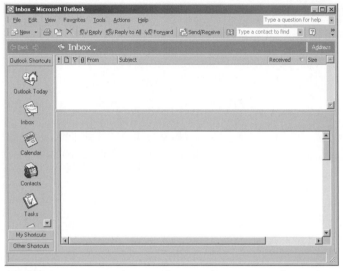

Figure 2-1.   Here's what you'll see at first startup after a clean installation.

The Startup Wizard is the same wizard you use to configure e-mail accounts after Outlook is installed. For that reason, you'll encounter this wizard again in the following section.

If you upgraded Outlook over a previous version, Outlook automatically migrates your accounts, preferences, and data the first time you run it. This means you don't have to perform any other tasks before working with Outlook 2002, unless you want to add other accounts or take advantage of features not provided by your current profile settings. In the following section, you'll learn how to add other services and accounts to your current Outlook profile.

newfeature!
Configuring Accounts and Services

Outlook 2002 provides a wizard to help simplify setup and configuration of e-mail accounts, data stores, and directory services. You use the same Startup Wizard that installs Outlook to add new e-mail accounts. When you start Outlook for the first time after a clean installation (that is, not an upgrade), Outlook runs the wizard automatically.

Follow these steps to get started setting up e-mail accounts:

1   Start Outlook. When the Outlook 2002 Startup Wizard appears, click Next.

Chapter 2: Advanced Setup Tasks

2 On the E-Mail Accounts page, click Yes, indicating that you want to set up an e-mail account, and then click Next. The wizard displays the Server Type page (see Figure 2-2).

3 Select the type of e-mail service for which you want to add an account and click Next.

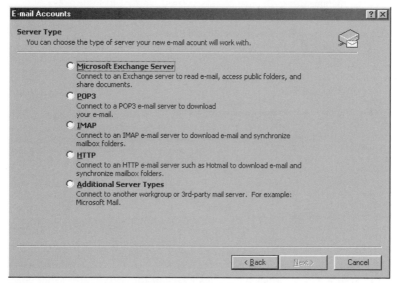

Figure 2-2. Select the type of server for the e-mail account you want to add.

> For a discussion of user profiles and how Outlook uses them to store your account settings, see "Understanding User Profiles," page 44.

The action the wizard takes at this point depends on the type of account you select. Rather than cover account configuration here outside the context of using each type of account, this book covers the specifics of each account type in the associated chapter. The following list will help you locate the appropriate chapter and section:

- **Exchange Server.** See Chapter 32, "Configuring the Exchange Server Client."

- **Internet Mail (POP3).** See "Using Internet POP3 E-Mail Accounts," page 154.

- **IMAP.** See "Using IMAP Accounts," page 161.

- **HTTP (including Hotmail and others).** See "Using Hotmail and Other HTTP-Based Services," page 165.

- **CompuServe.** See "Using Outlook with CompuServe," page 163 (includes CompuServe Classic and CompuServe 2000).

- **Fax Transport.** See "The Native Windows Fax Service," page 261.

Chapter 2

You can easily add an e-mail account to your Outlook profile after Outlook is installed.

Follow these steps to do so:

1 Right-click the Outlook icon on the desktop, choose Properties, and then click E-Mail Accounts. Or, with Outlook open, choose Tools, E-Mail Accounts to display the E-Mail Accounts Wizard, shown in Figure 2-3.

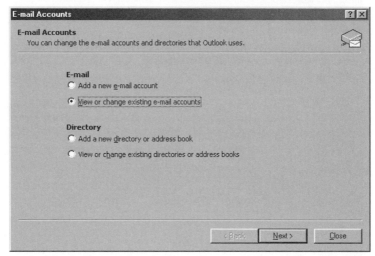

Figure 2-3. Outlook provides a wizard for adding and modifying accounts.

> **note** If your system includes multiple profiles, select the one to which you want to add accounts. Right-click the Outlook icon on the desktop and choose Properties. Click Show Profiles, locate and select your profile, and click Properties. Then select E-Mail Accounts.

2 Select Add A New E-Mail Account and click Next if you want to add an account. Select View Or Change Existing E-Mail Accounts to modify existing accounts.

3 Select the type of e-mail service to add and click Next. (As noted on the previous page, you can refer to other chapters for information about configuring specific account types.)

Testing Your E-Mail Account

Outlook offers a new feature to help you set up your e-mail account. You can now test the new account while you create it, rather than setting it up first and testing later. This helps you quickly identify problems with the account settings, such as an incorrect password or the wrong Domain Name System (DNS) name specified for the incoming or outgoing server.

Chapter 2: Advanced Setup Tasks

When you run the E-Mail Accounts Wizard, enter the settings for the account on the Settings page (see Figure 2-4). Then click Test Account Settings. Outlook locates the incoming and outgoing mail servers, logs on to the incoming mail server, and sends a test message (see Figure 2-5). If all steps are completed successfully, your account settings are correct. Difficulty with a particular step will help you identify problems with your settings, a connectivity problem, and so on. Although Outlook doesn't start a troubleshooter for you or recommend a fix, specific types of difficulties point to certain common problems. For example, if Outlook indicates that it can't find your e-mail server, the most likely problem is that you have specified the wrong DNS name (assuming that your Internet or intranet connection is working).

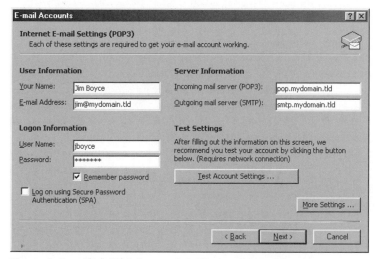

Figure 2-4. Click Test Account Settings when setting up a new account to test the account.

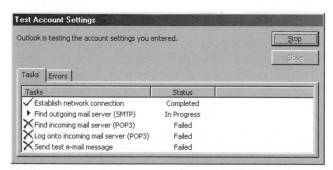

Figure 2-5. Outlook performs several tasks to check your account settings.

43

Troubleshooting

Outlook can't find your e-mail server.

If Outlook can't seem to locate your e-mail server, you can check a handful of settings to determine the problem. First, make sure your computer is connected to the network or the Internet, depending on where the server is located. If you're specifying a server on the Internet, make sure you have specified the correct, fully qualified domain name (FQDN) of the server, such as mail.proseware.tld. If you specify the correct name but Outlook still can't find the server, try pinging the server by name. Open a command console and type the following command where *<server>* is the FQDN of the server:

> *PING* <server>

If this results in an *unknown host* error, it's likely that DNS is not configured or working properly on your computer. Check the DNS settings for your TCP/IP protocol to make sure you are specifying the correct DNS server. If you know the IP address of the server, ping the address. If you are able to ping, you definitely have a DNS problem or are specifying the wrong DNS name. If the ping fails, you have a network connectivity or TCP/IP stack problem. At this point, it would be best to consult your network support staff. Your configuration will need to be verified (and changed, if an incorrect value has been specified). If you have faulty hardware, it will need to be replaced.

Understanding User Profiles

In Outlook, *user profiles* store the configuration of e-mail accounts, data files, and other settings you use in a given Outlook session. For example, your profile might include an Exchange Server account, an Internet mail account, and a set of personal folders. Outlook either prompts you to select a profile at startup or selects one automatically, depending on how you've configured it.

In most cases, you'll probably use only one profile and will configure Outlook to select it automatically. In some situations, however, multiple profiles can be useful. For example, you might prefer to keep your work and personal data completely separate on your notebook computer because of privacy concerns or office policies. In this situation, you maintain two profiles: one for your work data and a second for your personal data. You then configure Outlook to prompt you to choose a profile at startup. Choosing the profile controls which set of data files and configuration settings to use for that specific session. For example, when you're working at the office, you use the office profile—and when you're using the computer at home, you use the personal profile.

It's important to understand that Outlook profiles have no relationship to the other types of profiles you'll find in a Microsoft Windows operating system, which include *hardware profiles* and *user profiles*. Hardware profiles store hardware settings and allow you to switch between different hardware configurations without having to reconfigure your system. User profiles store the unique working environment (Desktop, My Documents, and so on) that you see when you log on to your computer. Outlook profiles, in contrast, apply only to Outlook.

> **note** Unless otherwise noted, the term *profile* in this book refers to an Outlook profile.

Each profile can contain multiple accounts and services, which means you can work with different e-mail servers at one time and use multiple sets of data files (such as a personal folders, or PST, file). The following list describes the items stored in an Outlook profile:

- **Services.** These include e-mail accounts and data files, along with their settings. For example, your profile might include an Exchange Server account, two Internet e-mail accounts, a PST file, and a directory service account. When these accounts are in a single profile, you can use all of them in the same Outlook session.

- **Delivery settings.** The profile specifies the store to which Outlook should deliver new mail when it arrives. With the exception of Internet Access Message Protocol (IMAP) accounts, which use their own PST files, all accounts use the same store location. You also can specify the order in which Outlook processes accounts.

To learn how to configure these delivery properties for a given profile, see "Setting Delivery Options," page 55.

- **Address settings.** You can specify which address book Outlook displays first; specify where Outlook should store personal addresses; and specify the order of the address books Outlook uses to check e-mail addresses when the profile includes multiple address books. In earlier versions of Outlook, you accessed these settings through the profile properties, but in Outlook 2002 you configure addressing in the Address Book window.

For detailed information on configuring and using address books in Outlook, see Chapter 5, "Managing Address Books and Distribution Lists."

The first time you run Outlook, it creates a profile called Outlook if you don't add any e-mail accounts to the profile. If you do add an e-mail account, Outlook uses the name you specify in the account settings as the name for the profile.

As explained previously, you can use multiple profiles. The following sections explain how to create new profiles, copy existing profiles to new profiles, and perform related operations.

Chapter 2

Creating Profiles

You don't have to be in Outlook to create a profile; in fact, you can't create one in Outlook. You create profiles from the desktop or via Control Panel. In addition to specifying a profile name, you can also (optionally) add e-mail and other services to the profile. You can create a profile from scratch or copy an existing profile to create a new one.

Creating a Profile from Scratch

When you have no existing Outlook profile or no profile that contains the accounts or settings you need, you must create a profile from scratch.

Follow these steps to create a new profile:

1 On the desktop, right-click the Outlook icon and choose Properties. Alternatively, open Control Panel and double-click the Mail icon.

2 In the Mail Setup dialog box (shown in Figure 2-6), click Show Profiles.

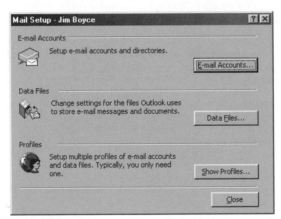

Figure 2-6. You access the current profile's settings as well as other profiles through the Mail Setup dialog box.

3 Click Add, specify a name for the profile in the New Profile dialog box, and click OK.

4 The E-Mail Accounts Wizard starts. Add accounts and other services to the profile. To create a new profile without adding any services (useful if you are not using Outlook for e-mail), click Close. In this situation, Outlook automatically creates a set of personal folders (a PST file) to store your Outlook data.

Chapter 2

Copying a Profile

In addition to creating profiles from scratch, you can also copy an existing profile to create a new one. When you copy a profile, Outlook copies all the settings from the existing profile to the new one, including accounts and data files.

Follow these steps to copy an existing profile:

1 On the desktop, right-click the Outlook icon and choose Properties. Alternatively, open Control Panel and double-click the Mail icon.

2 In the Mail Setup dialog box, click Show Profiles.

3 Select the existing profile that you want to use as the basis for the new profile and then click Copy.

4 In the Copy Profile dialog box, specify a name for the new profile and click OK.

Modifying or Removing a Profile

You can modify a profile at any time in order to add or remove services. You can also remove a profile altogether if you no longer need it.

Follow these steps to modify or remove an existing profile:

1 On the desktop, right-click the Outlook icon and choose Properties. Alternatively, open Control Panel and double-click the Mail icon.

2 In the Mail Setup dialog box, click Show Profiles.

3 Select the profile to be modified or removed.

4 Click Remove if you want to remove the profile, or click Properties to modify its settings.

Switching Profiles

You can configure Outlook either to use a specific profile automatically or to prompt you to select a profile at startup. If you want to change profiles, you need to exit Outlook and restart, selecting the appropriate profile.

Follow these steps to specify the default profile and use it automatically when Outlook starts:

1 On the desktop, right-click the Outlook icon and choose Properties. Alternatively, open Control Panel and double-click the Mail icon.

2 In the Mail Setup dialog box, click Show Profiles.

Chapter 2

47

Part 1: Working with Outlook

3 On the General tab (shown in Figure 2-7), select Always Use This Profile. In the drop-down list, select the default profile you want Outlook to use.

4 Click OK.

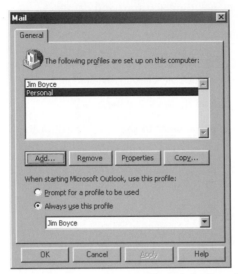

Figure 2-7. You can specify a default profile on the General tab.

Specifying the Startup Profile

If you work with multiple profiles and switch relatively often, you'll probably want to configure Outlook to prompt you to choose a profile at startup. This saves you the trouble of changing the default profile each time you want to switch. For example, assume that you use one profile for your personal accounts and another for your work accounts. Have Outlook prompt you for the profile when the program starts, rather than configuring the settings each time to specify the default profile.

Follow these steps to configure Outlook to prompt you to choose a profile:

1 On the desktop, right-click the Outlook icon and choose Properties. Alternatively, open Control Panel and double-click the Mail icon.

2 In the Mail Setup dialog box, click Show Profiles.

3 Select Always Use This Profile, select the profile you want Outlook to display as the initial selection in the list, and then select Prompt For A Profile To Be Used.

4 Click OK.

> **tip**   **Set the initial profile**
>
> You probably noticed in step 3 that you enabled an option and then immediately disabled it by selecting Prompt For A Profile To Be Used. In effect, you're accomplishing two tasks: setting the default profile and also configuring Outlook to prompt you for a profile. In the drop-down list, select the profile you use most often, which will save you the effort of selecting it when prompted at startup.

Configuring Online and Offline Data Storage

The previous section explained how to add e-mail account services and discussed data stores. This section provides a more detailed look at storage options in Outlook and how to configure those options.

Like earlier versions of Outlook, Outlook 2002 offers three options for storing data: your Exchange Server mailbox, PST files, and Offline Folder (OST) files. A store holds your Outlook data, including your Contacts, Calendar, and other folders. You can have only one default store. This means your e-mail, contacts, schedule, tasks, and other information are all stored in the same set of folders. Outlook directs all incoming e-mail to your default store. The single exception to this is an IMAP account, which stores its e-mail folders and messages separately from your other data.

> For detailed information on configuring and using IMAP accounts and how Outlook stores IMAP folders and messages, see "Using IMAP Accounts," page 161.

Although you can have only one default store, you can add other store files to a profile. You can use the other stores to organize or archive your data. For example, if you have a profile with an Exchange Server account and a POP3 account, the profile might be configured to deliver all mail to the Exchange Server mailbox. You might want to add another set of folders that you can use to separate your Internet mail from your workgroup mail, or perhaps you want to use a different store to separate your personal messages from your work-related messages. Another use for a second store file is to share data with others without exposing your default store. Whatever the situation, you need to decide which type of store is most appropriate for your default store as well as for your additional stores.

Personal Folders and Offline Folders

A PST file in Outlook 2002 is the same as the default store type in Outlook 97, 98, and 2000. You can password-protect PST files for greater security, although utilities available on the Web can bypass the password security. PST files offer encryption, providing an additional level of security. PST files do not have a built-in capability for synchronization with an Exchange Server mailbox, although you can work offline if the PST rather than the Exchange Server mailbox is configured as the default store location. If the Exchange Server mailbox is your default store, however (which is recommended), you must use an OST file to work offline.

> **tip** **Make your PST available when you're roaming**
>
> If you use a roaming Windows profile to provide a common desktop configuration regardless of the computer from which you log on, consider placing the PST (if you use one) on a network share that is available from all your logon locations. This eliminates the need to copy your PST across the network each time you log on, reducing network utilization and speeding logon time.

The format for PST files in this version of Outlook is the same as for Outlook 97, 98, and 2000, which means those systems can share a PST file created with Outlook 2002, and vice versa. This is a significant consideration if you need to share a local data file with other Outlook users who have not yet upgraded to Outlook 2002.

Adding Other Data Stores

While Outlook uses a particular store as your default store to contain your Outlook data and e-mail, you can add other store files to help you organize, separate, or archive your data.

Adding another store is easy. Just follow these steps:

1 Right-click the Outlook icon on the desktop, choose Properties, and then click Data Files. (Select the profile first, if necessary.) Or, if Outlook is running, choose Tools, Data File Management. The current storage files are listed in the Outlook Data Files dialog box.

2 Click Add, select Personal Folders file, and then click OK.

Chapter 2: Advanced Setup Tasks

3 Outlook prompts for the name and location of the file. You can specify a new file or select an existing file to add it to your current profile. Click OK after you specify the file and path.

4 Outlook next displays the Create Microsoft Personal Folders dialog box, shown in Figure 2-8. Configure settings as necessary based on the following list:

- **Name.** Specify the name by which you want the folders to be known in Outlook. This is not the file name for the store file, but you can use the same name for both if you want.

- **Encryption Setting.** Specify the encryption level for the folder file. Choose No Encryption if you don't want Outlook to encrypt your PST file. Choose Compressible Encryption if you want Outlook to encrypt the file with a format that allows compression to conserve space. Outlook does not compress the file. Instead, you must use the compression capabilities offered by your operating system (such as NTFS compression) or by a third-party application. Choose Best Encryption for highest security. PST files formatted using Best Encryption can be compressed, but not as efficiently as those that use Compressible Encryption.

- **Password.** Specify an optional password to protect your PST file from access by others.

- **Save This Password In Your Password List.** Select this option to have Outlook save the password for your PST file in your local password cache. This eliminates the need for you to enter the password each time you open the PST file. Clear this option if you want Outlook to prompt you each time (providing greater security).

5 Click OK to close the Create Microsoft Personal Folders dialog box.

Figure 2-8. Use the Create Microsoft Personal Folders dialog box to add a PST file.

> **tip** **Securing your PST file**
>
> It's possible for others to gain access to your PST file and bypass the password, even if
> you use a compression option. For best security, keep your sensitive data on the Ex-
> change Server rather than in a PST file. You can also employ NTFS permissions to se-
> cure the folder where your PST file is located, granting applicable permissions only to
> those users who need access to that folder or your PST file.

Removing Data Stores

Occasionally, you might want to remove a data store from a profile—perhaps you've
been using a PST file as your primary store and are now moving to an Exchange Server
with an OST file for offline use.

To remove a data store from a profile, you use steps similar to those you followed to
add a store:

1 Right-click the Outlook icon on the desktop, choose Properties, and then
click Data Files. (Select the profile first if necessary.) Or, if Outlook is running,
choose Tools, Data File Management. The current storage files are listed in
the Outlook Data Files dialog box.

2 Select the data file to remove from the profile and click Remove; then click
Yes to verify the action.

3 Click Close and then close the remaining dialog boxes.

When you remove a data file from a profile, Outlook does not delete the file itself. This
means you can later add the file back to a profile if you need to access its contents. If
you don't need the data stored in the file or if you've already copied the data to a different store, you can delete the file. Open the folder where the file is located and delete it
as you would any other file.

Configuring Offline Storage

Configuring an offline store allows you to continue working with data stored in your
Exchange Server mailbox when the server is not available (if your computer is disconnected from the network, for example). As soon as the server becomes available again,
Outlook synchronizes the data either automatically or manually—according to the way
you have configured Outlook.

For a detailed explanation of folder synchronization, see "Controlling Synchronization and
Send/Receive Times," page 190.

As in earlier versions of Outlook, Outlook 2002 supports the use of an OST file to
serve as an offline cache for Exchange Server. This method is compatible with all versions of Exchange Server, including Exchange Server 2000.

Chapter 2: Advanced Setup Tasks

Using an OST File

You can use an OST file to provide offline capability for your Exchange Server mailbox. You do not need to use a PST file in conjunction with the OST file—the OST file can be your only local store file, if you want. However, you can use other PST store files in addition to your OST file.

> **note** The OST file does not appear as a separate set of folders in Outlook. In effect, the OST file is hidden and Outlook uses it transparently when your computer is offline. For more information, see "Working Offline with Exchange Server," page 859.

Follow these steps to configure offline storage with an OST file:

1 Right-click the Outlook icon on the desktop, choose Properties, and then click E-Mail Accounts. If Outlook is running, choose Tools, E-Mail Accounts.

2 Select View Or Change Existing E-Mail Accounts and click Next, and then select the Exchange Server account and click Change.

3 Click More Settings to display the Microsoft Exchange Server dialog box. Click the Advanced tab, and then click Offline Folder File Settings to open the dialog box shown in Figure 2-9.

Figure 2-9. Specify the file name and other settings for the OST file.

4 Specify a path and name for the OST file in the File box, select the encryption setting, and click OK.

5 Click OK to close the Offline Folder File Settings dialog box.

6 Click Next and then click Finish.

Part 1: Working with Outlook

Changing Your Data Storage Location

On occasion, you might need to move a data file from one location to another. For example, perhaps you've been using a local PST file and now want to place that file on a network share for use with a roaming profile, so that you can access the file from any computer on the network.

Moving a PST file is a manual process. You must shut down Outlook, move the file, and then reconfigure the profile accordingly.

Follow these steps to move a PST file:

1 Shut down Outlook, right-click the Outlook icon on the desktop, and choose Properties.

2 Select a profile if necessary, and then click Data Files to display the Outlook Data Files dialog box (see Figure 2-10).

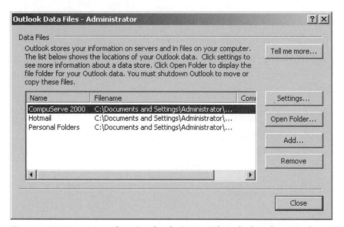

Figure 2-10. Use the Outlook Data Files dialog box to locate the existing PST.

3 Select the PST you want to move and click Open Folder. Outlook opens the folder where the PST is located and highlights the file's icon.

4 Drag the file or use the clipboard to move the file to the desired location; then close the folder.

5 Back in the Outlook Data Files dialog box, click Settings. Click OK at the error message.

6 Browse to the new location of the PST, select it, and click Open; then click OK.

7 Click Close to close the Outlook Data Files dialog box; then click Close again to close the Mail Setup dialog box.

newfeature!
Setting Delivery Options

Outlook uses one data store location as the default location for delivering messages and storing your other Outlook items. You can change the store location if needed. You also can specify the order in which Outlook processes e-mail accounts, which determines the server Outlook uses (where multiple servers are available) to process outgoing messages. The order also determines the order in which Outlook checks the servers for new messages.

For example, assume that you have an Exchange Server account and a POP3 account for your personal Internet mail. If the Exchange Server account is listed first, Outlook will send messages destined for Internet addresses through the Exchange Server. In many cases, however, this might not be what you want. For example, you might want all personal mail to go through your POP3 account and work-related mail to go through your Exchange Server account.

You have two ways to change the e-mail service that Outlook uses to send a message: you can configure the service order, or you can specify the account to use when you create the message.

Follow these steps to configure the service order for your e-mail:

1 Right-click the Outlook icon on the desktop and choose Properties. Alternatively, with Outlook open, choose Tools, E-Mail Accounts to display the E-Mail Accounts Wizard.

2 If your system includes multiple profiles, select the one to which you want to add accounts. Click Show Profiles, locate and select your profile, and click Properties. Then select E-Mail Accounts.

3 Click View Or Change Existing E-Mail Accounts and click Next.

4 Select accounts and use the Move Up and Move Down buttons to change the order of the accounts in the list (see Figure 2-11 on the next page).

5 Click Finish.

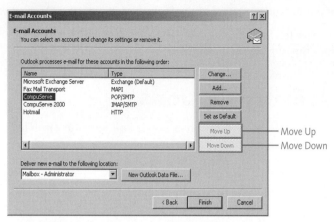

Figure 2-11. Use Move Up and Move Down to configure account order.

When you compose a message, you can override the default e-mail service that Outlook uses to send messages simply by selecting the account before sending the message.

To select the account, follow these steps:

1 Compose the message. Before sending it, click the Accounts button on the toolbar.

2 Select the account you want to use to send the message, make any other changes to options as needed, and click Send.

Chapter 3

Working in and Configuring Outlook

If you've used earlier versions of Microsoft Outlook, you'll find that the interface in Outlook 2002 hasn't changed that much, and you should have no problem getting started. If you're new to Outlook entirely, however, you need to become familiar with its interface, which is the main focus of this chapter.

Outlook presents your data using different views, and this chapter shows you how to customize the way those views look. The chapter also examines other standard elements of the interface, including toolbars, the Outlook Bar, the folder list, and the preview pane. You'll also learn how to use multiple Outlook windows and views and navigate your way through the Outlook interface.

This chapter looks at the various ways you can configure Outlook, explaining settings that control a broad range of options, from e-mail and spelling to security. In addition, you'll learn about settings in your operating system that affect how Outlook functions. Where appropriate, the text refers you to other chapters where configuration information is discussed in detail in the context of a particular feature or function.

Web access has been expanded and improved in Outlook, and this chapter examines that Web integration. You'll learn about browsing the Web with Outlook, using the desktop conferencing options available in Outlook, and accessing your Microsoft Exchange Server e-mail through a Web browser. The chapter finishes with a discussion of add-ins, which can enhance Outlook's functionality.

Understanding the Outlook Folders

Outlook uses a standard set of folders to organize your data. Once you're comfortable working with these standard folders, you'll be able to change their location, customize their appearance, or even create additional folders, as you'll learn throughout this book.

The following list describes the default Outlook folders:

Calendar This folder contains your schedule, including appointments, meetings, and events.

Contacts This folder stores information about people, such as name, address, phone number, and a wealth of other data.

Deleted Items This folder stores deleted Outlook items and can contain items of various types (contacts, messages, and tasks, for example). You can recover items from the Deleted Items folder, giving you a way to "undelete" an item if you've made a mistake or changed your mind. If you delete an item from this folder, however, the item is deleted permanently.

Drafts Use this folder to store unfinished drafts of messages and other items. For example, you can use the Drafts folder to store a lengthy e-mail message you haven't had a chance to finish yet. Or you might start a message, have second thoughts about sending it, and place it in the Drafts folder until you decide whether to send it.

Inbox Outlook delivers your e-mail to this folder. Keep in mind that, depending on the types of e-mail accounts in your profile, you might have more than one Inbox in locations other than your default information store. For example, if you have an IMAP account and an Exchange Server account, you'll have an Inbox folder for each.

Journal The Journal folder stores your journal items, allowing you to keep track of phone calls, time spent on a project, important e-mail messages, and other events and tasks.

Notes The Notes folder stores and organizes notes. You can move or copy notes to other folders in Outlook as well as to folders on disk (such as your desktop). You can also create shortcuts to notes.

Outbox The Outbox stores outgoing messages until those messages are delivered to their destination servers. You can configure Outlook to deliver messages immediately after you send them or have the messages wait in your Outbox until you process them (by synchronizing with the Exchange Server or performing a send/receive operation through your POP3 account, for example).

Sent Items The Sent Items folder stores a copy of messages you have sent. You can configure Outlook to automatically store a copy of each sent item in this folder.

Tasks The Tasks folder lists tasks that have been assigned to you or that you have assigned either to yourself or to others.

Working with the Standard Outlook Views

Before you can become proficient at using Outlook, you need to be familiar with its standard views and other elements of its interface. This section introduces you to Outlook's standard views, including information on how to work with them and customize them to meet your needs.

Outlook Today

Outlook provides default views of its standard folders as well as one additional view that is a summary of your schedule, tasks, and e-mail for the current day. This view, called Outlook Today, is the default view when you perform a clean installation of Outlook. To switch to this view if you have selected a different default view or if you are in another folder, click Outlook Today on the Outlook Bar (under Outlook Shortcuts). Figure 3-1 shows a typical Outlook Today view. In the calendar section on the left, Outlook summarizes your schedule for the current day, showing each appointment with time and title. You can easily view the details of a particular appointment by clicking the appointment time or title to open it.

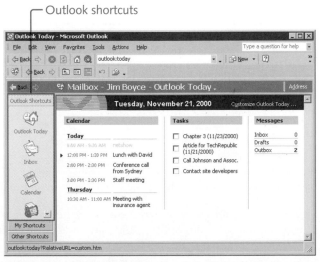

Figure 3-1. Outlook Today, the default Outlook view, lets you see your day at a glance.

In the middle column, Outlook Today lists your tasks for the current day, including overlapping tasks whose duration is longer than one day. The list includes a title and completion date for each task, along with a check box. You can mark the task as completed by selecting the check box; doing so crosses out the task in the list. If the check box is cleared, the task is incomplete.

The third column in Outlook Today lists the number of messages in your Inbox, Drafts, and Outbox folders. If the number appears in bold, the associated folder contains unread messages.

> For details on customizing the Outlook Today view to display additional information (including the use of HTML code in such customization), see "Customizing Outlook Today View," page 623.

Inbox

The Inbox displays your default message store (see Figure 3-2). For example, if you use an Exchange Server account and store your data on the Exchange Server, the Inbox view shows the Inbox folder on the Exchange Server. If you've configured Outlook to deliver messages to a local store (such as a PST file), the Inbox view shows the contents of the Inbox folder in that store.

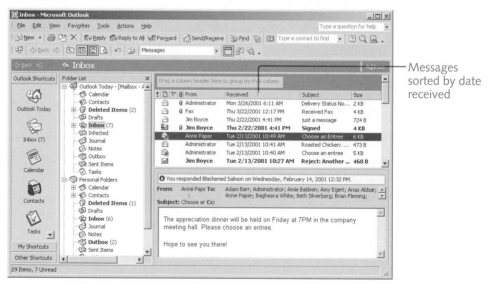

Messages sorted by date received

Figure 3-2. The Inbox view shows the contents of the Inbox folder of your default store.

As you can see in Figure 3-2, the Inbox view shows the message header for each message, including such information as sender, subject, and date and time received in various columns. You can easily sort messages by clicking on the column header for the column you want to use as the sort criterion. For example, to quickly locate messages from a specific sender, you can click the From column header to sort the list alphabetically by sender. To switch between ascending and descending sort, simply click the column header again. An up arrow beside the column name indicates an ascending sort (such as A to Z), and a down arrow indicates a descending sort (such as Z to A).

To learn how to add and remove columns and change their appearance and order, see "Customizing the Inbox View," page 63.

By default, Outlook shows the following columns in the Inbox view:

- **Importance.** This column indicates the level of importance, or priority, the sender has assigned to a message—Low, Normal, or High. A High priority message is accompanied by an exclamation mark, while a down arrow marks a Low priority message. No icon is displayed for a message of Normal importance.

tip After you've received a message, you can change its priority status by right-clicking the message, choosing Options, and specifying a new importance level.

- **Icon.** The icon column indicates the type of message and its status. For example, unopened messages are accompanied by a closed envelope icon, and read messages are accompanied by an open envelope icon.

- **Flag Status.** In this column, you can flag messages for follow-up action. For example, you can flag a message that requires you to place a call, to forward the message, or to respond at a particular time. You specify the action, date, and time for follow-up. Outlook displays a reminder for flagged items based on the flag settings you specify. To flag a message, right-click the message header and choose Follow Up. To mark the follow-up task as completed and change the flag icon, right-click the flagged message and choose Flag Complete. Choose Clear Flag to remove the follow-up.

For detailed information on flagging messages for follow-up and other ways to manage and process messages, see "Flagging and Monitoring Messages and Contacts," page 226.

- **Attachment.** The Attachment column displays a paper clip icon if the message includes one or more attachments. Right-click a message and choose View Attachments to view the attachments, or simply double-click an attachment in the preview pane.

caution Although Outlook provides protection against viruses and worms by preventing you from opening certain types of attachments, this is no guarantee against infection. Your network administrator might have modified the blocked attachments lists, or you might have modified your blocked attachments list locally, to allow a specific attachment type susceptible to infection to come through. So you should still exercise caution when viewing attachments, particularly from unknown sources. It's a good practice to save attachments to disk and run a virus scan on them before opening them.

Chapter 3

61

- **From.** This column shows the name or address of the sender.

- **Subject.** This column shows the subject, if any, assigned by the sender to the message.

- **Received.** This column indicates the date and time the message was received

- **Size.** This column indicates the overall size of the message, including attachments.

Time Is Relative

The date and time displayed in the Inbox's Received column can be a little deceiving. This data reflects the time the message was placed in your message store. If you're working online with an Exchange Server account, for example, Outlook shows the time the message was placed in the Inbox folder for your mailbox on the Exchange Server. If the time on your computer isn't coordinated with the time on the server, the time you actually receive the message could be different from the time reflected in the message header. For sent messages (in the Sent Items folder), the time indicated is the time the message was placed in your Outbox. If you're working offline, that time could differ from the time the message is actually sent.

Previewing Messages

Another part of the Inbox view is the preview pane, which appears at the bottom of the view. You can use the preview pane to preview messages without opening them in a separate window. The scroll bar on the right of the preview pane lets you scroll through the message. The top of the preview pane presents information about the message, such as sender, recipient, subject, and attachments. You can double-click most of the items in the preview pane header to see detailed information about the item. For example, you can double-click the name in the From field to display information about the sender (see Figure 3-3). Use this method to quickly copy contact information about the sender from the message to your Personal Address Book. You can also double-click attachments to open them. Right-clicking an item opens its shortcut menu, from which you can choose a variety of actions to perform on the item—for instance, you can right-click an attachment and choose Save As to save the attachment to disk. Experiment by right-clicking items in the preview pane to see which actions you can take for specific items.

tip If a message has been flagged for follow-up, information about the follow-up (the specific action, the date due, and so on) also appears in the preview pane header.

Chapter 3: Working in and Configuring Outlook

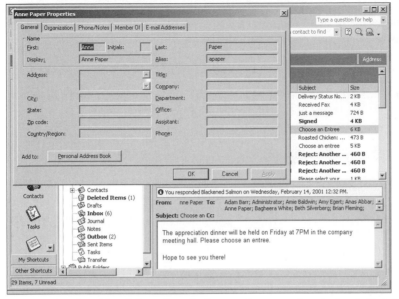

Figure 3-3. Double-click an item in the preview pane header to view detailed information about the item.

> **tip** To turn the preview pane on or off, choose View, Preview Pane.

> For detailed information on using and customizing the preview pane in various folders, see "Using the Preview Pane," page 86.

The AutoPreview feature also allows you to preview your messages. With message folders such as the Inbox, AutoPreview displays the first three lines of a message below its message header in the main folder window. This leaves you free to preview the first few lines of a message without opening the message or even selecting it. You can use AutoPreview in conjunction with or instead of the preview pane.

> For additional information on configuring and using AutoPreview, see "Using AutoPreview," page 87.

Customizing the Inbox View

Outlook offers a wealth of settings that you can use to control messaging. In addition, you also have quite a bit of control over the appearance of the Inbox and other message folders. For example, you can change the column headings included in the Inbox or add and remove columns. The following sections explore specific ways to customize the Inbox (which apply to other message folders as well).

> For detailed information on configuring messaging and other options, see "Configuring Outlook Options," page 88.

Adding and removing columns   By default, Outlook displays only a small subset of the available fields for messages. You can add columns for other fields, such as CC or Sensitivity, to show additional information.

To add and remove columns, follow these steps:

1 Open the folder you want to modify, right-click the column header bar, and choose Field Chooser to display the Field Chooser dialog box, shown in Figure 3-4.

Figure 3-4.   Add or remove columns by using the Field Chooser dialog box.

2 Locate the name of the field you want to add, and then drag the field to the desired location on the column header bar. Outlook displays arrows on the top and bottom of the column header bar to indicate where the column will be inserted.

3 Add other fields if necessary.

4 To remove a field, drag the field from the column header bar to the Field Chooser dialog box.

5 Close the Field Chooser dialog box.

You can choose other types of fields by selecting a type from the drop-down list at the top of the Field Chooser dialog box. You can also use this dialog box to create custom fields.

Outlook also provides another method for adding and removing columns in message folders:

1 Right-click the column header bar, choose Customize Current View, and then click Fields to display the Show Fields dialog box (see Figure 3-5).

Chapter 3: Working in and Configuring Outlook

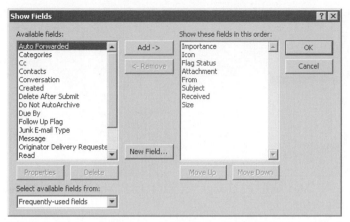

Figure 3-5. You can also use the Show Fields dialog box to add or remove columns.

2 To add a column, select the field from the Available Fields list and click Add.

3 To remove a column from the folder view, select the field from the Show These Fields In This Order list and click Remove.

4 Click OK to have your changes take effect.

Changing column order   In a message folder, Outlook defaults to displaying columns in a specific order, but you can easily change the order. The simplest way is to drag a column header to the desired location. You also can right-click the column header bar, choose Customize Current View, click Fields to display the Show Fields dialog box (shown in Figure 3-5), and use the Move Up and Move Down buttons to change the column order.

Changing column names   Outlook uses a default set of names for the columns it displays in message folders. However, you can change those column names—for example, you might want to rename the From column to Sender.

To change a column name, follow these steps:

1 Right-click the column header bar and choose Format Columns to display the Format Columns dialog box, shown in Figure 3-6 on the next page.

2 From the Available Fields list, select the field whose column header you want to change.

3 In the Label box, type the label you want displayed in the column header for the selected field.

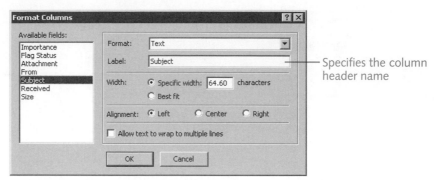

Specifies the column header name

Figure 3-6. You can change several column characteristics, including column header name.

4 Repeat steps 2 and 3 for other fields you want to change.

5 Click OK to apply the changes.

> **tip** **Make other changes in column display**
>
> You can't change the name of the Importance, Flag Status, or Attachment column. However, you can switch between using a symbol or text in the Importance and Flag Status columns. You can change the Attachment column to display either the paper clip icon or the text True/False, On/Off, or Yes/No, depending on whether the message has an attachment.

Changing column width   If a column isn't wide enough to show all the information for the field or if you need to make room for more columns, you might want to change the column width. The easiest way to change the width of a column is to drag the edge of the column header in the column header bar to resize it. Alternatively, you can right-click the column header bar, choose Format Columns, and specify a column width in the Format Columns dialog box (see Figure 3-6).

> **tip** **Automatically size columns**
>
> Use the Best Fit option in the Format Columns dialog box to automatically size the selected column, based on the amount of data it needs to display. Outlook examines the data for the field in the existing messages and resizes the column accordingly.

Changing column alignment   By default, all the columns are left-aligned in message folders, including the Inbox. You can, however, justify the columns to display to the left, right, or center. For example, you might want to change the format

Chapter 3

for the Size column to show only numbers and then display it right-justified. Simply right-click the column header bar and choose Format Columns. In the Format Columns dialog box (shown earlier in Figure 3-6), select the column to change and click Left, Center, or Right, depending on the type of justification you want.

Changing column data format Each default column in a message folder displays its data using a particular format. For example, the From column shows only the sender, not the recipient. Although in most cases the specified recipient is you, that isn't the case when the message you've received is a carbon copy. You might, then, want to change the data format of the From column to also display the person specified in the To field of the message. Other columns also offer different formats. For example, you can change the data format used by time and date fields such as Received or Sent to show only the date rather than date and time.

To change the data format used for a particular column, right-click the column header bar and choose Format Columns. In the Format Columns dialog box (shown in Figure 3-6), select the column whose format you want to change and then select the format from the Format drop-down list. The available formats vary according to the field selected.

Grouping messages Outlook offers many ways to organize and display your data. A good example of this flexibility is the option of grouping messages based on a hierarchy of criteria. For example, you might want to group messages in your Inbox first by subject, and then by sender, and then by date received, as shown in Figure 3-7.

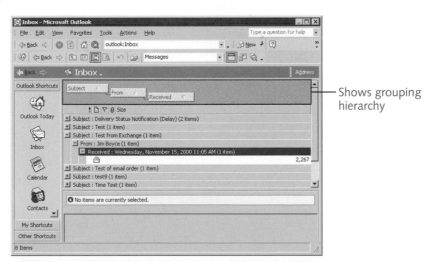

Shows grouping hierarchy

Figure 3-7. These messages are organized by three fields.

To organize your messages based on a particular column, you can simply right-click the column and choose Group By This Field.

For more complex groupings, follow these steps:

1 Right-click the column header bar and choose Group By Box to display the Group By box above the column header bar.

2 To set up a grouping, drag a column header from the column header bar to the Group By box.

3 To set up an additional level of grouping, drag another column header to the Group By box. Repeat this process until you have as many levels of grouping as you need.

To hide or show the Group By box, right-click the column header bar and choose Group By Box again. To expand or collapse your view of a group of messages, click the plus sign (+) and minus sign (–) icons next to the group or message.

> For a detailed explanation of grouping and sorting, along with several other topics that will help you organize your data, see "Grouping Messages by Customizing the Folder View," page 230.

Calendar

In the Calendar folder, you can look at your schedule in several different ways. By default, the calendar view shows the current day's schedule as well as the Date Navigator (a monthly calendar) and the TaskPad, which displays tasks that overlap or fall on the current day (see Figure 3-8).

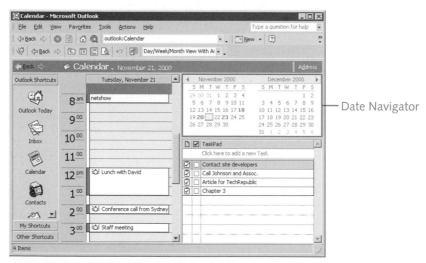

Figure 3-8. The default calendar view shows your schedule and tasks.

Your schedule shows the subject for each scheduled item—a brief description of a meeting or an appointment, for example—beside its time slot, blocking out the time assigned to the item. Items that overlap in the schedule are displayed side by side, as shown in Figure 3-9.

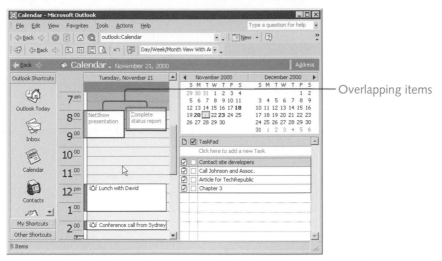

Figure 3-9. Overlapping items appear side by side in your schedule.

Working with the Schedule

The calendar view by default shows only the subject for each item scheduled in the period displayed. You can open the item to modify it or view details about it by double-clicking the item, which opens its form, shown in Figure 3-10.

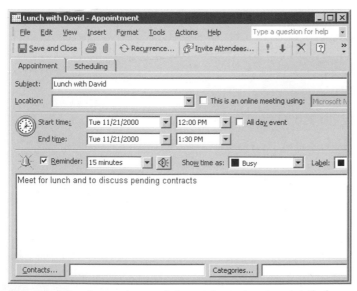

Figure 3-10. A sample appointment form showing details for a selected appointment.

You can add an item to your schedule by using one of these methods:

- Double-click the time slot of the start time you want to assign to the item.

- Right-click a time slot and choose the type of item to create (an appointment, a meeting, or an event).

- Select a time slot and then choose File, New to select the item type.

- Click the down arrow beside New on the Standard toolbar and select the item type.

The first method opens an appointment form. The form opened by the other three methods depends on the type of item you select.

Changing the start or end time for an item in the schedule is also easy. To move an item to a different time without changing its duration, simply drag the item to the new time slot. To change start or end time only, place the pointer over the top or bottom edge of the item and drag it to the desired time.

Using the Calendar's Preview Pane

Like the Inbox and other message views, the calendar view has a preview pane that lets you preview appointments and other items in your schedule without opening them. Just click the item to have it appear in the preview pane (see Figure 3-11). To turn the preview pane on or off, choose View, Preview Pane. To display more or less information in the pane, drag the top edge of the preview pane to resize it. You can also make other changes to the displayed item—such as subject and times—through the preview pane.

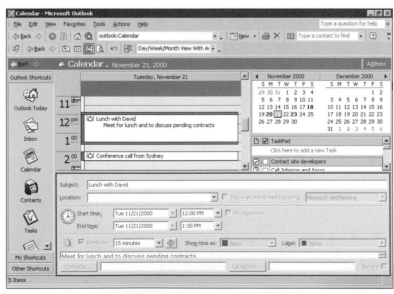

Figure 3-11. Use the preview pane in the Calendar view to preview scheduled items.

Using the TaskPad

The TaskPad, which appears at the bottom right of the default calendar view, displays a list of your tasks. By default, the TaskPad shows the tasks for the current day. However, you can change the types of tasks displayed by choosing View, TaskPad View and selecting the types of tasks you want Outlook to show, such as overdue tasks, tasks for the following week, or all tasks. You can mark a task as completed by selecting the check box beside the task name. As you can in the Inbox and other views, you can change the format of the columns displayed in the TaskPad: right-click the TaskPad column header bar and choose Format Columns.

> For more information about the TaskPad and the features Outlook provides for working with and assigning tasks, see Chapter 20, "Managing Your Tasks."

Using the Date Navigator

The monthly calendars in the upper right area of the calendar view are collectively called the Date Navigator. This feature is useful not only as a calendar but also as a way to provide a fast glance at how heavily scheduled your time is. Days with a scheduled item appear in bold, while those without scheduled items appear in a normal font. You can view a particular day by clicking it. Click the arrow at the left or right of the Date Navigator to change which months are displayed. You can also click the column header bar above either month to choose which month to view.

> **tip**   **Specify the Date Navigator's font**
>
> You can configure the Date Navigator to display all dates in normal text rather than using bold for days that contain items. Choose View, Current View, Customize Current View and click Other Settings. Clear the Bolded Dates In Date Navigator Represent Days Containing Items check box and then click OK.

You can change the number of months displayed by the Date Navigator by resizing the display, resizing the Calendar folder's window, or changing the font used by the Date Navigator. Assign a smaller font to show more months. (For details on how to change the Date Navigator's font, see "Setting Advanced Options," page 97.)

Customizing the Calendar View

Although the default calendar view shows only the subject for a scheduled item, you can configure the view to show additional detail—or you can change the view completely. For example, you can switch from a daily view to one that shows the work week, the calendar week, or the month. You can see an example of Work Week view in Figure 3-12, Week view in Figure 3-13 (both on the next page), and Month view in Figure 3-14 on page 73. To select a particular view, choose View and then choose Day, Work Week, Week, or Month, according to the type of view you want.

Chapter 3

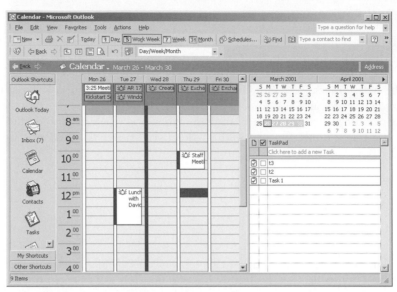

Figure 3-12. Use Work Week view to organize your work schedule.

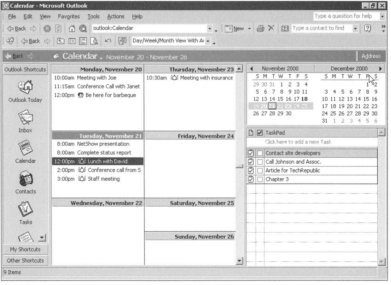

Figure 3-13. Week view can help you plan your entire week, both personal and work time.

Chapter 3: Working in and Configuring Outlook

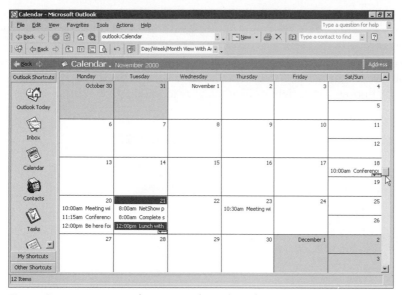

Figure 3-14. Use Month view to plan a broader range of time.

You have additional options for viewing your schedule in the Calendar folder. Choose the View command and then one of the following to change the view:

- **Day/Week/Month.** Shows the item title only in each view (Day, Work Week, Week, or Month).

- **Day/Week/Month With AutoPreview.** Includes AutoPreview in Day and Work Week views. With AutoPreview, Outlook displays as much of the data for the item as possible in the current view.

- **Active Appointments.** Shows only active appointments.

- **Events.** Shows only events.

- **Annual Events.** Shows only annual events.

- **Recurring Appointments.** Displays recurring appointments.

- **By Category.** Displays scheduled items grouped according to their assigned categories.

> For additional information on customizing the way Outlook displays information in the various calendar views, see Chapter 18, "Scheduling Appointments."

Contacts

The Contacts folder stores all your contact information. By default, the Contacts folder displays Address Cards view (see Figure 3-15 on the next page), which shows the name for each contact along with other selected fields (address and phone number, for

73

example). You can view the details for a contact by double-clicking the contact's address card, which opens the contact form, shown in Figure 3-16. Using this form, you can view or make changes to the contact's data or perform other tasks, such as calling the contact, generating a meeting request, or viewing a map of the contact's address. If you have a large number of contact entries stored in the Contacts folder, you can click the buttons at the right edge of the view to select which portion of the contacts list to show.

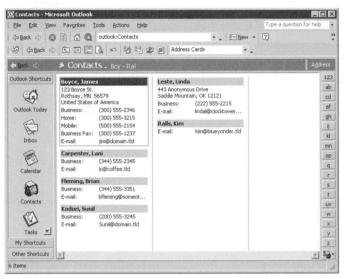

Figure 3-15. By default, the Contacts folder displays Address Cards view.

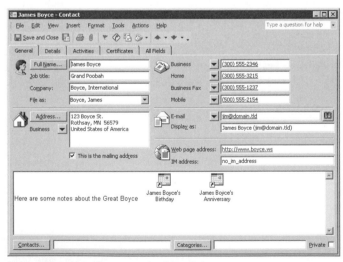

Figure 3-16. When you double-click a contact entry, you can view the contact form for that person.

> For a detailed discussion of working with contacts, including the actions you can take with the contact form, see Chapter 14, "Managing Your Contacts."

Outlook offers several other ways to view the contents of your Contacts folder. Choose View, Current View and then one of the following commands to change the view:

- **Address Cards.** Displays the name of each contact along with other selected data.

- **Detailed Address Cards.** Shows additional detailed information for each contact, including the person's title, the company the person works for, personal notes, and more.

- **Phone List.** Displays the contacts as a phone list.

- **By Category.** Groups contacts by their assigned categories.

- **By Company.** Groups contacts by the company with which they're affiliated.

- **By Location.** Groups contacts by country or region.

- **By Follow-Up Flag.** Groups contacts by the status of follow-up flags on their entries.

Adding contact entries to your Contacts folder is easy: Just right-click in the contacts view and choose New Contact, or click New on the toolbar. Either action opens the contact form, in which you enter the contact's data.

Customizing the Contacts View

Like other views in other folders, the view in the Contacts folder can be customized to suit your needs and preferences. For example, you can adjust the view to display additional fields of information or to remove fields you don't need. You can sort the view based on specific contact criteria or group like items together based on multiple criteria. For details about customizing the Contacts folder view, see Chapter 14, "Managing Your Contacts."

Tasks

The Tasks folder contains your task list. The default tasks view (see Figure 3-17 on the next page) lists each task in a simple list with subject, due date, and status. Double-click an existing task to open the task form, which displays detailed information about the task, including due date, start date, status, notes, and so on (see Figure 3-18 on the next page). To add a new task to the list, double-click a blank list entry to open a new task form, where you can enter all the details about the task.

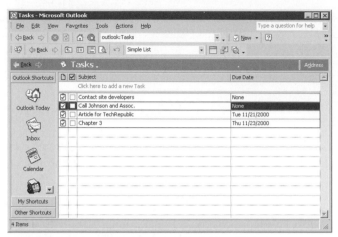

Figure 3-17. By default, the Tasks folder displays this view.

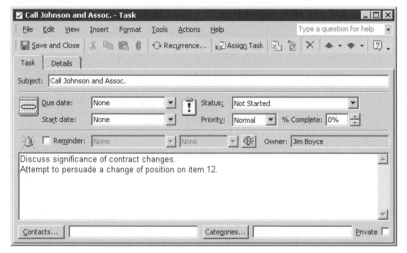

Figure 3-18. Use a task form to create a new task.

The task list shows tasks you've assigned to others as well as those tasks assigned to you (by yourself or by others). These assignments can be one-time or recurring, and the list shows both in-progress and completed tasks.

Like other Outlook views, the tasks view provides a preview pane you can use to view details for a task without opening the task item. To turn on the preview pane, choose View, Preview Pane. AutoPreview is also available in the Tasks folder; it displays notes about the task below the task name (see Figure 3-19).

Chapter 3: Working in and Configuring Outlook

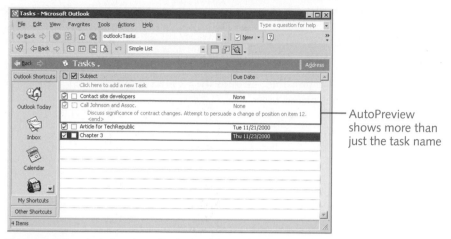

Figure 3-19. AutoPreview displays additional information about a task below the task name in the list.

Customizing the Tasks View

You can customize the view in the Tasks folder in a variety of ways—adding and removing columns, changing column names, or organizing tasks by category or other properties, to list a few. To customize the columns, right-click the column header bar and choose Format Columns. The resulting dialog box allows you to select the format for each column, change the name, apply justification, and so on. To change the order of columns in the view, simply drag the column headers into the desired positions, resizing as needed.

You can also organize your task list in various ways. You can click column headers to sort the columns in ascending or descending order, and you can group the columns based on a particular field or group of fields, just as you can in the Inbox and other Outlook folders.

You can also choose View, Current View and then one of the following commands to change the Tasks Folder view:

- **Simple List.** Shows whether the task has been completed, the task name, and the due date.

- **Detailed List.** Shows status, percent complete, and categories in addition to the information displayed in Simple List view.

- **Active Tasks.** Displays tasks that are active.

- **Next Seven Days.** Displays tasks for the next seven days.

● **Overdue Tasks.** Displays incomplete tasks whose due dates have passed.

● **By Category.** Organizes the task list by the categories assigned to tasks.

● **Assignment.** Shows the tasks assigned to specific people.

● **By Person Responsible.** Groups the view according to the person responsible for the various tasks.

● **Completed Tasks.** Shows only completed tasks.

● **Task Timeline.** Displays a timeline of all tasks.

> For more information on customizing the view in the Tasks folder, see "Viewing and Customizing the Tasks Folder," page 564.

Notes

With its notes feature, Outlook helps you organize your thoughts and tasks. Each note can function as a stand-alone window, allowing you to view notes on your desktop outside Outlook. The notes view provides a look into your Notes folder, where your notes are initially stored. From there, you can copy or move them to other locations (such as the desktop) or create shortcuts to them. By default, the initial notes view displays the notes as icons, with the first line of the note serving as the title under the note's icon (see Figure 3-20).

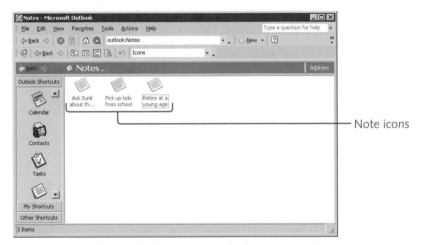

Figure 3-20. The standard notes view displays notes as icons.

As it does for other folders, Outlook offers several other ways to view the Notes folder. Choose Views, Current View and then one of the following:

- **Icons.** Displays an icon for each note, with the first line of the note serving as the icon's description (the default view).

- **Notes List.** Displays the notes as a line-by-line list.

- **Last Seven Days.** Resembles Notes List view, but restricts the display to only the past seven days, based on the current date.

- **By Category.** Groups the notes by their assigned categories.

- **By Color.** Groups the notes by their assigned color.

> **tip**   You can assign different colors to notes to serve as visual cues for the note's purpose, importance, or content.

You can use a preview pane in the Notes folder, displaying the text of a note when you click it in the list. You can also use AutoPreview in Notes List and Last Seven Days views to automatically display the contents of each note.

You can customize the views in the Notes folder the same way you can in other folders. You can, for example, drag columns to rearrange them, resize them, change column name and other properties, add other fields, and group notes based on various criteria.

> For a detailed explanation of how to work with the Notes folder, see Chapter 16, "Making Notes."

Deleted Items

The Deleted Items folder contains Outlook items that you've deleted, and it can include all the Outlook item types (such as messages, contacts, and appointments). The Deleted Items folder offers a way for you to recover items you've deleted, because the items remain in the folder until you manually delete them from that location or allow Outlook to clean out the folder. When you delete an item from the Deleted Items folder, that item is deleted permanently.

You can configure Outlook to automatically delete all items from the Deleted Items folder when you exit Outlook. To do so, choose Tools, Options and click Other. Select the check box Empty The Deleted Items Folder Upon Exiting and click OK.

Choosing the Startup View

Outlook uses Outlook Today view as the default startup view. However, you might want to change the view based on your type of work and the Outlook folders you use most. Or you might want to use another view as the initial view because it presents the information you need right away each morning to start your work day.

You can designate any of the Outlook folders as your startup view. Follow these steps:

1 In Outlook, choose Tools, Options.

2 Click the Other tab and then click Advanced Options.

3 From the Startup In This Folder drop-down list, select the view you want to see by default when Outlook starts.

4 Click OK, and then click OK again to close the Options dialog box.

Using Other Outlook Features

In addition to the various folders and views described in this chapter, Outlook incorporates several other standard components in its interface. The following sections explain these features and how to use them effectively.

> **note** This book assumes that you're familiar with your operating system and comfortable using menus. Therefore, neither the Outlook menu bar nor its individual menus are discussed in this chapter. Specific menus and commands are covered where applicable.

InsideOut

Outlook uses personalized menus, displaying only those menu items you've used most recently. You can click the double arrow at the bottom of a menu to see all of its commands. Although personalized menus unclutter the interface, they can be annoying if you prefer to see all available commands or are searching for a specific command that isn't displayed. To display all menu commands on a specific menu, right-click the menu or a toolbar and choose Customize. On the Options tab, select Always Show Full Menus.

Using the Outlook Bar

The Outlook Bar appears at the left edge of the Outlook window and contains shortcuts to the standard Outlook folders as well as shortcuts to folders you've created and to other important data folders (see Figure 3-21). For example, the Other Shortcuts group includes shortcuts to the My Documents folder, to My Computer, and to your Favorites folder. Just click an icon on the Outlook Bar to open that folder or item. The Outlook Bar therefore gives you quick access not only to Outlook folders but also to all your data.

Chapter 3: Working in and Configuring Outlook

Outlook Bar

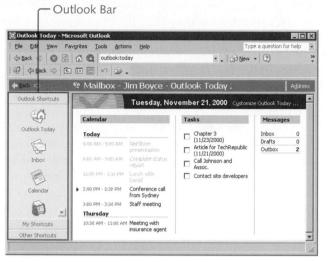

Figure 3-21. The Outlook Bar provides quick access to all Outlook data and other often-used resources and folders.

> For a detailed discussion of the Outlook Bar, including how to create your own groups and shortcuts, see "Customizing the Outlook Bar," page 605.

The following list summarizes the standard groups of shortcuts on the Outlook Bar and their contents:

- **Outlook Shortcuts.** This group contains shortcuts to each of your main Outlook folders, including Outlook Today, the Inbox, Calendar, Contacts, Tasks, Notes, and Deleted Items.

- **My Shortcuts.** This group provides quick access to some of your other Outlook folders, including Drafts, Outbox, Sent Items, and Journal. The My Shortcuts group also includes a shortcut to the Outlook Update Web site, a site maintained by Microsoft for updating your Microsoft Office application suite.

> For information about obtaining updates and finding troubleshooting resources for both Outlook and Office, see Appendix C, "Update and Troubleshooting Resources."

- **Other Shortcuts.** This group contains shortcuts to My Computer, My Documents, and your Favorites folder.

> **note** You can create new shortcuts in any of the existing groups on the Outlook Bar, and you can also create your own groups.

Chapter 3

Depending on your monitor's resolution and the number of shortcuts in each group, you might not be able to see all the icons in a group. If that's the case, you can use the up and down arrow buttons on the right edge of the Outlook Bar to scroll through the icons in the selected group.

Using Objects on the Outlook Bar

Most of the time, you'll probably just click an icon on the Outlook Bar to open its associated folder. However, you can also right-click an icon and use the resulting shortcut menu to perform various tasks with the selected object. For example, you might right-click the Calendar icon and choose Open In New Window to open a second window showing the calendar's contents. Or you might choose Advanced Find to carry out an advanced search in the selected folder. To view a different group, simply click the group's button on the Outlook Bar.

Controlling the Outlook Bar's Appearance

By default, Outlook displays the icons on the Outlook Bar using large icons, as shown previously in Figure 3-21. If your groups contain a lot of shortcuts, you might prefer to use small icons so that more items will fit in the visible portion of the Outlook Bar. To change the size of the icons, right-click the Outlook Bar and choose either Large Icons or Small Icons, depending on your preference. Figure 3-22 shows the Outlook Bar with small icons.

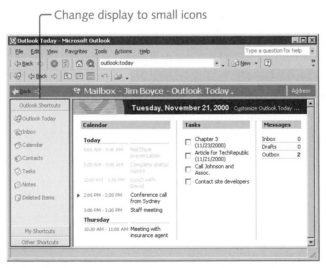

Change display to small icons

Figure 3-22.   You can configure the Outlook Bar to display small icons instead of large icons.

If you seldom use the Outlook Bar, you can turn it off to make room on the screen for the folder list or other data. Simply choose View, Outlook Bar to turn the display off or

Chapter 3

on. Alternatively, you can right-click the Outlook Bar and choose Hide Outlook Bar to turn off the display.

Using the Standard Outlook Toolbars

Outlook provides a Standard toolbar for the current folder that offers quick access to the tasks and functions you perform most frequently in that folder. Thus, the contents of the Standard toolbar change depending on the folder you have open. Certain items that appear on the toolbar for all folders work in specific ways in the context of the selected folder. For example, when you're working in the Inbox folder, clicking the New toolbar button starts a new e-mail message. With the Contacts folder open, clicking New opens a new contact form. You don't have to accept the default contextual action for these types of toolbar buttons, however—you can click the small down arrow next to a button to choose a specific command instead (see Figure 3-23). To display the Standard toolbar in a folder, choose View, Toolbars, Standard. Use the same process to turn off the toolbar display.

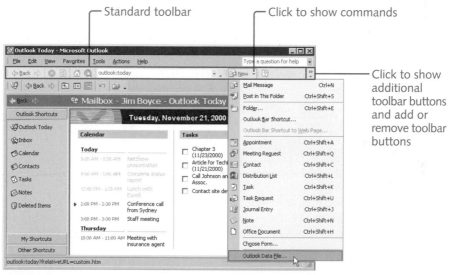

Figure 3-23. Click the down arrow beside a toolbar button to view additional command options.

> **note** Outlook 2002 and other Office XP applications now also refer to both menus and toolbars as *command bars*. However, Outlook still refers to the individual bars as *toolbars*. This book uses the two terms synonymously.

> **tip** If you're not sure what function a toolbar button performs, rest the pointer over the button to have Outlook display a ScreenTip explaining the button's purpose.

If your display isn't wide enough to accommodate the entire toolbar, Outlook displays a double right arrow icon on the right edge of the toolbar. Click this icon to view the remaining toolbar buttons and add or remove buttons from the toolbar.

> For more information on customizing the Standard toolbar and other toolbars, see "Customizing Command Bars," page 612.

The Advanced toolbar, shown in Figure 3-24, provides additional commands and also works in the context of the current folder. In addition to navigation buttons, the Advanced toolbar contains buttons for opening and closing the preview pane and the folders list, printing, setting up rules, selecting the current view, and more. Turn the Advanced toolbar on or off by choosing View, Toolbars, Advanced.

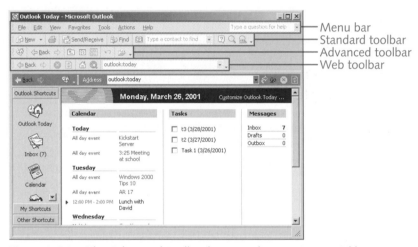

Figure 3-24. The Advanced toolbar lets you change views quickly.

The Web toolbar functions much as the navigation toolbar does in Microsoft Internet Explorer. It includes Web navigation buttons, a URL address box, buttons for stopping and refreshing the current page, and so on. Choose View, Toolbars, Web to show or hide the Web toolbar.

Using Multiple Outlook Windows

Although Outlook opens in a single window, it supports the use of multiple windows, which can be extremely useful. For example, you might want to keep your Inbox open while you browse through your schedule. Or perhaps you want to copy items from one folder to another by dragging them. Whatever the case, it's easy to use multiple windows in Outlook.

When you right-click a folder on the Outlook Bar, the shortcut menu for that folder contains the Open In New Window command. Choose this command to open the selected folder in a new window, keeping the existing folder open in the current window.

You also can open a folder from the folder list (discussed next) in a new window. However, the folder list uses an AutoHide feature to automatically hide the folder list after you select a folder. You must first lock the list so that it will stay open before you can right-click a folder and open the folder in a new window. To lock the folder list, click the push pin in the upper right corner of the folder list. Then right-click a folder and choose Open In New Window to open that folder in a new window.

Using the Folder List

When you need to switch between folders, you'll probably use the Outlook Bar most of the time. But the Outlook Bar doesn't include shortcuts to all your folders by default, and adding those shortcuts can clutter the bar, especially if you have multiple data stores. Fortunately, Outlook provides another quick way to navigate your folders: the folder list.

At the top of the folder window and below the toolbars and menu bar, you'll find a navigation bar. (See Figure 3-25.) To the right of the Back and Forward buttons is a drop-down menu with the current folder's name. Click the drop-down menu to display the folder list, as shown in Figure 3-25. In the list, click the folder you want to open. Outlook hides the folder list again after you select the folder.

Figure 3-25. Use the folder list to browse and select other folders.

In some cases, you might want to keep the folder list open rather than letting it close automatically. For example, you can't right-click a folder in the list without first locking the list so that it will stay open. To do so, click the push pin in the upper right corner of the folder list. The icon changes to an X. Click the X to close the folder list when you no longer need it.

Using the Status Bar

The status bar appears at the bottom of the Outlook window (see Figure 3-26) and presents information about the current folder and selected items, such as the number of items in the folder. It can also include other status information, such as the progress of folder synchronization. If you don't need the information in the status bar, you can turn it off to gain a little more space for the current folder's display. To turn the status bar on or off, choose View, Status Bar.

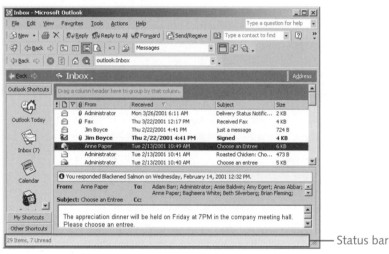

Figure 3-26. The status bar provides useful information, such as the number of items in the selected folder.

Using the Preview Pane

In earlier sections of this chapter, you read about the preview pane, which allows you to preview Outlook items without opening them. For example, you can preview an e-mail message in the preview pane simply by clicking the message header. To turn the preview pane on or off, choose View, Preview Pane or click the Preview Pane button on the Advanced toolbar.

To some degree, how the preview pane functions depends on how you configure it. For example, you can set up the preview pane to mark messages as read after they've been previewed for a specified length of time. To configure the preview pane, choose Tools, Options, click the Other tab, and click Preview Pane. Select options based on the following list:

- **Mark Messages As Read In Preview Window.** Select this option to have messages marked as read when they've been previewed for the time specified by the following option.

- **Wait *n* Seconds Before Marking Item As Read.** Specify the number of seconds a message must be displayed in the preview pane before it is marked as read.

- **Mark Item As Read When Selection Changes.** Select this option to have the message in the preview pane marked as read when you select another message.

- **Single Key Reading Using Spacebar.** Selecting this option allows you to use the Spacebar to move through your list of messages to preview them. Press Shift+Spacebar to move up the list. You also can use the Up and Down Arrow keys to move up and down the message list.

newfeature!

The preview pane in Outlook 2002 offers some new functionality, which includes the following:

- In a message folder, you can double-click an address in the preview pane to view details for the address.

- The InfoBar (discussed later in this section) now appears in the preview pane, giving you additional information about the selected item. The InfoBar was previously available only in message folders and the Calendar folder.

- The preview pane header displays the message's attachments. You can double-click an attachment to open it or right-click the attachment and choose other tasks from the shortcut menu (such as saving the attachment).

- The preview pane now displays Accept and Decline buttons so that you can accept or decline a meeting request in the preview pane without opening the request.

Using AutoPreview

AutoPreview, which is available in the Inbox, Notes, and Tasks folders, allows you to preview Outlook items without opening the preview pane. For example, with AutoPreview turned on in the Inbox folder, the first three lines of each message appear under the message header. To turn AutoPreview on or off for the current folder, choose View, AutoPreview. The AutoPreview state (on or off) is saved on a folder-by-folder basis, so you can have AutoPreview turned on for the Inbox and turned off for Notes and Tasks.

newfeature!
Using the InfoBar

In earlier versions of Outlook, the InfoBar appeared only in message and appointment forms, giving you additional information about the selected item. The InfoBar in a message form, for example, displays the From, To, Cc, and other fields. In Outlook 2002, however, the InfoBar also appears in the preview pane, as shown in Figure 3-27.

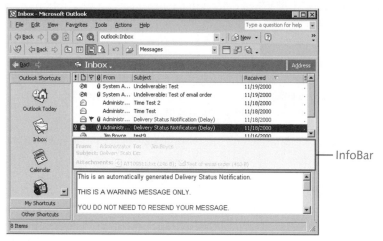

Figure 3-27. The InfoBar now appears in the preview pane as well as in message and appointment forms.

Some of the fields in the InfoBar simply display information, but others lead to more details. For example, you can double-click a name in the InfoBar to view the associated address and other contact information, or you can double-click attachments to open them.

Configuring Outlook Options

Because Outlook is a complex application with a broad range of capabilities, you have a good many options for controlling the way it looks and functions. This portion of the chapter is designed to help you configure Outlook to perform the way you need it to.

Each of the following sections describes a tab in Outlook's Options dialog box, providing an overview of the features listed on that tab. Because many of the options in this dialog box are best understood in the context of the feature they control, you'll find more detail about individual options in chapters that focus on a particular Outlook feature (messaging or scheduling, for example); be sure to consult the cross-references to the applicable chapters for more information.

To reach the Options dialog box described here, open Outlook and choose Tools, Options.

Preferences

The Preferences tab of the Options dialog box, shown in Figure 3-28, lets you configure general settings for all of Outlook's primary functions, from e-mail to scheduling to contact management.

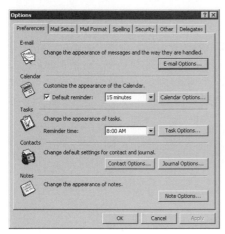

Figure 3-28. Use the Preferences tab of the Options dialog box to configure a broad range of general options.

Each of the option groups on the Preferences tab controls how a specific Outlook component works. The following list will help you locate specific settings:

E-Mail   You can specify how Outlook handles messages—for example, whether Outlook keeps a copy of sent items, saves unsent messages, or includes original message content in replies and forwards. Chapter 7, "Sending and Receiving Messages," provides extensive coverage of e-mail configuration options.

Calendar   You can control the look of Outlook's calendar by, for example, defining the work week, changing the appearance of the Date Navigator, or setting background color. See Chapter 18, "Scheduling Appointments," for a discussion of options for the Calendar folder.

Tasks   You can set the color for completed and overdue tasks, set up reminders for tasks with due dates, and configure other task-related settings. Chapter 20, "Managing Your Tasks," covers task options in detail.

Contacts   You can control the way names are displayed in the Contacts folder, check for duplicate contact entries, configure journal options, and set other

Part 1: Working with Outlook

options for storing and managing your contact information. See Chapter 14, "Managing Your Contacts," for a complete explanation.

Notes   You can, for example, set the color, size, and font used for notes. Chapter 16, "Making Notes," covers options for notes.

Mail Setup

On the Mail Setup tab (see Figure 3-29), you'll find additional settings that control e-mail accounts and Outlook's messaging functions. For example, you can use the Mail Setup tab to create or modify e-mail accounts and configure how and when Outlook sends and receives messages.

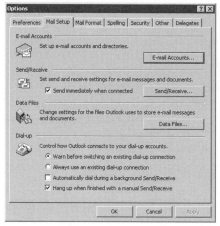

Figure 3-29.   Use the Mail Setup tab to configure e-mail accounts and general messaging properties.

The following list describes the major sections on the Mail Setup tab and directs you to the chapter where those settings are discussed:

E-Mail Accounts   These settings allow you to add, remove, or configure e-mail accounts. See Chapter 2, "Advanced Setup Tasks," and Chapter 6, "Using Internet Mail," to learn how to configure e-mail accounts.

Send/Receive   You can define groups of accounts, which Outlook then uses to determine when to process messages for specific accounts. You can configure settings separately for each group, providing a high degree of control over when and how Outlook processes messages. See Chapter 7, "Sending and Receiving Messages," for information about send/receive groups and send/receive options.

Data Files   These settings let you add, remove, and configure information stores (data files) for Outlook, including setting up offline access. See

Chapter 1, "Outlook Architecture, Setup, and Startup," to learn how to manage data files.

Dial-Up Here you can configure a handful of settings that determine how Outlook handles dial-up connections for sending and receiving messages. See Chapter 6, "Using Internet Mail," to learn about dial-up connection options.

Mail Format

Use the Mail Format tab (see Figure 3-30) to control the way your messages look and how you compose those messages. For example, you can use the Mail Format tab to specify either Word or Outlook as the default e-mail editor, to choose between plain-text and rich-text options, and to set international formatting options.

Figure 3-30. Use the Mail Format tab to select the default e-mail editor, mail format, and other properties.

The following list summarizes the option groups on the Mail Format tab. For details about the various settings in each group, consult Chapter 7, "Sending and Receiving Messages."

Message Format With these settings, you can choose between HTML, plain text, and rich text for outgoing messages; specify the default e-mail editor; specify the default e-mail viewer for rich-text messages; configure Internet and international options for messages; and set up other messaging features.

Stationery And Fonts You can set a default stationery (background) for messages, manage stationery, and specify font settings.

Signature These settings direct Outlook to add a text signature to all new messages and to replies and forwards. You can configure the two categories of messages separately. (Note that these signatures are different from digital signatures, which allow you to validate the authenticity of and encrypt messages.)

Spelling

The Spelling tab (see Figure 3-31) lets you specify how spelling should be checked in Outlook. The following sections summarize by function the settings available on this tab.

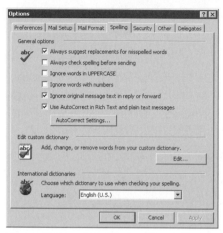

Figure 3-31. Use the Spelling tab to set options for checking spelling.

Checking Spelling

The General Options section of the Spelling tab allow you to set general guidelines for the spell checker. The options include the following:

- **Always Suggest Replacements For Misspelled Words.** When you select this option, the spell checker will display suggested changes for any misspelled words it finds.

- **Always Check Spelling Before Sending.** Select this option to have Outlook automatically check spelling before you send a message. You also can check spelling manually.

- **Ignore Words In UPPERCASE.** You can instruct the spell checker to skip over words that appear in all uppercase letters. This option is useful, for example, if your document contains numerous acronyms and you don't want the spell checker to waste time checking them.

- **Ignore Words With Numbers.** When you select this option, the spell checker will not attempt to check the spelling of words that include numbers, such as *some342*.

- **Ignore Original Message Text In Reply Or Forward.** Selecting this option specifies that Outlook will check spelling only in your message text, not in the original message text included in a reply or forward.

● **Use AutoCorrect In Rich Text And Plain Text Messages.** Selecting this option allows Outlook to use AutoCorrect in rich-text and plain-text messages to automatically correct certain common errors. See the following section for details.

Using AutoCorrect

Outlook, like other Office applications, supports AutoCorrect, a feature that allows Outlook to correct common spelling and typing errors and to replace characters with symbols. You also can use AutoCorrect as a shortcut, which means you can type a small string of characters and have those characters replaced by a longer string. For example, if you frequently type the words **Windows 2000**, you might set up AutoCorrect to replace your shorthand typed phrase **w2k** with **Windows 2000**. See the tip on page 98 for a handy use for smart tags and AutoCorrect entries.

Clicking the AutoCorrect Options button on the Spelling tab displays the AutoCorrect dialog box, shown in Figure 3-32. You can use this dialog box to add new AutoCorrect entries or change existing entries. Click Exceptions to specify exceptions to AutoCorrect rules.

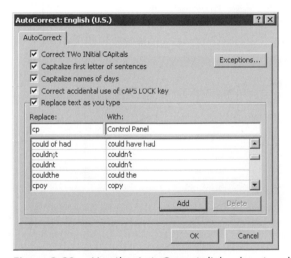

Figure 3-32. Use the AutoCorrect dialog box to add and modify AutoCorrect entries.

Editing a Custom Spelling Dictionary

When Outlook is checking spelling in a document and finds a word it considers misspelled, the program gives you the option of adding the word to a custom dictionary. This option lets you specify the correct spelling of words not found in Outlook's standard dictionary. For example, you might want to add your name to the custom dictionary if Outlook doesn't recognize its spelling. You can also add the correct spelling of special words or terms you use often to the custom dictionary.

Chapter 3

> **tip** **Use custom dictionaries throughout Office**
>
> All Office applications use the same spelling features, including the custom dictionary. Words you add to the dictionary from other applications are available in Outlook, and vice versa. This is also true for new dictionaries that you create: if you add another dictionary to Outlook, that new dictionary is available in other Office applications.

Click Edit on the Spelling tab to open the custom dictionary (Custom.dic) in Notepad to change or add entries. Enter one word per line. The custom dictionary file is stored in the Application Data\Microsoft\Proof folder of your profile folder (which varies according to your operating system).

You can add other dictionaries to Outlook. To add a new dictionary, follow these steps:

1 Open a message form (start a new message, for example) and choose Tools, Spelling And Grammar.

2 Click Options in the Spelling And Grammar dialog box and then click Custom Dictionaries.

3 In the Custom Dictionaries dialog box (see Figure 3-33), select the dictionary files you want to add and click OK.

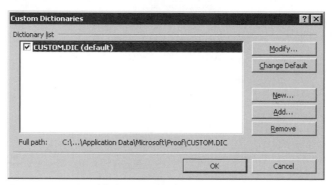

Figure 3-33.   Add dictionaries by using the Custom Dictionaries dialog box.

Using International Dictionaries

The International Dictionaries section on the Spelling tab allows you to specify the language that Outlook uses when checking spelling. Simply select the appropriate language from the drop-down list and click OK.

Security

The Security tab (see Figure 3-34) lets you configure a range of options that help you secure your messages, validate your identity to others, and protect your system against viruses and worms.

Figure 3-34. Use the Security tab to configure digital signatures and other security properties.

The Security tab includes the following groups of options.

> For details about the specific options on the security tab, see Chapter 12, "Securing Your System, Messages, and Identity."

Secure E-Mail   You can choose to encrypt outgoing messages, add digital signatures to outgoing messages, and configure other options for digital signatures and encryption.

Secure Content   These options help you define security zones, which determine how Outlook handles HTML messages.

Digital IDs (Certificates)   The settings accessed through this area help you manage digital certificates and signatures, which allow you to share encrypted messages and validate your identity to message recipients.

Other

The Other tab (see Figure 3-35 on the next page) provides a selection of settings that apply to various aspects of Outlook. The following sections explain how to configure specific features and behavior using this tab.

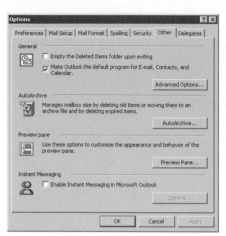

Figure 3-35. The Other tab gives you access to properties for several features.

Defining the Default Program for E-Mail, Contacts, and Calendar

One setting on the Other tab lets you specify that Outlook is the default application for creating and viewing e-mail, contacts, and calendar items. Select the option Make Outlook The Default Program For E-Mail, Contacts, And Calendar if you want Outlook to open when you open e-mail messages, contact entries, or calendar data from other sources.

Processing Deleted Items

You can use the Other tab to determine how Outlook processes deleted items. The first of the following two options is located on the Other tab; click the Advanced Options button to access the second.

- **Empty The Deleted Items Folder Upon Exiting.** Select this option to have Outlook automatically delete all items from the Deleted Items folder when you exit the program. This action permanently deletes the items.

- **Warn Before Permanently Deleting Items.** Select this option if you want Outlook to warn you before it permanently deletes items from the Deleted Items folder.

Setting Up AutoArchive

The options accessed by clicking the AutoArchive button on the Other tab let you control how Outlook archives data, processes deleted and expired items, and implements other backup properties, such as the retention policy. See Chapter 27 "Delegating Responsibilities to an Assistant," for more information on backup and archival options and procedures for Outlook.

Customizing the Preview Pane

Clicking the Preview Pane button on the Other tab provides access to options that determine the way the preview pane functions. These options are explained in detail earlier in this chapter; see "Using the Preview Pane," page 86.

Setting Up Instant Messaging

Use the Instant Messaging area on the Other tab to enable and configure MSN Messenger and use instant messaging (sending or receiving pop-up messages in communication with other users). See "Using Instant Messaging," page 217, for more information on instant messaging.

Delegates

The Delegates tab of the Options dialog box lets you specify other persons who have delegate access to your folders and can send items on your behalf (meeting requests, for example). See Chapter 27, "Delegating Responsibilities to an Assistant," for detailed information on using delegation and specifying delegates.

Setting Advanced Options

The Other tab of the Options dialog box lets you access a set of special advanced options for configuring Outlook. Click Advanced Options on the Other tab to display the Advanced Options dialog box, shown in Figure 3-36. You can use the options in this dialog box to configure various aspects of Outlook's behavior and appearance, as described in the list on the next page.

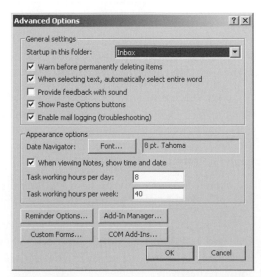

Figure 3-36. The Advanced Options dialog box controls several advanced features.

● **Startup In This Folder.** This option lets you specify which folder Outlook opens by default when you start the program. Select the folder in the drop-down list.

● **When Selecting Text, Automatically Select Entire Word.** Select this option to have Outlook automatically select the entire word and the following space when you highlight any portion of a word. This behavior simplifies selecting words and blocks of text. This option is unavailable if you have configured Word as your default e-mail editor.

● **Provide Feedback With Sound.** You can direct Outlook to play a sound when you perform actions such as opening a file or deleting a message.

newfeature!

● **Show Paste Options Buttons.** When this option is selected, Outlook displays a smart tag when you paste data from the Clipboard, allowing you to change the paste format and other paste options. This method of changing these options is faster than using the Edit menu.

newfeature!

tip **Use smart tags to get quick access to features**

Smart tags are controls embedded in documents to provide quick access to commands and features without forcing you to navigate the application's menu. When you paste data from the clipboard, for example, Office adds a smart tag beside the pasted data. You can select other paste formats and fine-tune the data without repasting or using the Edit menu. Smart tags also come in handy with AutoCorrect entries. If you type some text referenced by an AutoCorrect entry, Office changes the text automatically but adds a smart tag beside the modified text so you can select other changes or undo the correction. Other types of smart tags provide similar quick access to document data and editing.

● **Enable Mail Logging (Troubleshooting).** This option allows Outlook to log e-mail event status to the OPMLog.log file, which is located in the Temp folder of your profile folder (for example, \Documents And Settings\<*user*> \Local Settings\Temp on a system running Microsoft Windows 2000).

● **Date Navigator.** Click Font to select the font used by the Date Navigator (the two-month calendar that appears in the Calendar folder). Changing the font changes not only the appearance of the Date Navigator but also the number of months displayed. Make the font smaller to show more months or larger to show fewer months.

● **When Viewing Notes, Show Time And Date.** You can have Outlook display the time and date a note was created or last modified at the bottom of the note.

● **Task Working Hours Per Day** and **Task Working Hours Per Week.** These two options define your work week for managing tasks. The default settings are 8 hours and 40 hours, respectively.

- **Reminder Options.** Click this button to access settings for reminders. You can direct Outlook to display a reminder and play a sound when the reminder is due.

Using Outlook on the Web

Outlook includes several features that integrate its functionality with the Internet. This section explores these features, including a look at browsing the Web with Outlook, using NetMeeting and NetShow to facilitate desktop conferencing and collaboration, and connecting to Exchange Server through the Web protocol (formerly known as WebDAV).

Browsing the Web with Outlook

Outlook's integration with Internet Explorer allows you to browse the Internet without leaving Outlook. This feature is handy when you need to retrieve a file, view online documents, or otherwise access data on the Web but don't want to open Internet Explorer. Outlook's ability to browse the Web allows you to continue working in a single interface and avoid switching between open applications.

The default toolbar for all Outlook folders includes an Address box in which you can enter the URL for a Web-related resource, such as a Web site or an FTP site (see Figure 3-37). To view a site in Outlook, type the URL in the Address box and press Enter or click Go. Alternatively, you can click the drop-down button beside the Address box to select a URL that you've visited previously. The Stop and Refresh buttons on the toolbar perform the same function they do in Internet Explorer. When you want to go back to working with your Outlook folders, simply select the folder you need from the Outlook Bar or the folder list.

Figure 3-37.   You can use Outlook to browse Web sites and other Web resources.

Using NetMeeting

Microsoft NetMeeting is a desktop conferencing application included with Internet Explorer that allows an unlimited number of people to participate in a virtual meeting across the Internet or an intranet. With NetMeeting, participants can speak with one another, exchange messages, view one another through video, share applications and files, and collaborate on documents using an electronic whiteboard. Some of the available features depend on the participants' system configurations. For example, video conferencing requires a video camera, and audio conferencing requires a sound card and microphone. Some features of NetMeeting are useful over dial-up connections, but effective conferencing—particularly with a larger number of participants—requires a higher-speed connection, such as DSL, ISDN, or dedicated T1.

NetMeeting is not a component of Outlook. Rather, NetMeeting is a separate application included with Internet Explorer. You can obtain NetMeeting and Internet Explorer from Microsoft's Web site at *http://www.microsoft.com/windows/ie/default.htm*.

> For a detailed discussion of NetMeeting, including installation and configuration, see "Holding an Online Meeting," page 536.

Using NetShow

Microsoft NetShow is a client/server desktop conferencing platform for broadcasting live and on-demand audio, video, and multimedia presentations across the Internet or an intranet. NetShow is a great tool to provide not only live presentations to remote participants but also streaming multimedia across the Web.

InsideOut

Microsoft's NetShow is a complex system that is beyond the scope of this book. Chapter 19, "Scheduling Meetings and Resources," explains how to use NetShow from the client side to participate in presentations. The Microsoft Internet Explorer Resource Kit, available from Microsoft and other retailers, provides a detailed technical explanation of the NetShow platform from both the client and server perspectives. It also offers detailed information regarding NetShow deployment, presentation development, and related topics.

If you don't need the whiteboard or document collaboration features offered by NetMeeting but instead primarily use only video and audio chat, check out Eyeball Chat from Eyeball Networks at *http://www.eyeball.com*. Eyeball Chat provides great video performance and the application is free, as is access to the Eyeball Chat server.

Accessing Your Mail Through a Browser

Outlook serves as a great client application for e-mail, but on occasion you might want to use a simpler method of accessing your messages. For example, you might be out of town unexpectedly, without your computer, and realize that you need to read an important message. Or perhaps you'd like to check your office e-mail from home but don't have your Outlook configuration installed on your home computer. Whatever the case, Exchange Server supports access to your Exchange Server mailbox through Outlook Web Access (OWA), a server-side feature of Exchange Server.

Using Outlook Web Access to access your mailbox on an Exchange Server doesn't require extensive configuration. You simply point your Web browser to the URL on the server that provides access to your mailbox. The URL varies according to how OWA is configured on the server, in addition to a few other considerations. For a detailed look at using OWA to access your Exchange Server mailbox, see Chapter 36, "Accessing Messages Through a Web Browser."

Configuring Windows Settings for Outlook

Although most of the settings you'll need to configure for Outlook are configured through the program itself, some settings in the underlying operating system have an impact on the way Outlook functions and displays your data. This section offers an overview of the settings you might consider reviewing or modifying for use with Outlook.

Display Settings

Because Outlook packs a lot of information into a relatively small amount of space, your display resolution has some impact on Outlook's usefulness. You should configure your system for at least an 800 x 600 desktop, preferably larger, depending on the size of your monitor. This is particularly important if you're using multiple Outlook windows at one time.

To configure properties for the display, you use the Display icon in Windows Control Panel. You can also right-click the desktop and choose Properties to open the Display dialog box.

> **tip** A handful of freeware and shareware applications are available that let you create multiple virtual desktops to expand your available desktop space. A search of your favorite shareware site should turn up at least one or two such utilities.

Regional Settings

The regional settings on your computer determine how the operating system displays time, dates, currency, and other localized data. Because Outlook uses these types of data extensively, configuring your regional settings properly is an important step in setting up for Outlook. This step is especially important for your calendar if you use multiple time zones. To configure regional settings, use the Regional Settings or Regional Options icon in Control Panel.

Time Synchronization

Much of your Outlook data is time-sensitive. For example, e-mail messages have sent and received times, and meetings are scheduled for specific periods. If your system's clock isn't accurate, some of that data won't be accurate. You should make sure that your clock is set correctly and that the system maintains the accurate time . You can set the time either by using the Date/Time icon in Control Panel or by double-clicking the clock in the system tray.

You also can use synchronization tools to synchronize your computer with a time server. Such tools are available as third-party utilities for use with all Microsoft Windows platforms, and a search of your favorite download site should turn up a few. In addition, Windows NT and Windows 2000 clients can take advantage of the Windows Time Service (W32Time) that allows client computers to synchronize their time with domain controllers on their network. If you're not familiar with W32Time, check with your system administrator for help in setting it up.

---

tip   **Synchronizing time in Windows NT domains**

When Windows 2000 clients update their time on Windows NT domains, some compatibility issues can arise. If your Windows NT domain controllers use the Timeserv service, you need to upgrade to the W32Time service to allow Windows 2000 clients to participate. In addition, you need to make a few registry modifications on the Windows NT domain controller functioning as the time server to allow Windows 2000 clients to synchronize their times. See the Microsoft Knowledge Base article Q258059 for more information.

Using Add-Ins

Outlook provides tremendous functionality right out of the box and could well serve all your needs. But if you need additional features not provided directly by Outlook, *add-ins* can help to extend Outlook's functionality. Outlook includes a handful of such add-ins, and third-party developers can produce others.

Outlook supports two types of add-ins: application-specific (standard) add-ins and COM add-ins. Standard add-ins are the type supported by earlier versions of Outlook, which allow a developer to add features to one Office application. Standard add-ins are not portable between Office applications. These add-ins are integrated into Outlook through dynamic-link libraries (DLLs).

COM add-ins use the Microsoft Component Object Model to allow shared functionality between the various Office applications. COM add-ins were added as new features in Office 2000 and are also available in Office XP. These add-ins are integrated into Office applications, including Outlook, through either DLLs or ActiveX controls.

You install add-ins when you install Office; the list of available add-ins depends on which options you select during installation. To view the installed add-ins, choose Tools, Options and click the Other tab. Click Advanced Options to open the Advanced Options dialog box. Click Add-In Manager to view, install, and enable or disable standard Outlook add-ins and click COM Add-Ins to view, install, and enable or disable COM add-ins and control their load behavior.

> For more information on different add-ins available for use with Outlook, see Appendix E, "Outlook Add-Ins."

Chapter 4

Using Categories and Types

One of the primary functions of Microsoft Outlook is to help you organize your data, whether that data is a collection of contacts, a task list, your schedule, or a month's worth of messages. To make this easier, you can use Outlook's *categories,* which are words or phrases you assign to Outlook items as a means of organizing the items. For example, you might assign the category Personal to a message from a family member, to differentiate it from your work-related messages, and then customize the view to exclude personal items.

This chapter explains how categories work in Outlook and shows you how to manage a Master Category List, add new categories, assign them to Outlook items, and use categories to arrange, display, and search Outlook data. You'll also learn about entry types, which work in concert with categories to give you even more flexibility in organizing your data.

Understanding Categories

If you've used a personal finance or checkbook program such as Microsoft Money or Intuit's Quicken, you're probably familiar with categories. In these programs, you can assign a category to each check, deposit, or other transaction and then view all transactions for a specific category, perhaps printing them on a report for tax purposes. For example, you might use categories to keep track of business expenses and separate them by certain criteria, such as reimbursement policy or tax deductions.

Outlook's categories perform essentially the same function: you can place data into categories and manipulate the data based on those categories. For example, you might use categories to assign Outlook items such as messages and tasks to a specific project. You could then quickly locate all items related to that project. Or you might use categories to differentiate personal contacts from business contacts. Whatever your need for organization, categories offer a handy and efficient way to achieve your goal.

What can you do with categories? After you assign a category to each relevant Outlook item, you can sort, search, and organize your data according to the category. Figure 4-1, for example, shows the Advanced Find dialog box after a search for all Outlook items assigned to the category Project Blue. Figure 4-2 shows the Contacts folder organized by category, displaying all contacts who work for ProseWare Corporation. The ability to search by category makes it easy to find all the items associated with a specific project, contract, issue, or general category.

Figure 4-1. The Advanced Find dialog box displays the results of a search for all Project Blue items.

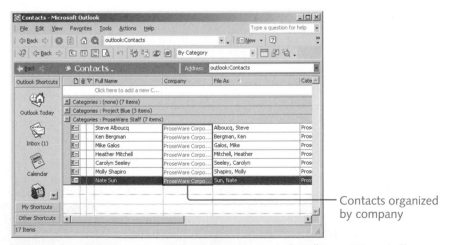

Contacts organized by company

Figure 4-2. You can group contacts by category to list all ProseWare staff.

Categories are useful only if you apply them consistently. After you become disciplined in using categories and begin to assign them out of habit, you'll wonder how you ever organized your day without them.

The Master Category List

Outlook maintains a Master Category List (MCL) that contains the default categories created by Setup when you install Outlook. The MCL is hard-coded and can't be changed. You can, however, modify your personal copy of the MCL, which is stored in the registry key

HKEY_CURRENT_USER\Software\Microsoft\Office\10.0\Outlook\Categories

The MCL serves as the basis for customizing your personal category list. The MCL contains several predefined categories that are useful in many situations, but your business or organization might need special categories not included with Outlook. You can customize the MCL to create your own category list with as many additional categories as you want, as the following section explains.

Customizing Your Personal Master Category List

Before you assign categories to Outlook items, you should go through the category list and add the categories you need. To determine which ones to add, spend some time thinking about how you intend to use them. Although you can always add categories later, creating the majority up front not only saves time but also helps you organize your thoughts and plan the use of categories more effectively.

Follow these steps when you're ready to create categories:

1 Open Outlook and then select any item (a message or a contact, for example).

2 Open the Categories dialog box by choosing Edit, Categories or by right-clicking the item and choosing Categories from the shortcut menu.

3 Click Master Category List to display the Master Category List dialog box, shown in Figure 4-3 on the next page.

Figure 4-3. You can add a new category in the Master Category List dialog box.

4 Type the new category name in the New Category box, and click Add. Repeat this step to add other categories as needed.

5 Click OK when you've finished adding categories, and then click OK to close the Categories dialog box.

> For information about creating new categories while you are assigning categories to an item, see the following section, "Assigning Categories to New Items."

The categories you add to your personal MCL depend entirely on the types of tasks you perform with Outlook, your type of business or organization, and your preferences. The following list suggests ways to categorize business-related data:

- Track items by project type or project name.

- Organize contacts by their type (for example, managers, assistants, technical experts, and financial advisors).

- Keep track of departmental assignments.

- Track different types of documents (for example, drafts, work in progress, and final versions).

- Track contacts by sales potential (for example, 30-day or 60-day).

- Organize items by priority.

The following list offers suggestions for categorizing personal data:

- Organize personal contacts by type (friends, family, insurance agents, legal advisors, and medical contacts, for starters).

- Track items by area of interest.

- Organize items for hobbies.

- Track items related to vacation or other activities.

Assigning Categories to New Items

Assigning categories to items is easy. You can assign multiple categories to each item if needed. For example, a particular contact might be involved in more than one project, so you might assign a category for each project to that contact. If you have a task that must be performed for multiple projects, you might assign those project categories to the task.

> To learn how to assign categories to existing items, see "Changing Category Assignments," page 112.

Follow these steps to assign categories to a new item:

1 Open the form to create the item. (Click New with the folder open, for example.)

2 Use one of the following methods to display the Categories dialog box, depending on the type of item you're creating:

   ■ **Message.** Click Options on the toolbar, and then click Categories.

   ■ **Calendar, contact, or task item.** Click Categories at the bottom of the form.

> **note** Depending on your screen resolution you might need to maximize the form to see the Categories button.

   ■ **Note.** You can't assign a category initially. Instead, add the note, right-click it, and choose Categories; or select the note and choose Edit, Categories.

3 In the Categories dialog box, select all the categories that pertain to the item. If you need to add a category, just click in the Item(s) Belong To These Categories box, type the category name, and click Add To List. This adds the category to your personal MCL.

4 Click OK to close the dialog box and continue creating the item.

As you can see in step 3, you don't have to open the MCL to create new categories. Instead, you can create a category on the fly when you're assigning categories to an item. Outlook will add the new category to your personal MCL. However, a drawback to

Chapter 4

creating categories on the fly is that you might not enter the category names consistently. As a result, you could end up with more than one version of a given category. As you might expect, Outlook treats category names literally, so any difference between two names, however minor, makes those categories different. Searching for one won't turn up items assigned to the other. For this reason, it's a good idea to always select categories from the MCL rather than creating them on the fly.

Assigning Categories Automatically

You can easily assign categories when you create an item, but you might prefer to simplify the process for items that will be assigned to the same category (or set of categories). For example, if you frequently create e-mail messages that have specific category assignments, you could bypass the steps involved in adding the categories to each new message. You can accomplish this by using an e-mail template.

For a detailed discussion of templates, see Chapter 22, "Using Templates."

You can use templates for other Outlook items as well. Simply create the template, assign categories to it as needed, and then save it with a name that will help you easily identify the category assignments or the function of the template. When you need to create a message with that specific set of category assignments, you can create it from the template rather than from scratch. Because the category assignments are stored in the template, new items created from the template are assigned those categories. Using templates to assign categories not only saves you the time involved in adding categories individually but also ensures that the category assignments are consistent. (For example, you won't misspell a name or forget to add a category.)

Modifying Categories and Category Assignments

At some point, you'll want to recategorize Outlook items—that is, you'll want to add, remove, or modify their category assignments. For example, when one project ends and another begins, some of your contacts will move to a different project, and you'll want to change the categories assigned to the contact items. Perhaps you've added some new categories to further organize your data and want to assign them to existing items. Or perhaps you made a mistake when you created an item or assigned categories to it, and now you need to make changes. Whatever the case, changing categories and category assignments is easy.

Changing Existing Categories

For one reason or another, you might need to change a category. For example, you might have misspelled the category when you created it, or you might want to change the wording a little. You can't edit an existing category, but you can remove the category and re-create it with modifications. For example, you might delete the category Fiends and create a new one named Friends to replace it (assuming that your friends are not really fiends).

Before you start changing categories, however, it's important to understand the ramifications. Changing a category doesn't modify the category for items to which it has already been assigned. If you remove the Fiends category from your MCL and replace it with Friends, any items previously assigned the Fiends category will still have that category assignment—Outlook won't automatically change them to the new category. However, Outlook also doesn't delete the category assignments of items whose categories are no longer in your MCL. Because the old categories remain associated with the item, you can still search based on the old category names. Therefore, when you change a category, you should search for all items using the old category and then change those items to assign the new category.

> **note** Think of the MCL as a list that simplifies the assignment of categories by allowing you to pick preset categories from the list rather than entering them manually each time. The category text itself is associated with the item, so changes to the MCL don't affect the items to which categories have been assigned.

An earlier section, "Customizing Your Personal Master Category List" (page 107), explained how to create new categories. Because you can't edit a category but instead must replace it, changing a category is much like adding a new one.

Follow these steps to replace one category with another:

1 In Outlook, select any item and choose Edit, Categories.

2 Click Master Category List to display the Master Category List dialog box.

3 Enter the new category in the New Category box and click Add.

4 Scan through the category list to find the old category, select it, and click Delete.

5 Click OK to close the dialog box.

Resetting the MCL to Its Default Version

Assume that you've made substantial changes to your personal MCL, modifying or removing most of the original categories, and now you want to restore them. Resetting the MCL to its default version copies the default MCL to your personal list, causing all your custom categories to be removed. (Keep in mind that although this removes the categories from your personal MCL, it doesn't remove them from the items to which they are assigned.) You can then re-create the custom categories as needed in your personal MCL.

Follow these steps to reset your personal MCL to the default copy:

1   In Outlook, select any item and choose Edit, Categories.

2   Click Master Category List.

3   Click Reset, and then click OK when prompted.

4   Click OK to close the MCL.

Changing Category Assignments

You can assign categories to an item at any time, adding and removing the ones you want.

To change the categories assigned to a specific item, follow these steps:

1   In Outlook, locate the item whose category assignment you want to change.

2   Select the item and choose Edit, Categories; or right-click the item and choose Categories from the shortcut menu.

3   In the Categories dialog box, add and remove categories as needed and click OK.

Changing Category Assignments of Multiple Items at One Time

In some cases, you'll want to change the category assignments of several items at one time. For example, assume that you've replaced a misspelled category name with the correct spelling. After you change the category list, any items to which you had assigned the old category will still have the incorrect spelling. You'll probably want to search for all items with the old category and assign the new one to them.

Follow these steps to do so:

1   In Outlook, choose Tools, Advanced Find.

2   In the Look For drop-down list, select the type of Outlook item for which you want to search.

3   In the Advanced Find dialog box, click the More Choices tab.

4   Type the old category name in the box beside the Categories button, and click Find Now.

5   In the search results area, select all the items whose categories you want to change. (Use Shift+Click or Ctrl+Click to select them.) Then click Edit, Categories.

6   In the Item(s) Belong To These Categories list, highlight the portion of the category you want to change, retype it, and click OK. Outlook reassigns the categories accordingly.

> **tip**   **Change a single category**
>
> If an item is assigned multiple categories, Outlook doesn't make changes to any categories that don't appear in the Item(s) Belong To These Categories list. You can change a single category without changing others.

Organizing Data with Categories

Now that you've created your personal MCL and faithfully assigned categories to all your data in Outlook, how do you put those categories to work for you? The previous section, which explained how to search for items with given categories, is a good example of how you can use categories to organize and sort your data: by specifying the categories in question in the Advanced Find dialog box, you can compile a list of items to which those categories have been assigned.

You also can sort items by category. To do so, follow these steps:

1   Open the folder containing the items you want to sort. If the Categories field isn't displayed, right-click the column bar and choose Field Chooser.

2   Drag the Categories field to the column bar.

3   Right-click the Categories column and choose Group By This Field.

Sharing a Personal Category List

If you work in a department, or if you share similar tasks and responsibilities with others, it's helpful to be able to share the same set of categories with those other users. Doing so helps to ensure that everyone is using the same categories, an important point when you're sharing items or receiving items from others that have categories assigned to them. For example, assume that your department is working on a handful of projects. Having everyone use the same project category names helps you organize your Outlook items and ensures that searches or sorts based on a given project will display all items related to the project, including those you've received from others.

Exporting Your Personal MCL

As mentioned earlier, Outlook stores your personal MCL in the registry rather than as a file. This means you can't simply share a file to share your categories. Instead, you must use one of two methods to share your category list:

- You can export the registry key containing the categories and have all other users import that key into their registries.

- You can use an e-mail to copy categories. For details on this method, see "An Alternative to the Registry Solution," page 115.

113

The following steps outline the registry method, which copies the entire MCL:

1 Choose Start, Run. Type **regedit** in the Run dialog box (see Figure 4-4), and then click OK.

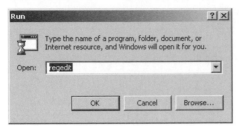

Figure 4-4. Start the Registry Editor in the Run dialog box.

2 Locate and select the key HKEY_CURRENT_USER\Software\Microsoft \Office\10.0\Outlook\Categories.

3 Choose Registry, Export Registry File.

4 Specify a path and file name to save the file, verify that the Selected Branch option is selected, and click Save.

At this point you have a registry file that other users can use to import the MCL to their systems, as explained in the next section.

> **caution**   It's important to exercise care when working with the registry. Incorrect changes could cause problems ranging from minor data loss to application crashes or the inability to boot your computer.

Importing Categories

Exporting a registry key to a file creates a text file with a REG file extension. Others can then import the Categories key into their systems by double-clicking the registry file containing the Categories key or by using the import function in the Registry Editor. However, the specific process for importing the categories depends on the version of Outlook used to create the registry file and the version into which the file is being imported.

If you view the registry file in a text editor such as Notepad or WordPad, you'll find that the file contains the registry key where the categories should be stored. For Outlook 2002, this key is

HKEY_CURRENT_USER\Software\Microsoft\Office\10.0\Outlook\Categories

For earlier versions of Outlook, the key is slightly different, distinguished by the value that immediately follows the Office value. For example, Outlook 2000 uses the registry key *HKEY_CURRENT_USER\Software\Microsoft\Office\9.0\Outlook\Categories* to store category entries.

Before you import a registry key containing categories into your own system, verify the Outlook version you're using and the key into which the categories need to be imported. For example, if you're importing categories from an earlier version of Outlook into Outlook 2002, you need to modify the registry file to place the information in the 10.0 key. If you're copying categories from Outlook 2002 into an earlier version, you need to change 10.0 to the version being imported.

To make the change before you import, open the registry file in Notepad or WordPad. As you can see in Figure 4-5, the registry key is specified near the beginning of the file. Change the key name to reflect the appropriate destination key, save the file, and then import it into the target system. You can import the key by double-clicking it, or you can open the Registry Editor as explained previously and choose Registry, Import Registry File.

Key name should reflect the Outlook version running on the target system

Figure 4-5. You can open a registry script in Notepad.

caution When you import the registry file, your existing categories are lost. See the following section for an alternative method if you want to retain your existing custom categories while also adding others from another user.

An Alternative to the Registry Solution

When you import a registry file, the existing categories in your MCL are replaced, not supplemented. This means you'll lose any custom categories you had added to your MCL before the import. To get around this problem, the person who originates the shared categories can create an e-mail message, assign all categories to the message, and then send it to others for import into their MCLs.

Chapter 4

To use this method of sharing categories, follow these steps:

1 On the source system for the categories, create a new mail message addressed to all users who need a copy of the categories.

2 In the message form, click Options and assign all custom categories (or only those to be shared) to the message.

3 Send the message.

4 On a receiving system, select the message and choose Edit, Categories; or right-click the message and choose Categories.

5 In the Categories dialog box, highlight all the categories in the Item(s) Belong To These Categories list and press Ctrl+C to copy them to the clipboard (see Figure 4-6).

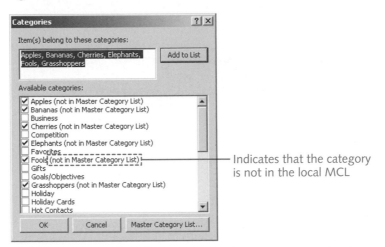

Indicates that the category is not in the local MCL

Figure 4-6. The selected categories are from a message being imported to the local MCL.

6 Click Master Category List, click in the New Category box, and press Ctrl+V to copy the categories to the box. Click Add to add them to the MCL.

tip To make sure everyone can import the categories successfully, include instructions in the body of the e-mail message explaining how to import the categories.

note As shown in Figure 4-6, Outlook identifies categories for the selected e-mail message that are not stored in the local MCL.

Using Entry Types

You can assign categories to all Outlook items to provide a means of sorting and organizing those items. The journal is no exception: each journal item can have multiple categories assigned to it. Journal items, however, can also be classified by *entry type*, which defines the purpose of the journal item. In many respects, entry types are like categories, because you can use them to sort and search for journal items.

When you create a journal item manually, Outlook assumes that you're creating a phone call journal entry and automatically selects Phone Call as the entry type. However, you can select a different entry type from the Entry Type drop-down list. Figure 4-7 shows the majority of the available entry types.

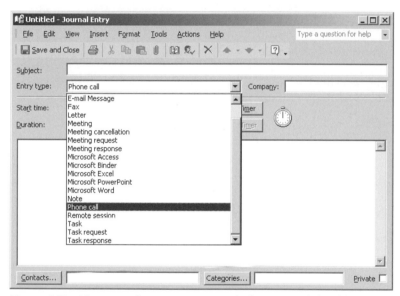

Figure 4-7. You can select entry types only from a predefined list.

Unlike categories, which you can create on the fly, journal entry types are limited to those types found in Outlook's predefined list. Although the default entry types cover a lot of bases, they don't offer much flexibility. For example, you might want to use the journal to track your activity in an application that isn't included on the list, or you might need to keep track of trips to the doctor, school programs, or other events. Although you don't have the ability to add entry types directly when you create a journal entry, you can modify the registry to add journal entry types.

Here's how:

1 Open the Registry Editor. (Choose Start, Run; type **regedit**; and click Open.)

2 Open the key HKEY_CURRENT_USER\Software\Microsoft\Shared Tools\Outlook\Journaling.

3 Right-click Journaling and choose New, Key.

4 Rename the key based on what the new entry type will be. For example, you might name it **Dr. Visit**.

5 Right-click the key you just created and choose New, String Value. Rename the string value **Description**.

6 Double-click the Description value just created, and set its value to the text you want to appear in the Entry Types drop-down list, such as **Dr. Visit**.

7 Close the Registry Editor.

After you have edited the registry to add the new entry type, it should appear on the journal entry form in the Entry Type drop-down list.

Part 2

Messaging

Managing Address Books and Distribution Lists

An e-mail program isn't very useful without the ability to store addresses. Microsoft Outlook, like other e-mail–enabled applications, has this storage ability. In fact, Outlook offers multiple address books that can help make sending messages easy and efficient.

This chapter explores how Outlook stores addresses and explains how Outlook interacts with Microsoft Exchange Server (which has its own address lists) to provide addressing services. You'll learn how to store addresses in Outlook's Contacts folder and use them to address messages, meeting requests, appointments, and more. You'll also learn how to create distribution lists to broadcast messages and other items to groups of users and how to hide the details of the distribution list from recipients. The chapter concludes with a look at how you can share your address books with others.

> Although this chapter discusses the Outlook Contacts folder in the context of address lists, it doesn't cover this folder in detail. For a detailed discussion of using and managing the Contacts folder, see Chapter 14, "Managing Your Contacts."

Understanding Address Books

As you begin working with addresses in Outlook, you'll find that you can store them in multiple locations. For example, if you're using an Exchange Server account, you have a couple of locations from which to select addresses. Understanding where these address books reside is an important first step in putting them to work for you. The following sections describe the various address books in Outlook and how you can use them.

Outlook Address Book

On all installations, including those with no e-mail accounts, Outlook creates a default Outlook Address Book (OAB). This address book consolidates all your Outlook contacts folders. With a new installation of Outlook, the OAB shows only one location for storing addresses: the default Contacts folder. As you add other contacts folders, those additional folders appear in the OAB, as shown in Figure 5-1. As you'll learn in "Removing Contacts Folders from the OAB," page 127, you can configure additional contacts folders so that they don't appear in the OAB.

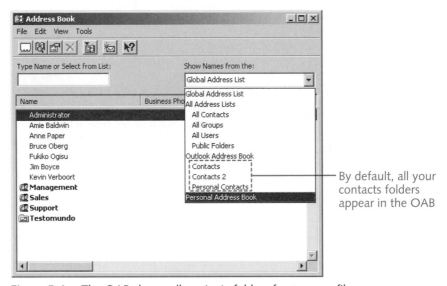

By default, all your contacts folders appear in the OAB

Figure 5-1.   The OAB shows all contacts folders for your profile.

> For detailed information on creating and using additional contacts folders, see "Creating Other Contacts Folders," page 386.

The OAB functions as a virtual address book rather than as a physical one because Outlook doesn't store the OAB as a file separate from your data store. Rather, the OAB provides a view into your contacts folders. When you add contact entries to the OAB, you're actually adding them to the Outlook Contacts folder. Because of this, you have all the same options for creating contact entries in the OAB as you do in the folder—the OAB and the Contacts folder are essentially one and the same.

Personal Address Book

You can add one Personal Address Book (PAB) to a profile and use the PAB to store additional contact information. Unlike the OAB, a PAB is a physical address book that Outlook stores on disk separate from your data store. The PAB uses a PAB file extension, and Outlook creates the file when you add the PAB to your profile.

To learn how to add a PAB to a profile, see "Adding a Personal Address Book," page 125.

The PAB doesn't function as a hook into your Contacts folder, so you don't have the same options for creating an entry in the PAB that you do in the Contacts folder. Figure 5-2 shows the New Internet Address Properties dialog box, which Outlook provides for creating new entries in a PAB. As you can see, you can't save the same amount of data for a contact in the PAB as you can in the Contacts folder.

For more information on creating contacts and their available options, see "Creating a Contact Entry," page 383.

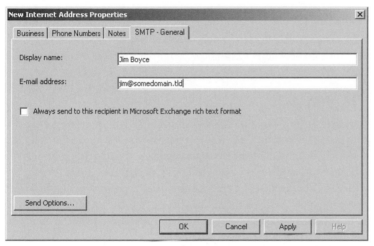

Figure 5-2. The form for creating a PAB entry doesn't include the same information as a form in the Contacts folder.

Even though the PAB doesn't store the same amount of information as an item in the Contacts folder, it's still a useful feature. You can use the PAB to store personal addresses or other contact information that you want to keep separate from your other Outlook data. Plus, you can use a PAB to share addresses with other users.

Global Address List

When you use a profile that contains an Exchange Server account, you'll find one other address list in addition to the OAB and PAB: the Global Address List (GAL). This address list resides on the Exchange Server and presents the list of mailboxes on the server as well as other address items created on the server, including distribution groups and external addresses (see Figure 5-3 on the next page). You can't create address information in the GAL, as you can in the other types of address books, however; only the Exchange Server system administrator can do this.

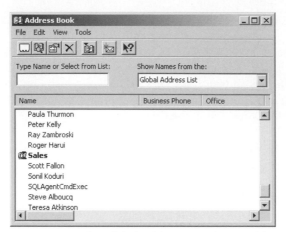

Figure 5-3. The Global Address List shows addresses on the Exchange Server.

Other Address Lists

In addition to the OAB, PAB, and GAL, you might see other address sources when you look for addresses in Outlook. For example, in an organization with a large address list, the Exchange Server system administrator might create additional address lists to filter the view to show only a selection, such as contacts with last names starting with the letters A through D or contacts external to the organization (see Figure 5-4). You might also see a list named All Address Lists. This list, which comes from Exchange Server, can be modified by the Exchange Server administrator to include additional address lists.

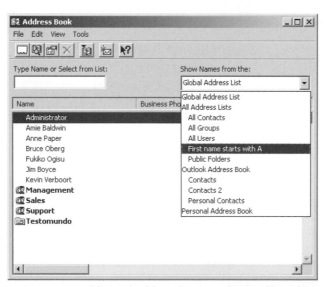

Figure 5-4. Additional address lists can display filtered lists of contacts.

124

Configuring Address Books and Addressing Options

Outlook offers a handful of settings you can use to configure the way your address books display contacts and address information. You also can add personal address books and choose which address book Outlook uses by default for opening and storing addresses and processing messages.

Adding a Personal Address Book

You might decide to add a personal address book to store addresses outside your Contacts folder. For example, you might use the PAB to store personal addresses separately from work addresses.

Follow these steps to add a PAB to your profile:

1 Close Outlook, right-click the Outlook icon on the desktop, and choose Properties. (Alternatively, you can use the Mail icon in Control Panel.)

2 Click E-Mail Accounts to start the E-Mail Accounts Wizard.

3 Select Add A New Directory Or Address Book and click Next.

4 Select Additional Address Books and click Next.

5 Select Personal Address Book and click Next.

6 Set properties for the new address book and click OK.

7 Click OK to close the Properties dialog box.

8 Restart Outlook to use the new address book.

Setting Options for the Outlook Address Book

You can set only one option for the OAB. This setting controls the order in which Outlook displays names from the OAB—either Firstname, Lastname or Lastname, Firstname.

Follow these steps to set this display option:

1 If Outlook is open, choose Tools, E-Mail Accounts to start the E-Mail Accounts Wizard. If Outlook is not open, right-click the Outlook icon on the desktop, choose Properties, and then click E-Mail Accounts.

2 Select View Or Change Existing Directories Or Address Books and click Next.

3 Select Outlook Address Book and click Change to display the Microsoft Outlook Address Book dialog box, shown in Figure 5-5 on the next page.

125

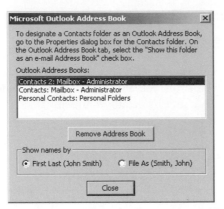

Figure 5-5. Select the format for OAB entries in the Microsoft Outlook Address Book dialog box.

4 In the Show Names By box, select the display format you prefer. Click Close, and then click Finish.

Setting Options for the Personal Address Book

For the PAB, you can select a format for displaying names, change the display name for the address book, specify a path to a different file, or include optional notes with the address book.

---

tip **Specify a different path**

When you need to place the PAB on a network share to make it available when you log on from other locations, and the file is not located in your Microsoft Windows profile folders, you might want to specify a path other than the default for the PAB. You might also change paths to select an existing PAB.

Follow these steps to configure the PAB:

1 If Outlook is open, choose Tools, E-Mail Accounts to start the E-Mail Accounts Wizard. If Outlook is not open, right-click the Outlook icon on the desktop, choose Properties, and then click E-Mail Accounts.

2 Select View Or Change Existing Directories Or Address Books and click Next.

3 Select Personal Address Book and click Change to display the Personal Address Book dialog box, shown in Figure 5-6.

4 To change the name of the address book that appears in Outlook, type the name you want to use in the Name box on the Personal Address Book tab.

5 In the Path box, type a path name or click Browse to specify the path to the PAB file.

Figure 5-6. The Personal Address Book dialog box offers several configuration choices.

6 Choose one of the Show Names By options to specify how you want the names displayed in the PAB.

7 On the Notes tab of the dialog box, add optional notes to be stored with the PAB. These notes are visible only in the Personal Address Book dialog box.

Removing Contacts Folders from the OAB

In most cases, you'll want all your contacts folders to appear in the Outlook Address Book. If you have several contacts folders, however, you might prefer to limit how many folders appear in the OAB. Or you might simply want to restrict the folders to ensure that specific addresses are used.

You can set the folder's properties to determine whether it appears in the OAB by following these steps:

1 Open Outlook and open the folders list. Then right-click the contacts folder in question and choose Properties.

2 Click the Outlook Address Book tab and clear the Show This Folder As An E-Mail Address Book option to prevent the folder from appearing in the OAB.

3 Change the folder name if necessary and then click OK.

Setting Other Addressing Options

You can configure other addressing options to determine which address book Outlook displays by default for selecting addresses, which address book is used by default for storing new addresses, and the order in which address books are processed when

Outlook checks names for sending messages. The following sections explain these options in detail.

Selecting the Default Address Book for Lookup

To suit your needs or preferences, you can have Outlook display a different address list by default. For example, for profiles that include Exchange Server accounts, Outlook displays the Global Address List by default. If you use the GAL only infrequently and primarily use your contacts folders for addressing, you might prefer to have Outlook show the OAB as the default address list rather than the GAL. Or you might want to display a filtered address list other than the GAL on the server.

Follow these steps to specify the default address list:

1 In Outlook, choose Tools, Address Book or click the Address Book icon on the toolbar. Outlook displays the Address Book window (see Figure 5-7).

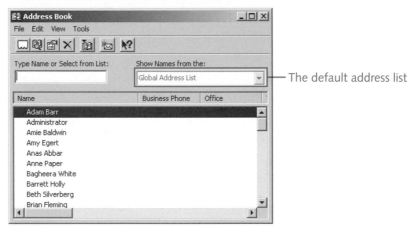

Figure 5-7. You can specify the default address list in the Address Book window.

2 Choose Tools, Options.

3 In the Addressing dialog box, select the default address list from the Show This Address List First drop-down list.

4 Click OK.

Specifying the Default Address Book for New Entries

You can choose which address book you want to use for personal addresses. Although you can't store these addresses in the GAL or other server address books, you can store them in either your OAB or PAB. When you create a new address in the New Entry dialog box, Outlook suggests storing the entry in the address book you have chosen as the default. If you want to store a particular address in a different address book, you can do so by clicking the In The option and selecting the address book from the drop-down list (see Figure 5-8).

> **note** The OAB is the default location for storing personal addresses because the profile will not include a PAB unless you add one. Keep in mind, however, that you don't actually store addresses in the OAB itself. Rather, you store addresses in your Contacts folder, which appears as your OAB.

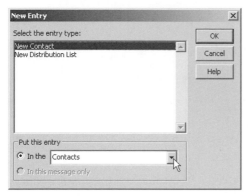

Figure 5-8.   Use the New Entry dialog box to determine where to store addresses.

Follow these steps to specify the default location for storing new personal addresses:

1   Open the Address Book window and choose Tools, Options.

2   Select the default address location for personal addresses from the Keep Personal Address In drop-down list.

3   Click OK.

Specifying How Names Are Checked

When you create a message, you can specify the recipient's name rather than specifying the address. Rather than typing **jimb@domain.tld**, for example, you might type **Jim Boyce** and let Outlook convert the name to an address for you. This saves you the time of opening the address book to look for the entry if you know the name under which it's stored.

When you click Send to process the message, Outlook checks the address book(s) to determine the correct address based on the name you entered. Outlook checks names from multiple address books if they are defined in the current profile. For example, Outlook might process the address through the GAL first, then through your OAB, and then through the PAB (assuming that all three are in the profile). If Outlook finds a match, it replaces the name in the message with the appropriate address. If it doesn't find a match or finds more than one, it displays the Check Names dialog box, shown in Figure 5-9, where you can select the correct address, create a new one, or open the address book to display more names and then select an address.

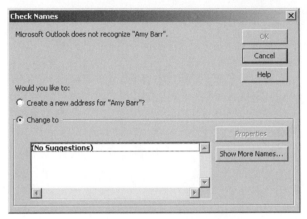

Figure 5-9. The Check Names dialog box helps you resolve address problems before you send a message.

Why change the order in which Outlook checks your address books? If most of your addresses are stored in an address book other than the one Outlook is currently checking first, changing the order can speed up name checking, particularly if the address book contains a lot of entries.

Here's how to change address book order:

1 In Outlook, open the Address Book window and choose Tools, Options.

2 Click the up and down arrow buttons that appear with the When Sending Mail list to rearrange the address book order in the list.

3 Click OK to close the dialog box.

Managing Contacts in the Personal Address Book

You can add entries for people and their corresponding addresses either in your contacts folders or in the PAB. You can add the address when you're creating a message, or you can work directly in the address book without opening or starting a message. This section of the chapter explains how to create address book entries in the PAB.

To learn how to create contact entries in your contacts folders, see "Creating a Contact Entry," page 383.

Creating Address Book Entries

To create an entry while you're composing a message, click the To, Cc, or Bcc button beside the corresponding box in the message form to display the Select Names dialog box (see Figure 5-10). Then click New to display the New Entry dialog box. You can also open the New Entry dialog box directly from the PAB. To do this, open the address book and click the New Entry button on the toolbar or choose File, New Entry.

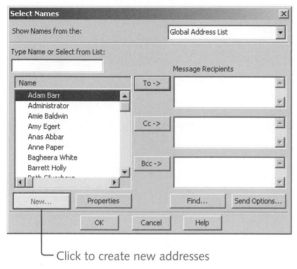

Click to create new addresses

Figure 5-10.   The Select Names dialog box leads you to the New Entry dialog box.

In the New Entry dialog box, select the type of address you want to create and click OK. The resulting dialog box depends on the type of address you selected. Figure 5-11 on the next page shows the dialog box for an Internet address.

> **note**   If you don't have the PAB set as the default location for new addresses, you won't be able to select an address type. You can change the default address location, create the entries, and then change the default location back if necessary.

Most of the address fields on Figure 5-11, such as name and phone number, are self-explanatory. After you enter the basic information, you can also set options for Internet address types that define how Outlook should send the message. On the SMTP-General tab, click Send Options to display the Send Options For This Recipient Properties dialog box shown in Figure 5-12 on the next page. Select I Want To Specify The Format For Messages To This Recipient, and then set options from the following list:

- **MIME.** Select this option to send the message using MIME. This is the default option and should work for most recipients.

- **Plain Text.** Select this option to always send the message body as plain text.

Chapter 5

- **Include Both Plain Text And HTML.** Select this option to send the message body as both plain text and HTML.

- **HMTL.** Select this option to send the message body using only HTML.

- **Plain Text/UUEncode.** Select this option to send the message using plain text and encoding for attachments rather than MIME.

- **BINHEX.** Select this option to use BINHEX for Macintosh attachments.

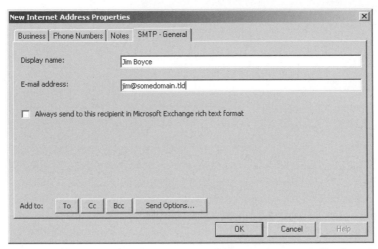

Figure 5-11. Use the New Internet Address Properties dialog box to enter information and set the format for a new Internet address.

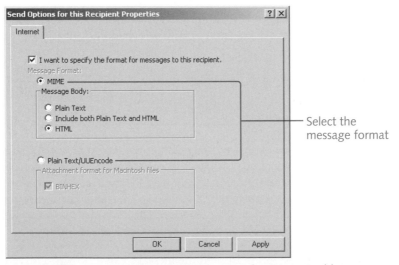

Figure 5-12. You can select sending options for Internet addresses.

Modifying Addresses

You can modify any addresses stored in your own address books, as well as in the address books of other users for which you have the appropriate access. You can modify an address while working with a form or while working directly in the address book. If you're using a message form, click the To, Cc, or Bcc button. Select the address you want to change and click Properties. If you're working in the address book instead, select the address and click Properties on the toolbar. Choose File, Properties or right-click the address and choose Properties. Outlook displays the same form you used to create the message. Make the changes you want and click OK.

Removing Addresses

Removing a contact from the PAB is much easier than creating one. Open the address book, select the address you want to delete, and click the Delete button on the toolbar or press the Delete key.

Finding People in the Address Book

If your address book contains a lot of addresses, as might be the case in a very large organization, it can be a chore to locate an address if you don't use it often. Outlook provides search capability in the address book to overcome that problem, making it relatively easy to locate addresses based on several criteria.

Follow these steps to locate an address in any address book:

1 Click the Address Book button on the toolbar to open the address book.

2 In the Show Names drop-down list, select the address book you want to search.

3 Click the Find Items button on the toolbar or choose Tools, Find to display the Find dialog box, shown in Figure 5-13 (for Exchange Server address lists) or Figure 5-14 (for the OAB and PAB) on the next page.

4 If you're searching an address list on the Exchange Server, decide what criteria you want to use and enter data in the fields to define the search. If you're searching an OAB or your PAB, specify the text to search for, which must be contained in the contact's name.

5 Click OK to perform the search.

Chapter 5

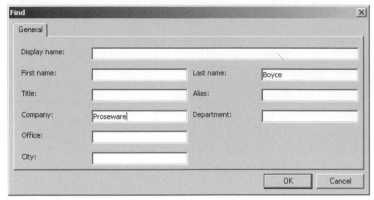

Figure 5-13. Use the Find dialog box to locate people in the address book.

Figure 5-14. The Find dialog box offers only a single search field for OAB and PAB searches.

When you click OK, Outlook performs a search in the selected address book based on your search criteria and displays the results in the Address Book window. You can revert to the full address book list by selecting the address book from the Show Names drop-down list. Select Search Results from the Show Names drop-down list to view the results of the last search.

---

tip **Use a directory service**

In addition to searching your address books, you also can search a *directory service* for information about contacts. A directory service is a server that answers queries about data (typically contact information) stored on the server. For detailed information on setting up and using directory services in Outlook, see "Configuring a Directory Service Account in Outlook," page 422.

134

Using Distribution Lists

If you often send messages to groups of people, adding all their addresses to a message one at a time can be a real chore, particularly if you're sending the message to a lot of recipients. As in other e-mail applications, *distribution lists* in Outlook help simplify the process, allowing you to send a message to a single address and have it broadcast to all recipients in the group. Rather than addressing a message to each individual user in the sales department, for example, you could address it to the sales distribution group. Outlook (or Exchange Server) takes care of sending the message to all the members of the group.

You can create distribution lists in either the OAB or your PAB. You also can use distribution lists that reside in the Exchange Server address lists, although you can't create distribution lists in the GAL or other Exchange Server address lists—only the Exchange Server system administrator can create the distribution lists on the server. However, you can modify distribution lists on the Exchange Server if you're designated as the owner of the list.

For a discussion of server-side distribution lists and how to create them, see "Creating Distribution Groups," page 772.

Creating Distribution Lists

Setting up a distribution list in your PAB or OAB is a relatively simple procedure. You can create a distribution list using addresses from multiple address books, which means, for example, that you might include addresses from the GAL on the Exchange Server as well as personal addresses stored in your Contacts folder and PAB. You can also include addresses of different types (for example, Exchange Server addresses, Internet addresses, and X.400 addresses). In general, it's easiest to set up a distribution list if all the addresses that will be included already exist, but you can enter addresses on the fly if needed.

Follow these steps to create a distribution list:

1 Open the address book.

2 Click the New Entry button or choose File, New Entry.

3 In the drop-down list, select the address book in which you want to store the distribution list.

4 In the Select The Entry Type list, select Personal Distribution List or New Distribution List (the option that is displayed varies according to address book type), and then click OK.

5 If you are creating the distribution list in the PAB, Outlook displays the dialog box shown in Figure 5-15 on the next page. If you are creating the distribution list in one of your contacts folders, you'll see a dialog box that is somewhat different, as shown in Figure 5-16.

135

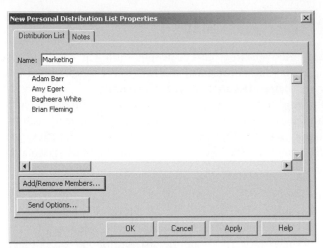

Figure 5-15. Use the Distribution List tab to set up a PAB distribution list.

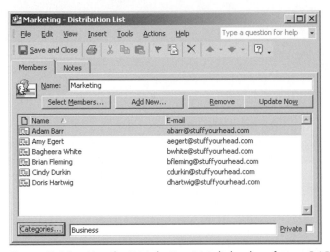

Figure 5-16. Use the Distribution List dialog box for an OAB distribution list.

6 In the Name box, specify a name for the list. This is the distribution list name that will appear in your address book.

7 For a PAB distribution list, click Add/Remove Members. For an OAB list, click Select Members. Either action opens the Select Members dialog box (see Figure 5-17).

8 Add members as needed, or click Add New in the Distribution List dialog box to enter new addresses if the addresses don't already exist in one of your address books. Click OK when you've finished adding members to the list.

9 Set other options as needed for the distribution list—for example, you can assign categories to the list.

10 For a PAB list, click OK on the Distribution List tab; for an OAB list, click Save And Close in the Distribution List dialog box.

Chapter 5

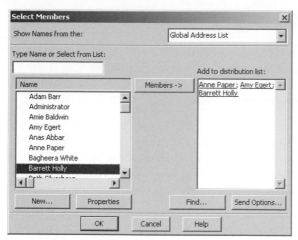

Figure 5-17. Add members to the distribution list by using the Select Members dialog box.

---

note You can't assign categories to a personal distribution group created in the PAB. However, you can assign certain other per-recipient properties depending on the address type for PAB entries.

Distribution lists appear in the address book with a group icon and a boldface name to differentiate them from individual addresses (see Figure 5-18).

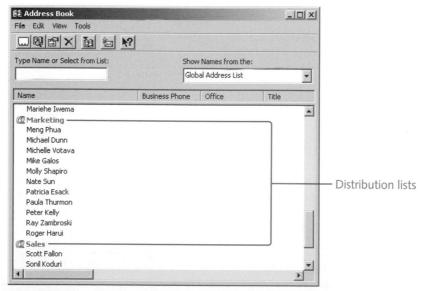

Distribution lists

Figure 5-18. Outlook differentiates between addresses and distribution lists in the address book.

Chapter 5

Creating a Contacts Distribution List

You can use the procedure just described to create a distribution list in your Contacts folder using addresses from the Contacts folder, your PAB, or address lists on Exchange Server. You also can create distribution lists within the Contacts folder rather than creating them through the address book.

To do so, open the Contacts folder, right-click any area of the folder other than a contact entry, and choose New Distribution List. Alternatively, with the Contacts folder open, click New, Distribution List on the toolbar or choose File, New, Distribution List. Any of these actions opens the Distribution List dialog box. Then continue by following the procedure described in the previous section.

> **note** In a contacts folder, distribution lists look just like addresses, although Outlook displays a distribution list in the address list with a group icon and with the distribution list name in bold.

Modifying a Distribution List

Your distribution lists will probably be dynamic rather than static, meaning you'll need to add or remove names. To modify the contents of a list, locate the distribution list in the address book or in your Contacts folder, open the list, and then use the Select Members button (for an OAB list) or the Add/Remove Members button (for a PAB list).

Renaming a Distribution List

You can change the name of a distribution list any time after you create it to reflect changes in the way you use the list, to correct spelling, or for any other reason. To rename a distribution list, locate the list in the address book, open it, and then change the name in the Name box. Close the distribution list to apply the change.

Deleting a Distribution List

You can delete a distribution list the same way you delete an address. Locate the distribution list in the address book or contacts folder, select it, and then click the Delete button on the toolbar or press Delete. Alternatively, you can right-click the list and choose Delete from its shortcut menu.

> **note** Deleting a distribution list doesn't delete the addresses associated with the list.

Hiding Addresses When Using a Distribution List

If you include a distribution list in the To or Cc box of a message, all the recipients of your message—whether members of the distribution list or not—can see the addresses of individuals in the list. Outlook doesn't retain the list name in the address field of the message but instead replaces it with the actual addresses from the list.

In some cases, the members of a distribution list might not want to have their addresses made public, even to other members of the list. In these situations, address the message using the Bcc box rather than the To or Cc box. To display the Bcc box in the message form, click the arrow beside Options on the toolbar and choose Bcc. Then enter in the Bcc box all addresses and distribution lists that should remain hidden.

Using Distribution Lists on a Server

You can use distribution lists on the Exchange Server—which are set up by the system administrator—the same way you use local distribution lists to simplify broadcasting messages to multiple recipients. (As mentioned earlier, you can't create distribution lists in the GAL or other Exchange Server address lists from Outlook, although you can modify such a list if you are designated as the list owner.)

You can use a server-side distribution list the same way you use a local distribution list. Select the list from the appropriate address list on the server. The list name will be converted to addresses when you send the message, just as a local distribution list is.

Differences Between Exchange Server 5.5 and Exchange 2000 Server

Distribution lists in Exchange 2000 Server are different from those in Exchange Server 5.5. Exchange Server 5.5 uses a dedicated directory structure and a distribution list object that is separate from security groups. Exchange 2000 Server uses the Active Directory and automatically uses security groups as distribution lists. With Windows 2000, you can also create distribution groups that function solely for the purpose of e-mail distribution (the equivalent of Exchange Server 5.5 distribution lists). Distribution groups in Windows 2000 cannot be used as security groups.

Chapter 31, "Exchange Server Overview and Setup," offers more information. For more information on Exchange 2000 Server, refer to *Microsoft Exchange 2000 Server Administrator's Companion* (Microsoft Press, 2000).

Chapter 5

Modifying a Server-Side Distribution List

If you are the designated manager of a distribution list on the Exchange Server, you can modify (but not create) the list through Outlook. To make changes, first open the address book and double-click the list. You will see a dialog box similar to the Marketing Properties dialog box shown in Figure 5-19.

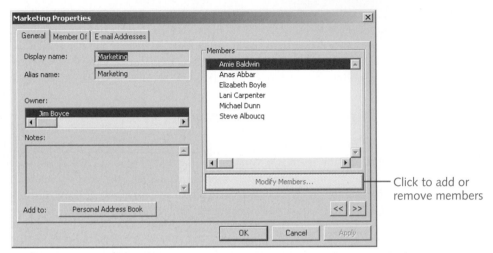

Click to add or remove members

Figure 5-19. Modify a server-side distribution list by using the General tab.

The three tabs of this dialog box allow you to view information about the selected list and its individual members:

- **General.** This tab displays general read-only information about the list, such as display name, alias, and owner.

- **Member Of.** This tab lists the other distribution groups of which the selected list is a member.

- **E-Mail Addresses.** This tab shows the e-mail addresses for the selected distribution list in all its available formats (SMTP and X.400, for example).

To modify the distribution list, click Modify Members on the General tab of the dialog box. You can add and remove members in the resulting Distribution List Membership dialog box.

> **tip** Use the arrow buttons in the lower right corner of the dialog box's General tab to display the next and previous items in the address book.

> **note** In Exchange 2000 Server, you don't grant ownership of a distribution group as you do over other objects such as files or folders. Rather, the user or group designated as the manager for the distribution group is considered the owner for the purposes of allowing modifications. You specify the manager on the Managed By tab of the group's dialog box in the Active Directory Users And Computers console.

Adding a Distribution List to a Local Address Book

If you prefer working through your local address books rather than the server address lists, you might want to add a server-side distribution list to your local address books. You can easily do so through the address book or the list's dialog box. Open the address book, locate the distribution list, and choose File, Add To Personal Address Book. If you have the list's dialog box open, click Personal Address Book on the Distribution List tab to add the list to the address book. Outlook adds the distribution list to whichever local address book is defined as the default location for personal addresses. (Choose Tools, Options in the address book if you want to redefine the default.)

If you add a server-side distribution list to a PAB, Outlook doesn't prompt for any additional information; it merely adds the list to the PAB. If you add the list to a contacts folder in the OAB, however, Outlook displays a form for the list that you can use to modify the group, assign categories, or mark it as private (see Figure 5-20). Make any changes as needed and click Save And Close.

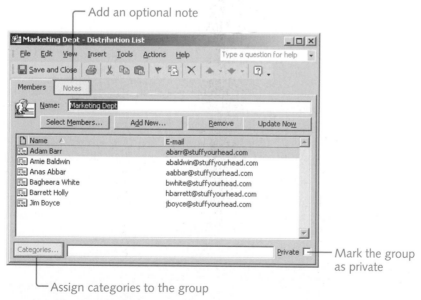

Figure 5-20. You can select various options for lists you store in the OAB.

Chapter 5

Automatically Adding Addresses to the Address Book

When you receive a message from a sender whose address you want to save in your local address books, you can add the address manually. Outlook also provides an easier method, however. With the message open, double-click the sender's address on the InfoBar. In the Properties dialog box, click Personal Address Book. Outlook adds the address to whichever local address book is specified as the default location for personal addresses. (Choose Tools, Options in the address book if you want to change this default.) If the dialog box doesn't offer a Personal Address Book button, right-click the address on the InfoBar and choose Add To Contacts instead to add the address to your Contacts folder.

Sharing Address Books

All users can view address lists on the Exchange Server, subject to how permissions are configured on the address lists. In effect, this means that all users can share a common address list through the server.

---

tip **Provide dynamic sharing**

You can share individual addresses with others by attaching the contact entries to an e-mail message and sending the message to all users who need the contact information. The recipients can then add the contact data to their own contacts folders. However, providing a dynamic means of sharing is much more efficient and effective, as explained in this section of the chapter.

You also can share your own address books, if needed. For example, you might have created an address book to store addresses for a specific project. Rather than have everyone who needs access to those addresses copy them to their own address books, you can manage the file yourself to keep it up-to-date and allow others to access it. This ensures that everyone will be using the current set of addresses.

How you share an address list depends on where the addresses are located. If they're located on the Exchange Server, you can share the folder to give others access to it. For local address books, the easiest solution is to use Net Folders, which means you can share an Outlook folder across the Internet or an intranet.

You can also make your data available by delegating access to your folders. For detailed information, see "Granting Access to Folders," page 687.

Sharing Contacts Through a Public Folder

If all the users who need to access the shared address book use Exchange Server, the easiest solution is to create a folder on the server and configure it to allow other users to access it. This method offers the benefit of providing access to remote users as well as local users.

> **note** It's possible for remote users to access a shared personal address book file. However, the network must provide remote access, and the computer or share where the address book file is located must be available to remote users.

Use the following method to share a folder containing contact information on the server:

1 Open the Public Folders branch and select All Public Folders.

2 In Outlook, choose File, Folder, New Folder or right-click All Public Folders and choose New Folder.

3 In the Create New Folder dialog box (see Figure 5-21), type a name for the new folder in the Name box.

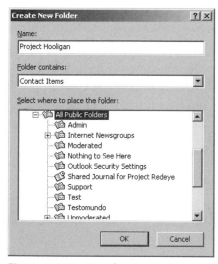

Figure 5-21. Use the Create New Folder dialog box to identify the folders.

4 Choose Contact Items from the Folder Contains drop-down list and click OK to create the folder as a root public folder.

> **note** You can create root-level public folders only if you've been given that right by the Exchange Server administrator.

5 Right-click the folder you just created and choose Properties, and then click Permissions to display the Permissions tab (see Figure 5-22).

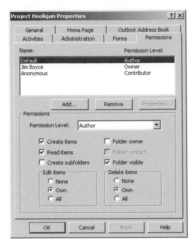

Figure 5-22. Use the Permissions tab to configure access to a public folder.

6 Configure the permissions based on the following explanation, and then click OK.

On the Permissions tab, you can specify the types of access that other users will have to the folder. Initially, in the Name box, the Default permission is set to None, making the folder visible but allowing no other access. When Anonymous is set to Contributor, all other users can create and read items in the folder, allowing them to create new contact entries and edit only those items they own (the ones they create).

You can configure permissions to grant individual users specific types of access. To do so, click Add, add the user, and then specify permissions as needed. However, you can use the Default and Anonymous settings to control access by most users and add individual users only if they need permissions that are more or less restrictive than those defined by Default and Anonymous.

Outlook gives you other ways to control permissions as well. For example, you can control the ability to edit and delete items separately from the ability to create items. You configure these permissions depending on what actions you want other users to be able to perform in the folder. You also can configure groups of permissions by using the Permission Level drop-down list or by specifying them individually.

> For a detailed discussion of creating and using public folders, see Chapter 34, "Sharing Information with Others."

Using Internet Mail

Not too many years ago, a person with an Internet e-mail address was the exception rather than the rule. Today, however, it seems as though everyone is using Internet e-mail. So it's a pretty good bet you'll want to use Microsoft Outlook to send and receive messages through at least one Internet e-mail account.

This chapter focuses on setting up both your operating system and Outlook to access Internet mail servers and accounts. For example, because Internet mail requires that your system use the TCP/IP protocol to connect to the Internet, this chapter explains how to add and configure TCP/IP on each of the Microsoft Windows operating systems (excluding Windows 3.*x* and Microsoft Windows NT 3.*x*).

In addition to configuring TCP/IP, you must configure a connection to the Internet. If your computer has a direct connection to the Internet—through a cable modem, DSL, or a local area network, for example—you can simply set up Outlook to include your Internet e-mail accounts. If your computer doesn't have a direct connection, you need to create a dial-up Internet connection. This chapter explains how.

The chapter also covers topics related to sending and receiving Internet e-mail. You'll learn how to create Internet e-mail accounts, use multiple accounts, and work with e-mail accounts for services such as Hotmail and CompuServe. You'll also learn how to ensure that your messages are available from different locations, what to do if your e-mail service won't accept outgoing mail from your dial-up location, and how to view full message headers in Internet e-mail.

Setting up TCP/IP isn't difficult, but before you start, you need to understand some background. The following section isn't intended to be a comprehensive guide to TCP/IP, but it does provide you with an overview and the information necessary to get up to speed with TCP/IP.

145

Understanding TCP/IP

Transmission Control Protocol/Internet Protocol (TCP/IP) is the standard network protocol for the Internet, providing connectivity between computers and other devices connected to the Internet. TCP/IP can also be used as a protocol for accessing a local area network (LAN).

Each device (called a *node*) on a TCP/IP network must have a unique IP address. (Devices can include workstations, servers, printers, and routers.) Like a house address, an *IP address* uniquely identifies a device and allows network traffic to be routed to and from the device. For example, when you browse to a Web site, your computer translates the site's URL (or Web address) into an IP address and uses that address to contact the remote server hosting the site. The site responds by sending traffic back to the IP address of your computer. The IP address takes the form of a dotted octet: four groups of numbers separated by periods, with a maximum of three digits in each group— 192.169.0.224, for example. Some parts of the address identify the network on which your computer resides, and other parts identify your computer on that network.

> **note** What's an octet? The groups of numbers in an IP address are called octets, not because they contain eight numbers (they don't), but because each group represents 8 bits, or 1 byte, of data.

You don't need to know how IP traffic moves across the Internet in order to use it, any more than you need to know how the engine in your car works in order to drive it. You do, however, need to know how to assign an IP address to your computer.

IP addresses can be assigned either statically or dynamically. With *static addressing,* you specify a unique address and a subnet mask. With *dynamic addressing,* a server automatically assigns you an IP address and a subnet mask, plus other settings that configure your computer properly to access the Internet. (Even if your computer uses a direct connection to the Internet, its address can still be assigned dynamically from a server on your network. Dynamic addressing is not exclusive to or required for dial-up connections, but it's the most common method of assigning addresses to dial-up clients.) Although some dial-up connections can use a static IP address, this chapter focuses on dial-up connections that typically use dynamic addressing to assign an IP address to your computer.

The *subnet mask* allows the network and host portions of your address to be identified, permitting a remote computer and your computer to locate each other on the Internet. You must assign the correct subnet mask so that your computer can have proper connectivity to the Internet. Like the address, the subnet mask takes the form of a dotted octet, such as 255.255.255.0.

> **note** Subnetting, the significance of subnet masks, and routing issues are beyond the scope of this book. For a detailed discussion of TCP/IP, subnetting, routing, and related issues, see *Microsoft TCP/IP Training* (Microsoft Press, 1997).

For our purposes, all you need to understand is that you must have both a valid IP address and an associated subnet mask for your computer. Unless you are using dynamic addressing, you'll also need the IP address of your *default gateway*. This is typically the address of the router that connects your local network to the Internet, but it could also be the IP address of a computer on your network that provides Internet connection sharing.

> **note** Because too many individual variables can come into play, this chapter cannot give you complete, precise instructions for configuring a direct Internet connection. Check with your system administrator if you need help setting up TCP/IP for a direct Internet connection.

Finally, your computer needs valid addresses for the Domain Name System (DNS) servers that will provide name-to-address mapping for your computer. For example, if you specify the DNS name mail.mydomain.tld as your incoming mail server, your computer needs some way to convert that to the IP address of the server. DNS performs this function. Like the IP address, subnet mask, and default gateway, the DNS server addresses can be configured on your computer statically or dynamically. For dial-up connections, the dial-up server usually assigns the DNS server addresses and all other TCP/IP configuration settings.

Now that you have a basic understanding of the information you need to configure an Internet connection, you're ready to dive in. The following section explains how to configure dial-up connections on various Windows platforms, including configuring TCP/IP settings for those connections. After your Internet connection is in place and working, you can start setting up and testing your Internet e-mail accounts.

> **tip** If your network provides a dedicated Internet connection, your computer might already be configured to access the Internet. If it isn't, call on your network administrator to help you add and configure TCP/IP on your computer.

Configuring Dial-Up Networking Options

Beginning with Windows 95, all versions of Microsoft Windows include a feature called Dial-Up Networking, which allows you to connect your computer to a remote network such as the Internet. You can also use Dial-Up Networking to connect to a private network such as your office LAN. If the LAN provides a direct connection to the Internet, you can access the Internet through that LAN dial-up connection, subject to how the network administrator has configured the dial-up server and other network properties.

Chapter 6

147

Before you start creating a dial-up connection, you need to determine the following:

- **IP address.** Most dial-up connections use dynamic addressing to auto-matically assign the appropriate address to your computer for the connection. If your dial-up server requires your computer to have a static IP address (unlikely), check with the dial-up server's administrator to determine the appropriate IP address. This address must not conflict with other addresses on the remote network.

- **Subnet mask.** Most dial-up connections automatically assign the subnet mask for the connection. If you need to assign a static IP address to your dial-up connection, check with the dial-up server's administrator to determine the proper subnet mask. The IP address and the subnet mask are assigned together, so if you use dynamic addressing you don't need to specify the subnet mask; it will be assigned automatically along with the IP address.

- **Default gateway.** This is typically the IP address of the router on the remote network. If your dial-up server assigns your address settings automatically, it will probably assign the default gateway address as well.

- **DNS servers.** You need the IP address of at least one DNS server to provide name-to-address mapping. If your server assigns your settings automatically, it might also assign the DNS server addresses. You can, however, specify different addresses if you have reason to do so. (DNS servers assigned by the remote server are sometimes unavailable, for example.)

- **Dial-up server number.** This is the phone number of the remote dial-up server.

- **User name and password.** This is the account name and password provided by the dial-up server. If you connect to an Internet service provider (ISP), the user account is almost always the part of your e-mail address to the left of the @ symbol in your e-mail address. For example, if your e-mail address is *jim@mydomain.tld,* your account name is *jim.*

- **Script required.** Most dial-up servers no longer require scripts to automate the connection process. A few services, however, including CompuServe, still require scripts to complete the connection. Windows provides a small selection of scripts for certain services.

When you've gathered all the necessary information for your dial-up connection, you're ready to create it. The following sections explain the process in each version of Windows.

> **note** This section assumes that you are creating a connection to a public ISP. Check with your system administrator if you need help creating a connection to your office network.

148

For detailed information on creating a dial-up connection to a remote private LAN, see "Establishing a Remote LAN Connection," page 850.

Dial-Up Networking in Windows 9*x* and Windows Me

If Dial-Up Networking isn't installed on your computer, you need to add it before creating a dial-up connection.

Follow these steps to add Dial-Up Networking (or to determine whether it is already installed):

1 Open Control Panel and double-click the Add/Remove Programs icon.

2 In the Add/Remove Programs dialog box, click Windows Setup.

3 Double-click Communications, or select it and click Details to display the Communications dialog box, shown in Figure 6-1.

Figure 6-1. Use the Communications dialog box to install Dial-Up Networking.

4 If Dial-Up Networking is selected in this dialog box, this feature is already installed on your computer. If Dial-Up Networking is not selected, select it and click OK.

Windows will copy the necessary files to your computer, prompting you for the location of the Windows files (Windows CD, for example), if necessary. You must restart Windows 9*x* or Windows Me to begin using Dial-Up Networking.

After you add Dial-Up Networking, you can create dial-up connections. Use the following procedure to add an Internet dial-up connection:

1 In Windows 9x, open My Computer, and then open the Dial-Up Networking folder. In Windows Me, click Start, Settings, Dial-Up Networking.

2 Double-click the Make New Connection icon to start the wizard.

3 In the Make New Connection Wizard, specify the name for the connection (as you want it to appear in the Dial-Up Networking folder), select the dial-up device from the drop-down list, and click Next.

4 Enter the area code and number of the server being dialed, select your location, and click Next.

5 Click Finish to complete the wizard.

6 In the Dial-Up Networking folder, right-click the connection you just created and choose Properties.

7 In Windows 9x, click the Server Types tab and clear Log On To Network. Clear NetBEUI and IPX/SPX Compatible, leaving TCP/IP selected. In Windows Me, click the Security tab and clear Log On To Network. Click the Networking tab and clear NetBEUI and IPX/SPX Compatible, leaving TCP/IP selected.

> **note** Leave the Log On To Network option selected if your dial-up server requires it. If you're unsure, you can leave it selected. Clearing it, however, will speed up the connection process slightly.

8 If you need to use dynamic addressing (in which the server assigns the IP address and other settings), skip to step 10. Otherwise, click TCP/IP Settings (on the Server Types tab in Windows 9x or on the Networking tab in Windows Me).

9 If you need to specify a static IP address or specify DNS servers, enter them in the TCP/IP Settings dialog box (see Figure 6-2) and click OK.

> **note** In the TCP/IP Settings dialog box, you can leave Use Default Gateway On Remote Network selected in almost all cases. This option causes the default gateway to be assigned by the server. If you need to specify a different default gateway, do so by using the properties for the TCP/IP protocol associated with the Dial-Up Adapter. Right-click Network Neighborhood and choose Properties to display these properties.

10 Click the Scripting tab if your dial-up server requires a script for logon completion. Click Browse to browse for the script file (which by default is stored in \Program Files\Accessories). Use the Cis.scp file for logging on to CompuServe.

11 Click OK to save the changes.

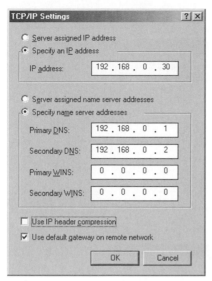

Figure 6-2. You can specify an IP address or DNS servers in the TCP/IP Settings dialog box.

---

tip **Use the Multilink tab**

If your system includes multiple dial-up devices and your ISP supports Multilink Point-to-Point Protocol, you can click the Multilink tab and configure the dial-up connection to use multiple devices for greater overall bandwidth. For a detailed discussion of Multilink, see *Microsoft Windows 2000 TCP/IP Protocols and Services Technical Reference,* by Thomas Lee and Joseph Davies (Microsoft Press, 2000).

Dial-Up Networking in Windows NT

Although Windows NT doesn't install Dial-Up Networking by default, it does create a Dial-Up Networking icon in My Computer.

If Dial-Up Networking is not already installed on your computer, follow these steps to add it:

1 Double-click the Dial-Up Networking icon in My Computer. Click Install and insert the Windows NT CD if prompted.

2 Windows NT copies the files. If no modem is installed, the Install New Modem Wizard appears. Install the modem by using the wizard.

3 In the Remote Access Setup dialog box (see Figure 6-3), select the dial-up device and click Configure to display the Configure Port Usage dialog box (see Figure 6-4).

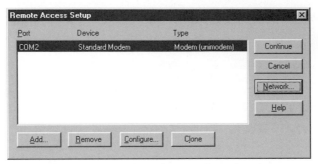

Figure 6-3. A standard modem is selected in this Remote Access Setup dialog box.

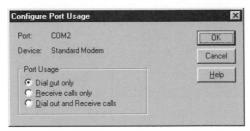

Figure 6-4. Specify dialing out, receiving calls, or both in the Configure Port Usage dialog box.

4 If you want to allow remote users to call your computer, select Dial Out And Receive Calls. If you don't want others to be able to dial your computer, select Dial Out Only and click OK.

5 In the Remote Access Setup dialog box, click Network.

6 If the NetBEUI and IPX options are selected, clear them, leaving only TCP/IP selected. Then click OK.

7 In the Remote Access Setup dialog box, click Continue.

8 After Windows NT completes the installation process, restart the computer.

After you have installed Dial-Up Networking, follow these steps to create a dial-up connection:

1 Open My Computer, and double-click Dial-Up Networking.

2 At the prompt, enter your area code and click Close.

3 Specify the name for the dial-up connection in the Name box and click Next.

4 Select I Am Calling The Internet. If you need to specify a script or a static IP address, select The Non-Windows NT Server I Am Calling and click Next.

5 Enter the phone number of the dial-up server and click Next.

6 Select Point-To-Point Protocol and click Next.

7 If you're prompted for a script, select the script and click Next.

8 If you're prompted for an IP address, enter the address and click Next.

9 If you're prompted for DNS and WINS (Windows Internet Naming Service) servers, enter the addresses and click Next.

10 Click Finish to create the connection.

Dial-Up Networking in Windows 2000

In Windows 2000, Dial-Up Networking (Remote Access Service, or RAS) is a core component that Setup installs by default. Unlike Windows 9x, Windows Me, and Windows NT, Windows 2000 collects all network connections—including dial-up connections—in a single place: the Network And Dial-Up Connections folder. You use this folder to create and configure Dial-Up Networking connections.

If you're running Windows 2000, follow these steps to create a dial-up account:

1 Right-click My Network Places on the desktop, and choose Properties to open the Network And Dial-Up Connections folder. Alternatively, choose Start, Settings, Network And Dial-Up Connections.

2 In the Network And Dial-Up Connections folder, double-click the Make New Connection icon to start the Make New Connection Wizard.

3 Click Next, select Dial-Up To The Internet, and click Next.

4 Select I Want To Set Up My Internet Connection Manually and click Next.

5 Select I Connect Through A Phone Line And A Modem and click Next.

6 Enter the area code and phone number of the dial-up server. If you need to specify IP addresses (instead of using dynamic addressing) or if you need to specify a logon script, click Advanced to open the Advanced Connection Properties dialog box. Select the script on the Connection tab, and specify IP addresses on the Addresses tab. Click OK to close the dialog box and then click Next.

7 Specify the user name and password for the connection and click Next.

8 Specify the connection name and click Next. When you're prompted to create an e-mail account, select No and click Next. Then click Finish.

Configuring Outlook for the Connection

You assign a dial-up connection by setting the properties of the account that will use the connection. If Outlook is open, choose Tools, E-Mail Accounts. Otherwise, right-click the Outlook icon on the desktop and choose Properties, and then click E-Mail Accounts.

> For help in creating e-mail accounts and assigning the dial-up connection, see "Configuring Accounts and Services," page 40.

Using Internet POP3 E-Mail Accounts

Most Internet-based e-mail servers use SMTP (Simple Mail Transfer Protocol) and POP3 (Post Office Protocol 3) to allow subscribers to send and receive messages across the Internet. (A few exceptions, such as CompuServe 2000, use IMAP; still other services, such as Hotmail and Yahoo!, use HTTP. These other protocols are covered in subsequent sections of this chapter.) If you have an account with a local ISP or other service provider that offers POP3 accounts, or if your office server is a non–Exchange Server system that supports only POP3, you can add an Internet e-mail account to Outlook to access that server.

> **tip** **Configure multiple accounts in one profile**
>
> You can configure multiple Internet e-mail accounts in a single Outlook profile, giving you access to multiple servers to send and receive messages. For additional information, see "Using Multiple Accounts," page 168.

Follow these steps to add an Internet e-mail account to Outlook:

newfeature!

1. In the Outlook 2002 Startup Wizard (which starts automatically the first time you start Outlook), move to the Server Type page. To reach this page if your profile already includes a mail account, right-click the Outlook icon on the desktop and choose Properties, and then click E-Mail Accounts. Choose Add A New E-Mail Account and click Next. You also can choose Tools, E-Mail Accounts in Outlook to add an e-mail account.

2. Select POP3 and click Next.

3. On the Internet E-Mail Settings (POP3) page (see Figure 6-5), specify the following information:

   - **Your Name.** Specify your name as you want it to appear in the From box of messages that others receive from you.

   - **E-Mail Address.** Specify the e-mail address for your account in the form **<account>**@**<domain>**—for example, *someone@domain.tld*.

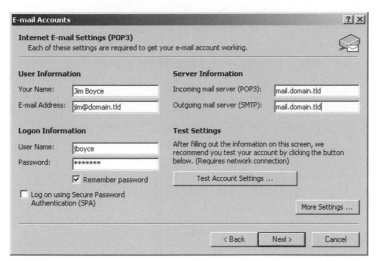

Figure 6-5. Use the Internet E-Mail Settings (POP3) page to configure the account settings.

■ **Incoming Mail Server (POP3).** Specify the IP address or DNS name of the mail server that processes your incoming mail. This is the server where your POP3 mailbox is located and from which your incoming mail is downloaded.

■ **Outgoing Mail Server (SMTP).** Specify the IP address or DNS name of the mail server that you use to send outgoing mail. In many cases, this is the same server as the one specified for incoming mail; but it can be different if your account requires it. Some organizations separate incoming and outgoing mail services onto different servers for load balancing, security, or other reasons.

Many servers don't support outgoing mail unless you connect to the server's network. To learn how to overcome that problem, see "My Mail Server Won't Accept Outgoing Messages," page 171.

■ **User Name.** Specify the user account on the server that you must use to log on to your mailbox to retrieve your messages. Do not include the domain portion of your e-mail address. For example, if your address is *someone@domain.tld*, your user name is *someone*.

■ **Password.** Specify the password for the user account entered in the User Name box.

■ **Remember Password.** Select this option to have Outlook maintain the password for this account in your local password cache, eliminating the need for you to enter the password each time you want to retrieve your mail. Clear this check box to prevent other users from downloading your mail while you are away from your computer. If the check box is cleared, Outlook prompts you for the password for each session.

■ **Log On Using Secure Password Authentication (SPA).** Select this option if your server uses SPA to authenticate your access to the server.

4 Click More Settings to display the Internet E-Mail Settings dialog box, shown in Figure 6-6. You can configure these settings based on the information in the following sections.

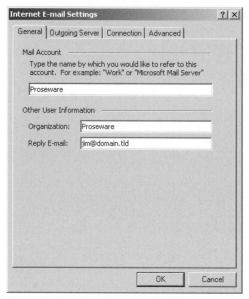

Figure 6-6. Use the Internet E-Mail Settings dialog box to configure additional Internet account settings.

Configuring General Settings for Internet Accounts

Use the General tab of the Internet E-Mail Settings dialog box (see Figure 6-6) to change the account name that is displayed in Outlook and to specify organization and reply address information:

● **Mail Account.** Specify the name of the account as you want it to appear in Outlook's account list. This name has no bearing on the server name or your account name. Use the name to differentiate one account from another—for example, you might have various accounts named CompuServe, Work, and Personal.

● **Organization.** Specify the group or organization name you want to associate with the account.

- **Reply E-Mail.** Specify a reply e-mail address that you want others to use when replying to messages that you send with this account. For example, you might redirect replies to another mail server if you are in the process of changing ISPs or mail servers. Enter the address in its full form—*someone@domain.tld*, for example. Leave this option blank if you want users to reply to the e-mail address you specified in the E-Mail Address box for the account.

Configuring Outgoing Server Settings for Internet Accounts

Use the Outgoing Server tab (see Figure 6-7) to configure a handful of settings for the SMTP server that handles the account's outgoing messages. Although in most cases you won't need to modify these settings, you will have to do so if your server requires you to authenticate in order to send outgoing messages. Some ISPs use authentication as a means of allowing mail relay from their clients outside their local subnets. This allows authorized users to relay mail and prevents unauthorized relay.

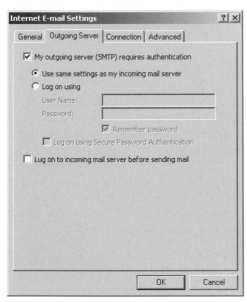

Figure 6-7. Use the Outgoing Server tab to configure authentication and other options for your SMTP server.

The Outgoing Server tab contains the following options:

- **My Outgoing Server (SMTP) Requires Authentication.** Select this option if the SMTP mail server that processes your outgoing mail requires your client session to authenticate. Connections that don't provide valid credentials are rejected. Selecting this option makes several other options on the tab available.

- **Use Same Settings As My Incoming Mail Server.** Select this option if the SMTP server credentials are the same as your POP3 (incoming) server credentials.

- **Log On Using.** Select this option if the SMTP server requires a different set of credentials from those required by your POP3 server. You should specify a valid account name on the SMTP server in the User Name box as well as a password for that account.

- **Remember Password.** Select this option to have Outlook save your password from session to session. Clear it if you want Outlook to prompt you for a password each time.

- **Log On Using Secure Password Authentication.** Select this option if your server uses SPA to authenticate your access to the server.

- **Log On To Incoming Mail Server Before Sending Mail.** Select this option to have Outlook log on to the POP3 server before sending outgoing messages. Use this option if the outgoing and incoming mail servers are the same server and if the server is configured to require authentication in order to send messages.

Configuring Connection Settings for Internet Accounts

Use the Connection tab (see Figure 6-8) to specify how Outlook should connect to the mail server for this Internet account. As with a Microsoft Exchange Server account, you can connect via the LAN, a dial-up connection, or a third-party dialer such as the one included with Microsoft Internet Explorer. Select the LAN option if your computer is hard-wired to the Internet (LAN, DSL, cable modem, or other persistent connection) or if you use a shared dial-up connection to access the Internet. Select the option Connect Via Modem If The LAN Is Not Available if you want Outlook to attempt a LAN connection first, followed by a dial-up connection if the first attempt fails (for example, when your notebook PC is disconnected from the LAN).

Select the option Connect Using My Phone Line to use an existing dial-up networking connection or create a new dial-up connection. Select the connection from the drop-down list, and then click Properties if you need to modify the dial-up connection. Click Add if you need to add a dial-up connection.

> If you need help configuring and using dial-up connections, see "Configuring Dial-Up Networking Options," page 147.

If you want to connect to the Internet or to your remote network using the dialer that is included with Internet Explorer or a dialer that is included with a third-party dial-up client, select the option Connect Using Internet Explorer's Or A 3rd Party Dialer.

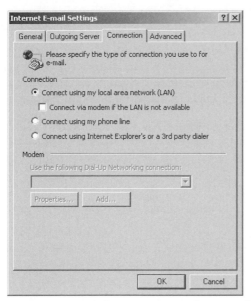

Figure 6-8. Use the Connection tab to specify how Outlook should connect to the server.

Configuring Advanced Settings for Internet Accounts

Although you won't normally need to configure settings on the Advanced tab (see Figure 6-9) for an Internet account, the settings can be useful in some situations. You can use the options on this tab to specify the SMTP and POP3 ports for the server, along with timeouts and other settings shown on the next page.

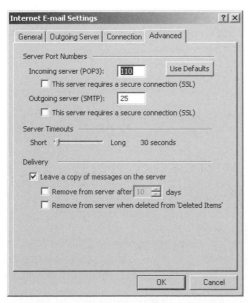

Figure 6-9. Use the Advanced tab to specify nonstandard TCP ports for the server.

159

Chapter 6

- **Incoming Server (POP3).** Specify the TCP port used by the POP3 server. The default port is 110. Specifying a nonstandard port works only if the server is listening for POP3 traffic on the specified port.

- **Outgoing Server (SMTP).** Specify the TCP port used by the SMTP server for outgoing mail. The default port is 25. Specifying a nonstandard port works only if the server is listening for SMTP traffic on the specified port.

- **Use Defaults.** Click to restore the default port settings for POP3 and SMTP.

- **This Server Requires A Secure Connection (SSL).** Select this option if the server requires the use of a Secure Sockets Layer (SSL) connection. With rare exceptions, public POP3/SMTP mail servers do not require SSL connections.

- **Server Timeouts.** Use this control to change the period of time Outlook will wait for a connection to the server.

- **Leave A Copy Of Messages On The Server.** Select this option to retain a copy of all messages on the server, downloading a copy of the message to Outlook. This is a useful feature if you want to access the same POP3 account from different computers and want to be able to access your messages from each one. Clear this check box if you want Outlook to download your messages and then delete them from the server. Some servers impose a storage limit, making it impractical to leave all your messages on the server.

- **Remove From Server After _n_ Days.** Select this option to have Outlook delete messages from the server a specified number of days after they are downloaded to your system.

- **Remove From Server When Deleted From 'Deleted Items'.** Select this option to have Outlook delete messages from the server when you delete their downloaded copies from your local Deleted Items folder.

Controlling Where Outlook Stores POP3 Messages

When you create a POP3 account, Outlook needs to know where to store your mail folders. By default, Outlook stores your POP3 mail folders in whatever location is currently specified as the default delivery location for new mail. For example, if you already have an Exchange Server account with the Exchange Server mailbox designated as the location for e-mail delivery, Outlook uses the same mailbox location for POP3 mail. Where Outlook stores the folders also depends on the other services, if any, you're using with Outlook. The following list summarizes the possibilities:

- **POP3 only or as a first account.** When you set up a POP3 account as your only Outlook e-mail account or as your first account, Outlook creates a personal folders (PST) file in which to store your POP3 e-mail folders. Outlook uses the same PST file to store your other Outlook data, such as contacts and calendar information.

- **POP3 added to a profile with an existing Exchange Server account.** In this scenario, Outlook uses the e-mail delivery location specified for your Exchange Server account as the location to deliver POP3 mail. For example, if you currently store your Exchange Server data in your Exchange Server mailbox on the server, your POP3 messages will be placed in your Exchange Server mailbox. In effect, this means your POP3 messages are downloaded to your computer from your Internet mail account and then uploaded to your Exchange Server mailbox. If you specify a local folder for Exchange Server instead, Outlook places your POP3 messages in that same local folder.

- **POP3 added after an IMAP account.** IMAP accounts are stored only in PST files, and Outlook automatically creates a PST file for the IMAP account. (The file is created when you first open Outlook using the profile that contains the IMAP account.) Outlook also creates a PST file for storing your other Outlook data, keeping your IMAP data and other Outlook data separate. Outlook designates the PST file as the default location for new mail, even though messages from your IMAP account are delivered to your IMAP PST file. If you later create a POP3 account, Outlook uses the same PST file for your POP3 account by default. This means your IMAP folders and mail are kept separate from your POP3 and Exchange Server mail. You can change the settings afterward if you want to designate a different file for storing your POP3 messages, but doing so also changes the location of your Contacts folder, Calendar folder, and other Outlook folders.

newfeature!
Using IMAP Accounts

Internet Mail Access Protocol (IMAP) is becoming more common on Internet-based e-mail servers because it offers several advantages over POP3. Outlook's support for IMAP means that you can use Outlook to send and receive messages through IMAP servers as well as through Exchange Server, POP3, and the other mail server types that Outlook supports.

For more information on IMAP and its differences from POP3, see "IMAP," page 19.

Configuring an IMAP account is a lot like configuring a POP3 account. The only real difference is that you select IMAP as the account type rather than POP3 when you add the account. You can refer to the previous section on creating POP3 accounts for a description of the procedure to follow when adding an IMAP account.

The one setting you might want to review or change for an IMAP account as opposed to a POP3 account is the root folder path. This setting is located on the Advanced tab of the account's Properties dialog box. Open this dialog box, click More Settings, and click Advanced. Specify the path to the specific folder in your mailbox folder structure that you want to use as the root for your mailbox. If you aren't sure what path to enter, leave this option blank to use the default path provided by the account.

Chapter 6

Controlling Where Outlook Stores IMAP Messages

When you create an IMAP account in an Outlook profile, Outlook doesn't prompt you to specify the storage location for the IMAP folders. Instead, Outlook automatically creates a PST file in which to store the messages. The folder branch for the account appears in Outlook with the name of the IMAP account as the branch name (see Figure 6-10). Each IMAP account in a profile uses a different PST file, so all your IMAP accounts are separate from one another and each appears under its own branch in the folders list.

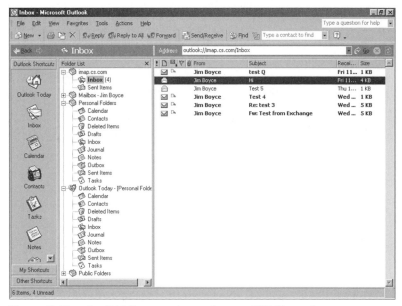

Figure 6-10.   An IMAP account uses its own PST file and appears as a separate folder branch.

How accounts are treated depends on the types of accounts you add to the profile. The following list summarizes the possibilities:

- **IMAP as the first or only account in the profile.** Outlook automatically creates a PST file to contain the IMAP folder set and a second PST file (which, for clarity, I'll call a *global PST file*) to contain your other Outlook data such as contacts and calendar information.

- **Multiple IMAP accounts in the profile.** Each IMAP account uses a separate PST file created by Outlook. Outlook also adds a separate global PST file to contain your other Outlook data.

● **IMAP first, followed by non-IMAP accounts.** The non-IMAP accounts default to storing their data in the global PST that is created when you add the IMAP account. The global PST is defined as the location where new mail is delivered. You can change the location after you set up the accounts, if you prefer. For example, if you add an Exchange Server account, you'll probably want to change the profile's properties to deliver mail to your Exchange Server mailbox instead of to the global PST file. IMAP mail is unaffected by the setting and is still delivered to the IMAP account's PST file.

● **Non-IMAP accounts followed by IMAP account(s).** The existing accounts maintain their default store location as defined by the settings in the profile. Added IMAP accounts each receive their own PST.

newfeature!
Using Outlook with CompuServe

You can use Outlook to send and receive CompuServe mail through either Classic CompuServe or CompuServe 2000 accounts. The following sections explain the differences between the two and how to configure Outlook to accommodate them.

Configuring Outlook for Classic CompuServe Accounts

Classic CompuServe accounts use e-mail addresses that end in *@compuserve.com* or *@csi.com*. Classic CompuServe accounts function as POP3 accounts, so configuring them in Outlook is much the same as configuring other POP3 accounts. However, you need to understand that the logon password you use for your POP3 account is not necessarily the same as the password you use to connect to CompuServe. Your connection password is associated with your user ID, which takes the form *nnnnn,nnnn*—for example, 76516,3403. Your POP3 password is associated with your CompuServe POP3 account name, which is the first part of your CompuServe address (without the domain). In the address *boyce_jim@compuserve.com*, for example, *boyce_jim* is the user name. Although you can set the two passwords to be the same, they do not have to match.

Before you can begin managing your CompuServe Classic e-mail account through Outlook, you must set your POP3 password. You can do this only by connecting to CompuServe through the CompuServe software. Click Go, enter **POPMAIL** as the destination, and press Enter to access the POPMAIL area, where you can set your POP3 password.

For details on configuring POP3 accounts, see "Using Internet POP3 E-Mail Accounts," page 154.

After you set the password, create a POP3 account in Outlook using the settings described in the following list:

- **Your Name.** Specify your name as you want it to appear in the From box of messages you send.

- **E-Mail Address.** Enter your CompuServe e-mail address in the form <user>@*compuserve.com* or <user>@*csi.com*, where <user> is your user account number in dotted format or your POP3 alias. The compuserve.com and csi.com domains are synonymous—you should be able to use either one.

- **Incoming Mail Server.** Enter **pop.compuserve.com** as the incoming mail server.

- **Outgoing Mail Server.** Enter **smtp.compuserve.com** as the outgoing mail server if you dial a CompuServe access number, or specify the SMTP server name for your local ISP account or for a server on your network that allows mail relay from your computer. The smtp.compuserve.com server does not support mail relay from outside the CompuServe network, in order to reduce spamming.

- **User Name.** Specify your CompuServe account.

- **Password.** Specify the password for your CompuServe account.

- **Log On Using Secure Password Authentication (SPA).** Do not select this option (leave it cleared).

Configure the remaining settings as you would for any other POP3 account.

note If you use CompuServe only for e-mail, you might not have the CompuServe software installed on your system. You can't use CompuServe 2000 software to configure your POP3 e-mail password because CompuServe Classic and CompuServe 2000 are separate services. You can download the necessary software from *ftp.csi.com/software/ windows/cs402/without_ie/cs495bn.exe*. It requires nearly 18 MB, however, so be prepared for a long download if you connect through dial-up.

Configuring Outlook for CompuServe 2000 Accounts

CompuServe 2000 accounts use addresses that end in @cs.com and use IMAP rather than POP3. CompuServe 2000 does not require a virtual key, so you can use Outlook to access your CompuServe 2000 accounts without any additional software. A virtual key is a hardware-independent number that uniquely identifies a key on the keyboard.

Configure an Outlook account for CompuServe 2000 by using the following settings in the E-Mail Accounts Wizard when you create the account:

- **Your Name.** Specify your name as you want it to appear in the From box of messages you send.

- **E-Mail Address.** Enter your CompuServe e-mail address in the form <user>@*cs.com*, where <user> is your user account screen name.

- **Incoming Mail Server.** Enter **imap.cs.com** as the incoming mail server.

- **Outgoing Mail Server.** Enter **smtp.cs.com** as the outgoing mail server if you dial a CompuServe access number, or specify the SMTP server name for your local ISP account or for a server on your network that allows mail relay from your computer. The smtp.compuserve.com server does not support mail relay from outside the CompuServe network, in order to reduce spamming.

- **User Name.** Specify your CompuServe account.

- **Password.** Specify the password for your CompuServe account.

Configure the remaining settings as you would for any other IMAP account.

newfeature!
Using Hotmail and Other HTTP-Based Services

Because Outlook supports the HTTP protocol, you can access your HTTP-based mail services (such as Hotmail) through Outlook rather than using a Web browser to send and receive messages. Using Outlook gives you the ability to compose and reply to messages offline, potentially saving you connect charges if you use metered Internet access. HTTP-based mail support also gives you the advantages of Outlook's composition, filtering, and other features you might not otherwise have when managing your mail with a Web browser.

The following section explains how to set up an account in Outlook to process your Hotmail account. You can use the same information for almost any HTTP-based account, changing the settings as needed to point to the appropriate URL for the server. Although the following assumes that you're setting up the account for Hotmail, it also provides additional information on configuring other HTTP-based accounts.

Using Outlook with Hotmail Accounts

Since Hotmail is a service owned and operated by Microsoft, it's no surprise that Outlook includes built-in support for sending and receiving messages through Hotmail.

Follow these steps to configure a Hotmail account in Outlook:

1 In the Outlook 2002 Startup Wizard, move to the Server Type page. To reach this page, if your profile already includes a mail account, right-click the Outlook icon on the desktop and choose Properties, and then click E-Mail Accounts. Choose Add A New E-Mail Account and click Next.

> If you want to use multiple profiles and want to learn how to configure settings and accounts for a specific profile, see "Understanding User Profiles," page 44.

2 Select HTTP and click Next.

3 On the Internet E-Mail Settings (HTTP) page, specify the following information:

■ **Your Name.** Specify your name as you want it to appear in the From box of messages that others receive from you.

■ **E-Mail Address.** Specify the e-mail address for your account in the form **<account>@<domain>**—for example, *someone@domain.tld*. For a Hotmail account, specify **<account>@*hotmail.com***, where **<account>** is your Hotmail account name.

■ **User Name.** Specify the user account on the server that you must use to log on to your mail box to retrieve your messages. Do not include the domain portion of your e-mail address. For example, if your address is *someone@domain.tld*, your user name is *someone*.

■ **Password.** Specify the password for the user account entered in the User Name box.

■ **Log On Using Secure Password Authentication (SPA).** Select this option if your HTTP-based e-mail server uses SPA to authenticate your access to the server. Hotmail does not use SPA, so you can leave this option cleared for Hotmail accounts.

■ **HTTP Mail Service Provider.** Select Hotmail from this drop-down list if you're setting up a Hotmail account, or choose Other if you're configuring Outlook for a different HTTP-based mail service. If you choose Hotmail, Outlook fills in the Server URL option with the appropriate URL for accessing Hotmail through Outlook.

■ **Server URL.** If you are setting up an account for an HTTP-based service other than Hotmail, specify the URL for the server's Web page that provides access to your mail account. This is not necessarily the same URL you would use when accessing your account by using a browser.

4 Click More Settings to access the settings shown in Figure 6-11 and described in the following sections.

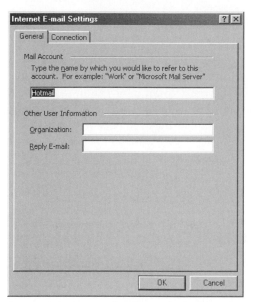

Figure 6-11. Use the General tab to configure general settings for the HTTP account.

> For more information on configuring properties for HTTP-based accounts, see "Using Internet POP3 E-Mail Accounts," page 154. Most of the settings for HTTP and POP3 are the same.

Understanding Where Outlook Stores HTTP Messages

Outlook stores mail messages for Hotmail and other HTTP e-mail accounts locally, just as it does for POP3. When you add a Hotmail or other HTTP account to a profile, Outlook creates a PST specifically for that account, regardless of whether the profile includes other accounts. Outlook delivers new messages to that PST, even if the default delivery location is elsewhere. For example, assume that you create a profile with an Exchange Server account as the default delivery location for new mail. You add a POP3 account, and that mail is delivered to your Exchange Server mailbox. You then add a Hotmail account and an IMAP account. Each of these last two accounts gets its own PST file, and Outlook delivers new messages for each account to its respective PST file.

Using Outlook with Prodigy

The Prodigy e-mail service functions as a standard POP3 server. You therefore can use Outlook to send and receive e-mail through your Prodigy account. Configure the account for pop.prodigy.net as the incoming mail server and smtp.prodigy.net as the outgoing mail server. Specify your Prodigy account and password for authentication, add a PST if you don't want to use the default delivery location (such as an Exchange Server mailbox), and configure other settings as you would for any other POP3 account.

Using Outlook with MSN

Although MSN mail accounts are available through the Hotmail Web site, you must configure Outlook with a different URL (not the Hotmail URL) in order to retrieve your MSN mail. Start the E-Mail Accounts Wizard and select HTTP as the account type. When the wizard prompts you for the account information, select MSN from the HTTP Mail Service Provider drop-down list, and specify your MSN account name and password in the Logon Information section of the dialog box. Outlook creates a PST in which to store the messages.

> For additional information on configuring HTTP account properties, see "Using Outlook with Hotmail Accounts," page 165.

Using Multiple Accounts

newfeature!

Although many users still have only one e-mail account, it's becoming much more common to have several. For example, you might have an e-mail account for work, a personal POP3 account with your ISP, and a Hotmail account. Although previous versions of Outlook sometimes made it difficult to use multiple accounts, Outlook 2002 accommodates multiple accounts with ease, all in the same profile, which means that you don't need to switch profiles as you use different accounts.

Setting up for multiple accounts is easy—just add the accounts, as needed, to your profile. However, working with multiple accounts in a single profile requires a few considerations, as explained here.

Sending Messages Using a Specific Account

When you send a message, Outlook uses the account specified as the default (see Figure 6-12). This can sometimes be a problem when you have multiple accounts in your profile. For example, you might want to send a personal message through your personal POP3 account, but if your Exchange Server account is designated as the default, your personal message will go through your office mail server. This might violate company policies or expose your personal messages to review by a system administrator. Additionally, the reply address comes from the account Outlook uses to send the message, which means replies will come back to that account. You might want to check your POP3 mail from home, for example, but you find that replies have been directed to your office account because the original messages were sent under that account.

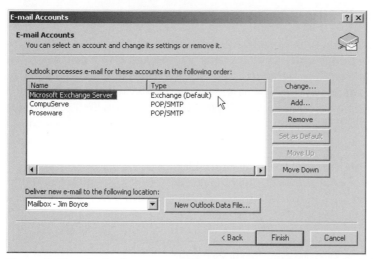

Figure 6-12. Outlook uses one of your e-mail accounts as the default account for outgoing messages.

Sending messages with a specific account is simple in Outlook. When you compose the message, click the down arrow beside Accounts on the message form toolbar (see Figure 6-13), and select the account you want Outlook to use to send the current message. Outlook then uses the reply address and other settings for the selected account for that message.

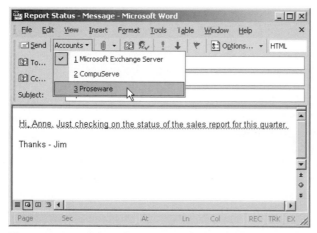

Figure 6-13. Select the account from which you want to send the message, using the Accounts button on the message form toolbar.

Chapter 6

2: Messaging

Separating Incoming Messages by Account

With the exception of mail for IMAP and HTTP accounts, Outlook delivers all mail to the default message store. (Outlook delivers IMAP and HTTP mail to the store associated with the respective accounts.) This can be a problem or an annoyance because all your e-mail could potentially wind up in the same Inbox, regardless of which account it came through. If you manage multiple accounts, it's useful to keep the messages separate. For example, you might want to keep personal messages that come through your POP3 account separate from those that come to your Exchange Server account.

You can separate messages into specific folders or stores using message rules, which allow you to specify actions Outlook should take for messages that meet specific criteria, including the account to which they were delivered. For a complete discussion of rules and automatic message processing, see "Processing Messages Automatically," page 231.

---

tip   **Keep messages separate on a shared computer**

If you share a computer with other users, you probably want to keep your messages separate from those of the other users. Although you could use the same logon account and create separate profiles or even use the same profile and set up message rules to separate the incoming messages, neither method is a very good solution. Instead, use different logon accounts on the computer, which will keep your Outlook profiles separate and therefore keep your messages separate.

Keeping a Copy of Your Mail on the Server

If you want to be able to retrieve your mail from different computers, you might want to keep a copy of your messages on the mail server. This makes all messages available no matter where you are or which computer you use to retrieve them. For example, if your computer at the office is configured to retrieve messages from your POP3 account every hour and you don't leave a copy of the messages on the server, you'll be able to see only the last hour's worth of messages if you connect from a different computer.

IMAP stores messages on the server by default. POP3 accounts, however, work differently. By default, Outlook retrieves the messages from the POP3 server and deletes them from the server. If you want the messages to remain on the server, you need to configure Outlook specifically to do so.

Here's how:

1 If Outlook is open, choose Tools, E-Mail Accounts. Alternatively, right-click the Outlook icon on the desktop and choose Properties, and then click E-Mail Accounts.

2 Select View Or Change Existing E-Mail Accounts and click Next.

170

3 Select the POP3 account and click Change.

4 Click More Settings and then click the Advanced tab.

5 Select Leave A Copy Of Messages On The Server, and then use the two associated options if you want Outlook to remove the messages after a specific time or after they have been deleted from your local Deleted Items folder.

6 Click OK, click Next, and then click Finish.

Troubleshooting

My mail server won't accept outgoing messages.

Your mail service might not accept mail relay (outgoing messages) unless you connect to the server's network. For example, POP3 Classic CompuServe accounts do not support mail relay from other servers. You must dial up a CompuServe point-of-presence to place your computer on CompuServe's network and establish a connection to CompuServe's outgoing mail server.

Connecting through the server's network isn't always practical, however. For example, if you live in a rural area, you might not have a local access number for your service. In this situation, you might use a local ISP account to connect to the Internet to retrieve your messages from other mail servers. Your ISP then invariably allows mail relay from your subnet, which lets you send messages through your own account on the ISP's mail server.

To make this work, simply specify your ISP's outgoing mail server instead of the mail server for the remote network; or, if you connect through your LAN and your organization provides a mail server with relay capability, specify that server for outgoing mail.

You specify the outgoing mail server through the e-mail account's dialog box:

1 If Outlook is open, choose Tools, E-Mail Accounts. Alternatively, right-click the Outlook icon on the desktop and choose Properties, and then click E-Mail Accounts.

2 Select View Or Change Existing E-Mail Accounts and click Next.

3 Select the POP3 account and click Change.

4 Specify the server in the Outgoing Mail Server (SMTP) box and click Next. Then click Finish.

Viewing Full Message Headers

Internet messages include routing information in their headers that specifies the sending address and server, the route the message took to get to you, and other data. In most cases, the header offers more information than you need, particularly if all you're interested in is the body of the message. But if you're trying to troubleshoot a mail problem or identify a sender who is spamming you, the headers can be useful.

---

tip   **Track down spammers**

You can't always assume that the information in a message header is accurate. Spammers often spoof or impersonate another user or server—or relay mail through another server—to hide the true origin of the message. The header helps you identify where the mail came from so you can inform the server's administrator that the server is being used to relay spam. To notify the administrator, you can send a message to *postmaster@<domain>.tld*, where *<domain>.tld* is the relaying mail server's domain.

To view the full message header, right-click the message and choose Options to display the Message Options dialog box, shown in Figure 6-14. The message header appears in the Internet Headers box. You can highlight the text and press Ctrl+C to copy the text to the clipboard for inclusion in a note or other message.

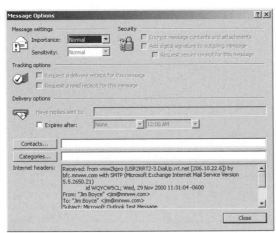

Figure 6-14.   View the full message header in the Message Options dialog box.

172

Sending and Receiving Messages

Of all the features in Microsoft Outlook, messaging is probably the most frequently used. Even if you use Outlook primarily for contact management or scheduling, chances are good that you also rely heavily on Outlook's e-mail and other messaging capabilities. Because many of Outlook's key features make extensive use of messaging for workgroup collaboration and scheduling, understanding messaging is critical to using the program effectively.

This chapter provides an in-depth look at a wide range of topics related to sending and receiving messages with Outlook. You'll learn the fundamentals—working with message forms, addressing, replying, and forwarding—but you'll also explore other, more advanced topics. For example, this chapter explains how to control when your messages are sent, how to save a copy of sent messages in specific folders, and how to work with attachments.

You'll discover how to add more than just plain text to your messages by working with graphics, hyperlinks, files, attachments, and electronic business cards. As this chapter explains, you can also spruce up your messages by using stationery, which allows you to assign a theme to your messages. Outlook provides a choice of stationery—or you can create your own. You'll also learn how to automatically attach a text signature or an electronic business card to each message you send.

Working with Messages

This section of the chapter offers a primer to bring you up to speed with Outlook's basic messaging capabilities. It focuses on topics that relate to all types of e-mail accounts. The Inbox is the place to start learning about Outlook, so fire up the program and open the Inbox folder. The next section explains how to work with message forms.

> If you haven't added e-mail accounts to your profile, see the appropriate chapter for details. Chapter 6, "Using Internet Mail," explains how to configure POP3, IMAP, and HTTP accounts; Chapter 32, "Configuring the Exchange Server Client," explains how to configure the Microsoft Exchange Server client.

Opening a Standard Message Form

You can begin a new message in Outlook using any one of these methods:

- Choose File, New, Mail Message.

- With the Inbox open, click New on the message form toolbar.

- Click the down arrow beside the New button on the message form toolbar and choose Mail Message.

- With the Inbox open, press Ctrl+N.

Outlook uses Microsoft Word as the default e-mail editor. When you begin a new message, Word starts and displays the Untitled Message form shown in Figure 7-1. If you've chosen Outlook as your default message editor instead of Word, Outlook displays the message form shown in Figure 7-2.

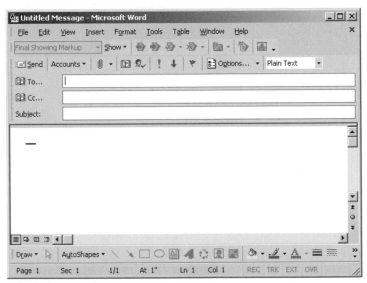

Figure 7-1.   You use this standard message form when Word is the default editor.

174

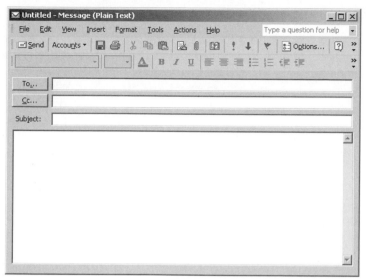

Figure 7-2. You use this standard message form when Outlook is the default editor.

Configuring Your E-Mail Editor and Viewer

You can specify the application you want to use for creating, editing, and viewing messages. To locate these settings, choose Tools, Options and click the Mail Format tab. By default, Outlook uses Microsoft Word as the e-mail editor for creating and editing messages. If you prefer, however, you can use Outlook as your editor. It takes slightly longer to begin composing a message when Word is the editor, because Outlook must start Word if it is not already running. If you work primarily with plain-text messages and don't use text formatting or graphics in messages, using Outlook as your default e-mail editor will speed up the process. You can also specify whether to use Word or Outlook for reading rich-text messages.

For an explanation of Plain Text and Rich Text formats, see "Formatting Text in Messages," page 202.

On the Mail Format tab of the Options dialog box, you can adjust the following settings:

● **Use Microsoft Word To Edit E-Mail Messages.** Select this option to specify Word as the default e-mail editor. Clear the option to use Outlook as the editor.

● **Use Microsoft Word To Read Rich Text E-Mail Messages.** Select this option to use Word to read rich-text messages. Clear the option to use Outlook instead.

Addressing Messages

Outlook's address books make it easy to address messages. When you want to send a message to someone whose address is stored in one of your local address books or in an address list on the server, you can click in the To box on the message form and type the recipient's name—you don't have to enter the entire address. When you send the message, Outlook checks the name, locates the correct address, and adds it to the message. If multiple addresses match the name you specify, Outlook shows all the matches and prompts you to select the appropriate one. If you want to send a message to someone whose address isn't in any of your address books, you need to type the full address in the To box. Alternatively, you can open a personal address book, add the address so that it will be available in the future, and then select it from there.

> For more information about Outlook address books, see Chapter 5, "Managing Address Books and Distribution Lists."

> **tip** Outlook can check the names and addresses of message recipients before you send the message. Enter the names in the To box and click the Check Names button on the message form toolbar to perform this action.

To open the address book (see Figure 7-3), click an Address Book icon beside an address box on the message form. Outlook opens the Select Names dialog box, which you can use to address the message.

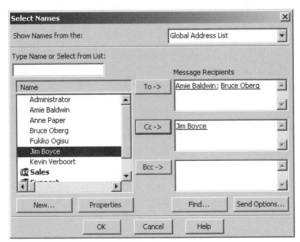

Figure 7-3. In the Select Names dialog box, you can select addresses from the address book.

Follow these steps to select addresses in this dialog box and add them to your message:

1 In the Show Names From The drop-down list, select the address list you want to view.

2 Select a name from the list, and click To, Cc, or Bcc to add the selected address to the specified address box.

3 Continue this process to add more recipients if necessary. Click OK when you're satisfied with the list.

> **tip** You can include multiple recipients in each address box on the message form. If you're typing the addresses yourself, separate them with a semicolon.

Including Carbon Copies and Blind Carbon Copies

You can direct a single message to multiple recipients either by including multiple addresses in the To box on the message form or by using the Cc (Carbon Copy) and Bcc (Blind Carbon Copy) boxes. The Cc box appears by default on message forms, but the Bcc box does not. To display the Bcc box, click the down arrow beside Options on the message form toolbar and choose Bcc. You use the Cc and Bcc boxes the same way you use the To box: type a name or address in the box, or click the Address Book icon beside the box to open the address book.

> **tip** **Hide addresses when necessary**
>
> The names contained in the To and Cc boxes of your message are visible to all recipients of the message. If you're using a distribution list, Outlook converts the names on the list to individual addresses, exposing those addresses to the recipients. If you want to hide the names of one or more recipients or don't want distribution lists exposed, place those names in the Bcc box.

Using Word to Compose Messages

Using Word as the default e-mail editor means you can take advantage of all Word's formatting, graphics, and other capabilities to create rich-text, multimedia messages. For example, you can use character and paragraph formatting, bulleted lists, automatic numbered lists, animated text, graphics, and other Word features to create dynamic messages (see Figure 7-4 on the next page). If Outlook is set up to use Word as your default editor, simply open a new message form and begin creating the message, using any Word features you need.

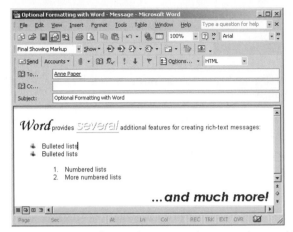

Figure 7-4. With Word as your editor, you have additional options for creating rich-text messages.

For information on specifying Word as the default e-mail editor, see the sidebar "Configuring Your E-Mail Editor and Viewer," page 175.

You can also create messages when you start Word outside Outlook:

1 With Word open, create the message in the body of the document.

2 Choose File, Send To, Mail Recipient. Word displays a message form with To, Cc, and Subject boxes.

3 Address the message and click Send when the message is complete.

Troubleshooting

The e-mail headers won't go away in Word.

When you're working in Word and you choose File, Send To, Mail Recipient, Word displays an e-mail toolbar with From, To, Cc, Bcc, and Subject headers. This lets you address a message and send the current document as the body of the message. If you decide not to send the message after all and want to continue editing the document, you could make the headers go away by shutting down Word, restarting, and reopening the document. But there is a much easier way: just choose File, Send To, Mail Recipient again. This command acts like a toggle to turn the e-mail toolbar on and off.

Specifying Message Priority and Sensitivity

By default, new messages that you create in either Outlook or Word have their priority set to Normal. You might want to change the priority to High for important or time-sensitive messages or to Low for nonwork mail or other messages that have relatively less importance. Outlook displays an icon in the Importance column of the recipient's Inbox to indicate High or Low priority. (For messages with Normal priority, no icon is displayed.)

The easiest way to set message priority is by using the toolbar in the message form. Click the High Priority button (which has an exclamation mark icon) to specify High priority. Click the Low Priority button (which has a down arrow icon) to specify Low priority. To set the priority back to Normal, click the selected priority again to remove the highlight around the button (see Figure 7-5). You can also click Options on the toolbar and set the message priority in the Message Options dialog box. In the Message Settings section of the dialog box, choose the priority level from the Importance drop-down list.

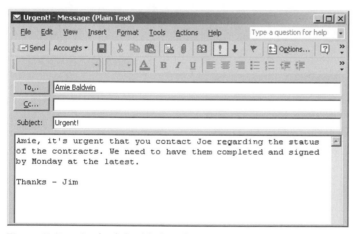

Figure 7-5. Outlook highlights the appropriate priority button to provide a visual indicator of the message's priority.

You also can specify a message's sensitivity, choosing a Normal (the default), Personal, Private, or Confidential sensitivity level. Setting sensitivity adds a tag to the message that displays the sensitivity level you've selected. This helps the recipient see at a glance how you want the message to be treated. To set sensitivity, click Options on the message form toolbar and select the sensitivity level from the Sensitivity drop-down list.

Saving a Message to Send Later

Although you can create some messages in a matter of seconds, others can take considerably longer—particularly if you're using formatting or special features or if you're composing a lengthy message. If you're interrupted while composing a message, or if you simply want to leave the message to finish later, you can save the message in your Drafts folder. Later, when you have time, you can reopen the message, complete it, and send it. Choose File, Save in the message form to have Outlook save the message to the Drafts folder (see Figure 7-6). When you're ready to work on the message again, open the Drafts folder and double-click the message to open it.

> To learn how to configure Outlook to automatically save a copy of messages you send, see "Saving Messages Automatically," page 198.

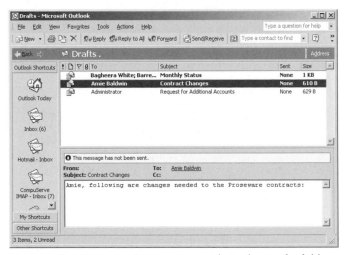

Figure 7-6. Messages in progress reside in the Drafts folder.

> **tip** You also can choose File, Save As to save a message as a Word document (or in another document format) outside your Outlook folders.

Setting Sending Options

In the Advanced E-Mail Options dialog box (see Figure 7-7), you can configure various options that affect how Outlook sends e-mail messages. To open this dialog box, choose Tools, Options and click E-Mail Options on the Preferences tab. In the E-Mail Options dialog box, click Advanced E-Mail Options.

> For details on specifying which account is used to send a message, see "Sending Messages Using a Specific Account," page 168.

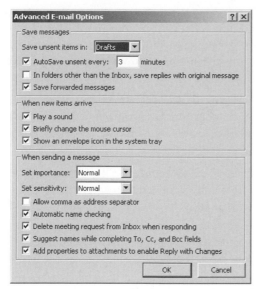

Figure 7-7. You can choose options for sending messages in the Advanced E-Mail Options dialog box.

In the Advanced E-Mail Options dialog box, you can modify the following settings:

- **Set Importance.** This option sets the default importance, or priority, level for all new messages. When you compose a message, you can override this setting by clicking the High Priority button or the Low Priority button on the toolbar in the message form or by clicking Options on the toolbar and setting the priority in the Message Options dialog box. The default setting is Normal.

- **Set Sensitivity.** This option sets the default sensitivity level for all new messages. When you compose a message, you can override this setting by clicking Options on the toolbar and setting the sensitivity level in the Message Options dialog box.

- **Allow Comma As Address Separator.** If this option is selected, you can use commas as well as semicolons in the To, Cc, and Bcc boxes of a message form to separate addresses.

- **Automatic Name Checking.** Select this option to have Outlook attempt to match names to e-mail addresses. Verified addresses are underlined, and those for which Outlook finds multiple matches are underscored by a red wavy line. When multiple matches exist and you've used a particular address before, Outlook underscores the name with a green dashed line to indicate that other choices are available.

- **Delete Meeting Request From Inbox When Responding.** Select this option to have Outlook delete a meeting request from your Inbox when you respond to the request. If you accept the meeting, Outlook enters the meeting in your calendar. Clear this check box if you want to retain the meeting request in your Inbox.

- **Suggest Names While Completing To, Cc, And Bcc Fields.** When this option is selected, Outlook completes addresses as you type them in the To, Cc, and Bcc boxes of the message form. Clear this check box to turn off this automatic completion.

- **Add Properties To Attachments To Enable Reply With Changes.** When this option is selected, Outlook adds properties to the attached documents of outgoing messages that allow the recipient to reply to the message with changes.

Controlling When Messages Are Sent

To specify when Outlook should send messages, choose Tools, Options and click Mail Setup to locate the following option:

- **Send Immediately When Connected.** With this option selected, Outlook sends messages as soon as you click Send, provided Outlook is online. If Outlook is offline, the messages go into the Outbox until you process them with a send/receive operation (which is also what happens if you do not select this option).

Requesting Delivery and Read Receipts

Regardless of which e-mail editor you use, you can request a *delivery receipt* or a *read receipt* for any message. Both types of receipts are messages that are delivered back to you after you send your message. A delivery receipt indicates the date and time your message was delivered to the recipient's mail server. A read receipt indicates the date and time the recipient opened the message.

Specifying that you want a delivery receipt or a read receipt for a message doesn't guarantee that you're going to get one. The recipient's mail server or mail client might not support delivery and read receipts. The recipient might have configured his or her e-mail client to automatically reject requests for receipts, or the recipient might answer No when prompted to send a receipt. If you receive a receipt, it's a good indication that the message was delivered or read. If you don't receive a receipt, however, you can't assume that the message wasn't delivered or read. A message receipt serves only as a positive notification, not a negative one.

To request receipts for a message you're composing, click the Options button on the message form toolbar to display the Message Options dialog box (see Figure 7-8). You'll find the delivery and read receipt options in the Voting And Tracking Options group.

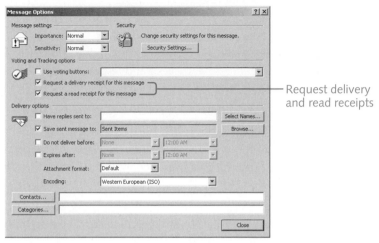

Request delivery
and read receipts

Figure 7-8. Use the Message Options dialog box to request a delivery receipt, a read receipt, or both.

Using Message Tracking and Receipts Options

You can set options to determine how Outlook handles delivery and read receipts by default. Choose Tools, Options and click E-Mail Options on the Preferences tab. In the E-Mail Options dialog box, click Tracking Options to display the Tracking Options dialog box, shown in Figure 7-9, where you'll find the options discussed in this section.

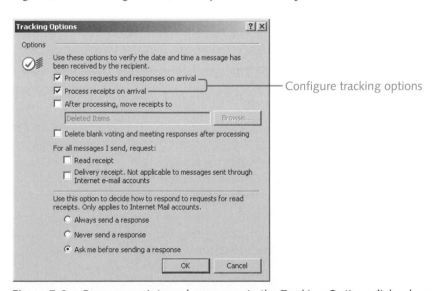

Configure tracking options

Figure 7-9. Process receipts and responses in the Tracking Options dialog box.

183

The following options control how Outlook requests read receipts and how the receipts are processed after they are received:

- **Process Requests And Responses On Arrival.** Select this option to have Outlook process all message receipt requests and responses when they arrive.

- **Process Receipts On Arrival.** Select this option to have Outlook generate received/read receipts when messages come in requesting them. Clear this check box to have Outlook prompt you for each receipt.

- **After Processing, Move Receipts To.** Select this option to have Outlook move receipts from the Inbox to the specified folder.

- **For All Messages I Send, Request Read Receipt.** Select this option to have Outlook request a read receipt for each message you send. When you compose a message, you can override this setting; to do so, click the Options button on the message form toolbar.

- **For All Messages I Send, Request Delivery Receipt.** Select this option to have Outlook request a delivery receipt for each message you send. (Note that this option is not available for messages that are sent through Internet e-mail accounts.)

These three options in the Tracking Options dialog box let you control how Outlook responds to requests from others for read receipts on messages you receive, and apply to Internet Mail accounts only:

- **Always Send A Response.** When this option is selected, Outlook always sends a read receipt to any senders who request one. Outlook generates the read receipt when you open the message.

- **Never Send A Response.** Select this option to prevent Outlook from sending read receipts to senders who request them. Outlook will not prompt you regarding receipts.

- **Ask Me Before Sending A Response.** Selecting this option lets you control, on a message-by-message basis, whether Outlook sends read receipts. When you open a message for which the sender has requested a read receipt, Outlook prompts you to authorize the receipt. If you click Yes, Outlook generates and sends the receipt. If you click No, Outlook doesn't create or send a receipt.

Sending a Message for Review

If you compose a message from Word (that is, you started Word outside Outlook), you have the ability to send the message as a document for review. You might use this feature if you're collaborating on a document with others or incorporating their comments into the final draft. Recipients can review the document and add comments, which they send back to you. They also can incorporate the changes directly in the document, which lets them take advantage of Word's revision marks feature. To send a document for review, open the document in Word and choose File, Send To, Mail Recipient (For Review).

> **note** For more detailed information on sending documents for review, see *Microsoft Word Version 2002 Inside Out,* by Mary Millhollon and Katherine Murray (Microsoft Press, 2001).

Sending a Message as an Attachment

If you compose a message using Word as the e-mail editor, you can send the message as an attachment rather than as the body of the message. For example, you might be working on a long document that you would prefer to send as an intact DOC file. If that's the case, with the document open in Word, choose File, Send To, Mail Recipient (As Attachment).

Sending to a Routing Recipient

Another option that's available when you use Word as your e-mail editor is routing a document to a group of users, either one at a time or all at the same time. For example, you might need to send a document to three recipients for each person's approval. Or you might want to route a document to all the members of a group in a specific sequence, giving each member a chance to review both the document and the comments of earlier reviewers. Routing slips allow you to accomplish either of these tasks.

Follow these steps to use a routing slip:

1 In Word, compose the message and choose File, Send To, Routing Recipient.

2 Outlook displays a message indicating that another program (Word) is attempting to access addresses you have stored in Outlook. When you click Yes to allow Word to read your addresses, the Routing Slip dialog box is displayed (see Figure 7-10 on the next page).

3 Click Address and add the addresses of all recipients to whom you want to send the message. If you want the message to be routed to the recipients in sequence (the One After Another option at the bottom of the dialog box), select the addresses in the order in which you want the recipients to receive the message.

> **tip** If you prefer, you can add the addresses to the Routing Slip dialog box in any order. Then you can use the Move arrow buttons to change the routing order, as indicated in Figure 7-10.

Chapter 7

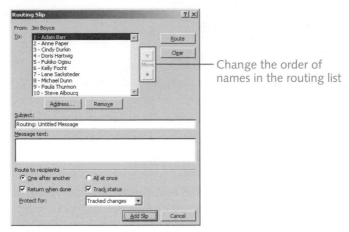

Change the order of
names in the routing list

Figure 7-10. Use the Routing Slip dialog box to route a message to
multiple recipients.

4 Specify the subject and the message text for the routing slip, and then select
from the following options:

▓ **One After Another.** Outlook sends the message only to the first recipient on the list. That recipient then uses the routing slip to route the
message to the next person on the list.

▓ **All At Once.** Outlook sends the message to all recipients on the routing list at the same time.

▓ **Return When Done.** Outlook automatically returns the routed document to you when the last recipient closes it.

▓ **Track Status.** Outlook delivers an e-mail message to you each time a
recipient sends the document to another person on the routing list.

▓ **Protect For.** In the drop-down list, select Comments to allow recipients
to insert comments but not to modify the document. Select Tracked
Changes to turn on revision marks and allow recipients to insert
changes using revision marks. Select Forms if you're routing a form
that you want recipients to fill out, but you don't want them to modify
the form itself. Select None if you don't want to track any changes.

5 Click Add Slip to add the routing slip, and then click Send to send the
document.

> **note** To learn more about sending documents using a routing slip, see *Microsoft Word Ver-
> sion 2002 Inside Out,* by Mary Millhollon and Katherine Murray (Microsoft Press, 2001).

186

Replying to Messages

When you reply to a message, Outlook sends your reply to the person who sent you the message. Replying to a message is simple: select the message in the Inbox, and then click the Reply button on the Standard toolbar; choose Actions, Reply; or press Ctrl+R. Outlook opens a message form and, depending on how you have configured Outlook for replies, can also include the original message content in various formats.

If the message to which you're replying was originally sent to multiple recipients and you want to send your reply to all of them, click Reply All; choose Actions, Reply To All; or press Ctrl+Shift+R.

> For more information about message replies, see "Using Other Reply and Forwarding Options," page 188.

> **tip** **Hide the recipients list**
>
> When you use Reply All, Outlook places all the addresses in the To box. If you don't want the recipients list to be visible, use the Bcc box to send blind carbon copies. To do this, click Reply All, highlight the addresses in the To box, and cut them. Then click in the Bcc box and paste the addresses there.

Forwarding Messages

In addition to replying to a message, you can forward the message to one or more recipients. To forward a message, select the message header in the message folder (Inbox or other), and then click Forward on the message form toolbar; choose Actions, Forward; or press Ctrl+F. Outlook opens a new message form and either incorporates the original message in the body of the current one or attaches it to the new message.

If you forward a single message, Outlook by default forwards the original message in the body of your new message, and you can add your own comments. If you prefer, however, you can configure Outlook to forward messages as attachments rather than including them in the body of your messages.

> For information about options for forwarding, see "Using Other Reply and Forwarding Options," page 188.

> **note** If you select multiple messages and click Forward, Outlook sends the messages as attachments rather than including them in the body of your message.

Using Other Reply and Forwarding Options

You can change how Outlook handles and formats message replies and forwarded messages. These options reside in the E-Mail Options dialog box, shown in Figure 7-11.

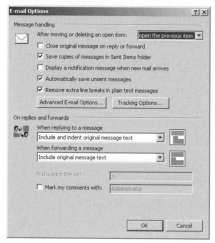

Figure 7-11. You can set options for message replies and forwarded messages in the E-Mail Options dialog box.

To open this dialog box, choose Tools, Options and click E-Mail Options on the Preferences tab. You can then view or set the following options:

- **Close Original Message On Reply Or Forward.** Select this option to have Outlook close the message form when you click Reply or Forward. Clear this option to have Outlook leave the message form open. If you frequently forward the same message with different comments to different recipients, it's useful to have Outlook leave the message open so that you don't have to open it again to perform the next forward.

- **When Replying To A Message.** Use this drop-down list to specify how Outlook handles the original message text when you reply to a message. You can choose to have Outlook generate a clean reply without the current message text, include the text without changes, or include but indent the text, for example. Note that you can either include the original message text in the body of your reply or add it to the message as an attachment.

- **When Forwarding A Message.** Use this drop-down list to specify how Outlook handles the original message text when you forward a message. You can, for example, include the message in the body of the forwarded message or add it as an attachment.

- **Prefix Each Line With.** If you select Prefix Each Line Of The Original Message in the When Replying To A Message option or the When Forwarding A Message option, you can use this box to specify the character Outlook uses to prefix each line of the original message in the body of the reply or the forwarded message. The default is an angle bracket (>) and a space, but you can use one or more characters of your choice.

- **Mark My Comments With.** Select this option and enter a name or other text in the associated box. Outlook will add the specified text to mark your typed comments in the body of a message that you are replying to or forwarding. This option has no effect if you're using Word as your e-mail editor, because Word uses revision marks for document annotation.

For more details on replying to and forwarding messages, see "Replying to Messages" and "Forwarding Messages," page 187.

Troubleshooting

You can't forward a single message as an attachment.

In Outlook 2002, you can send documents from other Microsoft Office applications as attachments, and you can forward multiple messages in Outlook as attachments. However, sending a single message as an attachment rather than including it in the body of the message in Outlook requires either that you reconfigure Outlook's default behavior before forwarding the message or that you use a workaround.

To change Outlook's default behavior so that it sends a single message as an attachment when you forward it, choose Tools, Options, E-Mail Options. In the When Forwarding A Message drop-down list, select Attach Original Message and click OK. This setting now applies to all messages you forward, not just to the current one.

If you want to override Outlook's default behavior for the current message only, use one of these two workarounds. One method is to select *two* messages to forward and then, in the message form, delete the attached message that you don't want to include. A second method is to compose a new message and choose Insert, Item to insert the message (or any other Outlook item).

Controlling Synchronization and Send/Receive Times

Outlook uses *send and receive groups* (or *send/receive groups*) to control when messages are sent and received for specific e-mail accounts. You can also use send/receive groups to define the types of items that Outlook synchronizes. *Synchronization* is the process in which Outlook synchronizes the local copy of your folders with your message store on the Exchange Server. For example, assume that while you've been working offline you have created several new e-mail messages and scheduled a few events. You connect to the Exchange Server and perform a synchronization. Outlook uploads to your Exchange Server the changes you made locally and also downloads changes from the server to your local store, such as downloading messages that have been delivered to your Inbox on the server.

Send/receive groups allow you to be flexible in controlling which functions Outlook performs for synchronization. For example, you can set up a send/receive group for your Exchange Server account that synchronizes only your Inbox and not your other folders, for those times when you simply want a quick check of your mail.

Send/receive groups also are handy for helping you manage different types of accounts. For example, if you integrate your personal and work e-mail into a single profile, you can use send/receive groups to control when each type of mail is processed. You might create one send/receive group for your personal accounts and another for your work accounts. You can also use send/receive groups to limit network traffic to certain times of the day. For example, if your organization limits Internet connectivity to specific times, you could use send/receive groups to schedule your Internet accounts to synchronize during the allowed times.

Think of send/receive groups as a way to collect various accounts into groups and assign to each group specific send/receive and synchronization behavior. You can create multiple send/receive groups, and you can include the same account in multiple groups if needed.

Setting Up Send/Receive Groups

To set up or modify send/receive groups in Outlook, choose Tools, Send/Receive Settings, Define Send/Receive Groups. Outlook displays the Send/Receive Groups dialog box, shown in Figure 7-12. By default, Outlook sets up one group named All Accounts and configures it to send and receive when online and offline. You can modify or remove that group, add others, and configure other send/receive behavior in the Send/Receive Groups dialog box.

190

Chapter 7

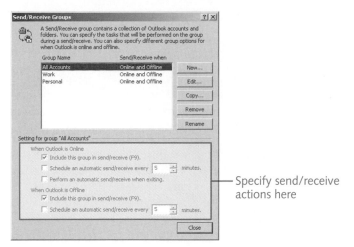

Figure 7-12. You can specify send/receive actions in the Send/Receive Groups dialog box.

When you select a group from the Group Name list, Outlook displays the associated settings in the Setting For Group area of the dialog box:

- **Include This Group In Send/Receive.** Select this option to have Outlook process accounts in the selected group when you click Send/Receive on the message form toolbar or press F9. Outlook provides this option for both online and offline behavior.

- **Schedule An Automatic Send/Receive Every *n* Minutes.** Select this option to have Outlook check the accounts in the selected group every *n* minutes. The default is 5 minutes. Outlook provides this option for both online and offline behavior.

- **Perform An Automatic Send/Receive When Exiting.** Select this option to have Outlook process the accounts in the selected group when you exit Outlook from an online session.

Creating New Groups

Although you could modify the All Accounts group to process only selected accounts, it's better to create other groups as needed and leave All Accounts "as is" for those times when you do want to process all your e-mail accounts together.

Follow these steps to create a new group:

1 In Outlook, choose Tools, Send/Receive Settings, Define Send/Receive Groups.

2 Click New, type the name for the group as you want it to appear on the Send/Receive submenu, and click OK. Outlook displays the Send/Receive Settings dialog box, shown in Figure 7-13 on the next page.

191

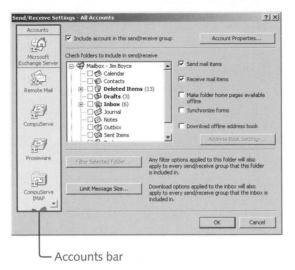

Accounts bar

Figure 7-13. You can configure account processing in the Send/Receive Settings dialog box.

3 In the Accounts bar on the left, click the account you want to configure. By default, all accounts in the group are excluded from synchronization, indicated by the red X on the account icon.

4 Select the Include Account In This Send/Receive Group check box to activate the remaining options in the dialog box and to have the account included when you process messages for the selected group.

5 In the Check Folders To Include In Send/Receive list, click the box beside each folder that you want Outlook to synchronize when processing this group.

6 Select other settings, using the following list as a guide:

   ■ **Send Mail Items.** Select this option to have Outlook send outgoing mail for this account when a send/receive action occurs for the group.

   ■ **Receive Mail Items.** Select this option to have Outlook retrieve incoming mail for this account when a send/receive action occurs for the group.

   ■ **Make Folder Home Pages Available Offline.** This option has Outlook cache folder home pages offline so that they are available to you any time.

   ■ **Synchronize Forms.** Select this option to have Outlook synchronize changes to forms that have been made locally as well as changes that have been made on the server.

192

■ **Download Offline Address Book.** When this option is selected, Outlook updates the offline address book when a send/receive action occurs for the group.

■ **Get Folder Unread Count.** For IMAP accounts only, you can select this option to have Outlook get the number of unread messages from the server.

7 If you need to apply filters or message size limits, do so. Otherwise, click OK and then click Close to close the Send/Receive Groups dialog box.

For information on how to apply filters or message size limits, see "Filtering Folders During Synchronization," below or "Limiting Message Size," page 195.

Modifying Existing Groups

You can modify existing send/receive groups in much the same way you create new ones. Choose Tools, Send/Receive Settings, Define Send/Receive Groups. Select the group you want to modify and click Edit. The settings you can modify are the same as those discussed in the preceding section.

Filtering Folders During Synchronization

Although you'll probably want to synchronize all items for each folder when you send and receive, you might occasionally want to filter a folder to process only items that meet certain criteria. For example, perhaps you want to download only incoming messages that have no attachments, because a large attachment in your Inbox is choking your Internet connection and preventing you from retrieving an important message.

Outlook provides a means of filtering the send/receive process for each folder. When you set a filter for a folder, the filter applies not just to the selected send/receive group but to that folder in all send/receive groups to which it belongs. In other words, the filter follows the folder, not the selected group.

Follow these steps to filter a folder:

1 Choose Tools, Send/Receive Settings, Define Send/Receive Groups.

2 Select a group to modify and click Edit.

3 From the Accounts bar, select the account containing the folder you want to filter.

4 In the Check Folders To Include In Send/Receive list, select the folder to filter.

5 Click Filter Selected Folder to open the Filter dialog box, shown in Figure 7-14 on the next page.

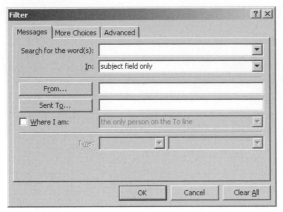

Figure 7-14. You can filter folder actions using the Filter dialog box.

6 Set up the filter criteria by entering the relevant information and choosing options on the various tabs of the Filter dialog box. Click OK.

7 Make other changes to accounts and folders as needed, and click OK to close the Send/Receive Settings dialog box. Then close the Send/Receive Groups dialog box.

As you browse through the options in the Filter dialog box, you'll find that Outlook gives you considerable flexibility for defining the filter criteria.

Clearing a Filtered Selection

Filter criteria that you have specified will continue to be applied until you clear the filter.

Follow these steps to clear the filter and allow unfiltered synchronization:

1 Choose Tools, Send/Receive Settings, Define Send/Receive Groups.

2 Select a group to modify and click Edit.

3 From the Accounts bar, select the account containing the folder you want to filter.

4 In the Check Folders To Include In Send/Receive list, select the folder to filter.

5 Click Filter Selected Folder to open the Filter dialog box.

6 Click Clear All, and then click OK.

Limiting Message Size

You can also use the Send/Receive Settings dialog box to specify a limit on message size for messages downloaded from the Inbox of the selected Exchange Server account. This provides an easy way to control large messages that arrive in your Exchange Server account. Rather than downloading messages that are larger than the specified limit, Outlook places them in a folder on the server named Large Messages (a subfolder of the Inbox) and notifies you of that action. You can then go online and open the Large Messages folder to view the messages or include the Large Messages folder in your next synchronization.

> **note** Specifying a message size limit in the Send/Receive Settings dialog box doesn't affect the size of messages that you can receive on the server. It simply directs Outlook to copy large messages to a different folder on the server rather than downloading them.

Follow these steps to specify a message size limit for an Exchange Server account:

1 Choose Tools, Send/Receive Settings, Define Send/Receive Groups.

2 Select a group to modify and click Edit.

3 From the Accounts bar, select the Exchange Server account containing the folder for which you want to set a message size limit.

4 Click Limit Message Size to display the Download Options dialog box, shown in Figure 7-15 on the next page.

5 Specify the criteria you want to use to limit message download and click OK. Notice that you can also specify exceptions to the limits—for example, you can have Outlook download any High priority message, no matter how large.

When you create a message size limit by using this procedure, Outlook creates a message rule named Large Message Rule. If you need to configure more advanced options or exercise a finer degree of control over the size limit criteria, choose Tools, Rules Wizard. The Rules Wizard allows you to modify the Large Message Rule to suit your requirements.

> For more details about working with message rules, see "Processing Messages Automatically," page 231.

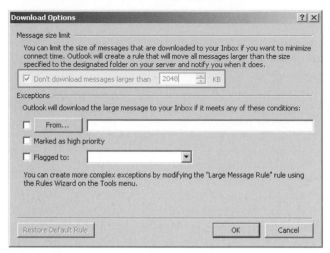

Figure 7-15.   Use the Download Options dialog box to control downloading of large messages.

You can use a similar mechanism to control downloading of large messages from POP3 accounts. In this case, you can choose to download only message headers for messages larger than a specified size.

Follow these steps to configure POP3 message size filtering:

1   Choose Tools, Send/Receive Settings, Define Send/Receive Groups.

2   Select a group to modify and click Edit.

3   From the Accounts bar, select the POP3 account for which you want to set a message size limit.

4   Select Download Only Item Descriptions For Items Larger Than *nn* KB, specify the size limit, and click OK.

To retrieve a message with a large attachment from a POP3 server, mark the message to be downloaded.

For details on using remote mail with POP3 accounts, see "Working with Message Headers," page 368.

Scheduling Send/Receive Synchronization

You can schedule synchronization for each send/receive group separately, giving you quite a bit of control over when Outlook processes your Inbox, Outbox, and other folders for synchronization. You can configure Outlook to process each send/receive group on a periodic basis as well as to process specific groups when you exit Outlook. For example, you might schedule the All Accounts group to synchronize only when you exit Outlook, even though you've scheduled a handful of other groups to process messages more frequently during the day. Because you can create as many groups as needed and can place the same account in multiple groups, you have a good deal of flexibility in determining when each account is processed.

Configuring Send/Receive Schedules

Follow these steps to configure synchronization for each send/receive group:

1 Choose Tools, Send/Receive Settings, Define Send/Receive Groups.

2 In the Send/Receive Groups dialog box, select the group whose schedule you want to modify.

3 In the Setting For Group area, select Schedule An Automatic Send/Receive Every *n* Minutes, and then specify the number of minutes that should elapse between send/receive events for the selected group. Set this option for both online and offline behavior.

4 If you want the group to be processed when you exit Outlook, select Perform An Automatic Send/Receive When Exiting.

You can use a combination of scheduled and manually initiated send/receive events to process messages and accounts. For example, you can specify in the Send/Receive Group dialog box that a given group (such as All Accounts) must be included when you click Send/Receive or press F9 and then configure other accounts to process as scheduled. Thus some accounts might process only when you manually initiate the send/receive event, and others might process only by automatic execution. In addition, you can provide an overlap so that a specific account processes manually as well as by schedule—simply include the account in multiple groups with the appropriate settings for each group.

Disabling Scheduled Send/Receive Processing

On occasion, you might want to disable scheduled send/receive events altogether. For example, assume that you're working offline and don't have a connection through which you can check your accounts. In that situation, you can turn off scheduled send/receive processing until a connection can be reestablished.

To disable scheduled send/receive processing, choose Tools, Send/Receive Settings, Disable Scheduled Send/Receive. Select this command again to enable the scheduled processing.

Chapter 7

197

2: Messaging

Managing Messages and Attachments

Using Outlook's e-mail features effectively requires more than understanding how to send and receive messages. This section of the chapter helps you get your messages and attachments under control.

Saving Messages Automatically

You can configure Outlook to save messages automatically in several ways—for example, saving the current message periodically or saving a copy of forwarded messages. You'll find most of the following options in the E-Mail Options dialog box (shown earlier in Figure 7-11) and in the Advanced E-Mail Options dialog box (shown earlier in Figure 7-7).

- **Automatically Save Unsent Messages (in the E-Mail Options dialog box).** Use this option to have Outlook save unsent messages in the Drafts folder. Outlook by default saves unsent messages to the Drafts folder every 3 minutes. Clear this option if you don't want unsent messages saved in this folder.

- **Save Unsent Items In (in the Advanced E-Mail Options dialog box).** Specify the folder in which you want Outlook to save unsent items. The default location is the Drafts folder.

- **AutoSave Unsent Every *n* Minutes (in the Advanced E-Mail Options dialog box).** Specify the frequency at which Outlook automatically saves unsent items to the folder specified by the Save Unsent Items In option.

- **In Folders Other Than The Inbox, Save Replies With Original Message (in the Advanced E-Mail Options dialog box).** With this option selected, Outlook saves a copy of sent items to the Sent Items folder if the message originates from the Inbox (new message, reply, or forward). If the message originates from a folder other than the Inbox—such as a reply to a message stored in a different folder—Outlook saves the reply in the same folder as the original. If this option is cleared, Outlook saves all sent items in the Sent Items folder.

You can also use rules to control where Outlook places messages. For more information on creating and using rules, see Chapter 8, "Filtering, Organizing, and Using Automatic Responses."

- **Save Forwarded Messages (in the Advanced E-Mail Options dialog box).** Select this option to save a copy of all messages that you forward. Messages are saved in either the Sent Items folder or the originating folder, depending on how you set the previous option.

Retaining a Copy of Sent Messages

Keeping track of the messages you send can often be critical, particularly in a work setting. Fortunately, with Outlook, you can automatically retain a copy of each message you send, providing a record of when you sent the message and to whom you sent it.

By default, Outlook stores a copy of each sent message in the Sent Items folder. You can open this folder and sort the items to locate messages based on any message criteria. You can view, forward, move, and otherwise manage the contents of Sent Items just as you can with other folders.

If you allow Outlook to save a copy of messages in the Sent Items folder, over time the sheer volume of messages can overwhelm your system. So you should implement a means—whether manual or automatic—to archive or clear out the contents of the Sent Items folder. With the manual method, all you need to do is move or delete messages from the folder as your needs dictate. If you want to automate the archival process, you can do so; for details on how to automatically archive messages from any folder, see "Configuring the Automatic Archiving of Items," page 716.

Follow these steps to specify whether Outlook retains a copy of sent messages in the Sent Items folder:

1 Choose Tools, Options and click E-Mail Options on the Preferences tab.

2 In the E-Mail Options dialog box (see Figure 7-16), select the Save Copies Of Messages In Sent Items Folder check box to have Outlook retain sent messages. If you want to prevent Outlook from keeping a copy of sent messages, clear this check box. Click OK.

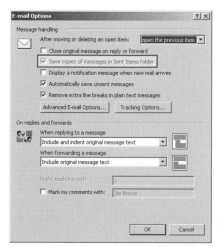

Figure 7-16. In the E-Mail Options dialog box, you can choose whether Outlook saves copies of sent messages.

> **tip** If you need to change Outlook's behavior for a single message, you can override the setting. With the message form open, choose File, Properties and then select the action you want Outlook to take.

Saving Attachments to a Disk

It's a sure bet that some of the messages you receive include attachments such as documents, pictures, or applications. In general, you can work with these attachments in Outlook without saving them separately to disk. For example, you can double-click an attachment in the InfoBar to open the attachment. The next step then depends on the attachment's extension and the application with which that extension is registered on your system.

But in many instances, it's necessary to save attachments to disk. For example, you might receive a self-extracting executable containing a program you need to install. In that case, the best option is to save the file to disk and install it from there.

You can save attachments using either of these methods:

- If you're using the preview pane, right-click the attachment in the InfoBar and choose Save As.

- Choose File, Save Attachments if you want to save one or more attachments or if the preview pane is not available. This option is handy when you want to save all attachments.

Saving Messages to a File

Although Outlook maintains your messages in your store folders, occasionally you might need to save a message to a file. For example, you might want to archive a single message or a selection of messages outside Outlook or save a message to include as an attachment in another document.

You can save a single message to a file or combine several messages into a single file. When you save a single message, Outlook gives you the option of saving it in one of the following formats:

- **Text Only.** Save the message as a text file, losing any formatting in the original message.

- **Rich Text Format.** Save the message in RTF format, retaining the original message formatting.

- **Outlook Template.** Save the message as an Outlook template that you can use to create other messages.

- **Message Format.** Save the message in MSG format, retaining all formatting and attachments within the message file.

When you save a selection of messages, you can store the messages only in a text file, and Outlook combines the body of the selected messages in that text file. This then allows you to concatenate the various messages (that is, to join them sequentially) into a single text file. You might use this capability, for example, to create a message thread from a selection of messages.

To save one or more messages, open the Outlook folder where the messages reside and select the message header(s). Choose File, Save As and specify the path, file name, and file format.

Configuring Message Handling

Outlook provides several options that let you control how Outlook handles and displays messages. In the E-Mail Options dialog box (shown earlier in Figure 7-16), you can change either of these two settings:

- **After Moving Or Deleting An Open Item.** Use this option to control what action Outlook takes when you move or delete an open item, such as a message. You can set Outlook to open the previous message, open the next message, or return to the Inbox without opening other messages.

- **Remove Extra Line Breaks In Plain Text Messages.** Select this option to have Outlook automatically remove extra line breaks from plain-text messages that you receive. Clear the check box to leave the messages as they are.

Moving and Copying Messages Between Folders

Managing your messages often includes moving them to other folders. For example, if you're working on multiple projects, you might want to store the messages related to each specific project in the folder created for that project. The easiest method for moving a message between folders is to drag the message from its current location to the new location. If you want to copy a message rather than moving it, right-click the message, drag it to the folder, and then choose Copy.

If you can't see both the source and destination folders in the folder list, or if you prefer not to drag the message, you can use a different method of moving or copying. Select the message in the source folder and choose Edit, Move To Folder or Copy To Folder, depending on which action you need. Outlook displays a dialog box in which you select the destination folder.

> **tip** You can use the shortcut menu to move a message to a specified folder by right-clicking the message and choosing Move To Folder.

Deleting Messages

When you delete messages from any folder other than the Deleted Items folder, the messages are moved to the Deleted Items folder. You can then recover the messages by moving them to other folders, if needed. When Outlook deletes messages from the Deleted Items folder, however, those messages are deleted permanently.

You can set Outlook to automatically delete all messages from the Deleted Items folder whenever you exit the program, which helps keep the size of your message store manageable. However, it also means that unless you recover a deleted message before you exit Outlook, that message is irretrievably lost. If you seldom have to recover deleted files, this might not be a problem for you.

To change what happens to items in the Deleted Items folder when you exit Outlook, choose Tools, Options and click the Other tab. Select or clear Empty The Deleted Items Folder Upon Exiting.

Including More Than Text

The majority of your messages might consist of unformatted text, but you can use formatted text and other elements to create rich-text and multimedia messages. For example, you might want to use character or paragraph formatting for emphasis, add graphics, or insert hyperlinks to Web sites or other resources. The following sections explain how to accomplish these tasks.

Formatting Text in Messages

Formatting text in messages is easy, particularly if you're comfortable with Microsoft Word. Even if you're not, you should have little trouble adding some snap to your messages with character, paragraph, and other formatting.

Your options for rich text depend in part on whether you use Word or Outlook as your e-mail editor. Outlook offers some rich-text capabilities, but Word offers many more. For example, you can apply paragraph formatting to indent some paragraphs but not others, create bulleted and numbered lists, and apply special color and font formatting. Regardless of which editor you use, the formatting options are available on the editor's Format menu. These options are simple to use. Understanding the underlying format in which your messages are sent, however, requires a little more exploration.

By default, Outlook uses Hypertext Markup Language (HTML) as the format for sending messages. HTML format lets you create multimedia messages that can be viewed
directly in a Web browser and an e-mail client. Depending on the capabilities of the
recipient's e-mail client, however, you might need to use a different format. Plain Text
format doesn't allow any special formatting, but it offers the broadest client support—
every e-mail client can read plain-text messages. Alternatively, you can use Rich Text
format to add paragraph and character formatting and to embed graphics and other
nontext media in your message.

> **note** Using HTML format for messages doesn't mean that you need to understand HTML to
> create a multimedia message. Outlook takes care of creating the underlying HTML
> code for you.

You choose the format for the current message from the message form's Format menu,
selecting Plain Text, Rich Text, or HTML. If Word is your editor, choose one of those
options from the drop-down list on the message form toolbar. To set the default message format for all new messages, choose Tools, Options on the Outlook menu bar and
click the Mail Format tab (see Figure 7-17). Select the format from the Compose In
This Message Format drop-down list.

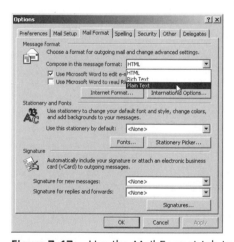

Figure 7-17. Use the Mail Format tab to set the default message format.

On the Mail Format tab of the Options dialog box, you can click Fonts to display the
Fonts dialog box, shown in Figure 7-18. Use the options in this dialog box to control
which fonts Outlook uses for specific tasks, such as composing new messages, replying
to or forwarding a message, and composing or reading plain-text messages. You can
specify the font as well as the font size, color, and other font characteristics.

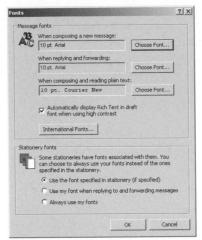

Figure 7-18. Use the Fonts dialog box to control the appearance of fonts in Outlook for specific tasks.

Including Graphics in Messages

Your ability to insert graphics in a message depends in part on which editor and message format you use. You can't insert embedded graphics in a message that uses Plain Text format in either editor. If Outlook is your default editor, you can insert embedded graphics only when using HTML format. With Word as the editor, you can insert graphics using either Rich Text or HTML format.

> **note** Although you can't insert embedded graphics, you can attach graphics files to a plain-text message with either Outlook or Word as the editor.

The process you use to insert graphics and the options that are available also vary according to which editor you use. The following sections explain the differences.

Attaching Graphics Files to Plain-Text Messages

With either Outlook or Word as your editor, follow these steps to attach a graphics file to a plain-text message:

1 In the message form, choose Insert, File.

2 In the Insert File dialog box, locate the file you want to attach and click Insert.

Inserting Graphics with Outlook as the Editor

With Outlook as the default editor, follow these steps to insert a graphic in a message:

1 In the message form, choose Format, HTML to use HTML format for the message.

2 Choose Insert, Picture to display the Picture dialog box, shown in Figure 7-19.

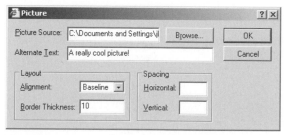

Figure 7-19. Use the Picture dialog box to specify a border and other properties for the picture you want to insert in your message.

3 In the dialog box, enter the following information:

- **Picture Source.** Specify the path to the graphics file that contains the picture or click Browse to locate the file.

- **Alternate Text.** Enter optional text that will appear in place of the picture for recipients whose e-mail clients don't support HTML or whose clients are configured not to show graphics.

- **Alignment.** Specify how you want the image aligned in the message and how text will flow with the graphic. For example, you would select Texttop if you wanted the top of the image to be in line with the top of the text to its right. Click the question mark on the title bar and then click this drop-down list to view explanations of the available options.

- **Border Thickness.** Add an optional border around the graphic, with a specified pixel width.

- **Spacing.** Enter the amount of spacing, in pixels, that should be added to the horizontal and vertical sides of the image.

4 Click OK to insert the graphic.

Inserting Graphics with Word as the Editor

When Word is your default editor, you have additional options for inserting a graphic in a message:

1 Begin composing a new message using HTML or Rich Text format, and place the cursor in the body of the message where you want the picture placed.

2 Choose Insert, Picture and then choose one of the following commands:

- **Clip Art.** Insert a clip art image from disk.

- **From File.** Insert a graphics file from disk.

- **From Scanner Or Camera.** Import a picture from your scanner or digital camera.

- **Organizational Chart.** Insert an organizational chart (which you can modify). Figure 7-20 shows an example.

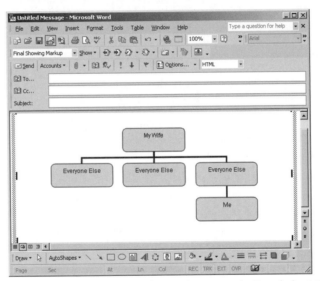

Figure 7-20. You can easily insert an organizational chart that you can modify as needed.

- **New Drawing.** Insert a Drawing Canvas object in which you can draw using Word's built-in drawing tools.

- **AutoShapes.** Insert a Word AutoShape symbol from Word's AutoShape library.

- **WordArt.** Insert a WordArt object. WordArt provides special formatting and other text effects that allow you to create dynamic text.

- **Chart.** Insert a Microsoft Graph chart object.

At this point, the next steps depend on which command you have chosen. If you need help with a particular procedure, consult the Word online Help feature or see *Microsoft Word Version 2002 Inside Out,* by Mary Millhollon and Katherine Murray (Microsoft Press, 2001).

> **tip**   You can insert various types of editable diagrams in a message by choosing Insert, Diagram.

Inserting Hyperlinks

With either Outlook or Word as your e-mail editor, you can easily insert hyperlinks (links) to Web sites, e-mail addresses, network shares, and other items in a message. When you type certain kinds of text in a message, Outlook automatically converts the text to a hyperlink, requiring no special action from you. For example, if you type an e-mail address, an Internet URL, or a UNC (Universal Naming Convention) path to a share, Outlook converts the text to a hyperlink. To indicate the hyperlink, Outlook underlines it and changes the font color.

When the recipient of your message clicks the hyperlink, the resulting action depends on the type of hyperlink. With an Internet URL, for example, the recipient can go to the specified Web site. With a UNC path, the remote share opens when the recipient clicks the hyperlink. This is a great way to point the recipient to a shared resource on your computer or on another computer on the network.

> **tip**   **Follow a hyperlink**
>
> You can't follow (open) a hyperlink in a message you're composing by clicking the hyperlink. This action is restricted to allow you to click the hyperlink text and edit it. To follow a hyperlink in a message you're composing, hold down the Ctrl key and click the hyperlink.

Inserting Hyperlinks with Outlook as the Editor

When Outlook is your e-mail editor, you have another option for inserting a hyperlink in a message:

1   Locate the cursor where you want to insert the hyperlink, and choose Insert, Hyperlink to display the Hyperlink dialog box, shown in Figure 7-21.

2   From the Type drop-down list, select the type of hyperlink you want to insert. Outlook adds the appropriate prefix to the URL field.

3   Complete the URL and click OK.

207

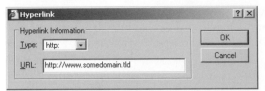

Figure 7-21. Use this dialog box to insert a hyperlink when Outlook is your e-mail editor.

Inserting Hyperlinks with Word as the Editor

When you use Word as your e-mail editor, you have many more options for inserting hyperlinks. Locate the cursor where you want to insert the hyperlink, and choose Insert, Hyperlink to display the Insert Hyperlink dialog box, shown in Figure 7-22.

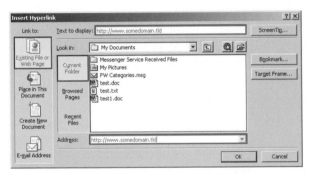

Figure 7-22. Use the Insert Hyperlink dialog box to insert a hyperlink in a message when Word is your e-mail editor.

The options displayed in the Insert Hyperlink dialog box vary according to the type of hyperlink you're inserting, as the following sections explain.

Inserting hyperlinks to files or Web pages   To insert a hyperlink to a file or to a Web page, select Existing File Or Web Page in the Link To bar. Then provide the following information in the Insert Hyperlink dialog box:

- **Text To Display.** In this box, type the text that will serve as the hyperlink in the message. Outlook underlines this text and changes its color to indicate the hyperlink.

- **Look In.** If you are linking to a file, use this drop-down list to locate and select the file on the local computer or on the network. (If you want to insert a hyperlink to a file you've used recently, click Recent Files to view a list of most recently used files in the document list of the dialog box.)

- **Browse The Web.** To browse for a URL to associate with the hyperlink, click the Browse The Web button to open your browser. (If you want to insert a hyperlink to a page you've recently viewed in your Web browser, click Browsed Pages. The document list in the dialog box changes to show a list of recently browsed pages.)

- **Address.** Type the local path, the Internet URL, or the UNC path to the file or Web site in this box.

- **ScreenTip.** Click this button to define an optional ScreenTip that appears when the recipient's pointer hovers over the hyperlink.

- **Bookmark.** Click this button to select an existing bookmark in the specified document. When the recipient clicks the hyperlink, the document opens at the bookmark location.

- **Target Frame.** Click this button to specify the browser frame in which you want the hyperlink to appear. For example, choose New Window if you want the hyperlink to open in a new window on the recipient's computer.

Troubleshooting

Recipients of your messages can't access linked files.

If you're setting up a hyperlink to a local file, bear in mind that the recipient probably won't be able to access the file using the file's local path. For example, linking to C:\Docs\Policies.doc would cause the recipient's system to try to open that path on his or her own system. You can use this method to point the recipient to a document on his or her own computer. But if you want to point the recipient to a document on your computer, you must either specify a UNC path to the document or specify a URL (which requires that your computer function as a Web server).

The form of the UNC path you specify depends on your operating system as well as that of the recipient. UNC paths in Microsoft Windows 9x, Windows Me, and Windows NT are limited to \\<server>\<share>\<document>, where <server> is the name of the computer sharing the resource, <share> is the share name, and <document> is the name of the document to open. In Windows 2000, you can specify a deeper UNC path, such as \\<server>\<share>\<subfolder>\<sub-subfolder>\<document>.doc. For the hyperlink to work properly, however, the recipient must also be using Windows 2000.

Chapter 7

Inserting a hyperlink to a place in the current message If you click Place In This Document in the Link To bar, the Insert Hyperlink dialog box changes, as shown in Figure 7-23. The Select A Place In This Document area shows the available locations in the open document: headings, bookmarks, and the top of the document. Select the location to which you want to link, provide other information as necessary (the text to display in the hyperlink, for example, or perhaps a ScreenTip), and then click OK.

Link to a place in the current document

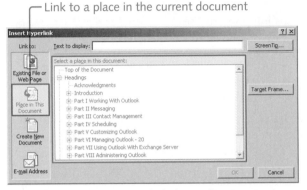

Figure 7-23.   You can easily link to a location in the current document.

> **note** This method is most commonly used when you have opened a document in Word and are inserting a hyperlink in that document rather than in a separate e-mail message.

Inserting a hyperlink to a new document If you select Create New Document in the Link To bar of the Insert Hyperlink dialog box, you can specify the path to a new document and choose to either edit the document now or insert the hyperlink for later editing. You'll most often use this method for inserting hyperlinks in a Word document rather than in an e-mail message.

Inserting a hyperlink to an e-mail address If you select E-Mail Address in the Link To bar, you can easily insert an e-mail address as a hyperlink in a message. When recipients click the hyperlink, their e-mail programs will open a new e-mail message addressed to the person you have specified in the hyperlink. Although you can simply type the e-mail address in the message and let Outlook convert it to a mailto: link, you might prefer to use the Insert Hyperlink dialog box instead (when Word is your e-mail editor). As Figure 7-24 shows, you can use this dialog box to select from a list of e-mail addresses you have recently used on your system and to specify the subject for the message as well as the address.

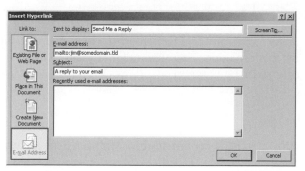

Figure 7-24. You can insert a mailto: hyperlink with extra options when Word is your e-mail editor.

Removing a hyperlink   To remove a hyperlink, right-click in the hyperlink and then choose Remove Hyperlink from the shortcut menu. Outlook retains the underlying text but removes the hyperlink.

Inserting Files in the Body of a Message

Occasionally, you'll want to insert a file in the body of a message rather than attaching it to the message. For example, you might want to include a text file, a Word document, or another document as part of the message.

Follow these steps to insert a file:

1 Place the cursor where you want to insert the file, and choose Insert, File to open the Insert File dialog box.

2 Locate and select the file to insert, and click the arrow beside the Insert button.

3 Click Insert As Text to insert the file in the body of the message.

---

tip   **Use the clipboard to insert a file**

In some cases, you'll find it easier to use the clipboard to insert a file in a message, particularly if the file is already open in another window. (Just select the file and copy and paste or cut and paste it into the message.) You can also use the clipboard when you need to insert only a portion of a file, such as a few paragraphs from a document.

Attaching Files

To attach a file to a message, you can use the steps described in the preceding section for inserting a file, with one difference: in step 3, click Insert rather than Insert As Text. Alternatively, you can click the paper clip icon on the toolbar to insert a file as an attachment, or you can simply drag the file into the message window.

211

Attaching a Business Card to a Message

With Outlook, you can send a copy of a contact item in vCard format, a standard format for exchanging contact information. This allows the recipient to import the contact data into a contact management program, assuming that the recipient's program supports the vCard standard (as most do).

Here's how to share your contact information with others using a vCard:

1 In Outlook, open the Contacts folder and select the contact item you want to send.

2 Choose Action, Forward As vCard. Outlook inserts the vCard into the message.

3 Complete the message as you normally would and click Send.

---

tip   **Send data as an Outlook item**

If you know that the recipient uses Outlook, you can right-click the contact and choose Forward—or select the contact and choose Action, Forward—to send the contact data as an Outlook contact item. Outlook users can also use vCard attachments.

For more details on using and sharing vCards, see "Sharing Contacts with vCards," page 415.

Customizing Your Messages with Stationery

By default, Outlook uses no background or special font characteristics for messages. However, it does support the use of stationery, so you can customize the look of your messages.

With Outlook stationery, you use a set of characteristics that define the font style, color, and background image for messages. In effect, stationery can give your messages a certain look and feel (see Figure 7-25). You can easily switch from one stationery to another—you're not locked into using the same stationery for all messages, and you don't need to change Outlook options each time you want to use a different stationery.

---

note   To use stationery, you must use HTML format for the message. When you use stationery, you're actually adding HTML code to the message to control its appearance.

If you're like the majority of Outlook users, you use the program mostly for business purposes and probably won't use stationery on a regular basis. But it's useful to know the basics about this feature, which can add creativity, punch, or even some humor to your personal mail.

212

Figure 7-25. Stationery gives your messages a thematic look.

Using Predefined Stationery

Outlook provides several predefined stationery themes that you can use in your messages. To view these themes, choose Tools, Options and click the Mail Format tab. Click Stationery Picker to display the Stationery Picker dialog box, shown in Figure 7-26.

Figure 7-26. Use the Stationery Picker dialog box to preview stationery.

> **note** The Stationery Picker button on the Mail Format tab is unavailable if you have selected either Plain Text or Rich Text as your default message format.

213

You can edit most of the stationery listed in this dialog box, changing background image and font, although a few—such as Currency and Jungle—cannot be edited. To edit stationery, open the Stationery Picker dialog box, select the stationery you want to modify, and click Edit to display the Edit Stationery dialog box, where you can make changes as you like.

You can assign a default stationery to be used in all your messages. To do so, choose Tools, Options and click the Mail Format tab. Select the default stationery in the Use This Stationery By Default drop-down list and then click OK. If you don't want your messages to use stationery, or if you want to use it only infrequently, follow the same procedure but set the default stationery to None.

If Word is your e-mail editor, you can specify which stationery to use when you compose a message. This allows you to override the default stationery or to assign a stationery to that particular message, even though none of your other messages include it. To choose a stationery for a single message, open the message form, click the down arrow beside the Options button, and then choose Stationery. Outlook displays the Personal Stationery tab of the E-Mail Options dialog box, which you can use to assign a theme.

Creating Your Own Stationery

You can create your own stationery using the background image, font, and color settings of your choice. You can either use an existing stationery theme as a starting point or create one from scratch.

Follow these steps to create a new stationery theme:

1. Choose Tools, Options and click the Mail Format tab.

2. Click Stationery Picker, and then click New. Outlook provides a wizard to step you through the process of creating stationery.

3. In the wizard, specify a name for the stationery, select an existing stationery to use as a template or start a blank one, and then click Next.

4. In the Edit Stationery dialog box, specify font characteristics and background and click OK.

After you add your new stationery, it appears in the Stationery list in the Stationery Picker dialog box. To use the stationery, simply select it and click OK.

---

tip   **Select additional stationery themes**

You'll find additional stationery themes at the Microsoft Office Update Web site. To find the right page, choose Tools, Options, Mail Format. Click Stationery Picker, and then click the Get More Stationery button.

Using Signatures

Outlook supports two types of signatures that you can add automatically (or manually) to outgoing messages: standard signatures and digital signatures. This chapter focuses on standard signatures, which can include text and graphics, depending on the mail format you choose.

> To learn about digital signatures, which allow you to authenticate your identity and encrypt messages, see "Protecting Messages with Digital Signatures," page 332.

Understanding Message Signatures

Outlook can add a signature automatically to your outgoing messages. You can specify different signatures for new messages and for replies or forwards. Signatures can include both text and graphics as well as vCard attachments. Both Rich Text and HTML formats support vCards, but you can include graphics only if you use HTML as the message format. If your signature contains graphics and you start a new message using either Plain Text or Rich Text format, the graphics are removed, although any text defined by the signature remains. When you start a message using Plain Text format, any vCard attachments are also removed.

Why use signatures? Many people use a signature to include their contact information in each message. Still others use a signature to include a favorite quote or other information in the message. Regardless of the type of information you want to include, creating and using the signature is easy.

Defining Signatures

To define a signature, you use Outlook's Mail Format options. If you want to include a graphic, check before you start to ensure that you already have that graphic on your computer or that it's available on the network.

Follow these steps to create a signature:

1 In Outlook, choose Tools, Options and click the Mail Format tab.

2 Click Signatures to open the Signatures dialog box, and then click New to open the Create New Signature Wizard.

3 Specify a name for the signature as it will appear in Outlook. Select the option to start a new signature or select one to use as a template, and then click Next to open the Edit Signature dialog box (see Figure 7-27 on the next page).

Figure 7-27. Format the text of your signature in the Edit Signature dialog box.

4 In the Signature Text box, type the text you want to include in the signature, and use the Font and Paragraph buttons to format the text. (These two buttons aren't available if you have specified Plain Text as the default format on the Mail Format tab.)

5 To attach a vCard from an Outlook contact item, click New vCard From Contact. Select the contact item, click Add, and click OK. You also can select existing vCards from the Attach This Business Card (vCard) To This Signature drop-down list.

6 Create other signatures, and then click OK in the Create Signature dialog box.

Adding Signatures to Messages

The signature Outlook adds to new messages and the signature it adds to replies and forwards don't have to be the same. To set up different signatures for these different kinds of messages, choose Tools, Options and click the Mail Format tab. Use the Signature For New Messages and the Signature For Replies And Forwards drop-down lists to select the appropriate signature for each kind of message.

> **tip**   **Specify the default message format**
>
> Keep in mind that the signature data Outlook adds to the message depends on the default message format specified on the Mail Format tab. Set the default format to HTML if you want to create or edit signatures that contain graphics.

Other than letting you specify the signature for new messages or for replies and forwards, Outlook does not give you a way to control which signature is attached to a given message. For example, if you want to use different signatures for personal and business messages, you must switch signatures manually. Outlook will not differentiate between the types of accounts, nor can you create a rule to automatically add a signature to specific types of messages.

You can change the signature to be used by choosing Tools, Options, Mail Format and selecting a signature from the drop-down lists in the Signature area of the Mail Format tab. You also can change the signature when composing a message. If Word is your e-mail editor, click the arrow beside the Options button and choose E-Mail Signature. If Outlook is your editor, click the Signature button on the Standard toolbar and select the signature you want to use as the new default signature.

newfeature!
Using Instant Messaging

Outlook integrates support for MSN Messenger Service, referred to as *Instant Messaging*, which allows you to send instant messages to others across the Internet. In effect, Instant Messaging functions something like online chat does—you send and receive messages in real time with other online users. This section of the chapter explains how to configure and use MSN Messenger Service with Outlook.

When you use Instant Messaging in Outlook, Outlook checks the online status of a contact when you open the person's contact item or open an e-mail item from the contact. You can then click the online indicator for that person on the InfoBar, which opens MSN Messenger Service's Instant Message dialog box (see Figure 7-28 on the next page). In this dialog box, you can compose and send an instant message. The message then appears on the recipient's desktop (see Figure 7-29 on the next page), and he or she can reply by clicking the message.

> **note**   Outlook checks the online status of the other person only once, when you open the contact or e-mail item. It doesn't check periodically for a change in online status after the item has been opened.

Figure 7-28. Use the Instant Message dialog box to send and receive instant messages.

Figure 7-29. Incoming instant messages appear on the desktop; click the message to answer.

Outlook by itself doesn't extend MSN Messenger Service functionality—rather, it hooks into the existing MSN Messenger Service, which you must install separately. In addition, to have others appear online in Outlook, you need to add those contacts to your MSN Messenger Service list of contacts.

> **caution** You should never give out your password, credit card information, or other personal data in an Instant Message conversation because IM is not secure. This is particularly important if you don't really know the person with whom you're conversing.

Installing MSN Messenger Service

If MSN Messenger Service isn't installed on your system, Outlook can help you locate and install the software. Choose Tools, Options and click the Other tab. Select Enable Instant Messaging In Outlook and click OK. Outlook opens a browser at the MSN Messenger Service download site so that you can download the software. If you prefer to download the software yourself, point your browser to *http://www.msn.com*, and look for the MSN Messenger Service download link.

Adding Contacts for MSN Messenger Service

Outlook itself doesn't check the online state of your contacts; instead, it relies on the MSN Messenger Service application to perform this task. Before you can start using MSN Messenger Service with Outlook, you need to add contacts to your MSN Messenger Service contact list:

1 Double-click the MSN Messenger Service icon in the system tray to display the MSN Messenger Service window, shown in Figure 7-30.

Figure 7-30. You can add, send, call, or page by using the MSN Messenger Service window.

2 Click Add to open the Add A Contact Wizard (see Figure 7-31 on the next page).

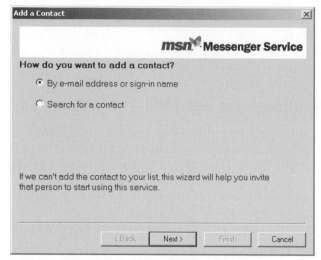

Figure 7-31. Use the Add A Contact Wizard to add contacts in MSN Messenger Service.

3 Select By E-Mail Address Or Sign-In Name and click Next.

4 Enter the contact's e-mail address and click Finish.

note If the contact doesn't have a passport from passport.com, you won't be able to add that contact in MSN Messenger Service.

Repeat these steps to add other contacts with whom you want to be able to communicate via MSN Messenger Service. The MSN Messenger Service window will show the online or offline state of each contact.

Setting Instant Messaging Options

Outlook has only one setting of its own related to MSN Messenger Service: the Enable Instant Messaging In Microsoft Outlook option on the Other tab of the Options dialog box. However, you can configure several options for MSN Messenger Service through the service itself. You can find these options either by clicking Options in the Instant Messaging area on the Other tab in Outlook or by choosing Tools, Options in the MSN Messenger Service window. These options are specific to MSN Messenger Service, not to Outlook, so you should consult the MSN Messenger Service Help documentation for details about the various settings.

Sending Instant Messages in Outlook

When you click a message header in your Inbox, Outlook checks MSN Messenger Service to determine whether the e-mail address matches a contact defined in your MSN Messenger Service contact list. If it finds a match, Outlook checks the contact's online status. If the person is online, Outlook indicates that in the InfoBar (see Figure 7-32). Click the status indicator on the InfoBar to open the MSN Messenger Service window and begin chatting.

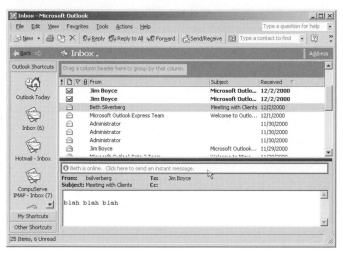

Figure 7-32.   Click the online status indicator in the InfoBar to begin chatting.

Configuring Other Messaging Options

This section of the chapter provides an explanation of additional options in Outlook that control messaging features and tasks. You can specify how you want to be notified when new mail arrives, configure how Outlook connects for e-mail accounts that use Dial-Up Networking, and control the formatting of Internet and international e-mail messages.

Setting Up Notification of New Mail

You might not spend a lot of time in Outlook during the day if you're busy working with other applications. However, you might want Outlook to notify you when you receive new messages. The first of the following options is located in the E-Mail Options dialog box (shown earlier in Figure 7-16). The remaining options are located in the Advanced E-Mail Options dialog box (shown earlier in Figure 7-7).

- **Display A Notification Message When New Mail Arrives (in the E-Mail Options dialog box).** Select this option to have Outlook display a pop-up message to alert you to a new message in your Inbox.

- **Play A Sound.** Select this option to have Outlook play a sound when a new message arrives. By using the Sounds icon in Control Panel, you can change the New Mail Notification sound to use a WAV file of your choosing.

- **Briefly Change The Mouse Cursor.** Select this option to have Outlook briefly change the pointer to a mail symbol when a new message arrives.

- **Show An Envelope Icon In The System Tray.** Select this option to have Outlook place an envelope icon in the system tray when new mail arrives. You can double-click the envelope icon to open your mail. The icon disappears from the tray after you've read the message(s).

Controlling Dial-Up Account Connections

The Mail Setup tab of the Options dialog box (choose Tools, Options) includes a handful of options that determine how Outlook connects when processing mail accounts that use Dial-Up Networking:

- **Warn Before Switching An Existing Dial-Up Connection.** Select this option to have Outlook warn you before it disconnects the current dial-up connection in order to dial another connection specified by the account about to be processed. This warning gives you the option of having Outlook use the current connection instead of dialing the other one.

- **Always Use An Existing Dial-Up Connection.** Select this option to have Outlook use the active dial-up connection rather than dialing the one specified in the account settings.

- **Automatically Dial During A Background Send/Receive.** When this option is selected, Outlook dials without prompting you when it needs to perform a background send/receive operation.

- **Hang Up When Finished With A Manual Send/Receive.** When this option is selected, Outlook hangs up a dial-up connection when it completes a manual send/receive operation (one you initiate by clicking Send/Receive).

For details on setting up Dial-Up Networking in each Windows operating system, see "Configuring Dial-Up Networking Options," page 147.

Formatting Internet and International Messages

The Mail Format tab of the Options dialog box (choose Tools, Options) provides access to a handful of settings that control how Outlook processes Internet and international messages.

Setting Internet Format

To control how Outlook formats messages sent to Internet recipients, click Internet Format on the Mail Format tab to open the Internet Format dialog box, shown in Figure 7-33.

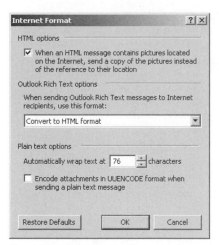

Figure 7-33.   Use the Internet Format dialog box to control the format of outgoing Internet messages.

The following list explains the options in the Internet Format dialog box:

- **When An HTML Message Contains Pictures Located On The Internet, Send A Copy Of The Pictures Instead Of The Reference To Their Location.** With this option selected, Outlook inserts a copy of the pictures in the message. Clear this check box to have Outlook insert a hyperlink to the graphics instead.

- **When Sending Outlook Rich Text Messages To Internet Recipients, Use This Format.** Use this drop-down list to specify how Outlook converts rich-text messages when sending those messages to Internet recipients.

- **Automatically Wrap Text At *n* Characters.** In this box, enter the number of characters per line that Outlook should use for Internet messages.

- **Encode Attachments In UUENCODE Format When Sending A Plain Text Message.** When this option is selected, attachments to messages sent as plain text are encoded within the message as text rather than attached as binary MIME attachments. The recipient's e-mail application must be capable of decoding UUEncoded messages.

- **Restore Defaults.** Click this button to restore Outlook's default settings for Internet messages.

Setting International Options

Click International Options on the Mail Format tab to display the International Options dialog box (see Figure 7-34 on the next page), which lets you specify whether Outlook uses English for message headers and flags and control the format for outgoing messages.

Figure 7-34. Use the International Options dialog box to configure language options for Outlook.

The International Options dialog box includes the following options:

- **Use English For Message Flags.** Select this option to use English for message flag text, such as High Priority or Flag For Follow-Up. If you use a different language and this option is not selected, message flags appear in the selected language rather than in English.

- **Use English For Message Headers On Replies And Forwards.** When you're using a non-English version of Outlook, you can select this option to display message header text—such as From, To, or Subject—in English rather than in the default language.

- **Preferred Encoding For Outgoing Messages.** Use this drop-down list to specify the encoding character set Outlook should use for outgoing messages. Select the setting to take into account the requirements of the majority of messages you send (based on their destination and the language options you use).

Filtering, Organizing, and Using Automatic Responses

Without some means of organizing and filtering e-mail, most people would be inundated with messages, many of which are absolutely useless. In addition, when you're out of the office for an extended period—on vacation, for example—and are still being bombarded with new messages, Microsoft Outlook's ability to automatically process and respond to incoming messages can be critical.

This chapter examines the features in Outlook that allow you to automatically manage messages based on a variety of factors, including sender, account, and size of message. For example, you can have Outlook move messages sent by a specific account to a specific folder, giving you an easy way to organize and separate messages from different accounts. This chapter also shows you how to customize your message folder views, which can aid you in organizing and managing your work.

Outlook helps you handle unwanted mail, such as junk and adult content messages (often referred to as *spam*). This chapter explains how to manage and filter out those types of messages. You'll also examine Outlook's ability to automatically respond to messages, which lets you generate Out Of Office replies to incoming messages.

225

Flagging and Monitoring Messages and Contacts

Outlook allows you to *flag* a message, in order to draw the recipient's attention to the message. Perhaps you're sending a message to an assistant, who needs to follow up on the message by a certain day the following week. In that case, you would flag the message for follow-up and specify the due date. When your assistant receives the message, the flag appears in the message header, as shown in Figure 8-1.

Flag messages for pending actions

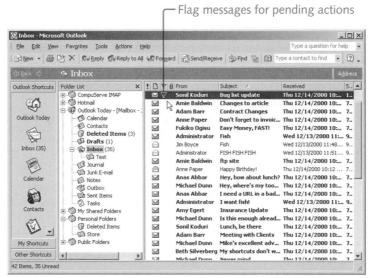

Figure 8-1. You can flag a message to highlight it or to include additional information.

Flagging Outgoing Messages

A flag gives you a means of including additional information or instructions with a message. The information stands out more if you include the flag text in the header rather than in the body of the message, where it might be overlooked. Perhaps most important, the flag can set a reminder on the recipient's system to help ensure that your instructions, whatever they are, are carried out. For example, if you want the recipient to phone you by a specific date regarding the message, the reminder will appear on the recipient's system at the appropriate time (assuming that he or she uses Outlook). Outlook provides several predefined flag messages, or you can create your own message.

Use the following steps to flag a message you send:

1 With the message form open, choose Actions, Follow Up, or click the Follow Up button on the form's Standard toolbar. Either action displays the Flag For Follow Up dialog box, shown in Figure 8-2.

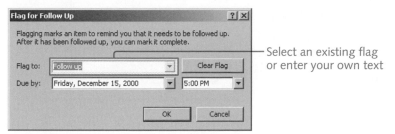

Figure 8-2.   Select the flag text or type your own message in this dialog box.

2   From the Flag To drop-down list, select the text you want to include with the flag, or type your own text in this box.

3   If you want to include a due date and a subsequent reminder, select the date in the Due By drop-down list, which opens a calendar you can refer to. Alternatively, you can enter a date, day, time, or other information as text in the Due By box.

4   Click OK and then send the message as you normally would.

Troubleshooting

Reminders don't work for flagged messages you have moved.

Incoming messages typically go in the Inbox folder, and the same is true for flagged messages. Outlook displays reminders for flagged messages as long as those messages reside in the Inbox. But if a flagged message is moved to another folder, either manually or by a message rule, Outlook won't display the reminder at the designated time. If you must move flagged messages, try to move them to a common folder so that they'll be easier to spot. Or you might create a rule that assigns them a High priority level, which will give you a further visual clue when you're searching for flagged messages.

Viewing and Responding to Flagged Messages

When you receive a flagged message, a flag icon appears next to the message header in the message folder. If you have configured Outlook to display the preview pane, the flag text appears in the preview pane header above the addresses (see Figure 8-3 on the next page). The flag icons help you identify flagged messages when the preview pane is turned off. You can sort the view in the folder using the Flag column, listing all flagged messages together to make them easier to locate. To view the flag text when the preview pane is turned off, simply open the message. The flag text appears above the addresses.

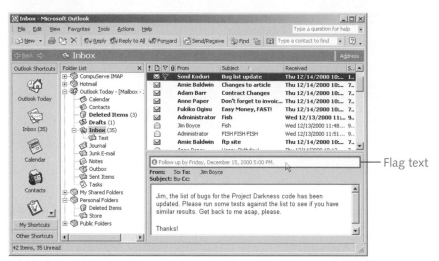

Figure 8-3. Flagged messages display a flag icon in the message folder, and the flag text appears in the preview pane header.

Outlook has no special mechanism for processing flagged messages other than the reminders previously discussed. You simply call, e-mail, or otherwise respond based on the flag message. Flagged messages to which you have responded by e-mail automatically display a white flag icon in the message folder. A red flag indicates you haven't responded yet. To change the flag status, right-click a flagged message and choose Flag Complete. To remove the flag from the message, right-click a flagged message and choose Clear Flag.

Flagging Sent and Other Messages

In addition to flagging your outgoing messages, you also can flag messages that you've already sent. Although this action can't display a flag after the fact on the recipient's system, it does give you a way to flag and follow up messages from your end. You can flag messages in any message folder, including the Sent Items folder. You can work with these flags and flagged messages the same way you work with the flagged messages you receive from others.

note When you send a flagged message, Outlook also flags the copy of the message that it saves in the Sent Items folder (assuming that you have configured Outlook to save a copy of sent messages).

In addition to flagging items that you send, you might also want to flag messages you have received from others that didn't originally include flags. For example, you might flag a message that you need to follow up, or you might use the flag text to indicate other tasks you must perform in connection with the message or its subject.

> **tip** **Add notes to received messages**
>
> You can use flags to add notes to messages you receive from others, giving yourself a quick reminder of pending tasks or other pertinent information. If the messages reside in your Inbox folder, Outlook can generate a reminder for you concerning the flagged item. To set up Outlook to do so, right-click the message, choose Follow Up, and then set a due date and time.

Flagging Contact Items

You can flag contact items as well as messages, marking them for follow-up or adding other notations to an item. For example, you might flag a contact item to remind yourself to call the person by a certain time or date or to send documents to the contact. A flag you add to a contact item shows up in all contacts views, but it isn't always readily apparent—for instance, the flag shows up as text in Address Cards and Detailed Address Cards views. In other views, Outlook uses a flag icon (see Figure 8-4). As you can for messages, you can use one of Outlook's predefined flags to mark a contact item, or you can specify your own flag text.

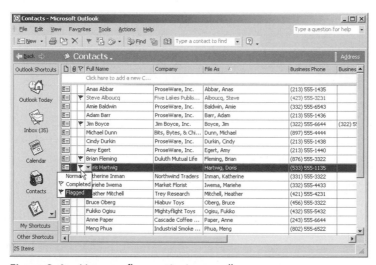

Figure 8-4. You can flag contacts as well as messages.

To assign a flag to a contact item, follow these steps:

1 Right-click the contact item and choose Follow Up.

2 In the Flag For Follow Up dialog box, select the flag type in the Flag To drop-down list, or type in your own text.

3 Specify the due date and time, and then click OK.

229

Outlook uses the same icons for flagged contact items as it does for messages. A red flag icon indicates a pending action, while a white flag indicates a completed action. To change the flag status for a contact item, right-click the item and choose Flag Complete or Clear Flag.

You'll sometimes find it helpful to view the Contacts folder sorted by flag, so you can see at a glance which contacts are flagged and what action is required. You can group by flag in several different views, but Outlook also provides a standard view that sorts contacts by flag, as shown in Figure 8-5. To display this view of the Contacts folder, choose View, Current View, By Follow-Up Flag.

Figure 8-5. You can list items in the Contacts folder by flag.

Grouping Messages by Customizing the Folder View

To help you organize information, Outlook allows you to customize various message folder views. By default, Outlook displays only a small selection of columns for messages, including From, Subject, Received, Size, Flag, Attachment, and Importance columns.

> For details on how to add and remove columns from a folder view to show more or less infor- mation about your messages, see "Working with the Standard Outlook Views," page 59.

You can easily sort messages using any of the column headers as your sort criterion. To view messages sorted alphabetically by sender, for example, click the column header of the From column. To sort messages by date received, click the column header of the Received column. Click the Attachment column header to view all messages with attachments.

In addition to managing your message view by controlling columns and sorting, you can *group* messages based on columns. Whereas sorting allows you to arrange messages in order using a single column as the sort criterion, grouping allows you to display the messages in groups based on one or more columns. For example, you might group messages based on sender, and then on date received, and finally on whether they have attachments. This method helps you locate messages more quickly than if you had to search through a message list sorted only by sender.

Grouping messages in a message folder is a relatively simple process:

1 In Outlook, open the folder you want to organize by grouping the messages it contains.

2 Right-click the column header and choose Group By This Field if you want to group based only on the selected field. Choose Group By Box if you want to group based on multiple columns.

Processing Messages Automatically

If you're like most people, you are often swamped by messages that are useless or annoying, including sales pitches, announcements, and possibly adult content messages, all of which you probably didn't request. Outlook gives you the means to block those messages or process them automatically to unclutter your Inbox.

If you receive a lot of messages, you might want to have the messages analyzed as they come in, to perform actions on them before you read them. For example, you can have all messages from a specific account sent to a specific folder. Or perhaps you want messages that come from specific senders to be assigned High priority. Whatever the case, Outlook lets you manipulate your incoming messages to accomplish the result you want. This section of the chapter shows you how, starting with an overview of message rules.

---

tip   **Limit the number of message rules you create**

Because of a limitation in MAPI (Message Application Programming Interface), Outlook allocates only 32 KB for storing rules. Although this is fine for most users, you could bump your head on the ceiling if you create too many rules.

Understanding Message Rules

A *message rule* defines the action Outlook takes for a sent or received message if the message meets certain conditions specified by the rule. For example, you might create a rule that tells Outlook to move all messages from a specific POP3 account into a specified folder rather than leaving them in your default Inbox. Or you might want Outlook to place a copy of all outgoing High priority messages in a special folder.

In Outlook, you use several *conditions* for defining a message rule. These conditions can include the account from which the message was received, the message size, the sender or recipient, specific words in various fields or in the message itself, and the priority assigned to the message. In addition, you can combine multiple conditions to refine the rule and further control its actions. For example, you might create a rule that moves all your incoming POP3 messages to a folder other than the Inbox and also deletes any messages that contain certain words in the subject field. Although not a complete list, the following are some of the most common tasks you might perform with message rules:

- Organize messages based on sender, recipient, or subject.
- Copy or move messages from one folder to another.
- Flag messages.
- Delete messages automatically.
- Reply to, forward, or redirect messages to individuals or distribution lists.
- Respond to messages with a specific reply.
- Monitor message importance (priority).
- Print a message.
- Play a sound.
- Execute a script or start an application.

For details on how to generate automatic replies to messages, see "Creating Automatic Responses with the Out Of Office Assistant," page 253.

Whatever your message processing requirements, Outlook probably offers a solution through a message rule, based on either a single condition or multiple conditions. You also can create multiple rules that work together to process your mail. As you begin to create and use message rules, keep in mind that you can define a rule to function either when a message is received or when it is sent. When you create a rule, you specify the event to which the rule applies.

You create all message rules in the same way, regardless of the specific purpose of the rule. Rather than focusing on defining rules for specific tasks, this chapter explains the general process of creating rules. With an understanding of this process, you should have no problem setting up rules for a variety of situations. In fact, creating message rules is relatively easy, thanks to Outlook's Rules Wizard.

To start the wizard in Outlook, choose Tools, Rules Wizard. You'll first see the Rules Wizard dialog box, shown in Figure 8-6. The Rules Wizard list contains all the existing rules that you have defined. Outlook applies the rules in the order in which they are listed, an important fact to consider when you're creating rules.

For more information about determining the order in which message rules execute, see "Setting Rule Order," page 243.

Troubleshooting

Rules don't work for some of your accounts.

If some of your rules work only for certain accounts and not for others, the problem could be that some of those accounts are HTTP-based mail accounts. Outlook's message rules do not process messages sent to or received from HTTP-based mail accounts, such as Microsoft Hotmail, nor can you manually apply rules to process messages in the Inbox sent from HTTP accounts after the messages have been received. Check with your HTTP mail service provider to determine whether it offers server-side message rules that you can use in place of Outlook's rules to process your messages.

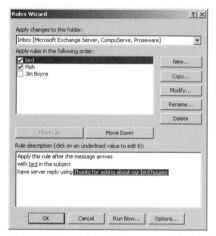

Figure 8-6. The Rules Wizard dialog box displays existing rules and allows you to create and modify message rules.

You might use certain rules all the time but use others only at special times. Each rule includes a check box beside it. Select this check box when you want to use the rule; clear it when you want to disable the rule.

InsideOut

I can understand why Outlook isn't able to use rules to process messages from HTTP-based servers, but it's difficult to understand why you can't run rules in HTTP mail folders after the fact. You can run a rule manually in any other folder to perform the rule's action at any time after messages are downloaded. The ability to do this in HTTP mail folders would give you a means of cleaning out and processing HTTP mail manually, if not during send/receive operations. It would be great to see this feature in a future release.

Creating Client-Side and Server-Side Rules

In Outlook, you can create either *client-side* or *server-side* rules. Outlook stores client-side rules locally on your computer and uses them to process messages that come to your local folders, although you also can use client-side rules to process messages on Microsoft Exchange Server. A client-side rule is needed when you're moving messages to a local folder rather than to a folder on Exchange Server. For example, if messages from a specific sender that arrive in your Exchange Server Inbox must be moved to one of your personal folders, the rule must function as a client-side rule, because the Exchange Server computer is not able to access your personal folders.

Server-side rules reside on the Exchange Server rather than on your local computer, and they can usually process messages in your Exchange Server mailbox whether or not you're logged on and running Outlook. The Out Of Office Assistant (discussed later in this chapter) is a good example of how server-side rules can be used. It processes messages that come into your Inbox on the server even when your computer is turned off and you're a thousand miles away. As long as the Exchange Server is up and functioning, the server-side rules can perform their intended function.

When you create a rule, Outlook examines the rule's logic to determine whether it can function as a server-side rule or as a client-side rule. If it can function as a server-side rule, Outlook stores the rule on the Exchange Server and treats it as a server-side rule. If the rule must function as a client-side rule, Outlook stores it locally and appends the parenthetical phrase *(client-only)* after the rule name to designate it as a client-side rule. Figure 8-7 shows a selection of rules in Outlook, some of which function as client-side rules and others that function as server-side rules.

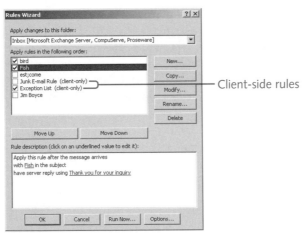

Figure 8-7. Outlook supports server-side rules as well as client-side rules.

Troubleshooting

Your server-side rules don't execute.

Server-side rules, which process messages that come into your Exchange Server Inbox, usually can execute when Outlook isn't running. In some cases, however, server-side rules can't function unless Outlook is running and you're connected to the server.

When a server-side rule is unable to process a message because Outlook is offline (or for other reasons), the Exchange Server generates a DAM (deferred action message), which it uses to process the message when Outlook comes back online. When Outlook goes online, it receives the DAM, performs the action, and deletes the DAM.

For information on how to apply client-side rules to specific folders or to all accounts, see "Applying Rules to Specific Folders," page 240.

Creating New Rules

When you create a message rule, you must first specify whether you want to create the rule from a predefined template or from scratch. Because the templates address common message processing tasks, using a template can save you a few steps. When you create a rule from scratch, you set up all conditions for the rule as you create it. You can use many different conditions to define the actions the rule performs, all of which are available in the Rules Wizard. With or without a template, you have full control over the completed rule and can modify it to suit your needs. Outlook's templates are a great way to get started, however, if you're new to using Outlook or message rules.

Let's look first at the general procedure for creating rules and then at more specific steps. The general process is as follows:

1 Select the folder in which the rule will apply. For example, if you have an Exchange Server account and an IMAP account, you must choose the Inbox to which the rule will apply.

note If you have only one account, or an Exchange Server account and one or more POP3 accounts, you have only one Inbox to choose as the target for the rule. IMAP accounts, however, use their own Inbox folders, which means you can apply rules to these accounts separately from your Exchange Server and POP3 accounts. For example, if you have an Exchange Server account, two POP3 accounts, and an IMAP account in the same profile, you'll see two Inboxes listed as possible targets for the rule: one for the Exchange Server and POP3 accounts and one for the IMAP account.

2 Specify when the rule applies—that is, when a message is received or when it is sent.

3 Specify the conditions that define which messages are processed—for example, account, sender, priority, or content.

4 Specify the action to take for messages that meet the specified conditions—for example, move, copy, or delete the message; change its priority; flag it for follow up; or generate a reply.

5 Create other message rules to accomplish other tasks as needed, including possibly working in conjunction with other rules.

6 Set the order of rules as needed.

Troubleshooting

You have conflicting message rules.

Outlook's support for multiple accounts, combined with its ability to use both client-side and server-side rules, can pose certain problems. For example, assume that you have a POP3 account that delivers messages to your Exchange Server mailbox rather than to a local store. Also assume that you create a client-side rule to process certain POP3 messages but that you also have a server-side rule for processing messages. The server-side rule takes precedence because the client-side rule doesn't execute until the message arrives in the Inbox, even though the message came through your computer before it was placed in your Exchange Server mailbox. Thus the message is processed by the server-side rule, potentially bypassing the local rule. If the server-side rule deletes the message, for example, the message will never make it back to your personal folders to allow the client-side rule to act on it.

The order of rule precedence is important for the same reason—two rules, even on the same side, can perform conflicting actions. Keep this in mind when you're creating rules and working with non-Exchange accounts that store messages in your Exchange Server mailbox.

note When you specify multiple conditions for a rule, the rule combines these conditions in a logical AND operation—that is, the message must meet all of the conditions to be considered subject to the rule. You also can create rules that use a logical OR operation, meaning that the message is subject to the rule if it meets any one of the conditions. For details, see "Creating Rules That Use OR Logic," page 242.

The following steps guide you through the more specific process of creating a message rule:

1 In Outlook, choose Tools, Rules Wizard to display the Rules Wizard dialog box.

2 In the Apply Changes To This Folder drop-down list, select the folder to which you want to apply the rule. If you have only one Inbox, you don't need to make a selection.

3 Click New to display the wizard page shown in Figure 8-8.

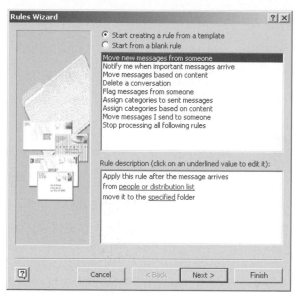

Figure 8-8. To create a rule, you can use a template or start from scratch.

4 If you want to use a template to create the rule, select the template from the list and click Next. To create a rule from scratch, choose Start From A Blank Rule and continue with step 5.

5 If you're starting a rule from scratch, Outlook prompts you to select when you want the rule to execute. Select Check Messages When They Arrive to apply the rule to incoming messages, or select Check Messages After Sending to apply the rule to sent messages. If you're creating the rule from a template, Outlook skips this step, because the processing event is already defined by the template.

6 In the conditions list in the top half of the wizard page shown in Figure 8-9 on the next page, select the conditions that define the messages to which the rule should apply. For template-based rules, a condition is already selected, but you can change the condition and add others as necessary.

7 In the Rule Description area of the wizard page, click the underlined words that specify the data for the condition(s). For example, if you're creating a rule to process messages from a specific account, click the word *specified*, which is underlined, and then select the account from the Account dialog box. Click OK and then click Next.

Chapter 8

237

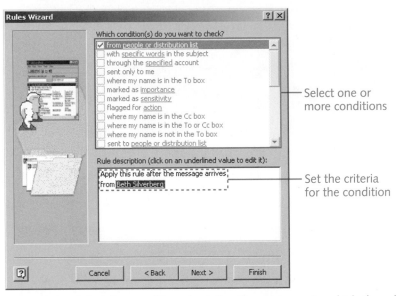

Figure 8-9. Select the conditions to define the messages to which the rule will apply.

8 In the upper half of the new wizard page, select the actions you want Outlook to apply to messages that satisfy the specified conditions (see Figure 8-10).

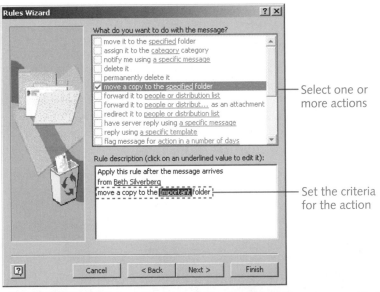

Figure 8-10. Select the actions Outlook should take for messages that meet the rule's conditions.

9 In the lower half of the wizard page, click each underlined value needed to define the action and specify the data in the resulting dialog box. Click OK to close the dialog box and then click Next.

10 Select exceptions to the rule if needed, and specify the data for exception conditions (see Figure 8-11). Click Next.

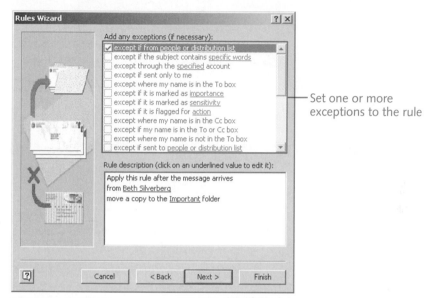

— Set one or more exceptions to the rule

Figure 8-11. You can specify exceptions to the rule to fine-tune message processing.

11 On the final page of the Rules Wizard (see Figure 8-12 on the next page), specify a name for the rule as you want it to appear in Outlook.

12 Select options according to the following list, and click Finish:

- **Run This Rule Now On Messages Already In "Inbox."** Select this option if you want Outlook to apply the rule to messages that you have already received and that currently reside in the Inbox folder in which the rule applies. For example, if you have created a rule to delete messages from a specific recipient, any existing messages from the recipient are deleted after you select this option and click Finish to create the rule.

- **Turn On This Rule.** Select this option to begin applying the rule you have created.

- **Create This Rule On All Accounts.** Select this option to apply the rule to all applicable folders. For example, if you have three folders listed in the Apply Changes To This Folder drop-down list at the top of the initial Rules Wizard page, selecting this check box causes Outlook to apply the rule to all three folders rather than only to the selected folder.

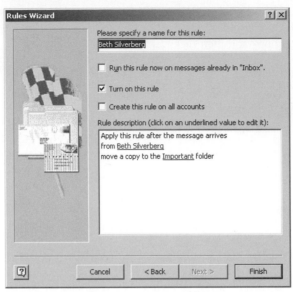

Figure 8-12. Configure a name and options for the rule.

> For more details about using rules in various folders, see the following section, "Applying Rules to Specific Folders."

tip To create a rule that operates on all messages, don't specify a condition that Outlook must check. Outlook prompts you to verify that you want the rule applied to all messages.

Applying Rules to Specific Folders

When you first open the Rules Wizard, it displays the rules that have already been defined for your profile, both client-side and server-side, as shown earlier in Figure 8-7 on page 234. You might recall that you use the Apply Changes To This Folder drop-down list at the top of the dialog box to select the folder for which you want to create or modify a rule.

Regardless of the folder you select, the rules list in the wizard always displays your server-side rules. The client-side rules that appear in the list depend on the folder you select. The list for a selected folder contains only the client-side rules for that particular folder, unless you've copied a rule to multiple folders or created a rule expressly for all folders.

To apply a rule to a specific folder, select that folder in the Apply Changes To This Folder drop-down list when you begin creating the rule. To apply a rule to all folders, select the Create This Rule On All Accounts option at the completion of the wizard (as explained in step 12 on page 239).

Copying Rules to Other Folders

By default, Outlook doesn't create rules for all folders; instead, it creates the rule only for the selected folder. If you have created a rule for one folder but want to use it in a different folder, you can copy the rule to the other folder.

Follow these steps to do so:

1 Choose Tools, Rules Wizard to start the Rules Wizard.

2 Select the rule you want to copy and click Copy.

3 When you're prompted, select the destination folder for the rule and click OK.

For details on sharing rules with other Outlook users, see "Sharing Rules with Others," page 245.

Creating Rules Based on Existing Messages

In some situations, you'll want to create rules from specific messages. For example, if you frequently receive unwanted messages from a particular sender, you might want to delete the messages without downloading them. You can specify the address when you begin to create a rule in the Rules Wizard, but in this case it would be easier to create the rule from the message instead, saving you the trouble of typing the sender's name or address. Or perhaps the subject of a particular group of messages always contains a unique string of text, and you want to build the rule around that text. Rather than typing the text yourself, you can create the rule from one of the messages.

Here's how to create a rule from a specific message:

1 In Outlook, open the folder containing the message.

2 Right-click the message header and choose Create Rule.

3 Outlook adds several new conditions to the Rules Wizard that reflect the properties of the selected message—sender and subject, for example. Select a condition and complete the rule as you normally would if you were creating it from a template or from scratch.

note Remember that HTTP accounts don't support Outlook rules. If you right-click a message stored in a folder for an HTTP-based mail account, you'll see that the Create Rule command is not available. Also, rules are always created in the Inbox, not in other folders. You can, however, run rules in other folders.

Creating Rules That Use OR Logic

Up to this point, you've explored relatively simple rules that function based on a single condition or on multiple AND conditions. In the latter case, the rule specifies multiple conditions and applies only to messages that meet all the conditions. If a rule is defined by three AND conditions, for example, Outlook uses it only on messages that meet condition 1, condition 2, and condition 3.

You also can create rules that follow OR logic. In this case, a rule specifies a single condition, but multiple criteria for that condition. The rule will then act on any message that meets at least one of the criteria for the condition. For example, you might create a rule that deleted a message if the subject of the message contained any one of three words. If one of the conditions is met (that is, if the subject of a message contains at least one of the three words), Outlook will delete that message.

With Outlook, you can create several rules that use OR logic within a single condition, but you can't create a single rule that uses OR logic on multiple conditions. For example, you might create a rule that deletes a message if the message contains the phrase *MLM*, *Free Money*, or *Guaranteed Results*. However, you can't create a message rule that deletes the message if the subject of the message contains the words *Free Money* (condition 1), or if the message is from a specific sender (condition 2), or if the message is larger than a given size (condition 3). OR must operate within a single condition. When you create a rule with multiple conditions, Outlook always treats multiple conditions in the same rule using AND logic. You would have to create three separate rules to accommodate the latter example.

InsideOut

Outlook Express beats Outlook hands down when it comes to creating rules that use OR logic. The interface in Outlook Express is much more intuitive, and the ability to create such rules is obvious to the user because of the way Microsoft designed the interface. It would be great if, for example, you could create a single rule with multiple OR conditions in Outlook as easily as you can in Outlook Express.

If you have a situation where you need to check for more than one piece of data in a single condition, you can do so easily enough, however: when you create the rule and define the condition, specify multiple items. For example, if you need a rule that processes messages based on four possible strings in the subject of the messages, click Specific Words in the Rule Description area of the Rules Wizard. In the Search Text dialog box, enter the strings separately. As you can see in Figure 8-13, the search list includes the word *or* to indicate that the rule applies if any one of the words appears in the subject.

Figure 8-13. Specify data separately to create a rule that uses OR logic.

While you can't create a single rule with OR logic operating on multiple conditions in Outlook, you can create rules that combine AND and OR logic. For example, you might create a rule that applied if the message was from a specific sender and the subject contained the words *Free Money* or *Guaranteed Results*. Keep in mind that you must specify two conditions—not one—to build the rule. The first condition would check for the sender and the second would check for the words *Free Money* or *Guaranteed Results*.

Modifying Rules

You can modify a rule at any time after you create it. Modifying a rule is much like creating one. To modify a rule, choose Tools, Rules Wizard to open the Rules Wizard. Select the rule you want to modify and click Modify. Outlook presents the same options you saw when you created the rule, and you can work with them the same way.

Setting Rule Order

Outlook executes rules for incoming messages when the messages arrive in the Inbox, whether on the server or locally (depending on whether the rules are client-side or server-side). Outlook executes rules for outgoing messages when the messages arrive in the Sent Items folder.

As mentioned earlier, the order in which rules are listed in Outlook determines how Outlook applies them. In some situations, the sequence could be important. Perhaps you have one rule that moves High priority messages to a separate folder and another rule that notifies you when High priority messages arrive. For the latter rule to work properly, it needs to execute before the one that moves the messages, because the notification rule won't execute if the messages are no longer in the Inbox.

You can control the order of Outlook rules quite easily by taking the following steps:

1 In Outlook, choose Tools, Rules Wizard to open the Rules Wizard.

2 Select a rule to be moved.

3 Use the Move Up or Move Down button to change the order in the list (see Figure 8-14). Rules execute in the order listed, the one at the top executing first and the one at the bottom executing last.

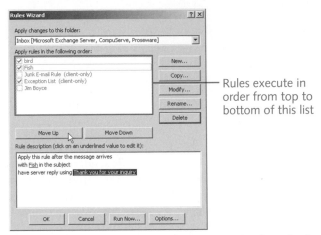

Rules execute in order from top to bottom of this list

Figure 8-14. You can control execution order for rules by rearranging the rules list.

Stopping Rules from Processing

In certain cases, you might want your message rules to stop processing altogether. Perhaps someone has sent you a very large message that is causing your dial-up connection to time out or is taking a long time to download. You would like to create a rule to delete the message without downloading it, but you don't want any of your other rules to execute. In this case, you would place a new rule at the top of the list and define it so that the last action it takes is to stop processing any other rules. In effect, this allows you to bypass your other rules without going to the trouble of disabling them.

You can also use the Stop Processing More Rules action to control rule execution in other situations. To stop Outlook from executing other rules when a message meets a specific condition, include the action Stop Processing More Rules as the last action for the rule. You'll find this action in the What Do You Want To Do With The Message list in the wizard.

Disabling and Removing Rules

In some cases, you might want message rules to execute only at certain times. Perhaps you use a rule to do routine cleanup on your mail folders but don't want the rule to run automatically. Or perhaps you want to create a rule to use only once or twice but would like to keep it in case you need it again later. In those cases, you can disable the rule. Choose Tools, Rules Wizard and then clear the rule's check box in the list. Only those rules whose check boxes are selected will apply to incoming or outgoing messages.

Because the amount of space allocated for message rules in Outlook is finite, removing unused rules can make room for additional ones, particularly if you have several complex rules. If you don't plan to use a rule again, you can remove it by choosing Tools, Rules Wizard, selecting the rule, and clicking Delete.

Sharing Rules with Others

By default, Outlook stores server-side rules on the Exchange Server and stores client-side rules on your local system. Regardless of where your message rules are stored, you can share them with others by exporting the rules to a file. You can then send the file as an e-mail attachment or place it on a network share (or a local share) to allow other users to access it.

Follow these steps to export your message rules to a file:

1 In Outlook, choose Tools, Rules Wizard.

2 In the Rules Wizard, click Options.

3 Click Export Rules (see Figure 8-15), and then select a path for the file in the resulting Save Exported Rules As dialog box (a standard file/save dialog box).

Figure 8-15. Use the Options dialog box to import and export rules.

4 To save the rules using either Outlook 2000 or Outlook 98 format, select a format in the Save As Type drop-down list.

5 Click Save.

You can export your rules in any of three formats, depending on the version of Outlook used by the people with whom you want to share your rules. If you need to share with various users, export using the earliest version of Outlook. Later versions will be able to import the rules because they are forward-compatible.

Using the Organizer Pane to Create Rules

The Rules Wizard isn't the only method you can use to create message rules in Outlook. Using the Organize command provides an easier way to create certain types of rules, making it an attractive alternative for novice users. With this method, however, you do have fewer options and less flexibility.

When you choose Tools, Organize with the Inbox open, Outlook changes the view to include the organizer pane at the top of the view, as shown in Figure 8-16. The organizer pane includes four modes, three of which allow you to create rules:

● **Using Folders.** Use this mode to create a rule that moves messages with a specific sender or recipient into a specified folder.

● **Using Colors.** Use this mode to create a rule that applies a specified color to messages with a specific sender or recipient. Outlook changes the color of the message header in the Inbox accordingly.

● **Junk E-Mail.** Use this mode to create a rule that colors junk and adult content messages with specified colors.

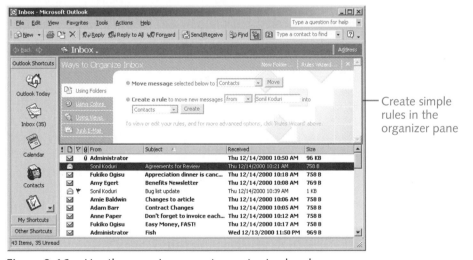

Create simple rules in the organizer pane

Figure 8-16. Use the organizer pane to create simple rules.

> For more details about using Junk E-Mail mode, see "Managing Junk and Adult Content Mail," page 248.

Creating rules with the organizer pane is generally self-explanatory; it's included here only to identify it as an alternative to the Rules Wizard. If you provide support for other Outlook users, you might want to recommend the organizer pane to those users you believe will have difficulty creating rules with the Rules Wizard.

Using Rules to Move Messages Between Accounts

One common task users often want to perform is to move messages between accounts. Assume that you have two accounts: an Exchange Server account for work and a POP3 account for personal messages. You have specified the Exchange Server mailbox as the delivery location for new mail, so all your POP3 messages go into your Exchange Server Inbox. But you now want those messages to go into an Inbox in a local PST rather than your Exchange Server mailbox. In this case, it's a simple matter to move the personal messages from the Exchange Server Inbox to the POP3 Inbox. Just create a rule that moves messages that meet the specified conditions to your POP3 Inbox.

Here's how to accomplish this:

1 In Outlook, choose Tools, Rules Wizard to start the wizard.

2 Click New, select Start From A Blank Rule, and click Next.

3 Select Through The Specified Account. In the Rule Description area, click the underlined word *specified* and select your POP3 account. Then click OK.

4 Click Next. Select Move It To The Specified Folder, and click the underlined word *specified* in the Rule Description area.

5 Select the folder in your PST to which the messages should be moved and click OK.

6 Click Next. Specify any exceptions to the rule and then click Next again.

7 Specify a name for the rule and other options as needed and then click Finish.

Running Rules Manually and in Specific Folders

Normally you use message rules to process messages when they arrive in your Inbox or are placed in the Sent Messages folder. However, you also can run rules manually at any time. Perhaps you have created a rule that you want to use periodically to clean out certain types of messages or move them to a specific folder. You don't want the rule to operate every time you check mail; instead, you want to execute it only when you think it's necessary. In this case, you can run the rule manually.

You might also want to run a rule manually when you need to run it in a folder other than the Inbox. For example, assume that you've deleted messages from a specific sender and now want to restore them, moving the messages from the Deleted Items folder back to your Inbox. In this situation, you could create the rule and then execute it manually in the Deleted Items folder.

It's easy to run a rule manually and in a specific folder:

1 Choose Tools, Rules Wizard to open the Rules Wizard.

2 Select the rule you want to run (one that has already been defined), and click Run Now. Outlook displays the Run Rules Now dialog box, shown in Figure 8-17.

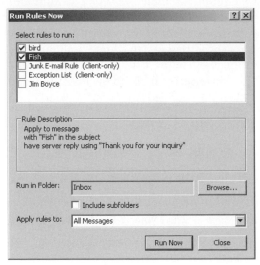

Figure 8-17. Use the Run Rules Now dialog box to run a rule manually in a specified folder.

3 Select the rule you want to run in the list. By default, Outlook will run the rule in the Inbox unless you specify otherwise. Click Browse to browse for a different folder. If you also want to run the rule in subfolders of the selected folder, select the Include Subfolders check box.

4 In the Apply Rules To drop-down list, select the type of messages on which you want to run the rule.

5 Click Run Now to execute the rule, or click Close to cancel.

Managing Junk and Adult Content Mail

Tired of wading through all the junk mail? Anyone with an e-mail account these days is hard-pressed to avoid the unsolicited ads, invitations to multilevel marketing schemes, or unwanted adult content messages. Fortunately, Outlook offers a couple of features to help you deal with all the junk coming through your Inbox.

Filtering Junk and Adult Content Mail

Although you can create message rules to deal with mail from specific junk and adult content senders based on, for example, sender address or subject, Outlook also provides an entirely different mechanism that makes it easier to block such unwanted messages. When you install Outlook, Setup adds a Filters.txt file that Outlook uses to define junk

Chapter 8

and adult content senders. This file defines common conditions such as subject text and sender address found in these types of messages. By default, the Filters.txt file is located in the folder \Program Files\Microsoft Office\Office10\1033. You can open the file and review it in Notepad or WordPad, but don't edit the file directly. Instead, you can use features in Outlook to modify the list.

The organizer pane, discussed earlier in this chapter, includes a Junk E-Mail mode, which lets you either color or move messages that fit Outlook's filter criteria, as defined by the Filters.txt file and any custom filter conditions you specify. Although you can take only two possible actions with these messages—coloring them or moving them—the organizer pane is the easiest way to start filtering junk mail because you don't need to manually create any rules.

> **tip**   Consider coloring any junk and adult content messages for a trial period before you start deleting them. This bit of caution will help you identify any useful exceptions and guard against lost messages.

To start filtering out unwanted messages, open Outlook and follow these steps:

1 Open the Inbox and choose Tools, Organize to display the organizer pane (see Figure 8-18).

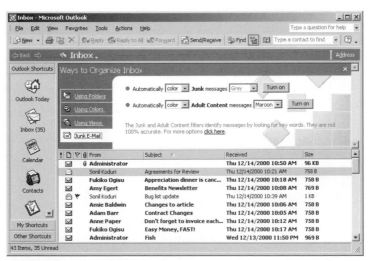

Figure 8-18. Use the organizer pane to quickly configure Outlook to filter unwanted messages.

2 Click Junk E-Mail in the organizer pane.

3 In the bulleted line concerning junk messages, select either Color or Move in the first drop-down list, depending on which action you want to take with messages that fit the junk message criteria.

4 In the associated drop-down list at the right, select a color or a folder, depending on your previous selection.

5 Click Turn On. If you chose to move junk mail messages and the Junk E-Mail folder doesn't exist, Outlook prompts you for a location in which to create the folder. Specify a location and click OK. Click Yes if you want Outlook to create a shortcut to the folder on the Outlook Bar.

6 In the bulleted line concerning adult content messages, select either Color or Move in the first drop-down list, depending on which action you want to take with messages that match the adult content criteria.

7 In the associated drop-down list at the right, select a color or a folder.

8 Click Turn On. If you chose to move adult content messages to the Adult Content folder and that folder doesn't exist, Outlook prompts you for a location in which to create the folder. Specify a location and click OK. Click Yes if you want Outlook to create a shortcut to the folder on the Outlook Bar.

Managing the Junk Senders and Adult Content Senders Lists

You can add your own filter conditions for Outlook to use when filtering junk and adult content messages in addition to the conditions specified in Filters.txt. For example, you can add senders to the Junk Senders list (or the Adult Content Senders list), which causes messages from those senders to be treated as junk mail.

Follow these steps to add other senders to the Junk Senders list:

1 Open Outlook and choose Tools, Organize to display the organizer pane if it isn't already displayed.

2 Click Junk E-Mail, and then click Click Here to view other options.

3 Click Edit Junk Senders to display the Edit Junk Senders dialog box (see Figure 8-19).

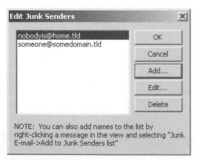

Figure 8-19. Edit or delete a junk mailer's address in the Edit Junk Senders dialog box.

4 Click Add to display the Sender dialog box, enter the e-mail address or the domain of the sender, and click OK.

5 Add other junk senders as necessary, and then click OK to close the Edit Junk Senders dialog box.

To edit the Adult Content Senders list, you follow the same procedure, with one difference: in step 3, click Edit Adult Content Senders to open the Edit Adult Content Senders dialog box, which works exactly the same way as the Edit Junk Senders dialog box does.

InsideOut

Because the Internet is so fluid, with domains coming and going every day, and because spammers change their tactics frequently to bypass filters, having an up-to-date Filters.txt file is important. Although Microsoft doesn't provide an update file at this point, it does provide documentation about the Filters.txt file. To view this information, open the organizer pane, click the Click Here link, and then click the Outlook Web Site link. You also can point your browser to *http://officeupdate.microsoft.com/Articles/newfilters.htm* to view the information.

Applying Exceptions to Junk and Adult Content Conditions

When you use the organizer pane to turn on junk and adult content filtering, Outlook automatically creates rules to perform the filtering. One of the items Outlook creates is the Exception List, which lets you specify exceptions to the filter conditions Outlook uses to screen junk and adult content messages. This list allows you to receive wanted messages that otherwise would be processed by the rule. For example, you might want to receive messages with certain subjects that otherwise would be filtered by Outlook.

Follow these steps to add exceptions to the junk and adult content filters:

1 In Outlook, first verify that you've turned on junk and adult content filtering, and then choose Tools, Rules Wizard.

2 In the Rules Wizard, click Exception List in the Apply Rules In The Following Order list.

3 In the Rule Description area, click Exception List to display the Edit Exception List dialog box.

4 Click Add, specify the e-mail address or domain of the sender you want excluded from processing by the rule, and click OK.

5 Add other exceptions as needed and click OK.

6 Close the Rules Wizard.

Creating Other Junk and Adult Content Rules

The junk and adult content message rules you set up in the organizer pane offer only two options for processing spam: coloring the message header or moving the message to a different folder. You could move the messages to the Deleted Items folder and then configure Outlook to empty Deleted Items on exit, but you might prefer a more direct approach to deleting these messages. Or perhaps you want to perform another task such as copying the message or sending an automatic reply. You can do so by creating custom rules that use the Junk Senders and Adult Content Senders lists to process the messages.

> **tip**   **Don't reply to spam**
>
> Although you might be tempted to have Outlook send an automatic nasty-gram reply to every piece of spam you receive, restrain the urge. In many cases, the spammer's only way of knowing whether a recipient address is valid is when a reply comes back from that address. You make your address that much more desirable to spammers when you reply, because they know there's a warm body at the other end of the address. The best course of action is to delete the message without looking at it.

You create rules to handle spam the same way you create other rules—by changing the conditions and actions accordingly:

1 In Outlook, choose Tools, Rules Wizard to open the Rules Wizard.

2 Click New to start a new rule.

3 Select Start From A Blank Rule, select Check Messages When They Arrive, and click Next.

4 Scroll through the condition list and select Suspected To Be Junk E-Mail Or From Junk Senders or Containing Adult Content Or From Adult Content Senders.

5 In the Rule Description list (see Figure 8-20), click Junk Senders or Adult Content Senders to edit the sender list as explained in previous sections, and then click Next.

6 Select the action you want Outlook to take with these messages and click Next.

7 Specify any exceptions to the rule and click Next.

8 Specify options for the rule as you would for any other and click Finish.

When you're creating custom rules to process spam, keep in mind that you can't create a single rule that uses OR logic with multiple conditions. Thus, in most cases, you won't define the Junk Senders and Adult Content Senders conditions in the same rule, because doing so would require that a message meet both conditions for the rule to apply. In most cases, only one condition or the other will apply, so you'll have to create two rules: one to handle junk mail and the other to handle adult content mail.

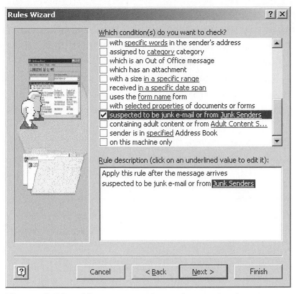

Figure 8-20. You can create custom rules to process spam.

Creating Automatic Responses with the Out Of Office Assistant

One of the key features in Outlook that makes it a great e-mail client is the Out Of Office Assistant, which lets you automatically generate replies to incoming messages when you aren't in the office. For example, if you're going on vacation for a couple of weeks and won't be checking your e-mail, you might want to have the Out Of Office Assistant send an automatic reply to let the senders know you'll respond to their messages when you get back.

To learn how to create automatic responses with custom rules, see "Creating Automatic Responses with Custom Rules," page 257.

Managing Mail When You're Out

Before you start learning about the Out Of Office Assistant, take a few minutes to consider a few other issues that relate to managing e-mail when you're out of the office.

First, the Out Of Office Assistant is a server-side component for Exchange Server. This means you can use it to process your Exchange Server account but not your POP3, IMAP,

HTTP, or other e-mail accounts, unless those accounts deliver incoming messages to your Exchange Server Inbox. You can create rules to process your other accounts and simulate the function of the Out Of Office Assistant, but you must do this by creating custom rules.

Second, keep in mind that because the Out Of Office Assistant functions as a server-side component, it processes your messages even when Outlook isn't running (a likely situation if you're scuba diving off the Great Barrier Reef for a couple of weeks). In order to process your other accounts with custom Out Of Office rules, Outlook must be running and checking your messages periodically. If you have a direct Internet connection, you can configure the rules, configure your send/receive groups to allow Outlook to periodically check messages for the non–Exchange Server accounts, and leave Outlook running. If you have a dial-up connection to these accounts, you'll have to also configure Outlook to dial when needed and disconnect after each send/receive operation.

> **caution**   Be sure to configure your dial-up connection to disconnect after a reasonable idle period, such as 15 minutes. Otherwise, if your Internet access is metered, you might come back from two weeks of sun and fun to find that your dial-up connection has been connected continuously for the last two weeks. Most ISPs implement an idle cut-off, but any activity on the line can cause it to remain connected, so it's important to configure the behavior from your side as well. Also be sure to configure Outlook to disconnect after the send/receive operation is completed.

For detailed instructions on configuring dial-up connections, see "Configuring Dial-Up Networking Options," page 147. For information on configuring send/receive groups, see "Controlling Synchronization and Send/Receive Times," page 190.

Using the Out Of Office Assistant

Using the Out Of Office Assistant is relatively easy. Here's the process in a nutshell:

1 Specify the text you want Outlook to use for automatic replies when you're out of the office.

2 If necessary, create custom rules for the Exchange Server to use to process incoming messages during your absence.

For information about custom Out Of Office rules, see "Creating Custom Out Of Office Rules," page 256.

3 Tell Outlook you're out of the office, which causes the Out Of Office Assistant to start responding accordingly.

4 When you get back, tell Outlook you're in the office, which turns off the Out Of Office Assistant rules processing.

> **note** When you start Outlook, it checks to see whether the Out Of Office Assistant is turned on. If it is, Outlook asks whether you want to turn it off.

After the Out Of Office Assistant is set up and functioning, messages that arrive in your Inbox receive an Out Of Office response with the message text you've specified. The Exchange Server keeps track of the send-to list and sends the Out Of Office response the first time a message comes from a given sender. Subsequent messages from that sender are sent to your Inbox without generating an Out Of Office response. This procedure cuts down on the number of messages generated and keeps the senders from becoming annoyed with numerous Out Of Office replies.

> **note** The Exchange Server deletes the send-to list for Out Of Office responses when you close the Out Of Office Assistant from Outlook.

Setting Up the Out Of Office Assistant

Follow these steps to specify the text for automatic replies and to tell Outlook you're out of the office:

1 In Outlook, select the Exchange Server Inbox and choose Tools, Out Of Office Assistant.

2 In the Out Of Office Assistant dialog box (see Figure 8-21), type the body of your automatic message reply in the AutoReply box. While the Out Of Office Assistant is active, the Exchange Server uses this message to reply to incoming messages.

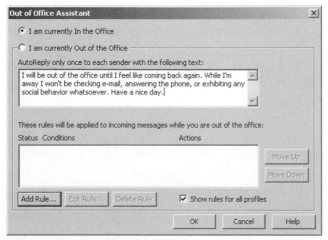

Figure 8-21. Use the Out Of Office Assistant dialog box to specify your automatic message reply.

3 Select I Am Currently Out Of The Office and click OK.

Creating Custom Out Of Office Rules

With the Out Of Office Assistant, you can create custom rules to use in addition to the basic automatic reply. To create a custom rule, open the Out Of Office Assistant and click Add Rule to display the Edit Rule dialog box, shown in Figure 8-22.

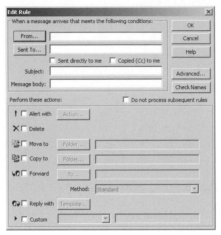

Figure 8-22. You can create custom rules to use with the Out Of Office Assistant.

The options in the Edit Rule dialog box are straightforward, particularly if you're now an old hand at creating rules. Specify the conditions the incoming messages should meet, and then specify the action the Exchange Server should perform if a message meets those conditions.

When you define the conditions, keep in mind that the Out Of Office Assistant conditions can be met by either full or partial matches. For example, you could enter **yce** in the Sent To box, and the rule would apply if the address contained Joyce, Boyce, or Cayce. If you want the condition to be met only if the full string is found, enclose the text in quotation marks—for example, enter **"yce"**.

Applying OR Logic in Out Of Office Assistant Rules

To understand how to apply OR logic in Out Of Office Assistant rules, consider two issues. First, unlike the Outlook rules discussed previously in this chapter, Out Of Office Assistant rules that contain multiple conditions using OR logic rather than AND logic can be processed by the Exchange Server. For example, if you enter **free money** as a condition for the Subject box and **Nate Sun** as a condition for the From box, the Exchange Server applies the rule if the message subject contains the words *free money* or if the sender is Nate Sun. This is in contrast to Outlook's rule behavior, which would apply the rule only if the subject contained the words *free money* and if the sender was Nate Sun.

Second, you can use semicolons within an Out Of Office rule to create an OR condition that addresses multiple possible matches. For example, if you want to create a rule that deletes messages containing the text *free money*, *MLM*, or *Trial Offer*, click Subject and enter the following text: **"free money"; "MLM"; "Trial Offer"**.

How Outlook evaluates the message depends on whether the condition data is enclosed in quotation marks. If you omit the quotes, partial-word matches satisfy the condition. If you enter **cat; car; amble**, for example, Outlook applies the rule to messages that include the words *cat, catapult, car, carpet, amble,* and *bramble.* If you enclose each string in quotes, Outlook matches only messages containing *cat, car,* and *amble.* In this example, Outlook will apply the rule to any message that has any one of those three strings in its subject.

You also can use this type of logic when addressing case sensitivity in your rules. For example, you might specify the following to allow Outlook to apply the rule to all messages that include the specified text in the subject using different case: **"No Worries"; "NO WORRIES"; "no worries".**

When you create rules for the Out Of Office Assistant to use, you can click Advanced in the Edit Rule dialog box to specify additional conditions for the rule. Outlook displays the Advanced dialog box, shown in Figure 8-23. You can specify multiple conditions for the rule in this dialog box.

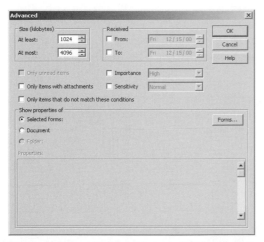

Figure 8-23. Use the Advanced dialog box to specify additional rule conditions.

> **tip** Although Microsoft's documentation indicates that you need to use a semicolon to define an OR condition, commas seem to work just as well.

Creating Automatic Responses with Custom Rules

The Out Of Office Assistant is great for generating automatic replies to messages that arrive in your Inbox when you're out of the office. However, the Out Of Office Assistant sends an Out Of Office response only the first time a message arrives from a given sender. Subsequent messages go into the Inbox without generating an automatic response (unless you set up a separate server-side rule).

In some cases, you might want Outlook to generate automatic replies to messages at any time and for other accounts—not only for messages that arrive in your Exchange Server mailbox. Perhaps you've set up an Internet e-mail account to take inquiries about a product or service you're selling. You can create a rule to automatically send a specific reply to messages that come in to that account. Or you might want people to be able to request information about specific products or topics by sending a message containing a certain keyword in the subject line. In that case, you can create a rule to generate a reply based on the subject of the message.

> **note** In Web jargon, applications or rules that create automatic responses are often called *autoresponders*.

You create automatic responses such as these not by using the Out Of Office Assistant but by creating custom Outlook rules with the Rules Wizard. As with other rules, you specify conditions that incoming messages must meet to receive a specific reply. For example, you might specify that an incoming message must contain the text *Framistats* in its subject in order to generate a reply that provides pricing on your line of gold-plated framistats.

> **note** You aren't limited to specifying conditions only for the subject of an incoming message. You can use any of the criteria supported by Outlook's rules to specify the conditions for an automatic response.

Setting Up the Reply

When you use a custom rule to create an automatic response, you don't define the reply text in the rule. Rather, you have two options: specifying a template on your local computer or setting up a specific message on the server. If you opt to use a template on your local computer, you create the message in Outlook and save it as a template file.

Follow these steps to create the template:

1 Configure Outlook as your default e-mail editor. To do so, choose Tools, Options and click the Mail Format tab. Clear the Use Microsoft Word To Edit E-Mail Messages option and click OK.

2 Begin a new message and enter the subject and body, but leave the address boxes blank.

3 Choose File, Save As.

4 In the Save As dialog box, specify a path and name for the file, and then select Outlook Template in the Save As Type drop-down list. Click Save.

Using a template from your local system causes the rule to function as a client-side rule. As a result, Outlook can use the rule to process accounts other than your Exchange Server account (such as a POP3 account), but the Exchange Server can't generate automatic responses when Outlook isn't running or is offline.

If you opt to store the message on the server, you select or create the message when you create the rule. Outlook stores the message on the server, which allows the rule to function as a server-side rule even when Outlook is offline. Outlook can continue generating automatic responses to messages that arrive in your Inbox even when Outlook isn't running. In many respects, this is the best option, because it helps ensure that the rule can function all the time. In addition, client-side responses are generated only once per session for a given sender, but server-side responses execute for all messages that meet the rule conditions.

Troubleshooting

Your autoresponse rule executes only once.

When you create a rule using the Reply Using A Specific Template action, Outlook executes the rule only once for a given sender in each Outlook session. Outlook keeps track of the senders in a list and checks incoming messages against the list. For the first message from a given sender that matches the rule conditions, Outlook generates the response; for subsequent messages, Outlook doesn't generate the response. Closing and restarting Outlook refreshes the sender list, and the next message from that sender that meets the criteria generates a response. This prevents Outlook from sending repetitive responses to a person who sends you multiple messages that satisfy the rule conditions. The Out Of Office Assistant uses the same process—and this behavior is by design.

If you create a server-side rule that uses Have Server Reply Using A Specific Message, the Exchange Server creates an autoresponse for all messages that meet the specified conditions, regardless of whether the message is the first from a particular sender.

Creating Automatic Responses from Local Templates

Follow these steps to create a client-side rule that responds to incoming messages with a reply from a template stored locally on your computer:

1 Using Outlook as your e-mail editor, compose the reply message and save it as a template (OFT) file.

2 Choose Tools, Rules Wizard to open the Rules Wizard.

3 Select the folder where you want the rule applied and click New.

4 Select Start From A Blank Rule and click Next.

5 Specify the conditions for the rule and click Next.

6 Select Reply Using A Specific Template.

7 In the Rule Description area, click A Specific Template.

8 From the Select A Reply Template dialog box (see Figure 8-24), select the template you want to use for the reply and click Open.

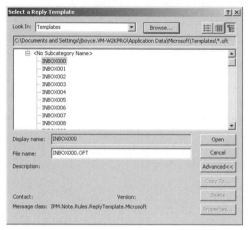

Figure 8-24. Select the message template to use as the reply.

9 Click Next and specify exceptions, if any, for the rule.

10 Click Next, specify final options for the rule, and click Finish.

Creating Automatic Responses from the Server

Follow these steps to create a server-side rule to generate automatic responses using a message stored on the server:

1 Choose Tools, Rules Wizard to open the Rules Wizard.

2 Select the folder where you want the rule applied and click New.

3 Select Start From A Blank Rule and click Next.

4 Specify the conditions for the rule and click Next.

5 Select Have Server Reply Using A Specific Message.

6 In the Rule Description area, click A Specific Message.

7 Create the message using the resulting message form, specifying the subject and text but no addresses, and then click Save and Close.

8 Click Next and specify exceptions, if any, for the rule.

9 Click Next, specify final options for the rule, and click Finish.

Sending and Receiving Faxes

Although Microsoft Outlook 2002 doesn't include its own fax service, it does support faxing through third-party applications such as WinFax. This means that most MAPI-enabled fax applications can deliver incoming faxes to your Inbox. In addition, Outlook supports the fax service provided by Microsoft for Windows 2000.

Although Microsoft Fax is not supported in Outlook 2002, you might still be able to use the version of Microsoft Fax included with Microsoft Windows 95 to receive faxes in your Outlook Inbox. For this to work, the fax service must already be installed and functioning, and a previous version of Outlook must be installed and configured to use the fax service. Then you can upgrade to Outlook 2002, and the fax service should continue to work. Success with this method can be spotty, however, so don't be surprised if incoming fax capability suddenly fails after the upgrade. If that's the case, you'll need to switch to a third-party application to integrate faxing with Outlook.

Covering the configuration of third-party fax applications in this book isn't practical because of the number of applications available. Instead, this chapter explains how to install, configure, and use the Windows 2000 fax service in conjunction with Outlook.

The Native Windows Fax Service

Previous versions of Outlook included the WinFax Starter Edition from Symantec (WinFax SE) for faxing in Internet-Only Mail mode and relied on the native Windows fax service for faxing from Corporate/Workgroup mode. Outlook 2002 integrates messaging into a single mode and no longer includes

261

WinFax SE. Instead, Outlook now relies solely on the native Windows fax service. Although you can use third-party fax applications with Outlook, many users don't need the extended features these programs offer, such as fax broadcast or the extensive selection of cover pages. Instead, the ability to print to the fax printer driver to send and receive faxes in your Inbox—the limit of what the Windows fax service can do—is enough. For that reason, this chapter focuses primarily on using the native Windows 2000 fax service with Outlook. If you need help using a third-party fax application with Outlook, check that fax application's documentation, Web site, or support center for more information.

Configuring the Fax Service

Installing and configuring the Windows 2000 fax service to work with Outlook 2002 is relatively easy. This section explains how to work through that process.

Installing Under Windows 2000

Setup automatically installs Microsoft Fax when you install Windows 2000. In fact, Windows 2000 doesn't even provide a way to remove the service. The fax service is already installed on your system and ready to use with Outlook. You do, however, need to take some steps to configure your system.

Adding Microsoft Fax to Your Profile

Adding the Windows 2000 Microsoft Fax Transport provider in Outlook requires more effort than simply configuring a few fax settings. The additional security provided by Windows 2000 requires you to also modify the user account under which the fax service operates and the service's startup properties.

In order for Microsoft Fax to work with Outlook in Windows 2000, the following conditions must be met:

- The user's account, whether local or domain, must be a member of the local Administrators group.

- The fax service must be configured to use the user's account to log on rather than the system account.

- The user's account must have the right to log on as a service.

Follow these steps to configure these properties on a computer that is a member of a workgroup:

1 Log on as Administrator, right-click My Computer, and choose Manage.

2 Expand the Local Users And Groups branch and select the Users node (see Figure 9-1).

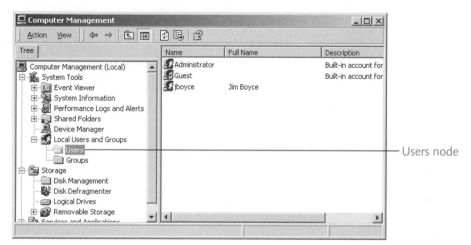

Figure 9-1. Configure group membership through the Local Users And Groups branch.

3 Double-click the user account used to log on with Outlook.

4 Click the Member Of tab. If the Administrators group isn't listed, click Add, select Administrators, click Add, and click OK.

5 Close the Computer Management console.

If the user is a member of a domain, the process is somewhat different because in this case you need to make the user's domain account a member of the local Administrators group:

1 Log on as Administrator, right-click My Computer, and choose Manage.

2 Expand the Local Users And Groups branch and select the Groups node.

3 Double-click the Administrators group.

4 In the Administrators Properties dialog box, click Add.

5 In the Select Users Or Groups dialog box, select the target domain in the Look In drop-down list.

6 Select the user's domain account in the list (see Figure 9-2 on the next page), click Add, and click OK.

Chapter 9

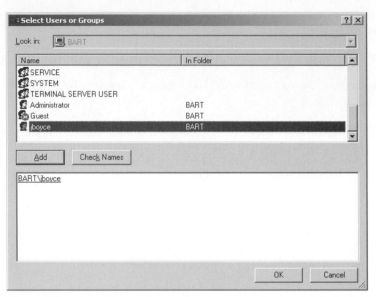

Figure 9-2. Add the user's domain account to the local Administrators group.

7 Click OK to close the Administrators Properties dialog box, and then close the Computer Management console.

Follow these steps to accomplish the next part of the task—adding the fax transport to your profile:

1 Close Outlook, right-click the Outlook icon on the desktop, choose Properties, and click E-Mail Accounts.

2 Select Add A New E-Mail Account and click Next.

3 Select Additional Server Types and click Next.

4 Select Fax Mail Transport and click Next (see Figure 9-3.)

5 Click Close.

Next configure the fax service to log on using the user's account rather than the system account:

1 Choose Start, Programs, Administrative Tools, Services to open the Services console. (Alternatively, open the Services branch of the Computer Management console.)

2 Locate and double-click Fax Service.

3 In the Fax Service Properties dialog box, select Automatic in the Startup Type drop-down list, as shown in Figure 9-4.

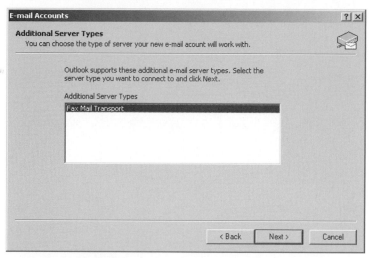

Figure 9-3. Outlook uses the Fax Mail Transport to deliver incoming faxes to your Inbox.

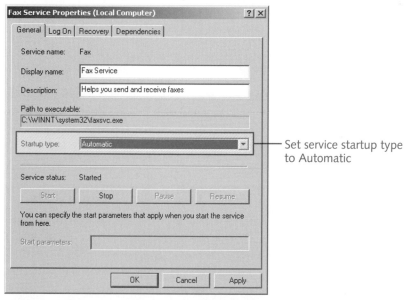

Set service startup type to Automatic

Figure 9-4. Configure the service to start automatically.

4 Click the Log On tab (see Figure 9-5 on the next page). Select This Account and click Browse.

265

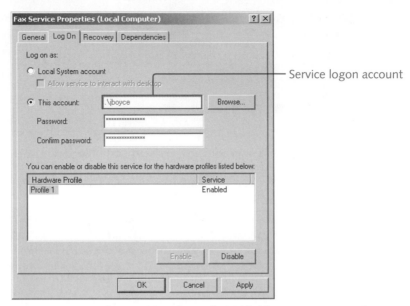

Figure 9-5.   On the Log On tab, configure the fax service to use the user's account.

5 Select the user's local account or domain account in the Select User dialog box and then click OK.

6 In the Password box, type the password associated with the specified user account. Verify the password and click OK. Windows 2000 automatically grants the account the right to log on as a service.

7 Stop and restart the fax service.

Troubleshooting

Adding a user to Domain Admins doesn't work.

In order for the fax service to deliver messages to the user's profile, the user's domain or local account must be a direct member of the local Administrators group. Adding the user's domain account to the Domain Admins group, and then adding the Domain Admins group to the local Administrators group won't work. This approach is appropriate only for domain administrators and presents a security risk, even if it's successful.

The last phase configures the fax service to log on using the user's account and selects the profile to which faxes should be delivered:

1 Click Start, Programs, Accessories, Communications, Fax, Fax Service Management to open the Fax Service Management console.

2 Click Devices and then double-click the fax modem.

3 Select Enable Receive, set the number of rings before answer, and click the Received Faxes tab.

4 Select Send To Local E-Mail Inbox, and then select the profile to which faxes should be delivered (see Figure 9-6).

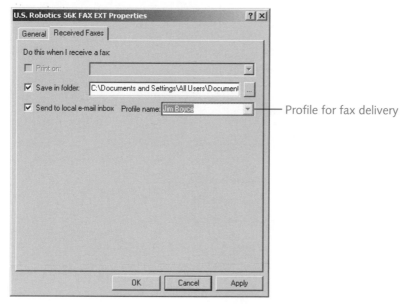

Figure 9-6. Choose the profile for fax delivery.

5 Click OK and close the Fax Service Management console.

Configuring Microsoft Fax Under Windows 2000

The interface in Windows 2000 is completely different from the one in Windows 9x, so you'll need to use the Fax Service Management console to configure the fax service settings.

Follow these steps to configure Microsoft Fax in Windows 2000:

1 Log on as Administrator.

2 Click Start, Programs, Accessories, Communications, Fax, Fax Service Management to open the Fax Service Management console, shown in Figure 9-7 on the next page.

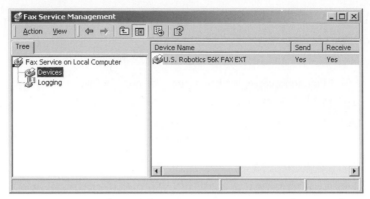

Figure 9-7. Use the Fax Service Management console to configure fax properties in Windows 2000.

3 Right-click Fax Service On Local Computer and choose Properties to display the dialog box shown in Figure 9-8.

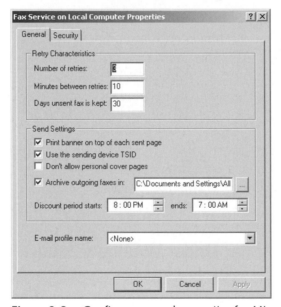

Figure 9-8. Configure general properties for Microsoft Fax on the General tab.

4 Configure options on the General tab using the following list as a guide:

- **Retry Characteristics.** Use these three options to specify the way Microsoft Fax attempts to resend faxes after a failure.

- **Print Banner On Top Of Each Sent Page.** Select this option to include your name, fax number, and other information as a banner at the top of each outgoing fax page. You can use the Fax icon in Control Panel to configure the user properties; see "Configuring User Properties," page 270.

268

- **Use The Sending Device TSID.** Select this option to include on the cover page the Transmission Station Identifier (TSID) of the fax device rather than the fax number specified in your user properties. Clear this option to use the fax number specified on the User tab.

- **Don't Allow Personal Cover Pages.** Select this option to prevent users from sending faxes with cover pages other than the default cover pages provided with Microsoft Fax. Clear this option to allow users to use any cover page.

- **Archive Outgoing Faxes In.** Use this option to archive all outgoing faxes to a specified folder. The default location is \Documents And Settings\All Users\Documents\Faxes\My Faxes\Sent Faxes, but you can click the button beside the text box to select a different folder. Clear this option if you don't want to save a copy of each fax.

---

tip   On systems running Windows 2000 that have been upgraded from Windows NT, the root folder for profiles is %systemroot%\Profiles rather than \Documents And Settings.

- **Discount Period.** Use these two options to set the start and stop times that indicate a period when outgoing calls are less expensive.

5 Click the Security tab, shown in Figure 9-9, and configure security as needed. Add accounts or groups, specifying the permissions each should have, and then click OK.

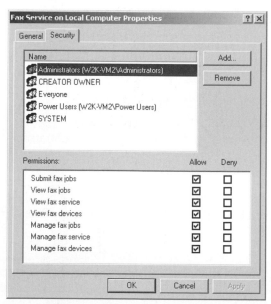

Figure 9-9. Use the Security tab to control the actions users can perform with the fax service.

6 Close the Fax Service Management console.

Configuring User Properties

You can configure additional properties for Microsoft Fax, such as user information and cover pages, through Control Panel. When you double-click the Fax icon in Control Panel, Windows 2000 opens a dialog box with four tabs. The following sections explain the options on each tab.

User Information Tab

The User Information tab (see Figure 9-10) provides spaces for name, fax number, e-mail address, and other information that Microsoft Fax can include in the banner and cover pages of outgoing faxes. You can enter details as you like, including your company and department affiliation, your job title, and a billing code for faxes.

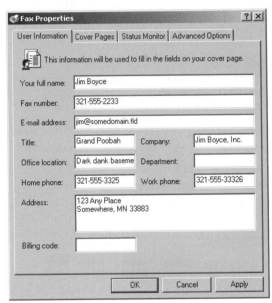

Figure 9-10.   Enter information about yourself on the User Information tab.

Cover Pages Tab

You can use the Cover Pages tab of the dialog box to add and modify your own cover pages. For all the details about using this tab, see "Using Cover Pages," page 274.

Status Monitor Tab

The Status Monitor tab, shown in Figure 9-11, provides options that determine how the fax service notifies you of incoming faxes. The available options include the following:

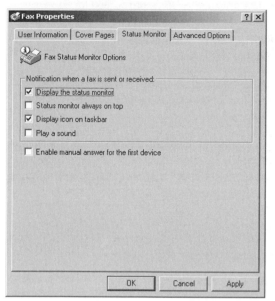

Figure 9-11. Use the Status Monitor tab to specify how the fax service notifies you of incoming faxes.

- **Display The Status Monitor.** With this option selected, Microsoft Fax displays the Status Monitor dialog box when a call comes in.

- **Status Monitor Always On Top.** Select this option to have the Status Monitor dialog box appear on top of all other application windows, even when the Status Monitor does not have focus (is not the active window).

- **Display Icon On Taskbar.** Select this option to include a Status Monitor icon on the system tray to quickly access the fax queue and other fax service properties.

- **Play A Sound.** Select this option to have Fax play a sound when a fax comes in. Use the Sounds And Multimedia icon in Control Panel to configure the WAV file used for incoming fax notification. The sound is specified by the Windows Explorer/Incoming Fax item (by default, Ringin.wav).

- **Enable Manual Answer For The First Device.** Select this option if you share a line for voice and fax calls on the fax modem and want to be able to answer calls manually rather than let Windows answer the call. When a call comes in, you can answer the call manually and, if it's a fax call, direct Microsoft Fax to pick up the call to receive the fax.

Advanced Options Tab

The Advanced Options tab provides three buttons that open the Fax Service Management console, open the Fax Service Management Help file, or add a fax printer driver.

Sending Faxes

Regardless of which operating system you use, you can send faxes from any application because Microsoft Fax functions as a printer driver. To send a fax, just print the document to the Fax printer icon (see Figure 9-12). To do so, choose File, Print to open the Print dialog box. Select Fax in the Name drop-down list (which lists all available printers) and click OK.

Figure 9-12. Send a fax from any application by using the Fax printer icon.

You also can send a cover page fax outside an application in those situations where you need to send only a quick note as a fax, rather than a document.

Follow these steps to send a cover page fax in Windows 2000:

1 Click Start, Programs, Accessories, Communication, Fax, Send Cover Page Fax. After the Send Fax Wizard starts, click Next.

2 In the Send Fax Wizard, enter the information for the recipient (see Figure 9-13). Alternatively, click Address Book to add the recipient to the address book or select an existing recipient.

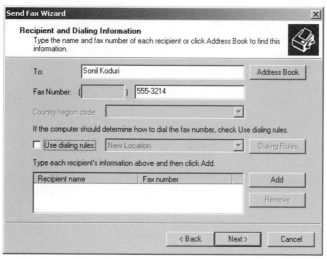

Figure 9-13. Specify recipient information for the fax.

3 Select Use Dialing Rules if you want Windows 2000 to dial the call using the dialing rules defined by the selected location. Clear this option to dial the call as a local call (using only the number specified in the phone number portion of the Fax Number boxes).

4 Click Add to add the recipient to the list.

5 If you want to include other recipients, add them and then click Next.

6 Select the cover page to use for the fax, enter a subject, and type the body of your fax in the Note box. Click Next.

7 On the Scheduling Transmission page of the wizard (see Figure 9-14 on the next page), specify when you want the fax sent and enter an optional billing code, if needed. Windows 2000 logs an event containing the billing code to the fax event log. You can use the log and the codes to track fax costs by project and account.

---

tip   **View fax event logs**

You can use the Event Viewer to view the fax event logs in the Windows 2000 Application log. Look for events with Fax Service as the source. To easily locate fax events, sort the Application log view by the Source field.

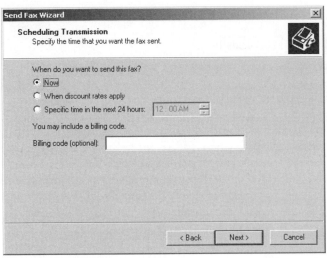

Figure 9-14. Specify send time and an optional billing code.

8 Click Next and then click Finish to submit the fax to the queue.

Using Cover Pages

As the previous steps illustrated, you can use a cover page as the only page of the fax for a simple message. The fax service can automatically include information on the cover page, such as your user information and the time the fax was sent. You also can include cover pages with other data. For example, you might need to fax a Word document and include a cover sheet. The following section explains how.

The first step in using cover pages with Microsoft Fax under Windows 2000 is to add or create them. Windows 2000 includes four basic cover pages; you can either use them without modification or change them to suit your needs. You also can create your own cover pages from scratch.

Adding Default Cover Pages

When you first configure Microsoft Fax, none of the default cover pages appear in your list of personal cover pages.

Follow these steps to add the four default cover pages to your list:

1 Double-click the Fax icon in Control Panel.

2 Click the Cover Pages tab and click Add.

3 Browse to \Documents And Settings\All Users\Documents\My Faxes\Common Coverpages.

> **tip** The root for user profiles on systems that have been upgraded from Windows NT is %systemroot%\Profiles rather than \Documents And Settings.

4 Select a cover page and click Open to add it to the list.

5 Repeat to add other cover pages, pulling them from other locations if available on your local computer or on the network.

Creating New Cover Pages

Windows 2000 includes an application called the Fax Cover Page Editor that lets you create and save custom fax cover pages to use with the fax service. Essentially, the Fax Cover Page Editor is a lot like a page layout tool for desktop publishing. If you have experience using Word, Web site development applications, or even Paint, you shouldn't have any trouble creating your own cover pages. Rather than explaining the Fax Cover Page Editor in detail, this section covers the main points to get you started.

First, to start the editor, double-click the Fax icon in Control Panel. On the Cover Pages tab, click New to open the editor (see Figure 9-15). Although you can create cover pages from scratch, you might find it easier to modify one of the existing pages to suit your needs, saving it under a different file name.

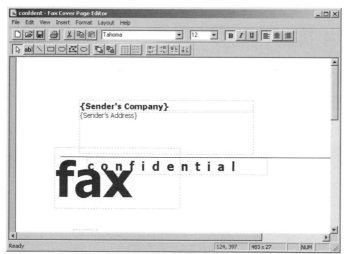

Figure 9-15. The Fax Cover Page Editor functions as a simple page layout tool.

You can insert graphics, text, and basic shapes on a cover page with the tools the editor provides. For example, you might want to include your company's logo on your fax cover pages. More important, perhaps, is your ability to insert dynamic fields on the cover page that Fax automatically fills in when you send a fax. These fields include your user name, fax number, time sent, and recipient name. Choose Insert, followed by Recipient, Sender, or Message, to view the types of fields you can insert on the cover page.

InsideOut

Unfortunately you can't insert a graphic from a file from the Fax Cover Page Editor's interface. This would be a handy feature to include in future versions of the Fax Cover Page Editor. You can insert graphics, but you have to use the clipboard to do so.

After you complete the layout of your cover page, save it to a disk. To do so, choose File, Save As. Then specify a path and name and click OK.

Receiving Faxes

Assuming that you've set up Microsoft Fax and Outlook properly, incoming faxes should be routed directly to your Inbox, where you can handle them just as you handle e-mail messages. Figure 9-16 shows a few faxes in the Inbox. Note that the message header's subject is always Received Fax, not the subject described in the fax. Because the fax comes through as a bitmap, the fax service has no way to extract the subject from the fax itself.

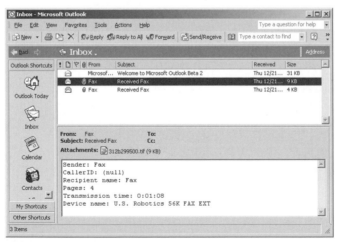

Figure 9-16. Faxes appear as messages with attachments in the Inbox.

If you've configured the fax service for manual reception, the service displays a dialog box when a call comes in. Click Yes to answer the call and receive the fax. As with automatic reception, the fax service delivers the fax to your Inbox.

Viewing Faxes

The fax comes through as an attachment in TIF format, which you can view with the application that is associated with TIF files on your system. To view a fax, open the attached TIF file as you would open any other attachment. By default, Outlook associates TIF files with the Microsoft Office Document Imaging application. The application is located by default in \Program Files\Common Files\Microsoft Shared\ MSPaper\Mspview.exe. If Document Imaging is the default application for TIF files, you should see something similar to Figure 9-17 when you open a fax TIF attachment.

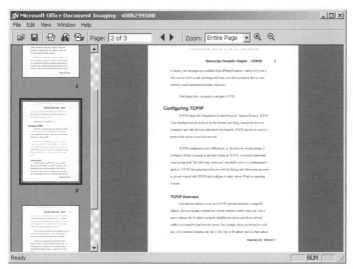

Figure 9-17. Use the Document Imaging application to view and manipulate received faxes.

The Document Imaging application shows the fax pages as thumbnails in the left pane and shows the selected page in the right pane. You can rotate pages, zoom in, print, and perform a handful of other tasks that make it easier to view and print the fax. You also can move individual pages to a new file by first selecting the page and then choosing Edit, Move Pages To New File. Document Imaging is a simple application, and a few minutes exploring its interface should make you comfortable using it.

Controlling the View

The Document Imaging application supports two viewing modes: Reading view and Page view. The default is Page view, which displays the fax as shown in Figure 9-17. You also can press F11 or choose View, Reading View to switch modes. Reading view displays the fax one page at a time, as shown in Figure 9-18 on the next page. Click the up or down arrows to scroll through the document and view other pages. Click the down arrow beside the fax document name, and choose Return To Page View or press Esc to return to Page view.

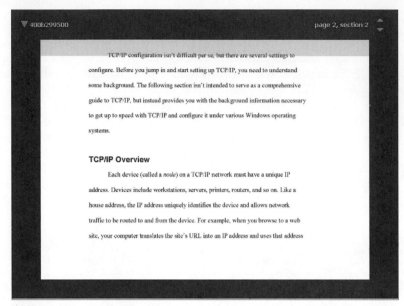

Figure 9-18. You can view the fax one page at a time in Reading view.

Troubleshooting

Fax images are displayed with a different application and show only the first page.

Outlook uses the application defined by the system's TIF document association to display faxes. Your system might be configured to use a different application to view TIF files. Because not all graphics applications support viewing multipage TIF documents, you might see only the first page of a fax. If that's the case, you need to associate TIF files with an application that supports multipage TIF documents. The following section explains how to restore Document Imaging as the default viewer for TIF files.

Restoring Document Imaging as the Default Viewer

If you install other graphics applications on your system, it's a strong possibility that one of these programs might change document associations on the system and that TIF files might now be associated with the new application rather than with Document Imaging. If you're seeing only the first page of faxes or want to use Document Imaging for other reasons, you need to reassociate Document Imaging with TIF files.

Follow these steps to do so:

1 Open any folder in Windows Explorer (such as My Computer).

2 Choose Tools, Folder Options and click the File Types tab, shown in Figure 9-19.

278

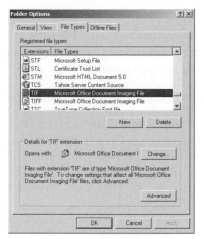

Figure 9-19. Use the File Types tab to change document association.

3 Scroll through the document list, locate TIF, select it, and click Change.

4 Select Microsoft Office Document Imaging and click OK.

5 Click OK to close the Folder Options dialog box.

---

tip **Set file association manually**

If you want to specify the application manually, click Advanced on the File Types tab after you select TIF from the list. Select Open, click Edit, and enter the following in the Application box (include the quotation marks and be sure to change the path if the file is located in a different folder or volume):

"C:\Program Files\Common Files\Microsoft Shared\MSPaper\Mspview.exe" "%1"

Printing Incoming Faxes

When a fax arrives, you have four options for processing the fax: print it, place it in your incoming fax queue folder, place it in your Inbox, or perform any combination of those three actions.

If you want Outlook to act like a fax machine, printing each fax as soon as it arrives, follow these steps:

1 Choose Start, Programs, Accessories, Communication, Fax, Fax Service Management.

2 Click the Devices node, and then double-click the fax modem to open its Properties dialog box.

3 Click the Received Faxes tab, select Print On, and then select the printer from the drop-down list.

4   Click OK and close the Fax Service Management console.

> **note**   In addition to printing the fax, you also should have it delivered to your Inbox or to a folder as specified by the other two options on the Received Faxes tab. This ensures that you have a backup copy if something goes wrong with the print job.

You can print individual faxes at any time. Simply open the fax in Document Imaging (or other application) and choose File, Print to print it just as you would print any other document.

Managing Faxes

You can manipulate faxes that have been delivered to your Inbox the same way you manipulate other messages in the Inbox. For example, you can move them from one folder to another or delete them. Having faxes delivered to your Inbox is a good way to easily recognize when new faxes come in, but you might want them delivered to another folder instead.

You can do so by creating a rule:

1   In Outlook, create the folder in which you want faxes to be stored, making sure that it's a standard message folder. Using another folder type will cause Outlook to handle the faxes differently than it handles e-mail messages, making them more difficult to retrieve.

2   Choose Tools, Rules Wizard to start the Rules Wizard.

3   Click New, select Start From A Blank Rule, and click Next.

4   Select With Specific Words In The Subject.

5   In the Rule Description area, click Specific Words, type **Received Fax** in the Specify Words box, click Add, and click OK.

6   Click Next and select Move It To The Specified Folder.

7   In the Rule Description area, click Specified, select the destination folder, and click OK.

8   Click Next, specify any exceptions to the rule, and click Next.

9   If you want to move existing faxes to the folder, select Run This Rule Now On Messages Already In Inbox.

10   Click Finish to create the rule.

> For a detailed explanation of message rules and how to create and manage them, see "Understanding Message Rules," page 231.

Integrating Outlook Express and Outlook

Microsoft Outlook is a good application for situations in which you need contact management, scheduling, task management, and the other features it offers in addition to messaging. But if you need only POP3 e-mail support (for many Internet e-mail programs, for example) and don't use the other features, Outlook might be more application than you need. In those situations, Outlook Express, which is included with Microsoft Internet Explorer, is a better option.

note POP3 is a standard e-mail protocol used by many Internet-based e-mail services. For example, most local Internet service providers (ISPs) use POP3, as do other services such as CompuServe and Prodigy.

Even if you do use all of Outlook's features in your everyday work, you'll still encounter times when Outlook will be more than you need. You might be going out of town, for example, and want to check e-mail while you're gone but not use any of Outlook's other features. Outlook Express is probably already on your notebook computer, has a smaller footprint than Outlook, and is a good choice as a POP3 client—with a few features even Outlook doesn't match.

Because this book focuses specifically on Outlook, the following chapter doesn't cover all the details of how to use Outlook Express. Rather, it explains how to integrate the two programs, moving messages and addresses between them. Information about integrating the two programs can be particularly useful if you're switching from one to the other or if you need to use Outlook Express for a short period and want your addresses and selected messages on hand.

281

---

tip   **Use POP3 with Microsoft Exchange Server**

If you have an Exchange Server account, you can connect to it by using Outlook Express if the Exchange Server is running the POP3 connector or a virtual POP3 server. You might also be able to access your Exchange Server account via a Web browser. Check with your system administrator for details, or see Chapter 36, "Accessing Messages Through a Web Browser," for information on accessing the Exchange Server through a browser.

Outlook vs. Outlook Express

If you've read the early chapters of this book, you should be fairly familiar with Outlook's features and capabilities. Outlook Express provides three primary features, outlined in the following sections.

E-Mail

Unlike Outlook, Outlook Express does not support Exchange Server, IMAP, or HTTP accounts, but it does support POP3 accounts (see Figure 10-1). If the Exchange Server is configured for POP3 access, you can use Outlook Express to send and receive messages through your Exchange Server account. However, you won't have access to your schedule or other Exchange Server account capabilities through Outlook Express.

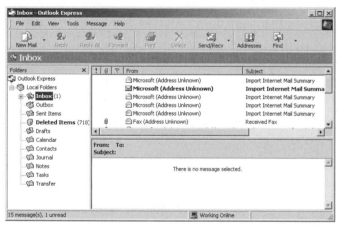

Figure 10-1.   Outlook Express is a good alternative to Outlook for POP3-only users.

---

tip   You can use Outlook Express with any POP3 account, including Classic CompuServe, Prodigy, and other services that support POP3.

Although it's limited to POP3 support, Outlook Express is still a very useful e-mail application. Like Outlook, Outlook Express allows you to manage multiple accounts at one time, perform scheduled send/receive operations, and specify which accounts are used in automatic send/receive operations. It supports message rules and is even easier to use than Outlook for creating rules.

Outlook Express also supports rich-text messages (see Figure 10-2). You can insert graphics, format fonts and paragraphs, automatically insert and indent message text in replies and forwards, and use many of the same editing and viewing features found in Outlook. In short, using Outlook Express for e-mail is a good alternative to Outlook if you need only POP3 support or need a temporary, lower-overhead alternative to Outlook.

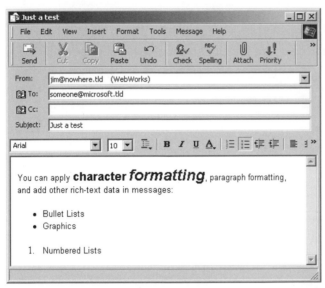

Figure 10-2. Like Outlook, Outlook Express supports rich-text messages.

Newsgroups

Outlook Express functions as a newsgroup reader, which means you can use it to read and post messages to public and private newsgroup servers (see Figure 10-3 on the next page). Microsoft chose to use Outlook Express as the default newsgroup reader rather than to incorporate news features into Outlook.

Chapter 10

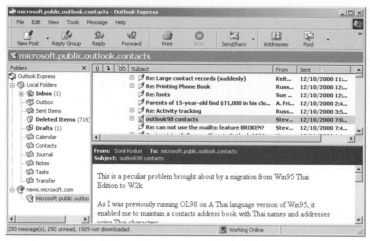

Figure 10-3. Outlook Express is the default newsgroup application for Outlook.

> For details about using Outlook Express for newsgroups, see Chapter 11, "Using Outlook Express for Public and Private Newsgroups."

LDAP Searches

The third function Outlook Express performs is Lightweight Directory Access Protocol (LDAP) searches. You can use Outlook Express to query LDAP directory services for information about people listed in the directory. Outlook Express sets up several directory service accounts automatically (see Figure 10-4), allowing you to query popular services—Bigfoot, InfoSpace, VeriSign, WhoWhere, and Yahoo!, for example. You can also add your own directory service accounts.

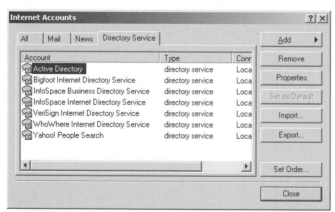

Figure 10-4. Outlook Express creates several directory service accounts automatically.

> For a detailed discussion of LDAP in both Outlook and Outlook Express, see Chapter 15, "Using LDAP Directory Services."

The Bottom Line

Outlook Express is a good alternative to Outlook for POP3 accounts—or even for your Exchange Server account—for those times when you're out of the office and need to access your messages but don't want the larger Outlook application. It serves as a reasonably good newsgroup reader, and its LDAP capabilities are useful for searching directory services. If you're looking for a newsreader that provides additional options for offline processing and message management, you might consider a third-party application such as Forte's Agent.

If Outlook is your choice for messaging, you'll probably use Outlook Express only for newsgroups and the occasional instance when you need to access your e-mail from your notebook computer when you're away from the office or at home. The following sections focus on how to move messages, addresses, and accounts between Outlook and Outlook Express to simplify migration from one to the other and to allow you to share your message-related data between the two applications.

Copying Messages and Addresses to Outlook

You can move messages from Outlook Express to Outlook, and vice versa. This is extremely useful if you're making a permanent switch from Outlook to Outlook Express or want to transfer messages from Outlook to Outlook Express for use out of the office. The following sections explain how to transfer messages between the two programs.

Understanding How Outlook Express Stores Messages

Outlook Express stores messages grouped in database files, not in individual files. Each database file represents an Outlook Express folder. (Outlook uses a single store file.) The Outlook Express Inbox, for example, resides in the Inbox.dbx file. Other folders have their own files.

You don't really need to know where the Outlook Express folders are stored to migrate your messages to Outlook. However, it's a good idea to know where they are in case you want to back them up or in case you need to move your messages between two Outlook Express installations or to a disk with more space. It's also important because you might need to move your Outlook Express files from one computer to another before exporting them to Outlook.

Migrating Messages Between Systems

You can move your messages from Outlook Express to Outlook, provided that the Outlook Express message store exists on the same system that holds your Outlook profile. Thus the first task is to get your Outlook Express messages on the computer where Outlook is installed, if they aren't there already. Then you can easily export them to your existing Outlook profile.

> **tip** Don't bother trying to place the Outlook Express store on a shared network if you're changing the location of your store or moving to another computer. The Outlook Express store must be stored locally.

You can copy individual folders to Outlook if you don't need to import all your Outlook Express folders. For example, if you're interested only in the Inbox, you can copy only the Inbox.dbx file. If you want to perform a selective copy but want to include folders other than the Inbox, however, make sure that you also copy the Folders.dbx file from your Outlook Express store folder to your Outlook system.

Follow these steps if your Outlook Express messages are not already located on the computer where Outlook is installed:

1 On the system containing your Outlook Express data, choose Tools, Options to open the Options dialog box. Click the Maintenance tab, shown in Figure 10-5.

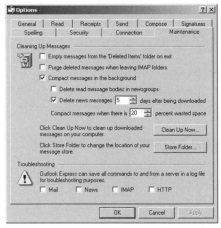

Figure 10-5. Use the Maintenance tab to locate your Outlook Express information store folder.

2 Click Store Folder to display the location of your Outlook Express information store (see Figure 10-6).

Figure 10-6. Each user has an information store folder based on the user profile.

3 Note the path to your store folder and click Cancel.

4 Configure Windows Explorer to show hidden files and folders. (The Outlook Express folder is by default located in a hidden folder.)

5 Copy the entire Outlook Express folder to the system where Outlook is installed. You can copy across the network, use a Zip disk or CDR, or use a direct-cable connection if the computers aren't networked. The destination really doesn't matter because you'll be using the folders only temporarily. Make sure to copy the entire folder as a whole, rather than as individual files.

6 On the system where Outlook is installed, open Outlook Express. If Outlook Express prompts you to create an e-mail account, click Cancel.

7 Choose Tools, Options and click Maintenance.

8 Click Store Folder and click Change.

9 Locate and select the folder you copied in step 5 and then click OK.

10 Click OK in the Store Location dialog box.

11 Outlook Express detects that files are present in the specified location and asks whether you want to use them or replace them with the messages from your old store location. Click Yes to switch to that store.

12 Shut down and restart Outlook Express to have the change take effect.

> **note** Copying the message files to the system where Outlook is installed doesn't also copy the Outlook Express Address Book, which is stored separately. See the following section if you need to move your address book from one computer to another.

Migrating Your Windows Address Book Between Systems

Outlook Express uses the Windows Address Book to store addresses. The address book file has the same name as your Windows logon name with a WAB file extension. The address book file is located by default in the Application Data\Microsoft\Address Book folder of your profile (for example, \Documents And Settings\<*user*>\Application Data\Microsoft\Address Book on computers running Windows 2000). Outlook can't use the WAB file directly, but you can easily import the addresses from a WAB into Outlook's Personal Address Book (PAB). Before you can import the address book, however, it must reside on the same system as Outlook.

If your Outlook Express data is located on another computer, follow these steps to copy the address book to the system where Outlook is installed:

1 On the system where your Outlook Express data resides, locate your WAB file as explained earlier. If you're not sure where to look, perform a search on ***.wab** to locate all WAB files on the system. Yours will be the one whose file name matches your Windows logon name.

2 Copy the WAB file to the same location on the computer where Outlook is installed, either across the network or by disk or other means.

3 Open Outlook Express on the target system (where Outlook is located), and verify that all your addresses are intact.

Copying Messages, Addresses, and Rules to Outlook from Outlook Express

Before you transfer addresses, you might need to perform one more advanced step. Although Outlook includes a Personal Address Book option as the destination for incoming addresses, selecting that option results in no addresses being imported in the majority of cases. Instead, you have two options: import the addresses into your Contacts folder or export the addresses from Outlook Express to a PAB.

Exporting Addresses from Outlook Express

If you want to store your Outlook Express addresses in an Outlook PAB, the easiest method is to export the addresses directly from Outlook Express to the PAB. To accomplish the same task from Outlook, you must import the addresses into the Contacts folder and then move them to the PAB.

Follow these steps to export addresses from Outlook Express to your Outlook PAB:

1 Add the PAB to your Outlook profile if it isn't already there.

> For details about adding the PAB to your profile, see "Configuring Address Books and Addressing Options," page 125.

2 In Outlook, choose Tools, Address Book to open the Address Book window.

3 In the Address Book window, choose Tools, Options.

4 On the Addressing tab, select Personal Address Book in the Keep Personal Addresses In drop-down list. Then click OK and close the Address Book window.

5 Open Outlook Express and choose File, Export, Address Book.

6 In the Address Book Export Tool dialog box, select Microsoft Exchange Personal Address Book and click Export.

7 If Outlook isn't running, Outlook Express prompts you to select the profile. Select the profile in which you want the addresses stored and click OK.

8 Click Close after the export is completed.

9 Open the Address Book window again and, if needed, change the location for storing personal addresses from the PAB back to the location you want.

Importing Addresses Within Outlook

If you're not using a PAB and don't want the incoming addresses mingled with your existing contacts list, you need to do a little planning. You also need to use the following procedure if you *are* using a PAB but want to perform the import from Outlook.

Let's first look at an overview of the process and then examine the specific steps involved. You begin by adding a PAB to your profile, if that's where you want the addresses to go. You could also add them to a subfolder of your Contacts folder. Because the addresses always move into the Outlook Contacts folder, you need to move the existing contacts temporarily, import the addresses, move them to the location you want, and then restore your original contacts. If you want the incoming messages stored in a subfolder of the Contacts folder, create two folders: one as a temporary haven for your existing contacts and a second for the incoming addresses. In this example, assume that the first is called Temp and the second is called My Addresses.

Move the existing contacts from the Contacts folder to the Temp folder. Perform the import to add the incoming addresses to the Contacts folder. Move them to the My Addresses folder. Move the contacts from the Temp folder back to the Contacts folder, and then delete the Temp folder.

If you want the incoming messages placed in your PAB, don't create the My Addresses folder. Instead, select the PAB as the destination when you import the addresses.

> **tip**   **Clean house before importing**
>
> Be sure to clean out unwanted messages and folders from Outlook Express before importing the messages, especially if Outlook Express contains a lot of messages. You also should clean up the names and addresses in the Outlook Express address book, adding names to any addresses that include only the e-mail address. Otherwise, Outlook uses the domain from the user's e-mail address as the name.

After you have located your Outlook Express messages and address book on the same computer as Outlook, the hard work is done, and you can quickly and easily import those items into Outlook. You can accomplish the task either from Outlook or from Outlook Express.

Because you can copy the messages and address book at the same time in Outlook, the following steps describe this particular approach:

1 Make sure that your Outlook Express messages (and, optionally, your address book) reside on the same computer as Outlook.

2 If you need to separate incoming addresses from your existing contacts, create folders as necessary and add the PAB. For example, create subfolders of the Contacts folder named My Addresses and Temp.

3 Move the existing contacts to the temporary folder.

4 In Outlook, choose File, Import And Export.

5 In the Import And Export Wizard, select Import Internet Mail And Addresses and click Next.

6 Select Outlook Express 4.x, 5 in the list, and select the items you want to import (see Figure 10-7). Then click Next.

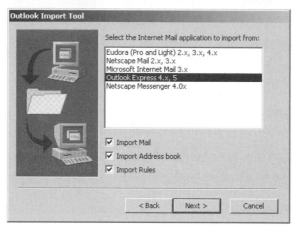

Figure 10-7. You can import mail, addresses, and rules.

7 If you are importing addresses, select Outlook Contacts Folder, as shown in Figure 10-8. Specify how you want duplicate items to be handled and click Finish.

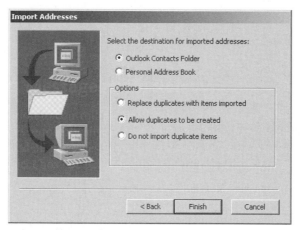

Figure 10-8. Specify the location for incoming addresses and how duplicates should be handled.

8 If you want to separate the incoming addresses from your existing contacts, move the newly imported addresses from the Contacts folder to the location you want to use (such as My Addresses). Then move the original contacts back to the Contacts folder.

9 Delete the Temp folder.

Depending on the number of addresses and messages you have, copying your data from Outlook Express to Outlook could take a long time. That's why it's a good idea to clean out old messages and any other unwanted items from Outlook Express before you begin importing the data in Outlook.

Troubleshooting

Some contacts don't appear in the Outlook Address Book.

You might run across a situation in which items in your Contacts folder don't appear in the Outlook Address Book, even when you select the contact items under Outlook Address Book in the Show Names drop-down list. This isn't a bug—it's by design. The Address Book shows only addresses that contain an e-mail address or a fax number. Any contact item that lacks both of those fields won't show up in the Outlook Address Book.

Copying Addresses and Messages to Outlook Express

In addition to moving addresses and messages from Outlook Express to Outlook, you also can move them the other way. You might do this if you're going to be out of the office and need to check your e-mail but don't want to install Outlook on your notebook computer.

In order to copy addresses from Outlook to Outlook Express, you must run Outlook Express on the same system as Outlook. After copying the addresses to Outlook Express, you can copy the WAB file to another computer to make it available on that system. Then simply locate the appropriate WAB file and copy it to the appropriate location on the other computer.

For details on this method, see "Migrating Your Windows Address Book Between Systems," page 287.

Copying Addresses from Outlook to Outlook Express

You can copy addresses from an Outlook PAB to your Outlook Express address book. If your Contacts folder contains any contact items, you must first copy them to the PAB before importing them into Outlook Express—Outlook Express will not import addresses from your Contacts folder, even if it is stored in a local PST file.

Follow these steps to import addresses from Outlook into Outlook Express:

1 In Outlook, copy the contact items from your Contacts folder to a PAB.

2 Open Outlook Express and choose File, Import, Other Address Book.

3 Select Microsoft Exchange Personal Address Book and click Import.

4 If Outlook isn't running, Outlook Express prompts you to select the profile from which to import addresses. Click OK to begin the import operation.

5 If the Outlook Express address book already contains an entry that is being imported, Outlook Express displays the Confirm Replace dialog box shown in Figure 10-9. Click the appropriate button to specify how you want Outlook Express to treat duplicates.

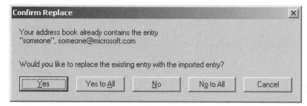

Figure 10-9. Outlook Express prompts you to specify how to handle duplicates.

6 Click Close. Then open the address book in Outlook Express to verify that your addresses were imported correctly.

Copying Messages from Outlook to Outlook Express

You can import messages to Outlook Express from Outlook by using a wizard provided with Outlook Express for that purpose. Outlook Express imports from your default message store (that is, the store you've configured in Outlook as the location for incoming mail). This means you might need to change the default store in order to import messages.

For example, assume that you have an Exchange Server account and have configured Outlook to deliver mail to your Exchange Server mailbox, but you want to import messages from your personal folders to Outlook Express. In that situation, you would configure the personal folders as the default store in Outlook, import the messages into Outlook Express, and then reconfigure Outlook to use the Exchange Server mailbox as the default store.

---

tip **Import from multiple message stores**

You can import from multiple stores by performing multiple imports, changing the default store in Outlook before each import. Keep in mind that Outlook Express won't differentiate between stores, however; the messages in the Inbox folders for two different Outlook stores will all show up in the same Inbox in Outlook Express.

Follow these steps to import messages into Outlook Express from Outlook:

1 If you need to import messages from a store other than your current default store, configure Outlook to use that store for new message delivery.

2 Open Outlook Express, and choose File, Import, Messages.

3 Select Microsoft Outlook in the Select Program list, and click Next.

4 If Outlook isn't running, Outlook Express prompts you to select the profile from which to import the messages. Select a profile, and click OK.

5 Outlook Express prompts you to specify which folders to import (Figure 10-10). Select All Folders to import all messages, or select Selected Folders, and then select the folders to include. (You can use the Shift or Ctrl key to select multiple folders.)

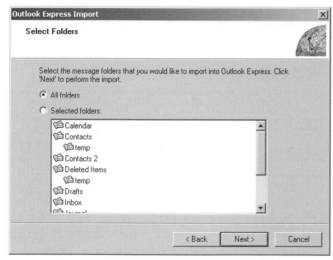

Figure 10-10. Outlook Express prompts you to specify which folders to import.

6 Click OK to start the import, and then click Finish.

7 If you changed the default Outlook store in step 1, change it back.

If you import folders other than your message folders, you might not see what you expect in Outlook Express after the import is completed. Outlook Express imports everything as messages. Contact items, tasks, and calendar items all come in as messages because Outlook Express doesn't support these other item types. Figure 10-11 on the next page shows the results of importing the Contacts folder into Outlook Express.

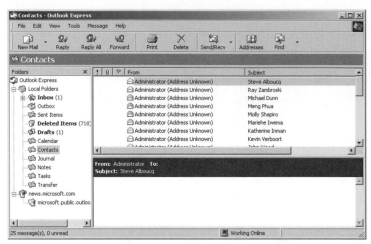

Figure 10-11. Nonmessage items are imported into Outlook Express as messages.

Copying Accounts

In most cases, it's as easy to create accounts from scratch as it is to copy them from Outlook to Outlook Express, or vice versa. If you want to save yourself a little typing, however, importing the account is the way to go.

---

tip   **Import accounts automatically**

Outlook checks for new Outlook Express accounts on startup. If one exists, Outlook asks whether you want to import the account. Outlook prompts only once, so if you click No, it won't prompt you again. Instead, you must use the procedure outlined in the following section.

Copying Accounts to Outlook

Copying accounts from Outlook Express to Outlook is simple, thanks to a wizard in Outlook:

1 In Outlook, choose File, Import And Export.

2 Select Import Internet Mail Account Settings and click Next.

3 Outlook prompts you to select the e-mail client from which to import accounts. Select Outlook Express and click Next.

4 If more than one account exists in Outlook Express, Outlook prompts you to select one (see Figure 10-12). Select the account you want to import and click Next.

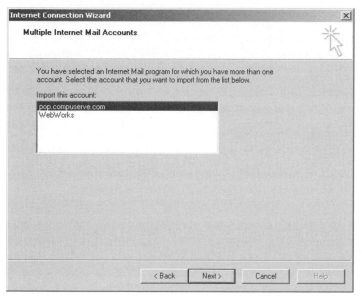

Figure 10-12. Outlook prompts you to select the account to import.

5 Outlook then presents a series of wizard pages that include the account information. Verify the information and click Next on each page, and then click Finish.

Copying Accounts to Outlook Express

The process for importing accounts from Outlook into Outlook Express is also easy, thanks to the wizard Outlook Express provides for that purpose.

Follow these steps to import Outlook accounts into Outlook Express (keeping in mind that you can import only POP3 accounts):

1 In Outlook Express, choose File, Import, Mail Account Settings.

2 Select the option Microsoft Windows Messaging or Exchange or Outlook and click Next.

3 Select an account to import and click Next.

4 In the Confirm Settings dialog box, verify the settings for the account. If they are correct, click Next and then click Finish. If you need to make changes, select Change Settings, click Next, and modify settings as needed.

Chapter 10

295

Using Outlook Express for Public and Private Newsgroups

Like its predecessors, Microsoft Outlook 2002 doesn't include a newsgroup reader. Instead, Outlook relies on Outlook Express as its default newsgroup reader. Outlook Express is included with Microsoft Internet Explorer 4.0 and later. Although other newsgroup applications are available—most notably Forte's Agent, which offers some additional benefits—Outlook Express is a good choice for occasional forays into newsgroups and situations where you're not dealing with a large number of encoded attachments.

This chapter explores the newsgroup features in Outlook Express and shows you how to use Outlook Express to read newsgroup messages, post new messages, handle attachments, and process items automatically.

> You'll find additional discussion of Outlook Express in Chapter 10, "Integrating Outlook Express and Outlook," which explains how to move messages, address books, and accounts between Outlook and Outlook Express.

Overview of Newsgroups and News Servers

Newsgroups are the Internet's equivalent of a huge bulletin board. Each newsgroup focuses on a specific area of interest, and you can post messages to a newsgroup and view other people's posting. Newsgroups are *threaded*, which means that you can easily follow a specific discussion within the group.

Outlook Express organizes all messages related to a specific topic in an expandable and collapsible hierarchy. Each newsgroup has a unique name not only to help you identify its topic but also to help you locate the group among the other newsgroups hosted by the server.

Public Internet newsgroups number in the tens of thousands, and many businesses provide their own news servers that allow customers to obtain support or provide feedback. Microsoft, for example, maintains public news servers where you can get support for various products and interact with other users. It also maintains private news servers for participation by beta testers.

In addition, many organizations implement private news servers where employees can share information and collaborate on projects. You can use Outlook Express as a newsreader for both public and private newsgroups. The only real difference between the two types of groups is access—private news servers restrict access while public news servers do not.

> **note** News servers use a standard protocol called Network News Transfer Protocol (NNTP) to support connection from news clients such as Outlook Express. Microsoft Windows 2000 Server includes an NNTP service you can use to set up your own news server. If you're interested in setting up your own news server for private newsgroups, see "NNTP + Outlook = Internet Newsgroups," page 842.

Configuring Outlook Express for Newsgroups

This chapter assumes that you have some degree of familiarity with newsgroups but don't necessarily have a lot of experience working with them. This section, which focuses on setting up Outlook Express to access your news server, should help you get started.

> **note** Before you can begin using Outlook Express to view Internet newsgroups or other public or private newsgroups outside your local area network (LAN), you need to establish an Internet connection. For details on setting up a Dial-Up Networking connection, see "Configuring Dial-Up Networking Options," page 147.

Starting Outlook Express to Read Newsgroups

You can start Outlook Express in two ways: either from Outlook or from the Windows desktop. To start Outlook Express from Outlook, choose View, Go To, News. Outlook Express opens (if it isn't already running) but doesn't open a specific news account or newsgroup.

You also can open Outlook Express from the Windows desktop. Windows automatically places an Outlook Express icon on the Quick Start menu, just to the right of the Start menu. Alternatively, you can start the program by choosing Start, Programs, Outlook Express.

Setting Up a News Account

Setting up a news account is the first step in using Outlook Express to access a news server. The process is simple, but it requires some preparation. In particular, you need to have the following information available:

- **News server name or IP address.** You need to know the Domain Name Service (DNS) name or the Internet Protocol (IP) address of the news server so that Outlook Express can connect to it.

- **Logon information.** Most public news servers don't require logon. Many private servers, however, do require that you specify valid account credentials (user name and password).

- **Port, if not standard.** The default Transmission Control Protocol (TCP) port for NNTP is 119. Almost all news servers use the default, so you will rarely need to specify a nonstandard port.

- **Whether the server requires Secure Sockets Layer (SSL).** Most public servers do not require SSL, although some private servers do. If you're unable to connect without SSL, try enabling it and then retest the connection.

- **Whether Secure Password Authentication (SPA) is required.** Most news servers do not require SPA. If you are unable to connect, however, enable SPA and try again.

Follow these steps when you're ready to set up your news accounts:

1 Create the Internet connection for your computer (if you don't already have one).

2 Open Outlook Express and choose Tools, Accounts to open the Accounts dialog box.

3 Click the News tab and then click Add, News to start the Internet Connection Wizard.

4 Specify your name, e-mail address, server name, and other information as prompted by the wizard and then click Finish.

5 In the Internet Accounts dialog box, double-click the account you just created or select it and click Properties.

6 Configure settings for the account, as explained in the following four sections.

General Tab

On the General tab (see Figure 11-1), you can change the account name, specify your name and e-mail addresses, and determine whether the account is included when checking for new messages.

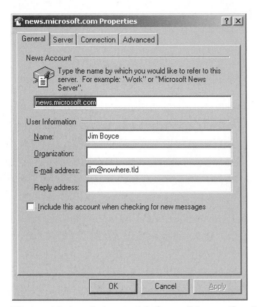

Figure 11-1. Enter user information on the General tab for a news account.

Configure settings on the General tab using the following list as a guide:

- **News Account.** Specify the name for the account as you want it to appear in Outlook Express. This account name appears in the Internet Accounts dialog box and in the folder list in Outlook Express.

- **Name.** Specify your name as you want it to appear in the header of messages that you post.

- **Organization.** Specify an optional organization name (such as a company name).

- **E-Mail Address.** Enter your e-mail address as you want it to appear in messages that you post. Leave this box blank if you don't want your e-mail address posted.

- **Reply Address.** Specify the address to which replies to your posts will be sent if a reader replies directly to you rather than to the newsgroup.

- **Include This Account When Checking For New Messages.** Select this option if you want Outlook Express to check the newsgroups to which you've subscribed and indicate the number of unread messages beside the group name in the folder list.

Server Tab

Use the Server tab (see Figure 11-2) to specify the server's DNS name or IP address and authentication settings, as explained in the following list:

- **Server Name.** Enter the fully qualified DNS name (FQDN) of the server or enter its IP address.

- **This Server Requires Me To Log On.** Select this option if the news server requires that you provide an account name and password to access the server.

- **Account Name.** Specify the account name to use if the server requires you to log on. If the server is hosted on a server in a Windows domain but uses accounts in a trusted domain for authentication, include the domain name before the user name, such as *MYDOMAIN\myusername*.

- **Password.** Specify the password associated with the account specified above.

- **Remember Password.** Select this option if you want Outlook Express to store the password for this news server in your password cache.

- **Log On Using Secure Password Authentication.** Select this option if the news server requires SPA for authentication.

Figure 11-2. You can specify server options on the Server tab.

Troubleshooting

You are unable to connect to a server that doesn't require authentication.

Many news providers opt to use *subnet exclusion* rather than authentication to control access to the news server. For example, an Internet service provider (ISP) will typically allow access to the news server only by clients within the ISP's own subnets. This method, which allows the ISP to restrict access to the news server to its customers only, is easier to implement than authentication, from an administration perspective.

If you're having problems connecting to a news server that doesn't require authentication, and you know your settings are correct, subnet exclusion could be the problem. The only way around the problem is to dial into the ISP's network using its access numbers or to establish a virtual private network (VPN) connection to a VPN server that resides within an allowed subnet.

Connection Tab

On the Connection tab, you specify the dial-up connection to use for the selected server. Clear the Always Connect Using This Account check box if you connect through a LAN or want to connect using whichever dial-up connection is active when you attempt the connection.

Advanced Tab

Use the Advanced tab (see Figure 11-3) to specify the port for the NNTP server and other advanced settings, as described in the list on the facing page.

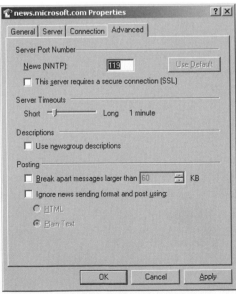

Figure 11-3. The Advanced tab includes the port setting and other newsgroup options.

- **News (NNTP).** Specify the TCP port used for the NNTP protocol on the news server. The default is 119. Most servers use the default settings, so you should not have to change this setting in most situations.

- **This Server Requires A Secure Connection.** Select this option if the server requires SSL for the connection. SSL provides higher security, but most servers don't require it.

- **Server Timeouts.** Specify the amount of time the server can be unresponsive before Outlook Express cancels the download of messages or groups. Use a shorter timeout if you have a fast Internet connection or the server is not relatively busy. Use a longer timeout for slow Internet connections and heavily used servers.

- **Use Newsgroup Descriptions.** In addition to its newsgroup name, each newsgroup also can have a longer description that helps you identify it. Select this option if you want Outlook Express to download newsgroup descriptions with the newsgroup names when you refresh the newsgroup list or download new newsgroups.

- **Break Apart Messages Larger Than n KB.** You can use this option to break messages into multiple messages smaller than the specified size. Most servers support large messages, so you'll rarely need to use this option.

- **Ignore News Sending Format And Post Using.** Select this option and specify the format for posting to the selected newsgroup if you want to override the default setting defined in the global properties of Outlook Express. To configure the default setting, choose Tools, Options and click the Send tab.

Managing the Newsgroup List

Each server maintains a certain number of newsgroups. A typical public Internet news server hosts 40,000 or more; other public and private news servers usually host fewer. Microsoft's public news server at *news.microsoft.com*, for example, currently hosts approximately 1,400 newsgroups. Other business and private news servers generally host a smaller number of groups.

When you first add a news account, Outlook Express asks whether you want to download the list of newsgroups from the server. You must download this list in order to be able to browse the newsgroups. This generally doesn't take very long, even when you're downloading from a public Internet news server. You can download the 40,000-plus newsgroup list in a matter of a few minutes, even on the slowest connections. Keep in mind that you're downloading only the newsgroup names (and, optionally, the group descriptions), but no message headers or messages.

Downloading and Updating the List

If you didn't let Outlook Express download the newsgroup list when you set up your account, you can download it at a later time. You also might want to reset the list if you think it might contain new newsgroups not included in your original list or if you want to download the newsgroup descriptions as well as the names.

Follow these steps to reset the newsgroup list, which downloads a new copy of the list:

1 Open Outlook Express, click the server in the folders list, and then click Newsgroups in the right pane to display the Newsgroup Subscriptions dialog box (see Figure 11-4).

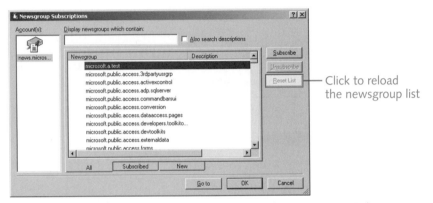

Click to reload the newsgroup list

Figure 11-4. Reset the newsgroup list by using the Newsgroup Subscriptions dialog box.

2 If you want to download descriptions as well as names, select the Also Search Descriptions check box.

> **note** If descriptions are not currently downloaded, Outlook Express asks whether you want to reset the list. Click Yes to do so.

3 Click Reset List to download the new copy of the list.

> **tip** If you don't want to download descriptions, you can reset the list quickly this way: right-click the news server in the folders list and choose Reset List.

Subscribing and Unsubscribing to Groups

You can view any newsgroup without subscribing to the group. But subscribing to a group you frequently visit can simplify access because Outlook Express includes subscribed newsgroups in the folders list (see Figure 11-5). You can then quickly open a specific group by clicking it in the folders list.

Subscribed newsgroups

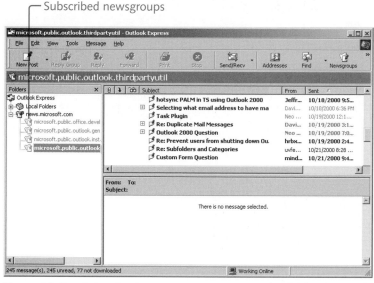

Figure 11-5. Subscribed newsgroups appear in the folders list, making them easily accessible.

Subscribing to a newsgroup has no effect on the server. You're not associating your user account, e-mail address, or any other information with any setting on the server. Nor can others who use a news server determine to which newsgroups you subscribe. Subscription is purely a client-side setting that makes it easier for you to access frequently used groups.

Follow these steps to subscribe to a newsgroup and add it to your folders list:

1 Open Outlook Express, click the news server in the folders list, and then click Newsgroups in the right pane.

2 In the Newsgroup Subscriptions dialog box, click the All tab, and then locate and select the newsgroup to which you want to subscribe.

3 Click Subscribe.

4 Repeat the process to subscribe to other newsgroups.

note To subscribe to multiple groups, hold down the Ctrl key and select multiple newsgroups.

Outlook Express displays a small icon beside each subscribed group on the All tab. You also can click the Subscribed tab in the Newsgroup Subscriptions dialog box to view a list that includes only your subscribed newsgroups, as shown in Figure 11-6 on the next page. The New tab shows new newsgroups.

Subscribed groups

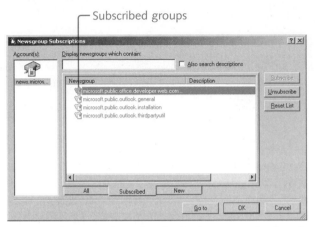

Figure 11-6. Use the Subscribed tab to view the list of newsgroups to which you have already subscribed.

Viewing a Group

You don't have to subscribe to a group to view its contents, but only those groups to which you've subscribed appear in the folder list by default.

To open other groups to read and post messages, follow these steps:

1 Click the Newsgroups button on the toolbar to open the Newsgroup Subscriptions dialog box, shown previously in Figure 11-4.

2 In the Display Newsgroups Which Contain box, enter the newsgroup name to view a specific newsgroup. To view all the newsgroups associated with a given topic, enter any portion of the newsgroup name; for example, enter **microsoft.public.access** to view all newsgroups about Microsoft Access. Enter a single word to view a list of all newsgroups that contain that word.

3 After you find the newsgroup you want, click it in the Newsgroup list and then click Go To.

Searching Descriptions

As explained previously, newsgroups can include optional descriptions that explain the content or intent of the newsgroup. When you search for a newsgroup on a particular topic, Outlook Express searches only on the newsgroup name by default. To include the description in the search, select the Also Search Descriptions check box in the Newsgroup Subscriptions dialog box. If you have not yet downloaded the descriptions, Outlook Express prompts you to reset the newsgroup list and download descriptions. Even with a full complement of Internet newsgroups, downloading generally takes only a few minutes over a dial-up connection and is considerably faster over a dedicated connection.

Reading Messages

Because of the way Outlook Express presents the newsgroup and its contents, reading messages in newsgroups is easy. Before you can read messages, however, you need to download message headers. You can then read messages, follow a discussion thread, and mark messages for offline processing.

Downloading Message Headers

After you select a newsgroup, Outlook Express downloads a certain number of message headers from the newsgroup by default. The message headers appear in the right pane, and you can sort the view based on the various columns—subject, size, or date and time posted, for example.

The number of message headers that Outlook Express downloads automatically when you open a newsgroup depends on how you've configured the program. Choose Tools, Options and click the Read tab to display the Read options shown in Figure 11-7. The Get *n* Headers At A Time check box specifies the number of headers that Outlook Express will download when you open the newsgroup and when you direct it to download message headers by choosing Tools, Get Next *n* Headers. If you clear the Get *n* Headers At A Time check box, Outlook Express downloads all headers from the newsgroup.

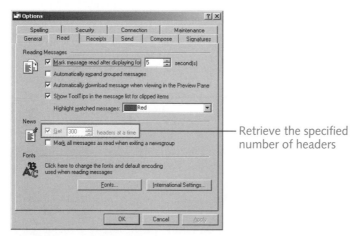

Retrieve the specified number of headers

Figure 11-7. Use the Read tab to determine how Outlook Express downloads message headers.

> **tip** If you clear the Get *n* Headers At A Time check box, the command on the Tools menu changes to Get New Headers.

Troubleshooting

You can't download message headers.

On occasion you might not be able to download message headers. This is because your message store is preventing Outlook Express from properly distinguishing between existing and new message headers. If that's the case, you can clear out all headers so that Outlook Express can download them again.

To do so, follow these steps:

1 Save any newsgroup messages or attachments you don't want to lose.

2 Open Outlook Express and choose Tools, Options. Click the Maintenance tab.

3 Click Clean Up Now, click Browse, and select the subscribed newsgroup (or the news server if you haven't subscribed to any groups).

4 Click Reset to delete all message headers and bodies, and then download the message headers again.

Viewing and Reading Messages

Reading a newsgroup message is about as easy as reading an e-mail message in your Inbox. Depending on how you have configured Outlook Express, it can be as simple as opening the newsgroup and clicking the message header to download the message and view it in the preview pane. You also can double-click a message header to open it in a message window.

Choose View, Layout to display the Window Layout Properties dialog box, shown in Figure 11-8. Use the options in the Preview Pane group to turn the preview pane on or off and to specify its location and whether it includes the preview pane header.

You can configure Outlook Express not to download messages when you click their headers. If a selected message hasn't been downloaded, Outlook Express tells you so in the preview pane, and you can then double-click the message to download it. (If the preview pane isn't displayed, Outlook Express takes no action.) You can select multiple message headers, open all of them, and mark them for later download.

Outlook Express displays a half-page icon beside the header of a message that hasn't been downloaded yet and shows a full-page icon beside a message that has been downloaded. The headers of unread messages appear in a bold font, and the headers of read messages appear in a normal font, giving you a quick indication of which messages have been read and which have not. If not all messages in a thread have been read, the first message in the thread retains the bold font when the thread is collapsed but not when you expand the thread. This helps you determine that the thread contains unread messages.

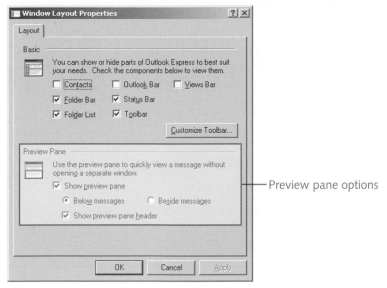

Figure 11-8. Use the Window Layout Properties dialog box to set preview pane options.

By default, Outlook Express marks as read any message that has been previewed for more than 5 seconds, but you can modify this behavior and set a different preview duration by following these steps:

1 In Outlook Express, choose Tools, Options and click Read.

2 On the Read tab, select the Mark Message Read After Displaying For *n* Seconds check box to have Outlook Express automatically mark as read all messages that are previewed for the specified duration. If you don't want Outlook Express to automatically mark messages as read unless you have actually opened them, clear this check box.

3 Change the preview period in the associated seconds box if you want to increase or decrease the duration of the preview.

> **tip** Increasing the preview period allows you to read part of a message and skip to another without the first being marked as read.

4 If you want Outlook Express to mark all messages in the newsgroup as read when you exit the newsgroup, select the Mark All Messages As Read When Exiting A Newsgroup check box.

5 Click OK to close the dialog box.

Working with Message Threads

Messages in a newsgroup are organized in Outlook Express by *thread*. A thread is a group of interrelated messages, or posts and replies to those posts. Message threads are also called *conversations*. Outlook Express indicates message threads by displaying a plus sign beside the first message in the thread. You can click the plus sign to expand the thread, which changes the icon to a minus sign. Click the minus sign to collapse the thread. As Figure 11-9 shows, Outlook Express also organizes the messages in a thread by indenting them to indicate the relationship between them in the thread.

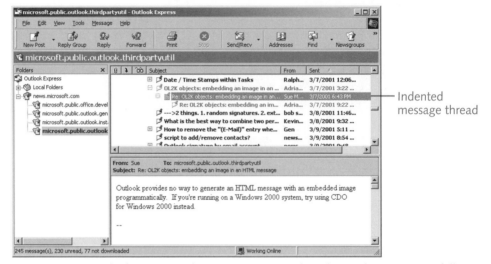

Figure 11-9. Outlook Express indents messages in a thread to make it easier to follow the conversation.

To learn how to "ungroup" messages from conversations and display them individually, see "Controlling Which Messages Are Shown," page 320.

Unscrambling Messages

Outlook Express supports a standard called ROT13 that allows you to unscramble messages. ROT13 doesn't provide actual security; it simply replaces each character in a message with a character 13 places later in the alphabet, which means that anyone can unscramble the message. However, scrambling messages can hide messages that might be considered offensive or ones the sender wants to make more difficult to read for other reasons.

You can't scramble messages in Outlook Express, but you can unscramble messages that others have posted to a newsgroup. Download the message, select its header, and choose Message, Unscramble.

Posting Messages

Posting messages to a newsgroup is a lot like sending an e-mail message. You can post a message to a single newsgroup or post to several at one time.

Posting a Message to a Single Group

To compose a message to post to a newsgroup, click the New Post button on the toolbar or choose File, New, News Message. Outlook Express displays a message form, as shown in Figure 11-10, and automatically includes the name of the current newsgroup in the Newsgroups box.

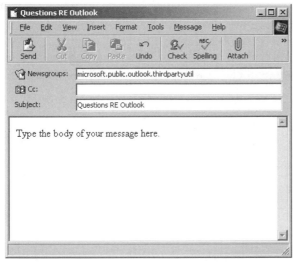

Figure 11-10. Composing a news message is much like composing an e-mail message.

Type the topic of your message in the Subject box, and then type your message in the message box. As you can in Outlook, you can post the message using HTML, which means you can create a rich-text message with character and paragraph formatting, bullets, and numbered lists. Click the Attach button if you want to attach a file to the message, and then click Send. Depending on how you've configured Outlook Express, the message is either posted immediately or sent to the Outbox until the next time you process messages. Outlook Express places a copy of the post in the Sent Items folder, if you've configured the program to do so (on the Send tab in the Options dialog box).

> **tip** Use the Cc box on the message form to send a copy of the message post to one or more e-mail addresses.

Chapter 11

Posting a Message to Multiple Groups

In some cases, you'll want to post the same message to more than one newsgroup. You might be looking for a particular item to buy, for example, and want to post an inquiry to several newsgroups all related to the same topic. Posting to multiple newsgroups is called *cross-posting*.

Composing the message, saving it, and then posting it separately to each newsgroup requires that you monitor each newsgroup for answers. If you cross-post the message, however, you can monitor all the replies in any one newsgroup as they appear in all. Only one instance of the message thread exists, but because you've assigned it to multiple newsgroups, it appears in each one.

To cross-post a message, address it to multiple newsgroups when you compose the message, separating the newsgroup names with a comma. Click the Newsgroups button on the message form to open the Pick Newsgroups dialog box (see Figure 11-11), in which you can select the newsgroups. Use the Show Only Subscribed Newsgroups button to select groups without having to type their names.

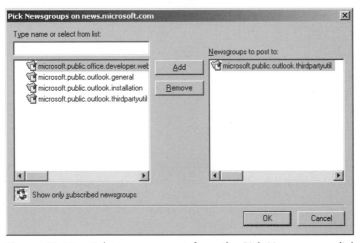

Figure 11-11. Select newsgroups from the Pick Newsgroups dialog box.

Processing Newsgroups and Working Offline

Outlook Express provides a good selection of features for automatic processing of messages and working with newsgroups offline. For example, you might want to review message headers offline—if you connect through a metered dial-up connection—and mark selected messages to be downloaded the next time you connect. The following sections explain how to process messages automatically and use Outlook Express offline.

Downloading a Selection of Messages

If you have a dedicated Internet connection, you'll probably do most of your work with Outlook Express online, downloading messages one at a time. If you want to download a large selection of messages or if you connect through a metered dial-up connection, you might prefer to mark messages for downloading and process them automatically. Handling messages this way allows you to process a large group of messages without having to manually download each one. Furthermore, you can review the message headers offline, decide which ones to download, and process them automatically the next time you go online.

> **note** A metered dial-up connection is one for which you are charged a per-hour or per-minute connect fee rather than a flat fee. More online time therefore equates to greater expense.

> **tip** If you're working online and have configured Outlook Express to download messages when previewed, you can select multiple messages and Outlook Express will download them one after another.

Follow these steps to download a selection of messages:

1 Choose Tools, Options. Click the Read tab and clear the Automatically Download Message When Viewing In The Preview Pane check box. Close the Options dialog box.

2 Beside each message you want to download, click the Download column, indicated by a down arrow. By default, the Download column is the second column from the left.

3 After you select all the messages you want to download, choose Tools, Synchronize Newsgroup. Then select Get Messages Marked For Download and click OK.

4 If you're currently working offline, Outlook Express prompts you to connect (unless you've configured it to connect automatically) and then displays a download dialog box that shows the status of the download.

> **tip** Hold down the Shift key and click the first and last messages in a range to select the range. Hold down the Ctrl key and click to select noncontiguous messages.

Selecting the first message in a thread for download automatically selects all other messages in the thread for download. If you don't want all the messages, expand the thread and cancel the selection of those messages you don't want Outlook Express to download.

> **tip**   You also can choose Tools, Mark For Offline, Download Message Later or Download Conversation Later to mark messages for download.

Creating Messages Offline

You can compose messages offline for later posting, which is particularly useful if you connect through a metered dial-up connection. Composing your posts offline can cut down your online time considerably. Outgoing messages wait in your Outbox until you connect and perform a send/receive operation.

You can compose messages offline without any special configuration. However, you'll probably want to set up Outlook Express so that it does not attempt to send messages immediately—that is, you'll want to prevent it from attempting to log on to your ISP and send messages as soon as you click the Post button after you compose the message. To do this, choose Tools, Options and click the Send tab. Clear the Send Messages Immediately check box and click OK. Then compose messages as you normally would. If Outlook Express prompts you to go online, select the option to work offline. When you're ready to post the message, choose Tools, Send And Receive, Send All.

Synchronizing Individual Newsgroups

In addition to letting you mark messages for later download, Outlook Express provides other features for synchronizing newsgroups. You can direct Outlook Express to perform the following actions:

- **Retrieve All Messages From A Newsgroup.** Select this option to have Outlook Express download all messages in the selected newsgroup.

- **Retrieve New Messages Only.** Use this option to retrieve new messages from the server. This option retrieves the message body as well as the message header.

- **Download Headers.** Select this option to download all message headers from the newsgroup.

To perform any of these actions, choose Tools, Synchronize Newsgroup; select the appropriate option from the Synchronize Newsgroup dialog box; and click OK. This action processes messages or headers only in the current newsgroup. If you have other newsgroups with messages or headers to download, you must synchronize those separately.

> **note** Synchronizing newsgroups helps you process them automatically, which means you'll spend less time manually reviewing message headers or marking messages for download. When you synchronize newsgroups, all messages that you have marked for download are processed and message headers for new messages are downloaded.

Synchronizing All Newsgroups and E-Mail Accounts

In addition to synchronizing selected newsgroups, you also can synchronize all newsgroups and e-mail accounts. If you choose Tools, Synchronize All, Outlook Express checks for new messages on your e-mail accounts and processes subscribed newsgroups according to their synchronization setting. For example, if a newsgroup's synchronization settings are configured to download new headers only, Outlook Express downloads marked messages in the newsgroup and any new headers. If the synchronization setting is configured to download all messages, Outlook Express downloads all messages for the newsgroup during the synchronization, regardless of whether the messages are marked for download.

To configure synchronization settings for a subscribed newsgroup, right-click the newsgroup in the folders list, choose Synchronization Settings, and then choose one of the following options:

- **Don't Synchronize.** Don't include this newsgroup in the synchronization process.

- **All Messages.** Download all messages from the newsgroup regardless of whether they're marked for download.

- **New Messages Only.** Download only new messages whose headers are not currently downloaded.

- **Headers Only.** Download only message headers not currently downloaded.

The synchronization settings for subscribed newsgroups are the best way to perform automatic processing on a global scale. You can configure each subscribed newsgroup separately to achieve the type of synchronization you need.

Monitoring and Managing Messages

Outlook provides tools for monitoring and managing e-mail messages; Outlook Express provides similar tools for monitoring and managing newsgroup messages. This section of the chapter examines these features, starting with message flagging.

Flagging Messages

You can flag messages in Outlook Express just as you do in Outlook. Outlook Express places a flag icon beside the message header. Unlike Outlook, however, Outlook Express provides no mechanism for generating reminders for flagged messages or for assigning follow-up actions to flagged messages. However, you can sort the display to view all flagged messages together, which means you can quickly identify messages that you've flagged.

By default, Outlook Express doesn't display the Flag column, but you can turn it on to flag messages by following these steps:

1 Choose View, Columns and select Flag from the list.

2 Use the Move Up and Move Down buttons to change the column order and then click OK.

3 To flag a message, click in the Flag column beside the message header. Click again to clear a flag.

> **tip** You can also simply drag column headers from one location to another to change the order in which the columns appear.

Watching a Conversation

With smaller newsgroups, you don't need to perform any special processing to monitor the group for messages that interest you. As the number of messages in a newsgroup grows, however, keeping track of specific messages and conversations becomes more difficult. For example, perhaps you've posted a message to a newsgroup and you want to monitor the group to determine when someone posts a reply. You can direct Outlook Express to monitor the particular conversation and notify you when new messages are added to it. This saves you the trouble of updating the message headers, scrolling through the newsgroup to locate your message, and checking it for new replies.

To direct Outlook Express to watch a conversation, click beside the message header in the Watch/Ignore column (indicated in the column bar by a pair of spectacles). Outlook Express places a similar icon beside the message to indicate that it is being watched, as shown in Figure 11-12. When you process message headers, Outlook Express colors the message thread red to indicate that it contains new replies. Outlook Express also colors the newsgroup name in the folders list red to indicate that it contains watched messages with new replies.

316

Watch flag

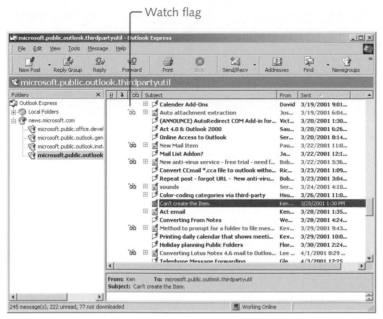

Figure 11-12. Outlook Express is watching several conversations in a newsgroup.

Ignoring a Conversation

In addition to flagging messages to be watched, you can flag messages to be ignored. Flagging a conversation to be ignored doesn't change the way Outlook Express handles it for synchronization, but it does exclude those messages from your current view. For example, you might not be interested in the majority of messages in a newsgroup and want to ignore them to focus on the rest. You can flag the conversation to be ignored and then configure Outlook Express to hide those ignored messages from the current view. This simplifies the view and lets you concentrate on those messages that interest you.

Follow these steps to ignore a conversation:

1 Click in the Watch/Ignore box beside the message header to set it to Watch. Click it again to set it to Ignore.

2 Outlook Express places a circle and slash icon beside the message header to indicate that it's being ignored (see Figure 11-13 on the next page).

3 Configure the view to hide read and ignored messages by choosing View, Current View, Hide Read Or Ignored Messages.

Chapter 11

Ignore flag

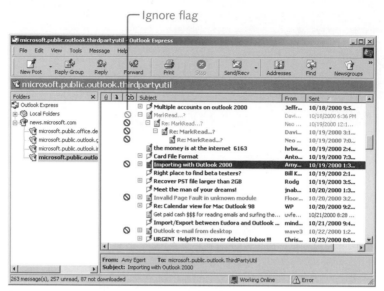

Figure 11-13. Conversations are flagged to be ignored.

Finding Messages

Outlook Express provides a search feature that finds messages based on various search criteria you specify—for example, words in the subject or the body of the message, the sender, or the date. Choose Edit, Find, Message In This Folder to display the Find dialog box, shown in Figure 11-14. Specify the text to search for in the Look For box. If you want to also search the message bodies of all downloaded messages, select the Search All The Text In Downloaded Messages check box.

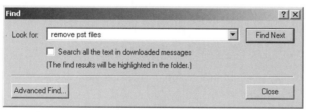

Figure 11-14. Use the Find dialog box to locate messages that fit specific search criteria.

If you need to perform a more extensive search, click Advanced in the Find dialog box or choose Edit, Find, Message. Outlook Express displays the Find Message dialog box, shown in Figure 11-15, which provides several additional fields you can use to refine the search. You also can click the Browse button to specify the root of the search location. For example, you might select the news server as the root to search all subscribed newsgroups for messages that fit your search criteria. In the Find Message dialog box, select the Include Subfolders check box to have Outlook Express search all subfolders of subscribed newsgroups within the news server.

Chapter 11

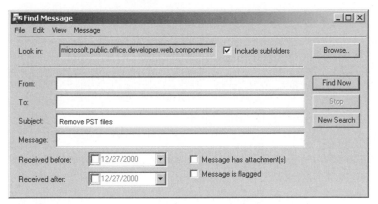

Figure 11-15. Use the Find Message dialog box to perform advanced searches.

Filtering and Controlling the Message View

With newsgroups that contain a lot of messages (typical of many Internet newsgroups and common even with many other private newsgroups), it's often useful to sort or filter the view so that you can focus on specific messages or threads. You can sort the message headers in Outlook Express based on any of the displayed columns. To do so, simply click the appropriate column header. For example, click the From column header if you're trying to locate a message from a specific sender or click the Subject header if you want to locate messages with a specific subject. Click the column header a second time to switch between ascending and descending sort order.

> **tip** If you don't want to use the mouse, you can choose View, Sort By to sort the message headers.

Adding and Removing Columns

Outlook Express provides additional columns you can display in addition to the default set. For example, you can include a Flag column (explained earlier) to keep track of specific messages. You can also exclude certain columns if you're not interested in the information they provide. For example, if you aren't interested in the size of messages, you can turn off the Size column to make room for other columns.

To change the columns Outlook Express displays, choose View, Columns or right-click a column header and choose Columns to display the Columns dialog box. Select the columns you want to include, use the Move Up and Move Down buttons to change their display order, and then click OK. You can resize columns or change their order by dragging the column headers.

Controlling Which Messages Are Shown

By default, Outlook Express shows all messages, whether or not they've been down-loaded. You can set up the view to show all messages, to show only downloaded mes-sages, or to hide read messages. Choose View, Current View, and then one of the following commands:

- **Show All Messages.** Select this option to show all message headers, whether or not the message bodies have been downloaded.

- **Hide Read Messages.** Select this option to show only those messages that are marked as unread.

- **Show Downloaded Messages.** Select this option to show only those messages whose message bodies have been downloaded.

- **Hide Read Or Ignored Messages.** Select this option to hide messages that are marked as read or marked to ignore.

- **Show Replies To My Messages.** Select this option to show replies to messages that you have posted.

- **Group Messages By Conversation.** Select this option to group messages according to thread; clear the option to display messages individually.

Using Rules

Outlook Express supports the use of rules for processing e-mail and newsgroup mes-sages. In addition, you can use rules to create custom views to show or hide messages based on specific criteria.

Creating Custom Views

Although the views included by default with Outlook Express are useful in many situa-tions, you might occasionally need to filter the view in other ways. For example, you might want to create a view that hides ignored messages but not read messages. You can accomplish this by creating a custom view, which applies a rule that you define to filter the newsgroup folder.

Follow these steps to create a custom view:

1 In Outlook Express, choose View, Current View, Define Views.

2 In the Define Views dialog box (see Figure 11-16), click New to display the New View dialog box (see Figure 11-17).

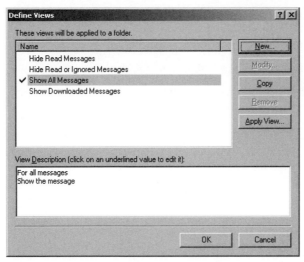

Figure 11-16. The Define Views dialog box shows currently defined views and allows you to create custom views.

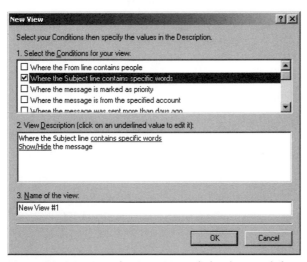

Figure 11-17. Use the New View dialog box to define a rule that filters the newsgroup folder view.

3 Select the rule condition that will apply to the new view. For example, to hide all ignored messages, select Where The Message Is Watched Or Ignored.

4 In the View Description area, click the underlined word that specifies the condition and then specify the criteria. For example, click Watched Or Ignored to specify Ignore Threads if you're creating a rule that hides ignored messages.

5 In the View Description area, click the underlined word that specifies the action to take and then select an action. For example, to hide all ignored messages, click Show/Hide and select Hide Messages.

6 Enter a name for the rule in the Name Of The View box and click OK.

7 To apply the view, select the view rule you just created, click Apply View, select either The Currently Selected Folder or All Of My Folders, and click OK. Outlook Express filters the view accordingly, and the applied view appears as a command on the Current View menu.

> **tip** You can modify the rule that defines the current view by choosing View, Current View, Customize Current View.

Processing Messages with Rules

In addition to controlling the view through message rules, you can use rules to process messages automatically. For example, you might create a message rule that marks for download all messages from specific senders or messages containing certain words in the Subject box. Or perhaps you want to use certain colors to identify messages from specific senders.

You can either apply rules when message headers and messages are downloaded or apply them manually afterward.

In either case, the first task is to create the rule, as follows:

1 In Outlook Express, choose Tools, Message Rules, News and click New.

2 In the New News Rule dialog box, select the condition or conditions to apply to the message in the Conditions list.

3 In the Actions list, select the action or actions you want Outlook Express to take on messages that fit the conditions.

4 Click the underlined words in the Rule Description area to define the condition and the action.

5 In the Name Of The Rule box, enter a name for the rule as you want it to appear in the rules list and click OK.

News rules that you select on the News Rules tab of the Message Rules dialog box are applied automatically when Outlook Express downloads message headers and messages. You can turn off a rule by canceling the selection in the list.

You can apply a message rule manually at any time. For example, you might create a rule that deletes read messages with dates older than a given date. Rather than applying the rule automatically, you can apply it any time you want to clean out old messages.

Follow these steps to apply a rule manually:

1 Choose Tools, Message Rules, News.

2 Click Apply Now to display the Apply News Rules Now dialog box (see Figure 11-18).

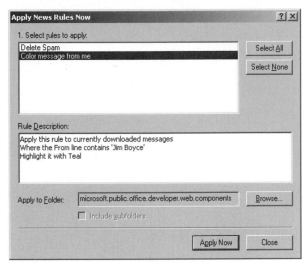

Figure 11-18. Select which rules to apply from the Apply News Rules Now dialog box.

3 Select the rules you want to apply.

4 Check the Apply To Folder box to determine whether the correct folder is displayed. If it isn't, click Browse and select it. Select the news server if you want to apply the rule to all messages that fit the conditions in all subscribed newsgroups.

5 Click Apply Now.

Working with Attachments

Internet newsgroups are a very popular means of sharing all sorts of files—from images to sound files to video clips. With Outlook Express, you can post newsgroup messages that include attachments. The following sections cover viewing, saving, and manipulating attachments to newsgroup messages.

Previewing Attachments

Outlook Express examines the attachment for a message when you preview the message and, if the file type is supported, includes the attachment in the preview pane. Click a message containing a JPG attachment, for example, and Outlook Express shows the

JPG below the message in the preview pane. Regardless of whether Outlook Express can preview the attachment, it includes a paper clip icon in the preview pane header. Click the paper clip icon and select the attachment to open it.

Saving Attachments

To save one or more attachments to disk, you can click the paper clip icon and choose Save Attachments. You also can choose File, Save Attachments. In either case, Outlook Express prompts you for the location where the file should be saved.

Posting Messages with Attachments

Posting a message with an attachment is as easy as sending an e-mail message with an attachment:

1 Click New Post and compose your message.

2 Click the Attach button on the toolbar or choose Insert, File Attachment.

3 Locate and select the file and click Attach.

4 Post the message as you would any other.

Decoding Attachments

Most news servers impose a maximum size limit on messages, so certain types of messages—particularly those containing larger video clips—are often split into multiple messages. To read the message or view the attachment, you must recombine the multiple messages into one. To do so, select all the messages in the set after downloading them, and then choose Message, Combine And Decode.

Outlook Express displays a dialog box containing the messages and prompts you to arrange them in order. Typically, the messages' titles indicate their order. Use the Move Up and Move Down buttons to arrange them, with the first at the top of the list and the last at the bottom, and then click OK. Outlook Express combines and decodes the message and displays it in a separate window. Choose File, Save As to save the entire message to disk.

Archiving and Restoring Messages

Outlook Express doesn't provide an easy means for archiving and restoring messages, whether from newsgroups or e-mail. However, you can save messages to disk, move messages between Outlook Express installations, and retain your messages during a reinstallation of Outlook Express if it becomes necessary.

Archiving Messages

As it does with e-mail messages, Outlook Express stores messages and attachments not as individual files but collectively in folder files, one newsgroup per file. Because all messages are stored together, there is no easy way to archive groups of messages from within a newsgroup. However, you can save messages and attachments individually to keep an archive copy, which means you can save important messages and attachments outside Outlook Express.

To save a message, select the message in Outlook Express and choose File, Save As. Specify the path and file name for the message and click Save. By default, Outlook Express uses the message header name as the file name, but you can specify any name you like. To save attachments, select the message and choose File, Save Attachments. Specify a path for the attachments and click Save.

Archiving a Newsgroup

Although the Outlook Express interface doesn't provide a way to archive a newsgroup, you can archive a newsgroup manually by copying the newsgroup file to a backup location. For example, suppose that you want to archive all messages in a particular newsgroup as of the current date, clearing the newsgroup file to start with messages from that date.

Here's how to accomplish this without saving individual messages and attachments:

1 In Outlook Express, choose Tools, Options and click the Maintenance tab.

2 Click Store Folder and note the location of your Outlook Express message store (see Figure 11-19).

Figure 11-19. Note the location of your Outlook Express message store folder.

3 Close Outlook Express.

4 Open the folder identified in step 2 and change the file extension for the newsgroup file you want to archive from DBX to something else, such as BAK.

> **tip** You can move the file to a backup location, but you must move it back to the original folder if you want to use it later.

325

Chapter 11

5 Start Outlook Express and open the archived newsgroup. Outlook Express re-creates the missing folder file by replacing it with an empty one and, depending on how you have configured the program, downloads the headers from the newsgroup but not the messages.

How do you use the archived file? Unfortunately, it isn't an easy process. You need to change the file extension of the current newsgroup file, restore the DBX extension to the backup file, and then restart Outlook Express. When you open Outlook Express, you'll find the old message file in place, complete with downloaded messages and attachments.

---

tip **Archive newsgroup messages selectively**

An alternative to this procedure is to copy individual newsgroup files or the entire contents of your Outlook Express store folder to a backup location and then delete messages from the current store. When you need to work with the archive copy, choose Tools, Options. Click the Maintenance tab, click Store Folder, and point Outlook Express to the archive location. Point it back to the original location when you're finished working with the archived messages.

Moving Your Message Store

You can move your Outlook Express message store, which is useful for archival purposes, as just explained; it's also useful when you want to move your newsgroups and messages from one computer to another or to a disk with more space.

Moving the message store is relatively easy:

1 Open Outlook Express and choose Tools, Options. Click the Maintenance tab and then click Store Folder to identify the current location of your store folder.

2 Close Outlook Express and copy the store folder to its new location.

3 Open Outlook Express and choose Tools, Options. Click the Maintenance tab, click Store Folder, and then click Change. (If you're moving your message store to a different computer, perform this step and step 4 on the computer to which you moved or copied your store file.)

4 Select the new location and click OK. Outlook Express informs you that the specified location already includes a store and asks whether you want to use that store. Click Yes.

Retaining Accounts and Messages During a Reinstallation

Although it doesn't happen often, you might occasionally need to reinstall Outlook Express. Or perhaps you're moving to a new computer and want to retain your accounts and messages.

Retaining Accounts

The easiest way to retain accounts during a reinstallation or move is to make a backup copy of the appropriate registry key before installation and then restore the key after you reinstall Outlook Express (or move to another computer):

1 Close Outlook Express and click Start, Run. Enter **regedit** and click OK.

2 In the Registry Editor, open the branch HKEY_CURRENT_USER\
Software\Microsoft\Internet Account Manager.

3 Choose Registry, Export Registry File.

4 Specify a file name and path, verify that the Selected Branch option is selected, and click Save.

5 On the system to which you are moving Outlook Express, or after performing a reinstallation, double-click the REG file created in step 4 to add the registry settings to your registry.

6 Open Outlook Express and verify that your accounts are working.

Retaining Messages

You can retain existing newsgroups and messages by copying your entire message store to the other computer or, in the case of reinstalling Outlook Express, backing it up and then restoring the message store:

1 Open Outlook Express and choose Tools, Options. Click the Maintenance tab and then click Store Folder to identify the current location of your store folder.

2 Close Outlook Express and, if you're moving to a different computer, copy the store folder to its new location. If you're preparing to reinstall Outlook Express, copy the store folder to a backup location.

3 Install or reinstall Outlook Express, and then open Outlook Express. Use the Maintenance tab to locate your current store, as you did in step 1.

4 Close Outlook Express, copy your backup store in the location determined in step 3, and then restart Outlook Express.

327

Securing Your System, Messages, and Identity

Microsoft Outlook includes features that can help protect your system from computer viruses and malicious programs, prevent others from using e-mail to impersonate you, and prevent the interception of sensitive messages. Some of these features—such as the ability to block specific types of attachments—are new in Outlook 2002.

This chapter begins by examining security zones, which allow you to specify how Outlook should handle HTML-based messages. Because HTML messages can contain malicious scripts or even HTML code that can easily affect your system, Outlook's ability to handle these messages is extremely important.

This chapter also discusses the use of both digital signatures and encryption. You can use a digital signature to authenticate your messages, proving to the recipient that a message indeed came from you and not from someone trying to impersonate you. Outlook allows you to encrypt outgoing messages to prevent them from being intercepted by unintended recipients; you can also read encrypted messages sent to you by others. In this chapter, you'll learn how to obtain and install certificates to send encrypted messages and how to share keys with others so that you can exchange encrypted messages.

Virus protection is another new and important feature in Outlook. You can configure Outlook to automatically block specific types of attachments, thus helping prevent virus infections. Outlook provides two levels of attachment protection, one for individual users and one for system administrators.

Using Security Zones

Outlook's support for HTML-based messages poses certain security risks. It's relatively easy, for example, for someone to embed in an HTML message scripts that extract data from your system, delete data, or insert a Trojan horse virus. Because of this, restricting the actions that HTML messages can perform can have a significant impact on your system's security.

Outlook uses the security zones defined by Microsoft Internet Explorer. By default, Outlook assigns HTML messages to the Restricted Sites zone. This zone prevents HTML messages from carrying out most potentially dangerous actions, such as downloading unsigned ActiveX controls or files, active scripting, or scripting of Java applets.

In most cases, you'll want to continue to use the Restricted Sites zone for Outlook. In some situations, however, you might need to use a different zone or perhaps modify the settings to create a custom zone. For example, you might want to eliminate the restrictions if you don't receive messages from outside your intranet (which, of course, implies trust of the other users on the intranet).

> **tip** Regardless of which zone you select for Outlook, it deactivates ActiveX controls and does not run scripts.

To select the security zone you want Outlook to apply to HTML messages, choose Tools, Options and click Security. In the Secure Content section of the Security tab (see Figure 12-1), select a zone in the Zone drop-down list.

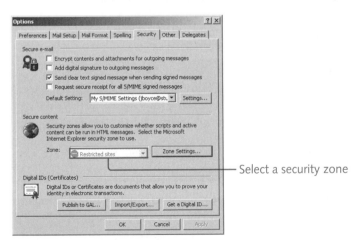

Select a security zone

Figure 12-1. Use the Security tab to select the security zone you want Outlook to apply to HTML messages.

If you need to change the zone settings, click Zone Settings to display the Security dialog box, shown in Figure 12-2. Use the slider to set a general security level, or click Cus-

Chapter 12

tom Level to display the Security Settings dialog box (see Figure 12-3), in which you can specify custom settings.

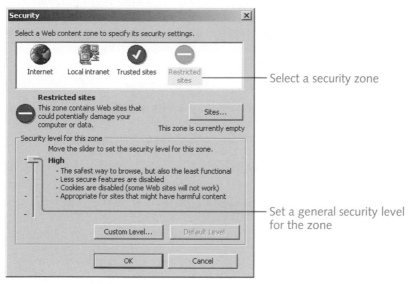

Select a security zone

Set a general security level for the zone

Figure 12-2. Use the Security dialog box to select a zone or change its settings.

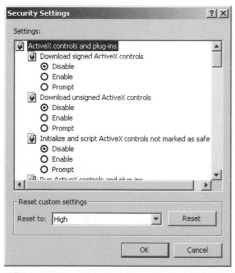

Figure 12-3. Use the Security Settings dialog box to define custom security settings.

It's important to understand that when Outlook processes messages, it uses the security settings from the security zone you've selected—it does not consider settings you might have made in other zones. For example, assume that you've specified several restricted domains in the Restricted Sites zone but have configured Outlook to use the Internet zone. When an HTML message arrives that originated in one of the domains specified in your Restricted Sites zone, Outlook applies the security settings for the Internet zone, ignoring the restriction you've placed on that domain. Because Outlook treats all HTML messages the same, adding sites to other security zones in Outlook doesn't provide additional security. Instead, you should consider the security zone you select to be the main determinant of how HTML messages are handled globally. (For that reason, this book doesn't cover the topic of adding sites to security zones.)

> **note** Unlike Outlook, Internet Explorer does consider the settings in all zones when determining how to handle pages from specific domains and security zones. If you're using Internet Explorer, it's therefore a good idea to add domain restrictions for various zones as needed. Keep in mind, however, that Outlook considers only the zone, not the domains it might specify.

Protecting Messages with Digital Signatures

Outlook supports the use of *digital signatures* to sign messages and validate their authenticity. For example, you can digitally sign a sensitive message so that the recipient can know with relative certainty that the message came from you and that no one is impersonating you by using your e-mail address. This section of the chapter explains digital certificates and signatures and how to use them in Outlook.

Understanding Digital Certificates and Signatures

A *digital certificate* is the mechanism that makes digital signatures possible. Depending on its assigned purpose, you can use a digital certificate for a variety of tasks, including the following:

- Verifying your identity as the sender of an e-mail message
- Encrypting data communications between computers—between a client and a server, for example
- Encrypting e-mail messages to prevent easy interception
- Signing drivers and executable files to authenticate their origin

A digital certificate binds the identity of the certificate's owner to a pair of keys, one public and one private. At a minimum, a certificate contains the following information:

- The owner's public key
- The owner's name or alias

- A certificate expiration date
- A certificate serial number
- The name of the certificate issuer
- The digital signature of the issuer

The certificate can also include other identifying information, such as the owner's e-mail address, postal address, country, or gender.

The two keys are the aspect of the certificate that enables authentication and encryption. The private key resides on your computer and is a large unique number. The certificate contains the public key, which you must give to recipients to whom you want to send authenticated or encrypted messages. Think of the keys in a literal sense, as two keys that open a lock with two keyholes. The only way to open the lock is to have both keys.

Outlook uses slightly different methods for authenticating messages with digital signatures and for encrypting messages, as you'll see later in the chapter. Before you begin either task, however, you must first obtain a certificate.

Obtaining a Digital Certificate

Digital certificates are issued by certification authorities (CAs). In most cases, you obtain your e-mail certificate from a public CA such as VeriSign or Thawte. However, systems based on Microsoft Windows NT Server and Microsoft Windows 2000 Server running Certificate Services can function as CAs, providing certificates to clients who request them. Check with your system administrator to determine whether your enterprise includes a CA. If it doesn't, you need to obtain your certificate from a public CA, usually at a minimal cost. Certificates are typically good for one year and must be renewed at the end of that period.

If you need to obtain your certificate from a public CA, point your Web browser to the CA's Web site, such as *http://www.verisign.com* or *http://www.thawte.com*. Follow the instructions provided by the site to obtain a certificate for signing and encrypting your e-mail (see Figure 12-4, for example). The certificate might not be issued immediately; instead, the CA might send you an e-mail message containing a URL that links to a page where you can retrieve the certificate. When you connect to that page, the CA installs the certificate on your system.

> **tip** You can click the Get A Digital ID button on the Security tab of the Options dialog box to display a page from Microsoft's Web site that includes links to several certification authorities.

Chapter 12

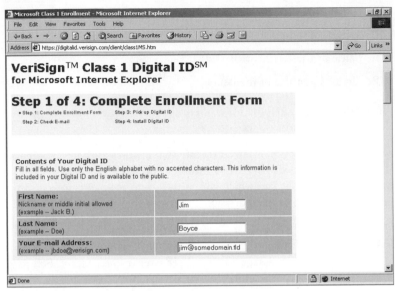

Figure 12-4. You can use the Web to request a digital certificate from a public CA.

If you're obtaining a certificate from a CA on your network, the method you use depends on whether the network includes an enterprise CA or a stand-alone CA and whether you're running Microsoft Windows 2000.

If you're using Windows 2000 on a network with an enterprise CA, follow these steps to request a certificate:

1 Choose Start, Run and type **MMC**. Click OK.

2 In the Microsoft Management Console (MMC), choose Console, Add/Remove Snap-In.

3 In the Add/Remove Snap-In dialog box, click Add.

4 In the Add Standalone Snap-In dialog box, select Certificates and click Add.

5 In the Certificates Snap-In dialog box, select My User Account and click Finish.

6 Click Close, and then click OK to return to the MMC.

7 Expand the Certificates–Current User branch.

8 Expand the Personal branch, right-click Certificates, and choose All Tasks, Request New Certificate. You can also right-click the Personal branch and choose All Tasks, Request New Certificate.

9 Follow the prompts provided by the enterprise CA to request your certificate. The certificate should install automatically.

To request a certificate from a stand-alone CA on your network, point your Web browser to *http://<server>/certsrv*, where <server> is the name or IP address of the CA. The CA provides a Web page with a form that you must fill out to request the certificate (see Figure 12-5). Follow the CA's prompts to request and obtain the certificate. The site includes a link that you can click to install the certificate.

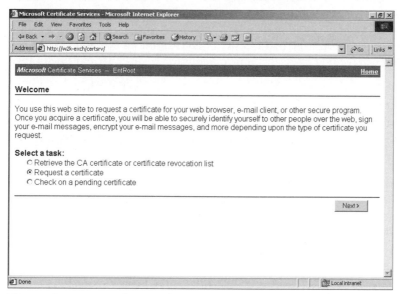

Figure 12-5. A Windows 2000 CA presents a Web form that you can use to request a certificate.

Copying a Certificate to Another Computer

You can copy your certificate from one computer to another, which means that you can use it on more than one system. The process is simple: you first export (back up) your certificate to a file and then import the certificate into the other system. The following sections explain how to export and import certificates.

> **note** As you use the Certificate Import Wizard and the Certificate Export Wizard (discussed in the following sections), you might discover that they don't precisely match the descriptions presented here. Their appearance and operation might vary slightly, depending on the operating system you're running and the version of Internet Explorer you're using.

Backing Up Your Certificate

Whether you obtained your certificate from a public CA or from a CA on your network, you should back it up in case your system suffers a drive failure or the certificate is lost or corrupted. You also should have a backup of the certificate so that you can export it to any other computers you use on a regular basis, such as a notebook computer or your home computer. In short, you need the certificate on every computer from which you plan to digitally sign or encrypt messages. To back up your certificate, you can use Outlook, Internet Explorer, or the Certificates console (available in Windows 2000). Each method offers the same capabilities; you can use any one of the three.

Follow these steps to use Outlook to back up your certificate to a file:

1 In Outlook, choose Tools, Options and click the Security tab.

2 Click Import/Export to display the Import/Export Digital ID dialog box, shown in Figure 12-6.

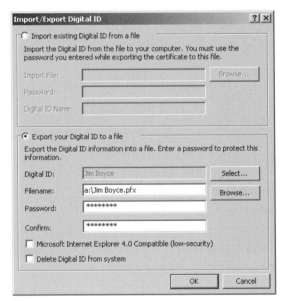

Figure 12-6. You can export certificates in the Import/Export Digital ID dialog box.

3 Select the option Export Your Digital ID To A File. Click Select and select the certificate to be exported.

4 Click Browse and specify the path and file name for the certificate file.

5 Optionally, you can enter and confirm a password.

6 If you plan to use the certificate on a system with Internet Explorer 4, select the Microsoft Internet Explorer 4.0 Compatible check box. If you use Internet Explorer 5 or later, clear this check box.

7 Click OK to export the file.

If you want to use either Internet Explorer or the Certificates console to back up a certificate, you use the Certificate Export Wizard, as follows:

1 If you're using Internet Explorer, begin by choosing Tools, Internet Options. Click the Content tab and then click Certificates. In the Certificates dialog box, shown in Figure 12-7, select the certificate you want to back up and click Export to start the wizard. If you're using the Certificates console, begin by opening the console and expanding Certificates–Current User/Personal/ Certificates. Right-click the certificate to export, and choose All Tasks, Export to start the wizard.

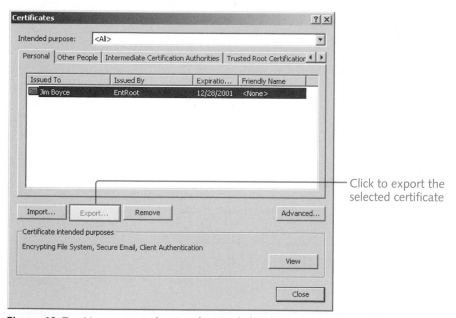

Click to export the selected certificate

Figure 12-7. You can use the Certificates dialog box to export a certificate.

2 In the Certificate Export Wizard, click Next.

3 On the wizard page shown in Figure 12-8, select Yes, Export The Private Key and then click Next.

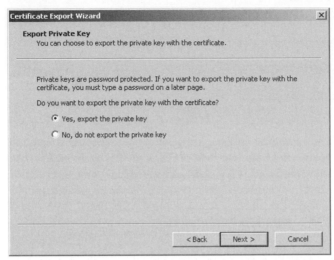

Figure 12-8. This wizard allows you to export the private key.

4 Select Personal Information Exchange, and then clear the Enable Strong Protection option. If other options are selected, clear them as well. Click Next.

tip If you're using Internet Explorer version 5 or later, you do not need to clear the Enable
Strong Protection option. You should clear the other options, however.

5 Specify and confirm a password to protect the private key and click Next.

6 Specify a path and file name for the certificate and click Next.

7 Review your selections and click Finish.

Troubleshooting

You can't export the private key.

In order to use a certificate on a different computer, you must be able to export the
private key. If the option to export the private key is unavailable when you run the
Certificate Export Wizard, it means that the private key is marked as not exportable.
Exportability is an option you choose when you request the certificate. If you request
a certificate through a local CA, you must select the Advanced Request option in order to request a certificate with an exportable private key. If you imported the certificate from a file, you might not have selected the option to make the private key
exportable during the import. If you still have the original certificate file, you can import
it again, this time selecting the option that will allow you to export the private key.

Installing Your Certificate from a Backup

You can install (or reinstall) a certificate from a backup copy of the certificate file by using Outlook, Internet Explorer, or the Certificates console (available in Windows 2000). You must import the certificate to your computer from the backup file.

The following procedure assumes that you're installing the certificate using Outlook:

1 In Outlook, choose Tools, Options and click the Security tab.

2 Click Import/Export to display the Import/Export Digital ID dialog box, shown earlier in Figure 12-6.

3 Click Browse to locate the file containing the backup of the certificate.

4 In the Password box, type the password associated with the certificate file.

5 In the Digital ID Name box, type a name by which you want the certificate to be shown. Typically, you'll enter your name, mailbox name, or e-mail address, but you can enter anything you want.

6 Click OK to import the certificate.

You can also import a certificate to your computer from a backup file by using either Internet Explorer or the Certificates console, as explained here:

1 If you're using Internet Explorer, begin by choosing Tools, Internet Options. Click the Content tab, click Certificates, and then click Import to start the Certificate Import Wizard. If you're using the Certificates console, begin by opening the console. Then right-click Certificates–Current User/Personal and click All Tasks, Import to start the wizard.

2 In the Certificate Import Wizard, click Next.

3 Browse and select the file to import and then click Next.

4 Select the option Automatically Select The Certificate Store Based On The Type Of Certificate and click Next.

5 Click Finish.

Signing Messages

Now that you have a certificate on your system, you're ready to start digitally signing your outgoing messages so that recipients can verify your identity. When you send a digitally signed message, Outlook sends the original message and an encrypted copy of the message with your digital signature. The recipient's e-mail application compares the two versions of the message to determine whether they are the same. If they are, no one has tampered with the message. The digital signature also allows the recipient to verify that the message is from you.

Chapter 12

Understanding S/MIME and Clear-Text Options

Secure/Multipurpose Internet Mail Extensions (S/MIME), an Internet standard, is the mechanism in Outlook that allows you to digitally sign and encrypt messages. The e-mail client handles the encryption and decryption required for both functions.

Users with e-mail clients that don't support S/MIME can't read digitally signed messages unless you send the message as clear text (unencrypted). Without S/MIME support, the recipient is also unable to verify the authenticity of the message or to verify that the message hasn't been altered. Without S/MIME, then, digital signatures are relatively useless. However, Outlook does offer you the option of sending a digitally signed message as clear text to recipients who lack S/MIME support. If you need to send the same digitally signed message to multiple recipients—some of whom have S/MIME-capable e-mail clients and some of whom do not—digitally signing the message allows those with S/MIME support to authenticate it, while including the clear-text message allows the others to at least read it.

The following section explains how to send a digitally signed message, including how to send the message in clear text for those recipients who require it.

Adding Your Digital Signature

Follow these steps to digitally sign an outgoing message:

1 Compose the message in Outlook.

2 Click the Options button on the message form toolbar to open the Message Options dialog box.

3 Click Security Settings to open the Security Properties dialog box, shown in Figure 12-9.

4 Select Add Digital Signature To This Message, and then select other options as indicated here:

- **Send This Message As Clear Text Signed.** Select this check box to include a clear-text copy of the message for recipients who don't have S/MIME-capable e-mail applications. Clear this check box to prevent the message from being read by mail clients that don't support S/MIME.

- **Request Secure Receipt For This Message.** Select this check box to request a secure receipt to verify that the recipient has validated your digital signature. When the message has been received and saved and your signature verified (even if the recipient doesn't read the message), you receive a return receipt. No receipt is sent if your signature is not verified.

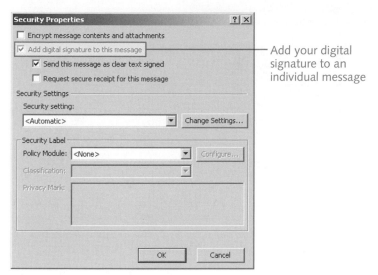

Add your digital signature to an individual message

Figure 12-9. You can add a digital signature by using the Security Properties dialog box.

5 If necessary, select security settings in the Security Settings drop-down list. (If you have not yet configured your security options, you can do so by clicking Change Settings; for details, see "Creating and Using Security Profiles," page 343.

6 Click OK to add the digital signature to the message.

---

tip **Speed up digital signing**

If you send a lot of digitally signed messages, you'll want to configure your security options to include a digital signature by default; see the following section for details. In addition, you might want to add a button to the toolbar to let you quickly sign the message without using a dialog box. For details about how to add such a button, see the Troubleshooting sidebar "You need a faster way to digitally sign a message," page 344.

Setting Global Security Options

To save time, you can configure your security settings to apply globally to all messages, changing settings only as needed for certain messages. In Outlook, choose Tools, Options and then click Security. On the Security tab, shown in Figure 12-10, you can set security options using the list on the next page as a guide.

Chapter 12

Figure 12-10.   Use the Security tab of the Options dialog box to configure options for digital signing and encryption.

● **Encrypt Contents And Attachments For Outgoing Messages.** If most of the messages you send need to be encrypted, select this check box to encrypt all outgoing messages by default. You can override encryption for a specific message by changing the message's properties when you compose it. Clear this check box if the majority of your outgoing messages do not need to be encrypted.

For information about encryption, see "Encrypting Messages," page 354.

● **Add Digital Signature To Outgoing Messages.** If most of your messages need to be signed, select this check box to digitally sign all outgoing messages by default. Clear this check box if most of your messages do not need to signed; you will be able to digitally sign specific messages as needed when you compose them.

● **Send Clear Text Signed Message When Sending Signed Messages.** If you need to send digitally signed messages to recipients who do not have S/MIME capability, select this check box to send clear-text digitally signed messages by default. You can override this option for individual messages when you compose them. In most cases, you can clear this check box because most e-mail clients support S/MIME.

● **Request Secure Receipt For All S/MIME Signed Messages.** Select this check box to request a secure receipt for all S/MIME messages by default. You can override the setting for individual messages when you compose them. A secure receipt indicates that your message has been received and the signature verified. No receipt is returned if the signature is not verified.

● **Settings.** Click the Settings button to configure more advanced security settings and create additional security setting groups. For details, see the following section, "Creating and Using Security Profiles."

- **Publish To GAL.** Click this button to publish your certificates to the Global Address List (GAL), making them available to other Exchange Server users in your organization who might need to send you encrypted messages. This is an alternative to sending the other users a copy of your certificate.

Creating and Using Security Profiles

Although in most cases you need only one set of Outlook security settings, you can create and use multiple security profiles. For example, you might send most of your secure messages to other Exchange Server users, only occasionally sending secure messages to Internet recipients. In that situation, you might maintain two sets of security settings: one that uses Exchange Server security and another that uses S/MIME, each with different certificates and hash algorithms (the method used to secure the data).

You can configure security profiles by using the Change Security Settings dialog box, which you access through the Security tab of the Options dialog box. One of your security profiles acts as the default, but you can select a different security profile any time it's needed.

Follow these steps to create and manage your security profiles:

1 In Outlook, choose Tools, Options and click the Security tab.

2 Click Settings to display the Change Security Settings dialog box, shown in Figure 12-11. Set the options described on pages 344 and 345 as needed.

Figure 12-11. Configure your security profiles in the Change Security Settings dialog box.

343

■ **Security Settings Name.** Specify the name for the security profile that should appear in the Default Setting drop-down list on the Security tab.

■ **Secure Message Format.** In this drop-down list, select the secure message format for your messages. The default is S/MIME, but you also can select Exchange Server Security. Use S/MIME if you're sending secure messages to Internet recipients. You can use either S/MIME or Exchange Server Security when sending secure messages to recipients on your Exchange Server.

Troubleshooting

You need a faster way to digitally sign a message.

If you don't send a lot of digitally signed messages, you might not mind the steps you need to go through to get to the Security Properties dialog box to sign the message when you compose it. However, if you frequently send digitally signed messages but don't want to configure Outlook to sign all messages by default, all the clicking involved in signing the message can seem like a very long trip.

To digitally sign your messages faster, consider adding a toolbar button that lets you toggle a digital signature with a single click:

1 Open the Inbox folder in Outlook.

2 Click New to display the message form for a new message.

3 In the message form, choose View, Toolbars, Customize and then click the Commands tab, shown in Figure 12-12.

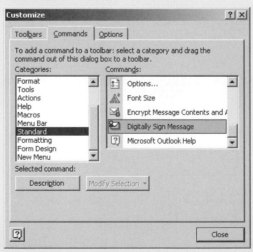

Figure 12-12. Use the Commands tab to add the Digitally Sign Message command to the toolbar.

■ **Default Security Setting For This Secure Message Format.** Select this check box to make the specified security settings the default settings for the message format you selected in the Secure Message Format drop-down list.

■ **Default Security Setting For All Secure Messages.** Select this check box to make the specified security settings the default settings for all secure messages for both S/MIME and Exchange Server Security.

newfeature!

■ **Security Labels.** Click to configure security labels, which display security information about a specific message and restrict which recipients can open, forward, or send that message. Security labels rely on security policies implemented in Windows 2000.

■ **New.** Click to create a new set of security settings.

■ **Delete.** Click to delete the currently selected group of security settings.

■ **Password.** Click to specify or change the password associated with the security settings.

■ **Signing Certificate.** This read-only information indicates the certificate being used to digitally sign your outgoing messages. Click Choose if you want to choose a different certificate.

> You assign the default signing and encryption certificates through Outlook's global security settings; for information, see "Setting Global Security Options," page 341.

■ **Hash Algorithm.** Use this drop-down list to change the hash algorithm used to encrypt messages.

4 Click Standard in the Categories list, and then drag the Digitally Sign Message command to a location on the toolbar.

note In order to modify the Standard toolbar, you must be using Outlook as your e-mail editor. If you switch to using Microsoft Word as the e-mail editor, changes you make to the toolbar are not carried over to Word.

5 If you frequently encrypt messages, you can also drag the Encrypt Message Contents And Attachments command to the toolbar.

6 Click Close and then close the message form.

Now whenever you need to digitally sign or encrypt a message, you can click the appropriate button on the toolbar when you compose the message. Outlook displays a blue outline around the button to indicate that the command has been selected, so you can tell at a glance whether the message will be signed, encrypted, or both.

- **Encryption Certificate.** This read-only information indicates the certificate being used to encrypt your outgoing messages. Click Choose if you want to specify a different certificate.

- **Encryption Algorithm.** Use this drop-down list to change the encryption algorithm used to encrypt messages. The encryption algorithm is the mathematical method used to encrypt the data.

- **Send These Certificates With Signed Messages.** Select this check box to include your certificate with outgoing messages. Doing so allows recipients to send encrypted messages to you.

3 Click OK to close the Change Security Settings dialog box.

4 In the Default Setting drop-down list on the Security tab, select the security profile you want to use by default and then click OK.

If you later want to switch security profiles, you can select the profile you want to use in the Default Setting drop-down list on the Security tab.

Reading Signed Messages

When you receive a digitally signed message, Outlook displays the encrypted version of the message as an attachment. The Inbox displays a Secure Message icon in place of the standard envelope icon (see Figure 12-13) and shows a Secure Message button in the preview pane. The message form also includes a Secure Message button (see Figure 12-14). You can click the Secure Message button in either the preview pane or the form to display information about the certificate.

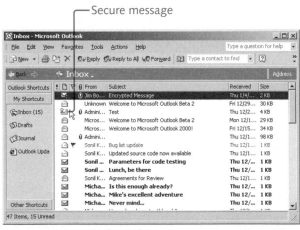

Figure 12-13. Outlook displays a different icon in the Inbox for secure messages.

Chapter 12

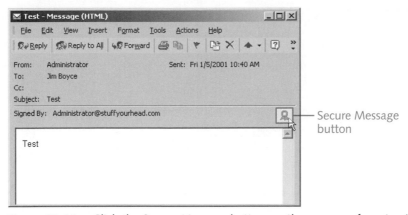

Figure 12-14. Click the Secure Message button on the message form to view information about the certificate.

Because Outlook supports S/MIME, you can view and read a digitally signed message without taking any special action. How Outlook treats the message, however, depends on the trust relationship of the associated certificate. If the certificate is not explicitly distrusted, Outlook displays the message in the preview pane. If the certificate is not trusted, you'll see an error message in the preview pane header, as shown in Figure 12-15. You can open the message, but you've been alerted that there's a problem with the sender's certificate. Outlook also displays a dialog box noting the error when you open the message (see Figure 12-16).

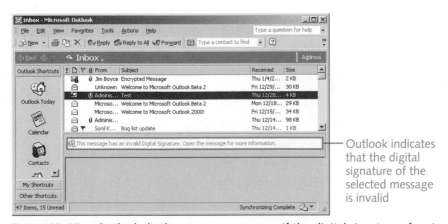

Figure 12-15. Outlook displays an error message if the digital signature of an incoming message is untrusted.

Figure 12-16. Outlook warns you when you open a message that has a certificate problem.

There is no danger in opening a message with an invalid certificate. However, you should verify that the message really came from the person listed as the sender and is not a forged message.

Changing Certificate Trust Relationships

To have Outlook authenticate a signed message and treat it as being from a trusted sender, you must add the certificate to your list of trusted certificates. An alternative is to configure Outlook to inherit trust for a certificate from the certificate's issuer. For example, assume that you have a CA in your enterprise. Rather than configuring each sender's certificate to be trusted explicitly, you can configure Outlook to inherit trust from the issuing CA—in other words, Outlook will implicitly trust all certificates issued by that CA.

Follow these steps to configure the trust relationship for a certificate:

1 In Outlook, select the signed message. If the preview pane displays an error message, or if you aren't using the preview pane, open the message and click the Secure Message button to view the Message Security Properties dialog box (see Figure 12-17). Otherwise, click the Secure Message button in the preview pane.

2 In the Message Security Properties dialog box, click the Signer line, and then click Edit Trust to display the Trust tab of the View Certificate dialog box, shown in Figure 12-18.

Chapter 12

Figure 12-17. Use the Message Security Properties dialog box to view status and properties of the certificate.

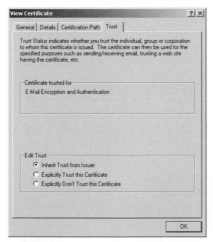

Figure 12-18. Use the Trust tab to configure the trust relationship for the certificate.

3 Select one of the following options:

- **Inherit Trust From Issuer.** Select this option to inherit the trust relationship from the issuing CA. See the following section, "Configuring CA Trust," for detailed information.

349

- **Explicitly Trust This Certificate.** Select this option to explicitly trust the certificate associated with the message if you are certain of the authenticity of the message and the validity of the sender's certificate.

- **Explicitly Don't Trust This Certificate.** Select this option to explicitly distrust the certificate associated with the message. Any other messages that you receive with the same certificate will generate an error message in Outlook when you attempt to view them.

4 Click OK, and then click Close to close the Message Security Properties dialog box.

For more information on viewing a certificate's other properties and configuring Outlook to validate certificates, see "Viewing and Validating a Digital Signature," page 351.

Configuring CA Trust

Although you might not realize it, your computer system by default includes certificates from several public CAs (typically VeriSign, Thawte, Equifax, GTE, or several others), which were installed when you installed your operating system. Outlook and other applications by default trust certificates issued by those CAs without requiring you to obtain and install each CA's certificate.

The easiest way to view these certificates is through Internet Explorer:

1 In Internet Explorer, choose Tools, Internet Options and click the Content tab.

2 Click Certificates to open the Certificates dialog box (see Figure 12-19). Click the Trusted Root Certification Authorities tab, which contains a list of the certificates.

Figure 12-19. You can view a list of certificates in Internet Explorer's Certificates dialog box.

If you have a personal certificate issued by a specific CA, the issuer's certificate is installed on your computer. Messages you receive that are signed with certificates issued by the same CA inherit trust from the issuer without requiring the installation of any additional certificates. If you're working in a large enterprise with several CAs, however, you'll probably receive signed messages containing certificates issued by CAs other than the one that issued your certificate. Thus you might not have the issuing CA's certificate on your system, which prevents Outlook from trusting the certificate. In this case, you need to add that CA's certificate to your system.

If you need to connect to a Windows 2000–based or Windows NT–based enterprise CA in order to obtain the CA's certificate and install it on your system, follow these steps:

1 Point your Web browser to *http://<machine>/certsrv,* where <machine> is the name or IP address of the CA.

2 After the page loads, select Retrieve The CA Certificate Or Certificate Revocation List, and then click Next.

3 Click Install This CA Certification Path to install the CA's certificate on your system.

The procedure just outlined assumes that the CA administrator has not customized the certificate request pages for the CA. If the pages have been customized, the actual process you must follow could be slightly different from the one described here.

> **tip** If you prefer, you can download the CA certificate rather than installing it through the browser. Use this alternative when you need to install the CA certificate on more than one computer and must have the certificate as a file.

Viewing and Validating a Digital Signature

You can view the certificate associated with a signed message to obtain information about the issuer, the person to whom the certificate is issued, and other matters.

To do so, follow these steps:

1 Open the message and click the Secure Message button in either the preview pane or the message form to display the Message Security Properties dialog box, whose Description box provides information about the certificate's validity.

2 Click Signer in the list to view additional signature information in the Description box, such as when the message was signed (see Figure 12-20).

Chapter 12

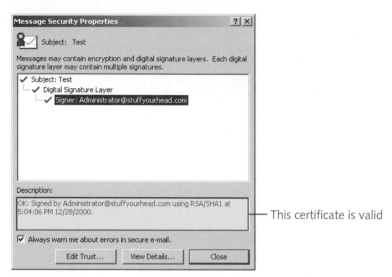

This certificate is valid

Figure 12-20. The Description box offers information about the validity of the certificate.

3 Click View Details to open the Signature dialog box, shown in Figure 12-21, which displays even more detail about the signature.

Figure 12-21. Use the Signature dialog box to view additional properties of the signature and to access the certificate.

4 On the General tab of the Signature dialog box, click View Certificate to display information about the certificate, including issuer, certification path, and trust mode.

5 Click OK and then click Close to close the Message Security Properties dialog box.

The CA uses a certificate revocation list (CRL) to indicate the validity of certificates. If you don't have a current CRL on your system, Outlook can treat the certificate as trusted but won't be able to validate the certificate and will indicate this when you view the signature.

You can locate the path to the CRL by examining the certificate's properties:

1 Click the Secure Message button for the message, either in the preview pane or in the message form.

2 Click Signer and then click View Details.

3 On the General tab of the Signature dialog box, click View Certificate and then click the Details tab (see Figure 12-22).

Figure 12-22. Use the Details tab to view the CRL path for the certificate.

4 Scroll through the list to find and select CRL Distribution Points.

5 Scroll through the list in the lower half of the dialog box to locate the URL for the CRL.

When you know the URL for the CRL, you can point your browser to the site to download and install the CRL. If the certificate was issued by a CA in your enterprise, you can obtain the CRL from the CA.

To obtain and install the CRL, follow these steps:

1 Point your browser to *http://<machine>/certsrv*, where <machine> is the name or IP address of the server.

2 Select the option Retrieve The CA Certificate Or Certificate Revocation List and click Next.

3 Click Download Latest Certificate Revocation List and save the file to disk.

4 After downloading the file, locate and right-click the file, and then choose Install CRL to install the current list.

Troubleshooting

You need a faster way to validate certificates.

If you often work with digitally signed messages and frequently need to verify certificates, consider adding the Verify Digital Signature command to the toolbar to give you a one-click method of viewing the certificate properties.

To add the command to the toolbar, follow these steps:

1 Open any existing message.

2 Right-click the toolbar in the message form and choose Customize.

3 Click Standard in the Categories list, and then drag Verify Digital Signature from the Commands list to the toolbar. Note that you can do this only if Outlook—not Word—is your e-mail editor.

4 Click Close, and then close the message form.

The next time you want to validate a certificate, all you need to do is click the button on the toolbar.

Encrypting Messages

You can encrypt messages to prevent them from being read by unauthorized persons. It is, of course, true that with enough computing power and time (significant amounts of both) any encryption scheme can probably be broken. But the chances of someone investing those resources in your e-mail are pretty remote. So you can be assured that the e-mail encryption Outlook provides offers a relatively safe means of protecting sensitive messages against interception.

Before you can encrypt messages, you must have a certificate for that purpose installed on your computer. Typically, certificates issued for digital signing can also be used for encrypting e-mail messages.

For detailed information on obtaining a personal certificate from a commercial CA or from an enterprise or stand-alone CA on your network, see "Obtaining a Digital Certificate," page 333.

354

Getting Ready for Encryption

After you've obtained a certificate and installed it on your system, encrypting messages is a simple task. Getting to that point, however, depends in part on whether you're sending messages to an Exchange Server recipient on your network or to an Internet recipient.

Swapping Certificates

Before you can send an encrypted message to an Internet recipient, you must have a copy of the recipient's certificate. To read the message, the recipient must have a copy of your certificate, which means you first need to swap certificates.

> **note** When you are sending encrypted messages to an Exchange Server recipient, you don't need to swap certificates. Exchange Server takes care of the problem for you.

The easiest way to swap certificates is to send a digitally signed message to the recipient and have the recipient send you a signed message in return, as outlined here:

1 In Outlook, choose Tools, Options and click the Security tab.

2 Click Settings to display the Change Security Settings dialog box.

3 Verify that you've selected S/MIME in the Secure Message Format drop-down list.

4 Select the option Send These Certificates With Signed Messages and click OK.

5 Click OK to close the Options dialog box.

6 Compose the message and digitally sign it. Outlook will include the certificates with the message.

When you receive a signed message from someone with whom you're exchanging certificates, you must add the person to your Contacts folder in order to add the certificate:

1 Open the message, right-click the sender's name, and then choose Add To Contacts. If the preview pane is displayed, you can right-click the sender's name in the pane and choose Add To Contacts.

2 Outlook displays the General tab of the contact form (see Figure 12-23). Fill in additional information for the contact as needed.

Chapter 12

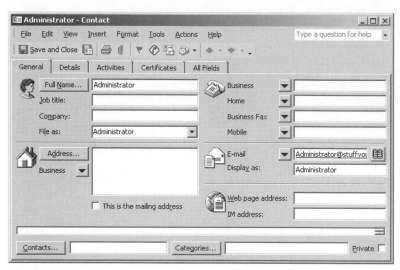

Figure 12-23. Use the contact form to add the sender's certificate to your system.

3 Click the Certificates tab. You should see the sender's certificate listed (see Figure 12-24), and you can view the certificate's properties by selecting it and clicking Properties. If no certificate is listed, contact the sender and ask for another digitally signed message.

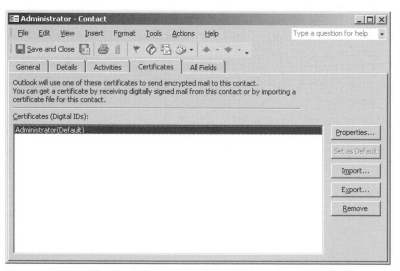

Figure 12-24. The Certificates tab of the contact form displays the sender's certificate.

4 Click Save And Close to save the contact item and the certificate.

Obtaining a Recipient's Public Key from a Public CA

As an alternative to receiving a signed message with a certificate from another person, you might be able to obtain the person's certificate from the issuing CA. For example, if you know that the person has a certificate from VeriSign, you can download that individual's public key from the VeriSign Web site. Other public CAs offer similar services. To search for and download public keys from VeriSign (see Figure 12-25), connect to *https://digitalid.verisign.com/services/client/index.html*. Check the sites of other public CAs for similar links that allow you to download public keys from their servers.

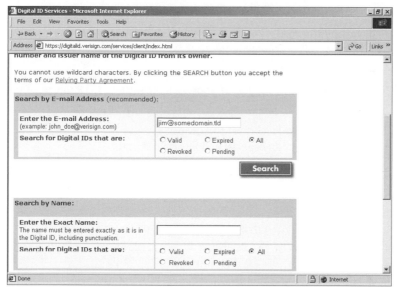

Figure 12-25.   VeriSign, like other public CAs, provides a form you can use to search for and obtain the public keys for certificate subscribers.

The process for downloading a public key varies by CA. In general, however, you enter the person's e-mail address in a form to locate the certificate, and the form provides instructions for downloading the certificate. You should have no trouble obtaining the public key after you locate the certificate on the CA.

Save the public key to disk, and then follow these steps to install the key:

1 Open the Contacts folder in Outlook.

2 Locate the contact for whom you downloaded the public key.

3 Open the contact item, and click the Certificates tab.

4 Click Import. Browse to and select the certificate file obtained from the CA and click Open.

5 Click Save And Close to save the contact changes.

Sending Encrypted Messages

When you have everything set up for sending and receiving encrypted messages, it's a simple matter to send one:

1 Open Outlook and compose the message.

2 In the message form, click Options, and then click Security Settings.

3 Select Encrypt Message Contents And Attachments, and then click OK.

4 Click Close, and then send the message as you normally would.

5 If the message is protected by Exchange Server security, you can send it in one of three ways, depending on your system's security level:

- If the security level is set to Medium (the default), Outlook displays a message informing you of your security setting. Click OK to send the message.

- If the security level is set to Low, Outlook sends the message immediately, without any special action on your part.

- If the security level is set to High, type your password to send the message.

> **tip** To make it easier to encrypt a message, you can add the Encrypt Message Contents And Attachments command to the toolbar in the message form. For details about the process involved in doing this, see the Troubleshooting sidebar "You need a faster way to digitally sign a message," page 344.

Reading Encrypted Messages

When you receive an encrypted message, you can read it as you would read any other message, assuming that you have the sender's certificate. Double-click the message to open it. Note that Outlook uses an icon with a lock, rather than the standard envelope icon, to identify encrypted messages.

> **tip** You can't preview encrypted messages in the preview pane. Also, the ability to read encrypted messages requires an S/MIME-capable mail client. Keep this in mind when sending encrypted messages to other users who might not have Outlook or another S/MIME-capable client.

> You can verify and modify the trust for a certificate when you read a message signed by that certificate. For information on viewing and changing the trust for a certificate, see "Changing Certificate Trust Relationships," page 348.

Importing Certificates from Outlook Express

If you have used Microsoft Outlook Express to send and receive secure messages, your Outlook Express address book contains the public keys of the recipients. You can import those certificates to use in Outlook if they are not already included in the Contacts folder. Unfortunately, Outlook Express doesn't export the certificates when you export its address book; instead, you must export the certificates one at a time.

Follow these steps to move certificates from Outlook Express to Outlook:

1 Open Outlook Express and choose Tools, Address Book.

2 In the address book, double-click the name of the person whose certificate you want to export.

3 Click the Digital IDs tab.

4 Select the certificate to export and click Export.

5 Save the certificate to a file. (Outlook Express uses the CER file extension.)

6 Open Outlook, open the Contacts folder, and open the contact item for the person who owns the certificate you're importing.

7 Click the Certificates tab, click Import, select the file created in step 5, and click Open.

8 Save and close the contact form.

newfeature!
Virus Protection

Outlook provides a handful of features to help protect your system against viruses and other malicious system attacks. For example, Outlook 2000 introduced attachment virus protection, which is continued in Outlook 2002. Outlook also offers protection against Office macro viruses.

For information about protecting against malicious HTML-based messages, see "Using Security Zones," page 330.

This section examines two client-side antivirus technologies: attachment blocking and macro security. The discussion of attachment blocking focuses on how Outlook sends and receives messages with specific types of attachments.

For information on server-side antivirus technologies, including how to configure attachment blocking at the server, see Chapter 39, "Backup Strategies and Virus Protection."

Chapter 12

Protecting Against Viruses in Attachments

In the "old days," infected boot floppies were the most common way computer viruses were spread. Today, e-mail is by far the most common infection mechanism. Viruses range from mostly harmless (but irritating) to severe, sometimes causing irreparable damage to your system. Worms are a more recent variation, spreading primarily through e-mail across the Internet. Worms can bog down a system by consuming the majority of the system's resources, and they can cause the same types of damage as viruses.

Outlook provides protection against viruses and worms by letting you block certain types of attachments that are susceptible to infection. Executable programs (EXE, COM, and BAT files) are good examples of attachments that are primary delivery mechanisms for viruses. Many other document types are equally susceptible—HTML documents and scripts, for instance, have rapidly become favorite delivery tools for virus terrorists. Outlook provides two levels of protection for attachments, Level 1 and Level 2. The following sections explains these two levels, the file types assigned to each, and how to work with attachments.

Level 1 Attachments

When you receive a message containing an attachment in the Level 1 group, Outlook displays the paper clip icon beside the message header, indicating that the message has an attachment, just as it does for other messages with attachments. When you click the message header, Outlook displays a message in the InfoBar informing you that it has blocked the attachment (see Figure 12-26.) Table 12-1 lists the Level 1 file types.

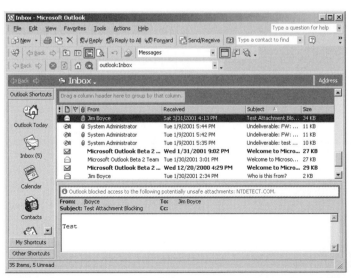

Figure 12-26. Outlook displays a message informing you that it has blocked the attachment.

Table 12-1. Level 1 attachments

File Extension	Description
ADE	Microsoft Access project extension
ADP	Microsoft Access project
BAS	Microsoft Visual Basic class module
BAT	Batch file
CHM	Compiled HTML Help file
CMD	Microsoft Windows NT/Windows 2000 command script
COM	Microsoft MS-DOS program
CPL	Control Panel extension
CRT	Security certificate
EXE	Program
HLP	Help file
HTA	HTML program
INF	Setup Information File
INS	Internet Naming Service
ISP	Internet Communication settings
JS	Microsoft JScript file
JSE	Microsoft JScript Encoded Script file
LNK	Shortcut
MDA	Microsoft Access add-in program
MDB	Microsoft Access program
MDE	Microsoft Access MDE database
MDZ	Microsoft Access wizard program
MSC	Microsoft Common Console document
MSI	Microsoft Windows Installer package
MSP	Microsoft Windows Installer patch
MST	Microsoft Visual Test source files
PCD	Photo CD image or Microsoft Visual Test compiled script
PIF	Shortcut to MS-DOS program

(continued)

Chapter 12

Table 12-1. *(continued)*

File Extension	Description
REG	Registration entries
SCR	Screen saver
SCT	Microsoft Windows Script Component
SHS	Shell Scrap Object
URL	Internet shortcut
VB	Microsoft VBScript file
VBE	Microsoft VBScript Encoded script file
VBS	Microsoft VBScript file
WSC	Microsoft Windows Script Component
WSF	Microsoft Windows Script file
WSH	Microsoft Windows Script Host settings file

You cannot open Level 1 attachments that are blocked by Outlook. You can open and view the messages, but Outlook disables the interface elements that otherwise would allow you to open or save the attachments. If you forward a message with a blocked attachment, Outlook strips the attachment from the forwarded message.

note If you use Exchange Server, the Exchange Server administrator can configure attachment blocking at the server. In addition, you can configure Outlook to allow certain Level 1 attachments (essentially removing them from the Level 1 list) by modifying the registry. For details on virus protection in Exchange Server and how to have Outlook open blocked attachments, see "Configuring Blocked Attachments," page 969.

You have another option for accessing blocked attachments if your Exchange Server has Outlook Web Access (OWA). OWA doesn't provide any attachment blocking, which makes it possible to retrieve the messages—with attachments—through your Web browser. Point your browser to *http://<server>/Exchange*, where <server> is the IP address or name of your server. Use your Exchange Server account to log on and open the message with the attachment, and then save the attachment to disk.

Your server might use a different URL for Outlook Web Access depending on how your administrator has configured the server. For coverage of OWA, see Chapter 36, "Accessing Messages Through a Web Browser."

If Outlook Express is installed on your computer, you have an additional method for opening blocked attachments. Outlook doesn't strip out the attachments—rather, it simply prevents you from opening or saving them. You can, then, import the messages into Outlook Express and open the attachments there.

Here's how to import an attachment for opening:

1 Create a new folder in Outlook, and move the message with the blocked attachment to that folder. You could leave the message in the Inbox, but that would require you to import all messages from the Inbox to Outlook Express. Moving the message to a different folder lets you import only one message.

2 Open Outlook Express and choose File, Import, Messages.

3 Choose Microsoft Outlook in the Outlook Express Import Wizard and click Next.

4 Select the folder from step 1 and click Next to begin the import.

5 Click Finish when the messages have been imported.

Level 2 Attachments

Outlook also supports a second level of attachment blocking. Level 2 attachments are defined by the administrator at the server level (and therefore apply to Exchange Server accounts). You can't open Level 2 attachments directly in Outlook; but Outlook does allow you to save them to disk, and you can open them from there.

To open a Level 2 attachment this way, follow these steps:

1 Open the message and choose File, Save Attachments. Select the attachment you want to save.

2 In the Save Attachment dialog box, specify the folder in which you want to save the file and click Save.

3 Outside Outlook, browse to the folder and open the file.

Because the Level 2 list is empty by default, no attachments are blocked as Level 2 attachments unless the Exchange Server administrator has modified the Level 2 list.

For detailed information on configuring attachment blocking under Exchange Server, see "Configuring Blocked Attachments," page 969.

Protecting Against Office Macro Viruses

Like other Microsoft Office applications, Outlook allows you to use macros to auto-mate common tasks. Macros have become an increasingly popular infection mecha-nism for viruses because most inexperienced users don't expect to have their systems infected by common Office documents. However, Office macros can contain viruses that cause just as much damage as any other virus. Protecting yourself against macro viruses is an important step in safeguarding your system overall.

You can guard against macro viruses by implementing a virus scanner on your system that checks your documents for macro viruses, by installing a virus scrubber on your e-mail server, or by using both methods. Another line of protection is to control how and when macros are allowed to run. Outlook provides three security levels for macros that determine which macros can run on the system. To set the level, choose Tools, Macro, Security and select one of these three levels:

- **High.** Only signed macros from sources you've designated as trusted will run. Outlook disables unsigned macros, preventing them from running.

- **Medium.** For each macro, Outlook prompts you to decide whether to run the macro.

- **Low.** All macros are allowed to run.

> For additional information on configuring macro security and specifying trusted sources, see "Setting Macro Security," page 661.

Processing Messages Selectively

Like previous versions of the program, Microsoft Outlook 2002 includes a feature called *remote mail* that allows you to manage your e-mail messages without downloading them from the server. Although you might not believe that you need yet another way to retrieve your messages, remote mail offers advantages that you'll come to appreciate over time.

Although remote mail is primarily a feature for Microsoft Exchange Server, other e-mail accounts can take advantage of similar capabilities (which, for the sake of simplicity, this chapter refers to generically as remote mail). For example, with POP3, IMAP, and HTTP accounts, you can download message headers only, to review your messages before downloading the message bodies and attachments. The process is similar for all these types of accounts, although POP3 and Exchange Server accounts offer additional options.

This chapter focuses specifically on using remote mail for non–Exchange Server accounts. It explains how to set up your system to use remote mail for IMAP, HTTP, and POP3 accounts; how to manage your messages through remote mail; and how to use alternatives to remote mail, such as send/receive groups.

For detailed information on configuring and using the remote mail feature for Exchange Server accounts, see "Using Remote Mail," page 865.

Understanding Remote Mail Options

The primary advantage of using remote mail is the ability to work with message headers of waiting messages without having to download the messages themselves. You can simply connect to the e-mail server, download the headers for new messages, and disconnect. You can then take your time reviewing the message headers to decide which messages to download, which ones to delete without reading, and which ones to leave on the server for later. After you've made your decisions and marked the headers accordingly, you can connect again and download those messages you've marked to retrieve, either leaving the others on the server or deleting them.

Remote mail is extremely useful when you're pressed for time but have a message with a large attachment waiting on the server. You might want to retrieve only your most critical messages without spending the time or connect charges to download that message and its attachment. To accomplish this, you can connect with remote mail and select the messages you want to download, leaving the one with the large attachment on the server for a less busy time when you can download it across the network or through a broadband Internet connection.

Remote mail is also useful when you discover a corrupt message in your mailbox that might otherwise prevent Outlook from downloading your messages. You can connect with remote mail, delete the offending message without downloading it, and then continue working normally.

> **note** Remote mail works only for the Inbox; you can't use it to synchronize other folders.

newfeature! Remote Mail in a Nutshell

Outlook 2002 offers remote mail for several types of accounts, with differing capabilities. All of the following accounts allow you to download and mark message headers without downloading the messages themselves:

Exchange Server. By marking the message headers, you can indicate which messages to download and which to delete from the server. In addition, you can specify conditions that determine which messages are downloaded— for example, those with particular subjects, those from certain senders, those smaller than a specified size, or those without attachments. You can mark messages offline.

POP3. By marking the message headers, you can indicate which messages should be moved from the server to your system, which messages should be downloaded with a copy left on the server, and which messages should be deleted from the server without being downloaded. You also can specify a size limit and download only messages that are smaller than the specified size; for messages that exceed the size limit, you can download headers only. You can mark messages offline.

IMAP and HTTP. By marking the message headers, you can indicate which messages to download and which to delete from the server. Both types of accounts store mail on the server, so marking to download a copy isn't relevant (as it is for a POP3 account) because a copy of the message stays on the server anyway. With an HTTP account, you must be online in order to mark message headers for deletion; IMAP accounts allow you to mark for deletion while offline. You don't have any special options for selective or conditional processing with either type of account.

Using Remote Mail with Hotmail

Remote mail is a good choice for managing your POP3, IMAP, or Exchange Server mailbox remotely. With Microsoft Hotmail accounts, remote mail doesn't offer any real advantage because Hotmail accounts download the headers without the full messages anyway; the message bodies are downloaded only when you view the messages. However, you can't delete messages from Hotmail without being online, although you can delete unread messages without downloading them as long as you don't have the preview pane turned on. You also can connect through your Web browser to Hotmail to delete messages without downloading them.

Setting Up for Remote Mail

Non–Exchange Server accounts generally deliver messages to a personal folders (PST) file, although you can configure POP3 accounts to deliver messages to your Exchange Server mailbox. If your POP3 account delivers mail to your Exchange Server mailbox, you can use remote mail with the account as long as you're connected to the Exchange Server while you're using remote mail on the POP3 account. For example, assume that you connect over the local area network (LAN) to the Exchange Server but connect to a POP3 account by modem. In that scenario, you'd be able to use remote mail for the POP3 account.

In another scenario, assume that you dial into your LAN to work with your Exchange Server account, and the remote access server also provides connectivity to the Internet. Your POP3 account delivers mail to your Exchange Server mailbox. In this case, you can use remote mail for both accounts because you have access to your mail store. The key is that in order to use remote mail, you must have access to your mail store so that Outlook has a place to deliver the downloaded message headers.

If you don't use Exchange Server, you don't need to do anything special to configure your system to use remote mail. Because your mail store is local, you have access to it all the time (unless the server is down or offline).

367

To use remote mail, you naturally need a connection to the remote server. Generally this takes the form of a dial-up connection, either to the server's network or to the Internet. If you haven't already done so, you'll need to set up a dial-up connection to the appropriate point.

> For detailed instructions on setting up a dial-up connection, see "Configuring Dial-Up Networking Options," page 147.

newfeature! Working with Message Headers

The following sections explain the specific steps to follow as you perform various tasks with message headers through remote mail. You'll learn how to download the headers, how to selectively mark them, and how to process them.

Downloading Message Headers

When you want to process messages selectively, you first download the message headers and then decide what action you want to perform with each message, based on its header. Downloading message headers for an account is easy. In Outlook, choose Tools, Send/Receive, Work With Headers, Download Headers From, and then select one of the following:

- **This Folder.** Select this option to download the message headers for the currently selected folder.

- **All Accounts.** Select this option to download message headers for all accounts. (Outlook downloads only headers in the account's Inbox folder.)

- **<Account Name>.** This option allows you to select a specific account whose headers you want to download.

> **note** The three options under Download Headers From appear only if you have multiple accounts configured in your profile.

After you select one of these three options, Outlook performs a send/receive operation but downloads only message headers from the specified account or accounts. If you want to save on connect charges, you then can disconnect from the server to review the headers and decide what to do with each message.

Outlook displays the downloaded message headers in the Inbox. The icon for a message header whose associated message has not been downloaded is slightly different from the standard envelope icon. In addition, Outlook displays an icon in the Header Status column to indicate that the message has not yet been downloaded (see Figure 13-1).

Message body not yet downloaded

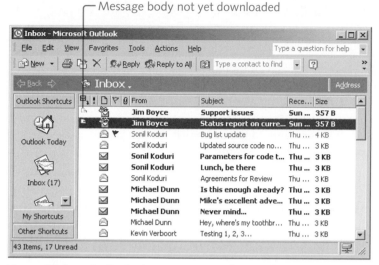

Figure 13-1. Outlook places an icon in the Header Status column to indicate that the message itself has yet to be downloaded.

Marking and Unmarking Message Headers

After you download the headers, you can decide what to do with each message: retrieve it, download a copy, or delete it.

Marking to Retrieve a Message

With a POP3 account, you can mark a message header to have Outlook retrieve the message, remove it from the server, and store it in your local store. With IMAP or HTTP mail accounts, you can mark a message header to have Outlook download the message, but those accounts continue to store the message on the server until you delete it.

To mark a message to be downloaded from the server to your local store, select the message header, right-click it, and choose Mark To Download Message(s). Alternatively, you can choose Tools, Send/Receive, Work With Headers, Mark/Unmark Messages, Mark To Download Message(s).

> **tip** To quickly select multiple message headers, hold down the Ctrl or Shift key while you click the message headers.

Marking to Retrieve a Copy

In some cases, you might want to download a copy of a message but also leave the message on the server—for example, you might need to retrieve the same message from a different computer. To mark a message header to have Outlook retrieve a copy, select the message header, right-click it, and choose Mark To Download Message Copy. Alternatively, you can select the message header and choose Tools, Send/Receive, Work With Headers, Mark/Unmark Messages, Mark To Download Message Copy. Outlook indicates in the Header Status column of the Inbox that the message is marked for download and changes the message icon accordingly (see Figure 13-2).

> **note** As explained earlier, it isn't necessary to download a copy from an IMAP or HTTP server, as those servers continue to store a copy of the message on the server. Downloading a copy is applicable only to POP3 and Exchange Server accounts.

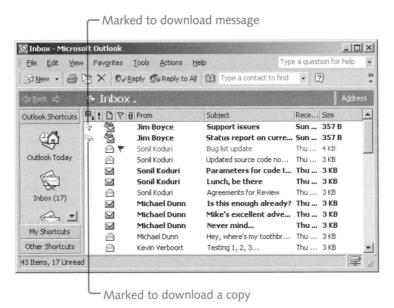

Figure 13-2. These messages are marked to have Outlook retrieve a copy.

> **tip** So that you can easily identify the pending action, Outlook displays different icons in the Header Status column of the Inbox for messages marked to download and messages marked to download a copy.

370

Marking to Delete a Message

You also can mark messages to be deleted from the server without downloading. You might do this for junk mail or messages with large attachments that you don't need and don't want choking your download session.

To mark a message for deletion, select the message header, right-click it, and choose Delete or press the Delete key. Outlook strikes through the message header and changes the download icon to indicate that the message will be deleted the next time you process messages (see Figure 13-3).

Marked to delete

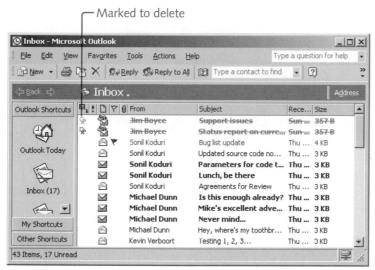

Figure 13-3. A strikethrough indicates that the message will be deleted without downloading.

Unmarking a Message

As you work with message headers, you'll occasionally change your mind after you've marked a message. In that case, you can unmark the message. Select the message header, right-click it, and choose Unmark Selected Headers. Alternatively, you can choose Tools, Send/Receive, Work With Headers, Mark/Unmark Messages, Unmark Selected Headers.

You also can unmark all message headers, clearing all pending actions. To do so, choose Tools, Send/Receive, Work With Headers, Mark/Unmark Messages, Unmark All Messages.

Chapter 13

Processing Marked Headers

After you've reviewed and marked the message headers, you can process the messages to apply the actions you've chosen. When you do so, for example, messages marked for download are downloaded to your system, and messages marked for deletion are deleted from the server.

To process marked messages, choose Tools, Send/Receive, Work With Headers, Process Marked Headers From. Then select either All Accounts or the account for which you want to process messages. Outlook connects and performs the specified actions (see Figure 13-4).

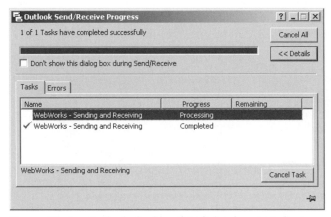

Figure 13-4. Outlook displays this dialog box to indicate progress status for remote mail, as it does for other send/receive operations.

Troubleshooting

You can't find the remote mail commands.

As you work with remote mail, you'll probably come to wish for an easier, faster way to access the remote mail commands. The remote mail commands are buried deep in the Tools menu, making it difficult to locate them quickly. Outlook also doesn't provide a toolbar for remote mail commands. Fortunately, you can create your own toolbar if you're someone who finds remote mail useful.

Follow these steps to create your own toolbar for remote mail:

1 In Outlook, choose View, Toolbars, Customize to open the Customize dialog box. Click the Toolbars tab, shown in Figure 13-5.

2 Click New. Type the name **Remote Mail** in the New Toolbar dialog box and click OK. Outlook opens an empty toolbar.

Figure 13-5. Use the Toolbars tab to create your own toolbar for remote mail.

3 Click the Commands tab in the Customize dialog box and select Tools from the Categories list.

4 Drag the commands you want to include on the toolbar from the Commands list to the new toolbar. At a minimum, the following commands are useful:

- Download Headers From

- Mark/Unmark Messages

- Mark To Download Message(s)

- Mark To Download Message Copy

- Delete

- Unmark Selected Headers

- Unmark All Headers

- Process Marked Headers From

Selective Downloading for POP3 Using Send/Receive Groups

Using send/receive groups in Outlook gives you additional options for selective message processing with POP3 accounts. You can configure a POP3 account in a send/receive group to download only headers, for example, or to download only those messages smaller than a specified size while retrieving only headers for larger messages. If you prefer to process your POP3 account selectively—perhaps because you connect over a dial-up connection, or because you want to delete unwanted messages before they arrive in your Inbox, or because you need to control which messages are downloaded—you can use a send/receive group to process the account.

> For details on setting up send/receive groups, see "Controlling Synchronization and Send/ Receive Times," page 190.

Let's assume that your profile includes two POP3 accounts, a Hotmail account, and an Exchange Server account. You want to process messages normally for the Hotmail and Exchange Server accounts but would like to process the POP3 accounts selectively. You can configure a send/receive group (either the default All Accounts group or another that you create) to perform a send/receive operation for the other accounts that processes all messages. You can also configure the POP3 accounts in the send/receive group to download only message headers. When you perform a send/receive operation with the group, the POP3 accounts download only headers and the other accounts download messages.

> **tip**   You can't use send/receive groups for selective processing with Hotmail and HTTP accounts. You can apply a filter to Exchange Server folders to selectively process messages and other items from those folders. For details, see "Controlling Remote Mail Through Send/Receive Groups," page 868.

You can configure multiple send/receive groups, using different settings for each (although some settings, such as Exchange Server filters, apply to all send/receive groups to which the folder belongs). For example, you might configure your POP3 accounts in the All Accounts send/receive group to download message bodies and attachments but create a second send/receive group named POP3 Remote that processes only message headers for your POP3 accounts when that group is executed.

Retrieving Only Message Headers

After you decide which combination of send/receive groups makes the most sense for you, follow these steps to configure a POP3 account to retrieve only message headers and then process the headers:

1   In Outlook, choose Tools, Send/Receive Settings, Define Send/Receive Groups.

2   Select the existing send/receive group in which you want to configure POP3 accounts for headers only (or create a group for that purpose) and then click Edit.

3   On the Accounts bar of the Send/Receive Settings dialog box (see Figure 13-6), click the POP3 account.

4   Select the option Download Item Description Only.

5   If you don't want the group to send messages from the selected POP3 account, clear the Send Mail Items check box.

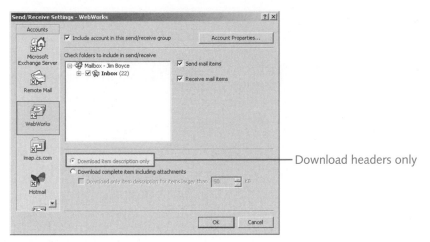

Figure 13-6. You can configure a POP3 account to download only headers.

6 Click OK and then close the Send/Receive Groups dialog box.

7 Choose Tools, Send/Receive, and select the group to have Outlook process it according to the settings you specified in the previous steps. Outlook then downloads message headers.

8 Review and mark the downloaded message headers and then process the group again. Alternatively, choose Tools, Send/Receive, Work With Headers, Process Marked Headers From and select the appropriate account.

Retrieving Based on Message Size

You can configure a POP3 account in a send/receive group to specify a message size limit. Messages that meet or are below the specified size limit are downloaded in their entirety, complete with attachments. For messages larger than the specified size, only headers are downloaded. This is an easy way to restrict the volume of incoming POP3 mail and keep large messages from choking a low-bandwidth connection such as a dial-up.

Follow these steps to configure a POP3 account in a send/receive group to download headers only for messages over a specified size:

1 In Outlook, choose Tools, Send/Receive Settings, Define Send/Receive Groups.

2 Select or create the send/receive group and click Edit.

3 Select the POP3 account on the Accounts bar of the Send/Receive Settings dialog box, and then select the option Download Complete Item Including Attachments.

4 Select Download Only Item Description For Items Larger Than *n* KB, as shown in Figure 13-7 on the next page.

375

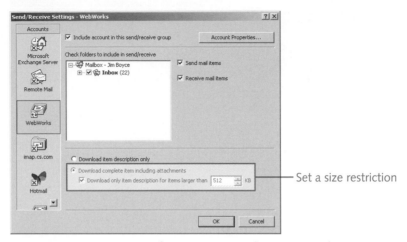

— Set a size restriction

Figure 13-7. You can specify a message size limit to control connect time and mail volume.

5 Enter a value to define the message size limit and then click OK.

6 Click Close to close the Send/Receive Groups dialog box.

Keeping Messages on the Server

Often you'll want to keep a copy of your messages on the server and download a copy. For example, you might be checking your messages from the office but want to be able to retrieve them from home or from your notebook computer. Or perhaps you're using remote mail to process a few important messages and want to leave copies on the server for safekeeping. You can configure the account to leave a copy of all messages on the server, allowing you to retrieve the messages again from another system.

When you configure a POP3 account to retain messages on the server, you also can specify that the messages must be removed after they've been on the server for a designated period of time. Alternatively, you could have Outlook delete the messages from the server when you delete them from your Deleted Items folder, which prevents the messages from being downloaded again from the server after you've deleted your local copies.

Here's how to configure these options for POP3 accounts:

1 In Outlook, choose Tools, E-Mail Accounts; or right-click the Outlook icon on the desktop, choose Properties, and click E-Mail Accounts.

2 Choose View Or Change Existing E-Mail Accounts and click Next.

3 Select the POP3 account and choose Change.

4 Click More Settings and then click the Advanced tab (see Figure 13-8).

376

Chapter 13

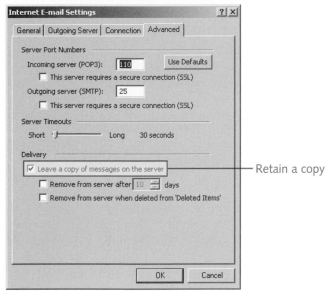

Retain a copy

Figure 13-8. Use the Advanced tab to configure the account to leave messages on the server.

5 Select the option Leave A Copy Of Messages On The Server, and then select one of the two associated options if needed. Click OK.

6 Click Next and then click Finish.

Part 3

Contact Management

Managing Your Contacts

The Contacts folder in Microsoft Outlook is an electronic tool that can organize and store all the thousands of details you need to know to communicate with people, businesses, and organizations. Use the Contacts folder to store e-mail addresses, street addresses, multiple phone numbers, and any other information that relates to a contact, such as a birthday or an anniversary date.

From a contact entry in your list of contacts, you can click a button or choose a command to have Outlook address a meeting request, an e-mail message, a letter, or a task request to the contact. If you have a modem, you can have Outlook dial the contact's phone number. You can link any Outlook item or Microsoft Office document to a contact to help you track activities associated with the contact.

Outlook allows you to customize the view in the Contacts folder to review and print your contact information. You can sort, group, or filter your contacts list to better manage the information or to quickly find entries.

Outlook also supports the use of vCards, the Internet standard for creating and sharing virtual business cards. You can save a contact entry as a vCard and send it in an e-mail message. You can also add a vCard to your e-mail signature.

This chapter introduces Outlook's contact management ability. Outlook's Contacts feature provides powerful tools to help you manage, organize, and find important contact information.

Working with the Contacts Folder

The Contacts folder is one of Outlook's default folders. This folder stores information such as name, physical address, phone number, and e-mail address for each contact. You can use the Contacts folder to quickly address e-mail messages, place phone calls, distribute bulk mailings through mail merge (in Microsoft Word), and perform many other communication tasks. The Contacts folder is not, however, the same as your address book. Your Outlook Address Book (OAB) lets you access the Contacts folder for addressing messages, but the OAB also lets you access addresses stored in personal address books and Microsoft Exchange Server address lists.

> For detailed information about working with address books in Outlook, see Chapter 5, "Managing Address Books and Distribution Lists."

You can open the Contacts folder either by clicking the Contacts icon in the Outlook Shortcuts group on the Outlook Bar or by opening the folder list and clicking Contacts. When you open the folder, you'll see its default view, Address Cards, which displays contact entries as address cards that show name, address, phone number, and a handful of other items for each contact (see Figure 14-1). Outlook provides seven predefined views for the Contacts folder that offer different ways to display and sort the contacts list.

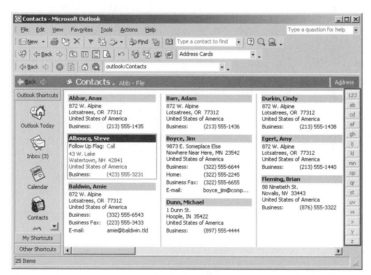

Figure 14-1. Use the Contacts folder to manage contact information such as address, phone number, and fax number for your business associates and friends.

> For details about the available views in the Contacts folder and how to work with them, see "Viewing Contacts," page 404.

> **tip** You can use the button bar at the right of the folder (see Figure 14-1) to quickly jump to a specific area in the Contacts folder. For example, click the M button to jump to the list of contacts whose names begin with M.

When you double-click a contact entry in the Contacts folder, Outlook opens a contact form similar to the one shown in Figure 14-2. This multi-tabbed form lets you view and modify a wealth of information about the person. You also can initiate actions related to the contact. For example, you can click the AutoDialer button on the form's toolbar to dial the contact's phone number. You'll learn more about these tasks throughout the remainder of this chapter. The following section explains how to create a contact entry and also introduces the tabs on the contact form to help you understand the types of information you can store.

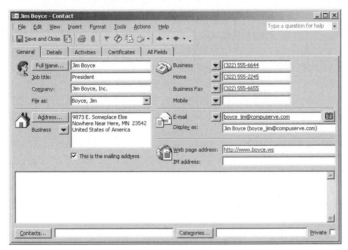

Figure 14-2.   The General tab of a contact form shows address, phone, and other information about the contact.

Creating a Contact Entry

To create a contact entry, you can start from scratch, or you can base the new entry on a similar, existing entry—for example, the entry for a contact from the same company.

You can open a contact form and create a new entry from scratch in any of the following ways:

- Choose File, New, Contact.
- Right-click a blank area in the Contacts folder (not a contact entry), and choose New Contact.

- With the Contacts folder open, press Ctrl+N.

- If the Contacts folder is not open, click the arrow beside the New button on the toolbar and choose Contact.

When the contact form opens, type the contact's name in the Full Name box and enter all the other information you want to include for the contact, switching tabs as needed. To save the entry, click Save And Close.

Filling in the information on the contact form is a fairly straightforward process. You might find a few of the features especially useful. For example, the File As drop-down list allows you to specify how you want the contact to be listed in the Contacts folder. You can choose to list the contact under his or her own name in either Lastname, Firstname format or Firstname Lastname format; to list the contact by company name rather than personal name; or to use a combination of contact name and company name.

You can also store more phone numbers in the contact entry than the four that are displayed on the form. When you click the drop-down button by a phone number entry (see Figure 14-3), you see a list of possible phone numbers from which you can select a number to view or modify; the checked items on the list are those that currently contain information. When you select a number, Outlook shows it on the form.

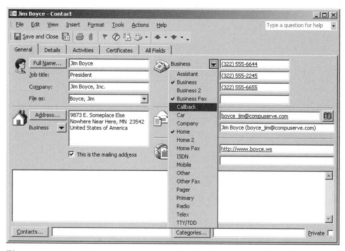

Figure 14-3. You can store multiple phone numbers for a contact, but only four appear on the form at one time.

In addition to storing multiple phone numbers for a contact, you also can store multiple physical addresses. Click the drop-down button under the Address button on the form to select a business, home, or other address. The E-Mail box can also store multiple data items; click the drop-down button to choose one of three e-mail addresses for the individual. For example, you might list both business and personal addresses as well as an HTTP-based address (such as a Microsoft Hotmail address) for the contact.

Chapter 14: Managing Your Contacts

The Details tab of the contact form (see Figure 14-4) lets you add other information, such as the contact's department, office number, birthday, and anniversary. The Online NetMeeting Settings area of the form lets you specify the default directory server to use when establishing a NetMeeting session with the contact and the e-mail alias that NetMeeting uses to locate the contact. You can click Call Now to open NetMeeting and start a session with the contact.

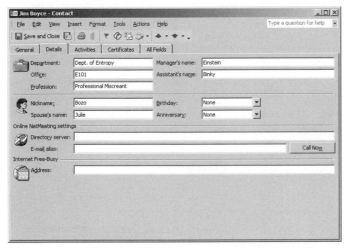

Figure 14-4. The Details tab stores additional information—both business and personal—about the contact.

> For detailed information on configuring and using NetMeeting, see "Holding an Online Meeting," page 536.

The Activities tab of the contact form is useful for locating e-mail messages, logged phone calls, and other items or activities associated with a specific contact. For information about using the Activities tab, see "Associating a Contact with Other Items and Documents," page 389.

---

tip **Add contacts quickly**

When you use one of the table views to display your Contacts folder, you'll see a row at the top of the list labeled Click Here To Add A New Contact. This is a handy way to enter a contact's name and phone number quickly—simply type the information directly in the row, and Outlook will add the contact entry to the folder.

Creating Contact Entries from the Same Company

If you have several contacts who work for the same company, you can use an existing contact entry to create a new entry. Simply open the existing entry and choose Actions, New Contact From Same Company. Outlook opens a new contact form with all the company information (name, address, and phone numbers) supplied—all you have to do is fill in the personal details for that individual.

> You can also use a template to create multiple contact entries that share common data such as company affiliation. For information about working with templates in Outlook, see Chapter 22, "Using Templates."

Creating a Contact Entry from an E-Mail Message

When you receive an e-mail message from someone you'd like to add to your contacts list, you can create a contact entry directly from the message. In the From box of the message form or on the InfoBar of the preview pane, right-click the name and choose Add To Contacts on the shortcut menu. Outlook opens a new contact form with the sender's name and e-mail address already entered. Add any other necessary data for the contact, and click Save And Close to create the entry.

Copying an Existing Contact Entry

In some cases, you might want to create a copy of a contact entry. For example, although you can keep both personal and business data in a single entry, you might want to store the data separately. You can save time by copying the existing entry rather than creating a new one from scratch.

To copy a contact entry in the Contacts folder, right-drag the entry to an empty spot in the folder and choose Copy. Outlook creates a new entry containing all the same information as the original. You also can copy contact information to another folder. Open the folder where the contact entry is stored, and then locate the destination folder on the Outlook Bar or in the folder list. Right-drag the contact entry to the destination folder and choose Copy from the shortcut menu.

Creating Other Contacts Folders

In addition to providing its default Contacts folder, Outlook allows you to use multiple contacts folders to organize your contacts easily. For example, you might use a shared contacts folder jointly with members of your workgroup for business contacts and keep your personal contacts in a separate folder. Or you might prefer to keep contact information you use infrequently in a separate folder to lessen the clutter in your main Contacts folder. The process of creating a contact entry in any contacts folder is the same regardless of the folder's location—whether it is part of your Exchange Server account or in a personal folders (PST) file, for example.

You can create six types of folders in Outlook, each designed to hold a specific type of data. A Contact Items folder stores contacts.

To create a new folder for storing contacts, follow these steps:

1 Choose File, New, Folder. Alternatively, you can right-click the folder list and choose New Folder to open the Create New Folder dialog box (see Figure 14-5).

Figure 14-5. Use the Create New Folder dialog box to create new Outlook folders.

2 In the Name box, type a name for the folder. This is the folder name that will be displayed in Outlook (on the Outlook Bar and in the folder list, for example).

3 Select Contact Items in the Folder Contains drop-down list.

4 In the Select Where To Place The Folder list, select the location for the new folder.

5 Click OK.

6 Answer the prompt when Outlook asks whether you want to place a shortcut to this folder on the Outlook Bar.

When you create a new contacts folder using this method, Outlook sets up the folder using default properties for permissions, rules, description, forms, and views. If you want to create a new contacts folder that uses the same custom properties as an existing folder, you can copy the folder design, as explained in the following section.

Copying the Design of a Folder

Another way to set up a new contacts folder is to copy the design of an existing contacts folder to the new one. Folder design properties include permissions, rules, description, forms, and views.

> **note** You can copy a folder design as described here only for folders that are contained in an Exchange Server mailbox.

> For information about various folder properties, see "Setting Folder Properties," page 700.

To copy the design of an existing contacts folder, follow these steps:

1 In the folder list, click the contacts folder to which you want to copy the folder properties.

2 Choose File, Folder, Copy Folder Design.

3 In the Copy Design From dialog box (see Figure 14-6), click the folder whose design you want to copy.

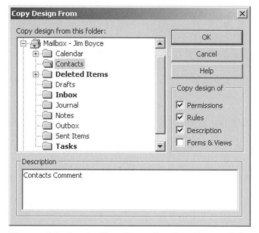

Figure 14-6. In the Copy Design From dialog box, select the folder whose design you want to copy.

4 In the Copy Design Of area, select the specific properties you want to copy.

5 Click OK. An Outlook prompt warns you that the existing properties of the current folder will be replaced with properties from the source folder. Click Yes to perform the copy or No to cancel.

Copying a folder's properties this way does not copy the contents of the folder—it copies only the selected properties. It is also different from copying the folder itself, which copies the contents of the folder to a new location.

> For more information about copying folders, see "Copying and Moving a Folder," page 698.

Working with Contacts

You can do much more with your Outlook contacts list than just viewing address and phone information. Outlook provides a set of tools that make it easy to phone, write, e-mail, or communicate with contacts in other ways. This section of the chapter explains these tools.

Associating a Contact with Other Items and Documents

As you work with contacts, it's useful to have e-mail messages, appointments, tasks, documents, or other items related to the contact at your fingertips. You can relate items to a contact by creating links. For example, if you create a task to call several of your contacts, you can use the Contacts button on the task form to link the task to those contacts: click Contacts on the task form, and then select the contacts in the resulting Select Contacts dialog box (see Figure 14-7).

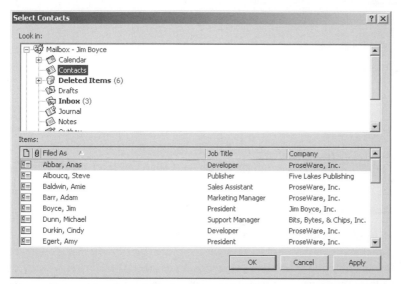

Figure 14-7. Use the Select Contacts dialog box to associate contacts with a task.

For details on setting up tasks, see "Creating a Task," page 550.

E-mail messages that you send to a contact are automatically linked to that contact and show up on the Activities tab of the contact form (discussed shortly). In addition, most items you create by using the Actions menu are automatically linked to the contact entry and appear on the Activities tab. For example, if you choose Actions, New Task For Contact to create a new task for a contact, Outlook links the task to the contact.

Part 3: Contact Management

Troubleshooting

Creating a new letter doesn't create a contact link.

If you choose Actions, New Letter To Contact, Outlook starts a new letter to the contact but does not link the document to that contact item. You can work around the problem by manually linking the document and the contact item. For details on creating the link, see "Linking a Contact to a Document," page 391.

The Activities tab of any contact form displays all the items related to that contact, as shown in Figure 14-8. Outlook searches for links to items in the main Outlook folders, including Contacts, e-mail (Inbox and other message folders), Journal, Notes, Tasks, and Calendar.

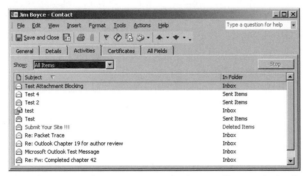

Figure 14-8. The Activities tab shows all items linked to the contact.

---

tip **Open linked contacts**

You can open a contact item from within another item linked to it by double-clicking the contact name in the Contacts box on the other item's form. For example, if you have linked an appointment to a contact, you can open the contact item by double-clicking the contact name shown on the appointment form.

What good is the Activities tab? It's extremely useful for finding items associated with a specific contact. For example, you could sort the Inbox by sender to locate an e-mail message from a particular person, or you could use the Activities tab in his or her contact form to achieve the same result. You could also view a list of the tasks assigned to an individual by checking the Activities tab. Although you can view these associations in other folders, the Activities tab not only offers an easier way to view the links but also lets you see all linked items, not just specific types of items.

Linking a Contact to Existing Outlook Items

As mentioned previously, Outlook automatically links contacts to most Outlook items if you create the item by using the Actions menu. For those items that aren't linked automatically, you can create the link manually. For example, you might want to create a link from a contact entry to a message that did not come from the contact.

To link a contact entry to an existing Outlook item, such as a task or an appointment, follow these steps:

1 Select or open the contact entry.

2 Choose Actions, Link, Items to display the Link Items To Contact dialog box (see Figure 14-9).

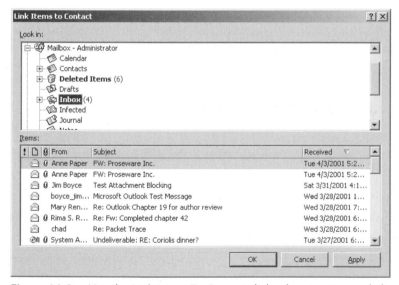

Figure 14-9. Use the Link Items To Contact dialog box to set up a link.

3 In the Look In list, select the folder that contains the item you want to link to the contact.

4 In the Items list, select the specific item(s) you want to link to the contact.

5 Click OK to create the links.

Linking a Contact to a Document

In many cases, you might want to create a link between a contact and one or more documents. For example, assume that you manage contracts for several individuals or companies. You can create a link from a contract document to the contact who is covered by the contract, to make it easier to open the document from the contact form.

With this link, you don't need to remember the document name if you know the name of the contact with which it is associated.

Follow these steps to create a link between a document and a contact:

1 Open the Contacts folder, right-click the contact item, and choose Link, File to display the Choose A File dialog box (a standard file selection dialog box).

2 Locate the file(s) you want to associate with the contact and click Insert.

3 Outlook opens a new journal entry form with a link to the document inserted in the item. Click Save And Close to create the link.

When you want to open the document, open the contact form and click the Activities tab. Locate the linked document and double-click it to open the journal entry. Then double-click the document shortcut to open the document.

Linking a Contact to a New Message

When you send an e-mail message to a contact, Outlook automatically links that message to the contact. But you can also link a message to a contact even if that person is not one of the recipients of the message. For example, every time you send a message regarding a particular client to your sales staff, you can associate the message with the client's contact entry.

Here's how to establish the link:

1 Create a new e-mail message.

2 Click Options on the message form, and then click Contacts to display the Select Contacts dialog box.

3 Select the name of the person to whom the message should be linked and click OK.

4 Click Close to return to the message form.

5 Complete the message and send it.

Removing a Link

Occasionally you'll want to remove a link between a contact and another item. For example, perhaps you've accidentally linked the wrong document to a contact, or perhaps the contact who had been associated with a particular project has taken a different job.

To remove a link from a contact to an item, follow these steps:

1 Open the contact item and click the Activities tab.

2 Double-click the link to the item you want to remove.

- If the linked item is an e-mail message, choose View, Options. In the Contacts box, select the linked contact and press Delete.

- For any other type of linked item, open the item and delete the contact name from the Contacts box at the bottom of the form.

> **note** Although you can remove the contact association in a task, doing so removes the task from the contact's Activities tab only if the task is assigned to someone other than the linked contact. If the contact owns the task, the task continues to be listed on the Activities tab even after the task is marked as completed.

Assigning Categories to Contacts

A *category* is a keyword or a phrase that helps you keep track of items so that you can easily find, sort, filter, or group them. Use categories to keep track of different types of items that are related but stored in different folders. For example, you can keep track of all the meetings, contacts, and messages for a specific project when you create a category named after the project and assign items to it.

Categories also give you a way to keep track of contacts without putting them in separate folders. For example, you can keep business and personal contacts in the same contacts folder and use the Business and Personal categories to sort the two sets of contacts into separate groups.

One quick way to assign categories to a contact is to right-click the contact item and choose Categories. Then, in the Categories dialog box, you can select the check boxes next to the categories you want to assign to the contact. Alternatively, you can open the contact item and click the Categories button on the contact form to open the Categories dialog box. This dialog box is useful not only for assigning categories but also for reviewing the categories you've already assigned to an item.

> For more information about how to assign a category to a contact; how to use categories to sort, filter, and group contact items; and how to create your own categories, see Chapter 4, "Using Categories and Types."

Resolving Duplicate Contacts

If you create a contact entry using the same name or e-mail address as an entry that already exists in your Contacts folder, Outlook displays a dialog box in which you can choose to either add the new contact entry or update your existing entry with the new information (see Figure 14-10 on the next page).

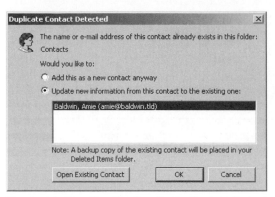

Figure 14-10. Use the Duplicate Contact Detected dialog box to tell Outlook how to handle the duplicate contact.

If you select the first option, Outlook adds the new contact to your Contacts folder, and you'll now have two entries listed under the same name or e-mail address. In that case, you'll probably want to add some additional information to the contact forms—perhaps company affiliation or a middle initial—to distinguish the two entries.

If you select the second option, to update the existing entry with information from the new one, Outlook compares the fields containing data in both entries and copies the data from the new entry into any fields that have conflicting data. For example, if you have a contact named Amie Baldwin whose phone number is 555-5655, and you create a new contact entry for Amie Baldwin with a new phone number, Outlook copies the new number into the existing entry and leaves the other fields the same.

Not all data is simply copied, however. Outlook does not copy any categories you've assigned to the new entry or any text that appears in the message box of the new entry. If you want to copy data from these fields from a new entry into an existing entry, you must copy them manually. Likewise, if you've added links to items other than contacts on the Activities tab of the new contact form (links to tasks or appointments, for example), Outlook does not copy them. Certificates and links to contacts on the Activities tab are copied from the new entry and added to the existing entry without replacing the original information.

In case you need to revert to the information in the original contact entry, a copy of the original entry is stored in your Deleted Items folder whenever Outlook copies new data.

> **note** If you are adding many contacts, Outlook can save the information faster if you do not require the program to detect duplicates. To turn off duplicate detection, choose Tools, Options. Click Contact Options, and clear the Check For Duplicate Contacts check box.

Phoning a Contact

If you have a modem, you can use Outlook to dial any phone number you specify, including phone numbers for contacts in your contacts list. Before Outlook can make phone calls for you, however, you must set up your computer and a modem for automatic phone dialing.

To set up automatic dialing, follow these steps:

1 Install a modem through Control Panel, and verify that the modem works. (Dial your Internet service provider or use the Phone Dialer application on the Accessories menu to dial a number.)

2 Open the Phone And Modem Options icon in Control Panel, and use the Dialing Rules tab to specify your area code and other dialing properties so that Outlook will know how to dial the phone numbers (what number to dial for an outside line, whether to use a credit card to dial, and other dialing properties).

To make a phone call to a contact using Outlook, follow these steps:

1 Open the Contacts folder.

2 Right-click a contact item and choose Call Contact to open the New Call dialog box with the contact's phone number already entered (see Figure 14-11).

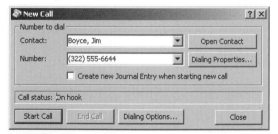

Figure 14-11.   Select the number to call and other options in the New Call dialog box.

■ If you want Outlook to use a phone number associated with a different contact, type the contact's name in the Contact box and press Tab or click in the Number box. Alternatively, you can simply enter the phone number in the Number box.

■ If the contact entry for the person you're calling already includes phone numbers, select the phone number in the Number box. If the contact entry doesn't specify a phone number, type the number in the Number box.

3   To keep a record of the call in the journal, select the Create New Journal Entry When Starting New Call check box. If you select this check box, a journal entry opens with the timer running after you start the call. You can type notes in the text box of the journal entry while you talk.

4   Click Start Call.

5   Pick up the phone handset and click Talk.

6   If you created a journal entry for the call, click Pause Timer to stop the clock when you've finished the call. Then click Save And Close.

7   Click End Call and hang up the phone.

---

tip   **Keep track of phone calls**

If you want to time a call and type notes in Outlook while you talk, you can create a journal entry for the call as you dial. The journal entry form contains a timer that you can start and stop and also provides space to type notes. For example, you might want to use this option if you bill clients for time spent on phone conversations. For more information about using the journal for phone calls, see Chapter 17, "Keeping a Journal."

---

note   If you omit the country code and area code from a phone number, the automatic phone dialer uses settings from the Dialing Properties dialog box, which you can access through the Phone And Modem icon in Control Panel or by clicking Dialing Properties in the New Call dialog box. If you include letters in the phone number, the automatic phone dialer does not recognize them.

Setting Up Speed Dial Entries

If you make frequent calls to particular phone numbers, you can create a speed dial list of those phone numbers and quickly make calls from the list. Before you become enamored of the idea of Outlook's speed dialing feature, however, you should understand that it suffers from a bug that renders it only moderately useful. Although you can add names and numbers to the speed dial list, Outlook keeps only the numbers and loses the names. If you remember who a particular number belongs to, this isn't a problem. But if you have more than a few numbers on the list, the speed dial feature won't do you much good.

Follow these steps to create entries in the speed dial list:

1   Open the Contacts folder and choose Actions, Call Contact, New Call to open the New Call dialog box.

2 Click Dialing Options to display the Dialing Options dialog box (see Figure 14-12).

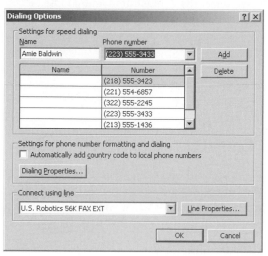

Figure 14-12. Use the Dialing Options dialog box to add speed dial numbers.

3 If the person's contact information is stored in the Contacts folder, type the name in the Name box and press Tab to move to the Phone Number box, where Outlook automatically fills in the phone number from the contact entry. If you need to use a different number, select it from the drop-down list or type the number in the Phone Number box.

4 Click Add to add the entry to the speed dial list.

5 Repeat these steps to add other numbers as needed and then click OK.

6 Click Close to close the New Call dialog box.

Redialing Recently Dialed Numbers

In addition to using the speed dial list, you also can select a phone number from a list of numbers you've recently dialed. To do so, choose Actions, Call Contact, Redial and select the number you want to dial from the menu.

Sending an E-Mail Message to a Contact

If you're working in the Contacts folder, you can send an e-mail message to one of your contacts without switching to the Inbox folder. This is a handy feature that can save a lot of time over an average work day.

Here's how to send a message from the Contacts folder:

1 In the Contacts folder, select the contact item and choose Actions, New Message To Contact. Or simply right-click the contact and choose New Message To Contact.

2 In the Subject box, type the subject of the message.

3 In the message body, type the message.

4 Click Send.

Sending a Letter to a Contact

Although it's a digital world, you still occasionally need to send a paper letter through the mail. But you can use Outlook technology to make it easier. Rather than retyping a contact's information in a Word document when you need to write a letter, use the data from the Contacts folder and let Outlook enter that data for you.

Follow these steps to use contact information in a Word letter:

1 Open the Contacts folder.

2 Select the contact item for the person to whom you're writing the letter.

3 Choose Actions, New Letter To Contact.

4 Follow the instructions in the Letter Wizard in Word to create the letter.

Connecting to a Contact's Web Site

It seems everyone has a Web site these days, whether it's the company site or a collection of family photos. If you have the URL for a contact's Web page recorded in the contact entry, you can connect to that site directly from Outlook. This is particularly handy for linking to business sites from a company contact entry—for example, you might create a link to the company's support or sales page. Associating Web sites with contacts is often more meaningful than simply storing a URL in your Favorites folder.

With the Contacts folder and the contact item open, you can connect to the contact's Web site by performing one of the following actions:

● Choose Actions, Explore Web Page.

● Press Ctrl+Shift+X.

● Click the hyperlink that appears in the Web Page Address box in the contact entry.

Scheduling Appointments and Meetings with Contacts

Many Outlook users believe that the Calendar folder is the only place you can easily schedule a new appointment or meeting, but that's not the case. You can schedule an appointment or a meeting in any Outlook folder. The Contacts folder, however, is a logical place to create new appointments and meetings because those events are often associated with one or more contacts stored in the Contacts folder.

Scheduling an Appointment with a Contact

In Outlook, an appointment involves only your schedule and time, whereas a meeting involves inviting others and coordinating their schedules. Also, when you set up a meeting, Outlook generates a meeting request, which it doesn't do for an appointment. In most other respects, appointments and meetings are the same.

Although you can schedule an appointment in the Calendar folder, you might prefer to schedule it from the Contacts folder instead. The primary advantage is that you don't have to leave the Contacts folder to create the appointment. Outlook automatically adds the contact to the Contacts box on the appointment form.

To schedule an appointment with one of your contacts, follow these steps:

1 In the Contacts folder, open the contact item for the person with whom you want to schedule the appointment and choose Actions, New Appointment With Contact. Or simply right-click the contact and choose New Appointment With Contact.

2 Enter any applicable information on the appointment form such as subject, location, or time.

3 Click Save And Close to create the appointment.

> **note** Using this method to schedule an appointment with a contact places the appointment on your calendar. It does not notify the contact of the appointment.

> For details about setting up appointments, see Chapter 18, "Scheduling Appointments."

Scheduling a Meeting with a Contact

As mentioned previously, meetings differ from appointments in that they are collaborative efforts that involve the schedules of all the attendees. When you set up a meeting, Outlook creates and sends meeting requests to the individuals you want to invite. You can create meeting requests for any number of contacts through the Contacts folder, saving the time of switching folders.

To send a meeting request to one or more of your contacts from the Contacts folder, follow these steps:

1. Open the Contacts folder and select the contact entries for those people you want to invite to the meeting. (To select multiple entries, hold down the Ctrl key and click the entries.)

2. Choose Actions, New Meeting Request To Contact.

3. In the Subject box, type a description of the proposed meeting.

4. In the Location box, enter the location.

5. Enter the proposed start and end times for the meeting.

6. Select any other options you want.

7. Click Send.

> For details about setting up meetings and sending meeting requests, see Chapter 19, "Scheduling Meetings and Resources."

Assigning a Task to a Contact

The Tasks folder in Outlook offers a handy way to keep track of your work as well as the work you delegate to others. For example, if you manage a group of people, you probably use the Tasks folder to assign tasks to the people who work for you. But if you need to assign a job to one of your contacts, you can do this directly from the Contacts folder. Doing so adds the contact's name to the Contacts box in the task request.

Follow these steps to assign a task to a contact:

1. In the Contacts folder, open the contact item and then choose Actions, New Task For Contact. Or simply right-click the contact and choose New Task For Contact.

2. Outlook opens a new task form. Enter the subject and other information about the task and then click Assign Task. Outlook adds the contact's e-mail address in the To box.

3. Click Send to send the task request.

Flagging a Contact for Follow-Up

You can flag a contact item for follow-up to have Outlook remind you to call or e-mail the contact. For example, suppose that you want to make a note to yourself to call a colleague at 10:00 A. M. tomorrow to ask about the status of a project. You could create

Chapter 14: Managing Your Contacts

a note in the Notes folder, create a task, or add an appointment to your schedule—but an easy way to create the reminder is to add a follow-up flag to the contact entry in the Contacts folder.

Flagging a contact item adds an additional field to the contact data. The flag appears in the contacts list (see Figure 14-13) and shows up as a message on the contact form (see Figure 14-14). You can also organize the view in the Contacts folder to show contacts sorted by flag: choose View, Current View, By Follow-Up Flag.

Follow-up flag

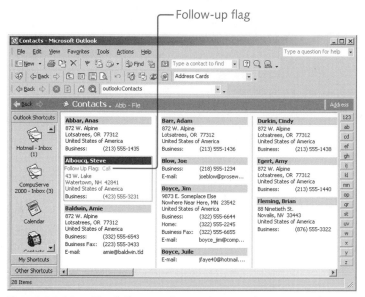

Figure 14-13. The follow-up flag appears in the contacts list.

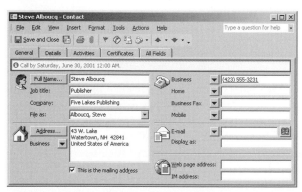

Figure 14-14. Outlook displays a message on the contact form indicating that a follow-up is needed for the contact.

If you specify a particular date and time for follow-up when you add the flag, Outlook generates a reminder at the appointed time. Adding a reminder helps ensure that you don't forget to follow up with the contact and ensures that you do it at the appropriate time.

Follow these steps to flag a contact for follow-up:

1 In the Contacts folder, select the contact item you want to flag and choose Actions, Follow Up. Or right-click the contact and choose Follow Up.

2 In the Flag To box of the dialog box (see Figure 14-15), select the type of flag you want Outlook to use or type your own.

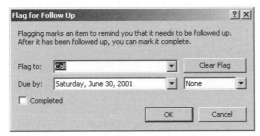

Figure 14-15. Use the Flag For Follow Up dialog box to specify the flag text and set an optional reminder.

3 Enter a date in the Due By box, and select a time in the drop-down list if you want Outlook to generate a reminder for the follow-up.

4 Click OK. Outlook adds the flag text to the contact item, as shown in Figure 14-13.

> **tip** You can flag a contact item in any view by right-clicking it and choosing Follow Up.

When you have completed your follow-up action, you can remove the flag from the contact item (clear the flag) or mark the follow-up as completed. If you clear the flag, Outlook removes it from the contact item. If you prefer to have the flag remain, you can mark the follow-up as completed. In this case, the flag remains but the contact form includes a message indicating that the follow-up was accomplished (and the date). When you choose View, Current View, By Follow-Up Flag to view the Contacts folder sorted by flag, the completed items are grouped together.

Use one of the following methods to mark a follow-up flag as completed:

● Select the flagged contact item, choose Actions, Follow Up, and select the Completed check box.

● Right-click the contact item and choose Flag Complete.

Use one of the following methods to clear a flag, which removes it from the contact item:

- Right-click the contact item in the Contacts folder and choose Clear Flag.

- Select the contact item, choose Actions, Follow Up, and click Clear Flag in the Flag For Follow Up dialog box.

Finding Contacts

If you store only a small list of contacts, finding a particular one is usually not a problem. As the number of contacts grows, however, it becomes more and more difficult to locate information, especially if you aren't sure about a name. For example, you might remember that a person works for a certain company but can't recall the person's name. Outlook provides a handful of features to help you quickly and easily locate contact information.

Perhaps the easiest method of locating a contact if you know the name is to type the name in the Find A Contact box on Outlook's Standard toolbar and then press Enter. Outlook locates the contact and displays the contact form. If more than one contact matches the data you've entered, Outlook displays a dialog box listing all the matches to allow you to select the appropriate one (see Figure 14-16).

Figure 14-16. Use the Choose Contact dialog box to select the correct contact after a search.

You also can choose Tools, Find to open a Find Bar above the Contacts folder, as shown in Figure 14-17 on the next page. You can use this Find Bar to locate other information in addition to contacts (such as e-mail messages or tasks).

> **tip** Choose Tools, Find a second time to close the Find Bar.

Finally, if you need to perform an advanced search, choose Tools, Advanced Find to open the Advanced Find dialog box (see Figure 14-18 on the next page). You can use this dialog box to perform more complex searches based on multiple conditions, such as searching for both name and company.

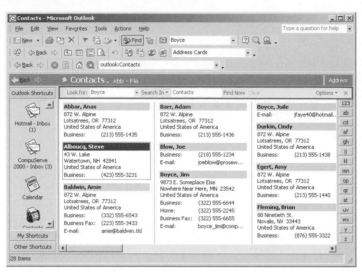

Figure 14-17. Use the Find Bar to locate contacts and other information in Outlook.

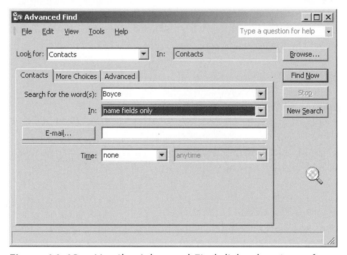

Figure 14-18. Use the Advanced Find dialog box to perform more complex searches using multiple conditions.

> For a detailed discussion of how to perform both simple and complex searches in Outlook, see Chapter 29, "Finding and Organizing Data."

Viewing Contacts

Outlook provides predefined views for reviewing your contacts list in the Contacts folder. For example, Address Cards view displays names and addresses of contacts in blocks that look like address labels. This view is a convenient way to look up a contact's mailing address. In Phone List view, Outlook displays contact entries in table rows with details such as phone, job title, and department name in columns. This view is helpful for quickly finding a contact's phone number or job title. You can customize the various standard views to control the amount of detail or to help you organize and analyze information.

Using Standard Views in the Contacts Folder

The Contacts folder offers seven standard formats for viewing contacts. To change views, choose View, Current View and select the view you want to use. Two of the standard formats are card views and five are table views, as described in the following list:

- **Address Cards.** This view (the default) displays contact entries as individual cards with name, one mailing address, and business and home phone numbers.

- **Detailed Address Cards.** This view also displays individual cards, which show name, business and home addresses, phone numbers, and additional details such as job title, company, and Web address.

- **Phone List.** This table view displays a list with the contact's name, the company name, business phone number, business fax number, home phone number, mobile phone number, categories, and a check box to enable or disable journaling for the contact.

- **By Category.** This view groups contacts by their assigned categories.

- **By Company.** This view groups contacts by company, which is helpful when you're trying to find a contact who works for a particular company.

- **By Location.** This view groups contacts by country or region.

- **By Follow-Up Flag.** In this view, you can easily locate all the contact entries that are flagged for follow-up. Outlook groups them together and also shows the due date for follow-up action.

> **tip** You can easily resize address cards by dragging the vertical dividing line between cards. This changes the width of all card columns.

Customizing the Contacts View

The methods of customizing the view in Outlook folders are generally the same for all folders. This section examines a handful of specific ways you might customize the Contacts folder to make it easier to locate and work with contacts. For example, you might have Outlook use a specific color for contacts who work for a particular company.

You can also change the fonts used for the card headings and body, specify card width and height, and have Outlook automatically format contact entries based on rules.

> For more details about customizing views (applicable to the Contacts folder), see "Customizing the Inbox View," page 63. In addition, Chapter 24, "Creating Custom Views and Print Styles," covers additional ways to customize views.

Filtering the Contacts View

You can filter the view in the Contacts folder to show only those contacts that meet the conditions you specify in the filter. For example, you can use a filter to view only those contacts who work for a particular company or who live in a particular city.

Follow these steps to set up a view filter in the Contacts folder:

1 Open the Contacts folder and choose View, Current View, Customize Current View.

2 Click Filter in the View Summary dialog box.

3 In the Filter dialog box, specify the conditions for the filter. If you don't see the items you need to specify for the condition, use the Field drop-down list on the Advanced tab to select the necessary field.

4 Click OK to close the Filter dialog box, and then click OK in the View Summary dialog box to apply the filter.

When you want to view the entire contents of the folder again, you can remove the filter, as detailed here:

1 Choose View, Current View, Customize Current View.

2 Click Filter.

3 In the Filter dialog box, click Clear All and then click OK.

4 Click OK to close the View Summary dialog box.

Configuring Fonts and Card Dimensions

You can change the font Outlook uses for card headings and the card body text in the card views (Address Cards view and Detailed Address Cards view). You can also change the font style, size, and script, but not the color.

Follow these steps to change the font for card headings and body test:

1 Choose View, Current View, Customize Current View.

2 In the View Summary dialog box, click Other Settings to display the Format Card View dialog box (see Figure 14-19).

Figure 14-19. Use the Format Card View dialog box to specify the font for card headings and body text.

3 Click Font in the Card Headings or Card Body areas of the dialog box to open a standard Font dialog box in which you can select font characteristics.

4 Make your font selections and click OK in the Font dialog box.

5 Specify options according to the following list and then click OK:

- **Allow In-Cell Editing.** Selecting this check box allows you to modify contact data by clicking a field in the view without opening the contact form.

- **Show Empty Fields.** Select this check box if you want Outlook to show all fields for all contacts, even if the fields are empty. Clear this option to simplify the view of your Contacts folder. Note that when this option is selected, Outlook displays all fields defined for the view, not all contact fields.

- **Card Width.** Set the card width (in number of characters) using this option.

- **Multi-Line Field Height.** Use this option to specify the number of lines you want Outlook to display on the card for multiline fields.

6 Click OK to close the View Summary dialog box.

Using Automatic Formatting

Outlook performs some limited automatic formatting of data in the Contacts folder. For example, it uses bold for distribution list items, regular font for unread contacts, and red for overdue contacts (contact entries with an overdue follow-up flag).

You can make changes to these automatic formatting rules, and you can even create your own rules. For example, you might want to display overdue contacts in blue rather than in red, or you might want to use a particular color for all contacts who work for a certain company.

Follow these steps to modify an existing rule or create a new one:

1 In Outlook, open the Contacts folder and choose View, Current View, Customize Current View.

2 Click Automatic Formatting in the View Summary dialog box to display the Automatic Formatting dialog box, shown in Figure 14-20.

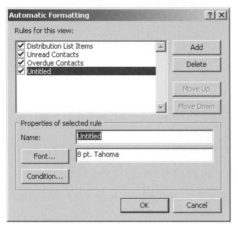

Figure 14-20. Use the Automatic Formatting dialog box to create custom rules that control how Outlook displays contacts.

3 If you want to modify an existing rule, select the rule and click Font to change the font characteristics or click Condition to modify the condition for the rule (see step 5).

> **note** You can modify a rule condition only for rules that you have created. You cannot change the condition for the three predefined rules.

4 Click Add if you want to add a new rule. Outlook creates a new rule named Untitled, as shown in Figure 14-20.

5 Type a new name in the Name field, click Font and specify font characteristics, and then click Condition to open the Filter dialog box, shown in Figure 14-21.

6 Specify the criteria to define the rule condition. For example, click Advanced, click Field, click Frequently Used Fields, and click Company. Then select Contains in the Condition drop-down list and type a company name in the Value box. This causes Outlook to automatically format all contacts from the specified company using the font properties you specify in the next step.

7 Click OK to close the Filter dialog box, Click Font in the Automatic Formatting dialog box, specify the font properties, and click OK.

8 Close the Automatic Formatting and View Summary dialog boxes to view the effects of the new rule.

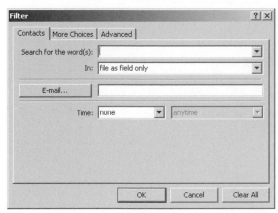

Figure 14-21. You can specify complex conditions using the Filter dialog box.

> **note** Automatic formatting rules follow the hierarchy in the list shown in the Automatic Formatting dialog box. Use the Move Up and Move Down buttons to change the order of rules in the lists and thereby change the order in which they are applied.

Printing Contacts

As an experienced user of Microsoft Windows, you probably need little if any explanation of how to print. So rather than focusing on basic printing commands, this section offers some insight into why you might print from the Contacts folder and what your options are when you do print.

Why print? If you're like most people, you probably try to work from your computer as much as possible and reduce the amount of paper you generate. The completely paperless office is still a distant goal for most people, however, and there will be times when you want to print your contacts list. For example, you might need to take a copy of your contacts with you on a business trip, but you don't have a notebook computer. A hard copy of your contacts is the solution.

Outlook supports several predefined paper types that allow you to print contact information using various formats, including preprinted sheets for several popular day planners. You can print a single contact entry, a selection of entries, or all entries. To print a selection (one or more), first select the contact entries to print by holding down the Ctrl key and clicking each one. If you want to print all contacts, choose Edit, Select All. Then choose File, Print to open the Print dialog box (see Figure 14-22).

In the Print Style area of the Print dialog box, you can select one of five print styles, each of which results in a different printed layout. You can use the styles as listed, modify them, or create new styles. To modify an existing style, select the style and click Page Setup to display the Page Setup dialog box, which resembles the one shown in Figure 14-23.

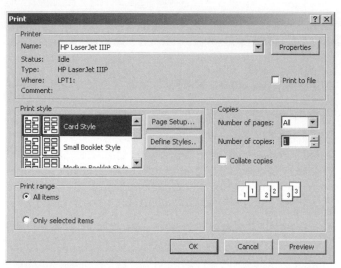

Figure 14-22. You can select several predefined styles from the Print dialog box.

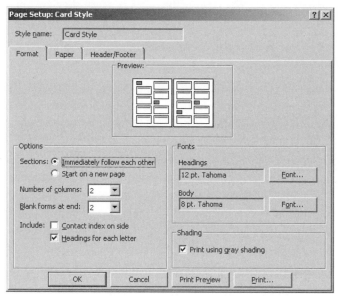

Figure 14-23. Modify a print style in the Page Setup dialog box.

Use the Format tab of this dialog box to specify fonts and shading and to set options such as printing a contact index on the side of each page, adding headings for each letter, and setting the number of columns. Use the Paper tab to select the type of paper, such as a preprinted sheet for your day planner, as well as to set up margins, paper source, and orientation. Use the Header/Footer page to add a header, a footer, or both to the printout.

If you need a custom layout but don't want to modify the existing styles, you can create your own style. In the Print dialog box, click Define Styles to display the Define Print Styles dialog box (see Figure 14-24). Select a style to use as the basis for your new style, and click Copy to open the Page Setup dialog box. Modify settings as needed and click OK to save the new style. Outlook uses the same name but prefixes the name with Copy Of—Copy Of Card Style, for example. You can change the name in the Style Name box in the Page Setup dialog box.

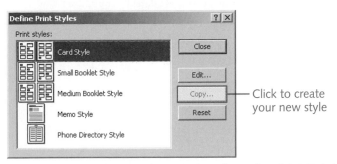

Click to create your new style

Figure 14-24. Select a style to copy in the Define Print Styles dialog box.

> For a detailed discussion of printing in Outlook and creating custom print styles, see "Printing in Outlook," page 645.

Working with Distribution Lists

A distribution list is a collection of contacts. It provides an easy way to send messages to a group of people. For example, if you frequently send messages to the marketing team, you can create a distribution list called Marketing Team that contains the names of all members of this team. A message sent to this distribution list goes to all recipients who belong to the distribution list. Outlook converts the address list to individual addresses, so recipients see their own names and the names of all other recipients in the To box of the message instead of seeing the name of the distribution list. You can use distribution lists in messages, task requests, and meeting requests.

> **tip** **Use nested distribution lists**
>
> Distribution lists can contain other distribution lists as well as individual addresses. For example, you might create a distribution list for each of seven departments and then create one distribution list containing those seven others. You could use this second list when you need to send messages to all seven departments.

You can create distribution lists in your Contacts folder using your contacts list. You also can create distribution lists in a personal address book, which is separate from your Contacts folder and stored in a PAB file. You can have one PAB per profile but any number of contacts folders. There is essentially no difference between distribution lists in PABs and contacts folders. You can store addresses from any available source (the Global Address List, a personal address book, contacts list, and so on). In general, you should create your distribution lists in the location where you store the majority of your addresses. This chapter assumes that you're creating distribution lists in your Contacts folder.

> For details on creating distribution lists in a personal address book and working with address books, see "Using Distribution Lists," page 135.

Creating a Personal Distribution List

As mentioned previously, you can create a distribution list either in a personal address book or in your Contacts folder.

Follow these steps to create a new distribution list in the Contacts folder:

1 In Outlook, choose File, New, Distribution List to open a distribution list form similar to the one shown in Figure 14-25.

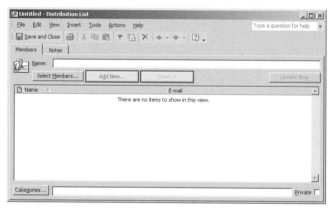

Figure 14-25. Add and remove members for a distribution list on the distribution list form.

2 Type the name of the list in the Name box. This is the name by which the list will appear in your Contacts folder. If you're creating a distribution list for the marketing department, for example, use the name Marketing.

3 Click Select Members to open the Select Members dialog box (see Figure 14-26).

4 In the drop-down list, select the location from which you want to select addresses (the Global Address List or the Contacts folder, for example).

5 In the Type Name Or Select From List box, type a name you want to include, which locates the name in the list. Or select the name in the Name list. Then click Members.

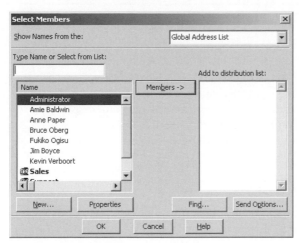

Figure 14-26. Use the Select Members dialog box to select addresses to include in the list.

6 Repeat step 4 to add all addresses to the list and then click OK when finished.

7 If you want to add a longer description of the distribution list, click the Notes tab and type the text.

8 Click Save And Close.

Adding or Deleting Names in a Distribution List

You can easily add and delete names from a distribution list. For example, assume that your department has added a few new employees and you need to add their addresses to the department distribution list.

Follow these steps to add or remove names from a distribution list:

1 In your Contacts folder, open the distribution list to display the distribution list form.

2 Perform one or more of the following actions:

- To add an address from an address book or a contacts folder, click Select Members.

- To add an address that is not in a contacts folder or an address book, click Add New.

- To delete a name, click the name and then click Remove.

3 Click Save And Close.

> **tip** **Fine-tuning distribution lists**
>
> You can assign categories to a distribution list, mark it as private, or add notes to it by using the distribution list form. Also, you can update addresses in a distribution list if their source addresses have changed. For example, if you've changed a colleague's e-mail address in the contact entry and now want to update the corresponding address in the distribution list, you can open the distribution list, select the address, and click Update Now on the distribution list form.

Sharing Contacts

Outlook lets you share contacts with others by sending vCards via e-mail or by sharing a contacts folder. The former method lets you share contacts with people who don't use Outlook or who don't have access to your network or Exchange Server to be able to share your Contacts folder. The latter method—sharing your Contacts folder—is a good solution when you need to provide access to contacts for others on your network. This chapter explains how to share contacts through vCards and offers a brief overview of sharing the Contacts folders.

> For a complete discussion of sharing Outlook folders, using public folders, and other methods of sharing data with other Outlook users, see Chapter 34, "Sharing Information with Others."

Sharing Your Contacts Folders

If you are running Outlook with Exchange Server, you can assign permissions to a folder stored in your Exchange Server mailbox to give other users access to that folder. You can grant permissions on a group basis or a per-user basis. Outlook provides two groups by default—Anonymous and Default—that you can use to assign permissions on a global basis. You also can add individual users to the permissions list as well as use distribution lists to assign permissions.

Follow these steps to set permissions on your Contacts folder to allow other users access to your contacts:

1 Open the folder list, right-click the Contacts folder, and choose Properties on the shortcut menu to display the Properties dialog box for the folder. You also can right-click the Contacts folder on the Outlook Bar and choose Properties to open the dialog box.

2 Click the Permissions tab (see Figure 14-27).

3 Click Add to display the Add Users dialog box.

Chapter 14: Managing Your Contacts

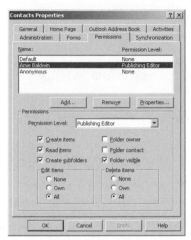

Figure 14-27. Configure permissions on the Permissions tab.

4 Select the person for whom you want to configure permissions and click Add. Then click OK to return to the Permissions tab.

5 In the Name box, click the name of the person you just added.

6 In the Permission Level drop-down list, select a level of permission according to the tasks the user should be able to do with your Contacts folder. When you select a permission level, Outlook selects one or more individual permissions in the Permissions area. You also can select or clear individual permissions as needed.

7 Click OK to save the permission changes.

You can grant several permissions for a folder, and you can assign them in any combination you need. For example, you should select the Folder Visible and Read Items permissions if you want someone to be able to view the contacts but not modify them or add new ones. Add the Create Items permission if you want the user to be able to add new contact items. Use the Edit Items and Delete Items groups of options to specify whether the user can edit existing or delete existing items.

For a complete explanation of permissions and folder sharing, see "Granting Access to Private Folders," page 687.

Sharing Contacts with vCards

A vCard presents contact information as an electronic business card that can be sent via e-mail. vCards are based on an open standard, allowing any application that supports vCards to share contact information. In addition to sending a vCard as an attachment, you also can include it with your message signature.

When you receive a message with a vCard attached, a paper clip icon appears in the preview pane to indicate the attachment. Use one of the following methods to add the data in the vCard as a contact entry:

- From the preview pane, select the paper clip icon and click the filename that appears.

- If you've opened the message, right-click the business card icon in the message and click Open.

After you can view the information sent in the vCard, click Save And Close to add the information to your contacts list.

> **tip** You can drag a vCard from a message to your Contacts folder to add the contact information.

Creating a vCard from a Contact Entry

As mentioned previously, one way to send contact information to someone else is to attach the contact entry to a message as a vCard. You can use this method to share your own contact information or to share one or more other contact entries with another person.

Follow these steps to attach a vCard to a message:

1 In the Contacts folder, select the contact item you want to send as a vCard.

2 Choose Actions, Forward As vCard. Outlook opens a new message form with the contact entry attached as a vCard.

3 Specify an address, complete the message as you would any other, and then click Send to send it.

Including a vCard with Your Signature

The second method of sharing a contact is useful when you want to share your own contact information. Rather than attaching it to a message, you can have Outlook send it along with your message signature. This ensures that the vCard is sent with all outgoing messages.

> You can attach text (such as a favorite quote) and graphics to each outgoing message as part of your signature. For complete details on using signatures with Outlook, see "Using Signatures," page 215.

Follow these steps to add your contact information as a vCard to your message signature:

1 Create your own contact entry if you have not already done so.

2 Choose Tools, Options.

3 On the Mail Format tab, click Signatures.

4 Click New.

5 Enter a name for your signature.

6 Select Start With A Blank Signature.

7 Click Next.

8 In the Edit Signature dialog box (see Figure 14-28), click New vCard From Contact.

Type in your text here

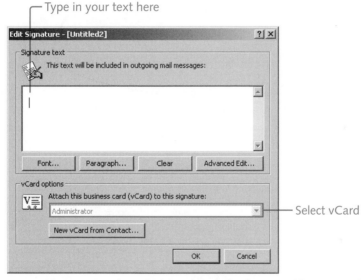

Select vCard

Figure 14-28. Use the Edit Signature dialog box to add text, graphics, and a vCard to your outgoing messages automatically.

9 In the Select Contacts To Export As vCards dialog box, select your name from the contact list, click Add, and then click OK.

10 Click Finish and then click OK twice.

From now on, your contact information will be attached to outgoing messages.

---

tip **Turn off signatures**

To prevent signatures from being added to your outgoing messages, choose Tools, Options and click the Mail Format tab. Select None in the Signature For New Messages drop-down list.

Saving a Contact Entry as a vCard

In addition to sending vCards as e-mail attachments, Outlook allows you to save a contact entry to a file as a vCard. You might do this if you want to link to vCards on a Web site so that others can download the vCards directly rather than receiving a message with the vCards attached. Or perhaps you want to save a large number of contacts as vCards and send them to someone via a Zip disk or other removable media rather than through e-mail.

Follow these steps to save a contact item as a vCard file:

1 In Outlook, open the contact item you want to save as a vCard.

2 Choose File, Export To vCard File.

3 Type a name in the File Name box and then click Save

Saving a vCard Attachment to Your Contacts Folder

When you receive a message containing a vCard attachment, you'll probably want to save the vCard as a contact item in your Contacts folder.

Follow these steps to save a vCard attachment as a contact item:

1 Open the message containing the attached vCard.

2 Double-click the attachment to open it.

3 In the open contact form, click Save And Close. The information in the vCard is saved to your Contacts folder by default.

Setting Contact Options

Outlook provides a handful of options that control how it stores and displays contacts. To view these options, choose Tools, Options and click Contact Options on the Preferences tab. In the Contact Options dialog box (see Figure 14-29), configure the options on the facing page.

Figure 14-29. Configure options for contacts in the Contact Options dialog box.

- **Default "Full Name" Order.**   This option specifies how Outlook creates the Full Name field when you click Full Name in the new contact form and enter the contact's first, middle, and last names, along with suffix and title.

- **Default "File As" Order.**   This option specifies the name Outlook creates in the card title. Outlook uses the information you specify for first, middle, and last name—as well as company—to create the card title based on how this option is set.

- **Check For Duplicate Contacts.**   Select this option if you want Outlook to check for duplicate contacts when you create new contacts.

Chapter 15

Using LDAP Directory Services

Lightweight Directory Acces s Protocol (LDAP) is a standard for querying directory services. For example, you can query LDAP servers for the address, phone number, or other information associated with an entry in the directory. Microsoft Windows 2000 Server uses LDAP as the primary mechanism for searching the Active Directory (AD). Microsoft Exchange Servers also can act as LDAP servers, allowing users to look up addresses and associated information in the directory.

This chapter explores LDAP and explains how to configure LDAP directory service accounts in Microsoft Outlook and Microsoft Outlook Express. The last section of the chapter explains how to configure your own LDAP server using Exchange Server 5.*x* and Exchange 2000 Server.

Overview of LDAP Services

LDAP was designed to serve with less overhead and fewer resource requirements than its predecessor, the Directory Access Protocol, which was developed for X.500. LDAP is a standards-based protocol that allows clients to query data in a directory service over a TCP connection. Microsoft's Active Directory and other directory services on the Internet such as Bigfoot, InfoSpace, and Yahoo! employ LDAP to implement searches of their databases.

> **note** For additional information regarding LDAP, refer to "MS Strategy for Lightweight Directory Access Protocol (LDAP)," available in the NT Server Technical Notes section of Microsoft TechNet or on the Web at *http://www.microsoft.com/ TechNet/winnt/Winntas/technote/ldapcmr.asp*.

newfeature!

Configuring a Directory Service Account in Outlook

In addition to supporting e-mail accounts, Outlook 2002 also allows you to add LDAP-based directory service accounts to query for subscriber information in the remote server's directory. The LDAP server might be internal to your organization, might be hosted by another company, or might be one of several LDAP directories located on the Internet. With an LDAP account in your profile, you can look up names, addresses, and other information stored in the directory.

To set up and configure an LDAP account in Outlook, follow these steps:

1 Right-click the Outlook icon on the desktop and choose Properties. Then click E-Mail Settings (and select the profile if necessary). Alternatively, if Outlook is already open, choose Tools, E-Mail Accounts.

2 Select Add A New Directory Or Address Book in the E-Mail Accounts Wizard and click Next.

3 Select Internet Directory Service (LDAP) and click Next.

4 On the Directory Service (LDAP) Settings page of the wizard (see Figure 15-1), type the server name or the IP address in the Server Name box.

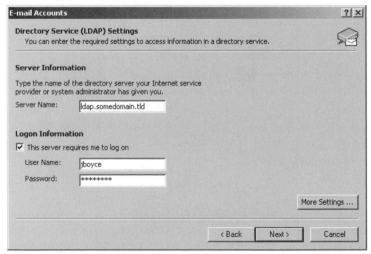

Figure 15-1. Specify the server name, and supply logon credentials if the server requires authentication.

5 If the server requires authentication, select the check box This Server Requires Me To Log On. Specify the logon credentials in the User Name and Password boxes. If you're authenticating on a Windows NT or Windows 2000 domain controller, include the domain by entering **<domain>\<user>** in the User Name box, where *<domain>* is the domain name and *<user>* is the user account.

Chapter 15

6 Click More Settings to open the Microsoft LDAP Directory dialog box, shown in Figure 15-2.

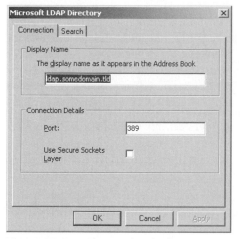

Figure 15-2. Change the display name, port, and other properties as needed.

7 Change the name in the Display Name box to the name you want Outlook to display in the address book for the directory service.

8 In the Port box, type the port number required by the LDAP server. The default port is 389, although you can use 3268 for most searches in an Active Directory's global catalog.

---

tip **Use two ports**

Port 3268 is the default port for the Active Directory global catalog. Certain types of data are available through one specific port, while other types of data are accessed through the other. For example, read-only copies of data from other domains are available only through the global catalog port. For that reason, you might create two directory services, one for each port. For details, see "Configuring an LDAP Server" page 429.

---

9 You can select the User Secure Sockets Layer (SSL) option to connect to the LDAP server through SSL. In most cases, SSL won't be required. This option works only if the server allows an SSL connection.

10 In the Microsoft LDAP Directory dialog box, click the Search tab, shown in Figure 15-3 on the next page.

11 Specify the search timeout and the maximum number of entries you want returned in a search. In the Search Base box, type the root for your search in the directory. If you're searching the Active Directory, for example, you might enter **dc=<*domain*>,dc=<*suffix*>**, where <*domain*> is your domain name (without the domain suffix). Specify the domain suffix (*net, com, org,* for example) as the last data item.

12 Click OK to close the dialog box. Then click Next and click Finish to complete the account setup.

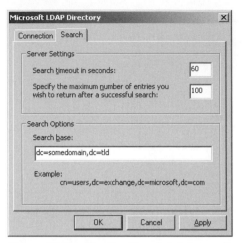

Figure 15-3. Use the Search tab to configure timeout, number of hits to return, and the search base.

> **note** Queries to the Active Directory using Secure Sockets Layer (SSL) should be directed to port 636. Global catalog queries using SSL should be directed to port 3269.

You can use the directory service accounts created in Outlook to perform LDAP queries from within Outlook. Outlook Express accounts can also be used for these types of searches. However, you can't use these accounts from the search/find feature of your operating system.

> **tip** You can make changes to a directory service account in Outlook and query using the new settings without having to restart Outlook.

Troubleshooting

Your LDAP query returns this error message: *There Are No Entries In The Directory Service That Match Your Search Criteria.*

Sooner or later, you'll attempt to query an LDAP server that you know contains at least one item meeting your search criteria—but you'll receive an error message telling you that no entries in the directory service match your criteria. One possible cause of this problem is that the search option specified at the LDAP server might be preventing the query from completing successfully. For example, you might be issuing an "any" query, but the server is configured to treat such queries as initial queries.

> For a detailed discussion of query types and how to configure the search option, see "Configuring Exchange Server 5.*x* LDAP Properties," page 430.

You might also receive this error message if you've incorrectly set LDAP directory service account properties—for example, you might have configured the account to use port 389 when the server requires SSL. Check your directory service account settings to ensure that you have specified the proper server name or address, port, and search base.

Configuring a Directory Service Account in Outlook Express

You can use Outlook Express as well as Outlook to perform LDAP searches. This capability can be handy when you're working on a system that does not have Outlook installed, such as a notebook computer that you use infrequently. You can access LDAP queries by using the Outlook Express address book or by using the search/find feature of your operating system.

> For an explanation of how to perform LDAP queries through your operating system, see "Searching from Windows," page 429.

To configure Outlook Express LDAP directory services, follow these steps:

1 In Outlook Express, choose Tools, Accounts.

2 In the Internet Accounts dialog box, click Directory Service to display the Directory Service tab (see Figure 15-4).

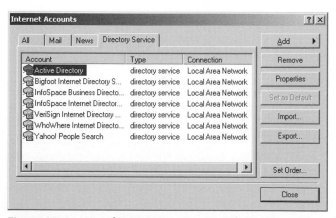

Figure 15-4. Use the Directory Service tab to view, add, and change directory service accounts.

3 Choose Add, Directory Service to start the Internet Connection Wizard.

4 In the Internet Directory (LDAP) Server box, type the DNS name or the IP address of the LDAP server. If the server requires authentication, select the option My LDAP Server Requires Me To Log On and click Next.

5 If you selected authentication, specify the account name and password for the directory server. If you're authenticating using a domain account outside your current domain, enter the account in the form *<domain>\<account>*. Specify the password and, if you're using Secure Password Authentication, select the option Log On Using Secure Password Authentication (SPA) and click Next.

6 The wizard asks whether you want to check addresses using this directory service. Choose Yes and click Next.

7 Click Finish to complete the account's setup.

8 On the Directory Service tab of the Internet Accounts dialog box, select the account you just created and click Properties to display the Properties dialog box for the account (see Figure 15-5).

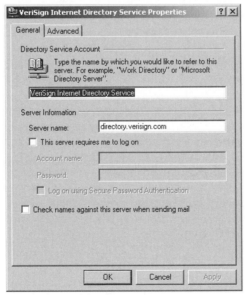

Figure 15-5. Use the General tab to specify name, server location, and other LDAP server properties.

9 Click Advanced. On the Advanced tab (see Figure 15-6), specify the port you want to use, the search timeout, and other properties. Click OK.

10 Close the Internet Accounts dialog box.

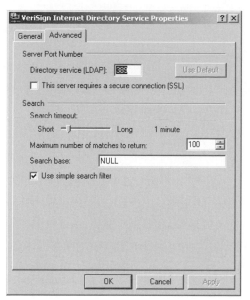

Figure 15-6. Use the Advanced tab to configure the port and other search properties.

Using LDAP to Find People

LDAP directory services that you create within Outlook can be searched through the Outlook Address Book only. Outlook Express comes preconfigured with several LDAP directory service accounts. You can query these directory services by using the Outlook Express address book or by using your operating system's search/find feature. The following sections explain the different ways you can perform LDAP queries through directory service accounts.

Searching from Outlook

You can perform LDAP queries in Outlook by using directory service accounts you add to Outlook. You can't search these directory service accounts outside Outlook, as you can with Outlook Express.

Follow these steps to perform an LDAP query with an LDAP server in Outlook:

1 In Outlook, click the Address Book icon to open the Address Book window. Alternatively, you can choose Tools, Address Book.

2 In the Outlook Address Book, choose the directory service from the Show Names drop-down list. Depending on how the directory service account is configured, Outlook might display the contents of the directory immediately in the address book.

427

Part 3: Contact Management

3 To search using specific criteria, click the Find Items button on the toolbar or choose Tools, Find. Either action opens the Find dialog box (see Figure 15-7).

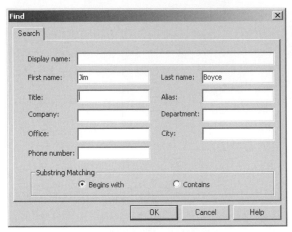

Figure 15-7. Use the Find dialog box to specify the criteria for the LDAP query.

4 Specify the criteria for the search and click OK.

Searching from Outlook Express

You can perform queries from within Outlook Express using LDAP directory service accounts you create in Outlook Express.

Follow these steps to do so:

1 In Outlook Express, click the Addresses icon on the toolbar or choose Tools, Address Book to open the address book.

2 In the address book, click the Find People button on the toolbar or choose Edit, Find People to display the Find People dialog box (see Figure 15-8).

Figure 15-8. Use the Find People dialog box to perform LDAP queries in Outlook Express.

3 In the Look In drop-down list, select the directory service account to use.

4 Specify the criteria for the search (such as name or e-mail address), click Advanced to specify additional parameters if needed, and click Find Now.

Searching from Windows

You can perform LDAP queries from Microsoft Windows using directory service accounts you create in Outlook Express.

Follow these steps to do so:

1 In Windows 9x or Windows NT, click Start, Find, People. In Windows 2000, click Start, Search, For People. Either action opens the Find People dialog box.

2 In the Look In drop-down list, select the directory service to query.

3 Enter the search criteria and click Find Now.

Configuring an LDAP Server

As you read the previous sections about directory services, you might have come to the conclusion that you'd like to enable LDAP queries on your own directory service. This section of the chapter isn't intended as an in-depth explanation of the LDAP services offered by Exchange Server or the Windows 2000 Active Directory, but it does discuss the most common configuration issues you'll encounter as you get your LDAP service on line and configure its primary settings.

> For more information on configuring Microsoft Exchange Server and Exchange 2000 Server, see Chapter 31, "Exchange Server Overview and Setup."

Adding Global Catalog Servers

When you promote a computer running Windows 2000 Server to a domain controller (DC), Windows 2000 automatically installs the Active Directory (AD) on the server. The Active Directory uses LDAP as its primary lookup mechanism, listening on the standard port 389 for LDAP queries and on port 636 for secure queries through SSL. Thus, to enable LDAP lookups, you need only install a Windows 2000 domain controller. However, you should consider whether you need to add another global catalog (GC).

The global catalog is an important part of the AD's structure. The GC is the mechanism through which searches occur in the AD and therefore is critical to all AD functions, including authentication. In the simplest terms, the GC functions much like a key database does, simplifying searches of the AD. The GC contains a full writable replica of all objects in the AD for its host domain. It also contains a partial read-only replica of the other domains in the forest. This read-only replica contains a copy of all objects in the domain forest, minus all but the attributes useful for searching. In essence, the GC serves as a flat database of the objects in the forest that allows quick location of any object in the directory—in other words, it's the directory's directory. The GC is built automatically by the AD's replication mechanisms.

By default, the first DC in a domain forest is designated as the GC server. Status as a DC does not equate to being a GC server—the only DC that functions by default as a GC server is the first one in the domain forest. Other DCs that come on line do not function as GC servers unless you configure them as such. Why configure a DC to act as a GC server? Redundancy is a primary reason, and availability is a close second. Because a GC server is necessary for authenticated logon, it's a good design practice to include a GC server at each site, particularly when the domain spans a wide area with links susceptible to failure. Having a local copy of the GC allows users to log on through the AD if the link to the other GC servers is down. If the GC is unavailable, Windows 2000 uses cached credentials for logon.

A network segment that is subject to disconnection from the site where the GC is hosted should have its own GC server. If the network connection is down and no GC server is available, clients will have difficulty logging on. Native-mode DCs require access to the GC to determine complete group membership access levels for each user, and if the GC is unavailable, the DC denies logon. So having spare GC servers is crucial.

To configure a computer as a GC server, you must first install it as a DC and then follow these steps:

1   Open the Active Directory Sites And Services console, expand the target site to locate the DC in the Servers node, and then expand the server.

2   Right-click NTDS Settings and choose Properties.

3   Select the Global Catalog check box and click OK.

> **note**   You can use ports 3268 and 3269 (SSL) only after the Active Directory is installed successfully, the server becomes a domain controller, and the Global Catalog option is set. DCs that do not host a copy of the GC will respond only to ports 389 and 636 (SSL).

Configuring Exchange Server 5.x LDAP Properties

When you install Exchange Server 5.x, Setup installs the LDAP protocol. If Exchange Server 5.x is installed on a Windows 2000 domain controller, or if Site Server is also installed on the same server, you'll experience problems because the AD and Site Server both use the default ports 389 and 636 (SSL) for LDAP queries. In either situation, you need to change the ports used by Exchange Server. You might want to change LDAP properties in other situations as well—for example, if your Exchange Server resides on the Internet, you might want to prevent anonymous LDAP queries and require users to authenticate.

You can configure the LDAP protocol at the site level and at the server level. By default, all servers in a site use the site's LDAP protocol settings. You can, however, modify individual servers to configure their LDAP properties differently. For example, you might allow anonymous queries on one but not another, require SSL on one but not another, and so on. In general, you'll want to configure global settings at the site level and then apply server-specific settings at the server level.

Follow these steps to configure LDAP settings at the site level for Exchange Server 5.*x*:

1 Open the Exchange Administrator and expand the site. Click Protocols in the left pane (see Figure 15-9).

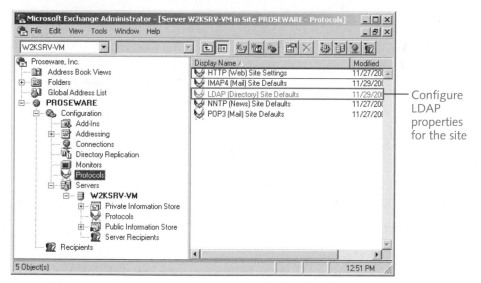

Configure LDAP properties for the site

Figure 15-9. You can configure LDAP at the site level to define defaults for all servers in the site.

2 Double-click LDAP (Directory) Site Defaults in the right pane to open the dialog box shown in Figure 15-10 on the next page.

3 To enable LDAP, select the Enable Protocol option. (To disable LDAP, clear this check box.)

4 In the Port Number box, specify the default port number for non-SSL queries.

5 Click Authentication. On the Authentication tab (see Figure 15-11 on the next page), select the authentication methods that will be allowed.

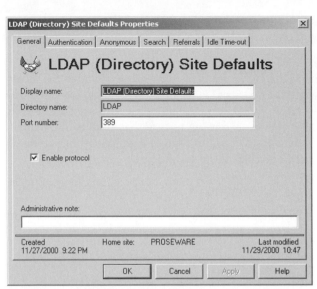

Figure 15-10. Use the LDAP (Directory) Site Defaults Properties dialog box to configure sitewide LDAP properties.

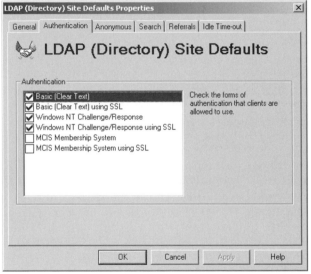

Figure 15-11. Use the Authentication tab to specify authentication methods used by servers in the site.

6 To allow anonymous LDAP queries, click the Anonymous tab and select the Allow Anonymous Access option. To prevent anonymous queries, clear this check box.

7 Click the Search tab and select one of the following options:

- **Treat "Any" Substring Searches As "Initial" Substring Searches (Fast).** Select this option to have Exchange Server treat all partial string searches as initial substring searches. (See the sidebar "Using Substring Searches" below, for further explanation.) For example, specifying the substring *Bo* would return the results *Boyce* and *Boris* but would not return the result *Placebo* or *Hobo*.

- **Allow Only Initial Substring Searches (Fast).** Select this option to have Exchange Server perform only initial substring searches and not perform final substring searches. For example, Exchange Server would perform a substring search for *Bo* and return *Boyce* but would not perform a substring search of *ce* that would return the result *Boyce*.

- **Allow All Substring Searches (Slow).** Select this option to allow Exchange Server to perform *initial*, *final*, and *any* substring searches. This option generally provides slower performance than the other two, so use it judiciously if you're running Exchange Server on a slow server or one that receives a significant number of LDAP queries.

8 For the option Maximum Number Of Search Results Returned, specify the largest number of search results that should be returned for a given query.

9 Click Referrals. Use the Referrals tab to create LDAP referral entries. (See the following section, "Setting Up Referrals," for details.)

10 Click the Idle Time-Out tab to specify whether Exchange Server closes idle LDAP connections and to specify the timeout period.

11 Click OK to apply the changes and close the dialog box.

Using Substring Searches

LDAP clients can perform three types of substring searches: *initial*, *final*, and *any*. With an initial substring search, the LDAP server attempts to match the string provided in the query against the beginning of entries in the directory. For example, an initial substring query for *Ji* would return *Jim*, *Jill*, and *Jiggle*. With a final substring search, the LDAP server attempts to match the string provided against the end of the entries in the directory. For example, a final substring search for *st* would return *Last*, *Best*, and *Most*. With an any substring query, the LDAP server attempts to match the string against any characters in the attributes. Such a search for *re* would return *Rebrovich*, *Bare*, and *Arena*.

You can perform substring searches by using the Advanced tab of the Find People dialog box in Outlook Express or by using the Begins With and Contains options in the Find dialog box in Outlook.

InsideOut

Querying LDAP servers is an area where Outlook Express beats Outlook. Outlook Express provides several additional options for performing queries, including Is, Contains, Starts With, Ends With, and Sounds Like. Outlook provides only the Contains and Begins With options. This means it's much easier to perform complex LDAP queries with Outlook Express than with Outlook.

You can also configure individual servers in a site with nondefault settings, as follows:

1 Open the Exchange Administrator and expand the Servers branch. Expand the server you want to modify and select the Protocols branch in the left pane.

2 In the right pane, double-click LDAP (Directory) Settings.

3 Clear the Use Site Defaults For All Properties option.

4 Configure settings for the server as needed. The options are the same as those discussed for the site level earlier in this section.

Setting Up Referrals

You can configure Exchange Server 5.5 to use up to 350 LDAP referral servers to perform LDAP queries on behalf of clients for information not found (or for additional information) in response to a client query. For example, a client might query the server for *Jim Boyce*, but no items in the directory match that name. However, the server can then submit the query to a referral server to obtain information about the queried data.

Follow these steps to set up LDAP referral servers in Exchange Server 5.*x*:

1 Open the Exchange Administrator.

2 Open the Protocols branch at the site level to specify a referral server at the site level. To specify a referral server at the server's level, open the Protocols branch of a specific server.

3 Click Referrals in the LDAP (Directory) Site Defaults Properties dialog box to open the Referrals tab, and then click New.

4 In the Referral Details dialog box (see Figure 15-12), specify the name or the IP address of the LDAP server, the directory name (search base), and the port number. If the server requires SSL, select the Connect Over SSL check box.

5 Click OK and then add any other referral servers you need.

6 Close the LDAP dialog box, and then close the Exchange Administrator.

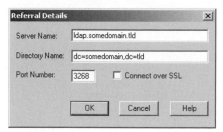

Figure 15-12. Use the Referral Details dialog box to specify the server properties for the LDAP referral server.

Configuring Exchange 2000 Server LDAP Properties

Unlike Exchange Server 5.*x*, Exchange 2000 Server integrates with the Active Directory rather than providing its own directory service. For that reason, you don't need to configure Exchange 2000 Server LDAP separately from the Active Directory, nor will you encounter the conflicts that are possible with Exchange Server 5.*x* (discussed in the preceding section). A few other common issues might affect you, however. The following sections explain these issues and how to address them with Windows 2000 AD and Exchange 2000 Server.

Creating External Referrals

Like Exchange Server 5.*x*, the Windows 2000 AD can use LDAP referrals to help clients locate queried information. References for referrals within the AD forest are created automatically and replicated across the directory, allowing domain controllers to offer referrals for directory partitions in the forest that the domain controllers don't hold (partitions located on other DCs.) These cross-reference objects are created automatically when the DCs are promoted, and they are replicated across the directory.

If you need to have the AD provide query referrals to external directory services, you can add *external cross-references*. In order for clients to be able to use the referrals, they must support *chase referrals,* which allow a client to receive a referral to an external service and follow that referral to complete the query. Both the Windows Address Book (Outlook Express) and Outlook support chase referrals.

Unlike Exchange Server 5.*x*, Windows 2000 Server doesn't by default provide an easy means of adding external cross-references. However, you can use the ADSI Edit console, one of the optional support tools included with Windows 2000 Server. To install the support tools, run Setup.exe from the \Support\Tools folder on the Windows 2000 Server CD.

Part 3: Contact Management

Then follow these steps to use the ADSI Edit console to add a cross-reference to an external LDAP service:

1 After installing the support tools, click Start, Run and start the Microsoft Management Console (MMC).

2 In the MMC, choose Console, Add/Remove Snap-In. Click Add, select ADSI Edit, click Add, click Close, and click OK.

3 Choose Action, Connect To.

4 In the Connection dialog box (see Figure 15-13), select the Naming Context option, and then select Configuration Container from the associated drop-down list.

Figure 15-13. Use the Connection dialog box to specify how to connect to the directory.

5 If you're connecting to the domain controller to which you're logged on, select Default. Otherwise, select the option Select Or Type A Domain Or Server, and then select the appropriate domain or server. Click OK.

6 Expand the Configuration Container branch, and then expand the CN= Configuration branch.

7 Right-click CN=Partitions and click New, Object.

8 By default, crossRef is selected, so click Next.

9 In the Value box, type a name to describe the location and click Next.

10 In the Value box, type the distinguished name for the external domain and click Next.

> **note** For an external LDAP server, you must specify a value for the external domain's distinguished name that matches the actual external directory name.

11 In the Value box, type the DNS name for the server hosting the directory partition or type the domain name, and then click Next.

12 Click Finish when you're satisfied with the settings.

Securing Global Address Lists

In some situations, you might want to apply access control lists (ACLs) to certain address lists to prevent LDAP queries for those address lists. For example, you might host multiple organizations on your Exchange Server and want to prevent users in one from browsing the addresses in another.

You can control access to address lists by setting ACLs on the list to restrict access, as explained here:

1 Open the Exchange System Manager, and expand the branch containing the address list in question.

2 Right-click the list and choose Properties. Then click Security.

3 On the Security tab, configure the permissions as needed (see Figure 15-14), and then click OK to close the dialog box.

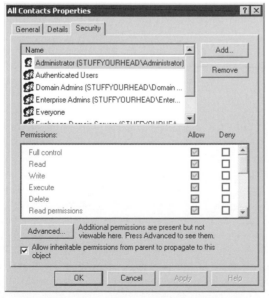

Figure 15-14. Use the Security tab to configure permissions for an address list and control access to it.

Chapter 15

Chapter 16

Making Notes

If you're like most people, there's at least one note stuck to your monitor, lying on your desk, or tucked in a drawer, keeping some critical piece of information relatively safe until you need it again—safe, that is, until you lose the note. If you're looking for a better way to keep track of all the small bits of information you receive every day, you can use Microsoft Outlook to create electronic notes for quick to-do lists, phone numbers, shopping lists—you name it. Notes reside in the Notes folder by default, but you can copy or move notes to other Outlook folders, use them in documents, place them on the desktop, or place them in your other file system folders.

This chapter examines notes and explores how to use them effectively in Outlook as well as how to integrate them in your other applications.

Understanding Outlook Notes

You can use Outlook notes to keep track of any kind of text-based information. For example, you might make a note as a reminder to call someone, to pick up a few things from the store on the way home, or to jot down a phone number. Outlook notes are really just simple text files, which you can create and view in the Outlook Notes folder (see Figure 16-1 on the next page).

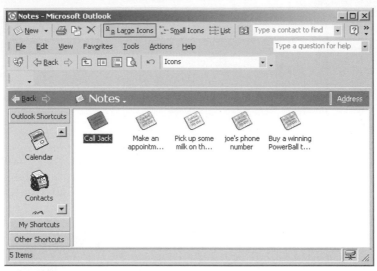

Figure 16-1. You can create and view your notes in the Notes folder.

When you create a new note, Outlook opens a window similar to the one shown in Figure 16-2. The note window is essentially a text box. As you type, the text wordwraps, and the window scrolls to accommodate the text. At the bottom of the note window, Outlook displays the date and time you created the note.

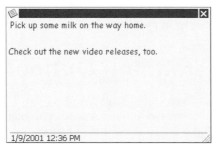

Figure 16-2. To create a new note, type in a note window.

You don't have to save the note explicitly—just close the note window and Outlook adds the note you've created to the Notes folder. You can copy or move a note to another Outlook folder or to a file system folder (such as your desktop), copy the text to the clipboard for inclusion in another document, or save the note to a text file. The following sections explain not only how to perform these actions but also how to use notes in other ways.

InsideOut

Although you can use notes in Outlook to keep track of just about any kind of information, a note is not always the best approach. Be sure you're not using the note in place of a more effective Outlook feature. For example, if you need to remind yourself to make a casual phone call some time during the day, a note might suffice. But if you need to set up an important conference call, it's better to create a task and have Outlook provide a reminder at the appropriate time. Likewise, the Contacts folder is the best place to keep track of contact information, rather than recording it on scattered notes. Notes are great when you need speed and convenience, but when another Outlook feature is suitable, you should view a note as a stopgap. For example, you might create a note for a quick to-do list now, and then add each item as a task in your Tasks folder later on when you have the time. As you become more familiar with notes, take a look at how you use them to make sure you're working effectively.

Configuring Note Options

Before you start creating notes, you might want to take a few minutes to configure the options that control the notes' default appearance.

To set these options, follow these steps:

1 Open Outlook and choose Tools, Options.

2 Click Note Options to display the Notes Options dialog box, shown in Figure 16-3.

3 Set the various options in this dialog box to determine the default color for notes (the color of the note window), the default size of the window, and the font used for the note text.

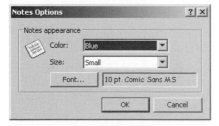

Figure 16-3. Use the Notes Options dialog box to control the size and color of the note window and the font used for notes.

You can change the window size of any individual note by dragging the note window's border. You also can change an existing note's color at any time (as explained in the following section).

> **tip** Because Outlook stores the date and time created for each note, you should check to make sure that your system time is accurate.

Working with Notes

Of all Outlook's features, notes are by far the easiest to use. The following sections explain how to create notes, change their color, copy them to other folders, and more.

Adding a Note

You create notes in the Notes folder. To open this folder, click the Notes icon on the Outlook Bar.

After you've opened the folder, follow these steps to create a note:

1 Right-click in the Notes folder and choose New Note or simply double-click in the folder window. Either action opens a blank note window.

2 Type your note directly in the window.

3 Click the Close button in the upper right corner of the note window to close and save it.

Outlook uses the first few dozen characters in the note as the title and displays it under the note's icon in the Notes folder.

> **tip** When you click a note to select it in the Notes folder, Outlook displays the entire note contents under the icon so that you don't have to open the note to read it.

Reading and Editing a Note

To read a note, you can double-click it to open the note window or click the note and read the text under the icon. To change the content of a note, open it as just described and edit it the same way you would edit a text file. Keep in mind, however, that you have no formatting options, so your notes are limited to plain text. To save your changes, simply close the note window.

Forwarding a Note

Although you'll probably create notes mainly for your own use, you might need to forward a note to someone. For example, a colleague might request a phone number or other contact information you've stored in a note. The easiest way to share the information is to forward the note as a message. Because Outlook sends the note as an attachment, the recipient can easily copy the note to his or her own Notes folder, place it on the desktop, or use the clipboard to copy the data to a new contact entry.

To forward a note, follow these steps:

1 Open the Notes folder, right-click the note, and choose Forward from the shortcut menu. Outlook opens a standard message form. If you are using Outlook as your e-mail editor, the note is shown as an attachment to the message (see Figure 16-4). If Microsoft Word is your e-mail editor, Word embeds the note as an icon in the body of the message.

2 Complete and send the message as you would any other message.

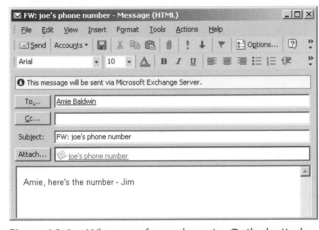

Figure 16-4. When you forward a note, Outlook attaches it to the message.

You can send notes in e-mail messages using other methods, too—you're not limited to embedding the note in the message or attaching it. For example, you can open the Notes folder and right-drag a note to the Inbox. The resulting shortcut menu allows you to create a message with the note as text in the body of the message, as a shortcut, or as an attachment.

Adding a Note Sent to You

When someone else sends you a note in an e-mail message, you can work with the note directly in the message. The note appears in the body of the message as an embedded object if it was sent using Word as the e-mail editor, with the note text under the icon, as shown in Figure 16-5. The note appears as an attachment to the message if the sender used Outlook as the e-mail editor. You can open the message and double-click the note to open it in a note window, but you'll probably prefer to copy the note to your own Notes folder.

Part 3: Contact Management

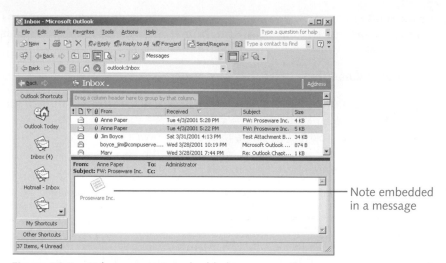

Note embedded
in a message

Figure 16-5. When a note is embedded in an e-mail message, you can open the note by double-clicking it.

To copy a note you've received to your Notes folder, follow these steps:

1 Open the Outlook Bar (if it is not already open) and scroll down so that the Notes icon is visible.

2 Open your Inbox, locate the note, and drag it to the Notes icon on the Outlook Bar. If the preview pane in the Inbox is open, you can drag the note from there; otherwise, open the message and drag the note.

Using a Note to Create a Task or an Appointment

If you've made a note about a task you must perform or an appointment you must keep, you can easily create an Outlook task or an appointment directly from the note. To do so, drag the note to the Tasks icon or the Calendar icon on the Outlook Bar, as appropriate. Outlook opens a new task form or a new appointment form with the note contents as the subject and contents of the task or appointment.

Moving and Copying Notes

You can move and copy notes to other folders. How Outlook treats the note depends on the destination folder itself. For example, if you copy a note to another notes folder, Outlook treats it as a note. But if you copy a note to the Calendar or Tasks folder, Outlook uses the note to create a new appointment or a new task.

If you right-drag a note to the Contacts icon on the Outlook Bar, Outlook creates a new contact and gives you several options for how to handle the note text. Outlook can add the text to the contact, add it as an attachment, or add it as a shortcut, depending on your selection. You can also copy the note as a journal entry by right-dragging it to the Journal icon on the Outlook Bar. You can choose to create the journal item with the note as an attachment or as a shortcut.

> **tip** Copying a note within the Notes folder is easy. Just right-drag the note to a new location in the folder, release the mouse, and choose Copy.

You can move or copy notes by dragging. To move a note to another notes folder, drag the note's icon to the destination folder. To copy a note instead of moving it, hold down the Ctrl key while dragging the note.

> **note** Dragging a note to a non-notes folder always copies the note rather than moving it—the original note remains in the Notes folder.

Copying a Note to the Clipboard

If you'd like to use the text of a note in another application or another Outlook folder, you can copy the note text to the clipboard. For example, you might copy a phone number from a note to a contact entry in the Contacts folder.

To copy the entire contents of a note to the clipboard, right-click the note and choose Copy. If you're working with the note in the Notes folder, you can select the note (or part of its text, such as a phone number) and choose Edit, Copy or press Ctrl+C. Then open the application or form where you want to use the note text and choose Edit, Paste or press Ctrl+V to paste the data from the clipboard.

> **note** If you copy a note from an e-mail message and then paste the note into another message, Outlook copies the note as an embedded OLE object rather than as text.

Copying a Note to the Desktop or Other Folder

In addition to moving and copying notes inside Outlook, you also can move or copy notes to your desktop or to another file system folder. Outlook creates an MSG file (an Outlook message file) to contain the note when you copy or move it outside Outlook. After you have copied or moved the note, you can double-click the file to open it.

To copy a note to the desktop or a file system folder, you need only drag it from the Notes folder to the desired destination. To move the note instead of copying it, hold down the Shift key while dragging.

> **tip** You can also move or copy a note from the desktop or a file system folder to your Notes folder. Just drag the note from its current location to the Notes folder.

Chapter 16

Changing Note Color

By default, Outlook notes are yellow (unless you've changed the default color in the Notes Options dialog box). But you can change the color of an individual note at any time. Open the Notes folder, right-click the note you want to change, and choose Color, followed by one of the five available colors: blue, green, pink, yellow, or white.

Why change color? Using a specific color for a specific type of note provides a visual cue about the purpose of the note. For example, you might use pink for notes whose contents are more urgent than others or for notes that have pending tasks associated with them. Perhaps you could use green to indicate personal notes and yellow for business-related notes.

For information about the Notes Options dialog box, see "Configuring Note Options," page 441.

Assigning Categories to Notes

You can assign categories to notes, just as you can to any other Outlook item. Categorizing helps you organize your notes, particularly if you choose to view your Notes folder by category. You can assign multiple categories to each note. For example, you might assign a project category to a note as well as an Urgent category.

For information on By Category view, see "Viewing Notes," page 448.

To assign categories to a note, follow these steps:

1 Right-click the note and choose Categories, or select the note and choose Edit, Categories.

2 In the Categories dialog box (see Figure 16-6), select the applicable categories.

3 If you don't see the categories you need, click Master Category List, create the required categories, and click OK.

> **tip** You can't directly edit an existing category, but you can achieve the same result by removing the existing category and replacing it with a new one.

4 Click OK in the Categories dialog box to close it and assign the selected categories.

You can view the categories assigned to a note using any one of several methods. For example, you can choose View, Current View, By Category to view the Notes folder organized by category. Or you can select a note and choose File, Print Preview—the printout contains the note's categories.

Chapter 16: Making Notes

For detailed information on working with categories, see Chapter 4, "Using Categories And Types."

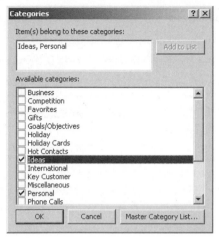

Figure 16-6. Use the Categories dialog box to assign categories to notes.

Printing a Note

To print a note, select the note and choose File, Print. Alternatively, you can right-click the note and choose Print from the note's shortcut menu. Outlook prints your name at the top of the page, followed by the date the note was created or last modified, the categories assigned to the note (if any), and the body of the note text. You also can choose File, Print Preview to preview the note.

Date and Time Stamping Notes

Outlook stamps each note with the date and time you created it and displays this information at the bottom of the note window. This date and time remain until you modify the note by adding or removing text. Then Outlook replaces the original date and time with the date and time you modified the text and stores this information with the note.

---

tip   **Change a note's time stamp**

Simply opening and reading a note does not change its time stamp. If you need to modify the note but retain the original time stamp, create a copy of the note and modify the copy. Drag the note to another location in the Notes folder to create the copy.

Deleting a Note

If you no longer need a note, you can delete it. Deleting a note moves it to the Deleted Items folder. What happens to it from there depends on how you have configured Outlook to process deleted items. If Outlook clears out the Deleted Items folder each time you exit the program, for example, the note is permanently deleted at that time. You can delete a note in any of the following ways:

- Right-click the note and choose Delete.

- Select the note and press the Delete key.

- Select the note and choose Edit, Delete.

- Drag the note to the Deleted Items folder on the Outlook Bar.

Viewing Notes

Outlook provides five predefined views for the Notes folder. To switch to a different view, choose Views, Current View. You can use any of the following predefined views:

- **Icons.** This default view displays an icon for each note with the first line of the note text serving as the icon's description.

- **Notes List.** This view displays the notes as a line-by-line list.

- **Last Seven Days.** This view is similar to Notes List view, but it displays only those notes created or modified within the past seven days, based on the current date.

- **By Category.** This view groups the notes as a list by their assigned categories. If more than one category is assigned to a single note, the note appears in each category group.

- **By Color.** This view groups the notes as a list by their assigned color.

You can use a preview pane in the Notes folder to display the text of a note when you click the note. When you use Notes List view or Last Seven Days view in the Notes folder, you can also use AutoPreview, which automatically displays the contents of each note in the list.

You can customize any of the views in the Notes folder the same way you customize the standard views in other folders. You can, for example, drag columns to rearrange them, resize columns, change column names and other properties, add other fields, and group notes based on various criteria.

> For information about customizing folder views, see "Customizing the Inbox View," page 63. For details about creating your own custom views, see Chapter 24, "Creating Custom Views and Print Styles."

Chapter 17

Keeping a Journal

Remembering everything you've done during the course of a busy day—e-mail messages sent, phone calls made, appointments set up—can be difficult. But the journal feature in Microsoft Outlook, which records your daily activities, can help you keep track of it all. In addition to tracking Outlook items such as e-mail messages and appointments automatically, you can use the journal to monitor every Microsoft Office document you create or modify. You can also manually record an activity that occurs away from your computer—a phone conversation, for example, or a handwritten letter you mailed or received.

The Journal folder provides a single place to track all your work and your daily interactions. For example, you can use the journal to list all items related to a specific contact: e-mail messages sent and received, meetings attended, and tasks assigned. You can track all the hours you've spent on activities related to a particular project. Or you can use the journal to retrieve detailed information based on when you performed an action—for example, if you know that you worked on a Microsoft Excel document last Tuesday but can't remember the path to the file, you can quickly look up the document if you've configured the journal to automatically record work on Excel files.

This chapter shows you how to record your work in the journal both automatically and manually. You'll also learn how to view and print your journal in standard and customized views.

Understanding the Outlook Journal

The Journal folder (see Figure 17-1 on the next page) provides you with tools to track and record daily activities. Journal entries can range in complexity from a manually created record of a phone call to an automatic entry generated every time an

449

e-mail message is sent to a specific contact or each time you work on a specific document. In addition to tracking Outlook items and Office documents, the journal also allows you to track a handwritten letter or the receipt of a courier package as well as any other event you choose to add to the journal manually, such as a conversation, a trip, or something you saw on the way to work.

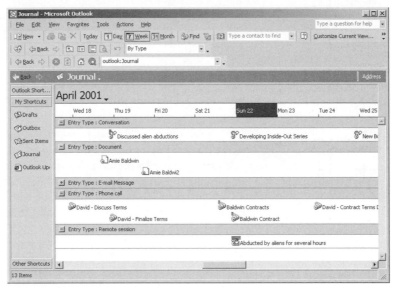

Figure 17-1. Use the Journal folder as an electronic diary of events, phone calls, tasks, and other daily items.

While other components of Outlook provide similar note-keeping abilities, only the journal provides a full (and optionally automatic) means to date and time stamp an activity, log the entry type (for example, a phone call or a meeting request), and even track the time spent on an activity for billing purposes.

Outlook records entries in your Journal folder based on when an action occurs. For example, a Microsoft Word document is recorded on the journal timeline when you create or modify the document. You can organize journal entries on the timeline into logical groups—such as e-mail messages, meetings, phone calls, or any items related to a specific project. You also can assign categories to journal items and organize the folder view by category. For example, you could assign a project name as a category to all journal items associated with that project, which would allow you to easily group journal entries by project.

You can open a journal entry form (see Figure 17-2) and review details about an activity, or you can use the journal entry as a shortcut to go directly to the Outlook item or the file referred to in the journal entry. For example, if you created a contract as a Word document that is associated with a journal entry, you could open the contract through that entry rather than locating it in the My Computer or My Documents folder.

Chapter 17: Keeping a Journal

Figure 17-2. The journal entry form contains many fields to help you organize, store, and find your journal entries.

Outlook's journal is an electronic diary. Everything that you normally write on your calendar or day planner (what you did, when you did it, and all the details you want to remember) you can record in the journal. But the journal is better than a paper diary, because it can automatically record activities such as e-mail messages you send to your boss, work you do on a Microsoft Access database, contracts you review or edit, and other items you work with in Office applications.

Some activities, such as a conversation in a trade show parking lot or a shopping excursion to find a new printer, can't be recorded automatically, but you can record anything manually. For example, you can record a phone call (not the voices, just the activity) and use the journal's timer to record the duration of the phone call in your journal entry. Or you could enter details about a conversation you had with a colleague during an impromptu lunch where you discussed a project on which you are collaborating.

To open the Journal folder, click the Journal icon on the Outlook Bar. If you're new to Outlook, you'll probably find a few entries in your journal already, because the journal records some items automatically by default. Figure 17-1 showed the journal's default view, which you see the first time you open the journal. Figure 17-3 on the next page shows Entry List view, another way of organizing your Journal folder.

For information about the views available to organize your Journal folder, see "Viewing the Journal," page 465.

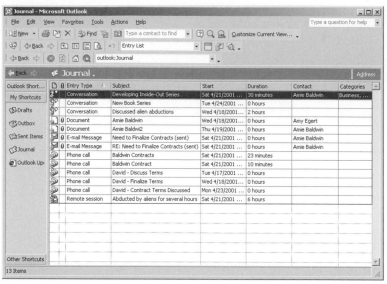

Figure 17-3. You can switch to Entry List view of the Journal folder.

Using Automatic Journaling

You can have Outlook create automatic journal entries for a wide range of items, including e-mail messages (both sent and received), task requests, and files you create or open in Microsoft Excel or Microsoft PowerPoint. In fact, you can use automatic journaling to record activities based on any contact, Office document, or Outlook item you select.

For example, suppose that you routinely exchange important e-mail messages with a business associate, and you want to track all exchanges for reference. Incoming messages from this associate arrive in your Inbox. You read them, reply to them, and then archive the incoming messages to another folder. But now your associate's messages are stored in one folder and your replies are in another. (By default, replies are stored in Outlook's Sent Items folder.) Configuring the journal to automatically track all of your e-mail exchanges with your associate places a record of all messages relating to this contact (both received and sent) in one convenient location. Instead of hunting for your response to your associate's question of two weeks ago, you can open the journal and find the entry associated with the message. Double-click the link embedded in the journal entry, and Outlook takes you to the message containing your response. Figure 17-4 shows a journal entry automatically added from an e-mail message.

Chapter 17: Keeping a Journal

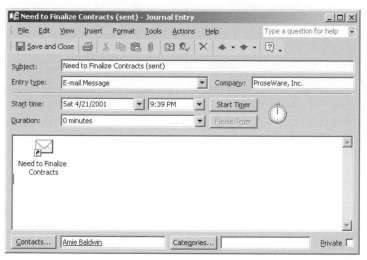

Figure 17-4. The journal can automatically note when you send or receive e-mail messages to or from specific contacts.

---

tip **Find e-mail items quickly**

To find e-mail items in the journal more quickly, select Entry List view and then click the Contact column to sort the view according to contact. This helps you see all journal items associated with a specific contact, including those items created automatically from e-mail messages.

Troubleshooting

E-mail messages are missing from the journal.

If you've set up automatic tracking for a contact who has more than one e-mail address, the journal will track only messages sent and received using the contact's default address—that is, the entry shown in the E-Mail box on the contact form, not an alternative e-mail address that might be entered in the E-Mail 2 or E-Mail 3 field. If you send a message to a contact using one of the alternative e-mail addresses in the E-Mail 2 or E-Mail 3 field, Outlook will not journal those messages. If you need to use one of these alternative addresses and want Outlook to journal the message, you must include the default address in the Cc line of the message form. This results in Outlook sending a duplicate message to the contact's default address, but it allows the item to be recorded.

As another example, consider a writer who uses Word every day to make a living. Turning on automatic document tracking for this application could provide some interesting insight into how the writer allocates the work day and which documents are the most demanding. The same holds true for other Office applications you use frequently.

If you use document tracking in such a scenario, however, you should be aware of the distinction between how Outlook tracks a document and how Word itself records editing time. (In Word, you can choose File, Properties and click the Statistics tab to locate the Total Editing Time field.) Outlook tracks the time a document is open, whereas Word tracks the time spent physically editing a document (that is, pressing keys). The Outlook journal automatically records the entire span of time a document is open, even if you are away from your desk tending to other matters.

If a record of the actual time spent working on a document is important to you (whether mulling a paragraph, reading a lengthy section, editing, or entering new text), the journal offers a more realistic record. But if you fail to close the document when you move on to other things, you'll end up adding time to the document's journal entry that wasn't really spent on the document. It's best to use a combination of Word's editing time field and the Outlook journal's tracking to get a realistic picture of how you spend your time.

Overall, the best choice is usually to use automatic tracking for your critical contacts and for specific applications that benefit from an automatic audit trail. You can place other items in the journal manually as required.

> **note** After you set it up, the journal's automatic tracking is always on. A piece of Outlook code runs in the background and monitors the Office applications you've selected to track—even if Outlook itself is closed.

Another issue to consider in relation to journaling is latency. When you use automatic tracking for documents, you'll often notice a significant lag between the time you close a document and the time the entry appears (or is updated) in the journal. Also keep in mind that if you've opened the document previously, the most recent tracking entry doesn't appear at the top of the list. By default, journal entries are ordered according to start date, which in this case would be the first time the document was opened or created, not the most recent.

> **note** Using automatic journaling can have a significantly negative impact on the performance of your applications because of the added overhead involved in journaling. This might not be apparent on your system, depending on your system's capabilities and the types of documents you use. But if you see a significant decrease in performance after turning on automatic journaling and can't afford the performance drop, you'll need to stop automatic journaling and resort to adding journal entries manually.

Setting Journal Options

The journal has many options that allow you to control what gets recorded, how it gets recorded, and when it gets recorded. To set journal options, choose Tools, Options. On the Preferences tab, click the Journal Options button to open the Journal Options dialog box, shown in Figure 17-5. The choices you make in this dialog box determine how your journal is set up and what it tracks.

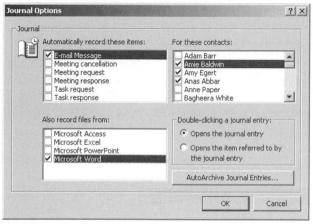

Figure 17-5. The Journal Options dialog box contains customization choices for the journal.

The following list summarizes the options in the Journal Options dialog box:

- **Automatically Record These Items.** Select from a list of Outlook items that can be tracked as journal entries. All options here involve three forms of messaging: regular e-mail, meeting notifications, and task delegation. Item types selected from this list are tracked for the contacts you choose in the For These Contacts list. Selecting an item to track without choosing an associated contact has no effect for that tracking option.

- **For These Contacts.** Here you link items you want to track with those contacts you want to track them for—task requests from your boss, for example. Outlook then automatically creates journal entries for the selected contacts and related items. Only contacts in your main Contacts folder can be selected for automatic journaling. You'll need to move (or copy) contact entries from subfolders to the main Contacts folder if you want to track items for them.

- **Also Record Files From.** Outlook creates an automatic journal entry every time an Office application selected in this list creates or accesses a document. The selections available depend on which Office applications are installed on your system. Documents from Access, Excel, PowerPoint, Word, and Microsoft Project can be tracked.

455

> **caution** When you set up automatic tracking for a particular document type (for example, Word documents), this setting applies to all documents you create, open, close, or save with the selected application. Thus it can also create many journal entries filled with information you might not need to preserve. Make this selection with care.

- **Double-Clicking A Journal Entry.** Double-clicking a journal entry can open either the entry itself or the item referred to by the entry, depending on your selection in this portion of the dialog box. Use this option to specify which action you prefer as the default. You can later override this setting by right-clicking the journal entry in any journal view.

- **AutoArchive Journal Entries.** Click to open the Journal folder's Properties dialog box and configure archive settings for the Journal folder.

> For details on archiving Outlook items, see Chapter 28, "Managing Folders, Data, and Archiving."

Turning Off Automatic Journaling

You won't find a one-click solution when you want to turn off automatic journaling. To turn this feature off, you must open the Journal Options dialog box and clear all the check boxes from the Automatically Record These Items and Also Record Files From lists. It's not necessary to clear contacts selected in the For These Contacts list. Because automatic journaling consists of tracking specific Outlook events for a contact as well as when specific types of Office files are accessed, breaking the link on the "items to track" end is enough.

Troubleshooting

Automatic journaling is causing delays.

Automatic journaling can cause very long delays during manual or automatic timed saves as well as when you exit the application. Although it might appear that the application has hung, in fact it is simply saving the journal information. If you experience apparent lock-ups during these procedures, check Outlook to see whether automatic journaling is turned on for the specific application involved. If so, wait a minute or two to give the application a chance to save your data, and then turn off automatic journaling if it has become too onerous to use. You can continue to add journal items manually for the application, if needed.

Automatically Recording E-Mail Messages

Recording e-mail to and from colleagues in the journal is a great way to keep track of discussions and decisions concerning a project, and it's easy to locate those messages later.

To record e-mail messages exchanged with a specific contact, follow these steps:

1 In Outlook, choose Tools, Options and then click Journal Options on the Preferences tab to open the Journal Options dialog box.

2 In the Automatically Record These Items list, select E-Mail Message.

3 In the For These Contacts list, select the contact whose e-mail you want to record.

4 Click OK twice, to close both dialog boxes.

Automatically Recording Contact Information

You can configure your journal to automatically keep track of your interactions with any one of your contacts. If you're working with a colleague on a specific project, for example, you might want to monitor your progress by recording every e-mail message, meeting, and task that involves this colleague.

To set up your journal to keep such a record based on the name of the contact, follow these steps:

1 In Outlook, choose Tools, Options and then click Journal Options on the Preferences tab to open the Journal Options dialog box.

2 In the Automatically Record These Items list, select the types of Outlook items you want to record in the journal.

3 In the For These Contacts list, select the relevant contact. (You can select more than one.)

4 Click OK twice, to close both dialog boxes.

---

tip   **Set up automatic journaling for a new contact**

When you create a new contact entry in your Outlook Contacts folder, click the All Fields tab on the contact form. In the Select From drop-down list, select All Contact Fields and then set the Journal field to Yes. Any activity related to the contact (meetings, appointments, phone calls, and so on) will now be recorded in the journal.

Automatically Recording Document Activity

Suppose you create and maintain custom Excel spreadsheets for the different divisions in your corporate enterprise. In the course of a busy day, it's easy to forget to write down whose file you worked on and for how long. There's a better way than keeping track on paper: you can have the journal automatically record every Office file you open, including when and how long you had each file open. Outlook can monitor your files and create a journal entry for every document you open and work on from Word, Excel, Access, PowerPoint, Microsoft Project, and Microsoft Office Binder.

> **note** Although the journal can automatically record work only in the Microsoft Office programs Word, Excel, Access, PowerPoint, Project, and Office Binder, you can enter your work from other programs manually.

Follow these steps to automatically record files you create or open:

1 In Outlook, choose Tools, Options and then click Journal Options on the Preferences tab to open the Journal Options dialog box.

2 In the Also Record Files From list, select the programs whose files you want to automatically record in your journal. The journal will record a new entry for each document from the selected programs when it is created, opened, closed, or saved.

3 By default, double-clicking an icon on the journal timeline opens the journal entry. If you'd rather be able to open the associated file when you double-click the icon, select the Opens The Item Referred To By The Journal Entry option.

InsideOut

If you've set up automatic journaling for all entries created by an application (Excel, for example), every document you create in that application generates a journal entry. If you right-click an entry and choose Open Item Referred To, Outlook opens the document that created the journal entry. However, this behavior can change. If you add a document item manually to the entry, and the icon for that item appears before the original document's icon in the entry, Outlook opens the manually added document. In other words, Outlook always opens the first document referenced in the entry when you choose Open Item Referred To from the entry's shortcut menu. This can be confusing because the subject continues to reference the original document. In addition, the manually added document will not appear in the View Attachments list on the entry's shortcut menu unless you inserted it as a file rather than as a shortcut. So, when you add entries manually, make sure to place the icon for the document added manually after the original document's icon and insert the document as a file.

> **tip** Regardless of which option you choose to be the default in the Journal Options dialog box, you can always right-click an icon on the journal timeline and then choose either Open Journal Entry or Open Items Referred To from the shortcut menu.

4 Click OK twice to close both dialog boxes.

> **note** Because journal entries contain links to your documents rather than copies of the actual documents, the entries might reference documents that no longer exist on your system. The journal has no way to record the deletion, moving, or renaming of files.

Adding Journal Items Manually

Automatic journaling can be tremendously useful. But what if some of the work you need to track is done in applications other than Office? You can't record the files automatically in your journal, but you can record them manually. Or what if you want to track your work only in a specific Word file rather than in every Word document? Instead of turning on automatic recording for all Word files, you can manually record your work only in specified files.

Likewise, if you want to record a nonelectronic event in your journal—a chat at the water cooler, a box of chocolates sent to a client, your approval of a printed proposal—you can add a journal entry manually. You can also use this method if you'd prefer to pick and choose which documents, messages, meetings, and task requests are entered in the journal rather than having Outlook routinely record all such items.

Recording Work in a File Manually

To keep a record of when and how long you worked in a file (along with any extraneous notes to yourself), follow these steps:

1 Locate the file you want to work in. You can navigate to the folder that contains the file using any technique you like, such as browsing My Computer or My Documents.

2 Drag the file icon in the folder window to the Journal icon on the Outlook Bar. It's easiest to drag the file if you resize both Outlook and the folder window so that you can clearly see both.

3 Click the Start Timer button to begin recording your working hours (see Figure 17-6 on the next page), and then double-click the file shortcut icon to open the file. At any time, you can enter notes to yourself in the box where the shortcut icon is located.

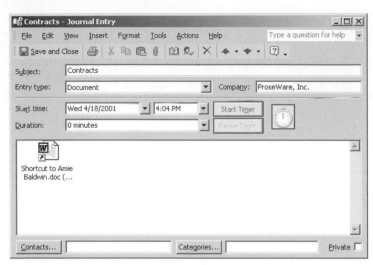

Figure 17-6. Click the Start Timer button to start recording time spent on a document.

4 When you finish working in the file, remember to stop the journal timer by clicking Pause Timer and then clicking the Save And Close button.

> **tip** If you need to take a temporary break in your work, click the Pause Timer button. When you return to work on the file, click Start Timer to continue recording your working hours.

Recording Outlook Items Manually

Recording an Outlook item such as a task in the journal is even easier than recording a file: open the Outlook window where the item is listed and drag it to the Journal icon on the Outlook Bar. For example, suppose that you want to record how much time you spend cleaning out your filing cabinets, a task you've entered in the Tasks folder. Open the Tasks folder, drag the task item to the Journal icon on the Outlook Bar. Click the Start Timer button and go to work. Then click Pause Timer to take a break. When you finish, click the Save And Close button.

Recording Other Activities Manually

Any activity you want to record can be entered in your journal. For example, you can monitor the time you spend on the Internet (which can be considerable) as well as re-cording any Web page addresses you want to save and other notes you need to jot down.

Chapter 17: Keeping a Journal

Follow these steps:

1 Double-click a blank area in your Journal folder. A new journal entry form opens.

2 In the Subject box, type a description of your activity.

3 In the Entry Type box, select an appropriate entry type for the activity. You can't create your own entry type, but you can choose among several available types. For example, you could classify an Internet search as Remote Session. Type any notes, including hyperlinks, in the large text box.

4 Click the Start Timer button to begin recording your activity.

5 When you're finished with your activity, click Pause Timer to stop the timer. Then click Save And Close to close the journal entry.

Manually Recording Phone Calls

When you use automatic dialing to call a contact, you can time the phone call, type notes in Outlook while you talk, and create a journal entry for the call. This feature can come in handy if, for example, you bill clients for your time spent on phone conversations.

Follow these steps to keep a record of an outgoing call in Journal:

1 Open the Contacts folder and select the contact entry for the person you want to call.

2 Click the Dial button on the Standard toolbar to open the New Call dialog box (see Figure 17-7).

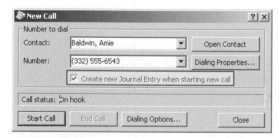

Figure 17-7. You can automatically start a new journal entry from the New Call dialog box.

3 Select the Create New Journal Entry When Starting New Call check box, and then click Start Call. A journal entry opens with the timer running. You can type notes in the body of the journal entry while you talk.

4 When you're finished with the call, click Pause Timer to stop the clock. Then click Save And Close.

You also can create journal entries for incoming calls, although Outlook currently offers no means of automatically creating the journal entries when you pick up the phone and start talking. Instead, when you answer the call and realize that you want to track it, you can open the journal as you begin the conversation, start a new journal item, and click Start Timer. Make notes as needed, and click Pause Timer when you hang up. Add any necessary details to the journal entry form, and then click Save And Close to create the item.

---

tip   **Use the journal as an inexpensive stopwatch**

You can start a new journal item and use the timer to time any activity, assuming that you don't need to-the-second timing. Just stop the timer and close the form without saving it unless you actually want to save the information in the journal.

For information about setting up automatic phone dialing and making calls from the Contacts folder, see "Phoning a Contact," page 395.

Changing Journal Entries

You can modify any details of a journal entry—for example, adding more notes to yourself, adding a contact's names or categories, or changing the duration of your activity. You can also move the entry to a different position on the journal timeline if you entered the wrong start date or time when you began recording the activity.

For information about timeline views in the Journal folder, see "Viewing the Journal," page 465.

Modifying an Entry

Suppose that in the middle of your boring department budget meeting, you realize that you didn't stop the journal timer when you stopped working on a spreadsheet to come to the meeting. You know that you worked on the spreadsheet for about three hours, however, so you can change the journal entry to reflect your actual work time.

To change the duration or any other property of an existing journal entry, follow these steps:

1   Open the Journal folder, and double-click the entry to open it.

2   Select the information you want to change and enter the correct data. For example, to change an incorrect record of how long you spent on an activity, double-click in the Duration box, change the value, and press Enter.

3   Make other changes as needed in the journal entry form.

4   Click Save And Close.

Moving an Entry on the Timeline

Suppose that you belatedly created a journal entry for a phone call you made yesterday and inadvertently entered the wrong date. When you later notice that the journal entry is in the wrong spot on the timeline, you can move the entry to the correct date.

Follow these steps to do so:

1 Open the Journal folder and double-click the entry to open it.

2 Click the arrow next to the Start Time box, and select the correct date.

3 Click Save And Close. Outlook will then move the entry to the correct spot on the timeline.

Deleting an Entry

Deleting a single entry from your journal timeline is easy: either click the entry's icon to select it and then press Delete, or right-click the entry's icon and choose Delete from the shortcut menu.

But what if you've been automatically recording your work in Excel workbooks but have also been experimenting with Excel, creating lots of test workbooks that you don't want to save or track. Now you have lots of useless entries cluttering up your Journal folder. You can delete them one at a time, but it's faster to switch to a table view of your entries, sort them so that all the useless entries are in one group, and delete them all at once.

> For information about the various views in the Journal folder, including table views and timeline views, see "Viewing the Journal," page 465.

Follow these steps to delete a group of entries:

1 In the Journal folder, choose View, Current View, Entry List. The view switches to a table view of all your journal entries.

2 To sort the entries so that all the ones you want to delete appear together, click the Entry Type column header. To sort specific entries by subject within a group of entry types, hold down the Shift key while you click the Subject column header.

> **tip** You can sort by as many as four categories using this method of holding down the Shift key while you click column headers.

3 To select and delete multiple journal entries, press Shift or Ctrl while you select the entries you want to delete and then click the Delete button on the toolbar. (Alternatively, you can press the Delete key to delete selected entries or right-click any of the selected entries and choose Delete from the shortcut menu.)

4 When you finish deleting the journal entries that you don't want, you can choose View, Current View and select the view you were using previously.

Connecting Journal Activities to Individual Contacts

If you work on a project with a colleague, you can associate your journal entries for the project with that colleague's contact entry. All the journal entries that are associated with the contact will appear on the Activities tab of the contact form.

For example, Figure 17-8 shows a journal entry for a Word letter to an associate. To connect a journal entry and document to a contact, click the Contacts button at the bottom of the journal entry form. In the resulting Select Contacts dialog box, click the names of the contacts with whom the journal entry should be associated and then click OK. The selected names appear in the Contacts box at the bottom of the journal entry form.

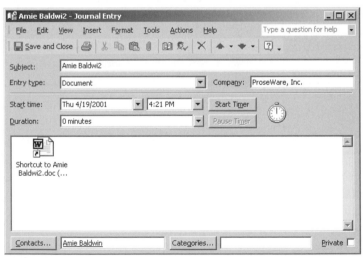

Figure 17-8. This journal entry shows a Word document associated with a contact.

So what does this do for you? When you open the contact entry for an associated contact and click the Activities tab (see Figure 17-9), you'll see a list of every Outlook item associated with that contact. You can open any of these items by double-clicking it. This is just one more way Outlook keeps all your information interconnected.

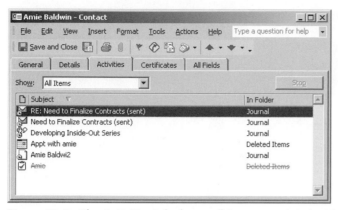

Figure 17-9. The Activities tab shows all items associated with the selected contact.

Viewing the Journal

When you look at the Journal folder in a monthly timeline view, you get a good overall picture of your recorded activities, but you must point to an individual icon to identify the activity. (When you point to an icon, a subject label appears.) You can make a few changes to a journal timeline view—for example, you can choose to always display the subject labels for icons in a monthly view, or you can specify a more useful length for the labels. You can also show week numbers in the timeline heading, which is useful for planning in some industries.

Because the Outlook journal creates a record of your activities, the six standard views available in the Journal folder differ considerably from the views in other types of Outlook folders. The following sections introduce you to each of the Journal folder views.

> **tip** You can choose whether to view a timeline in a journal view in day, week, or month increments by clicking the Day, Week, or Month button on the toolbar. These buttons are available only in the journal views that show a timeline and are not available in list views.

Using By Type View

The default view for the Journal folder is By Type view (see Figure 17-10). In this view, the journal entries are arranged in a timeline and are categorized by the entry type. To select By Type view, choose View, Current View, By Type.

Part 3: Contact Management

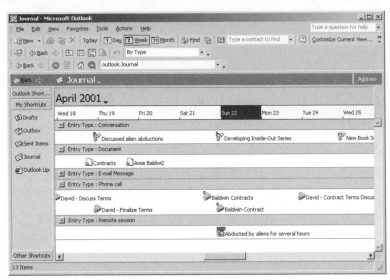

Figure 17-10. By Type view is the default Journal folder view.

Each entry type is indicated on a title bar. You can click the small box on the left edge of the title bar to expand or contract the type. A plus sign (+) in the box means that the type is collapsed, whereas a minus sign (–) indicates that the type is expanded. You might need to use the vertical scroll bar to see the complete list. When you expand a type, you can view any journal entries for that type in the area below the title bar.

> **tip** If you are surprised to find no entries when you expand a particular type, it's because Outlook displays the entries as a timeline. If no entries for the selected type were created recently, you might need to use the horizontal scroll bar to find the most recent entries.

By Type view is most useful if you want to find out which documents you worked on during a specific period. This view is not particularly useful for locating documents based on any other criteria. For example, you wouldn't want to use By Type view to locate all documents relating to a particular contact.

Using By Contact View

In By Contact view (see Figure 17-11), journal entries are also arranged in a timeline and are categorized by the contact associated with the entries.

Chapter 17

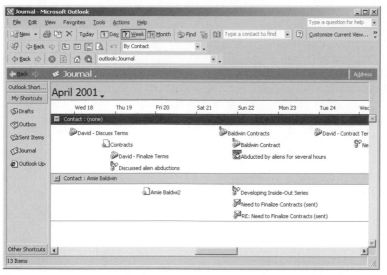

Figure 17-11. Use By Contact view to organize the journal by the contacts associated with each journal entry.

Each entry type is indicated by a title bar that shows the contact's name. Click the small box to expand or collapse the type. You might also need to use the horizontal scroll bar to view all items in a given entry type.

By Contact view makes it easy to find all documents and other journal items related to a specific contact. Any type of document can appear in the list, as can phone calls and other items associated with specific contacts.

InsideOut

Journal entries will appear in the correct category in By Contact view only if the entry is linked to the correct contact. Outlook does this automatically for items such as e-mail messages, but you must take care to see that Office documents are linked correctly. One way to ensure that documents are correctly linked is to select the contact in the Contacts folder and then choose File, New Office Document to create the file.

Using By Category View

In By Category view (see Figure 17-12 on the next page), journal entries are also arranged in a timeline and are organized by the categories you've assigned to them.

Chapter 17

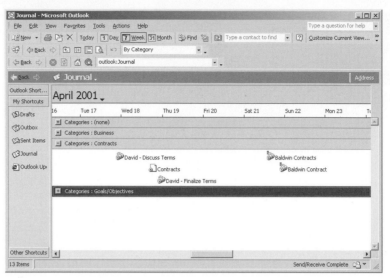

Figure 17-12. Use By Category view to organize the Journal folder based on the categories assigned to each journal item.

By Category view can be handy if you create categories that break down the journal entries by project. This view can be almost useless, however, unless you take the time to assign categories when you create documents. Outlook doesn't assign any categories by default. You can assign categories using Outlook's standard list, or you can create your own categories.

For information about assigning categories and creating custom categories, see Chapter 4, "Using Categories and Types."

tip **Assign categories to multiple entries**

You can access the Categories dialog box by right-clicking the journal entry and choosing Categories. To assign a category to multiple journal entries, select them all (by holding down the Shift or Ctrl key as you select), right-click the selection, and choose Categories.

Using Entry List View

Entry List view (see Figure 17-13) could be the most useful view of all. This view dispenses with the timeline and instead displays all journal entries in a table.

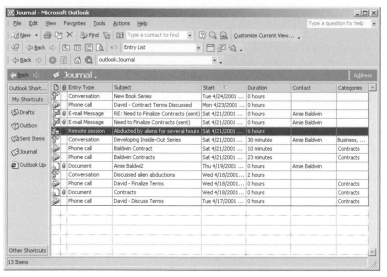

Figure 17-13. Entry List view displays journal entries in a table rather than on a timeline.

Because Entry List view does not use the timeline to display entries, it's much easier to view the list of entries—you don't have to use the horizontal scroll bar to locate the items. By default, this view is sorted in descending order based on the start date, but you can quickly sort the list using any of the column headers. Simply click a column header to sort the list; click the header a second time to reverse the sort order.

The paper clip icon in the second column of Entry List view indicates that an entry is a document. If this icon isn't displayed, the entry is a log of an activity that occurred within Outlook, such as an e-mail message.

Using Last Seven Days View

Last Seven Days view resembles Entry List view. This view is useful when you need to locate items you've worked on recently—especially if you can't quite remember the file name, contact, or category.

When you look closely at Last Seven Days view, you might notice that something doesn't look quite right: the dates shown for the journal entries clearly span much more than a week. The explanation is that the dates shown are the start dates for the journal entries, not the dates when the items were last accessed. Outlook is displaying the journal entries that have been created, accessed, or modified within the past week. Each entry shown in this view was accessed in some way during the past week, although the original entries might have been created quite some time ago.

> **tip** **Change the period of time shown in Last Seven Days view**
>
> You can customize Last Seven Days view to specify a different time period, such as the past month. To do so, choose View, Current View, Customize Current View. Click Filter in the View Summary dialog box and select the new time duration in the Time drop-down list.

Using Phone Calls View

Phone Call view (see Figure 17-14) displays only journal items that are associated with phone calls. Tracking phone calls and viewing them in the Journal folder can be extremely helpful. You can, for example, monitor the time you spend on billable calls. But even if you don't bill for your time, you'll find that phone call journal entries make it easier to recall phone conversations.

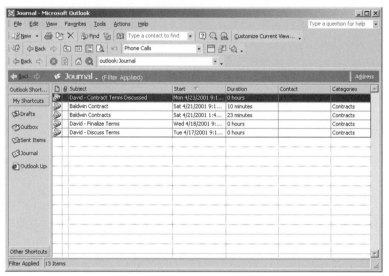

Figure 17-14. Use Phone Call view to organize the Journal folder according to journal items associated with phone calls.

Outlook will create journal entries for phone calls automatically only if you use the AutoDialer to begin the call. You must specify the duration yourself by entering the appropriate time on the phone call journal entry form. You can do so by actually entering a time.

> **tip** Remember to link your phone call journal entries to the appropriate contacts so that it will be easier to find all entries relating to specific contacts.

Customizing Journal Views

All the standard views in the Journal folder are customizable in a variety of ways. The changes you make to these views are persistent, however, so proceed with care. If you end up mangling a standard view beyond repair, it can be restored to its default by using the Reset button in the Define Views dialog box that you can open by choosing View, Current View, Define Views. (No such option exists for custom views.)

For information about creating custom views in Outlook, see Chapter 24, "Creating Custom Views and Print Styles."

Displaying Item Labels in the Monthly Timeline

A journal entry's label for a Journal entry designates where the file the journal entry references is located on your computer.

To display item labels on a monthly timeline, follow these steps:

1 In By Type view, right-click in an empty area of the Journal folder, and choose Other Settings on the shortcut menu.

2 In the Format Timeline View dialog box, select the Show Label When Viewing By Month check box.

note By default, the label width is 25 characters, but if you find that your labels are too short or too long, return to this dialog box and change the number in the Maximum Label Width box. The label width applies to the labels in the day and week timeline as well as the month timeline. To also hide the display of week numbers, you can clear the Show Week Numbers check box.

3 Click OK to close the dialog box.

Showing Week Numbers

In some industries, it's important to know schedules based on weeks of the year.

You can show week numbers in your timeline view by following these steps:

1 Right-click in an empty area of the Journal folder, and choose Other Settings on the shortcut menu.

2 In the Format Timeline View dialog box, select the Show Week Numbers check box.

3 Click OK to close the dialog box. In a monthly timeline, week numbers replace dates. In week and day views, both the week number and dates are displayed in the timeline header.

Printing Journal Items

The options available when you print from the Journal folder depend on whether a timeline view or a table (list) view is currently open. In a table view, you can open and print individual items, print the entire list, or print only selected rows. Printing the list is useful if you want a snapshot of the journal for a specific period of time. You can print table views using either Table or Memo print styles (explained shortly.)

> **tip** You don't have to open an item to print it. Simply right-click the item and choose Print from the shortcut menu.

In a timeline view, you can only open and print individual journal items. You can print individual items only in Memo style, but you can print attached files along with the journal entry details. To print the attached files, select the Print Attached Files check box in the Print dialog box.

> **For more information about printing views in Outlook and creating custom print styles, see Chapter 24, "Creating Custom Views and Print Styles."**

Table print style (see Figure 17-15) is available from any table view. It prints the selected view just as you see it in Outlook: each item on a separate row, and the fields displayed as columns. Table print styles have limited configuration options.

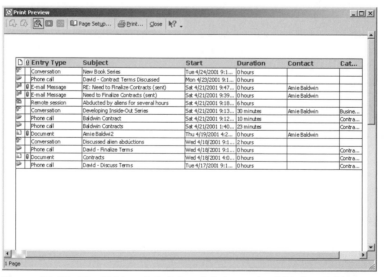

Figure 17-15. The Table print style prints journal entries in a table.

Memo style (see Figure 17-16) prints one item per page, with your name as the title and the details of the record following. Memo is a simple and quick, one-item-at-a-time print style. You can specify the title and field fonts, paper options, and the contents and fonts used by the header/footer.

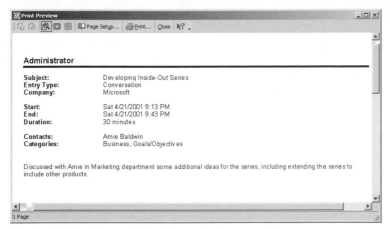

Figure 17-16. Memo style prints a single journal item per page.

Printing from the Journal folder is not a particularly difficult task for anyone who has used and printed from any Microsoft Windows–based application. However, you might be wondering how you can print just a selection of a table view. For example, you might need to print only the items that fall within a specific range or that are associated with a particular contact.

Follow these steps to print a selection of a table view:

1 Open the table view.

2 Click columns as needed to sort the data to help you locate the items you want to print. For example, click the Start column header to locate items that fall within a certain time range or click the Contact column header to locate items associated with a specific contact.

3 Select the first item in the range, hold down the Shift key, and select the last item in the range.

4 Choose File, Print to open the Print dialog box.

5 Select Table Style from the Print Style area and then select the Only Selected Rows option.

6 Set other print options as needed and click OK.

Sharing Journal Information

Because the Outlook journal keeps track of activities using a timeline, you might find that it is one of the most useful of Outlook's folders to share. If you're working on a project with several people, a shared Outlook Journal folder might be just what you need to make certain everyone is on track.

You can share a personal Journal folder (one that is contained in a set of personal folders, or PST file) and allow others to access that folder to view and create items in it, subject to the permissions you grant for the folder. Or, if you and all the people with whom you want to share the Journal folder use Microsoft Exchange Server, you can share the Journal folder as a public folder on the Exchange Server.

Follow these steps to share a personal Journal folder:

1 In Outlook, open the folders list and click the push pin to keep the list open.

2 Right-click the Journal folder and choose Properties to open the Journal Properties dialog box. Click the Permissions tab (see Figure 17-17).

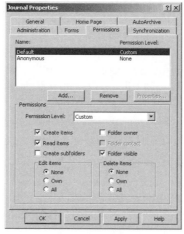

Figure 17-17. Share a folder by using the folder's Permissions tab in its Properties dialog box.

3 Click Default and select options in the Permissions area to specify the types of tasks all users can perform if they have no explicit permissions set (explained next.)

4 Click Add to open the Add Users dialog box, select a user (or more than one), and click OK to return to the Permissions tab.

Chapter 17: Keeping a Journal

5 With the user selected in the Name list, select permissions in the Permissions area to specify the tasks that user can perform.

6 Click OK to apply the permissions.

For details about sharing folders, see "Granting Access to Folders," page 687.

If everyone you want to share the folder with is using Exchange Server, it makes more sense to create a public Journal folder on the server and grant permissions as needed in that folder. This allows you to keep your private Journal folder private and inaccessible to others but allows everyone (assuming they are given the necessary permissions) to create and view items in the shared folder.

Follow these steps to create a shared public Journal folder:

1 In Outlook, open the folders list and click the push pin to keep the list open.

2 Expand the Public Folders branch, right-click the All Public Folders branch, and choose New Folder to open the Create New Folder dialog box (see Figure 17-18).

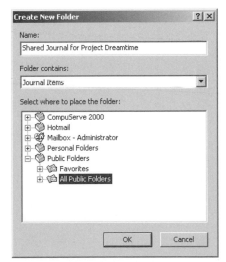

Figure 17-18. Use the Create New Folder dialog box to create a public Journal folder.

3 Specify a name for the new folder in the Name box.

4 Select Journal Items in the Folder Contains drop-down list.

5 Verify that All Public Folders is selected in Select Where To Place The Folder (or select a different location if needed) and click OK.

6 Right-click the newly created folder, choose Properties to open its Properties dialog box, and then click the Permissions tab. This tab is similar to the one shown previously in Figure 17-17.

7 Set permissions for the Default user to apply permissions for all users who won't have explicit permissions for the folder. Add users and set permissions for those who do need explicit permissions, and click OK to apply the permissions.

For a detailed discussion of creating public folders, see "Setting Up Public Folders," page 810.

Part 4

Scheduling

Chapter 18

Scheduling Appointments

For most of us, a calendar is a basic tool for organizing our lives, both at work and at home. With the calendar in Microsoft Outlook, you can schedule regular appointments, all day and multiday events, and meetings. You can view your schedule almost any way you want. In addition, you can share your calendar with others, which is a big help when scheduling organizational activities.

This chapter first describes the calendar and explains how to work with the basic Calendar folder view. Then you'll learn how to schedule and work with appointments and events. You'll also find information about the more advanced view options for the calendar and about how to share your calendar and free/busy information and how to view different time zones.

Both this chapter and the next focus on the features available in the Outlook Calendar folder. This chapter covers appointments and events; the following chapter discusses meetings and resources.

Calendar Basics

The Outlook Calendar folder provides a central location for storing vast amounts of information about your schedule. Figure 18-1 on the next page shows a basic one-day view of a calendar. You see this view when you first click the Calendar icon on the Outlook Bar to open the folder. This calendar contains no appointments yet, and no tasks are listed on the TaskPad.

479

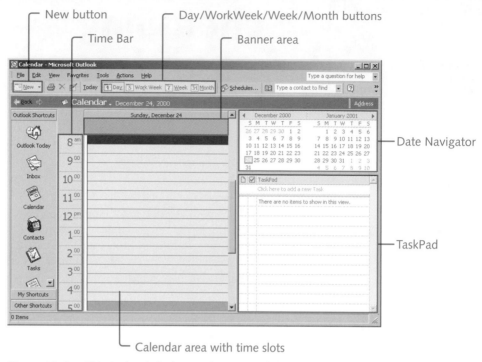

Figure 18-1. This is the default one-day view of the Outlook calendar.

Understanding Calendar Items

Outlook's calendar can contain three types of items: appointments, events, and meetings.

- An *appointment,* which is the default calendar item, involves only your schedule and time and does not require other attendees or resources. The calendar shows appointments in the time slots corresponding to their start and end times.

- When an appointment lasts longer than 24 hours, it becomes an *event.* An event is marked on the calendar not in a time slot but in a banner at the top of the day on which the event occurs.

- An appointment becomes a *meeting* when you invite other people, which requires coordinating their schedules, or when you must schedule resources. Meetings can be in person or set up online using Microsoft NetMeeting.

For in-depth information about meetings, see Chapter 19, "Scheduling Meetings and Re-sources." For information about using NetMeeting, see "Holding an Online Meeting," page 536.

You can create an appointment in any of these ways:

- Choose File, New, Appointment.

- When the Calendar folder is open, click the New toolbar button.

- When any other Outlook folder is open, click the arrow beside the New toolbar button and choose Appointment.

- Click a time slot on the calendar, and simply type the subject of the appointment in the time slot.

For detailed information about creating appointments and using the appointment form, see "Working with One-Time Appointments," page 487.

Using the Time Bar

When you choose a calendar display of six days or less, the Time Bar appears, displaying 30-minute time increments by default. Figure 18-2 shows the Time Bar set to 30-minute increments, with a 30-minute appointment on the calendar.

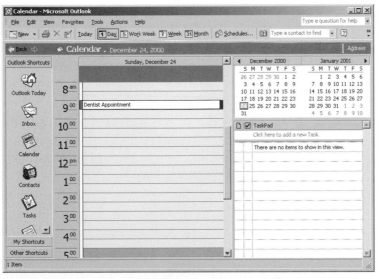

Figure 18-2. By default, the Time Bar is set to display 30-minute increments.

You can set the Time Bar to display different time increments. To do so, begin by right-clicking the Time Bar to display the menu shown in Figure 18-3 on the next page.

481

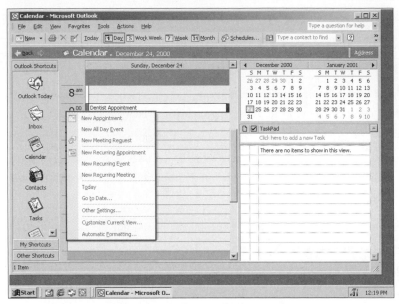

Figure 18-3.   Use this menu to change the time increment.

If you want to change the time scale to 10 minutes, click Other Settings to display the Format Day/Week/Month View dialog box. In the Time Scale drop-down list, choose 10 Minutes; the 30-minute appointment takes up three time intervals instead of one, as shown in Figure 18-4.

Now choose 60 Minutes from the drop-down list; Figure 18-5 shows the result. Note that when an appointment takes up less than a full Time Bar increment, as in this example, the scheduled time of the appointment is displayed with the appointment subject on the calendar.

If a time interval is not completely filled by an appointment, only the portion of the interval that is filled is highlighted to the left of the appointment on the calendar. For example, in Figure 18-5, only half the interval is highlighted because the 30-minute appointment takes up only half the 60-minute interval.

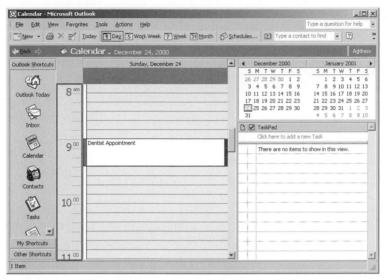

Figure 18-4. The Time Bar has been changed to display 10-minute increments.

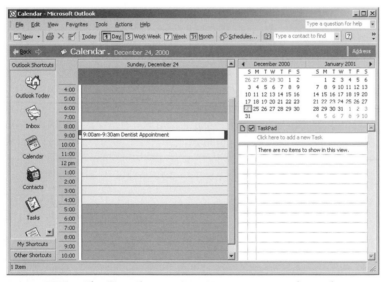

Figure 18-5. The Time Bar is set to 60-minute intervals, so the 30-minute appointment takes up half an interval.

Using the Date Navigator

The Date Navigator has several important uses. For example, you can use it to select the day to view on the calendar—in effect, jumping from one date to another. When you click a day in the Date Navigator, Outlook displays that day according to how you have set the view (by using the Day, Work Week, or Week toolbar buttons):

- In Day view, the selected day is displayed.

- In Work Week view (5 days), Outlook displays the week containing the day you clicked in the Date Navigator.

- In Week view (7 days), the calendar switches to a one-day view for the date you click.

By clicking the right and left arrows next to the month names in the Date Navigator, you can scroll forward and backward through the months.

> For information about Day, Work Week, and Week views, see "Setting the Number of Days Displayed," page 485.

Another use of the Date Navigator is to denote days that contain scheduled items. Those days appear in bold type; days with no scheduled items appear as regular text. This allows you to assess your monthly schedule at a glance.

Finally, you can use the Date Navigator to view multiple days on the calendar. In the Date Navigator, simply drag across the range of days you want to view; those days will all appear on the calendar. For example, Figure 18-6 shows what happens when you drag across three days in the Date Navigator. You can also view multiple consecutive days by clicking the first day and then holding down the Shift key and clicking the last day. To view multiple nonconsecutive days, click the first day you want to view and then hold down the Ctrl key and click each day that you want to add to the view.

> For more information on the Tasks folder and working with tasks, see Chapter 20, "Managing Your Tasks."

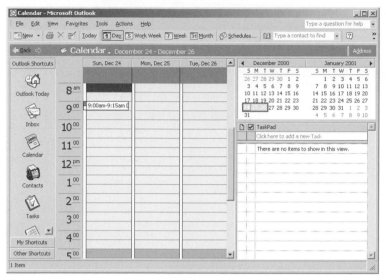

Figure 18-6. You can view multiple days by selecting them in the Date Navigator.

Using the TaskPad

The TaskPad offers an easy way of working with tasks from the Calendar folder. The TaskPad displays existing tasks from the Tasks folder and also allows you to add new tasks. Adding a new task is as simple as clicking in the TaskPad and typing the task subject. Double-click the task item to open the task form if you'd like to add more details. When you create a task on the TaskPad, Outlook automatically adds it to the Tasks folder.

One of the biggest advantages of having the TaskPad in the Calendar folder is that it gives you the ability to assess your schedule and fit tasks in where appropriate. When you drag a task from the TaskPad to the calendar, the appointment form appears, with the task information filled in. You need only set the schedule information for the appointment and save it to the calendar (as explained later in the chapter).

Setting the Number of Days Displayed

You can set the number of days displayed in the calendar in several ways. One way is to use the Date Navigator, as discussed on page 484. The easiest way, however, is to use the appropriate toolbar button. To select the number of days to view, click Day, Work Week, Week, or Month on the toolbar.

When the calendar displays six days or less, the days are shown side by side with the Time Bar (refer back to Figure 18-6, for example). Figure 18-7 shows the calendar when seven or more days are displayed.

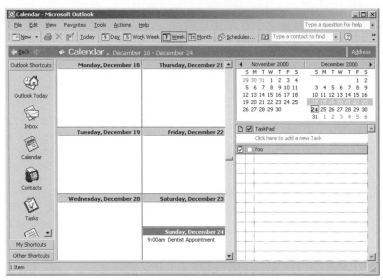

Figure 18-7. The calendar display changes depending on whether you are viewing six days or less or viewing seven days or more.

When you click the Month button on the toolbar, the view is slightly different from the view you see when you choose more than seven days in the Date Navigator. In particular, the Date Navigator and the TaskPad do not appear in Month view, as shown in Figure 18-8.

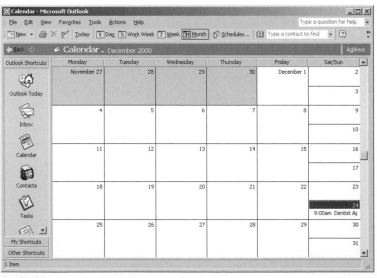

Figure 18-8. Month view doesn't include the Date Navigator or the TaskPad.

Selecting a Date

You can select a date in two ways. The first is by using the Date Navigator in Day, Work Week, or Week view. (The Date Navigator does not appear in Month view.) The second way to select a date is to click the Today button on the toolbar; this action takes you to the current day.

Working with One-Time Appointments

The most basic calendar item is the one-time appointment. You can create a one-time appointment in several ways:

- If the Calendar folder is not open, choose File, New, Appointment or click the down arrow next to the New toolbar button and choose Appointment. The appointment defaults to the next full 30 minutes (that is, if it's 1:50, the appointment is listed with a start time of 2:00 and an end time of 2:30).

- If the Calendar folder is open, click the New toolbar button or right-click the calendar and choose New Appointment. The appointment is scheduled for the time selected in the calendar.

When you take any of these actions, Outlook opens an appointment form, shown in Figure 18-9, where you can specify information for the new item.

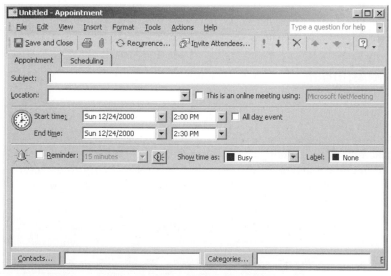

Figure 18-9. Use the appointment form to create a new appointment.

> **tip** **Create an appointment quickly**
>
> To quickly create an appointment, you can click a blank time slot on the calendar and type the subject of the appointment. When you use this method, however, Outlook doesn't automatically open a new appointment form. To add details to the appointment, you must double-click the new appointment to open the form.

Specifying the Subject and Location

Type the subject of an appointment in the Subject box at the top of the appointment form. Make the subject as descriptive as possible because it will appear on the calendar.

If you want, you can type a location for the appointment in the Location box. To view a list of all previously typed locations, click the drop-down arrow beside the Location box; rather than typing the location, you can select from this list. Outlook displays the location you specify in parentheses next to the appointment subject.

Specifying Start and End Times

You set the start and end times of the appointment by typing the date and time in the Start Time and End Time boxes or by clicking the drop-down arrows beside each box. If you click a drop-down arrow for a date, a calendar appears. Click a drop-down arrow for time, and a list of potential start and end times in 30-minute increments appears. The End Time drop-down list shows how long the appointment will be for each given end time.

Setting a Reminder

You can set a reminder for an appointment by selecting the Reminder check box on the appointment form. In the accompanying drop-down list, you can specify when the reminder should appear; the default is 15 minutes before the appointment. By default, a reminder both plays a sound and displays a reminder window, as shown in Figure 18-10. If you don't want the reminder to play a sound, or if you want to use a different sound, click the Sound button on the appointment form to change the settings.

> **note** To change the default behavior of appointment reminders, choose Tools, Options and click Preferences. In the Calendar section of the Preferences tab, you can select (or clear) the default reminder and set the default reminder time.

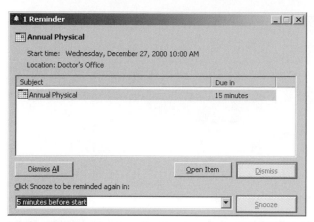

Figure 18-10. You can dismiss a reminder by clicking Dismiss or postpone it by clicking Snooze.

Classifying an Appointment

When you schedule an appointment on the calendar, it's displayed with one of four indicators:

- Busy (shaded black)
- Free (not shaded)
- Tentative (shaded with diagonal lines)
- Out Of Office (shaded gray)

The indicator appears on your local calendar and is also displayed when other users view the free/busy times of that calendar. By default, the time occupied by an appointment is classified as Busy. To reclassify an appointment, select the indicator from the Show Time As drop-down list, as shown in Figure 18-11 on the next page.

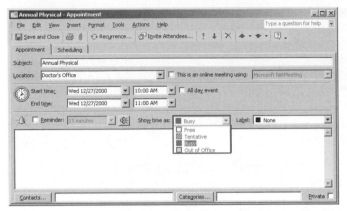

Figure 18-11. Use this drop-down list to select a classification for your appointment, which determines how it is displayed on your calendar.

Adding a Note

Sometimes an appointment requires more detail. You might need to remind yourself about documents you need to bring to the appointment, or perhaps you need to write down directions to an unfamiliar location. When that's the case, you can add a note by typing your text in the large text area of the form, as shown in Figure 18-12.

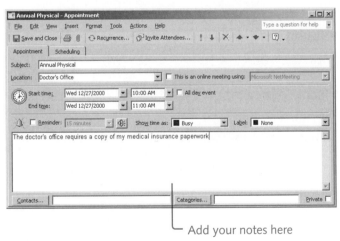

Add your notes here

Figure 18-12. You can write a note on the appointment form.

Assigning a Contact

After you create an appointment, you might decide that it would be helpful to include contact information. For example, if you scheduled a vet appointment, you might want to include the phone number and address. Rather than typing that information as a note, you can link to it (assuming that the data is stored in your Contacts folder).

> For more information about working with the Contacts folder, see Chapter 14, "Managing Your Contacts."

To assign a contact to an appointment, click the Contacts button at the bottom of the appointment form. This opens the Select Contacts dialog box, shown in Figure 18-13. Then select a folder, select a contact, and click OK to assign the contact to the appointment.

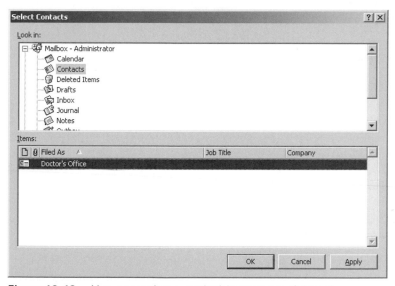

Figure 18-13. You can assign a contact to your appointment.

Categorizing an Appointment

Assigning an appointment to a category is simply another method of organizing your information. Outlook provides a number of categories by default (Business, Goals, and Ideas, for example), and you can add your own custom categories. Outlook allows you to categorize your appointments so that you can then filter or sort them before viewing. In this way, you can get an overview of all Outlook items based on a particular category. For example, you could view all appointments, meetings, messages, contacts, and tasks that have been assigned the same category—perhaps all the items related to a specific work project or objective.

Chapter 18

491

> For more information on working with categories in Outlook, see Chapter 4, "Using Categories and Types."

To assign a category to an appointment, click the Categories button at the bottom of the appointment form. In the Categories dialog box (see Figure 18-14), you can select one or more categories; click OK to assign them to the appointment.

Figure 18-14. You can assign one or more categories to your appointment.

Saving an Appointment

You can save an appointment in several ways. The most basic method is to click the Save And Close button on the toolbar of the appointment form. This saves the appointment to the Calendar folder and closes the appointment form. If you want to save the appointment but keep the form open, choose File, Save.

A more complex way to save appointments allows them to be transferred to other users (who might or might not use Outlook) and opened in other applications. To save your appointments in any of a number of file formats, choose File, Save As to display the Save As dialog box (see Figure 18-15).

The following formats are available:

- **Text Only** and **Rich Text Format.** These formats save the appointment in a file that text editors can read. Figure 18-16 shows an example of an appointment saved in Rich Text Format and then opened in WordPad.

> **tip** You can create a new appointment from an Outlook Template file by choosing File, New, Choose Form and selecting User Templates In File System from the Look In list.

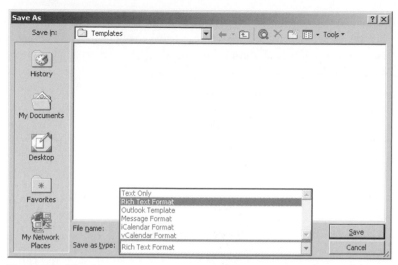

Figure 18-15. You can save your appointment in any of several formats so that the appointment can be opened with another application.

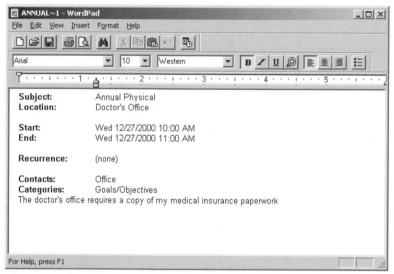

Figure 18-16. An appointment saved in Rich Text or Text Only format can be displayed in any application that supports those file types.

● **Outlook Template.** This format allows you to save an appointment and use it later to create new appointments.

● **Message Format.** Saving an appointment in this format is almost the same as saving an appointment to the calendar, except that the appointment is saved to a file in case you want to archive it or move it to another copy of Outlook. You can view the file in Outlook, and the data appears as it would if you had opened the item from the calendar.

- **iCalendar and vCalendar Format.** These formats are used to share schedule items with people who use applications other than Outlook. iCalendar is a newer version of the standard (maintained by the Internet Mail Consortium) and should be used if possible.

Changing an Appointment to an Event

To change an appointment to an event, select the All Day Event check box on the appointment form. When an appointment is converted to an event, the start and end times are removed and only the start and end dates are left because events by definition last all day. The event appears in the banner area of the calendar.

Working with One-Time Events

An event is an appointment that lasts for one or more entire days. You can create an event by right-clicking the calendar and selecting New All Day Event. Unlike appointments, events are not shown in time slots on the calendar. Instead, events are displayed as banners at the top of the calendar day. Figure 18-17 shows the calendar with a scheduled event—in this case, a trade show.

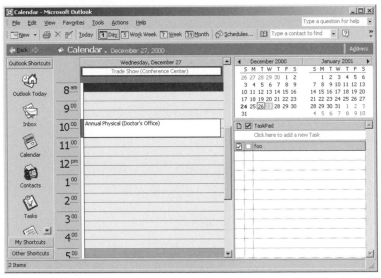

Figure 18-17. Outlook displays events as banners at the top of the calendar.

Chapter 18

---

tip **Create an event quickly**

A simple way to add an event is to click the banner area of the calendar and start typing the subject of the event. When you add an event this way, the event is automatically set to last for only the selected day. To add details and change the duration of the event, you must use the event form.

Using the Event Form

You can use an event form in much the same way you use an appointment form, with a few exceptions: you can set the start and end times only as dates, not times; the default reminder is set to 18 hours; and the time is shown by default as Free, as opposed to Busy. The event form and the appointment form look the same except that the All Day Event box is selected on the event form. You open an event form the same way you open an appointment form.

To create an event using the event form, type the subject, specify the start and end dates, add any optional information, and then click the Save And Close button on the toolbar. Figure 18-18 shows the event form for a trade show event.

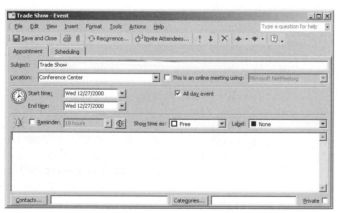

Figure 18-18.   Use the event form to specify the details of an event to be added to your calendar.

Changing an Event to an Appointment

To change an event to an appointment, clear the All Day Event check box on the event form. The boxes for start and end times reappear, and the event will now be displayed in time slots on the calendar, not in the banner area.

495

Creating a Recurring Appointment or Event

When you create a *recurring appointment* or a *recurring event,* Outlook automatically displays the recurrences in the calendar. A recurring appointment could be something as simple as a reminder to feed your fish every day or pay your mortgage every month. You can create a recurring calendar item by right-clicking the calendar and choosing New Recurring Appointment or New Recurring Event. Alternatively, you can open a normal (nonrecurring) item and click the Recurrence button on the toolbar. Either method displays the Appointment Recurrence dialog box, shown in Figure 18-19.

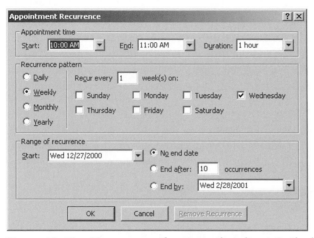

Figure 18-19. You can specify criteria that direct Outlook to display an appointment or event multiple times in the calendar.

In the Appointment Time area, you set the appointment time and duration. If you're creating the recurrence from an existing nonrecurring appointment, the time of that appointment is listed here by default.

The Recurrence Pattern area changes depending on whether you select the Daily, Weekly, Monthly, or Yearly option, as follows:

● **Daily.** Specify the number of days or every weekday.

● **Weekly.** Specify the number of weeks and the day (or days) of the week.

● **Monthly.** Specify the number of months as well as the day of the month (such as the 27th) or the day and week of the month (such as the fourth Wednesday).

● **Yearly.** Specify the date (such as December 27th) or the day and week of the month (such as the fourth Wednesday of each December).

Chapter 18

The last part of the Appointment Recurrence dialog box is the Range Of Recurrence area. By default, the start date is the current day, and the recurrence is set to never end. You can choose to have the appointment recur a specified number of times and then stop, or you can set it up to recur until a specified date and then stop—either method has the same effect. For example, to set up a recurring appointment that starts on the first Monday of a month and continues for four Mondays in that month, you could either set it to occur four times or set it to occur until the last day of the month.

Modifying an Appointment or Event

Changing an appointment or event is easy. First open the appointment or event by locating it in the calendar and either double-clicking the item or right-clicking it and choosing Open. Make the necessary changes in the form and then click the Save And Close button on the toolbar. The updated appointment or event is saved to the Calendar folder.

Deleting an Appointment or Event

You can delete an appointment or event in several ways. To send the item to the Deleted Items folder, right-click the item and choose Delete, or select the item and press the Delete key. To permanently delete the item, hold down Shift while choosing Delete or pressing the Delete key.

> **caution**   You cannot recover an item that has been deleted using the Shift key.

Using Color Effectively

You can use color as a tool to identify appointments and events. The easiest way to assign color to an appointment is to use the Label drop-down list in the appointment form. You can also create rules that direct Outlook to assign color labels automatically.

Assigning Color to an Appointment Manually

The Label drop-down list on the appointment form shows the different color labels you can assign to an appointment as a visual cue to indicate the purpose of the appointment, its importance, or its requirements. Simply select a color in the drop-down list when you fill in the appointment form. In Figure 18-20 on the next page, the appointment is a personal one, and it will be displayed on the calendar in the specified color.

Chapter 18

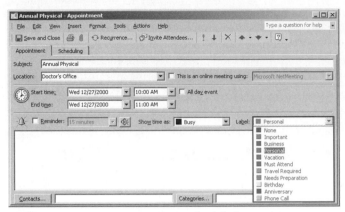

Figure 18-20. You can assign a color label to your appointment.

Assigning Color to an Appointment Automatically

To have Outlook automatically assign a color label to an appointment, you can create automatic formatting rules.

To create a Color rule, do the following:

1 Choose View, Current View, Customize Current View to open the View Summary dialog box.

2 Click Automatic Formatting to display the Automatic Formatting dialog box.

3 Click Add to add a new rule.

4 Type a name and assign a label to the new rule. Figure 18-21 shows a rule to automatically color all birthdays with a yellow Birthday label.

5 Click the Condition button to open the Filter dialog box (see Figure 18-22).

For details about using filters, see "Customizing the Current Calendar View," page 500.

Figure 18-21. This new rule will automatically assign a yellow label to all birthdays.

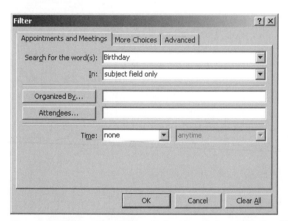

Figure 18-22. The Filter dialog box lets you set a filter that defines the condition on which the automatic color rule works.

6 In this dialog box, assign a condition to the rule. For example, you might use the most basic type of filter and look for the word *Birthday* in the subject line of all appointments.

7 Click OK to assign the condition to the new rule.

8 Click OK twice, once to close the Automatic Formatting dialog box and again to close the View Summary dialog box.

A rule is now in effect that all appointments with the word *Birthday* in their subject will be assigned the yellow Birthday label.

Chapter 18

Printing Calendar Items

You can print calendar items in two ways. The simplest method is to right-click the item and choose Print from the shortcut menu. This method prints the item using the default settings.

The other way to print an item is to first open it by double-clicking it or by right-clicking it and choosing Open. You can then click the Print button on the toolbar to print using the default settings, or you can choose File, Print to display the Print dialog box.

You can make selections in the Print dialog box to change the target printer, the number of copies, and the print style, if necessary. The print style defines how the printed item will look. Click Page Setup to change the options for the selected style. Use the Format tab to set fonts and shading; the Paper tab to change the paper size, orientation, and margin settings; and the Header/Footer tab to add information to be printed at the top and bottom of the page.

Customizing the Current Calendar View

Besides setting the number of days displayed, configuring the Time Bar, and color-coding your appointments, you can customize the standard view of the Calendar folder in other ways. You can redefine fields, set up filters that determine which items are displayed on your calendar, and control fonts and other view settings. To configure the view, begin by choosing View, Current View, Customize Current View to open the View Summary dialog box, shown in Figure 18-23.

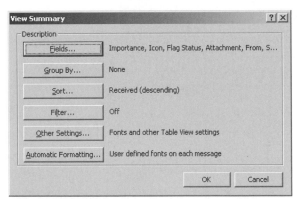

Figure 18-23. Use the View Summary dialog box to change view settings.

> **tip**   You can also customize views other than the current one. To do so, choose View,
> Current View, Define Views. Then select the view in the Define Views dialog box, and
> click the Modify button. This displays the View Summary dialog box, where you can
> change the options for the selected view.

Redefining Fields

Only two of the fields used for calendar items can be redefined: the Start and End fields. The values in these fields determine an item's precise location on the calendar—that is, where it is displayed. By default, the value contained in the Start field is the start time of the appointment, and the value contained in the End field is the end time of the appointment, which means that the item is displayed on the calendar in the time interval defined by the item's Start and End values.

To redefine either of the Start or End fields, click the Fields button in the View Summary dialog box to open the Date/Time Fields dialog box. In the Available Date/Time Fields list, select the field that you want to use for the Start field and click the Start button. Use the End button to change the End field. For example, if you redefine the Start field to Recurrence Range Start and the End field to Recurrence Range End, all recurring calendar items will display as a single item that starts on the date of the first occurrence and ends on the date of the last occurrence. This can be handy if you want to view the entire recurrence range for a given item graphically.

Filtering Calendar Items

You can filter calendar items based on their content, their assigned category, or other criteria. By filtering the current view, you can determine which calendar items are displayed on your calendar—for example, all items related to one of your work projects, all items that involve a specific coworker, or items with a particular importance level.

To filter calendar items, follow these steps:

1 Choose View, Current View, Customize Current View to open the View Summary dialog box.

2 Click Filter to open the Filter dialog box.

3 If the Appointments And Meetings tab isn't displayed (see Figure 18-24 on the next page), click it to bring it to the front.

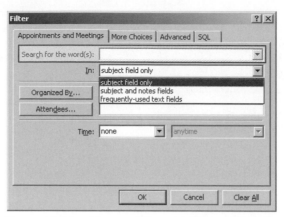

Figure 18-24. You can filter calendar items based on a specified word or phrase.

4 In the Search For The Word(s) box, type the word or phrase you want to use as the filter.

5 In the In drop-down list, select which areas of the calendar item to search— for example, you might have Outlook look only in the Subject field of your appointments.

6 When you click OK, Outlook displays on your calendar only those calendar items that contain the specified word or phrase.

To set additional criteria, you can use the three other tabs in the Filter dialog box— More Choices, Advanced, and SQL:

● **More Choices.** On this tab you can click Categories to select any number of categories. After you click OK, only calendar items belonging to the se- lected categories are displayed on the calendar. Using the check boxes on the More Choices tab, you can filter items based on whether they are read or unread, whether they have or do not have attachments, or their importance setting. The final check box on the tab enables or disables case matching for the word or phrase specified on the Appointments And Meetings tab. You can also filter items depending on size.

● **Advanced.** This tab allows an even wider range of filter criteria. You can specify any field, adding a condition such as Contains or Is Not Empty or a value for conditions that require one. Clicking the Add To List button adds the criteria to the list of filters.

● **SQL.** This tab has two purposes. In most cases, it displays the SQL code for the filter, based on the filter criteria you select on the other three tabs. If the Edit The Filter Directly check box is selected, however, you can manually type the SQL code for filtering calendar items directly on the SQL tab. This flexibility allows you to fine-tune your filters with a great degree of precision.

Controlling Fonts and Other View Settings

You can use the View Summary dialog box (see Figure 18-23, page 500) to make additional changes to the current view. In the View Summary dialog box, click the Other Settings button, which displays the Format Day/Week/Month View dialog box, shown in Figure 18-25.

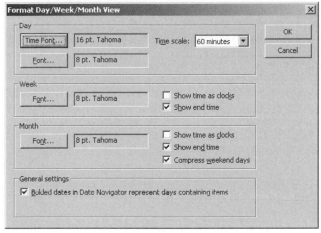

Figure 18-25. You can use the Format Day/Week/Month View dialog box to set font preferences for the Calendar folder as well as other options.

In the Format Day/Week/Month View dialog box, you can do the following:

● Set the fonts used in the calendar view.

● Set the calendar's time increments by selecting an option in the Time Scale drop-down list. This sets the amount of time represented by each interval in the Time Bar.

● Display weekend days in the calendar's Month view as smaller than week days by selecting the Compress Weekend Days check box.

● Decide whether days with scheduled items should appear in bold in the Date Navigator.

503

Creating a Custom View

Until now, this chapter has discussed only the customization of existing views, but you can also create completely new views as well as copy and modify views. If your current view is one you use often but nevertheless must change frequently to filter calendar items or modify fields, you might find it easier to create a new view.

To create a view or to see a list of already defined views, choose View, Current View, Define Views to open the Define Views dialog box, shown in Figure 18-26.

> **note** To work with Outlook's calendar views, you must open the Calendar folder.

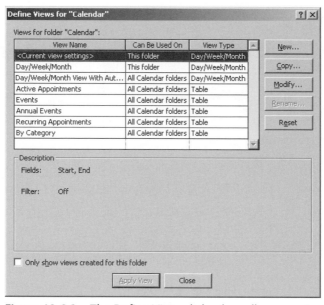

Figure 18-26. The Define Views dialog box allows you to see and work with the currently defined views as well as create new ones.

Creating a New View

To create a view, follow these steps:

1 Click the New button in the Define Views dialog box to open the Create A New View dialog box, shown in Figure 18-27.

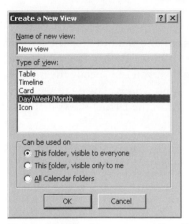

Figure 18-27. You can use the Create A New View dialog box to specify a name, a view type, the folder to which the view applies, and who is allowed to see the view.

2 Name the new view and select a view type. In the Can Be Used On section, specify the folder to which the view applies and who is allowed to see the view. You can select one of the following options:

- ■ **This Folder, Visible To Everyone.** Limits the view to the current folder and makes it available to any user.

- ■ **This Folder, Visible Only To Me.** Limits the view to the current folder but makes it available only to the current user.

- ■ **All Calendar Folders.** Allows the view to be used in any calendar folder by any user.

3 When you click OK to create the new view, the View Summary dialog box appears, in which you can set the options for the new view.

---

tip   **Change the availability of an existing view**

To change the availability of an existing view or who is allowed to see a view, first copy the view and assign a name to the copy. (See "Copying a View" on the next page for more information copying views.) Then select a new option in the Can Be Used On area. Finally, delete the original view and rename the new view using the name of the deleted view.

For information about setting view options in the View Summary dialog box, see "Customizing the Current Calendar View," page 500.

Chapter 18

Copying a View

If you want to modify an existing view but also want to keep the original, you can make a copy of the view. To copy a view, select it in the Define Views dialog box and click the Copy button. In the Copy View dialog box, you can specify the name of the new view, the folder to which the view will apply, and who is allowed to see the view. Click OK to create the copy, which is added to the list in the Define Views dialog box and the list on the View, Current View menu.

Backing Up Your Schedule

To back up items in your Calendar folder, you must export the data to a personal folders (PST) file.

To do so, follow these steps:

1 Choose File, Import And Export to start the Import And Export Wizard.

2 Choose Export To A File, as shown in Figure 18-28, and click Next.

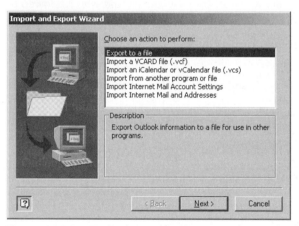

Figure 18-28. To back up calendar items, first open the Import And Export Wizard and select Export To A File.

3 On the Export To A File page (see Figure 18-29), select Personal Folder File (.pst) and then click Next.

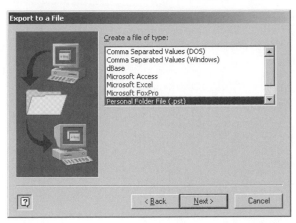

Figure 18-29. Calendar items should be backed up to a personal folders file.

4 On the Export Personal Folders page, select the folder to export (the Calendar folder, in the example shown in Figure 18-30). If you select the Include Subfolders check box, any subfolders of the selected folder are exported as well.

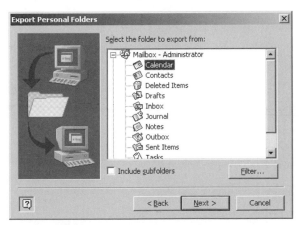

Figure 18-30. You use the Export Personal Folders page to specify the folder to export to a file.

5 Click the Filter button to open the Filter dialog box, in which you can specify the items to be exported. You can use the Filter dialog box if you want to export only specific items from your Calendar folder. If you choose not to use the Filter dialog box, all items will be exported.

For details about using the Filter dialog box, see "Filtering Calendar Items," page 501.

Chapter 18

6 Specify the exported file and the export options. The export options control how Outlook handles items that have duplicates in the target file. You can choose to overwrite duplicates, create duplicates in the file, or not export duplicate items.

7 Click Finish. The Create Microsoft Personal Folders dialog box (see Figure 18-31) displays the selected file name.

Figure 18-31. Type a password and choose encryption options before creating the PST file.

8 Specify a descriptive name for the personal folders file. You can also set encryption levels and a password for the file.

9 Click the OK button to create the file.

To restore data backed up to the personal folders file, follow these steps:

1 Choose File, Import And Export to start the Import And Export Wizard.

2 Choose Import From Another Program Or File and then click Next.

3 Select Personal Folder File (.pst) and click Next.

4 On the Import Personal Folders page, specify the backup file and how Outlook should handle duplicate items. You can choose to overwrite duplicates, create duplicate items, or not import duplicates. Then click Next.

5 Select the folder within the personal folders file to be imported (the Calendar folder in this case), decide whether to include subfolders, and select the target folder. (By default, the target folder is the folder with the same name in the current mailbox, as shown in Figure 18-32.) You can also click the Filter button to specify in the Filter dialog box which items are to be imported.

6 Click Finish to complete the import process.

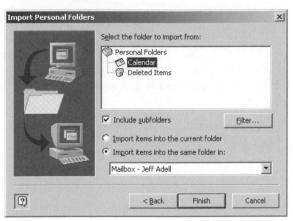

Figure 18-32. When you're importing items, you must select the folder to be imported from the personal folders file, whether to include subfolders, and the target folder.

Sharing Your Calendar

You can allow other users to access your entire calendar or selected calendar items. To share your calendar and its items, you must set permission levels for various users. In most cases, permissions are set by using built-in roles, as indicated in Table 18-1, but you can also set custom permissions for the rare cases when the built-in role does not fit the situation. Some permissions allow users to view your calendar; others allow users to add or even edit items. Table 18-1 explains these permissions.

Table 18-1.   Folder permissions

Permission	Description
Owner	The Owner role gives full control of the folder. An Owner can create, modify, delete, and read folder items; create subfolders; and change permissions on the folder.
Publishing Editor	The Publishing Editor role has all rights granted to an Owner, except the right to change permissions. A Publishing Editor can create, modify, delete, and read folder items and create subfolders.
Editor	The Editor role has all rights granted to a Publishing Editor, except the right to create subfolders. An Editor can create, modify, delete, and read folder items.
Publishing Author	A Publishing Author can create and read folder items and create subfolders but can modify and delete only folder items that he or she creates, not items created by other users.

(continued)

Chapter 18

Table 18-1. *(continued)*

Permission	Description
Author	An Author has all rights granted to a Publishing Author but cannot create subfolders. An Author can create and read folder items and modify and delete items that he or she creates.
Nonediting Author	A Nonediting Author can create and read folder items but cannot modify or delete any items, including those that he or she creates.
Reviewer	A Reviewer can read folder items but nothing else.
Contributor	A Contributor can create only folder items and cannot read items.
None	The None role has no access to the folder.

The first step in sharing the Calendar folder is to right-click it on the Outlook Bar and choose Properties. Then click the Permissions tab to view the current permissions for the folder. Figure 18-33 shows the Permissions tab with the Calendar folder's default permissions.

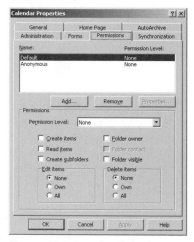

Figure 18-33. The default permissions for a folder are set to None.

To allow all users to view the calendar, you need to assign Reviewer permission to the default user. A *default user* is any user who is logged in. (An *anonymous user* is any user, whether they are logged in or not. Default users are a subgroup of anonymous users.) Select Default in the Name column and then change the permission level by selecting Reviewer in the Permission Level drop-down list.

You might assign a permission of Publishing Editor to users if they are colleagues who need to be able to schedule items for you as well as view and edit your calendar.

To give users Publishing Editor access to the calendar, follow these steps:

1 On the Permissions tab of the Folder Properties dialog box, click Add to open the Add Users dialog box, shown in Figure 18-34.

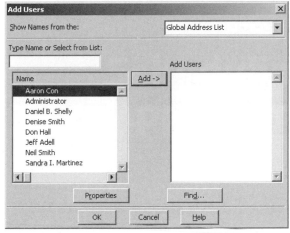

Figure 18-34. Add users to the Permissions tab so that you can specify their permissions for folder sharing.

2 Select a user from the list on the left and then click Add.

3 Repeat step 2 until you have selected all the users you want to add. Click OK.

4 By default, Outlook adds users to the Permissions tab with Reviewer permission. To change the permission of a newly added user to Publishing Editor, select the user's name and then select the permission in the Permission Level drop-down list. Figure 18-35 on the next page shows the Permissions tab after these changes have been made.

As you can see in Figure 18-35, the permissions granted to a user can be configured manually using the check boxes in the bottom half of the Permissions tab. However, this is usually unnecessary because you can set most combinations of settings by using the Permission Level drop-down list.

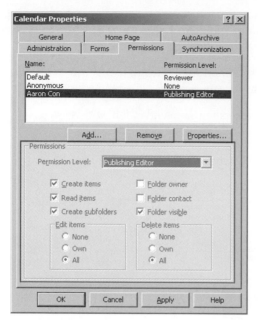

Figure 18-35. The default user's permission has been changed to Reviewer, and a user has been added and given Publishing Editor permission.

Managing Your Free/Busy Information

By default, if you're using Microsoft Exchange Server, your free/busy information is shared automatically with all other users on that server. If you want users who are not on your server to be able to view that information, you can share it. You share this data by using the Microsoft Office Internet Free/Busy Service, or another server, or both. When you're using a different server, HTTP, FTP, and file URLs are supported.

Troubleshooting

Other users don't see your schedule changes.

When you make changes to your schedule, those changes might not be visible right away to other users who need to see your free/busy times. By default, Outlook updates your free/busy times only every 15 minutes. To change the frequency of these updates, choose Tools, Options and click Calendar Options. Then click Free/Busy Options to locate the option Update Free/Busy Information On The Server Every *n* Minutes, which you can use to set the frequency of updates.

Publishing Your Schedule

The Microsoft Office Internet Free/Busy Service is a central place on the Internet where you can publish your schedule. Publishing your schedule allows anyone (or only those you specify) to access your free/busy information from anywhere on the Internet.

InsideOut

You can avoid publishing your free/busy information to any servers if you prefer. Choose Tools, Options and click Calendar Options. Then click the Free/Busy Options button. You can set the option Publish *n* Months Of Calendar Free/Busy Information On The Server to specify how much of your free/busy information is published. By setting this value to 0, no free/busy information is published, and your free/busy information will appear blank to other users.

To publish the schedule of your free/busy times using the Microsoft Office Internet Free/Busy Service, follow these steps:

1 Choose Tools, Options and click the Calendar Options. Then click the Free/Busy Options button to open the Free/Busy Options dialog box (see Figure 18-36).

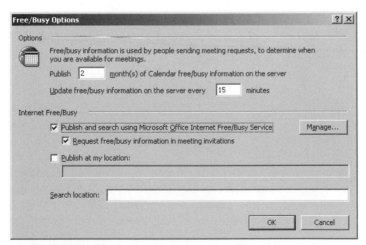

Figure 18-36. Configure the free/busy options and the location for publishing free/busy information.

2 Specify how much free/busy information you want to have published (two months is the default) and how often the free/busy information should be updated on the server (every 15 minutes is the default).

3 Specify the location where the free/busy information should be published (either the Microsoft Office Internet Free/Busy Service or a local location on your network provided by your system administrator).

4 Select the Publish And Search Using Microsoft Office Free/Busy Service check box.

5 To configure the service, click the Manage button. You must have an Internet connection to use the service. Figure 18-37 shows the sign-in page for the Microsoft Office Internet Free/Busy Service.

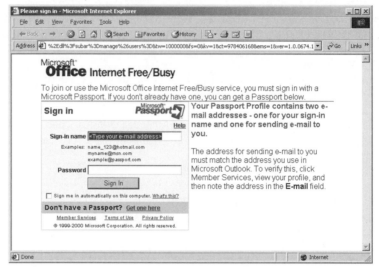

Figure 18-37. To use the Microsoft Office Internet Free/Busy Service, you must sign in using a Microsoft Passport login.

6 If you need to get a Microsoft Passport login, click Get One Here on the sign-in page. Fill out the form, including the e-mail address you are using with Outlook, and click Sign Up. You can then continue to the Free/Busy Service. After signing up, the service tells you how to configure Outlook for use.

7 From the screen shown in Figure 18-38, you can authorize other users to view your free/busy information by typing their e-mail addresses. Or select the All Microsoft Office Internet Free/Busy Service Members check box to allow all users to see your information.

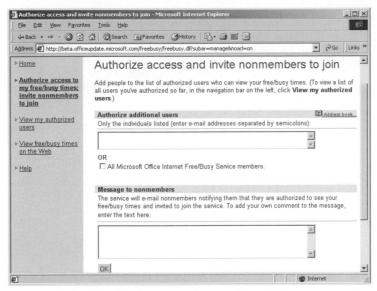

Figure 18-38. Specify the users who are allowed to access your free/busy information or select the check box to allow all users access.

8 If you want, type a personalized message to include in the e-mail sent by the Free/Busy Service. (The service sends an e-mail to all users who are not members of the service to notify them that they can view your free/busy information—and to invite them to join the service.)

9 Click OK to save your changes.

10 Continue clicking OK to close the Free/Busy Options, Calendar Options, and Options dialog boxes.

Your free/busy information is now shared using the Microsoft Office Internet Free/Busy Service, and other users who have joined the service can see that information.

Specifying the Schedule Server

You can also publish your free/busy schedule to another server using FTP, HTTP, or file URLs. Just follow these steps:

1 In the Free/Busy Options dialog box, select Publish At My Location.

2 In the text box, specify the fully qualified path to the server on which your free/busy information is to be published. The path must be in the form *ftp://<Myserver>/<directory>/<Myname>.vfb*. Free/busy files have an extension of .vfb. You can use the substitutions %SERVER%, which represents the server name in the e-mail address, and %NAME%, which represents the user name in the e-mail address. For example, for the address *user@example.tld*, %SERVER% represents *example.tld* and %NAME% represents *user*.

515

Chapter 18

3 In the Search Location text box, specify the server to search. This server will be used to view other users' free/busy information. The %SERVER% and %NAME% substitutions become more important here. As long as other users are using *ftp://%SERVER%/<directory>/%NAME% .vfb* to publish their free/busy information, you can use *ftp://%SERVER%/<directory>/%NAME% .vfb* to access it.

4 Click OK to close the Free/Busy Options dialog box.

Refreshing Your Schedule

Free/busy information is refreshed automatically at the intervals set in the Free/Busy Options dialog box. (Choose Tools, Options, click Calendar Options, and then click the Free/Busy Options button to access this dialog box).

You can refresh free/busy information manually as well. First, make sure that the Calendar folder is open. Then choose Tools, Send/Receive, Free/Busy Information.

Sending Your Free/Busy Information via E-Mail

To e-mail your free/busy information to others, you must first link that information to a vCard as follows:

1 Open a contact item containing your own contact information.

2 Click the Details tab of the contact form, shown in Figure 18-39.

3 In the Address box in the Internet Free-Busy area, type the address of the server containing your free/busy information.

4 Choose File, Save As and select vCard Files from the Save As Type drop-down list to save the contact information as a vCard.

5 Click OK to create the vCard.

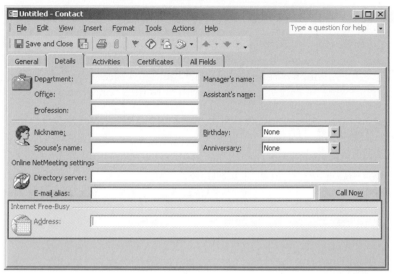

Figure 18-39. On the Details tab of a contact form, you can specify the Internet Free/Busy server.

You can now send the vCard to other users, and they can reference your free/busy information.

For details about using vCards, see "Sharing Contacts with vCards," page 415.

Changing the Free/Busy Status of an Item

You can change the free/busy status of an item easily. One method is to right-click the item and choose Show Time As, Free/Busy. The second method is to open the item (double-click or right-click it and choose Open), and choose Free/Busy from the Show Time As drop-down list.

Managing Time Zones

Outlook gives you a great deal of flexibility when it comes to time zones on your calendar. You can change time zones easily and even add a second time zone to the calendar. If you work for a corporation that has multiple offices in different time zones, being able to quickly reference your calendar with both time zones can make scheduling simpler.

Changing the Time Zone

To work with time zones, use the Time Zone dialog box (see Figure 18-40). To open this dialog box, right-click the Time Bar and choose Change Time Zone. (Alternatively, choose Tools, Options and click Calendar Options. Then click the Time Zone button.)

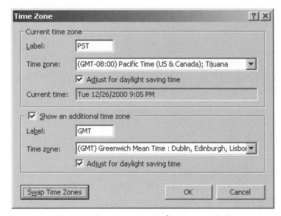

Figure 18-40. You can set the current time zone and display a second time zone.

In the Time Zone dialog box, you can specify a label for the current time zone, which is displayed above the Time Bar on your calendar. You can also set the time zone you want to use by selecting it from the Time Zone drop-down list, and you can choose whether to automatically adjust for daylight saving time.

> **note** Changing the time zone in the Time Zone dialog box has the same effect as changing the time zone by using the Date/Time icon in Control Panel.

When you change the time zone, the time of your appointments adjusts as well. Your appointments will stay at their scheduled time in the original time zone but will move to the appropriate time in the new time zone. For example, an appointment scheduled for 10:00 A.M. in the GMT+2 time zone will move to 8:00 A.M. if the time zone is changed to GMT (Greenwich Mean Time). Appointments are scheduled in absolute time, regardless of the time zone.

Using Two Time Zones

To add a second time zone to your calendar, follow these steps:

1 In the Time Zone dialog box, select the Show An Additional Time Zone check box.

2 Assign a label to the second time zone. This step is not necessary, but it can help to avoid confusion later on. (If your first time zone does not already have a label, adding one now will allow you to easily distinguish the two.)

3 In the second Time Zone drop-down list, select the second time zone.

4 Select the Adjust For Daylight Saving Time check box if you want Outlook to make this adjustment.

5 You can click Swap Time Zones to swap the current time zone with the second time zone. This feature is useful if you travel between corporate offices in different time zones.

Figure 18-41 shows the calendar after these changes have been applied.

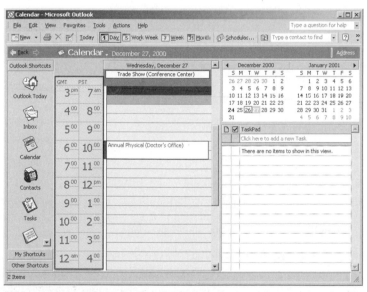

Figure 18-41. The calendar displays both time zones in the Time Bar under their respective labels.

Chapter 18

Publishing Your Calendar as a Web Page

If you want individuals who are not running Outlook or another scheduling program to be able to view your calendar, you can save it to a Web page. You can save the calendar to any Web server using FTP and to some using HTTP. For an example of a calendar saved as a Web page, see Figure 18-42.

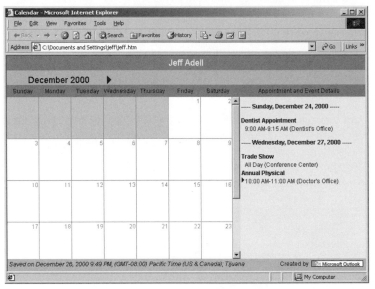

Figure 18-42. This is an example of a calendar published as a Web page.

To save a calendar to a Web page, follow these steps:

1 Ensure that the Calendar folder is open.

2 Choose File, Save As Web Page to open the Save As Web Page dialog box.

3 Specify the start and end dates of the schedule you want to publish.

4 Choose whether to include appointment details.

5 If you want, specify a background graphic in the text box.

6 Specify a title for the Web page and the location for saving the page. You can save the page to a file on the local drive or to an FTP or HTTP server specified by the URL.

7 Click Save to display the saved Web page by default. (If you do not want the Web page displayed by default, clear the Open Saved Web Page In Browser check box.)

Chapter 19

Scheduling Meetings and Resources

Before the introduction of workgroup software such as Microsoft Exchange and Microsoft Outlook, scheduling a meeting could be a difficult task. Now all it takes is a few simple steps to avoid those endless e-email exchanges trying to find a suitable meeting time for all invitees. Outlook provides you with a single place to schedule both people and resources for meetings.

Chapter 18, "Scheduling Appointments," tells you all about scheduling appointments. Meetings and appointments are similar, of course: both types of items appear on your calendar, and you can create, view, and store them in your Outlook Calendar folder. An appointment, however, involves only your schedule and time, whereas a meeting involves inviting others and coordinating their schedules. Another difference is that a meeting often requires you to schedule resources, such as a conference room or an overhead projector.

You can schedule meetings with other Outlook users as well as with those who use any e-mail or collaboration application that supports the vCal or iCal standards. This chapter takes you through the process of scheduling meetings and lining up resources. It also introduces online meetings, which can be set up through Microsoft NetMeeting, and another form of online collaborative communication, the broadcast of Microsoft PowerPoint presentations.

Sending a Meeting Request

To schedule a meeting, you begin by sending a meeting request. Choose File, New, Meeting Request or click the arrow beside the New button on the toolbar and choose Meeting Request. The meeting form opens, as shown in Figure 19-1.

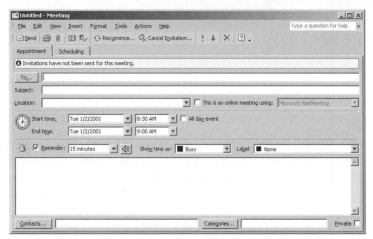

Figure 19-1. You use the meeting form to schedule meetings and send meeting requests.

A meeting request is like an appointment item, but with a few additional details—and you can work with it in much the same way you work with an appointment. This chapter describes only the parts of a meeting request that differ from an appointment.

> For details about creating and working with appointments in Outlook's Calendar folder, see Chapter 18, "Scheduling Appointments."

Selecting Attendees

To invite people to your meeting, start by selecting their names on either the Appointment tab or the Scheduling tab of the meeting form. To select them on the Appointment tab, you can type each name in the To box, separating them with a semicolon. When you enter the names manually, Outlook considers each person a required attendee. Alternatively, you can click the To button to open the Select Attendees And Resources dialog box (see Figure 19-2). In this dialog box, select a name in the Name list and click Required or Optional to designate whether or not that person's attendance is critical. (This choice will be reflected in the meeting request you send to these individuals.) After you have finished adding names, click OK to close the dialog box.

To add names using the Scheduling tab, shown in Figure 19-3, you can click in the designated box in the All Attendees column and type a name. Alternatively, you can click the Add Others button and select the location from which you want to add the names. For example, if you want to add individuals from the Global Address List, click Add Others and then select Add From Address Book to open the Select Attendees And Resources dialog box. As before, select a name, click Required or Optional, and then click OK.

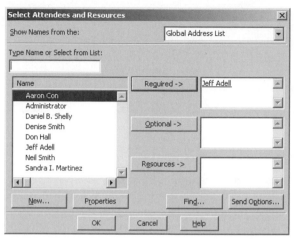

Figure 19-2. In the Select Attendees And Resources dialog box, you can add the names of the individuals you're inviting to your meeting.

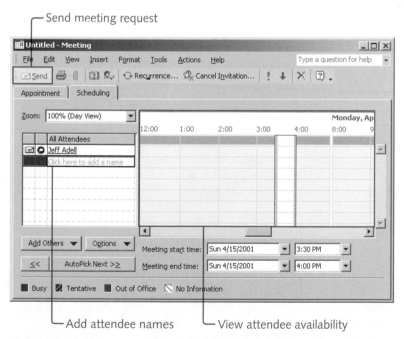

Figure 19-3. You can use the Scheduling tab to add meeting attendees and view their schedules.

523

InsideOut

Can't find the attendee you're looking for and you know that attendee is in the address book? Make sure that the correct address list is selected in the Show Names From The drop-down list. By default, the Global Address List, which shows all names from your Microsoft Exchange Server organization, is selected (if you're running Outlook with Exchange Server). It is possible to change the default address list, however, and yours could be set to something else.

Scheduling a Meeting

After you have added the names of the individuals you want to invite, you can schedule the meeting on the Scheduling tab of the meeting form, which now displays free/busy information for all the people you selected. In Figure 19-4, the Scheduling tab shows information for the meeting organizer (you), one required attendee, and one optional attendee.

The icons you see beside each name mean the following:

- The magnifying glass icon indicates the meeting organizer.

- The arrow indicates a required attendee.

- The icon containing the letter *i* indicates an optional attendee.

According to the free/busy information shown in Figure 19-4, everyone is available between 1:00 and 2:00 P.M., so you can schedule the meeting for that time slot using the Meeting Start Time and Meeting End Time drop-down lists.

If you want Outlook to fit the meeting into the next available time slot, click the AutoPick Next button. By default, AutoPick selects the next time slot in which all attendees and at least one resource are free.

---

tip   **Configure the AutoPick feature**

To change the default actions of AutoPick, click the Options button on the Scheduling tab and make your choices on the AutoPick menu. You can set AutoPick to select the next time slot in which all attendees and all resources are free, the next time slot in which all attendees and at least one resource are free (the default), a slot in which only required attendees are free, or a slot in which required attendees and at least one resource are free.

524

Add attendee names — View attendee availability

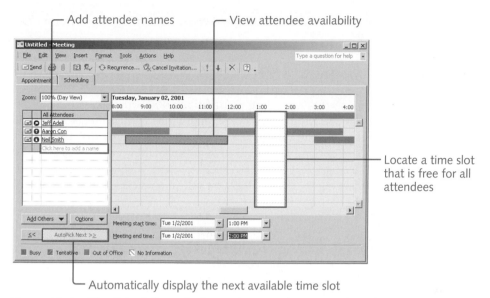

Locate a time slot
that is free for all
attendees

Automatically display the next available time slot

Figure 19-4. The Scheduling tab shows the attendees you selected along with their free/busy times.

You can decide whether the Scheduling tab's display of free/busy information should show only working hours (the default) or the entire day. To define working hours, choose Tools, Options in Outlook and click Calendar Options. Working hours are a way of displaying your time in the Calendar folder and controlling which hours are displayed on the Scheduling tab. In most cases, including nonworking hours on the Scheduling tab would become unmanageable.

After you have selected all the attendees, found an available time slot, and filled in all the necessary details on the message form, click the Send button on the form to send the meeting request to the attendees.

Scheduling a Meeting from the Contacts Folder

If it's more convenient, you can initiate meeting requests from the Contacts folder rather than the Calendar folder. Right-click the contact entry for the person you want to invite to a meeting and choose New Meeting Request To Contact. The meeting form opens, with the contact's name in the To box. From here, you can select more attendees and enter meeting details such as subject and location.

If the contact entry contains an address for an Internet free/busy server, you can download the contact's free/busy information by clicking the Options button on the Scheduling tab and selecting Refresh Free/Busy Information. You can also download the contact's free/busy information from the Microsoft Office Internet Free/Busy Service, if the contact uses that service.

> For details about the Microsoft Office Internet Free/Busy Service, see "Managing Your Free/Busy Information," page 512.

Changing a Meeting

To change any part of a meeting request, including attendees, times, or other information, first double-click the meeting item in the Calendar folder to open it and then make your changes. Click the Save And Close button to save the changes to the Calendar folder, or click Send Update to send an updated meeting request to the attendees. If you make changes that affect the other attendees, such as adding or removing attendees or changing the time or location, you should click Send Update so that the attendees get the new information.

Responding to a Meeting Request

When you click the Send button on a meeting form, a meeting request e-mail message is sent to the invited attendees. This message allows the attendees to accept, tentatively accept, or reject the meeting invitation; propose a new time for the meeting; and include a message in the reply.

Receiving a Request for a Meeting

The attendees you've invited to your meeting will receive a meeting request message similar to the one shown in Figure 19-5. When an attendee clicks the Calendar button, a copy of his or her calendar opens, showing the meeting tentatively scheduled.

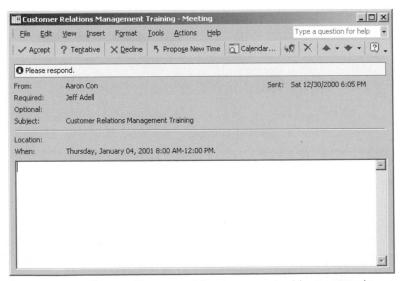

Figure 19-5. This meeting request has been received by an attendee.

An invited attendee has four options when replying to a meeting request:

- Accept the meeting outright.
- Tentatively accept the meeting.
- Decline the meeting.
- Propose a new time for the meeting.

When an attendee accepts, tentatively accepts, or declines the meeting, he or she can send the response immediately (which sends the default response), edit the response before sending (which allows the attendee to send a message with the response), or send no response.

newfeature!

To propose a new meeting time, the attendee can click the Propose New Time button. A dialog box appears that is essentially the same as the Scheduling tab of the meeting form. From here, the attendee can select a new time for the meeting and propose it to the meeting organizer by clicking Propose Time.

Troubleshooting

You have lost a meeting request.

When you respond to a meeting request, it is automatically deleted from your Inbox. If you accepted or tentatively accepted the meeting request, Outlook adds the meeting information to your Calendar folder. If you need to retrieve any of the data, check your Deleted Items folder for the meeting request itself and your Calendar folder for the meeting information.

To have Outlook keep meeting request messages in your Inbox even after you've responded, follow these steps:

1 Choose Tools, Options and click E-Mail Options.

2 Click Advanced E-Mail Options.

3 Clear the Delete Meeting Request From Inbox When Responding option.

newfeature!

Receiving a Response to Your Request

When an invited attendee responds to a meeting request, a message is returned to you, the meeting organizer. This message contains the response, including any message the attendee chose to include. In the meeting request response shown in Figure 19-6 on the next page, the attendee has tentatively accepted the meeting and included a message. Note that the response also lists the attendees who have accepted, tentatively accepted, and declined up to this point.

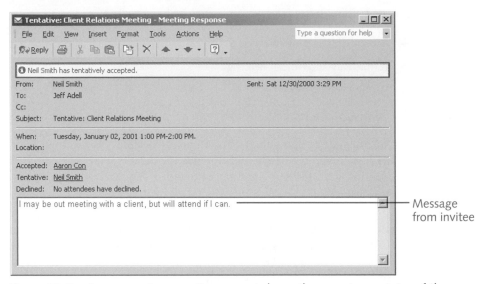

Figure 19-6. A response to a meeting request shows the acceptance status of the request and any message from the attendee.

Figure 19-7 shows a response in which the attendee has selected the Propose A New Time option on the meeting request.

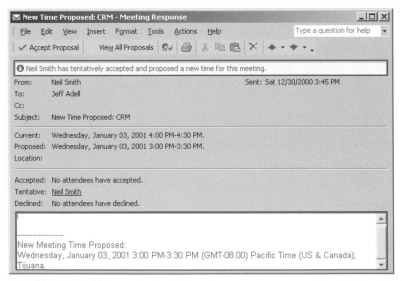

Figure 19-7. When an invited attendee proposes a new time for the meeting, the response to the meeting organizer looks like this.

When you receive a response proposing a new meeting time, you have two choices:

- Click the Accept Proposal button to accept the new time and open the meeting form. Verify any changes and then click the Send Update button to send the new proposed time to the attendees.

- Click the View All Proposals button to open the Scheduling tab of the meeting form, which displays a list of all proposed new times for the meeting suggested by any of the attendees (see Figure 19-8). You can select a new time from the list of proposed times and click Send Update to send the new time to the meeting attendees.

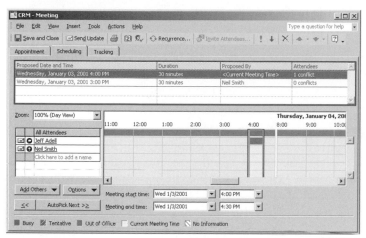

Figure 19-8. You can view the meeting times proposed by all attendees.

Checking Attendees

After you send a meeting request, you can check which attendees have accepted or declined by opening the meeting form in the Calendar folder and clicking the form's Tracking tab (see Figure 19-9). (The Tracking tab is not displayed on the initial meeting form; Outlook adds it after the meeting request has been sent.) The Tracking tab shows each invited attendee, along with whether their attendance is required or optional and the status of their response. The meeting organizer is the only person who can view the status of attendees.

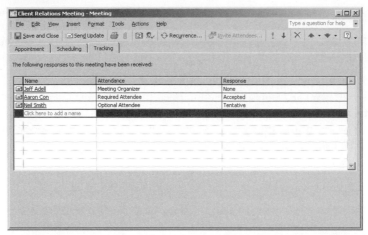

Figure 19-9. Only the person who scheduled the meeting can view the status of the attendees.

Scheduling Resources

To successfully plan and carry out a meeting, you'll usually need to schedule resources as well as people. *Resources* are items (such as computers and projectors) or locations (such as a meeting room) that are required for a meeting. You select resources in much the same way you select attendees.

The ability to schedule resources is typically most useful when you need to set up a meeting, but you might find other occasions when this capability comes in handy. For example, you might want to schedule laptop computers for employees to take home for the weekend or schedule digital cameras to take to building sites.

Setting Up Resources for Scheduling

You schedule a resource by sending a meeting request, adding the resource as a third type of attendee. (The other two types of attendees are Required and Optional, as previously mentioned; see "Selecting Attendees," page 522.) Because a resource is scheduled as a type of attendee, it must have a mailbox and a method of accepting or rejecting meeting requests. When you use Outlook and Exchange Server, a resource is almost identical to any other Exchange user except that it is configured to allow another user (the resource administrator) full access to its mailbox.

> **note** To use the process described here, you must be running Outlook 2000 or a later version.

The first step in setting up a resource for scheduling is to create (or have your system administrator create) a mailbox and an account for the resource. In many cases, resource account names are preceded by a symbol, such as # or &, so that the names, when alphabetized, appear as a group at the top or bottom of the Global Address List.

After creating the mailbox, you must grant permission for the user who will be the resource administrator to access that mailbox, as described here:

1 Choose Start, Programs, Administrative Tools In Windows and then select Active Directory Users And Computers.

2 Choose View, Advanced Features.

3 Click Users in the left pane and double-click the resource in the right pane.

4 On the Exchange Advanced tab, click Mailbox Rights and assign Full Mailbox Access to the resource administrator.

The resource administrator must now be able to log on to the resource's mailbox to set its resource scheduling options. The simplest way to approach this is to create a new Outlook profile for the resource's mailbox.

To create this profile, follow these steps:

1 In Control Panel, double-click Mail and then click the Show Profiles button.

2 Click Add to create a new profile, specify a name, and then click OK to continue.

3 Click E-mail Accounts. On the E-Mail Accounts Wizard page, select Add A New E-Mail Account (see Figure 19-10).

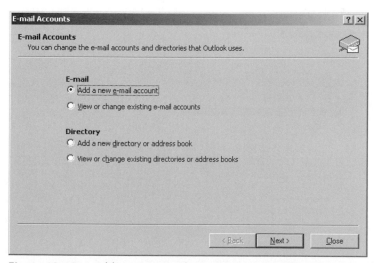

Figure 19-10.   Add a new e-mail account to the newly created profile.

4 For the server type, select Microsoft Exchange Server and then click Next.

5 On the next page of the wizard, shown in Figure 19-11, type the name of your Exchange Server and the name of the resource's mailbox, and then click Check Name to verify the resource name. After the name and the server have been verified, Outlook underlines them and the Check Names button becomes unavailable.

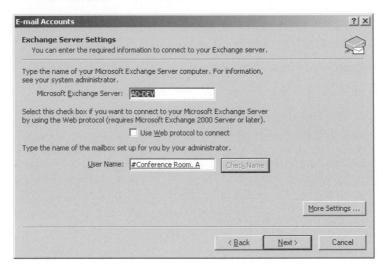

Figure 19-11. Specify the name of your Exchange Server and the name of the resource's mailbox, and then click Check Name to verify.

6 Click Next to save the new e-mail account settings, and then click Finish to save the profile. Figure 19-12 shows the new profile added to the list.

Figure 19-12. A new profile for resources has been added.

532

7 Because you will probably open this profile only once, to set the resource scheduling options, select the Always Use This Profile option. Then select the newly created profile from the drop-down list and click OK. (If you foresee having to open the resource's mailbox frequently to make changes, however, you can select Prompt For A Profile To Be Used. Each time you open Outlook, you will be prompted to select a profile.)

When you next open Outlook, you should see the resource's new mailbox in the folder list, as shown in Figure 19-13.

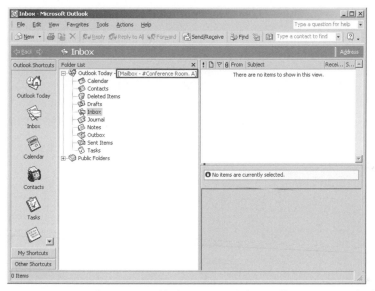

Figure 19-13. The new profile has opened the mailbox you specified for the resource when you created the profile.

tip If you want to configure more than one resource mailbox, each resource must have its own profile.

Now the resource administrator is able to configure the resource by following these steps:

1 In Outlook, choose Tools, Options and click Calendar Options.

2 Click the Resource Scheduling button to open the Resource Scheduling dialog box.

3 Select the Automatically Accept Meeting Requests And Process Cancellations option, which permits resource scheduling to work. (If you fail to select this option, you cannot schedule resources.) To avoid schedule conflicts, it's also a good idea to select Automatically Decline Conflicting Meeting Requests, which will cause the resource's mailbox to decline meeting requests when a

533

scheduling request overlaps with another meeting. The last option, Automatically Decline Recurring Meeting Requests, is useful if you don't want to allow a resource to be booked with recurring meetings.

> **tip** The Set Permissions button in the Resource Scheduling dialog box allows you to configure the permissions of the resource's Calendar folder so that users can book resources offline. In the steps outlined here, however, the actions in step 5 automatically configure the permissions.

4 Click OK to continue.

5 If resource permissions are not already set, the dialog box shown in Figure 19-14 opens, asking whether you want to automatically set permissions for all users for offline booking. Selecting this option gives users permission to view and edit the resource's calendar directly, which can get out of hand if you have a large user base. Set these permissions only if you think you can manage a situation in which users have the ability to directly edit the calendar. To set the permissions, click OK. Otherwise, click Cancel.

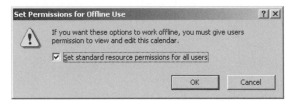

Figure 19-14. This dialog box automatically sets permissions so that users can view and edit the resource's calendar directly.

6 Click OK to close the Calendar Options dialog box, and click OK again to close the Options dialog box.

7 Close Outlook.

8 To change the profile back to the default, double-click Mail in Control Panel, and then click Show Profiles. Select the original profile from the drop-down list and click OK.

Using the Configured Resources

To schedule a resource after you have configured it, create a meeting request and fill in the details. When you add attendees to the meeting request using the Select Attendees And Resources dialog box, select the resource you want to add from the list and then click the Resources button (see Figure 19-15). Resources are added to the Resources box instead of to the Required or Optional box. When you have finished adding resources, click OK. Then complete and send the meeting request as you normally would.

Chapter 19

For details about creating and sending meeting requests, see "Sending a Meeting Request," page 522.

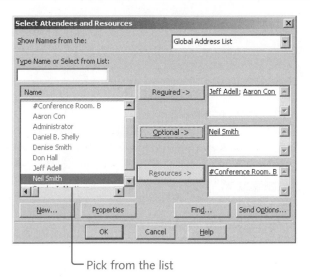

Pick from the list

Figure 19-15. Add a resource by selecting it from the list and clicking the Resources button.

After you send the meeting request, Outlook responds with a message about the resource's availability. If the resource is available during the time slot proposed for the meeting, Outlook notifies you that the resource has been booked successfully (see Figure 19-16).

Figure 19-16. Outlook notifies you if the resource was successfully booked.

Figure 19-17 shows the message that appears when you try to book a resource in a time that overlaps with an existing meeting in that resource's calendar. Click OK to return to the meeting form, where you must reschedule the meeting or choose a different resource.

Figure 19-17. When resources are already booked, you must change the meeting time or choose another resource.

Figure 19-18 shows the calendar for the resource being scheduled in the previous examples. The meetings shown have been scheduled automatically.

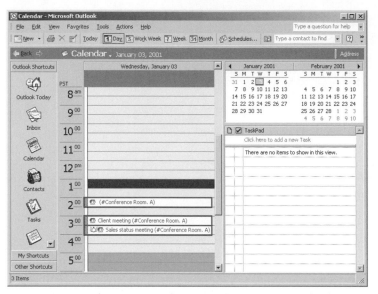

Figure 19-18. The meetings shown on the resource's calendar were booked automatically.

Holding an Online Meeting

So far in this chapter, you've seen how to schedule a face-to-face meeting in Outlook. You can also use Outlook to schedule online meetings using Microsoft NetMeeting (a multimedia collaboration application).

Setting Up NetMeeting

NetMeeting is installed with Microsoft Windows 2000 by default. If you have a different version of Windows, you can download NetMeeting from *http://www.microsoft.com/windows/netmeeting.*

To set up NetMeeting for the first time, follow these steps:

1 Start the program by clicking Start, Programs, Accessories, Communications, NetMeeting.

2 Click Next on the first NetMeeting Wizard page (an overview of NetMeeting's features).

3 Type your name and e-mail address information and then click Next.

4 Choose whether you want to log on to the NetMeeting directory server automatically each time NetMeeting starts (see Figure 19-19).

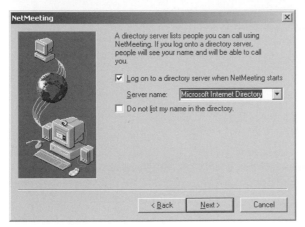

Figure 19-19. You can specify whether you want to log on to the NetMeeting directory server automatically and whether you want your name listed in the directory.

5 Choose whether you want your name advertised in the directory and click Next.

6 Select your connection speed in the list and then click Next to continue.

7 Choose whether to put a NetMeeting shortcut on your desktop and on the Quick Launch bar. Click Next to continue. The final page indicates the status of the NetMeeting setup. If you don't have a sound card, NetMeeting tells you that you can't use its audio features.

8 Click Finish to complete the NetMeeting configuration. NetMeeting opens, using its new configuration settings.

Scheduling a NetMeeting Conference

Scheduling a NetMeeting conference is similar to scheduling a face-to-face meeting: choose File, New, Meeting Request. Fill in the details of the meeting, including at least the start and end dates and times and the subject. Next select the check box This Is An Online Meeting Using, and then select Microsoft NetMeeting in the drop-down list. When you select the check box, more options become available (see Figure 19-20).

In the Directory Server box, you can specify the NetMeeting directory server to use for the scheduled online meeting. Outlook adds your e-mail address to the Organizer's E-Mail box. If you select the Automatically Start NetMeeting With Reminder check box, NetMeeting will start when the appointment reminder is displayed. The Office Document box allows you to specify a Microsoft Office document to be shared with the other meeting attendees.

537

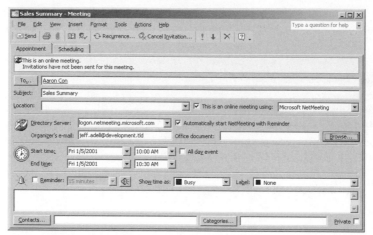

Figure 19-20. More options become available for online meetings that use NetMeeting.

Using NetMeeting

If the meeting has been set up to begin when Outlook displays the reminder, NetMeeting starts automatically when the reminder appears. Otherwise, you can open NetMeeting manually or by clicking the Start NetMeeting button in the reminder window. Figure 19-21 shows the initial NetMeeting screen.

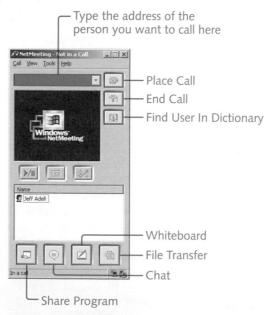

Figure 19-21. When the online meeting starts, you see the main NetMeeting screen.

Chapter 19

After NetMeeting starts, you must place a call to the other meeting participant. To place a call, choose Call, New Call or click the telephone icon to open the Place A Call dialog box (see Figure 19-22).

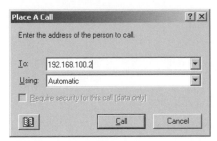

Figure 19-22. From this dialog box, you can connect to another NetMeeting user.

In the dialog box, type or select the e-mail address, computer name, or IP address of the user to call and then click the Call button. While NetMeeting is calling the other party, you'll see the status of the call in a window (see Figure 19-23).

Figure 19-23. NetMeeting displays the call status.

The receiving party's computer "rings" (the actual sound depends on how the user set the incoming call sound in Control Panel), and a window appears on the receiving party's screen (see Figure 19-24). This window shows who is calling and allows the receiver to accept or decline the call. If the receiver fails to make a choice within a short amount of time, your computer ends the call.

Figure 19-24. You can accept or decline a NetMeeting call.

When the call is established, you can speak to the other participant if both of you have sound cards, speakers, and microphones. You can also see each other if you have video capture devices. If only one party has any of these devices, they can still be used—but only one way.

note For in-depth information about using NetMeeting, see *http://www.microsoft.com/windows/netmeeting.*

NetMeeting gives you the tools to communicate with other people over the Internet. The four tools provided by NetMeeting are:

- Share Program
- Chat
- Whiteboard
- File Transfer

With the Share Program tool, you can share a program with the other parties in the meeting by following these steps:

1 Make sure the program you want to share is open on your desktop.

2 Click the Share Program button in NetMeeting to open the Sharing dialog box (see Figure 19-25).

Figure 19-25. You can share programs on your computer with other NetMeeting users.

3 Select the program to share in the list of open programs and then click the Share button. The shared program opens in a window on the desktop of the other parties (see Figure 19-26).

4 Using the options in the Sharing dialog box, shown in Figure 19-25, you can allow other users to control the application as follows:

- Clicking the Allow Control button allows other users to request control of the application; you can then choose to grant or deny that control.

- Selecting the Automatically Accept Requests For Control check box automatically grants control to users who request it.

540

- Selecting the Do Not Disturb With Requests For Control Right Now check box prevents control requests.

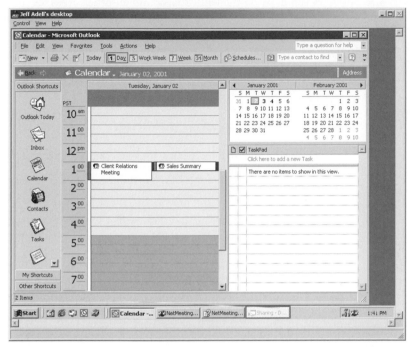

Figure 19-26. A program shared by another user is displayed in a window on the local desktop.

The Chat tool is a basic text chat in which those in a NetMeeting can chat by typing instead of by using audio and video capture devices. This can be useful when you're holding a NetMeeting with users who don't have sound or video devices. To open the Chat window (see Figure 19-27), simply click the Chat button in NetMeeting.

Figure 19-27. Use the NetMeeting Chat window to have text chat sessions with other parties in a call.

541

The Whiteboard tool is essentially a shared version of the Microsoft Paint accessory with a few extra features. Click the Whiteboard button in NetMeeting to open this feature. All users can draw on the whiteboard, and all other users see those changes unless one of them clicks the Lock Contents button, in which case only that user can make changes. The Remote Pointer button places on the whiteboard a hand icon that can be used to point out specific items during a meeting. The Select Area and Select Window buttons are used to paste the next area selected or the next window clicked, respectively, from your computer to the whiteboard. Figure 19-28 shows a whiteboard in use by two NetMeeting users.

To send one or more files, you can use NetMeeting's File Transfer tool as follows:

1 Open the File Transfer tool by clicking the File Transfer button in NetMeeting.

2 Click the Add Files button in the File Transfer dialog box to browse for the file you want to transfer.

3 Select the file to be transferred and click Add. The selected file appears in the File Transfer dialog box (see Figure 19-29). To remove a file in the list, select the file and click the Remove Files button.

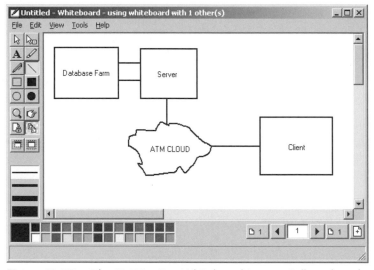

Figure 19-28. The NetMeeting Whiteboard is essentially a shared version of Paint with extra collaboration features.

4 In the drop-down list, select the user to whom you want to send the file (the default is Everyone).

5 Click the Send All button to send the file.

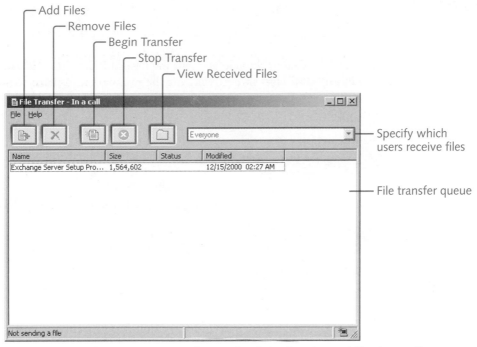

Figure 19-29. Use NetMeeting's File Transfer dialog box to send files to meeting participants.

Broadcasting a Presentation

You've thus far learned the ins and outs of scheduling both face-to-face and online meetings. This section explores how to schedule and conduct a special type of meeting: a broadcast presentation over the Web. Presentations are broadcast using Microsoft PowerPoint and Microsoft Windows Media Services. Online presentations can be viewed with a Web browser.

> **note** You must install Windows Media Presentation Broadcasting as part of PowerPoint during the Office XP installation. Windows Media Services must be installed with Microsoft Windows 2000 Server. (Or you can add either program later by using Add/Remove Programs in Control Panel.)

An Overview of Presentation Broadcasting

You can broadcast presentations live or from a saved recording. The first step is to create the presentation in PowerPoint and save it to a file. Next, still in PowerPoint with the saved presentation open, choose Slide Show, Online Broadcast and then choose either Record And Save A Broadcast or Start Live Broadcast Now.

543

> **note** For information about creating a PowerPoint presentation, see *Running Microsoft PowerPoint 2000,* by Stephen W. Sagman (Microsoft Press, 1999).

Clicking Record And Save A Broadcast opens the Record Presentation Broadcast dialog box (see Figure 19-30). This is where you type the summary information about the presentation. You can also configure the presentation by clicking Settings to open the Settings dialog box.

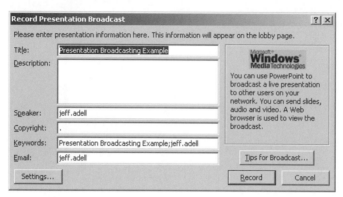

Figure 19-30. Type the summary information about the presentation before recording.

You use the Presenter tab of the Settings dialog box to specify whether you want to include with the recording the audio and video of the presenter, the audio only, or neither. You can also specify the slide show mode, resizable or full screen, the location for storing the broadcast files, and whether to include the speaker notes with the recorded presentation.

On the Advanced tab of the Settings dialog box, you can specify a remote Windows Media Encoder to encode the presentation as well as a Windows Media Server to use to broadcast the presentation. Note that by default the local computer broadcasts the presentation and only ten users can view it simultaneously.

> **note** If more than ten users will be viewing the presentation simultaneously, you must use a separate Windows Media Server.

After you click the Record button in the Record Presentation Broadcast dialog box (see Figure 19-30), the presentation is prepared for broadcast. Click Start to continue, and the slide show starts. You must click through the slide show as if you were showing it normally, adding audio and video if you want. After the slide show is complete, click in the dialog box to exit. A window appears containing the location of the saved presentation.

When you start a live presentation broadcast, the procedure is similar, with a few exceptions. First, the file location for the presentation files specified on the Presenter tab of the Settings dialog box must be a network share in the form \\\<server>\\<share>.

Second, you can specify a URL for an audience chat room on the Advanced tab of the Settings dialog box. In this way, viewers can give feedback and discuss the presentation. Finally, by clicking the Invite Audience button in the Live Presentation Broadcast dialog box, you can e-mail users and invite them to the presentation.

The Broadcast Presentation dialog box where the presentation is prepared for broadcast has two additional options not available for recorded presentations. You can click the Audience Message button to type a message that users will see when they enter the presentation. Click the Preview Lobby Page button to preview the Web page that users will see before the presentation starts. Clicking Start begins the live presentation with your live audio and video if you've chosen to include it. As you click through the presentation, the live online presentation follows suit. After the presentation is complete, click the final window to exit the slide show.

Scheduling a Presentation

To schedule a live presentation, choose Slide Show, Online Broadcast in PowerPoint and then click Schedule A Live Broadcast. This opens the Schedule Presentation Broadcast dialog box.

> **note** If this presentation has been broadcast live before, all instances of the word *Schedule* (as in "Schedule A Live Broadcast") are replaced with *Reschedule*.

Click the Settings button to configure the presentation broadcast settings. Then click the Schedule button to open a meeting form containing the details of the presentation as well as a link to the presentation. To schedule the presentation, type the names of the attendees and the details just as you would in a normal meeting request and then send it. The meeting reminders will contain a View Windows Media button that the recipients can click to view the presentation. When the organizer of the scheduled presentation clicks the View Windows Media button, however, a PowerPoint window opens asking whether the presentation should begin. Clicking Yes directs PowerPoint to prepare the presentation and count down until the scheduled presentation time. Clicking Start begins the presentation broadcast.

Viewing a Presentation

You view a presentation in a Web browser. To view a scheduled presentation, you must open the link to the presentation, which you can do in several ways. To view a saved presentation, open the link that you specified in the presentation broadcast settings dialog box when the presentation was saved.

To open a live presentation, you must either click the link that was included in the e-mail or the meeting request or click the View Windows Media button in the reminder for the scheduled presentation. Doing so opens the broadcast, showing the amount of time remaining until the broadcast begins. When the broadcast begins, the presentation is shown in the large window while the Windows Media Player on the page plays live audio and displays live video, if those are being broadcast. Figure 19-31 shows a presentation in progress.

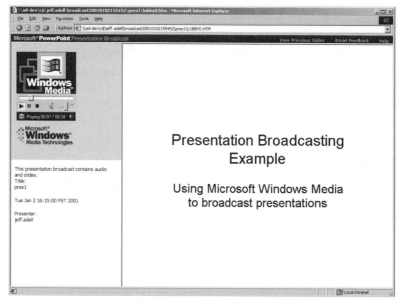

Figure 19-31.   Presentations are displayed in a Web browser while Windows Media Player plays any included live audio or video.

Troubleshooting

You can't view the presentation.

If you're unable to view a presentation, you might want to check your firewall settings. You need to make sure that your server and client both have the correct ports open. See Microsoft Knowledge Base article Q189416 for the required ports and for more information on firewall configuration and Windows Media Services.

Managing Your Tasks

Microsoft Outlook offers a broad selection of tools to help you manage your work day, including e-mail; a way to manage appointments, meetings, and events; a handy method of creating quick notes; and a journal for tracking projects, calls, and other items. All these tools are often related to creating and completing tasks. For example, writing this book was a long string of tasks to be completed: drawing up the outline, writing each chapter, and reviewing edits, for starters.

In your job, your tasks during the average day are no doubt different. Perhaps they include completing contracts, making sales calls, writing or reviewing documents, completing reports, developing Web sites, or developing program code. Some tasks take little time to complete, while others can take days, weeks, or even months.

Outlook provides the means not only to track your own tasks but also to manage tasks you need to assign to others. This feature is a much more efficient and effective way to manage tasks than using a notebook, sticky notes, or sheer memory power. You can set reminders and sort tasks according to category, priority, or status in order to help you view and manage them.

This chapter examines the Tasks folder and its related features. In addition to learning how to manage your own tasks, you'll also learn to assign and manage tasks for others.

Working with Tasks in the Tasks Folder

Outlook provides several ways for you to create and manage tasks. You can create one-time tasks or recurring tasks, set up reminders for tasks, and assign tasks to others. In this section, you'll see how to create tasks for yourself and how to use Outlook to manage those tasks effectively.

The default view in the Tasks folder, shown in Figure 20-1, offers a simple list that shows four columns: Icon, Complete, Subject, and Due Date.

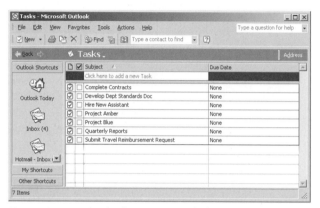

Figure 20-1. Outlook uses a simple list as the default Tasks folder view.

The following list summarizes these four columns:

- **Icon.** The Icon column indicates one of two states: either that the task is yours or that it's assigned to another person. The clipboard icon with a check mark indicates that the task is your own. A hand under the icon indicates that the task is assigned to someone else.

- **Complete.** Use this check box to indicate that a task has been completed. A check in the box indicates a completed task. Outlook crosses through the task's subject and due date when you mark the task as completed, offering another visual cue to help you distinguish completed tasks from those that are still outstanding.

- **Subject.** You can enter any text in the Subject column, but generally it should describe the task to be performed. You can also add notes to each task to further identify the purpose or goal of the task.

- **Due Date.** This column indicates the due date for the task and by default shows the day and date. You can specify different date formats if you want.

> For details on customizing the Tasks folder view, see "Viewing and Customizing the Tasks Folder," page 564. For additional information about features in Outlook that can help you use and manage views, see "Using Other Outlook Features," page 80.

You can view all the details of a task by double-clicking the task item. Doing so opens the task form, whose format varies depending on whether the task is yours or is assigned to someone else. Figure 20-2 shows the form for a task that belongs to you. Figure 20-3 shows the Task tab of a form for a task assigned to someone else.

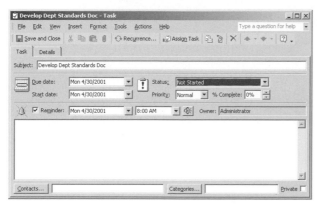

Figure 20-2. Create a new task with this standard task form.

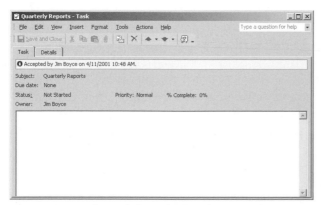

Figure 20-3. The task form for a task assigned to someone else shows less information than the task form for one of your own tasks.

The Details tab of the task form (see Figure 20-4 on the next page) shows additional information about the task such as date completed, total work required, actual work performed, and related background information.

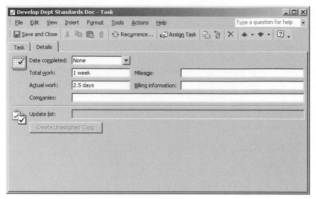

Figure 20-4. Use the Details tab to view additional information about the task.

---

tip Press Ctrl+Tab to switch between tabs in any multi-tabbed dialog box or form, including the task form.

Navigating Tasks Quickly

Although you can open tasks by double-clicking them in the Tasks folder, you might prefer to cycle through your tasks right in the task form. For example, when you want to review several tasks, opening and closing them from the task list one after another is a waste of clicks and effort. Instead, you can use the Next Item and Previous Item buttons on the form's Standard toolbar to display tasks in forward or reverse order (relative to the listed order in the Tasks folder). The list doesn't cycle from end to beginning or beginning to end, however, so clicking a button when you're at either of those points in the list closes the task form.

Creating a Task

Creating a task is mechanically much the same as creating any item in Outlook. Use any of the following methods to open a new task form:

- Between the column header bar and the first task in the list is a new task entry line labeled Click Here To Add A New Task. Click the line and start typing if you want to specify only the subject for the task, without initially adding details or selecting options. You can open the task at any time afterward to add other information.

- Double-click in an empty area of the task list.

- Right-click in an empty area of the task list and choose New Task.

- With the Tasks folder open, click New on the Standard toolbar.

- With any Outlook folder open, click the arrow beside the New button on the Standard toolbar and choose Task. This allows you to create a new task when another folder such as the Inbox or the Calendar folder is displayed.

The options on the task form are straightforward. Simply select the options you want and set the task properties (such as start date and due date). Opening the Due Date or Start Date drop-down list displays a calendar you can use to select the month and date for the task. If no specific date is required for the task, you can leave the default value None selected. If you currently have a date selected and want to set it to None, select None in the drop-down list.

InsideOut

As you'll learn a little later in this section, you can specify values for Total Work and Actual Work on the Details tab of the task form. Total Work indicates the total number of hours (days, weeks, and so on) required for the task; Actual Work lets you record the amount of work performed to date on the task. Unfortunately, the Percent Complete value on the Task tab is not tied to either of these numbers. Thus, if Total Work is set to 40 hours and Actual Work is set to 20 hours, the Percent Complete box doesn't show 50 percent complete. Instead, you must manually specify the value for Percent Complete.

note The Percent Complete value is tied to the Status field on the Task tab. If you set Percent Complete to 100, Outlook sets the status to Completed. If you set Percent Complete to 0, Outlook sets the status to Not Started. Any value between 0 and 100 results in a status of In Progress. Selecting a value in the Status drop-down list has a similar effect on Percent Complete. Select Not Started, for example, and Outlook sets the Percent Complete value to 0.

In addition to entering information such as the percentage of work that's completed, the priority, and the status, you can also set a reminder for the task. As it does for other Outlook items, such as appointments, Outlook can display a reminder window as well as play a sound as a reminder to start or complete the task. You can set only one reminder to a task, so it's up to you to decide when you want Outlook to remind you about the task. Click the speaker button on the task form to select the audio file you want Outlook to use for the reminder.

One key task setting on the Task tab is the Owner setting. When you create a task, you own that task initially. Only the owner can modify a task. Task ownership is relevant only to assigned tasks—that is, tasks you assign to others to perform.

For details about task ownership, see "Assigning Tasks to Others," page 557.

Other information you can specify on the Task tab includes contacts, categories, and the private/nonprivate status of the task. Assigning contacts to a task helps you to quickly access contact information for people associated with a task. For example, you might need to send e-mail or make a call to someone who's working on a task with you. In that case, you can open the task item and double-click the name in the text box beside the Contacts button. This opens the contact entry, from which you can initiate a call, open the person's Web site, quickly create a new e-mail message, or perform any of the other actions available through the contact form.

The ability to assign categories to tasks can help you organize your tasks. You can assign multiple categories to each task as needed and view the Tasks folder sorted by category. For example, you might assign project categories to tasks to help you sort the tasks according to project, allowing you to focus on the tasks for a specific project.

For details on working with categories, see "Assigning Categories to New Items," page 109.

The private/nonprivate status of a task allows you to control whether others who have delegate access to your folders can see a specific task. Tasks marked as private aren't visible unless you explicitly grant permission to the delegate to view private items. To control the visibility of private items, choose Tools, Options and click the Delegates tab. Double-click a delegate, and in the Delegate Permissions dialog box (see Figure 20-5) select or clear the option Delegate Can See My Private Items. Repeat the process for any other delegates as needed.

note The Delegates option is available only if you're using Microsoft Exchange Server and only if the Delegates add-in (Dlgsetp.ecf) is installed. Click Tools, Options, Other, Advanced Options, and click Add-In Manager to add or remove the Delegates add-in.

The Details tab of the task form (shown earlier in Figure 20-4) allows you to specify additional information about the task. The options on the Details tab include the following:

- **Date Completed.** Use this calendar to record the date the task is completed. This is the actual completion date, not the projected completion date.

- **Total Work.** Specify the total amount of work required for the task. You can enter a value in minutes, hours, days, or weeks by entering a value followed by the unit, such as 3 days.

552

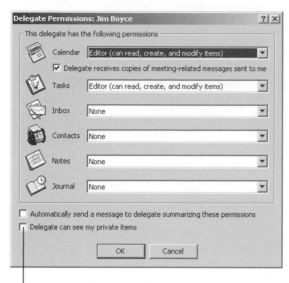

Allow or deny access to private items

Figure 20-5. Use the Delegate Permissions dialog box to control the visibility of private items.

- **Actual Work.** Record the total amount of work performed on the task to date. You can enter the data using the same units as in the Total Work box.

- **Companies.** List any companies associated with the task such as suppliers, customers, or clients.

- **Mileage.** Record mileage associated with the task if mileage is reimbursable or a tax-deductible expense.

- **Billing Information.** Record information related to billing for the task, such as rate, person to bill, and billing address.

- **Update List.** This option applies to tasks assigned to others. It shows the person who originally sent the task request and the names of all others who received the task request, reassigned the task to someone else, or elected to keep an updated copy of the task on their task list. When you send a task status message, Outlook adds these people as recipients of the status message.

- **Create Unassigned Copy.** Use this button to create a copy of an assigned task that you can send to another person.

For details on working with the update list, assigned tasks, and unassigned copies, see "Assigning Tasks to Others," page 557.

Troubleshooting

Others can't see your tasks.

In order for others to see your tasks, you must share your Tasks folder. If you're using Microsoft Exchange Server as your mail server, you can also allow others to see your tasks by granting them delegate access to your Tasks folder. The two methods are similar but with one major difference: granting delegate access to others allows them to send messages on your behalf. Sharing a folder simply gives others access to it without granting send-on-behalf-of permission.

To share your Tasks folder without granting send-on-behalf-of permission, right-click the Tasks folder icon on the Outlook Bar and choose Properties. Click the Permissions tab and add or remove users and permissions as needed.

For additional details on sharing folders and setting permissions, see "Granting Access to Private Folders," page 687. To learn how to set up delegate access to your folders, see Chapter 27, "Delegating Responsibilities to an Assistant."

Copying an Existing Task

You can quickly create a new task from an existing one by copying it through the clipboard. The new task has all the same information as the original task, but you can change any of the information as needed.

Follow these steps to copy a task:

1 Select the task by clicking the icon in the Icon column in the task list. The icon shows a clipboard with a check mark on it.

2 Choose Edit, Copy or press Ctrl+C to copy the task to the clipboard.

3 Choose Edit, Paste or press Ctrl+V to paste the contents of the clipboard as a new task.

Creating a Recurring Task

Earlier in the chapter, you learned several different ways to create a task that occurs once. You can also use Outlook to create recurring tasks. For example, you might create a recurring task for reports you have to submit on a weekly, monthly, or quarterly basis. Or perhaps you perform backup operations once a week and want Outlook to remind you to do this.

You create a recurring task much the same way you create a single-instance task, except that when the task form is open, you click the Recurrence button on the form's toolbar to display the Task Recurrence dialog box (see Figure 20-6).

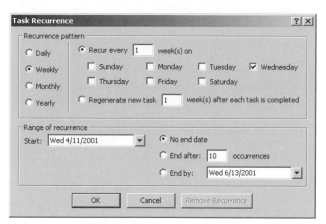

Figure 20-6. Create recurring tasks by using the Task Recurrence dialog box.

You can select daily, weekly, monthly, or yearly recurrence. Selecting one of these four options in the dialog box changes the options available in the dialog box, allowing you to select the recurrence pattern. For example, select Weekly and then select the days of the week on which you want the task to occur.

When you create a recurring task, one of the decisions you must make is whether you want the task to recur at a specified period regardless of the task's completion status. You can also choose to regenerate a new task after the existing task is completed. For example, you can create a task that recurs every Friday. The task will recur whether or not you marked the previous one as completed. If you need to complete the previous task before the next task is generated, however, you should configure the recurrence so that the new task is created only after the previous one is completed. For example, perhaps you run a series of reports, but each relies on the previous set being completed. In this situation, you would probably want to set up the task to regenerate only after the preceding one was completed.

The Regenerate option in the Task Recurrence dialog box allows you to configure the recurrence so that the new task is generated a specified period of time after the previous task is completed. Select the Regenerate option and then specify the period of time that should pass after completion of the task before the task is regenerated.

Other options for a recurring task are the same as for a one-time task. Specify subject, details, contacts, categories, and other information as needed. Remember to set up a reminder for the task if you want Outlook to remind you before the task's assigned completion time.

Adding a Reminder

You can add a reminder to a task when you create the task or after you create the task. As with reminders for appointments, you specify the date and time for the reminder as well as an optional sound Outlook can play along with the reminder.

Chapter 20

To add a reminder, follow these steps:

1 Open the task and select Reminder on the Task tab.

2 Use the calendar in the drop-down list beside the Reminder check box to select the date, and then select a time for the reminder. You can select a time in half-hour increments in the drop-down list or specify your own value by typing it in the box.

3 Click the speaker icon to open the Reminder Sound dialog box, in which you select a WAV file to assign to the reminder.

4 Click OK and close the task form.

> **note** Outlook uses a default time of 8:00 A.M. for the reminder. You can change this default value by choosing Tools, Options and setting the Reminder Time option on the Preferences tab.

Setting a Task Estimate

When you create a task, you might also want to estimate the time it will take to complete it. You can enter this estimate in the Total Work box on the Details tab of the task form. As the task progresses, you can change the value of Total Work to reflect your changing estimate or leave it at the original value to track time overruns for the task. For example, assume that you propose a 40-hour task to a client. As you work through the task, you continue to update the Actual Work box to reflect the number of hours you've worked on the task. You reach 40 hours of work on the task and haven't completed it. You then have to make a decision: do you update the Total Work value to show a new estimate for completion and bill the client accordingly, or do you leave it as is and absorb the cost overrun?

Unfortunately, the Total Work and Actual Work fields are simple, *nonreactive* data fields. Outlook provides no interaction between the two to determine an actual Percent Complete value for the task. For that reason—and because Outlook can't calculate job costs based on charge rates and the amount of work completed—Outlook by itself generally isn't a complete job tracking or billing application. You should investigate third-party applications to perform that task or develop your own applications using the Microsoft Office XP suite as a development platform.

> For details on how to get started developing your own Office applications, see Part 8, "Developing Custom Forms and Applications."

Marking a Task as Completed

Logically, the goal for most tasks is completion. At some point, therefore, you'll want to mark tasks as completed. When you mark a task as completed, Outlook strikes through the task in the task list to provide a visual cue that the task is finished. The easiest way to mark a task as completed is to place a check in the Complete column, which by default is the second column in the task list. You can also mark a task as completed on the Task tab. Simply select Completed in the Status drop-down list or set the Percent Complete box to 100.

Outlook by default sorts the task list by completion status. If you've changed the list to sort based on a different column, simply click that column header. For example, clicking the Complete column header will sort the task list by completion status. If you want to view only completed tasks, choose View, Current View, Completed Tasks. Viewing only incomplete tasks is just as easy: choose View, Current View, Active Tasks.

> For additional details on customizing the Tasks folder view, see "Viewing and Customizing the Tasks Folder," page 564.

Assigning Tasks to Others

In addition to creating tasks for yourself in Outlook, you can also assign them to others. For example, you might manage a staff of several people and frequently need to assign them projects or certain tasks in a project. The main benefit of using Outlook to assign those tasks is that you can receive status reports on assigned tasks and view these status reports in your Tasks folder. Outlook automates the process of sending task requests and processing responses to those requests. You'll learn more about assigning tasks in the sections that follow. First, however, you need to understand task ownership.

About Task Ownership

When you create a task, you initially own that task. Only a task's owner can make changes to it. This means that you can modify the properties (the percent complete, the status, the start date, and so on) of all tasks that you create and own. When you assign a task to someone else and that person accepts the task, the assignee becomes the owner of the task. You can then view the task's properties but can no longer change them. Similarly, you become the owner of tasks assigned to you when you accept them, and you can then make changes to those tasks.

A task's Owner property is a read-only value, which appears in the Owner box of the Task tab. The value has a gray background to indicate that it's read-only. You can click the value, but you can't change it directly. The only way to change owners is to assign the task and have the assignee accept it.

Making or Accepting an Assignment

Assigning a task to someone else is a simple process. In general, you create the task, add details, and specify options for the task. Then you tell Outlook to whom you want to assign the task, and Outlook takes care of generating the task request and sending it to the assignee.

Follow these steps to assign a task to someone else:

1 In Outlook, open the Tasks folder and create a new task.

2 Add information and set options for the task such as start date, due date, status, and priority.

3 Click Assign Task on the form's toolbar. Outlook changes the form to include additional options, as shown in Figure 20-7.

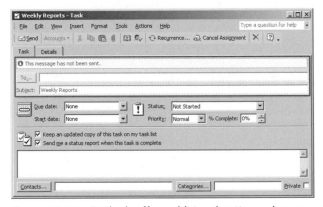

Figure 20-7. Outlook offers additional options when you assign a form to someone else.

1 In the To box, enter the address of the person to whom you're assigning the task, or click the To button to browse the address book for the person's address.

2 Outlook automatically selects the two options described in the following list. Set them as you want and click Send to send the task request to the assignee.

   ■ **Keep An Updated Copy Of This Task On My Task List.** Select this option if you want to keep a copy of the task in your own task list. You'll receive updates when the assignee makes changes to the task, such as a change in the Percent Complete status. If you clear this option, you won't receive updates, nor will the task appear in your task list.

   ■ **Send Me A Status Report When This Task Is Complete.** Select this option if you want to receive a status report on completion. The status report comes in the form of an e-mail message that Outlook generates automatically on the assignee's system when the assignee marks the task as completed.

For information about task updates and status reports, see "Tracking the Progress of a Task," page 562.

tip   Click Cancel Assignment in the task form to cancel an assignment and restore the original task form.

When you click Send, Outlook creates a task request message and sends it to the assignee. If you open the task, you'll see a status message indicating that Outlook is waiting for a response from the assignee (see Figure 20-8). This message changes after you receive a response and indicates whether the assignee accepted the task.

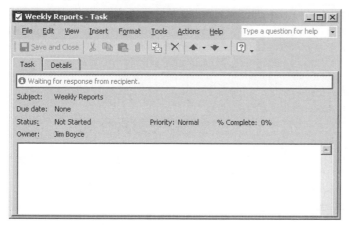

Figure 20-8.   Outlook indicates that it is waiting for a response to a task request for a selected task.

When you receive a task request from someone who wants to assign a task to you, the message includes buttons that allow you to accept or decline the task. Figure 20-9 on the next page shows the buttons in the InfoBar when the preview pane is displayed.

You can click either Accept or Decline to respond to the request. If the preview pane isn't open, you can open the message and click Accept or Decline on the message form toolbar. When you do so, Outlook displays a dialog box giving you the option of sending the message as is or editing it. For example, you might want to add a note to the message that you'll have to change the due date for the task or that you need additional information about the task. Choose Edit The Response Before Sending in the dialog box if you want to add your own comments; select Send The Response Now if you don't want to add comments. Then click OK to generate the message. The next time you synchronize your Outbox with the server, the message will be sent.

Chapter 20

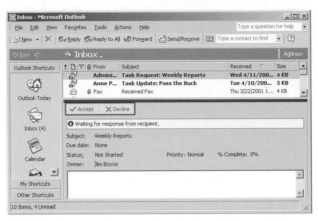

Figure 20-9.   You can easily accept or decline a task request by using the Accept or Decline button on the preview pane's InfoBar.

You have one additional option besides accepting or declining a task request that's waiting for your response—you can "pass the buck" and assign the task to someone else. For example, assume that you manage a small group of people. Your supervisor assigns a task to you, and you want to assign it to one of the people under you. When you receive the task request, open it, click Assign Task, and then select the person to whom you want to assign it. Outlook creates a task request and sends it to the assignee. When the assignee accepts the task, his or her copy of Outlook sends an acceptance notice to you and adds both the originator's address and your address to the update list on the Details tab of the task form. This means that changes to the task by the assignee are updated to your copy of the task and to the originator's copy.

Troubleshooting

Task requests keep disappearing.

After you accept or decline a task, Outlook automatically deletes the task request from your Inbox. Unlike meeting requests, task requests are always deleted—Outlook doesn't provide an option that allows you to control this behavior. Outlook does, however, keep a copy of the task request in the Sent Items folder. Outlook also deletes task update messages after you read them. These messages are generated automatically when someone modifies an assigned task. Outlook sends the task update message to the people listed in the update list on the Details tab of the task form. Although you can manually move these update messages out of the Deleted Items folder, Outlook provides no way to prevent them from being deleted.

When a response to a task assignment reaches you, Outlook doesn't automatically act on the response. For example, if someone accepts a task that you assigned, Outlook doesn't consider the task accepted until you open the response. Until that point, the InfoBar in the preview pane still indicates that Outlook is waiting for a response. When you open the response, the InfoBar in the message form shows whether the task has been accepted or declined, depending on the assignee's action. Outlook deletes the response when you close the message. You have no options for controlling this behavior—Outlook always deletes the response.

If an assignee declines your task request, you can easily assign the task to someone else (or reassign it to the same individual). Open the response, and click Assign Task in the form's toolbar just as you would when assigning a new task.

Reclaiming Ownership of a Declined Task

Your tasks won't always be accepted—you're bound to receive a rejection now and then. When you do, you have two choices: assign the task to someone else or reclaim ownership so that you can modify or complete the task yourself. To reclaim a task, open the message containing the declined task request and choose Actions, Return To Task List.

> **note** When you assign a task, the assignee becomes the temporary owner until he or she accepts or rejects the task. Reclaiming the task restores ownership to you so that you can modify the task.

Assigning Tasks to Multiple People

In some situations, you'll no doubt want to assign a task to more than one person. As a department manager, for example, you might need to assign a project to the people in your department or at least to a small group. Outlook is somewhat limited in task management: it can't track task status when you assign a task to more than one person. You can certainly assign the task, but you won't receive status reports.

What's the solution? You must change the way you assign tasks, if only slightly. Rather than assigning the whole project as a single task, for example, break the project into separate tasks and assign each one individually, or break a specific task into multiple tasks. Use a similar name for each task to help you recognize that each one is really part of the same task. For example, you might use the names Quarterly Report: Joe and Quarterly Report: Jane to assign the preparation of a quarterly report to both Joe and Jane.

InsideOut

While Outlook's task management features are certainly useful, a more comprehensive set of tools for distributing and managing tasks within a project would be a great addition to the program. For example, the ability to subdivide a task automatically would be helpful, as would the ability to assign a task to multiple people and still receive updates without having to subdivide the task. You can, however, work around this by adjusting the way you assign and manage tasks.

Assigning Multiple Tasks Through an Assistant or a Group Leader

If you manage more than one group, task assignment becomes a little more complex because you probably have more than one group or department leader under you. Ideally, you would assign a task to a group leader and the group leader would delegate portions of the task to members of his or her group. How you accomplish that delegation depends on whether you want to receive status updates directly from group members or only from the group leader.

If you want to receive updates from group members, divide the overall task into subtasks and assign them to the group leader. The leader can then assign the tasks as needed to individuals in the group. Task updates are then sent to both you and the group leader. If you prefer to receive updates only from the group leader, create a single all-encompassing task and assign it to the group leader, who can then divvy up the project into individual tasks to assign to group members as needed.

Tracking the Progress of a Task

When you assign a task, you can choose to keep an updated copy of the task in your task list. This copy allows you to track the status of the task. As the assignee adds or changes task information—such as changing the Total Work value—that assignee's copy of Outlook generates an update and sends it to the addresses listed in the task's update list (on the Details tab of the task form). Typically, the update list includes only one name—the name of the person who assigned the task. If the task was delegated (passed on from one person to another), the update list shows all persons in the assignment chain.

> **note** If you assign a task to multiple people, Outlook can no longer track task status. This limitation is one reason to subdivide a task, as explained in the previous section.

As mentioned, Outlook sends task status messages to the update list addresses when an assignee makes changes to a task. When you receive a status message, Outlook updates your copy of the task when you read the status message. Outlook then deletes the status message, with one exception: when the assignee marks the task as completed, Outlook sends a task completed message to the update list addresses. When you receive and read the message, Outlook marks your copy of the task as completed but does not delete the task completed message. Figure 20-10 shows a task completed message.

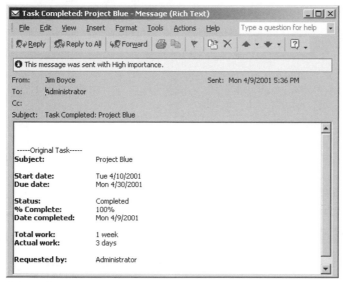

Figure 20-10. Outlook generates a task completed message when an assignee marks a task as completed.

Sending a Task Status Report

As you work on an assigned task, you'll probably want to send status updates to the person who assigned the task to you. Sending task status reports is more than easy—it's automatic. Outlook generates the updates each time you modify the task, such as when you change the Percent Complete value. Because you can't force another update without changing the task, you might want to make a small change in one of the task's properties—for example, increasing the Percent Complete value by 1 percent—to generate the update.

Creating an Unassigned Copy of an Assigned Task

Outlook allows you to create an unassigned copy of a task that you have assigned to someone else. This unassigned copy goes into your task list with you as the owner. You can then work on the task yourself or assign it to someone else. For example, suppose that you assigned a task to someone but you want to work on it, too. You can create a copy and then work on the copy, changing its dates, completion status, and other information as you go.

Creating an unassigned copy has one drawback, however: you will no longer receive updates for the assigned task. This makes it more difficult to track the other person's progress on the assigned task.

Follow these steps to create an unassigned copy of a task:

1 In Outlook, open the Tasks folder and then open the assigned task.

2 Click the Details tab, and then click Create Unassigned Copy.

3 Outlook displays a warning that creating the copy will prevent you from receiving updates to the assigned task. Click OK to create the copy or Cancel to cancel the process.

4 Outlook replaces the existing task with a new one. The new task has the same name except that the word *copy* is appended to the name in the Subject box. Make changes as needed to the task and then choose Save And Close to save the changes.

Viewing and Customizing the Tasks Folder

As mentioned at the beginning of this chapter, Outlook uses a simple list as the default Tasks folder view. Several other predefined views are also available, including those described in the following list. To use any of these views, choose View, Current View, and select the view you want.

- **Simple List.** Shows the task name, the due date, and whether the task is completed. This is the default view for the Tasks folder.

- **Detailed List.** Shows not only the information in a simple list but also status, percent complete, and categories.

- **Active Tasks.** Shows tasks that are active (incomplete).

- **Next Seven Days.** Shows tasks for the next seven days.

- **Overdue Tasks.** Shows incomplete tasks whose due dates have passed.

- **By Category.** Organizes the task list by the categories assigned to tasks.

- **Assignment.** Shows tasks assigned to specific people.

- **By Person Responsible.** Groups the view according to the person responsible for a task.

- **Completed Tasks.** Shows only completed tasks.

- **Task Timeline.** Shows a timeline of all tasks.

Outlook provides several ways to customize the view of the Tasks folder. These methods are the same as for other Outlook folders. For details on sorting, grouping by various columns, adding and removing columns, and customizing the folder view in other ways, see "Customizing the Inbox View," page 63.

> For information on using filters to locate and display specific tasks, such as those with certain text, dates, or other properties, see "Using Advanced Find," page 725.

In addition to using the customizing methods described in Chapter 3, you might also want to change the way Outlook displays certain items in the Tasks folder. For example, you could change the font or character size for the column names or change the color that Outlook uses to display overdue tasks (red by default). The following sections explain how to make these types of changes in the Tasks folder.

Changing Fonts and Table View Settings

Outlook by default uses an 8-point Tahoma font for column headings, rows, and AutoPreview text. You can select a different font or different font characteristics (point size, italic, color, and so on). You also can change the style and color for the grid lines on list views and specify whether to show the preview pane.

Follow these steps to customize your view settings:

1 Right-click the column header bar and choose Customize Current View, or choose View, Current View, Customize Current View.

2 In the View Summary dialog box, click Other Settings to display the Other Settings dialog box, shown in Figure 20-11 on the next page.

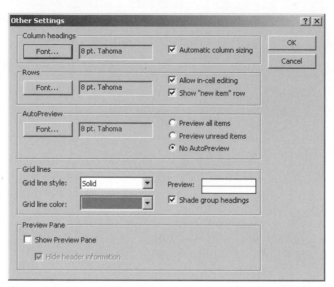

Figure 20-11. Configure font properties for the Tasks folder in the Other Settings dialog box.

3 Click Font in the Column Headings, Rows, or AutoPreview area of the dialog box to open a standard Font dialog box you can use to select font, size, and other settings for the specified text.

> **note** You can change color only for the AutoPreview text. Row and column text is displayed in a fixed color.

1 Use the options in the Grid Lines group to specify the line type and color you want Outlook to use for list views.

2 Set other options (use the following list as a guide), click OK to close the Other Settings dialog box, and then click OK to close the View Summary dialog box.

- **Automatic Column Sizing.** Sizes columns automatically and fits them to the display's width. Clear this option to specify your own column width (by dragging each column's header), and use a scrollbar to view columns that don't fit the display.

- **Allow In-Cell Editing.** Allows you to click in a cell and modify the contents. If this check box is cleared, you must open the task to make changes.

- **Show "New Item" Row.** Displays a row at the top of the list for adding new tasks. The New Item row appears only if in-cell editing is selected.

- **Preview All Items.** Turns on AutoPreview and causes Outlook to display the first three lines of the contents of all items.

- **Preview Unread Items.** Turns on AutoPreview and causes Outlook to display the first three lines of the contents of unread items only.

- **No AutoPreview.** Displays on the headings for items and does not display AutoPreview text.

- **Shade Group Headings.** Adds shading to headings when you view items in a grouped table view (where items are grouped by column value, such as all tasks with the same due date).

- **Show Preview Pane.** Shows the preview pane when selected. You also can choose View, Preview Pane to turn the preview pane on or off.

- **Hide Header Information.** Shows or hides the From, To, Cc, and Subject boxes in the InfoBar in the Inbox folder. However, this option has no effect in the Tasks folder.

Using Automatic Formatting

Outlook can perform automatic text formatting in the Task folder just as it can for other folders. For example, Outlook displays overdue tasks in red and uses gray strikethrough for completed and read tasks. Outlook has six predefined automatic formatting rules, and you can create additional rules if you want to set up additional automatic formatting. For example, you might create a rule to show in red all tasks that haven't been started and are due within the next seven days.

To create automatic formatting rules, choose View, Current View, Customize Current View. Then click Automatic Formatting to display the Automatic Formatting dialog box, shown in Figure 20-12.

Figure 20-12. Modify or create custom automatic formatting rules in the Automatic Formatting dialog box.

567

Follow these steps to create a new rule:

1 In the Automatic Formatting dialog box, click Add. This creates a new rule named Untitled.

2 Type a title for the rule and click Font. Use the resulting Font dialog box to specify the font characteristics you want Outlook to use for tasks that meet the rule's conditions. Click OK to close the Font dialog box.

3 Click Condition to open the Filter dialog box (see Figure 20-13). Specify the criteria for the condition. For example, select Not Started in the Status drop-down list, select Due in the Time drop-down list, and select In The Next 7 Days. This specifies that you want Outlook to use the font selections from step 2 to format any tasks that haven't been started and are due within the next seven days.

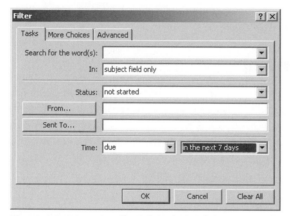

Figure 20-13. Use the Filter dialog box to specify conditions for the formatting rule.

4 Use the More Choices and Advanced tabs to set other conditions as needed, and then click OK.

5 Add other rules as needed. Click OK to close the Automatic Formatting dialog box, and then click OK to close the View Summary dialog box.

You can create fairly complex rules using the Filter dialog box, which can help you organize and identify specific types of tasks. Also note that you can change the order of the rules in the Automatic Formatting dialog box by using the Move Up and Move Down buttons. Outlook applies the rules in order from top to bottom, so it's possible for one rule to override another.

Setting General Task Options

Outlook provides a few options that control the appearance of items in the Tasks folder, reminders, and other task-related elements. To set these options, choose Tools, Options. On the Preferences tab of the Options dialog box, the Reminder Time option specifies the default reminder time for tasks. This option is set to 8:00 A.M. by default, but you can change the time if you like—perhaps you'd prefer to see reminders at 10:00 A.M. instead. Keep in mind that this setting is the default that Outlook uses for task reminders when you create a task, but you can change the reminder time for individual tasks as needed.

If you click Task Options, Outlook displays the Task Options dialog box, which includes the following options:

- **Overdue Task Color.** Select the color you want Outlook to use to display overdue tasks.

- **Completed Task Color.** Select the color you want Outlook to use to display completed tasks.

- **Keep Updated Copies Of Assigned Tasks On My Task List.** Select this option to have Outlook keep a copy of assigned tasks in your Tasks folder and update their status when assignees make changes to the tasks.

- **Send Status Reports When Assigned Tasks Are Completed.** Select this option to have Outlook send status reports to you when tasks you assigned to someone else are completed.

- **Set Reminders On Tasks With Due Dates.** Select this option to have Outlook set a reminder on tasks with due dates. Outlook bases the timer on the task's due date and the reminder time specified in the Options dialog box.

Working with Tasks in Other Ways

Outlook provides a few other ways to work with tasks in addition to the Tasks folder. The following sections explain how to set up and track tasks in the TaskPad and in Outlook Today view.

Working with Tasks on the TaskPad

If you use the calendar feature of Outlook, you'll find that the TaskPad appears in the Calendar folder's Day, Work Week, and Week views. Figure 20-14 on the next page shows Day view with the TaskPad highlighted. The TaskPad appears under the Date Navigator.

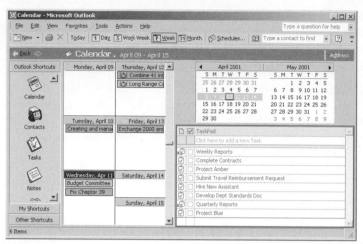

Figure 20-14. Use the TaskPad to work with tasks in your Calendar folder.

By default, Outlook shows only the Icon, Complete, and Subject columns for tasks in the TaskPad, but you can add and remove columns as needed. To do so, right-click the column header bar above the TaskPad and choose Field Chooser. Drag columns to and from the Field Chooser dialog box.

You can modify tasks directly in the TaskPad just as you can in the Tasks folder, depending on the view settings you've specified. For example, if you've turned on in-cell editing, you can make changes to a task simply by clicking it and typing the needed changes. You can mark a task as completed, change the Actual Work value, change the due date, and so on. The TaskPad is, in this respect, no different from the Tasks folder. The primary benefit of the TaskPad is that it allows you to work with your schedule and your tasks in a single window.

> **tip**   **Showing and hiding the TaskPad**
>
> You can drag the borders of the TaskPad to show it or hide it. If you drag the TaskPad's bottom border to the bottom of the view, the Date Navigator increases in size (and number of months displayed) to take up the space vacated by the TaskPad. Simply click in the bottom of the view and drag the mouse back up to restore the TaskPad. You also can drag the left edge of the TaskPad to the right edge of the display to hide it and the Date Navigator.

You can use the same methods that you use to create tasks in the Tasks folder to create a new task in the TaskPad. Right-click in the empty area of the TaskPad and choose New Task or New Task Request, depending on whether you're creating the task for yourself or assigning it to someone else. If both the Show New Item Row option and in-cell editing are enabled, you can click the Click Here row between the first task in the list and the column header to create a new task. Alternatively, you can click the arrow beside the New button on the toolbar and choose Task to create a new task.

Changing the TaskPad's View

Outlook offers seven options for viewing tasks in the TaskPad. In essence, these offer different TaskPad views. To select a TaskPad view, right-click in the empty area of the TaskPad and choose TaskPad View, followed by one of these selections:

- **All Tasks.** Shows all tasks regardless of status or due date.

- **Today's Tasks.** Shows all tasks active (incomplete) on the current date.

- **Active Tasks For Selected Days.** Shows active tasks on selected days. Select one or more dates, and then select this option to see which tasks are active.

- **Tasks For Next Seven Days.** Shows all tasks that are active during the next seven days from the current date.

- **Overdue Tasks.** Shows all overdue tasks.

- **Tasks Completed On Selected Days.** Shows completed tasks on selected days. Select one or more dates, and then select this option to see which tasks were completed.

The last option on the menu, Include Tasks With No Due Date, is not a view per se. Instead, selecting this option causes Outlook to include in the selected view those tasks that have no due date. Clear this option to hide tasks without due dates, excluding them from the list.

Setting TaskPad Options

Earlier this chapter explained how to customize the Tasks folder view by changing character formatting, columns display, and more. You can make some of these same changes in the TaskPad to customize its view. For example, you can add and remove columns, group by specific fields, sort the display, and set fonts and grid style. To configure these settings, right-click the TaskPad, choose TaskPad Settings, and then select the item you want to change.

For details on modifying the Task folder view, see "Viewing and Customizing the Tasks Folder," page 564.

Working with Tasks in Outlook Today

Chapter 3 explained in detail how Outlook Today gives you quick access to a useful selection of data (see Figure 20-15). The Calendar area displays meetings and events scheduled for the current day (and for subsequent days, if space allows). The Messages area indicates the number of unread messages in your Inbox, messages in the Drafts folder, and unsent messages in the Outbox. The Tasks area lists your tasks.

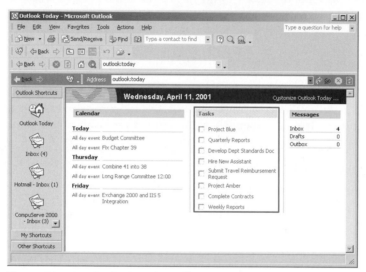

Figure 20-15. Outlook Today offers quick access to a range of information.

For detailed information on using Outlook Today, see "Outlook Today," page 59.

You can't create a task by clicking in the Tasks area of Outlook Today, but you can click the arrow beside the New button on the toolbar and choose Task to create a new task. To modify a task, click the task's name in the list to open the task form. Mark a task as completed by selecting the check box beside its name.

Integrating Microsoft Outlook and Microsoft Project

Software programs are designed to handle specific tasks or sets of tasks. For instance, Microsoft Outlook provides tools to perform several tasks, including creating and managing e-mail, setting up to-do lists, and organizing your contacts. You can even use Outlook to assign tasks, manage meetings, and keep track of events. When you need to manage a project, however, you might want to look into a project management program such as Microsoft Project 2000.

This chapter focuses on integrating Outlook and Project. For instance, you'll learn how to set up a resource list in Project using Outlook contacts. In addition, you can use Outlook's reminder feature to send yourself alerts about tasks during a project's lifetime.

Before you learn how to integrate Outlook and Project, you first need to look at what Project is and what you can do with it as a stand-alone program.

Overview of Microsoft Project

Microsoft Project is an electronic project management tool. You can use Project to perform the following tasks:

- Create project plans
- Track projects from start to finish
- Capture important milestones during a project

- Send announcements to team contacts about the status of a project

- Point out potential and actual problems during the course of a project

- Schedule meetings with important people

These are just a few examples of how Project makes it easy to view and manage your projects. Figure 21-1 shows one of the ways Project displays information related to your projects.

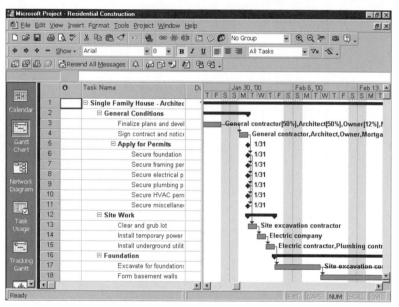

Figure 21-1. Use Project to organize, manage, and track projects for you, your team, or your entire organization.

Now let's look at some basic project management considerations as well as Project tasks and how to perform them.

Project Management Basics

Almost everyone—worker, homeowner, or organizational leader—works on some type of project. Some common projects include the following:

- Creating marketing material for an upcoming product launch

- Writing and publishing a book or newsletter

- Planning fundraising activities

- Renovating a room in your home

- Starting a new business

- Launching a Web site
- Managing employee training

Depending on the project you manage, you might need to keep track of a few or several hundred details. For instance, some projects are small enough that you need to keep track of only two or three employees, a few material resources (such as a load of gravel or a small shipment of computers), and start and finish dates. For larger projects, you might need to monitor not only your own employees but also the schedules of related firms' employees and include milestones to ensure that your schedule stays on track.

Some projects don't require a robust software tool such as Project. For instance, if you're put in charge of only one small project that can be finished in less than a day, you can probably track the project more efficiently with a scratchpad and pen. You shouldn't waste time starting Project, entering new project criteria, mapping a Gantt chart, and then starting the project. Simply get the resources you need and finish the project as quickly as you can.

On the other hand, suppose that you are assigned multiple small projects, a few medium-size ones, and a large project that must all be completed over several months. A project management tool such as Project can help ensure that you remember the details and maintain the schedule.

Keeping a Project in Balance

As a project gets under way and while it's in progress, you must strive to keep three things in balance: scope, schedule, and resources.

A project's *scope* is the set of tasks required to finish the project. If you are remodeling a bathroom in your home or office, for example, you must finish specific tasks before your bathroom is considered complete. Some of these tasks might include designing a new floor plan, ordering bathtub and sink fixtures, setting up a plumbing contractor, and demolishing the existing bathroom. All these tasks make up the scope of the project.

Your project's *schedule* is the time required to complete the project's tasks, and the order of those tasks. The schedule includes the obvious: projected start and finish dates. However, you must also consider scheduling other resource items, such as dates for the plumbing and heating personnel, the tile contractor, the electrician, and the inspector. Schedules should also include proposed receipt dates of any materials you need, such as custom faucet fixtures, lighting tracks, and a water filtration unit.

Finally, the *resources* for a project include the materials, equipment, and people necessary to complete the project. In many instances, you include not only contact information but also wage and benefit information for the people involved. (Benefits can include time off or holiday dates you must schedule around.) Likewise, materials and equipment connected with your project have related costs, operating expenses, and scheduling dynamics you must consider.

575

Another resource is where the project will take place. You must know the availability of the space throughout the project. In our example, the project's location is a bathroom, so you might not want to plan a renovation project to start when, for example, you are also hosting a large party. Similarly, if a project involves training employees, you don't want to schedule the training sessions to coincide with vacations or company-related events when an employee or group of employees will be out of town.

Microsoft Project's Four Project Management Steps

Microsoft Project helps you with the four main project management steps:

- Defining the project
- Creating the project plan
- Tracking the project
- Finishing the project

When you define the project, you outline the goals, define the scope, determine the necessary resources, and estimate how much time is needed to complete the project. You should also add milestones and internal deadlines, such as the date you want a wall demolished.

The *project plan* is the blueprint for your project. In short, the plan specifies exactly what needs to be accomplished, who will complete each task, how much time is estimated for each task, which tasks are dependent on others to finish before they can start, and any constraints you want applied to a task or a schedule. An example of a task constraint, or *dependency,* is that you might need to hire an electrician to rough in electrical outlets before your drywall contractor puts up your walls. Completing the drywall is dependent on the completion of the electrical work. Constraints might also include starting a task on a specific date (such as not on a weekend or holiday because of higher contracting costs).

Microsoft Project's strength is that it can track your project's history from start to finish as long as you enter correct data and keep the information up to date. Project can compare the actual time to complete a task with the time you estimated (and budgeted for). It also can analyze resource requirements to determine whether a resource is overloaded or whether you have scheduled a resource to complete more than one task at the same time. (Your plumber can work on only one part of the bathroom at a time, for instance.) This allows you to reformulate the plan to include additional resources, extend the project time, or redefine the scope of the project.

When a project is complete, that doesn't mean your work is finished. For instance, you might want to analyze the project so you can figure out how to manage a future project. Or you might have to gather project costs to review them with your manager or spouse. In addition, you might want to archive the project file for future reference.

Creating a Simple Project

To help you understand how Project works, this section shows you how to create a simple project plan for publishing a departmental newsletter.

Follow these steps to create the project:

1 Start Project 2000. If the Project Help window appears, click the Close button to turn it off.

2 Choose File, Close to close the blank project.

3 Choose File, New to display the New window.

4 Select Blank Project and click OK to display the Project Information dialog box (see Figure 21-2).

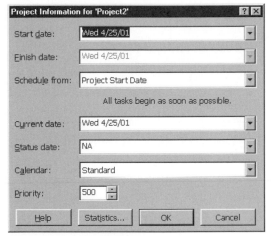

Figure 21-2. Use the Project Information dialog box to begin setting up your new Project file.

5 Enter a start or finish date. In this example, choose to start the project today. In the Schedule From drop-down list, select Project Start Date. In the Current Date drop-down list, select Today.

6 Click OK. A blank project appears.

7 Choose File, Save to save the project. Enter the project name **Issue 1** and click Save. Each time you save your project, you are prompted to create a baseline, which saves the project as a snapshot so that you can review it later against any changes. Click OK to do so.

Now you're ready to enter your task list. The task list for this example includes the following:

● **Write each article.** In this four-page newsletter, each page will include one article, named Page One Article, Page Two Article, and so on.

- **Create the author list.** Each article will have a separate author.

- **Define the editor and editor dates.** The newsletter will be edited by one editor.

- **Submit articles to the desktop publisher.** The newsletter will be desktop published by one person.

- **Submit the newsletter to the printer.** The edited and desktop published newsletter will be shipped to a printer on a specific date for printing.

- **Send out finished newsletter.** The printed newsletter will be mailed to subscribers by a specific date.

As you can see from the list, a simple four-page newsletter can include many tasks, dates, and resources.

Now add these tasks to your new project using Gantt Chart view:

1 In Project, click Gantt Chart on the View Bar.

note In Gantt Chart view, you can view your tasks as you enter them and see information that Project provides about the task.

2 In the Task Name box, type a task name, such as **Newsletter Issue 1**. Press Enter.

3 Continue adding tasks and durations. If you're following along with the example, you can refer to Table 21-1 for the list of tasks and their duration.

4 Order the tasks in the outline by indenting them as shown in Table 21-1. (For instance, indent the Write Page One Article task two times.) To indent a task, click the Indent button on the Formatting toolbar.

5 Add predecessors as indicated in Table 21-1. To do this, double-click a task and click the Predecessor tab. Click the Task Name column and select the predecessor in the drop-down list. Click OK to apply the change.

note In Project, a predecessor task is a task that must start or finish before another task can begin. For example, before an article can be edited, it first must be written. Thus all editing tasks have a predecessor task of writing. You can specify predecessor tasks using the Predecessors tab of the Summary Task Information dialog box.

6 Check to be sure that your entries match those shown in Figure 21-3.

7 Choose File, Save to save the project.

Table 21-1. Tasks for Newsletter Issue 1

Task Name	Duration	Indents	Predecessor
Write Articles	9 days	One	N/A
Write Page One Article	1 day	Two	N/A
Write Page Two Article	7 days	Two	N/A
Write Page Three Article	3 days	Two	N/A
Write Page Four Article	9 days	Two	N/A
Edit Articles	2 days	One	Write Articles
Edit Article One	1 day	Two	Write Page One Article
Edit Article Two	2 days	Two	Write Page Two Article
Edit Article Three	1 day	Two	Write Page Three Article
Edit Article Four	2 days	Two	Write Page Four Article
Desktop Publish Issue 1	3 days	One	Edit Articles
Print Newsletter	7 days	One	Desktop Publish Issue 1
Send Newsletter To Printer	2 days	Two	Desktop Publish Issue 1
Review and Approve Test Prints	1 day	Two	Send Newsletter To Printer
Print Copies Of Newsletter	2 days	Two	Review and Approve Test Prints
Receive Printed Newsletters	2 days	Two	Print Copies Of Newsletter
Mail Newsletter To Recipients	1 day	One	Receive Printed Newsletters

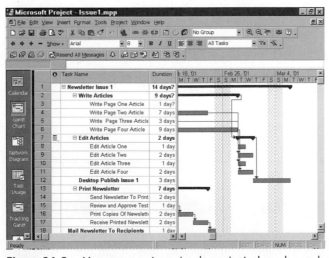

Figure 21-3. You can create a simple project plan, shown here in Project.

After you create your project plan, you can edit it for real data. For instance, suppose that the author of the article on page four needs an extra three days to complete it. Because everything that follows the authoring stage—editing, page layout, printing, and mailing—is dependent on the article being written, you must adjust your plan accordingly. To do this, change the duration date from 9 days to 12 days. Notice how this affects everything after the authoring stage.

This example, simple as it is, shows you how Project can manage and keep track of your projects. The next section looks at how you can integrate Project and Outlook.

> **note** For more information on using Project, visit the Microsoft Project 2000 Web site at *http://www.microsoft.com/office/project/*.

Troubleshooting

You're having trouble viewing and printing tasks and dependencies for projects.

If you're starting to have difficulties working with your projects, part of the problem might be that the project has gotten too large, which can happen pretty easily. In this section, you learned how to create a simple project. This small project could easily grow into a large project if you expanded it to include marketing and advertisement tasks. In general, as you're creating your projects, you might want to consider breaking large tasks into smaller multiple tasks to make them more manageable. To do this, follow these steps:

1 Choose Gantt Chart on the View bar.

2 Hold down Ctrl and click the row heading of each task you want to break out as a new project.

3 Choose Cut Task and then New.

4 Fill out the Start date box, choose OK, and then fill in the Task Name field. Click the first row and choose Paste.

5 Save your project and name it.

6 From the Window menu, select the project into which you want the new project file inserted. Choose Insert, Project and select where the project you want to insert is located. Then choose Insert.

Integrating Your Outlook Calendar

With the Outlook calendar, you can set up, manage, view, and set reminders for important meeting dates, events, and other activities. When you're working in Project, you can set Outlook reminders to alert you when tasks need to start or finish.

To set an alert with an Outlook reminder, do the following:

1 In Project, click the Gantt Chart button on the View Bar.

2 Select the task or tasks for which you want to set up reminders. Hold down the Ctrl key to select multiple tasks.

3 On the Workgroup toolbar, click the Set Reminder button to display the Set Reminder dialog box (see Figure 21-4). If the Workgroup toolbar is not visible, choose View, Toolbars, Workgroup.

Figure 21-4. Set a reminder in Project to alert you when a task needs to start or finish.

4 Set the reminder options you want for the tasks. For example, to get a reminder two days before a task is scheduled to finish, type **2**, select Days in the drop-down list, and then select Finish in the Before The *n* Of The Selected Tasks drop-down list.

5 Click OK.

> **note** Project warns you if you try to set a Start reminder after a task is scheduled to start or try to set a Finish reminder after a task is scheduled to finish.

Integrating Your Address Book

After you create an address book in Outlook, you don't need to waste time typing resource names each time a project plan requires them. Instead, just use an Outlook address book from within Project to add resource names, addresses, and e-mail information. This saves time and eliminates possible errors you might introduce when retyping resource information.

Creating a Resource List

A *resource list* is a list of names, distribution lists, or other contact information you use when assigning a task. For instance, if you want to assign a particular editor to edit your newsletter articles, you can add that editor's name to a resource list compiled from your Outlook Contacts folder and then assign that editor to the Edit Articles task.

Chapter 21

The following steps show how to create a resource list in Project using an Outlook address book:

1   In Project, click the Gantt Chart button on the View Bar.

2   On the Standard toolbar, click Assign Resources to display the Assign Resources dialog box (see Figure 21-5).

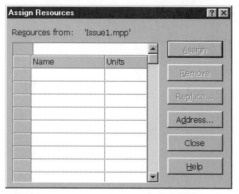

Figure 21-5.   Use the Assign Resources dialog box from within Project to assign Outlook contacts as resources.

3   Click Address to display the Select Resources dialog box (see Figure 21-6).

4   Select the resource you want to assign to project tasks.

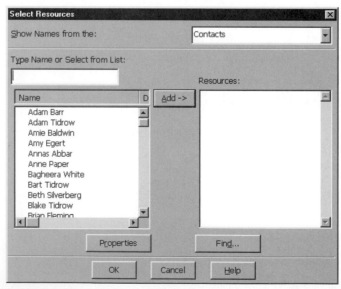

Figure 21-6.   Project's Select Resources dialog box looks similar to the Select Names dialog box you use when you're addressing an e-mail message in Outlook.

5 In the Name list, select a resource name or distribution list and click Add to add this name to the resource list. You can use this name as a resource for any task in Project.

For a detailed discussion of distribution lists, see Chapter 5, "Managing Address Books and Distribution Lists." For more on assigning tasks to and working with contacts, see Chapter 14, "Managing Your Contacts."

6 Continue adding names as necessary.

7 When you have finished adding names, click OK. The resources you selected are now part of the Assign Resources dialog box list.

8 Click Close to close the Assign Resources dialog box.

---

tip   **Use a distribution list**

In Project, you can use a distribution list as you would in Outlook to make your work easier. To use a distribution list as a resource in Project, create the distribution list in Outlook and then select the distribution list as shown in step 5 above. A distribution list is handy if you must assign a task to multiple resources, such as a task in which multiple team members must attend a training class or multiple resources must be used to finish a construction job.

Assigning a Resource to a Task

After you create your resource list, you can assign resources to any tasks in Project.

The following steps show you how:

1 In Project, click the Gantt Chart button on the View Bar.

2 In the Task Name column, select a task.

3 Click the Assign Resources toolbar button to display the Assign Resources dialog box.

4 Select a resource name or distribution list and then click Assign.

5 Continue assigning names as necessary.

6 When you've finished, click Close.

To see a list of resources assigned to a task, double-click the task in the Task Name list and then click the Resources tab (see Figure 21-7 on the next page). You can also select resources here. To do so, click a row in the Resources list, click the down arrow, and then select a resource in the drop-down list. Click OK to close the dialog box and apply any changes you've made to the list.

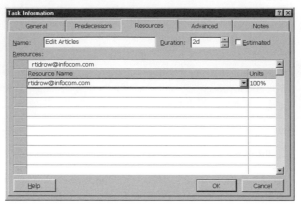

Figure 21-7. Click the Resources tab to review a list of resources assigned to a task.

Keeping Track of Your Progress

You can integrate Outlook's journal with Project to keep a record of all the work you do on a project, including when you opened, saved, and printed the project file. This feature comes in handy, for example, when you want to find out which project file you worked on yesterday or last week or which file you printed a few days ago.

To use the Outlook journal to track your project file work, do the following:

1 In Outlook, choose Tools, Options.

2 Click the Preferences tab.

3 Click Journal Options.

4 In the Also Record Files From list, select Microsoft Project (see Figure 21-8).

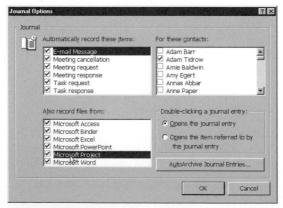

Figure 21-8. You can use Outlook's journal to keep journal information about your Project files.

584

5 Click OK to close the Journal Options dialog box, and then click OK again.

Now, as you use Project, the journal will automatically keep track of the work you do on your Project files.

> For more information about working with the Outlook journal, see Chapter 17, "Keeping a Journal."

Integrating Communication Features

One of the most difficult parts of managing a project is communicating with the people associated with a task or a set of tasks. If your company uses e-mail messages or the Internet, you can integrate Outlook's communication features with Project to help you effectively communicate with resources about task responsibilities.

You can use Project to send messages to workgroup system members, also called *teams*. Workgroups can then use Project to assign tasks, send and receive task updates, accept or decline task assignments, and submit status reports. Members of a team can use e-mail messages, the Web, or both to exchange Project information. Project files can include hyperlinks to other supporting documents so that resources can quickly and easily access related documents. These documents might include a Microsoft Word document describing the project in detail, a cost analysis worksheet in Microsoft Excel, or a related Web site you can view in Microsoft Internet Explorer.

> **note** The following section shows how to use Outlook's e-mail features to send and receive messages concerning task assignment, reporting status, and reporting updates. It's assumed that the workgroup functionality of Project is installed on your and your recipients' computers. To learn more about how to do this, consult the *User's Guide for Microsoft Project 2000*; this book ships with the Microsoft Project 2000 software.
>
> In addition, because e-mail systems and networks differ, the specific steps and features shown in this section might not work for your organization. Consult your network or e-mail administrator to find out whether your e-mail or LAN system can use Project's communication features.

Notifying Others That a Task Is Assigned

When you assign a task to a person who is part of your workgroup, you can send a notification to that person using e-mail. This is called a TeamAssign task request.

To send a TeamAssign task request, follow these steps:

1 Save your project file.

2 In Project, click Gantt Chart on the View bar.

Chapter 21

3 Select a task assigned to a resource you want to notify.

4 Choose Tools, Workgroup, TeamAssign to display the Workgroup Mail dialog box (see Figure 21-9).

5 Click Selected Task or, if you selected more than one task in step 3, click All Tasks.

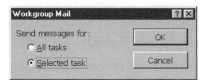

Figure 21-9. Send TeamAssign notifications to resources assigned to tasks.

6 Click OK and the TeamAssign dialog box opens (see Figure 21-10).

7 In the Subject box, type a subject if you want something other than TeamAssign as your subject.

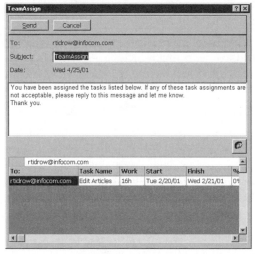

Figure 21-10. Fill out the TeamAssign dialog box before sending the notification to a recipient.

8 In the message area, type a message for the TeamAssign notification.

9 Scroll to the far right of the task information so that you can see the Comments box. Type any comments about the assignment.

10 Click Send.

11 If you receive a message telling you that another program is attempting to access your e-mail addresses, click Yes to continue.

Chapter 21

Outlook sends the TeamAssign notification. An envelope icon with a question mark appears next to the task related to the notification.

> **note** If you have Outlook configured to queue your messages in the Outbox folder before sending them, your TeamAssign notification is not sent until you click the Send/Receive button or activate the automatic send feature.

Sending an Update

After your project gets under way, you will have slips in the schedule, updates to tasks, and other events that require you to modify your Project file. When these events occur, you need to update your team members appropriately. You can do this using the TeamUpdate message feature.

You can send a TeamUpdate message to resources assigned to a specific task. For example, if Editor 1 is assigned to edit the newsletter, you can't send a TeamUpdate message to Author 1 about a change in the editing task. You can send your TeamUpdate message pertaining to the editing task only to the editor assigned to that task.

To send a TeamUpdate message, follow these steps:

1 In your project, update the task about which you want to send a TeamUpdate message. You cannot send a TeamUpdate message about a task unless the task has actually been updated first.

2 Save your project.

3 In Project, choose Tools, Workgroup, TeamUpdate.

4 In the Subject box, type a subject for your update.

5 In the message area, type your message.

6 If you have comments to make about the update, type them in the Comments box.

7 Click Send.

8 If you receive a message telling you that another program is attempting to access your e-mail addresses, click Yes to continue.

Outlook sends the TeamUpdate message. As you alert team members to updates in the project plan, they can also alert you to roadblocks that might keep them from completing tasks as planned or changes in their schedule that might affect your overall project schedule.

Chapter 21

Reporting the Status of a Task

Another workgroup-related function you can perform with Project and Outlook is to send TeamStatus messages. These are messages you send to resources requesting information about the status of a task.

To send a TeamStatus message, do the following:

1 In Project, select the task about which you want to send a TeamStatus message.

2 Choose Tools, Workgroup, TeamStatus to display the TeamStatus dialog box (see Figure 21-11).

3 In the Subject box, type a subject.

Figure 21-11.   Send a TeamStatus message to resources requesting status reports about tasks.

4 In the message area, type a message.

5 Click Send.

6 If you receive a message telling you that another program is attempting to access your e-mail addresses, click Yes to continue.

After you send the TeamStatus message, an icon appears next to the task name, indicating that you have not received a response yet.

Reading Workgroup Messages in Outlook

As a team member using Project and Outlook, you might receive a message from a project manager sending you a TeamAssign, TeamUpdate, or TeamStatus message. When you're running Outlook, you receive these types of messages the same way you receive regular e-mail messages. For example, if you receive all your e-mail messages in your Inbox, that's where you will receive your workgroup messages from Project. As you receive these messages, you can open them, read them, respond to them if necessary, and store them for later retrieval.

Similarly, as a project manager, you will receive responses to the TeamAssign, TeamUpdate, and TeamStatus messages that you send to other team members. You receive these responses in Outlook's Inbox. You might then need to respond to or act on these responses.

Opening and Viewing a Workgroup Message

To open and view a workgroup message sent to you, follow these steps:

1 Switch to Outlook and open the folder in which you receive new mail, such as the Inbox folder.

2 Double-click the workgroup message to open it. If Outlook can't recognize the file Project created, run Wgsetup.exe in the \wgsetup folder on the Project 2000 CD.

3 If you receive a message telling you that another program is attempting to access your e-mail addresses, click Yes to continue.

4 Read the Project workgroup message. An example of a reply to a TeamAssign message is shown in Figure 21-12.

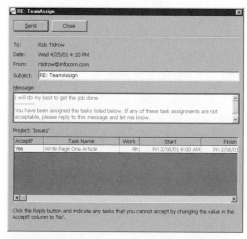

Figure 21-12. Read a reply to a Project TeamAssign message in Outlook.

589

Responding to a Workgroup Message

To respond to a workgroup message, such as a TeamAssign message, click the Reply button. To accept the task, check to be sure Yes is displayed in the Accept column at the bottom of the message window. Double-click in the Assign column to change from No to Yes, or vice versa. You also can enter text related to your reply in the message area. Click Send to send the message. When you accept a task from a workgroup message, it's added to your task list in Outlook.

For a TeamAssign message, you also have the option of declining the task. To decline a task, click Accept? in the TeamAssign message, click No, and then click Send.

Remember that when you receive a TeamStatus message, you need to reply with the requested information. For example, if your publisher asks for an update concerning any schedule changes regarding the completion of Issue 1 of the newsletter, you need to send that information in your reply to the TeamStatus message.

InsideOut

On systems on which you are running Microsoft Project Central, you can resend workgroup messages to workgroup members if you're upgrading from an earlier version of Project. This will update the workgroup members' task information in Project Central. If you do not do this, you will need to send individual TeamAssign messages for all tasks assigned to all workgroup members to update Project Central. To upgrade workgroup members' task information, follow these steps:

1 On the View bar, choose Gantt Chart.

2 Choose Tools, Workgroup, Resend All Messages.

3 Next, choose All Tasks or Selected Tasks, and then click OK.

4 Enter a subject in the Subject box, type a message and any comments you want to add, and then choose Send.

Reporting the Status of an Outlook Task

As you learned in the previous section, the tasks assigned to you in a workgroup message from a project manager appear in your Outlook tasks list. If you want to send an update message about the status of these tasks, make the changes in the Outlook Tasks folder before you send the status message.

You then can send a status message as outlined here:

1 In Outlook, choose Actions, New TeamStatus Report to display the New TeamStatus Report dialog box (see Figure 21-13).

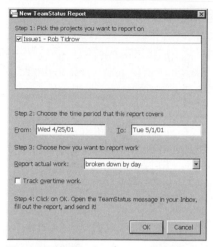

Figure 21-13. Send an updated status message about an Outlook task to a project manager.

2 If you receive a message telling you that another program is attempting to access your e-mail addresses, click Yes to continue.

3 Select the project or projects containing the tasks about which you want to send an update.

4 Type From and To dates for the period that your status report covers.

5 In the Report Actual Work drop-down list, select how you want to report the status. You can choose from the following options:

- As a total for the entire period

- Broken down by day

- Broken down by week

6 Select whether or not you want to track overtime work.

7 Click OK. Outlook creates a message for each project you specified in the New TeamStatus Report dialog box.

8 Click Inbox and then click New TeamStatus Report.

9 Click Reply and then click Send.

Sending and Routing Project Files

You can use Outlook to send and route entire Project files to other users. This section shows you how to send and route a Project file and how to forward a routed file.

Sending a Project File Using Outlook

One way you might want to share a Project file is to send it as a project file using Outlook e-mail. Recipients can then save the file to disk and open it in Project, allowing them to view, modify, or print the Project file. Of course, each person who receives the file must have Project 2000 installed on his or her computer.

To send a Project file this way, do the following:

1 In Project, choose File, Send To, Mail Recipient to display the message form (see Figure 21-14).

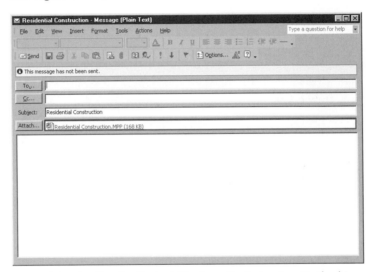

Figure 21-14. Send a Project file from Project using Outlook's e-mail features.

2 In the To box, type an e-mail address (or click the To button to access your address book). Add as many recipients as needed.

3 In the Subject box, type a subject. By default, Project uses the file name as the subject.

4 In the message area, type a message.

5 Click Send.

Routing a Project File Using Outlook

You can also use Outlook to route a Project file. With routing, you send a file sequentially from one team member to the next or to all team members at one time. Use the former method if you want only one version of the file to be seen by all team members in the routing slip list. In this way, one member can review and modify the file before sending it to the next person on the routing slip. Use the latter method if you want all individuals to review and modify the file and return it directly to you.

---

tip   **Use caution when routing sequentially**

One downside to routing a file to a list of team members sequentially is that if someone in the routing list is out of the office for an extended time, your routed file could get stuck in that person's Inbox until they return, delaying any work you want to do to the file.

To route a Project file, do the following:

1   In Project, choose File, Send To, Routing Recipient to display the Routing Slip dialog box.

2   Click Address to display the Address Book dialog box.

3   Select the recipients and then click OK. The addresses are added to the To list (see Figure 21-15).

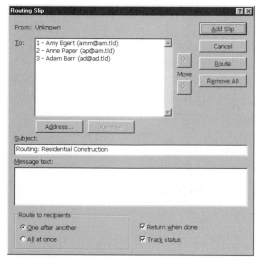

Figure 21-15.   You can route a Project file using Outlook's routing features.

4   Click the up and down arrows in the Move area to move recipients' locations in the list, specifying the order in which you want them to receive the routing slip. Or, if you want everyone to receive a copy simultaneously, select the All At Once option at the bottom of the dialog box.

5   In the Subject box, type a subject.

6 In the message area, type a message.

7 If you want the Project file returned to you after all recipients have received it, select Return When Done.

8 If you want Outlook to send you an e-mail notification each time the file is routed to the next recipient, select Track Status. This option allows you to keep track of where the file is in the routing sequence.

---

tip   **Save the routing slip**

You can save the routing slip with the Project file if you are not ready to send it out yet. To do so, click the Add Slip button. To route the file, choose File, Send To, Next Routing Recipient and then click OK.

---

9 When you're ready to start routing the file to specified recipients, click Route. If you receive a message telling you that another program is attempting to access your e-mail addresses, click Yes to continue. Outlook routes the file to the recipients.

Forwarding a Project File Using Outlook

If a Project file is routed to you, you must forward it to the next person in the list.

To forward a Project file, follow these steps:

1 Open Outlook and view the routed message.

2 Double-click the Project icon in the e-mail message to display the Project file.

3 In Project, view and modify the project as needed.

4 Choose File, Save to save your changes.

5 In Project, choose File, Send To, Next Routing Recipient.

6 Click OK when prompted to send the file to the specified person.

Part 5

Customizing Outlook

Chapter 22

Using Templates

If you use Microsoft Word frequently, you're probably familiar with templates. These useful tools can help you quickly and easily create documents that share standard elements—for example, boilerplate text, special font and paragraph formatting, and paragraph styles.

You can also use templates in Microsoft Outlook to streamline a variety of tasks. There is nothing magical about these templates; they are simply Outlook items that you use to create other Outlook items. For example, you might create an e-mail template for preparing a weekly status report that you send to your staff or management. Or perhaps you use e-mail messages to submit expense reports and would like to use a template to simplify the process.

This chapter not only discusses e-mail templates but also explores the use of templates for other Outlook items. For example, you'll learn how to use templates to create appointments, contact entries, task requests, and journal entries. The chapter also suggests some ways of sharing templates with others.

Working with E-Mail Templates

An e-mail template is really nothing more than a standard e-mail message that you have saved as a template. Here are some suggested uses for e-mail templates:

- Create an expense report form.

- Send product information to potential clients.

- Create status reports for ongoing projects.

- Send messages to specific groups of recipients.

- Create a form for information requests or product registration.

597

When you need to send similar messages frequently, creating a message template can save you quite a bit of time, particularly if the message contains a great deal of frequently used text, graphics, or form elements. You also reduce potential errors by reusing the same message each time rather than creating multiple messages from scratch. You can use the template to provide the bulk of the message, filling in any additional information required in each particular instance.

Creating an E-Mail Template

Creating an e-mail template is as easy as creating an e-mail message. You can start by opening a new message form, just as you would if you were sending a new message to a single recipient or group.

To create an e-mail template from scratch, follow these steps:

1 Be sure that you have specified Outlook as your e-mail editor. You can't save a message as a template with Microsoft Word as your editor.

2 With the Inbox folder open, click the New toolbar button to open a new message form. Enter the boilerplate text and any information that you want to include every time you send a message based on this template. For example, you can specify the subject, address(es), other headings, bullets, lists, and tables.

3 Choose File, Save As in the message form.

4 In the Save As dialog box, shown in Figure 22-1, specify a path and a name for the file. Select Outlook Template in the Save As Type drop-down list. Outlook adds an OFT extension to the file name.

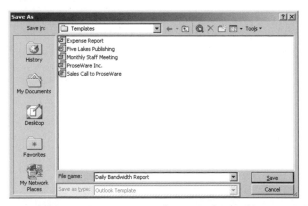

Figure 22-1. Save your newly created template as an OFT file.

Outlook opens your My Documents folder with HTML as the default file type. The default location for user templates, however, is the *<profile>*\Application Data\Microsoft\Templates folder, where *<profile>* is your user profile folder (such as

Documents And Settings*<user>* on a system running Microsoft Windows 2000). When you select Outlook Template as the file type, Outlook automatically switches to your templates folder.

---

tip   You don't have to create a message template from scratch. You can open an existing message, modify it as necessary, and then choose File, Save As to save it as a template.

You can create as many e-mail templates as you need, storing them on your local hard disk or on a network server. Placing templates on a network server allows other Outlook users to use them as well.

Using an E-Mail Template

After you create an e-mail template, it's a simple matter to use it to create a message, as shown here:

1   In Outlook, click the arrow beside New on the Standard toolbar and click Choose Form. Alternatively, choose File, New, Choose Form. Outlook opens the Choose Form dialog box (see Figure 22-2).

2   In the Look In drop-down list, select the location where the template is stored.

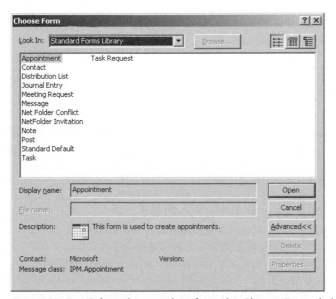

Figure 22-2.   Select the template from the Choose Form dialog box.

Chapter 22

599

3 Select the template from the list and click Open. This opens a message form based on the template data.

4 Fill out the message form to include any additional or modified information, and then send the message as you would any other.

Using a Template with a Distribution List

You can easily send messages to recipients in a distribution list without using a template: simply start a new message, select the distribution list from the address book, and send the message. If the messages you send to the members of the list are different each time you use it, you don't need a template. But if the messages contain much the same information time after time, they're good candidates for templates. For example, you might need to submit weekly reports to a group of administrators or managers, send task lists to people who work for you, or broadcast regular updates about products or services.

You create a template for a distribution list the same way you create any other e-mail template. The only difference is that you store the list of recipients within the template. To do so, simply select the distribution list in the appropriate address box when you create the template. If you don't want the various members of the group to see the addresses of other members on the list, be sure to insert the distribution group in the Bcc box rather than in the To or Cc box.

For more information about working with distribution lists, see Chapter 5, "Managing Address Books and Distribution Lists."

Using Other Outlook Template Types

E-mail messages are not the only Outlook item you can create from a template. In fact, you can create a template for any type of Outlook item. This section of the chapter explores some common situations in which you might use specific types of templates.

Appointments and Meetings

You might find it useful to create templates for setting up certain types of appointments and meetings. If you prefer to use a set of appointment properties that differ from Outlook's default properties, you can use a template that contains your preferred settings and then create each new appointment or meeting from that template. For example, if you have regular meetings with the same group of people, you can set up a template in which those individuals are already selected on the Scheduling tab so that you don't have to assemble the list each time you need to schedule a meeting. Or perhaps you prefer to have Outlook issue a reminder an hour before each appointment rather than the default 15 minutes. Or the majority of your meetings might be online meetings that use Microsoft NetMeeting and thus require a few specific settings.

You can create templates for appointments and meetings the same way you create e-mail templates. Open a new appointment form or meeting request and fill in all the data that will be standard each time you use the template. Then choose File, Save As and save the file as an Outlook template. When you want to use the template, choose File, New, Choose Form and follow the steps outlined earlier in "Using an E-Mail Template," page 599. You can also click the arrow beside the New button on the Standard toolbar and select Choose Form to select a form.

> For more information about using appointment forms and their settings, see Chapter 18, "Scheduling Appointments." For details about meeting requests, see Chapter 19, "Scheduling Meetings and Resources."

Contacts

In your Contacts folder, you're likely to add contact entries for people who work in or belong to the same organization, business, department, or other entity. These contacts might share the same company name, address, or primary phone number. In such a case, why not create a template to save yourself the trouble of entering the information for each contact entry separately (and potentially getting it wrong)? Or, for example, you might use the same directory server for all your NetMeeting sessions. Why not create a template that specifies the directory server, eliminating the chore of setting it each time you create a new contact?

As with other templates, you create a contact template by opening a new contact form and filling in the standard data. Then choose File, Save As and save the contact as an Outlook template.

> For more information about creating contact entries and working in the Contacts folder, see Chapter 14, "Managing Your Contacts."

tip **Create contacts from the same company**

You can create contact entries that share common company information by selecting a contact item and choosing Actions, New Contact From Same Company. However, this might not give you the results you need in all cases. For example, the New Contact from Same Company command uses the same address, company name, business phone, business fax, and Web page address for the new contact as for the selected one. If you also want to use the same directory server, categories, notes, or other properties for the new contacts, it's best to create a contact entry, save it as a template, and then create other contact entries from the template.

Tasks and Task Requests

If you perform the same task frequently, you can create a basic task as a template and then modify it as needed for each individual occurrence of the task. You also can create a task template with a specific set of properties and then use it to create various tasks. For example, you could create all your tasks with the status specified as In Progress rather than the default Not Started. Or perhaps you need to create many tasks with the same set of categories assigned to them.

In addition to creating task items from templates, you might also want to use templates to create task requests. A task request template is handy if you manage a group of people to whom you need to assign similar or identical tasks. Set up a template that incorporates the common elements and then create each task request from the template, filling in or modifying the unique elements, and addressing it to the specific person assigned to the task.

You use the same methods described earlier for e-mail templates to create and open templates for tasks and task requests.

> For more information about creating tasks and task requests, see Chapter 20, "Managing Your Tasks."

Journal Entries

You can use the Outlook journal to keep track of activities such as phone calls, remote sessions, or other actions that you want to record. Why use journal templates? Any time you find yourself adding a manual journal entry for the same type of activity with the same or similar properties, consider creating a template for the action. Perhaps you frequently record journal entries for phone calls to a particular individual, account, or company that contain the same phone number or company name or log the same duration. Rather than creating a journal entry from scratch each time, create a template and use the template instead.

> For more information about working with the Outlook journal, see Chapter 17, "Keeping a Journal."

Editing Templates

Outlook stores templates as OFT files when you save a template to disk. You can modify any template to make changes as needed.

To modify a template, follow these steps:

1 Choose Tools, Forms, Choose Form.

2 Outlook displays the Choose Form dialog box (shown earlier in Figure 22-2). In the Look In drop-down list, select the location where the template is stored.

3 Select the template and click Open.

4 Make changes as needed and choose File, Save to save the changes.

---

tip To find templates you've created so you can edit them, choose User Templates In File System from the Look In drop-down list in the Choose Form dialog box and then browse to the folder where you saved the template.

Sharing Templates

In some situations, you might find it useful to share templates with other users. For example, assume that you're responsible for managing several people who all submit the same type of report to you on a regular basis through e-mail. In that situation, you might create an e-mail template with the appropriate boilerplate information and your address in the To box and then have the staff use that template to generate the reports. This ensures that everyone is providing comparable information. In addition, whenever you need a different set of data from these employees, you need only modify the template.

By default, Outlook stores your template files in the Application Data\Microsoft\ Templates folder of your user profile. On a clean installation of Windows 2000, for example, this folder would be \Documents And Settings\<*user*>\Application Data\ Microsoft\Templates, where <*user*> is your user name. On systems upgraded from Microsoft Windows NT Workstation, the folder would be located in \WinntT\Profiles\ <*user*>\Application Data\Microsoft\Templates.

The easiest way to find the location where Outlook stores your templates is to save a template or at least go through the motions of saving it. Open a form, choose File, Save As, and then select User Templates In File System. Outlook displays the path to the folder just underneath the Look In drop-down list.

Why do you need to know where Outlook stores your templates? To share a template, you need to share the template file. This means placing the template in a shared network folder, sharing your template folder, or sending the template file to other users (the least desirable option). For any of these options, you need to know the location of the template file you want to share. After you locate the file, you can share the folder that contains it, copy the template to a network share, or forward it to other users as an attachment.

InsideOut

The best option for sharing a template, in my opinion, is to create a network share and place the template in that share. Configure permissions for the share so that you have full control and other users have read-only access to the folder. This allows you to make changes to the template, while allowing others to use but not modify the template.

Chapter 23

Customizing the Outlook Interface

Microsoft Outlook has a useful interface that serves most users well right out of the box. However, you probably perform certain tasks that are not readily available through the standard Outlook interface. For example, perhaps you use remote mail frequently and want quick access to the remote mail functions rather than drilling down through menus to find them.

As all Microsoft Office applications do, Outlook provides a way to tailor the interface to your needs. You can customize the Outlook Bar to add your own shortcuts, customize Outlook Today view and other standard views, and customize the way Outlook displays your folders. You can also create custom command bars.

This chapter focuses on the various ways you can fine-tune Outlook to the way you work. Some of the changes covered are minor; others are more significant. All of them can enhance your experience with Outlook and make it a more useful tool for bringing efficiency to your workday.

Customizing the Outlook Bar

Most people navigate through Outlook folders using the Outlook Bar. This section explains how you can customize the Outlook Bar to suit your preferences.

A Quick Tour of the Outlook Bar

The Outlook Bar, which appears on the left side of the Outlook window, contains shortcuts to your Outlook folders (see Figure 23-1 on the next page). The Outlook Bar also includes shortcuts to other common items, such as My Computer, My Documents, and your Favorites folder.

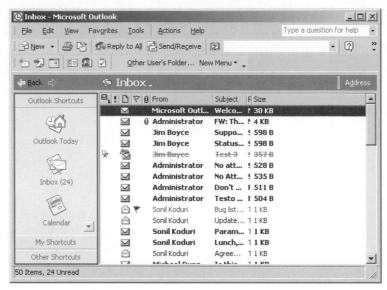

Figure 23-1. The Outlook Bar provides shortcuts to Outlook folders and other objects.

By default, the Outlook Bar displays three groups:

- **Outlook Shortcuts.** This group contains shortcuts to most of your Outlook folders, including Outlook Today, Inbox, and Contacts.

- **My Shortcuts.** This group contains shortcuts to Outlook folders you use less often, such as Drafts, Outbox, Sent Items, and Journal. It includes also a shortcut to the Microsoft Office Update Web site.

- **Other Shortcuts.** This group by default contains shortcuts to My Computer, My Documents, and Favorites.

You can make several changes to the Outlook Bar, including adding and removing groups, adding and removing shortcuts, and changing the appearance of its icons. The following sections explain these changes.

> **tip** You can change the width of the Outlook Bar by dragging its border.

Showing and Hiding the Outlook Bar

If you use the Outlook Bar often, you'll probably want it to remain open all the time. But if you work with a particular Outlook folder most of the time, you might prefer to have the additional space for the folder list or your favorite folder view. To that end,

Outlook allows you to hide and display the Outlook Bar as needed. Choose View, Outlook Bar to turn the Outlook Bar on and off. You also can right-click the Outlook Bar and choose Hide to hide it.

Changing the Size of Icons on the Outlook Bar

You can use small or large icons in each Outlook group. By default, the Outlook Shortcuts group uses large icons and the My Shortcuts and Other Shortcuts groups use small icons (see Figure 23-2).

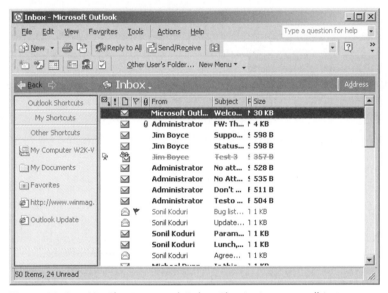

Figure 23-2. My Shortcuts and Other Shortcuts use small icons.

Each group maintains its own icon settings, so you can configure one group for large icons and another for small icons. To change the icon size, right-click the group and choose Large Icons or Small Icons.

Rearranging Icons on the Outlook Bar

Outlook arranges the icons on the Outlook Bar in a certain order. You can change the arrangement of the icons if you prefer a different order. For example, you might use the Inbox almost exclusively and prefer to have it rather than the Outlook Today icon at the top of the list. Or perhaps you want to move a rarely used icon to the bottom of the list.

To rearrange icons on the Outlook Bar, simply drag the icon you want to move to its new location (see Figure 23-3 on the next page).

Indicator

Figure 23-3. Outlook displays an indicator showing where the icon will be inserted.

Adding a Folder or Document to the Outlook Bar

You can create shortcuts to file system folders or Outlook folders. In addition, these shortcuts can be added to existing Outlook Bar groups or to new groups that you create. For example, if you use a particular document folder often, you might want to add that folder to one of your Outlook Bar groups. Or perhaps you've mistakenly removed a shortcut to one of your Outlook folders and now want to restore it.

The process is similar, regardless of the type of shortcut you're adding:

1 Open Outlook, and open the group in which you want to create the shortcut.

2 Right-click the Outlook Bar, and choose Outlook Bar Shortcut to open the Add To Outlook Bar dialog box (see Figure 23-4).

3 In the Look In drop-down list, select Outlook to add a shortcut to an Outlook folder or select File System to add a shortcut to a file system folder.

4 Select the folder from the directory tree or type the path in the Folder Name box. Click OK.

---

tip **Create shortcuts to network shares you use often**

You can specify UNC paths in addition to mapped drives. A UNC path takes the form \\<server>\<share>, where <server> is the computer sharing the folder and <share> is the folder's share name. On systems running Microsoft Windows 2000, you can specify longer UNC paths, such as \\<server>\documents\contracts\completed.

Chapter 23: Customizing the Outlook Interface

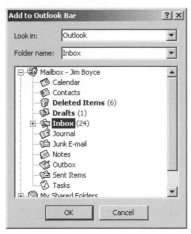

Figure 23-4. Use the Add To Outlook Bar dialog box to add shortcuts to the Outlook Bar.

Adding a Web Site to the Outlook Bar

You can add shortcuts to Web sites to the Outlook Bar. This lets you quickly open a site from Outlook to do research, check stock quotes, view news, and so on.

You have two ways to add Internet shortcuts to the Outlook Bar. One way is to open the site in Outlook and then add that currently displayed site to the My Shortcuts group. After you create the shortcut, you can move it to a different group, if necessary.

Follow these steps to use this method:

1 In Outlook, choose View, Toolbars, Web to display the Web toolbar.

2 In the Address field, type the URL for the site, such as ***http://www. microsoft.com***.

3 With the site displayed in Outlook, right-click the Outlook Bar and choose Outlook Bar Shortcut To Web Page. Outlook adds the shortcut to the bottom of the My Shortcuts group.

4 If you want to relocate the shortcut within the My Shortcuts group or to another group, drag the shortcut's icon to the new location.

The second way to add a Web site shortcut to the Outlook Bar is by dragging it. Open the Outlook Bar group in which you want to place the shortcut, and then simply drag an existing shortcut from the desktop or another folder to the Outlook Bar.

Chapter 23

> **tip**   **Create new Web shortcuts**
>
> You can create new Web shortcuts on the desktop or in a file system folder by right-clicking the location and choosing New, Shortcut. On the first page of the Create Shortcut Wizard, type the URL to the Web page, FTP site, or other Internet resource. Use *http://* as the URL prefix for Web pages, use *ftp://* for FTP sites, or use *https://* for secure sites that use Secure Sockets Layer (SSL).

Removing an Icon from the Outlook Bar

If you decide you no longer want a particular shortcut on the Outlook Bar, you can remove it easily. Simply right-click the icon and choose Remove From Outlook Bar. Click Yes to remove the shortcut or No to cancel.

Renaming an Icon on the Outlook Bar

In some cases, you'll want to change the name Outlook assigns to a shortcut on the Outlook Bar. For example, when you add a Web site shortcut, its name is the URL, which typically doesn't fit very well on the Outlook Bar. Or perhaps you simply want to change the shortcut's name to something more descriptive.

To change the shortcut name, right-click the shortcut's icon and choose Rename Shortcut. Type the new name and press Enter.

Working with Groups on the Outlook Bar

As mentioned, Outlook creates three groups by default on the Outlook Bar. You can also add your own groups, remove groups, and rename them. This section explains these tasks.

Adding a Group to the Outlook Bar

At some point, you might want to add your own groups of shortcuts to the Outlook Bar to help you reorganize existing shortcuts or organize new shortcuts. For example, you might want to create a group to contain all your Web shortcuts.

Adding a new group is easy. Simply right-click anywhere on the Outlook Bar and choose Add New Group. Outlook adds a new group named New Group and highlights the group name so that you can change it (see Figure 23-5). Type the group name and press Enter. Then click the group to open it and begin adding shortcuts or moving shortcuts to it from your other groups.

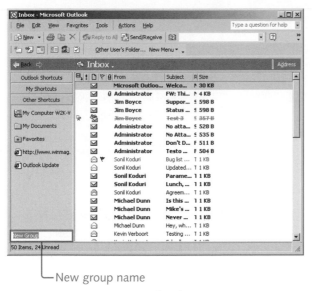

New group name

Figure 23-5. Type a name for the new group.

> **tip** You can copy shortcuts from one group to another. Simply drag the shortcut to the group button where you want the shortcut placed. Outlook expands the group so that you can drop the shortcut in place.

Renaming a Group on the Outlook Bar

You can rename a group as easily as you rename a shortcut. Open Outlook, right-click the group button on the Outlook Bar, and choose Rename Group. Type a new name for the group and press Enter.

Removing a Group from the Outlook Bar

If you decide that you want to remove a group from the Outlook Bar, you can do so at any time. Simply right-click the group button on the Outlook Bar and choose Remove Group. Click Yes to remove the group or No to cancel.

> **tip** If the group you remove contains shortcuts you've copied from other locations (such as the desktop), removing the group does not affect those shortcuts. Only the group is removed from the Outlook Bar.

Chapter 23

Customizing Command Bars

Microsoft now refers to menus and toolbars collectively as *command bars*. You can work with command bars as they're provided by Outlook, or you can customize their location and contents to suit your preferences. This section explains how to relocate command bars, add and remove commands, and configure custom options.

> **note** The terms *command bar* and *toolbar* are used synonymously throughout this chapter.

Working with Toolbars

Outlook includes the menu bar and three toolbars by default: Standard, Advanced, and Web. You can also create your own toolbars or command bars (see "Creating Custom Command Bars," page 614). Outlook makes it easy to rearrange your screen by displaying or hiding toolbars. You also can move command bars to different locations in the Outlook interface.

Displaying and Hiding Toolbars

You probably use the same one or two toolbars on a regular basis but sometimes need to display or hide a particular toolbar. By default, Outlook always displays the menu command bar—you can't turn it off. Outlook also displays the Standard toolbar by default, although you can turn it off if you don't use it.

To display or hide a toolbar, choose View, Toolbars and then select the toolbar in question. A check mark beside a toolbar indicates that it is displayed; no check mark indicates that the toolbar is hidden.

> **tip** You can right-click the menu bar or any toolbar and turn toolbars on or off by using the shortcut menu.

Moving and Docking Toolbars

All Outlook command bars—including the menu—are *dockable.* This means you can attach the command bar to any of the four sides of the Outlook window. You can also float a command bar. Figure 23-6 shows the menu bar docked at the right edge of the Outlook window. Figure 23-7 shows the menu bar floating on the desktop.

At the left edge of each command bar (if the bar is displayed at the top or bottom of the Outlook window) or at the top edge (if the command bar is docked at the right or left edge of the window) is an anchor you can use to move the command bar. Place the cursor over the anchor, and the cursor should change to a four-way arrow. Then drag the command bar to its new location. Drag the command bar away from a window edge to make it float. Drag it back to a window edge to dock it.

Chapter 23: Customizing the Outlook Interface

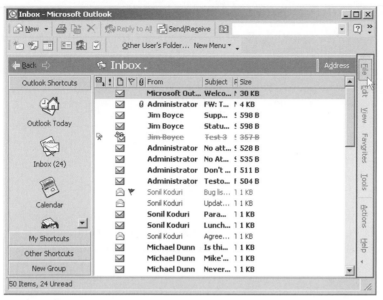

Figure 23-6. You can dock command bars at any of the four window edges.

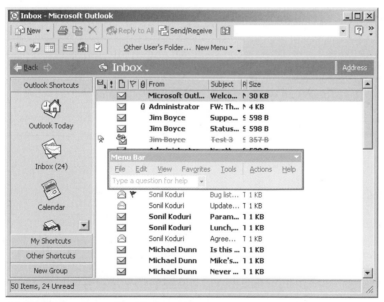

Figure 23-7. Command bars can also float on the desktop.

> **tip** If you need more vertical room in your folder views and don't use the menu often, consider docking the menu and toolbars at the right or left edge of the Outlook window.

Creating Custom Command Bars

Outlook gives you considerable control over the appearance and content of the command bars. Because Microsoft has combined menus and toolbars as a single type of command bar, you use a similar process to modify menus and toolbar items. The following sections explain how to make several types of changes to your command bars, including adding new ones.

> **tip**   If you wreak havoc with the default command bars in your zeal to customize them, you can restore them with relative ease. For details, see "Recovering the Default Command Bars," page 621.

You can modify the existing command bars, but in many cases you'll probably want to create your own. For example, you might want to create a command bar for remote mail. Or perhaps you use another group of commands to which you'd like quick access.

After you add a new command bar, you can add buttons and menus to it (explained in the following section). As mentioned, menus and toolbars are both considered command bars in Outlook 2002, so the process for creating a menu is the same as the one for creating a toolbar.

Follow these steps to create a command bar:

1   In Outlook, right-click any command bar and choose Customize to open the Customize dialog box. Alternatively, choose View, Toolbars, Customize.

2   In the Customize dialog box, click the Toolbars tab and then click New.

3   Type a name for the command bar and then click OK. Outlook opens a blank command bar.

Refer to the following section to add commands to your new command bar.

Adding Items

The default toolbars provided with Outlook cover the most commonly used commands, but they are not all-inclusive. Therefore, you might want to add frequently used commands to the existing toolbars or create custom toolbars.

In either case, you need to know how to add buttons to a toolbar:

1   In Outlook, right-click any toolbar and choose Customize to open the Customize dialog box. Alternatively, choose View, Toolbars, Customize.

2   Click the Commands tab (see Figure 23-8).

Chapter 23: Customizing the Outlook Interface

Figure 23-8. Use the Commands tab to add commands.

3 In the Categories list, select the command category containing the command you want to add.

4 In the Commands list, locate the command to add and drag it to the appropriate toolbar.

5 Repeat steps 3 and 4 to add other commands as needed.

6 Click Close to close the Customize dialog box.

> **tip** You can add a combination of menus and buttons to any command bar.

Removing Items

If you don't use certain commands on a toolbar, you might want to remove them to make room for others or to simplify the Outlook interface.

To remove a button, follow these steps:

1 In Outlook, open the Customize dialog box.

2 With any tab of the Customize dialog box displayed, drag the button out of its toolbar. You can release the button as soon as you see a small X appear by the pointer.

3 Click Close to close the Customize dialog box.

> **tip** **Reset toolbars to their defaults**
>
> You can reset any changes you made to a toolbar. Choose View, Toolbars, Customize, and then click the Toolbars tab. Select the toolbar to reset and click Reset. Click OK to reset the toolbar to its default state or Cancel to cancel the operation.

Reorganizing Items

You can reorganize the buttons on a command bar. The key point to understand is that whenever the Customize dialog box is open, any action you take on a command bar modifies that command bar. For example, drag a button or command out of the command bar and Outlook removes it.

Therefore, the basic method of reorganizing a command bar is to open the Customize dialog box and then simply drag the buttons or commands, as follows:

1 In Outlook, open the Customize dialog box.

2 With any tab in the Customize dialog box displayed, drag an item on a command bar from one location to another on the same command bar or on a different command bar.

3 Click Close to close the Customize dialog box.

Modifying Command Bar Items

Outlook inserts items on a command bar using a set of default characteristics. However, you can change these characteristics for any command bar item. For example, you can change the name of a menu, its shortcut key, or the icon assigned to a button. Following is a list of the modifications you can make:

● Change an item's name, reset it to its default properties, or delete the item.

● Modify the button image assigned to a command bar item by selecting a different image or editing the existing image.

● Change the style of the item so that it appears as text only, image only, or a combination of image and text.

● Assign a hyperlink to an item. When you click the item in Outlook, the document or site referenced by the link opens.

Follow these steps to modify an existing command bar item:

1 In Outlook, open the Customize dialog box.

2 Right-click the command button or menu item you want to change. Outlook presents a shortcut menu from which you can choose one of the following commands:

Chapter 23: Customizing the Outlook Interface

■ **Reset.** Resets the item back to its default properties (button image, name, for example).

■ **Delete.** Removes the item from the command bar.

■ **Name.** Changes the name of the item. Precede with the & character the key you want to use as the keyboard shortcut (the key you press instead of clicking the item). Note that some objects do not display their name by default.

■ **Copy Button Image.** Copies the button image of the selected item to the clipboard for use on a different button or in another program (or for documentation).

■ **Paste Button Image.** Pastes the contents of the clipboard on the item, for use as the button icon.

■ **Reset Button Image.** Resets the button to display its default image.

■ **Edit Button Image.** Opens the Button Editor dialog box (see Figure 23-9) so that you can edit the button image.

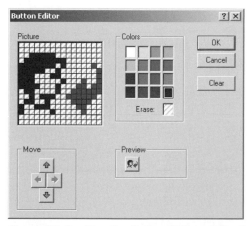

Figure 23-9. Use the Button Editor dialog box to edit the image assigned as a button's icon.

■ **Change Button Image.** Selects a different icon image from a set of predefined icons.

■ **Default Style.** Resets the button to its default style, such as image only or text only.

■ **Text Only (Always).** Shows the item as text without an image regardless of whether the item is on a toolbar or a menu.

■ **Text Only (In Menus).** Shows the item as text only (without an image) if it's used on a menu.

■ **Image And Text.** Shows the item as an icon with a text description beside it.

■ **Begin A Group.** Inserts a separator above a selected menu item or to the left of a selected toolbar button.

■ **Assign Hyperlink.** Assigns to the selected item a hyperlink that opens the linked site or document when you select the command bar item in Outlook.

3 Click Close to close the Customize dialog box.

Changing the Width of the Drop-Down List

Some Outlook command bar items use a drop-down list to display a list of information or to allow you to type information such as a search phrase or an address. If the drop-down list isn't wide enough to adequately display its information, you can widen it. You can also shrink lists that are too wide.

Here's how to change the width of a drop-down list:

1 In Outlook, open the Customize dialog box.

2 Select the drop-down list you want to modify.

3 Drag the left or right border of the drop-down list to resize it as needed.

4 Click Close to close the Customize dialog box.

Changing the Button Size

You can configure toolbars to display their buttons using either small icons (the default) or large icons. If your monitor is configured for a relatively high resolution, which can make the toolbar buttons hard to distinguish, configuring the toolbars for large icons can improve their readability considerably.

Follow these steps to configure button size:

1 In Outlook, open the Customize dialog box.

2 Click the Options tab (see Figure 23-10).

3 Select the Large Icons check box to turn on large icons, or clear the check box if you want to use the default small icon size. The change occurs immediately when you select or clear the option.

4 Click Close to close the Customize dialog box.

Chapter 23: Customizing the Outlook Interface

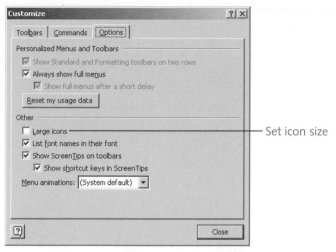

Figure 23-10. Configure icon size on the Options tab.

Troubleshooting

You can't add or remove separators on command bars.

Command bars can include separators. On a toolbar, the separator is a vertical gray line that separates one group of commands or menus from another. On a menu, the separator is a horizontal gray line that separates one set of commands on the menu from another. Separators are purely an aesthetic element—they serve no other purpose than to provide a visual separation between items on a toolbar or menu.

The process of adding or removing separators is as far from being intuitive as you can get in Outlook. No obvious feature in the user interface gives you the ability to drag separators into position or remove them. Actually, adding and removing them is easy, but you have to know the secret.

Follow these steps to add or remove a separator on a toolbar:

1 In Outlook, open the Customize dialog box.

2 Locate the two items you want to separate. Drag the item on the right slightly to the right. Outlook inserts a separator to the left of the item you dragged.

3 To remove a separator, drag the item just to the right of the separator slightly to the left.

4 Click Close to close the Customize dialog box.

(continued)

> **Troubleshooting** *(continued)*   You can also add a separator to a toolbar by using an item's shortcut menu. Open the Customize dialog box, right-click an item, and choose Begin A Group. Outlook inserts a separator to the left of the item.
>
> Follow these steps to add or remove a separator on a menu:
>
> **1** In Outlook, open the Customize dialog box.
>
> **2** Locate the two menu items you want to separate. Drag the bottom of the two items slightly downward. Outlook inserts a separator just above it.
>
> **3** To remove a separator, drag the menu item just below the separator slightly upward.
>
> **4** Click Close to close the Customize dialog box.

Restoring Default Command Bars

If you've made quite a few changes to the default command bars, the time might come when you want to reset them to their default state.

You can do so easily, as the following steps illustrate:

1 In Outlook, open the Customize dialog box.

2 Click the Toolbars tab.

3 Select the toolbar you want to reset and then click Reset. Outlook prompts you to verify that you want to reset the selected toolbar.

4 Click OK to reset the toolbar or Cancel to cancel the task.

Renaming a Custom Toolbar

Although Outlook doesn't allow you to rename the standard command bars, you can rename any custom command bars that you've created.

Follow these steps to rename a custom command bar:

1 In Outlook, open the Customize dialog box.

2 Select the command bar you want to rename and then click Rename.

3 Type a new name and click OK.

4 Click Close to close the Customize dialog box.

Deleting a Custom Command Bar

You can turn off any command bar to hide it. But if you no longer need a custom command bar you've created, you probably want to delete it.

Chapter 23: Customizing the Outlook Interface

Follow these steps:

1 In Outlook, open the Customize dialog box.

2 Click the Toolbars tab.

3 Select the command bar to delete and then click Delete.

4 Click OK to verify that you want to delete the command bar or Cancel to cancel the task.

Sharing a Custom Command Bar

Outlook stores your command bar definitions in the Outcmd.dat file. The data stored there includes changes you make to the default command bars as well as custom command bars you create. Outlook maintains a separate Outcmd.dat file for each user. If you share your computer with others who also use Outlook, there are probably multiple Outcmd.dat files stored on the system. By default, Outlook stores the file in the Application Data\Microsoft\Outlook folder under your profile folder (such as \Documents And Settings\<*user*> on a computer running Microsoft Windows 2000).

If you've spent quite a bit of time customizing the command bars and want to share those changes with others, you can do so by sharing your Outcmd.dat file. If someone else has customized such a file for you, you can easily install it on your system.

If you've received a customized Outcmd.dat file from another user, follow these steps to install it on your system:

1 Obtain the customized Outcmd.dat file from the other user (or, if you're sharing yours, give the file to others who need its customized toolbars).

2 To install the customized file on your system, exit Outlook and locate the Outcmd.dat file in your profile folder on your system.

3 Rename the existing Outcmd.dat file as Outcmd.old.

4 Copy the other user's Outcmd.dat file to your profile folder where the original Outcmd.dat file was located.

5 Restart Outlook.

> **caution**   If you made changes to your command bars before installing the other user's Outcmd.dat file, you'll lose those changes after installing the new file.

Recovering the Default Command Bars

As mentioned, Outlook stores command bar customization settings in the Outcmd.dat file, located in the Application Data\Microsoft\Outlook folder under your profile folder. If your Outcmd.dat file becomes corrupted, you can restore the default command bars by deleting or renaming the existing Outcmd.dat file. This process is also handy when you've made extensive changes to your command bars and want to restore them to their defaults.

Follow these steps:

1 Close Outlook.

2 Locate the Outcmd.dat file for your profile.

3 Rename the file Outcmd.old.

4 Restart Outlook. You should now see only the default command bars.

Controlling Command Bar Appearance and Behavior

Outlook lets you configure a handful of properties that control the way your command bars appear and function. To set these properties, open Outlook and choose View, Toolbars, Customize. Click the Options tab in the Customize dialog box (see Figure 23-10 on page 619).

The Options tab includes the following settings:

● **Show Standard And Formatting Toolbars On Two Rows.** Shows the Standard and Formatting toolbars on two rows when both toolbars are displayed.

● **Always Show Full Menus.** Turns off adaptive menus (those that show only the most frequently used commands) and shows all menu items. Clear this option to turn on adaptive menus.

● **Show Full Menus After A Short Delay.** Shows all menu items after you rest the pointer on a menu for a short delay period.

● **Reset My Usage Data.** Resets the usage data for adaptive menus. This command has no effect on the location of a command bar or on customized command bars (command bar modifications remain as they are).

● **Large Icons.** Shows large command bar icons.

● **List Font Names In Their Font.** Displays font names in their actual font to give you a sample of the font.

● **Show ScreenTips On Toolbars.** Shows ScreenTips when you rest the pointer over a toolbar button.

● **Show Shortcut Keys In ScreenTips.** Includes with the ScreenTip text the shortcut key (such as a function key), if any, assigned to each command bar item.

● **Menu Animations.** Lists a menu on which you can select a menu animation effect for Outlook to use when you open a menu. Select the (System Default) option to use your operating system's default menu effect.

> **tip** You can configure the operating system's menu animation effect by using the Effects tab of the Display dialog box. Right-click the desktop and choose Properties to display this dialog box. Select (System Default) and configure the system for no animation to turn off animations in Outlook.

Customizing Outlook Today View

Outlook uses Outlook Today view as its default view. Outlook Today synthesizes your most commonly used Outlook data into a single view, summarizing your schedule, tasks, and key e-mail folders for the current day. You can work with the view as is or modify it to suit your needs. This section explores how to customize Outlook Today view (see Figure 23-11).

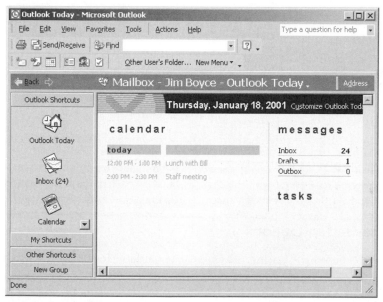

Figure 23-11. Outlook Today, which is the default Outlook view, summarizes your current day.

> For a basic description of how to use Outlook Today view, see "Outlook Today," page 590.

Although Outlook Today presents useful information, it might not show all the information you want or need to really keep track of your work day. You can customize Outlook Today view to show additional information and use HTML to present a truly customized interface. The following sections explain how.

Configuring Outlook Today

You can configure several options that control how this view looks as well as the data it displays. To configure the view, click the Customize Outlook Today link in Outlook Today view (in the upper right corner of the view). The screen shown in Figure 23-12 appears.

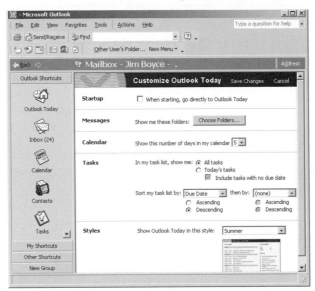

Figure 23-12. Use the settings shown here to configure Outlook Today view.

The following sections explain the changes you can make to Outlook Today view on this page. When you're satisfied with the changes, click Save Changes in the Customize Outlook Today title bar. Or click Cancel to close the page without applying the changes.

Specifying the Startup Option

If you select the When Starting, Go Directly To Outlook Today check box, Outlook opens Outlook Today view when you first start the program.

You also can specify the startup folder by using Outlook's options, as explained here:

1 In Outlook, choose Tools, Options.

2 Click Other.

3 Click Advanced Options.

4 In the Startup In This Folder drop-down list, select Outlook Today.

5 Click OK twice to close the dialog boxes.

The Startup In This Folder drop-down list specifies the folder Outlook will use by default when you start Outlook. Choosing Outlook Today in the list has the same effect as choosing When Starting, Go Directly To Outlook Today.

> **tip** If Outlook Today is configured as the default view and you clear the When Starting, Go Directly To Outlook Today check box without specifying a different startup folder in the Options dialog box, Outlook makes your Inbox the startup folder.

Specifying Folders to Show

Outlook Today view shows the Drafts, Inbox, and Outbox folders. If you seldom use the Drafts folder, you might prefer to remove it from Outlook Today. Or perhaps you want to add other folders to the view, such as Tasks and Contacts, to give you a quick way to open those folders without using the Outlook Bar.

To configure the folders that Outlook Today displays, click Choose Folders on the Customize Outlook Today page to open the Select Folder dialog box (see Figure 23-13). Select each folder you want to display, and then click OK.

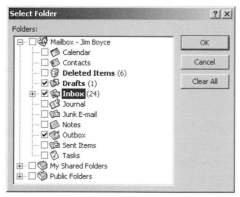

Figure 23-13.   Use the Select Folder dialog box to choose the folders you want Outlook Today to display.

Setting Calendar Options

The calendar portion of Outlook Today view displays a certain number of days from your calendar based on the current date. You can specify the number of days displayed by using the Show This Number Of Days In My Calendar option. Select a number from 1 to 7.

Setting Task Options

The tasks area of the Customize Outlook Today page lets you configure how Outlook Today displays your tasks. The following list summarizes these options:

- **All Tasks.** Shows all tasks regardless of the status or completion deadline.
- **Today's Tasks.** Shows overdue tasks and incomplete tasks that are due today.

Chapter 23

- **Include Tasks With No Due Date.** Shows tasks for which you've assigned no due date.

- **Sort My Task List By** *criteria* **Then By** *criteria.* Sort your task list according to the task's importance, due date, creation time, and start date. You can specify two sort conditions and also choose between ascending or descending sort order for both conditions.

Using Styles

Outlook Today by default displays its information using three columns on a white background. Outlook provides additional styles you can select to change the overall appearance of Outlook Today view. Use the Show Outlook Today In This Style dropdown list to select a style. The Customize Outlook Today page shows a sample of the style after you select it.

Customizing Outlook Today with HTML

If you have any experience with HTML development, you might have surmised that Outlook Today view is driven by HTML code. Therefore, this view is extensible, allowing you to customize it by modifying the HTML code that defines it. For example, you might want to add a stock ticker, a Web site, links to a database, or other information to your Outlook Today view.

The code for Outlook Today resides in the Outlwvw.dll file, which is normally located in the \Program Files\Microsoft Office\Office 10\1033 folder for an English installation. If you're not sure where the Outlwvw.dll file is located, choose Start, Find (or Start, Search) to search your system for the file. You need to know the location to extract the HTML code from the file for modification (explained shortly).

You have two options for customizing Outlook Today: you can create a custom Outlwvw.dll file, which requires programming ability and a compiler, or you can use an HTML document instead of the DLL file. This chapter focuses on the second option.

> **note** For more information on customizing Outlook Today, check the Microsoft Outlook Deployment Kit, which includes extensive documentation on customizing this view as well as other aspects of Outlook. The Outlook Deployment Kit is included on the Office XP CD in the \ORK folder. You'll find additional information at Microsoft's Web site at *http://www.microsoft.com/office/ork/pp*. Click Toolbox and then select Tools to view available options.

Extracting Outlook Today's HTML Code

Although you could write the HTML code for your Outlook Today view from scratch, doing so would take an in-depth understanding of not only HTML but also

Outlook. Most people find it easier to extract the HTML code from the default Outlwvw.dll file to use as the basis for their customization work. After you have the default code, you can begin customizing it to add the features you need.

Follow these steps to extract the HTML code from the Outlwvw.dll file:

1 Close Outlook and open Microsoft Internet Explorer.

2 Locate your Outlwvw.dll file by choosing Start, Search (or Start, Find) or by browsing for the file.

3 Click in the Address field in Internet Explorer, and type the following (replace the path to the file if yours is different):

Res://C:\Program Files\Microsoft Office\Office10\1033\Outlwvw.dll/outlook.htm

4 Internet Explorer might generate a script error, but the exact behavior depends on your version of Internet Explorer and whether you have the Script Editor installed. Just cancel the dialog box or click No if it appears.

5 In Internet Explorer, choose View, Source to open a Notepad window that displays the HTML code for Outlook Today view (see Figure 23-14).

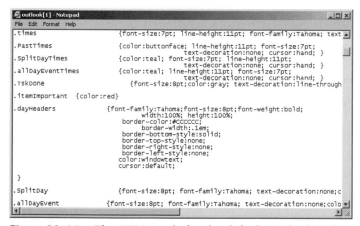

Figure 23-14. The HTML code for the default Outlook Today view is displayed in Notepad.

6 In Notepad, choose File, Save As and save the file with an HTM file extension (for example, Outlook Today.htm).

7 Use Notepad's Replace feature to perform a global search and replace operation in the file, searching for all instances of **display:none** and replacing them with **display:**. Then save the file.

Modifying Outlook Today

At this point, you have a functional Outlook Today.htm file. You can open the file in your favorite HTML editor and modify it as needed. For example, you might open the file in Microsoft FrontPage or Macromedia Dreamweaver to make your changes. You can also make the changes right in Notepad, but doing so requires an in-depth understanding of HTML programming and is the most difficult way to modify the file.

After you modify the file, you need to make a registry change to allow Outlook to use your custom file instead of the default DLL. The next section explains how.

Specifying Your Custom Outlook Today Page

Outlook by default looks to Outlwvw.dll for the Outlook Today view. For Outlook to use your custom HTML file instead, you must make a small change in the registry. Before you make the change, however, you should back up the Outlook registry key in case you have problems making the required change. If you do experience problems, you can restore the registry key to repair the problem.

Follow these steps to back up the Outlook registry key and make the change necessary to point Outlook to your new custom HTML file:

1 Choose Start, Run.

2 In the Run dialog box, type **regedit**.

3 In the Registry Editor, select the branch
   HKEY_CURRENT_USER\Software\Microsoft\Office\10.0\Outlook\Today.

4 Choose Registry, Export Registry File.

5 Verify that the Selected Branch option is selected in the Export Registry File dialog box, specify a file name (such as Today.reg), and click Save. If you later have problems getting your Outlook Today view to work, double-click this file to restore the Today registry key.

6 In the Today key, double-click the Url value or select the value and choose Edit, Modify. The Edit String dialog box opens (see Figure 23-15).

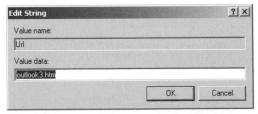

Figure 23-15. Change the registry value to point Outlook to a different Outlook Today view.

> **note** If the Url value doesn't exist, create it as a string value and then set its value according to the next step.

7 Type the path to your custom HTML file, preceding it with **File://**, as in the following example:

File://c:\My Documents\Custom\Outlook Today.htm

8 Click OK to save the changes.

9 Close the Registry Editor.

10 Open Outlook and select Outlook Today view to verify that Outlook is using your custom file and to test the code.

Sharing an Outlook Today Page

After you've gone to the trouble to use HTML to customize Outlook Today view, you might want to share that custom file with others or use it on a different computer. Simply copy the file to the other system, and make the same modification to the other system's registry to allow it to use the file.

Chapter 24

Creating Custom Views and Print Styles

Earlier chapters discussed the standard views Microsoft Outlook provides for its many folders and data types. Those chapters also discussed customizing standard views by grouping and sorting items and by adding and removing columns, changing column order and properties, filtering the view, and so on.

In this chapter, you'll learn how to create custom views in Outlook to present the information you want in a format that suits your needs. And because generating a printout of your data is often a by-product of creating a view, this chapter also focuses on how to create custom print styles in Outlook.

For more information on customizing existing views, see "Working with the Standard Outlook Views" page 59. You'll also find information about specific views in the chapters that cover them. For example, for more information on working with and customizing views in the Contacts folder, see "Viewing Contacts," page 404.

Creating and Using Custom Views

If the options for customizing existing Outlook views don't provide the information view you need, you can create your own views. You have two options for doing so: modifying an existing view or creating a new one from scratch.

Basing a New View on an Existing View

You can create a new, custom view from an existing view if the existing one offers most of the view elements you need. This is usually the easiest method because it requires the least amount of work.

Follow these steps to create a new, custom view from an existing view:

1 Open the folder whose view you want to modify, and then select the view to display it.

2 Choose View, Current View, Define Views to open the Define Views dialog box (see Figure 24-1).

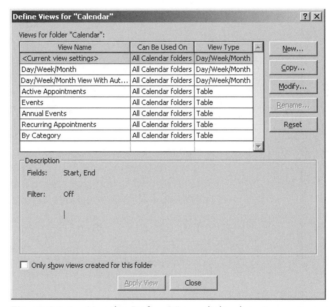

Figure 24-1. Use the Define Views dialog box to create a new view.

3 In the Views For Folder list, select the view you want to use as the basis for your new view, and then click Copy.

4 When Outlook prompts you to name the view, type a name.

5 Choose one of the following options:

- **This Folder, Visible To Everyone.** Makes the view available only in the folder from which it was created. Anyone with access to the specified folder can use the view.

Chapter 24: Creating Custom Views and Print Styles

■ **This Folder, Visible Only To Me.** Makes the view available only in the folder from which it was created. Only the person who created the view can use it.

■ **All** *type* **Folders.** Makes the view available in all folders that match the specified folder type. For example, when you create a custom view based on the Inbox, this option becomes All Mail And Post Folders, and Outlook makes the view available from the Inbox, Outbox, Drafts, Sent Items, and other message folders. If you base the new view on the Contacts folder, this option becomes All Contact Folders and makes the view available from all contacts folders.

6 Click OK to create the copy. The View Summary dialog box opens (see Figure 24-2).

Figure 24-2. The View Summary dialog box lets you access the functions you can use to define your custom view.

7 Use the options provided by the View Summary dialog box to customize the view.

> For details on all the options you can configure in the View Summary dialog box, see "Customizing a View's Settings," page 636.

8 After you've modified the settings as needed, click OK to close the View Summary dialog box and apply the view changes.

Creating a New View from Scratch

You can create an Outlook view from scratch if the view you want doesn't have much in common with any of the existing views. For example, perhaps you want to create an Inbox view that displays your messages as icons rather than headers (see Figure 24-3 on the next page). You can't modify a standard message view to display messages as icons, so you need to create the view from scratch.

Chapter 24

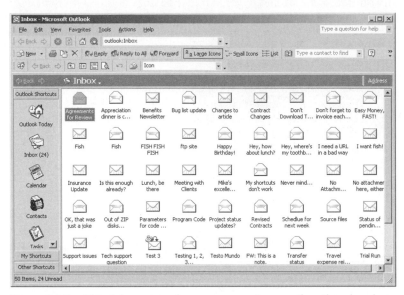

Figure 24-3. This Inbox view shows message icons rather than headers.

The process for creating a view from scratch is much like the process of modifying an existing view. When you create a new view, however, you have additional options for specifying the view.

Follow these steps to create a view from scratch:

1 In Outlook, open the folder or folder type for which you want to create a custom view.

2 Choose View, Current View, Define Views to open the Define Views dialog box.

3 Click New to open the Create A New View dialog box (see Figure 24-4).

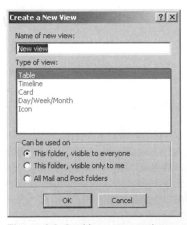

Figure 24-4. You can create several types of new views.

Chapter 24: Creating Custom Views and Print Styles

4 In the Name Of New View box, type a name for your new view.

5 In the Type Of View list, select the type of view you want to create, as follows:

- **Table.** Presents information in tabular form with one item per row and columns according to your selections. The default Inbox view is an example of a table view.

- **Timeline.** Displays items on a timeline based on the item's creation date (such as the received date for a message or the event date for a meeting). You might find this view type most useful for the Calendar folder.

- **Card.** Displays information using cards, as in Address Cards view (the default view in the Contacts folder).

- **Day/Week/Month.** Displays days in the left half of the window and monthly calendars in the right half. The actual view depends on the type of folder for which you create the view. Figure 24-5 shows a Day/Week/Month view created for the Inbox folder.

- **Icon.** Displays the items as icons, much as a file system folder does.

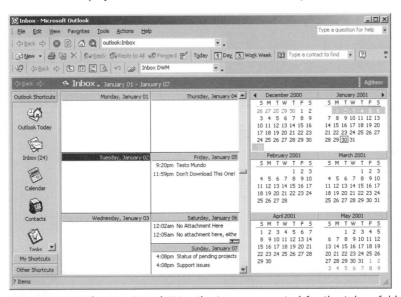

Figure 24-5. This Day/Week/Month view was created for the Inbox folder.

6 From the Can Be Used On group, select an option as described in the preceding section, and then click OK. The View Summary dialog box opens.

7 Customize the view as needed and then click OK.

8 Click Apply View to apply the view, or click Close to close the dialog box without applying the view.

Chapter 24

> For details on all the options you can configure in the View Summary dialog box, see "Customizing a View's Settings" below.

Modifying, Renaming, or Deleting a View

You can easily modify, rename, and delete custom views. For example, perhaps you want to apply a filter to a view in the Contacts folder to show only those contacts who work for a particular company. Maybe you want to have Outlook apply a certain label to appointments that have specified text in the subject.

To modify, rename, or delete a view, follow these steps:

1 Choose View, Current View, Define Views to open the Define Views dialog box.

2 In the Views For Folder list, select the view you want to change and do one of the following:

- To modify the view, click Modify. Use the options in the View Summary dialog box to apply changes to the view (as explained in the following section).

- To rename the view, click Rename and type the new name.

- To delete the view, click Delete. The Reset button changes to Delete if you select a custom view.

3 Click Close.

Customizing a View's Settings

Outlook gives you considerable control over the appearance and contents of a view. When you define a new view or modify an existing view, you end up in the View Summary dialog box, shown earlier in Figure 24-2. You can reach this dialog box in the following ways:

- Choose View, Current View, Customize Current View.

- Choose View, Current View, Define Views and then select a view and click Modify.

The options available in the View Summary dialog box change according to the folder selected. For example, the options for a contacts folder differ in some respects from the options for the Inbox. The same general concepts hold true for each type of folder, however. The following sections explain the various ways you can use these dialog box options to customize a view.

Configuring Fields

Clicking Fields in the View Summary dialog box in most cases opens the Show Fields dialog box (see Figure 24-6), which allows you to select the fields that you want to include in the view. (Exceptions to this behavior are discussed later.) For example, you might use the Show Fields dialog box to add the Cc or Sensitivity fields to the view.

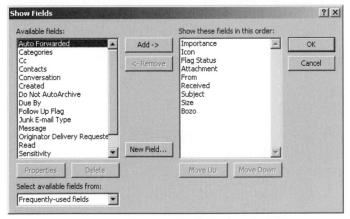

Figure 24-6. Use the Show Fields dialog box to add or remove fields in the view.

Adding fields in the Show Fields dialog box is easy. The available fields (those not already in the view) appear in the list on the left, and the fields already displayed appear in the list on the right. Select a field in the Available Fields list and click Add to add it to the view. To remove a field from the view, select the field in the Show These Fields In This Order list and click Remove. Use the Move Up and Move Down buttons to rearrange the order in which the fields are displayed in the view.

Troubleshooting

You need to restore a view to its original settings.

You've customized a view, and now you've decided that you need the old view back again. For the future, remember that you can copy an existing view. Rather than modifying an existing view, you can copy a view and then modify the copy. This way you'll still have the original view if you need it.

It's easy to restore a view to its previous settings, however. Choose View, Current View, Define Views. Select the view you want to restore and click Reset. Click OK when prompted to confirm the action.

tip　You can rearrange the order in which fields are displayed in a table view by dragging the column header for a field to a new location on the column header bar.

> You can click New Field in the Show Fields dialog box to create a custom field. For additional information on creating and using custom fields, see Chapter 40, "Designing and Using Forms," and Chapter 41, "Programming Forms with VBScript."

In some cases, clicking Fields in the View Summary dialog box opens a Date/Time Fields dialog box similar to the one shown in Figure 24-7. This occurs when you're working with a view that shows time duration, such as Day/Week/Month view in the Calendar folder, By Type view in the Journal folder, or Task Timeline view in the Tasks folder—in effect, nontable views that show time duration graphically.

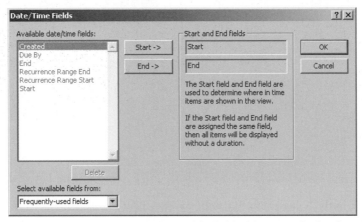

Figure 24-7. In the Date/Time Fields dialog box, specify the date fields used to show duration.

You use the Date/Time Fields dialog box to specify the fields Outlook will use to show item duration in the view. The default settings vary but are typically either Start and End or Start Date and Due Date. As an example, you might use the Date/Time Fields dialog box to change Task Timeline view in the Tasks folder to show the Date Completed field for the task's end rather than the Due Date field.

Grouping Data

Sometimes it's helpful to be able to group items in an Outlook folder based on specific data fields. For example, you might want to group tasks by owner so that you can see at a glance the tasks assigned to specific people. Or perhaps you want to organize contacts by country or region. In these and similar cases, you can modify an existing view or create a new one to organize the view based on the most pertinent data. To group data in a view, click Group By in the View Summary dialog box to open the Group By dialog box, shown in Figure 24-8.

Follow these steps to group data in a view:

1 In the Group By dialog box, select a field type in the Select Available Fields From drop-down list at the bottom of the dialog box. This selection controls the fields that appear in the Group Items By drop-down list.

Chapter 24: Creating Custom Views and Print Styles

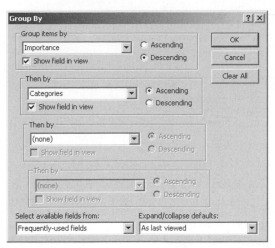

Figure 24-8. Use the Group By dialog box to specify criteria for grouping items in a view.

2 Select a field in the Group Items By drop-down list, and then select either Ascending or Descending depending on the sort order you want to use.

3 If you want to create subgroups under the main group, select a field in the Then By drop-down list. (The dialog box contains three such lists, providing three additional grouping levels.) For example, you might group tasks by Owner and then by Due Date.

4 After you've specified all the grouping levels you need, use the Expand/Collapse Defaults drop-down list to select how you want Outlook to treat the groups. Use the following list as a guide:

■ **As Last Viewed.** Collapses or expands the group according to its state in the previous session.

■ **All Expanded.** Expands all items in all groups.

■ **All Collapsed.** Collapses all items in all groups.

5 When you're satisfied with the group settings, click OK to close the Group By dialog box. Then click OK to close the View Summary dialog box.

Sorting Data

Sorting data in a view is different from grouping data. For example, you might group the Tasks folder by owner. Each group in the view then shows the tasks assigned to a particular person. You can then sort the data within the group as needed. For example, you might sort the tasks based first on due date and then on subject. Figure 24-9 on the next page shows the Tasks folder grouped by owner and sorted by subject.

Part 5: Customizing Outlook

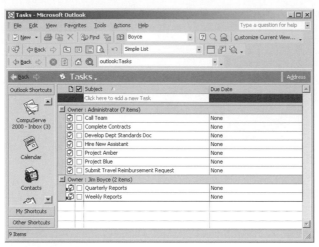

Figure 24-9. In this view, tasks are grouped by owner and sorted by subject, placing the tasks in alphabetical order by subject.

Sorting doesn't rely on grouping—you can sort a view whether it is grouped or not. For example, you might sort the Inbox based on the Received field to show messages in the order you received them.

---

tip   **Sort table views quickly**

You can quickly sort a table view by clicking the column header for the field by which you want to sort the view. Click the header again to change between ascending and descending sort order.

To create a sort order when you customize or define a view, click Sort in the View Summary dialog box to open the Sort dialog box (see Figure 24-10).

To configure sorting in the Sort dialog box, follow these steps:

1 In the Select Available Fields From drop-down list, select the type of field the sort should be based on.

2 In the Sort Items By drop-down list, select the specific field by which you want to sort the view.

3 Select Ascending or Descending, depending on the type of sort you need.

4 Use the Then By lists to specify additional sort levels, if necessary.

5 Click OK to close the Sort dialog box, and then click OK to close the View Summary dialog box.

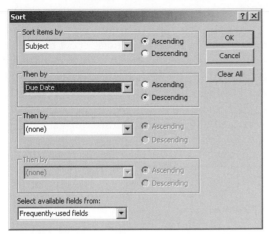

Figure 24-10. Configure sort order for the view in the Sort dialog box.

Applying Filters to the View

Outlook's ability to filter a view is an extremely powerful feature that gives you considerable control over the data displayed in a given view. For example, you might have hundreds of messages in your Inbox and need to filter the view to show only those messages from a particular sender. You could simply sort the Inbox by the From field and scan the list of messages, but you might want to refine the search a little, perhaps viewing only messages from a specific sender that have an attachment and were sent within the previous week. Filters allow you to do just that.

To configure a filter, click Filter in the View Summary dialog box to open the Filter dialog box, shown in Figure 24-11. This multi-tabbed dialog box lets you specify multiple conditions to define which items will appear in the view.

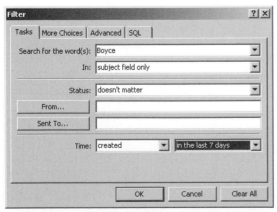

Figure 24-11. Use the Filter dialog box to specify multiple conditions that determine what data appears in the view.

The various tabs in the Filter dialog box include a broad range of options that let you specify multiple conditions for the filter. You can use conditions from more than one tab. For example, you might enter words to search for and a sender on the Messages tab, select categories on the More Choices tab, and specify a particular field and value on the Advanced tab. Note that the first tab of the dialog box varies according to the current folder type. For a contacts folder, for example, the first tab is labeled Contacts and offers options for creating filter conditions that apply to contacts. For a message folder, the first tab is labeled Messages and provides options for creating filter conditions specific to messages.

---

tip   **Use powerful filters**

The Advanced tab of the Filter dialog box gives you access to all available fields and several conditions (Contains, Doesn't Contain, and Is Empty, for example), making it the place to go to configure conditions not available on the other tabs. Use the SQL tab to perform Structured Query Language queries to retrieve data from the folder to show in the custom view.

Configuring Fonts and Other General Settings

When you click Other Settings in the View Summary dialog box, Outlook opens a dialog box that lets you configure some general settings for the custom view. These options vary from one folder type to another—the Contacts folder, the Inbox, and the Calendar folder, for example, all use different options. You can change such properties as the font used for column headers and row text, the grid style and shading for table views, and a handful of other general options.

Creating Rules for Automatic Formatting of Text

Click Automatic Formatting in the View Summary dialog box to display the Automatic Formatting dialog box, similar to the one shown in Figure 24-12. This dialog box lets you create rules that cause Outlook to automatically format data in the view based on the criteria you specify. For example, you might create an automatic formatting rule that has Outlook display in blue all tasks that you own and display all other tasks in black. Or perhaps you could create a rule to display in green all contacts from a specific company.

Figure 24-12. Use the Automatic Formatting dialog box to create rules that automatically format text in views based on the conditions you specify.

As you're working in the Automatic Formatting dialog box, keep in mind that you can't create task-oriented rules, as you can with the Rules Wizard. For example, you can't create a rule in this dialog box that moves messages from one folder to another. The rules you create in the Automatic Formatting dialog box control only the appearance (color, font, and font styles) of data in the view.

For information about the Rules Wizard, see "Processing Messages Automatically," page 231.

You can't modify the conditions for predefined rules, but you can specify the font characteristics to use for the rule. You can also create your own rules and change the order in which rules are applied to achieve the results you need.

To set up an automatic formatting rule for text, follow these steps:

1 Click Add in the Automatic Formatting dialog box to add a new rule named Untitled.

2 Click Font to open a standard Font dialog box in which you specify the font, font style, and color that will apply to text that meets the rule's condition.

3 Close the Font dialog box, and click Condition to open the Filter dialog box, shown in Figure 24-13 on the next page. This dialog box offers three tabs you can use to specify the condition for the rule. You can specify multiple conditions from multiple tabs, if needed.

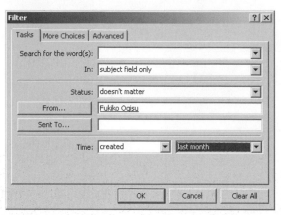

Figure 24-13. Specify conditions for the rule in the Filter dialog box.

4 Click OK when you're satisfied with the filter condition.

5 Click OK to close the Automatic Formatting dialog box, and then click OK to close the View Summary dialog box.

Troubleshooting

You need to restrict the available views.

In some situations, you might want to restrict the available views to only the custom views you've created, hiding the standard views that Outlook provides. For example, perhaps you created a custom calendar view that you want all employees to use rather than the standard calendar views because your custom view includes additional information the standard views don't contain. When you restrict Outlook's views to only custom views, the standard views no longer appear on the View menu.

You must configure each folder separately. For example, you might restrict the Calendar folder views without restricting the Inbox folder views. This would give users the ability to choose one of the standard Outlook views in the Inbox folder but would limit their choices to only custom views in the Calendar folder.

Follow these steps to restrict the views Outlook provides on the View menu:

1 In Outlook, select the folder whose views you want to restrict.

2 Choose View, Current View, Define Views to open the Define Views dialog box.

3 Select the Only Show Views Created For This Folder check box and click Close.

4 Repeat steps 2 and 3 to restrict other folders as necessary.

Printing in Outlook

Many users work in Outlook and never print any of the items they store in the program. For other users, however, the ability to print from Outlook is important. For example, if you use a hardcopy day planner rather than a notebook computer or a personal digital assistant to keep track of your daily schedule, you might prepare the schedule in Outlook and then print it for insertion in the day planner.

This section examines the options and methods for printing your Outlook data. It also explains how to customize the print styles provided by Outlook to create custom styles that better suit your preferences or needs.

Overview of Print Styles

Outlook offers several predefined print styles you can use to print information from various Outlook folders. The most common print styles are Table and Memo, as indicated in Table 24-1, which lists the standard print styles in Outlook.

Table 24-1. Outlook print styles by folder type

Folder Type	View	Print Styles
Calendar	Day/Week/Month Day/Week/Month with AutoPreview	Daily, Weekly, Monthly, Tri-Fold, Calendar Details, Memo
	Active Appointments Events Annual Events Recurring Appointments By Category	Table, Memo
Contacts	Address Cards Detailed Address Cards	Card, Small Booklet, Medium Booklet, Memo, Phone Directory
	Phone List By Category By Company By Location By Follow Up Flag	Table, Memo
Inbox	All except Message Timeline	Table, Memo
	Message Timeline	Print individual items only

(continued)

Table 24-1. *(continued)*

Folder Type	View	Print Styles
Journal	By Type By Contact By Category	Print individual items only
	Entry List Last Seven Days Phone Calls	Table, Memo
Tasks	All except Task Timeline	Table, Memo
	Task Timeline	Print individual items only

As Table 24-1 indicates, you can print only individual items when you're working with a timeline view. However, if you're scheduling a major project, a printout of a timeline view would be useful. If you need that capability, consider using Microsoft Project instead of Outlook. For details about how you can use Outlook to enhance your work in Project, see Chapter 21, "Integrating Microsoft Outlook and Microsoft Project."

Printing from Outlook

Printing from Outlook is just as easy as printing from any other application. Simply select the view or item you want to print and choose File, Print to print the document or File, Print Preview to preview it.

If you choose File, Print, Outlook displays a Print dialog box similar to the one shown in Figure 24-14. The contents of the dialog box vary according to the type of view from which you're printing.

In the Print Style list, select a print style. For example, select the Phone Directory style for the Contacts folder to print a phone list or select one of the two booklet styles if you want to print contact entries for a day planner. If you need to fine-tune the print settings, click Page Setup. Outlook displays a Page Setup dialog box similar to the one shown in Figure 24-15.

For additional details on printing contacts and using different print styles with the Contact folder, see "Printing Contacts," page 409.

Chapter 24: Creating Custom Views and Print Styles

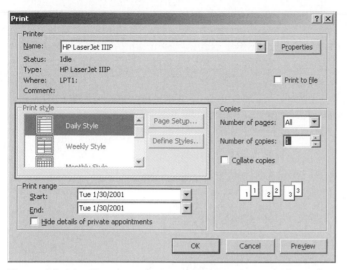

Figure 24-14. You can select an existing print style from the Print dialog box.

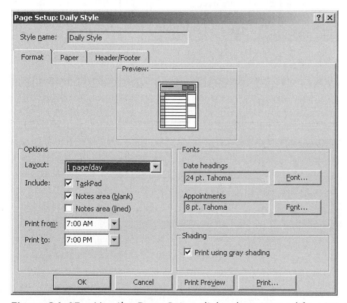

Figure 24-15. Use the Page Setup dialog box to modify print options for the selected style.

Use the Format tab of the Page Setup dialog box (see Figure 24-15) to specify the layout, fonts, and other general properties for the job. The options on the Format tab vary from one folder type to another. For example, you can use the Format tab to set the following options, some of which are specific to particular folder types:

- Whether Outlook keeps sections together or starts a new page for each section.

- The number of columns per page.

- The number of blank forms to print at the end of the job (such as blank contact forms).

- Whether Outlook prints a contact index on the page edge.

- Whether letter headings for each alphabetic section of a contact list are included.

- The font used for headings and for body text.

- Whether Outlook adds gray shading to headings.

- Whether the TaskPad and notes areas are displayed with a calendar.

- Whether weekends are printed in a calendar view.

- Whether Outlook prints one month of a calendar per page.

Use the Paper tab (see Figure 24-16) to select the page type, size, source, and other properties. For example, in the Type list on the Paper tab, you can select the type of day planner you use so that Outlook prints using that style.

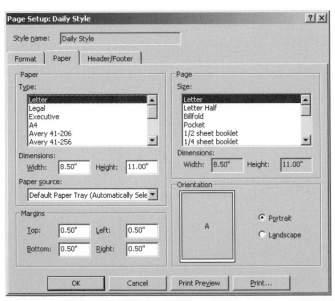

Figure 24-16. Use the Paper tab to select the paper source, size, type, and other paper settings.

Use the Header/Footer tab (see Figure 24-17) to specify the items you want printed in the header and the footer. This tab provides three boxes for the header and three for the footer. The left box specifies items that print on the left side of the page, the middle box specifies items that print on the middle of the page, and the right box specifies items that print on the right side of the page. You can enter text manually or use the buttons near the bottom to insert specific data such as page numbers, the user, the time, and other dynamic data.

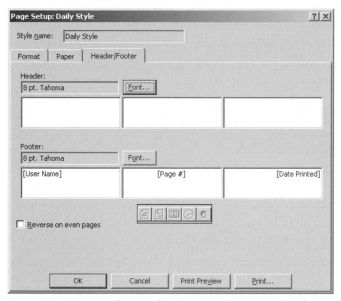

Figure 24-17. Use the Header/Footer tab to enter header and footer data.

After you select the page setup options, you can return to the Print dialog box or preview the document. The Print dialog box offers a handful of options that can help you further refine the printed data. For example, use the Start and End lists to specify a range of data to print. Select the Hide Details Of Private Appointments check box if you don't want the details of your private appointments printed. Set printer properties, the number of copies to print, and other general print settings. Then click OK to print or click Preview to preview the document.

Creating Custom Print Styles

Outlook provides a broad range of print styles, so it's likely that they will fit most of your needs. When these print styles don't quite offer what you need, however, you can create a custom print style.

> **tip** If you find yourself using an existing print style but frequently making the same option changes before printing, modify the existing print style to create a custom print style.

You can either modify an existing print style or copy a style and then modify it to incorporate the changes you need. If you always use the same modifications on a particular print style, you might prefer to simply modify that existing style rather than creating a new one. If you use the default style occasionally but modify its properties for most other print jobs, consider creating a custom print style based on the existing one so that both are available.

Follow these steps to modify or create a new print style:

1 Open Outlook, and then open the view whose print style you want to modify or on which you want to base your custom print style.

2 Choose File, Page Setup, Define Print Styles to open the Define Print Styles dialog box (see Figure 24-18).

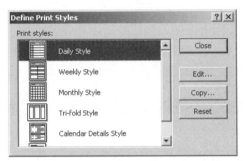

Figure 24-18. Use the Define Print Styles dialog box to modify and copy print styles.

3 If you want to create a new style, select an existing style and click Copy. Otherwise, select an existing style and click Edit. In either case, Outlook displays a Page Setup dialog box similar to the one shown in Figure 24-19.

4 Specify options as needed in the dialog box and then click OK to apply the changes.

5 Back in the Define Print Styles dialog box, click Close.

When you want to print with a particular style, open the view from which you want to print and choose File, Print. In the Print dialog box, select the style in the Print Style list, set other properties as necessary, and click OK to print.

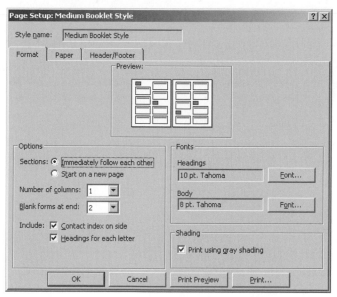

Figure 24-19. Specify properties for the print style.

Deleting Print Styles

If you've created some custom print styles but no longer use them, or if you've been experimenting with print styles and have a few samples you want to delete, removing them is a simple matter.

Follow these steps to remove a print style:

1 Choose File, Page Setup, Define Print Styles to open the Define Print Styles dialog box.

2 Select the style you want to remove and then click Delete.

3 When you have finished deleting print styles, click Close.

Resetting Print Styles

You can't delete the standard print styles provided by Outlook, but you can restore them to their default state. For example, suppose that you made several changes to the default Small Booklet style for the Contacts folder. Now you want to restore the print style to its default settings, but you don't remember what they are. Fortunately, Outlook remembers them for you.

To reset a print style, follow these steps:

1 Choose File, Page Setup, Define Print Styles to open the Define Print Styles dialog box.

2 Select the style you want to reset and click Reset. Outlook prompts you to verify the action.

3 Click OK to reset the style or Cancel to cancel the operation.

4 Click Close.

Automating Common Tasks

Microsoft Outlook is a feature-rich product and, as such, has an option, a wizard, or a graphical tool for accomplishing nearly anything you require from a personal information manager. If something does come up that the folks at Microsoft haven't planned for, though, you also have the option of customizing Outlook by using its built-in support for Microsoft Visual Basic code additions. Through the use of flexible Visual Basic for Applications (VBA) scripting options and built-in security controls, you can easily simplify and automate common tasks.

In this chapter, you'll learn how to create and use a macro. This includes creating the macro, stepping through a macro to test it, and deleting macros you no longer need. In addition, you'll find out about implementing security options for macros.

Understanding Automation Options

Outlook has a number of built-in automation options that allow the application to perform certain tasks for you. For example, the Rules Wizard automatically moves, copies, and forwards e-mail messages; and the organizer pane automatically color-codes e-mail messages and deals with junk and adult e-mail messages. The Out Of Office Assistant acts as an answering service when you're away.

For information about these examples of built-in automation options, see "Processing Messages Automatically," page 231; "Managing Junk and Adult Content Mail," page 248; and "Using the Out Of Office Assistant," page 254.

If a built-in option can accomplish the automated task you require, it should be your first choice. By using a built-in option instead of a custom one, you minimize problems that can occur if you need to reinstall Outlook or use Outlook on multiple machines. Using standardized options also guards against compatibility problems with upgrades to Outlook.

If none of the automation options does the trick, however, you can accomplish just about any customization by using Visual Basic for Applications. This chapter focuses on the use of VBA procedures known as macros to automate common tasks.

> For detailed information about using VBA with Outlook, see Chapter 42, "Using VBA in Outlook," and Chapter 43, "Integrating Outlook and Other Applications with VBA."

Understanding Macros

So just what is a macro? In general terms, a *macro* is a number of commands grouped together to execute a particular task. Macros are like small programs that operate within other programs. Macros have been around for a long time, and all Microsoft Office products support them at some level. In Outlook 2002, macros are implemented as Visual Basic for Applications procedures that are not linked to a particular form and are available from anywhere in Outlook. In Outlook, you manage macros by using the Tools menu, which contains a Macro submenu.

Using Macros

Macros are most useful for tasks that must be performed repeatedly without change. Even so, because a macro contains Visual Basic code, it can be flexible and can respond to variables or user input. With the power of scripting, a macro can accomplish a task in the most efficient way in response to specific conditions.

> **caution** Macros can be extremely powerful. This power can be a great asset for you, but it can also mean that any problems can become serious ones. Like many other things, macros can be dangerous when used improperly. Inexperienced programmers should take great care when writing and using macros in Outlook.

Following are the three basic programming elements you can work with in an Outlook macro:

- **Object.** An object is a particular part of a program, such as a button, a menu item, or a text field. Objects make up any element of Outlook that you can see or work with. An object has properties, and how you set these properties determines how the object functions. Visual Basic and VBA are object-oriented programming languages.

- **Property.** Any part of an object—its color, its width, and its value—is part of the set of attributes that make up its properties.

- **Method.** A method is a task that an object carries out. Methods can be modified based on user input or the value of certain properties.

In general, a VBA macro either determines or modifies the value of an object's property or calls a method. Macros, then, are nothing more than simple programs that use VBA to access or modify Outlook information.

---

note With the Macro Recorder in Microsoft Excel and Microsoft Word, you can simply record your mouse movements and keystrokes, and the computer plays them back when you execute the macro. Outlook 2002 doesn't include a macro recorder or any other graphical device for the nonprogrammatic creation of macros. As such, users familiar with programming basics and Visual Basic for Applications will have a head start in learning to create Outlook macros.

Creating a Macro from Scratch

The process for creating an Outlook macro is simple. The process for creating a *useful* macro, on the other hand, is more complex. Because of that, the discussion of advanced VBA is left for later chapters. In this chapter, I'll fall back on the most basic of functions, the Hello World dialog box macro. This macro creates a function that displays a message box containing the text *Hello World*. Clicking the OK button (the only button) closes the message box and ends the macro.

To create this macro, follow these steps:

1 Choose Tools, Macro, Macros to open the Macros dialog box.

2 In the Macro Name box, type a descriptive name for your new macro (no spaces are allowed). In Figure 25-1 on the next page, the macro is titled HelloWorldMsgBox.

3 Click Create. The Microsoft Visual Basic Editor starts, which allows you to add functionality to your macro. For those who are not programmers, creating VBA code might seem daunting, but simple tasks are actually quite easy.

4 Type the following (see Figure 25-2 on the next page):

```
MsgBox ("Hello World")
```

5 To test the code, choose Run, Run Sub/UserForm or click the Play button on the toolbar.

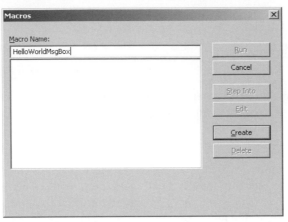

Figure 25-1. Enter the name for a new macro in the Macro Name box.

Play button

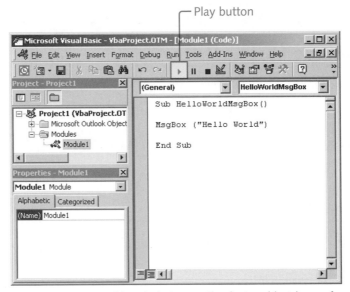

Figure 25-2. You add code between the first and last lines of a macro.

6 When you're prompted for which macro you want to run, select your macro and click Run. The message box shown in Figure 25-3 appears.

Figure 25-3. This is what you see when you run the macro.

7 Add an extra comma to the code, and test the macro. The Visual Basic Editor checks your VBA syntax and, because the extra comma causes a syntax problem with the code, an error message appears, as shown in Figure 25-4. Delete the extra comma to return the macro to a working state.

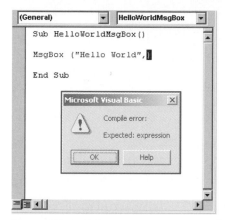

Figure 25-4. This error message is displayed because the Visual Basic Editor encountered incorrect syntax.

8 Verify that the macro runs properly (repeat step 5), and then choose File, Save. The default file name is VbaProject.OTM, but you can rename the file.

9 Close the Visual Basic Editor.

Running a Macro

After you save a macro, it is available for use. Choose Tools, Macro, Macros and select the HelloWorldMsgBox macro. When you click Run, the window appears as it did when you tested the macro in the Visual Basic Editor. Calling a macro this way is inconvenient, however. If you'll be using the macro often, you might want to add it as an item on your toolbar for easier access.

To add the macro to a toolbar, follow these steps:

1 Choose View, Toolbars, Customize to open the Customize dialog box.

2 Click the Commands tab.

3 In the Categories list, select Macros. The Hello World macro appears on the right (see Figure 25-5 on the next page).

4 Drag the Hello World macro to a location on the toolbar. Outlook adds a button to the toolbar, and clicking it runs the macro immediately.

Chapter 25

Figure 25-5. Locate the macro and add it to the toolbar.

Editing a Macro

After you create a macro, you can edit it by returning to the Macros dialog box:

1 In the Macros dialog box, select the HelloWorldMsgBox macro and then click the Edit button. The Visual Basic Editor starts and displays the selected macro.

2 Modify the macro so that it matches the following:

```
Sub HelloWorldMsgBox()
MsgBox ("Click OK to create a new message")
Set newMsg = Application.CreateItem(0)
    newMsg.Subject = "Sample Message from a Macro"
    newMsg.Body = "You can even add text automatically."
    newMsg.Display
End Sub
```

3 Verify that the changed macro works properly by clicking the Run Macro button on the Visual Basic Editor toolbar. Instead of your just seeing a simple message box as before, the macro should now present you with a new e-mail message window. The message should have information automatically filled in in the subject and body fields, as in Figure 25-6.

4 Save the changes and close the Visual Basic Editor.

5 When you return to the Macros dialog box, select the modified macro and click Run. You should see the same e-mail message that you saw in step 3.

> **tip** When you edit a macro, you'll eventually want to save it and test the changes. To ensure that you can return to the original macro in case of trouble, first export the project so that you can retrieve it later. For information about exporting, see "Sharing Macros with Others," page 660.

Chapter 25: Automating Common Tasks

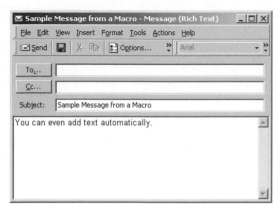

Figure 25-6. This is the new message created by running the macro.

Stepping Through a Macro

When you're creating a macro, it's often helpful to step through the code, which allows you to watch each line as it is being processed and see problems as they occur. To do this, open the sample macro for editing (as described in the preceding section), and then press the F8 key. The first line of the macro is highlighted, and its code is processed. To process the next line, press F8 again.

Step through the rest of the macro using the F8 key. Notice that clicking OK merely closes the message box rather than creating the e-mail message. This is because later steps are not followed automatically. The new e-mail message is created only after you press F8 through all the lines of the subprocedure.

note You can step through a macro only when it is being edited. When macros are executed from within Outlook, they automatically move through all procedures.

Troubleshooting

Your macro doesn't run properly.

If you are having problems getting a macro to run properly, you can try several different approaches to determine the source of the problem. The most common problem is incorrect syntax in your code. Finding errors in code can be a vexing job, but using the step-through process generally helps to find the line that is causing you problems.

If your syntax is correct, the problem might have to do with the way you're running the macro. Among the problems you should check are the security settings on the macro and the security settings on the computer. Also, if the macro has been deleted, but a toolbar button still remains, you might be trying to run a macro that no longer exists.

Deleting a Macro

Sometimes a macro outlives its usefulness. To delete a macro you no longer need, choose Tools, Macro, Macros. In the Macros dialog box, select the macro you want to remove and click Delete. When you're prompted to verify that you want to permanently delete the macro, click Yes to remove the macro from the list, making its code unavailable to Outlook.

> **note** If you have created a toolbar button for a macro that you subsequently delete, you must locate the button and remove it in a separate operation.

Sharing Macros with Others

If you're creating macros for use by a group of people, or even an entire organization, the macros must be installed separately for each user. Unfortunately, although the Macros dialog box has options for creating and deleting macros, it has no option for adding macros from other places. You can't share macros the same way you share files. Instead, sharing macros with other users is generally a two-step process: the user who creates the macro must export the macro code, and the other user must import the code.

To share a macro, follow these steps:

1 Choose Tools, Macro, Visual Basic Editor.

2 In the Visual Basic Editor, choose File, Export File to open the Export File dialog box (see Figure 25-7).

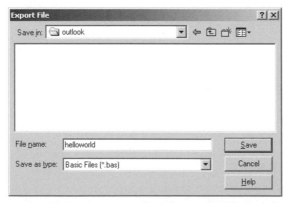

Figure 25-7. The macro file is being exported so that it can be shared.

3 In the Save As Type box, save the project as a BAS file. (By doing so, you can then e-mail the file to another user or make it available on the network.)

Once another user has access to the BAS file, the user can install the macro by following these steps:

1 Choose Tools, Macro, Visual Basic Editor.

2 In the Visual Basic Editor, choose File, Import File.

3 Browse to the file, open it, and save it to his or her machine.

4 The user can now access the macro through the Macros dialog box, as you do.

Setting Macro Security

Macros have several advantages, including their power, their flexibility, and their ability to run automatically, even without your knowledge. These advantages have a dark side, though, and poorly written or malicious macros can do significant damage to an Outlook message store. Because of the potential danger that macros pose, the Outlook Tools menu offers three security levels for Outlook macros:

- **High.** Your system can run only macros that are digitally signed. This means that some macros—even benign and potentially useful ones—are not available.

- **Medium.** You will be prompted as to whether you want to run untrusted macros.

- **Low.** Macros run automatically, regardless of their signature. This is the most dangerous setting.

For information about digital signatures, see "Protecting Messages with Digital Signatures," page 332.

Using Security Levels

To view or change the security level, choose Tools, Macro, Security and click the Security Level tab (see Figure 25-8 on the next page). The default setting is Medium, which is probably the best choice for most users.

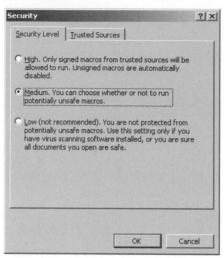

Figure 25-8. You can set the security level for macros on this tab.

InsideOut

When you create your own macros, they are not controlled by the security settings. User-created macros do not need to be signed and will run regardless of the security setting you have selected. This is nice for purposes of design and editing, but it assumes that you realize exactly what a macro will do. Moreover, it means that when you want to test macro security settings, you must run Outlook under a different user account.

Specifying Trusted Sources

To reduce the number of times you're prompted about whether to run a macro (if you've set a Medium security level) or to be able to run macros at all (if you've set a High security level), you can specify a trusted source.

When a digitally signed macro runs, Outlook displays the certificate attached to the macro. Besides choosing whether or not to run the macro, you're also given the choice of adding the certificate holder (the organization or individual who created the macro) to your list of trusted sources. Once the holder of the certificate is trusted, any macros signed with that certificate run without prompting at a Medium security setting and are among the macros that run at a High security setting.

To view the list of trusted certificates or to remove a trusted source, choose Tools, Macro, Security. Click the Trusted Sources tab to view the sources. To remove a trusted source, select one of the sources and then click Remove.

Part 6

Managing Outlook

Chapter 26

Integrating Outlook with Other Office Applications

Microsoft Outlook works well as a stand-alone application, but its real strength is realized when you integrate it with other Microsoft Office applications. Most of us spend our day working in one or two main programs, such as a word processor or a database program, so most of our information is saved in files designed for those programs. For instance, you probably save letters and other correspondence in Microsoft Word files, save contact information in Outlook, and save inventory, invoices, and other data in Microsoft Access or Microsoft Excel. With Office, you can integrate all this, which lets you choose the best tool for creating your information and the best tool for sharing or producing your data.

Some of the ways you can integrate Outlook with other Office applications include the following:

- Using Outlook contacts for a Word mail merge
- Exporting Outlook contacts to Word, Excel, or Access
- Importing contacts from Word, Excel, or Access into Outlook
- Using Outlook notes in other Office applications

In this chapter, you'll learn about using Outlook and other Office applications to share information between applications. Rather than employing standard copy-and-paste or cut-and-paste techniques, you'll find out about ways to reuse your information in Outlook or another file format without retyping or re-creating the data.

Using Contacts for a Mail Merge in Word

The Outlook Contacts folder allows you to create contact entries to store information about a person, a group, or an organization. You can then use that contact data to create e-mail messages, set up meetings or appointments, or complete other tasks associated with a contact. Your contacts list can also be used as the data source to provide names, addresses, phone numbers, and other pertinent data to your mail merge documents.

You perform a *mail merge* in Word when you want to create multiple documents that are all based on the same letter or document but that each have different names, addresses, or other specific information (referred to as *merge data*). For instance, you might perform a mail merge operation when you want to do a mass mailing to your customers about a new product launch.

You begin by creating and saving a standard letter. Next you place field codes where you want the recipient's address, the salutation, and other merge data to appear. *Field codes* are placeholders in documents where data will change. For instance, the name of the recipient should be a field code since it will change for each letter you send out.

You next create or assign a database to populate the field codes (that is, to insert the merge data). Word uses the database and contact information to create separate letters. You can then save these files or print each letter for your mass mailing.

> **tip** Before starting to set up a mail merge using your Outlook contact data, review your contact entries to make sure that the data is complete and current and that you don't have duplicate entries.

To perform a mail merge using Word 2002, follow these steps:

1 Start Word.

2 Choose Tools, Letters And Mailing, Mail Merge Wizard (see Figure 26-1).

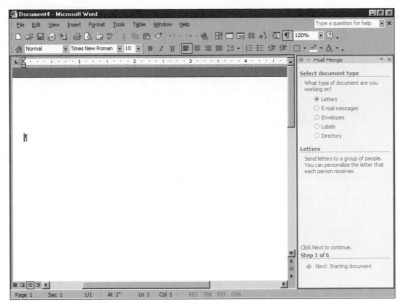

Figure 26-1. Start a mail merge by opening Word's Mail Merge Wizard, which appears in the task pane on the right.

3 In the task pane, click the type of document to create, such as Letters, and then click Next: Starting Document at the bottom of the pane.

4 Select the document to use—for example, the current document. Click Next: Select Recipients.

5 Click the Select From Outlook Contacts option.

6 Click the Choose Contacts Folder option to open the Select Contact List Folder dialog box (see Figure 26-2).

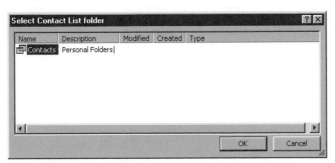

Figure 26-2. Select your Contacts folder here.

7 Select the folder that contains your contacts list and click OK to open the Mail Merge Recipients dialog box (see Figure 26-3).

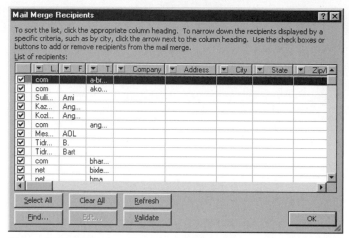

Figure 26-3. Select contacts to include in the mail merge from this dialog box.

8 Select the contacts you want to use to populate the mail merge document. You can use the following methods:

- Click Select All to select all contacts (the default).

- Click to clear the check boxes next to the names of those you do not want to include in the mail merge.

- Click Clear All and then select individual contacts.

tip If you want to create a mailing list that is a subset of your Contacts folder, you can filter the contacts list and then use the filtered list to perform a mail merge from Outlook.

9 Click OK.

10 Click Next: Write Your Letter.

11 Click Address Block to open the Insert Address Block dialog box (see Figure 26-4).

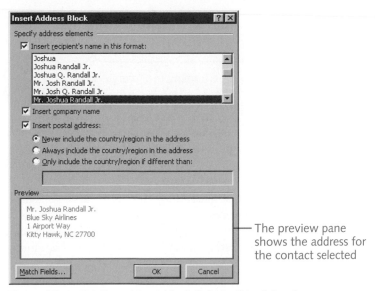

The preview pane shows the address for the contact selected

Figure 26-4. Set the address block field in this dialog box.

12 Using the options in this dialog box, specify the address fields and format you want to include in your letter. Click OK and then start writing your letter.

13 Click Next: Preview Your Letters to see how the Outlook contact data looks in your letter. Figure 26-5 shows an example.

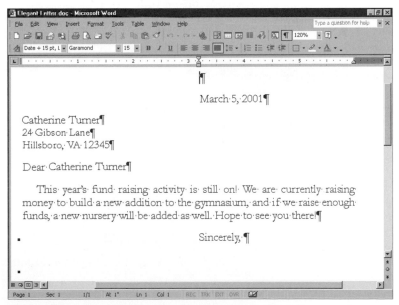

Figure 26-5. The address and salutation data in this letter came from an Outlook Contacts folder.

14 In the task pane, click Next: Complete The Merge to finish.

15 Finish editing your letter or print it.

> **note** For detailed information about performing mail merges in Word, as well as using other Word features, see *Microsoft Word Version 2002 Inside Out,* by Mary Millhollon and Katherine Murray (Microsoft Press, 2001).

Exporting Contacts to Access

Another way to use Outlook contact information is to export this data to Access. This is handy if you want to use contact data in database tables or reports. You could spend your time opening individual contact entries in Outlook, copying information from the contact form, and then pasting the information into Access where you want it. But Outlook makes the process much simpler. All you have to do is use the Import And Export Wizard and select Microsoft Access as the file to export to.

Here's how to export contact information to Access:

1 In Outlook, choose File, Import And Export to open the Import And Export Wizard.

2 Select Export To A File and then click Next.

3 On the wizard page shown in Figure 26-6, select Microsoft Access and then click Next.

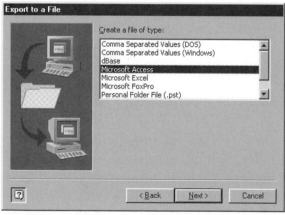

Figure 26-6. The Import And Export Wizard allows you to export to an Access file.

4 Select the folder from which to export data. In this case, select the Contacts folder (see Figure 26-7) or another folder that includes Outlook contact information. Click Next.

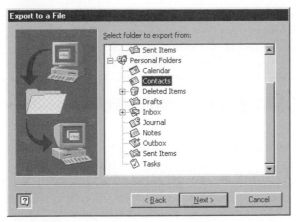

Figure 26-7. Select the folder from which you want to export.

5 Specify the folder and type a name for the export file. You can click the Browse button to navigate to a folder and then click OK to select that folder. When you do this, the file is given an MDB extension to denote an Access database file. Click Next.

6 Click Map Custom Fields. In this dialog box, you can add or remove field items, modifying the way the Outlook contacts list is saved in the new exported file (see Figure 26-8). Click OK when you finish.

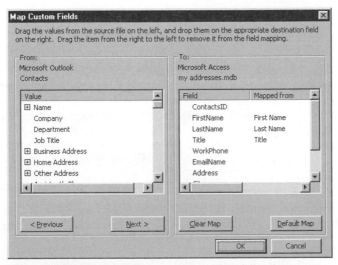

Figure 26-8. Modify field mappings in this dialog box.

671

7 Click Finish. Outlook exports the data from the Contacts folder and saves it in the specified file. You can now switch to Access and open the exported data as a table in that application.

> **note** For detailed information on working with Access, see *Microsoft Access Version 2002 Inside Out*, by Helen Feddema (Microsoft Press, 2001).

Importing Contacts from Access

Suppose you've collected and stored contacts in an Access database but now want to use them in Outlook. You can simply import the data to Outlook using the Import And Export Wizard. During the import process, Outlook can check to see whether duplicate entries are being added to your contacts list and can then create, ignore, or replace them.

Troubleshooting

After replacing a duplicate entry in Outlook, you find you've lost data.

Before you choose to allow Outlook to replace duplicate entries, you should make sure that the items really are duplicates. Entries might erroneously appear to be duplicates if, for example, you have two contacts whose names are the same. For that reason, you might want to allow Outlook to create duplicate entries and then, after the import process is finished, go into the Outlook Contacts folder and manually remove any true duplicates.

Before you begin, make sure that the database you want to import is closed in Access. If it's not, you'll receive an error message when Outlook tries to find the data source.

Then follow these steps to import the data:

1 Switch to Outlook and choose File, Import And Export to open the Import And Export Wizard.

2 Select Import From Another File Or Program and then click Next.

3 Select Microsoft Access and click Next.

4 In the File To Import box (see Figure 26-9), specify the Access file (MDB) that you want to import.

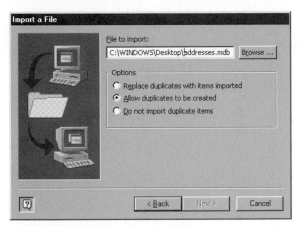

Figure 26-9. Specify the Access file to import and how Outlook should handle duplicates during the import process.

5 Specify how you want Outlook to handle duplicates, and then click Next.

6 Select the folder in which you want the imported data to be placed, such as the Contacts folder, and then click Next.

7 Click Map Custom Fields. In this dialog box, you can add or remove field items, modifying the way the Outlook contacts list is saved in the new imported file. Click OK when you finish.

8 Click Finish to start the import process.

---

tip **Avoid losing data during an import**

The import process can take several minutes or more if the database is a fairly large one. If the database is large, you should plan to import data during a break in your regular business. This can help to ensure that you don't run the risk of losing data if another running application or a process such as a mail merge operation interferes with the import and causes your system to crash.

Exporting Contacts to Excel

You might also find it useful to export Outlook contact information to Excel worksheets. In Excel, you can include the data in a spreadsheet of names and addresses for a contact management sheet, sort contact data in various ways, or perform other spreadsheet tasks with the data. Again, you simply use the Import And Export Wizard to create this Excel file.

Here's how to export contact information to Excel:

1 In Outlook, choose File, Import And Export to open the Import And Export Wizard.

2 Select Export To A File and then click Next.

3 Select Microsoft Excel and then click Next.

4 Select the folder from which to export data. In this case, select the Contacts folder or another folder that includes Outlook contact information. Click Next.

5 Specify the folder and type a name for the export file. You can click the Browse button to navigate to a folder and then click OK to select that folder. When you do this, the file is given an XLS file extension to denote an Excel worksheet file. Click Next.

6 Click Map Custom Fields. In this dialog box, you can add or remove field items, modifying the way the Outlook contacts list is saved in the new exported file. Click OK when you finish.

7 Click Finish. Outlook exports the data from the Contacts folder and saves it in the specified file.

---

tip Another reason to export contact information is that you might need to share this data with others who do not use Outlook but do use Excel. Simply export the data to an Excel worksheet, open the worksheet, and modify or edit any column information. Then save the file and send it to the other users.

---

note For detailed information on working with Excel, see *Microsoft Excel Version 2002 Inside Out*, by Mark Dodge and Craig Stinson (Microsoft Press, 2001).

Importing Contacts from Excel

You import contact information from an Excel worksheet the same way you import from an Access database. Suppose your coworker wants to send you contact information but is not running Outlook. Ask the coworker to save the data in an Excel worksheet and send that file to you. You can then use the Import And Export Wizard to import the new contact information into Outlook.

Before you begin the process, make sure that the worksheet you want to import is closed in Excel. If it's not, you'll receive an error message when Outlook tries to find the data source.

Then follow these steps to import the data:

1 Switch to Outlook and choose File, Import And Export to open the Import And Export Wizard.

2 Select Import From Another File Or Program and then click Next.

3 Select Microsoft Excel and then click Next.

4 In the File To Import box (see Figure 26-10), specify the Excel file (XLS) that you want to import.

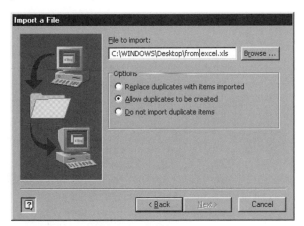

Figure 26-10. Select the Excel file to import and the options for handling duplicates during the import process.

5 Specify how you want Outlook to handle duplicates and then click Next.

6 Select the folder in which you want the imported data to be placed, such as the Contacts folder, and then click Next.

7 Click Map Custom Fields. In this dialog box, you can add or remove field items, modifying the way the Outlook contacts list is saved in the new imported file. Click OK when you finish.

8 Click Finish to start the import process.

You might want to review your contacts to ensure that the data was imported the way you need it. If it wasn't, modify it as necessary in Outlook.

Exporting Tasks to Office Applications

You can use the Import And Export Wizard to export other Outlook items. For example, you might want to export tasks to a Word or Excel file to view past or future assignments in a table format that can be easily edited or in a spreadsheet. You can then use this data in business correspondence, historical documents (such as a travel itinerary), event planning, work assignments, or presentations.

Follow these steps to export tasks to an Excel file:

1 In Outlook, choose File, Import And Export to open the Import And Export Wizard.

2 Select Export To A File and then click Next.

3 Select Microsoft Excel and then click Next.

4 Select the folder from which to export data. In this case, choose the Tasks folder or another folder that includes Outlook tasks. Click Next.

5 Specify the folder and type a name for the export file. You can click Browse to navigate to a folder and then click OK to select that folder. When you do this, the file is given an XLS file extension to denote an Excel worksheet file. Click Next.

6 Click Map Custom Fields. In this dialog box, you can add or remove field items, modifying the way Outlook task items are saved in the new imported file. Click OK when you finish.

7 Click Finish to start the import process and open the Set Date Range dialog box (see Figure 26-11).

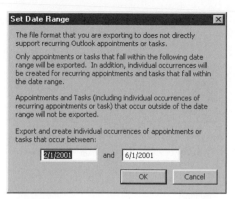

Figure 26-11. You might need to change the date range to include all the tasks you want to export.

8 Specify the date range for exported tasks. Also, some types of tasks are not directly exported or included, such as recurring tasks whose recurrences fall outside the date range you set. Modify the date range as necessary to include the tasks you want exported.

9 Click OK to start the export process. When it's finished, you can open the worksheet to review your tasks in Excel.

Using Notes in Other Applications

Outlook notes are great when you need to create electronic "sticky" notes as a reminder of things to do in a document or project or of messages to send out. But you are limited in how you can store information in notes and how you can use that information in other documents.

One way to reuse the information you've placed in notes is to export the Notes folder and use that file in another application. Suppose you have several notes that you want to archive and then remove from the Notes folder. Simply export the Notes folder to a tab-separated file and open the file in Word, creating a document that contains the information.

Here's how to export the file:

1 In Outlook, choose File, Import And Export to open the Import And Export Wizard.

2 Select Export To A File and then click Next.

3 Select Tab-Separated Value (Windows) and then click Next.

4 Select the folder from which to export data. In this case, select the Notes folder or another folder that includes Outlook notes. Click Next.

5 Specify the folder and type a name for the export file. You can click Browse to navigate to a folder and then click OK to select that folder. When you do this, the file is given a TXT extension to denote a text file (which you can open in Word). Click Next.

6 Click Map Custom Fields. In this dialog box, you can add or remove field items, modifying the way Outlook note items are saved in the new imported file. For example, you might want to remove the Note Color field because this field exports as a value. Click OK when you finish.

7 Click Finish to begin the export process.

Open the file in Word to see how the Notes file is displayed. In the example shown in Figure 26-12, the tab-separated items are converted from text to a table using the Word table feature.

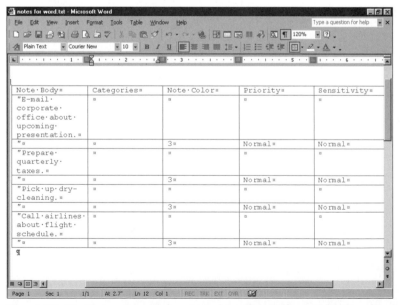

Figure 26-12. Your notes can be viewed in other Office applications, such as Word.

Delegating Responsibilities to an Assistant

Microsoft Outlook, when used with Microsoft Exchange Server, provides a handful of features that allow you to delegate certain responsibilities to an assistant. For example, you might want your assistant to manage your schedule, setting up appointments, meetings, and other events for you. Or perhaps you want your assistant to send e-mail messages on your behalf.

This chapter explains how to delegate access to your schedule, e-mail messages, and other Outlook data, granting an assistant the ability to perform tasks in Outlook on your behalf. This chapter also explains how to access folders for which you've been granted delegate access.

> For detailed information on other ways to share information through Outlook and public folders, see Chapter 34, "Sharing Information with Others."

Delegation Overview

Why delegate? You could simply give assistants your logon credentials and allow them to access your Exchange Server mailbox through a separate profile on their systems. The disadvantage to that approach is that your assistants then have access to all your Outlook data. By using Outlook's delegation features, however, you can selectively restrict an assistant's access to your data.

You have two ways of delegating access in Outlook. First, you can specify individuals as delegates for your account, which gives them send-on-behalf-of privileges. This means the delegated individuals can perform such tasks as sending e-mail messages and meeting requests for you. When an assistant sends a meeting request on your behalf, the request appears to the recipients to have come from you. You can also specify that delegates should receive copies of meeting-related messages that are sent to you, such as meeting invitations. This is a necessity if you want an assistant to be able to handle your calendar.

> **note** When a message is sent on your behalf, the recipient sees these words in the From box:
>
> <delegate> *on behalf of* <owner>
>
> where *<delegate>* and *<owner>* are replaced by the appropriate names. This designation appears in the header of the message form when the recipient opens the message but doesn't appear in the header in the Inbox. The Inbox shows the message as coming from the owner, not the delegate.

The second way you can delegate access is to configure permissions for individual folders, granting various levels of access within the folders as needed. This does not give other users send-on-behalf-of privileges but does give them access to the folder and its contents. The tasks they can perform in the folder are subject to the permission levels you grant them.

Assigning Delegates and Working as an Assistant

You can assign multiple delegates so that more than one individual can access your data with send-on-behalf-of privileges. You might have an assistant who manages your schedule and therefore has delegate access to your calendar and another delegate—your supervisor—who manages other aspects of your work day and therefore has access to your Tasks folder. In most cases, however, you'll probably want to assign only one delegate.

Adding and Removing Delegates

You can add, remove, and configure delegates for all your Outlook folders through the same interface.

Follow these steps to delegate access to one or more of your Outlook folders:

1 Choose Tools, Options to open the Options dialog box.

2 Click the Delegates tab (see Figure 27-1).

Figure 27-1. The Delegates tab shows the current delegates and lets you add, remove, and configure delegates.

3 Click Add to open the Add Users dialog box.

4 Select one or more users and click Add.

5 Click OK. Outlook displays the Delegate Permissions dialog box (see Figure 27-2).

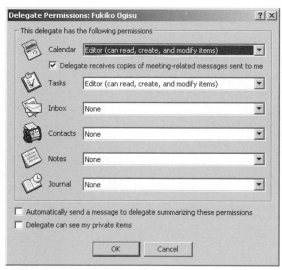

Figure 27-2. Configure delegate permissions in this dialog box.

Chapter 27

6 For each folder, select the level of access you want to give the delegate based on the following list:

- ▓ **None.** The delegate has no access to the selected folder.

- ▓ **Reviewer.** The delegate can read existing items in the folder but can't add, delete, or modify items. Essentially, this level gives the delegate read-only permission for the folder.

- ▓ **Author.** The delegate can read existing items and create new ones but can't modify or delete items.

- ▓ **Editor.** The delegate can read existing items, create new ones, and modify existing ones, including deleting them.

7 Set the other options in the dialog box using the following list as a guide:

- ▓ **Automatically Send A Message To Delegate Summarizing These Permissions.** Sends an e-mail message to the delegate informing him or her of the access permissions you've assigned in your Outlook folders (see Figure 27-3).

- ▓ **Delegate Can See My Private Items.** Allows the delegate to view items you've marked as private. Clear this option to hide your private items.

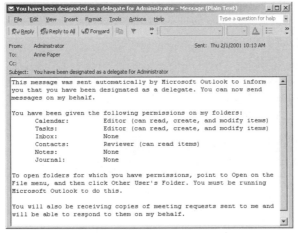

Figure 27-3. Outlook sends a message to delegates informing them of their access privileges.

8 Click OK to close the Delegate Permissions dialog box.

9 Add and configure other delegates as you want, and then click OK.

682

If you need to modify the permissions for a delegate, open the Delegates tab, select the delegate in the list, and click Permissions to open the Delegate Permissions dialog box. Then adjust the settings as needed, just as you do when you add a delegate. If you need to remove a delegate, select the delegate on the Delegates tab and click Remove.

> **tip** If the Permissions button appears dimmed or you are unable to assign delegate permissions for some other reason, the problem could be that you have designated a local PST as the default delivery location for your profile. Make sure you configure your profile to deliver mail to your Exchange Server mailbox instead.

Taking Yourself out of the Meeting Request Loop

If your assistant has full responsibility for managing your calendar, you might want all meeting request messages to go to the assistant rather than to you. That way, meeting request messages won't clog your Inbox.

Taking yourself out of the request loop is easy. Here's how:

1 With any folder open, choose Tools, Options.

2 Click the Delegates tab.

3 Select the option Send Meeting Requests And Responses Only To My Delegates, Not To Me.

4 Click OK.

> **note** This option appears dimmed if you haven't assigned a delegate.

Opening Folders Delegated to You

If you are acting as a delegate for another person, you can open the folders to which you've been given delegate access and use them as if they were your own folders, subject to the permissions applied by the owner. For example, suppose that you've been given delegate access to your manager's schedule. You can open his or her Calendar folder and create appointments, generate meeting requests, and perform the same tasks you can perform in your own Calendar folder. However, you might find a few restrictions. For example, you won't be able to view the contents of personal items unless your manager has configured permissions to give you that ability.

Follow these steps to open another person's folder:

1 Open Outlook with your own profile.

2 Choose File, Open, Other User's Folder to display the Open Other User's Folder dialog box (see Figure 27-4 on the next page).

683

Figure 27-4. Use the Open Other User's Folder dialog box to open another person's Outlook folder.

3 Type the person's name or click Name to browse the address list, and select a name.

4 In the Folder drop-down list, select the folder you want to open, and then click OK. Outlook generates an error message if you don't have the necessary permissions for the folder; otherwise, the folder opens in a new window.

Depending on the permissions set for the other person's folder, you might be able to open the folder but not see anything in it. If someone grants you Folder Visible permission, you can open the folder but not necessarily view its contents. For example, if you are granted Folder Visible permission for a Calendar folder, you can view the other person's calendar. If you are granted Folder Visible permission for the Inbox folder, you can open the folder, but you can't see any headers. Obviously, this latter scenario isn't useful. So you might need to fine-tune the permissions to get the effect you need.

tip When you click File, Open, the menu lists other users' folders that you've recently opened. You can select a folder from the list to open it.

When you've finished working with another person's folder, close it as you would any other window.

Scheduling on Behalf of Another Person

If you've been given delegate privileges for another person's calendar, you can schedule meetings and other appointments on behalf of that person.

To do so, follow these steps:

1 Open Outlook with your own profile.

2 Choose File, Open and open the other person's Calendar folder.

3 In the other person's Calendar folder, create the meeting request, appointment, or other item as you normally would for your own calendar.

As mentioned, the recipient of a meeting request sees the message as coming from the calendar's owner, not the delegate. When the recipient opens the message, however, the header indicates that the message was sent by the delegate on behalf of the owner. Responses to the meeting request come back to the delegate and a copy goes to the owner, unless the owner has removed himself or herself from the meeting request loop.

> For details about how to have meeting request messages go to the delegate rather than to the owner, see "Taking Yourself out of the Meeting Request Loop," page 683.

Sending E-Mail on Behalf of Another Person

If you've been given delegate permission for another person's Inbox, you can send messages on behalf of that person. For example, as someone's assistant, you might need to send notices, requests for comments, report reminders, or similar messages.

To send a message on behalf of another person, follow these steps:

1 Open Outlook with your own profile.

2 Start a new message. If the From box isn't displayed, choose View, From Field.

3 In the From box, type the name of the person on whose behalf you're sending the message.

4 Complete the message as you would any other, and then send it.

InsideOut

Microsoft recommends that you use Microsoft Word as your e-mail editor and even set it as the default editor. However, in this instance, Outlook actually works better as the editor. With Word as your editor, you can't display the From box directly. Instead, you must configure Outlook as your e-mail editor, display the From box, and then switch back to Word as your editor. The From box will then appear in Word.

Granting Send-on-Behalf-of Privileges to a Distribution List

In some situations, you might want to grant a distribution list send-on-behalf-of privileges. For example, you might want all members of the sales department to be able to broadcast messages to customers about promotions. Or perhaps a small team is working on a project and needs to funnel messages through a specific mailbox to communicate with others about the project. Granting delegate permission to the distribution group gives group members the ability to send messages on behalf of the specified mailbox. You could grant delegate permissions to individual users, but using the distribution list to assign permissions takes less time.

To allow a distribution list to send on behalf of a mailbox, you first need to set up the distribution group. Then you grant users delegate permissions for that group as needed.

Follow these steps:

1 In the Global Address List, create the distribution list.

For a discussion of setting up distribution lists in Outlook, see "Creating Distribution Lists," page 135.

2 Open Outlook, and log on to the mailbox for which you want to grant delegate access.

3 Choose Tools, Options.

4 Click the Delegates tab.

5 Click Add.

6 Select the distribution list and then click Add.

7 Click OK.

8 Configure delegate permissions for the Inbox to either Author or Editor. Fine-tune the permissions as necessary, and then click OK.

9 Click OK to close the Options dialog box.

Troubleshooting

You have problems granting delegate permissions for a distribution list.

If you're using Exchange Server 5.5 and try to delegate access for a mailbox to a distribution list, the members of that list might receive an error message stating that they don't have send-on-behalf-of permission for the mailbox. Microsoft offers a correction for this problem in the 5.5.2654.8 version of Store.exe. Obtain the fix from Microsoft's Web site at *http://www.microsoft.com/downloads/release.asp?ReleaseID=17142*.

Another problem you might run across is the inability to assign send-on-behalf-of privileges to a distribution group through the Exchange Server Administrator. This is because the distribution group doesn't appear in the address list when you attempt to select a delegate. This is by design. To assign the delegates, use Outlook instead as described at the beginning of this section.

Members of the distribution list can send messages on behalf of the mailbox just as they would when they have individual delegate access. Start a new message, specify the mailbox name in the From box, and send the message as you normally would. As long as you are a member of the distribution list, Exchange Server allows you to send the message.

Chapter 27

Granting Access to Folders

You can configure your folders to provide varying levels of access to other users according to the types of tasks those users need to perform within the folders. For example, you might grant access to your Contacts folder to allow others to see and use your contacts list.

Granting permissions for folders is different from granting delegate access. Users with delegate access to your folders can send messages on your behalf, as explained in earlier sections. Users with access permissions for your folders do not have that ability. Use access permissions for your folders when you want to grant others certain levels of access to your folders but not the ability to send messages on your behalf.

Configuring Access Permissions

Several levels of permissions control what a user can and cannot do in your folders. The permissions include the following:

- **Create Items.** Users can post items to the folder.

- **Read Items.** Users can read items in the folder.

- **Create Subfolders.** Users can create additional folders inside the folder.

- **Folder Owner.** The owner has all permissions for the folder.

- **Folder Contact.** The folder contact receives automated messages from the folder such as replication conflict messages, requests from users for additional permissions, and other changes to the folder status.

- **Folder Visible.** Users can see the folder.

- **Edit Items.** Users can edit all items or only those items they own.

- **Delete Items.** Users can delete all items or only those items they own.

Outlook groups these permissions into several predefined levels as follows:

- **Owner.** The owner has all permissions and can edit and delete all items, including those he or she doesn't own.

- **Publishing Editor.** The Publishing Editor has all permissions and can edit and delete all items but does not own the folder.

- **Editor.** Users are granted all permissions except the ability to create subfolders or act as the folder's owner. Editors can edit and delete all items.

- **Publishing Author.** Users are granted all permissions except the ability to edit or delete items belonging to others and the ability to act as the folder's owner.

687

- **Author.** This level is the same as Publishing Author except Authors can't create subfolders.

- **Nonediting Author.** Users can create and read items and delete items they own, but they can't delete others' items or create subfolders.

- **Reviewer.** Users can view items but can't modify or delete items or create subfolders.

- **Contributor.** Users can create items but not view or modify existing ones.

- **None.** The folder is visible but users can't read, create, or modify any items in the folder.

Follow these steps to grant permissions for a specific folder:

1 Open Outlook, right-click the folder whose permissions you want to set, and then choose Properties. (You can right-click the folder on the Outlook Bar or in the folders list.)

2 Click the Permissions tab (see Figure 27-5).

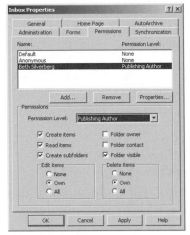

Figure 27-5. Use the Permissions tab to configure access permissions for the folder.

3 Click Default, and then set the permissions you want users to have if they are not explicitly assigned permissions (if their names don't appear in the Name list.)

4 Click Add to add a user with explicit permissions. Select the name from the Add Users list, click Add, and then click OK.

5 In the Name list, select the user you just added and set permissions as you want.

6 Click OK to close the folder's dialog box.

As you can see in Figure 27-5, you can remove users to remove their explicit permissions. Just select the user and click Remove.

To view (but not modify) a user's address book properties, select the user and click Properties (see Figure 27-6). If you want, you can add the user to your Personal Address Book.

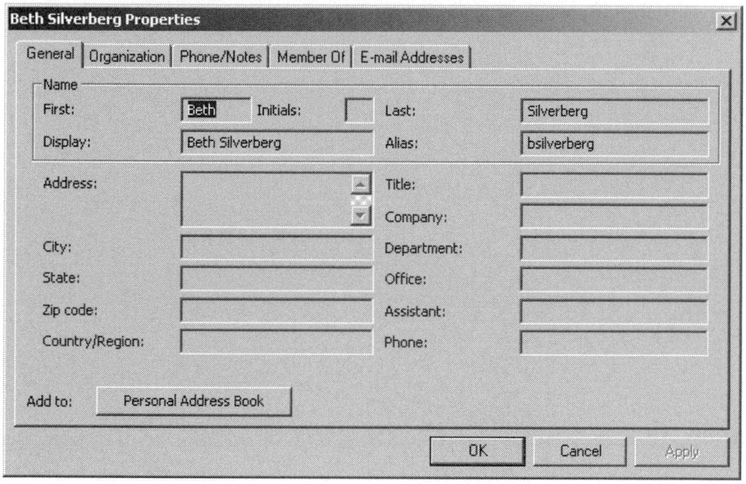

Figure 27-6. You can view a user's address book properties.

Accessing Other Users' Folders

After you've been granted the necessary permissions for another user's folder, you can open the folder and perform actions according to your permissions. For example, if you have only read permission, you can read items but not add new ones. If you've been granted create permission, you can create items.

To open another user's folder, choose File, Open, Other User's Folder. Specify the user's name and the folder you want to open, and then click OK.

For more information on opening and using another person's folder, see "Opening Folders Delegated to You," page 683.

Managing Folders, Data, and Archiving

Like any system, Microsoft Outlook can become overloaded with messages, contact information, appointments, and other data. If you can't manage all this data, you'll be lost each time you try to find a particular item. Outlook helps you manage information by providing folders for storing your data. You also can create your own folders, move data between folders, and set folder properties.

This chapter focuses on managing your Outlook folders and their contents. You'll learn how to create new folders to store e-mail messages, contact information, and other files. You'll also learn how to set up Outlook folders to use Web views so that you can display Web pages inside folders. In addition, you'll find out what it takes to archive your data, both manually when you want to archive data on the spot and automatically using AutoArchive.

Understanding Outlook Folders

Outlook folders are similar to folders you use in Windows Explorer or My Computer. You use Outlook folders to store items you work with, such as e-mail messages and attachments, contact entries, journal entries, tasks, appointments, and notes. Outlook includes default folders for each type of item—for example, the Calendar, Contacts, Journal, Inbox, and Tasks folders. Along with these item-type folders are other default folders, such as Deleted Items, Drafts, and Outbox.

These folders are all part of your personal folders, so they are private. If you are running Outlook with Microsoft Exchange Server, others on your network to whom you've assigned rights can view and manage items stored in these folders if you make the folders public. In addition, your Exchange Server administrator can set up public folders that appear in your folder list but are stored on the Exchange Server. You and others who have rights to these public folders will see a Public Folders icon in your folder list. If you have the correct rights, you can create and delete these public folders, store and manage items in them, and see content added to them by other users.

Working with the Folder List

If you move between folders frequently, you might want to navigate by using a combination of the Outlook Bar and the folder list. The Outlook Bar gives you quick access to the Outlook folders and the file system folders that the majority of people use most often. You, however, might use different Outlook and file system folders. For example, suppose that you have an Exchange Server account but also use a set of personal folders to store personal messages and contacts or other data. Because Outlook doesn't automatically add shortcuts on the Outlook Bar for your other folders, the best way to access these folders is usually through the folder list (see Figure 28-1).

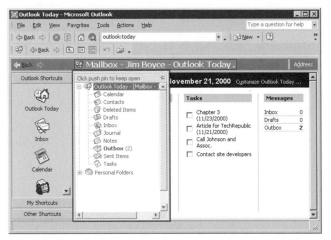

Figure 28-1. Use the folder list to move between folders not listed on the Outlook Bar or to see which folders are included in a given store.

You can display the folder list in several ways:

- Choose View, Folder List.
- Click the Folder List button on the Advanced toolbar.
- Click the folder name on the current folder's banner (at the top of the view).

After you select a folder from the list, the list is hidden again by default. (In other words, the folder list isn't "sticky. ") If you prefer to keep the folder list open because you want to move between several folders, click the push pin icon at the upper right corner of the folder list. The push pin changes to an X, and the folder list remains open even when you select a folder. Click the X to close the folder list.

> **tip** You can right-click a folder to display its shortcut menu, which gives you access to specific actions you can perform on the folder. Many of these actions, such as opening and deleting folders, are explained in the following sections.

Using and Managing Folders

When you perform an action in Outlook, you do so inside a folder. Outlook provides a handful of actions you can perform with folders to change their behavior, location, appearance, and so on, as described in the following sections.

Using a Folder

When you're ready to work with information in Outlook, you first go to the folder where that information is stored. For example, to read a new e-mail message downloaded to your Inbox folder, you must open the Inbox folder and then select the message to read. To open a folder, click its shortcut on the Outlook Bar or click the folder name in the folder list.

When you open the folder, its contents are displayed in the main Outlook window. To see the contents of a particular folder item, you must open it, using one of these methods:

- Double-click the item in the main Outlook window.
- Right-click the item and choose Open.
- Click the item and press Enter.

Depending on the type of folder you open, a preview pane might be available. The preview pane displays the contents of the currently selected item without requiring you to open a separate window for the folder item. The preview pane is handy because it provides a quick view and can help keep your desktop tidier. To display the preview pane, choose View, Preview Pane or click the Preview Pane button on the Advanced toolbar.

By default, the preview pane occupies half of the main Outlook window, as shown in Figure 28-2 on the next page. You can resize this pane by dragging the edge. To see an item in the preview pane, simply select the item in the folder.

Chapter 28

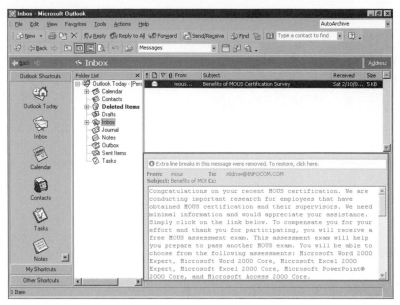

Figure 28-2. You can view the contents of a folder item in the preview pane.

For more information about working with the preview pane, see "Using the Preview Pane," page 86.

note A disadvantage of using the preview pane is that only one item can be open in the pane at any given time. If you want to open additional items, you must double-click them to display them in separate windows.

Creating a Folder

As you know, Outlook provides a basic set of folders in which you can store certain types of data, such as the Contacts folder for storing contact information. As you use Outlook more, you'll want to add other folders to organize your data. For example, you might add other message folders to store particular kinds of messages.

Each Outlook folder you add has a specific *type* based on the type of data it stores. For example, an e-mail message folder differs from a contacts folder because the former stores messages and the latter stores contact entries. Similarly, the Calendar folder stores appointments and events, and the Notes folder stores sticky notes. When you add a folder, you specify the folder type. You also specify the name of the folder and its location.

Follow these steps to create a folder:

1 Take one of the following actions to display the Create New Folder dialog box, shown in Figure 28-3.

- Choose File, New, Folder.

- Choose File, Folder, New Folder.

- Right-click a folder in the folder list and choose New Folder.

- Press Ctrl+Shift+E.

- Click the arrow beside the New button on the Standard toolbar and choose Folder.

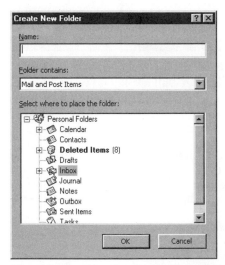

Figure 28-3. Use the Create New Folder dialog box to specify folder type, location, and other properties of the new folder.

2 In the Name box, type a name for the folder.

3 In the Folder Contains drop-down list, choose the type of item you want to store in this new folder.

4 In the Select Where To Place The Folder list, select the location for the new folder.

5 Click OK.

Adding a Folder Shortcut to the Outlook Bar

If you have a frequently used folder that isn't listed on the Outlook Bar, you can create a shortcut to the folder for the Outlook Bar, as explained here:

1 Open the folder list in Outlook.

2 On the Outlook Bar, click the Outlook Bar group to which you want to add the shortcut. For example, click My Shortcuts if you want to add a folder to the My Shortcuts group.

3 Right-click the folder and choose Add To Outlook Bar. Outlook adds a shortcut to the folder to the open Outlook Bar group.

When you want to remove a shortcut, right-click it, choose Remove From Outlook Bar, and then click Yes.

> **note** When you remove a folder shortcut from the Outlook Bar, you remove only the shortcut. You do not remove the folder from Outlook, nor do you delete the folder's contents. For information on deleting a folder and its contents, see "Deleting a Folder," page 699.

Another way to add a shortcut is to drag the folder from the folder list to the Outlook Bar. To move a shortcut on the Outlook Bar, simply drag it to its new location.

If you decide that a folder shortcut should be renamed, follow these steps:

1 Right-click the folder shortcut you want to rename.

2 Choose Rename Shortcut.

3 Type a new name and press Enter.

> **note** When you rename the folder shortcut, the folder name in the folder list does not change.

Renaming a Folder

Sometimes you need to change a folder's name, perhaps as a result of project modifications or a company name change. Unfortunately, you can't rename the default folders created by Outlook. You can, however, change the name of folders you create.

To rename a folder, begin with one of these actions:

- Open the folder list, right-click the folder, and choose Rename.
- Select the folder and then click the name to highlight it.
- Select the folder and choose File, Folder, Rename.

After taking one of these actions, simply type the new name and press Enter to have the change take effect.

Another way to change a folder's name is through its Properties dialog box (see Figure 28-4), which you can display by right-clicking the folder in the folder list and choosing Properties. On the General tab, type a new name in the top box. Click OK to save the name and to return to the folder list.

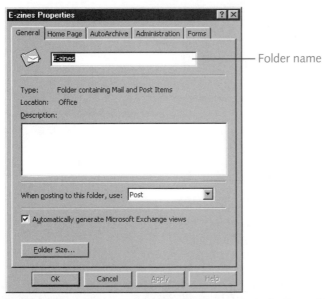

Figure 28-4. You can change a folder's name in its Properties dialog box.

InsideOut

When you change a folder's name, shortcuts to the folder on the Outlook Bar are not updated to reflect the change. You must rename any shortcuts separately (as described in the preceding section). In addition, if you right-click a shortcut on the Outlook Bar and choose Properties, you open the folder's properties, not the shortcut's properties. Thus, if you change the name in this Properties dialog box, it's the same as right-clicking the folder in the folder list and choosing Properties—that is, you change the folder's name, not the shortcut's name.

Copying and Moving a Folder

Occasionally, you might need to move or copy a folder from one location to another. For example, suppose that you've created some message folders in your Inbox to organize messages, but now you want to move those folders to a folder other than the Inbox. Or maybe you want to copy the Contacts folder from your Exchange Server mailbox to a set of personal folders.

Moving or copying folders is easy. Open the folder list, right-click the folder you want to move or copy, and choose either Move or Copy from the shortcut menu. Outlook displays a Move Folder dialog box (see Figure 28-5) or a Copy Folder dialog box. Select the folder in which you want to store the moved or copied folder and click OK, or choose New to create a new folder in which to store the moved or copied folder.

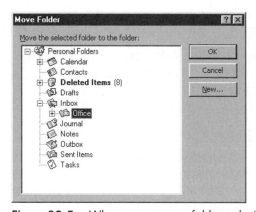

Figure 28-5. When you move a folder, select its new location in this dialog box.

Another way to move a folder is to drag it to a new location. You can copy a folder using a similar technique; just hold down the Ctrl key while dragging.

You can move one type of folder so that it becomes a subfolder of another type of folder. For example, suppose that you receive e-mail messages containing contact information. You can store these messages in a folder called, say, Contact Info. You then can store the Contact Info folder as a subfolder of Contacts. The type of data you can store in the subfolder is the type you originally established for that folder. (For example, when a message-type folder becomes a subfolder of a contacts-type folder, neither folder changes its type.)

If you want to move or copy a folder to the root of the folder store, move or copy the folder to the topmost folder in the list (such as Personal Folders). If you use the Edit, Cut or Edit, Copy commands to move or copy, select the topmost folder and choose Edit, Paste.

> **tip**   **Send a link to a public folder**
>
> When you're working with public folders, you might want to send another user a link to a folder rather than moving or copying the folder. To send the link, open the folder list, right-click the folder, and choose Send Link To This Folder. Outlook starts a new message containing a link to the folder. Address the message and send it as you would any other message.

Deleting a Folder

You can delete an Outlook folder the same way you delete a folder in Windows Explorer or My Computer. When you delete an Outlook folder, it's removed from the folder list and placed in the Deleted Items folder. This way, if you decide you want the folder back, you can retrieve it from the Deleted Items folder.

When you delete a folder, you delete the contents of the folder as well. The contents move with the folder to the Deleted Items folder and can be retrieved along with the folder later. You also can retrieve individual items from the Deleted Items folder, even if those items were deleted as part of a folder deletion. For example, if you delete a message folder named Project Alpha containing three messages, you can retrieve one, two, or all three messages individually without retrieving the Project Alpha folder.

To retrieve a folder from the Deleted Items folder, click Deleted Items and select the folder to retrieve. Move that folder from the Deleted Items folder to its original location or to another location.

Although you can't delete any of the default folders (the ones Outlook provides), you can delete folders you've added.

To do so, follow these steps:

1 Make sure the folder doesn't contain any data you need to keep or any data that you have not archived or backed up.

2 Open the folder list, right-click the folder, and choose Delete.

3 Click Yes to confirm the deletion or No to cancel.

> **tip** **Automatically delete folders of a specific date**
>
> Outlook can automatically remove items in a folder that match a specified date. If Outlook is configured to empty the Deleted Items folder on a certain date or whenever you quit the program, however, you might lose important items that you accidentally or prematurely sent to that folder. To see the deletion date of a folder, right-click the folder and choose Properties. On the AutoArchive tab, if the Archive This Folder Using These Settings option is selected, look to see whether the Permanently Delete Old Items option is also selected. If it is, the time in the Clean Out Old Items Older Than option specifies how much time you have to retrieve an item from that folder. Don't assume that the folder you deleted last year will still be around today.

Setting Folder Properties

Folders have several properties that control the way they appear and function, as well as others that control archiving, administration, and other activities. To view or set these properties, open the folder list, right-click the folder, and choose Properties to open a Properties dialog box for the folder. The following sections explain the options on each of the tabs in this dialog box.

Configuring General Folder Properties

You can use the General tab (see Figure 28-6) to locate information about a folder, name the folder, add a descriptive comment, and set other properties, as described in the following list:

Figure 28-6. Use the General tab of a folder's Properties dialog box to view information about the folder and set a few general properties.

- **Name.** In the top box, specify the name for the folder as you want it to appear in Outlook.

- **Type.** This property specifies the type of content the folder contains; it cannot be edited on this tab.

- **Location.** This property specifies the location in the folder hierarchy for the selected folder; it cannot be edited on this tab.

- **Description.** Use this box to type an optional description of the folder. The description appears only in the folder's Properties dialog box.

- **When Posting To This Folder, Use.** This drop-down list includes two selections. One is the default type of item you can store in the folder, such as Contact for a contacts folder. The other is Forms. If you select Forms in the list, Outlook opens the Choose Form dialog box (see Figure 28-7). Here you can select the form that the folder should use for new items added to the folder. For example, you might want to use the appointment form for a calendar folder.

- **Automatically Generate Microsoft Exchange Views.** Select this check box to have Outlook create views of public folders so that Microsoft Exchange users can view the folders.

- **Folder Size.** Click this button to view information about the amount of space a folder and its subfolders use.

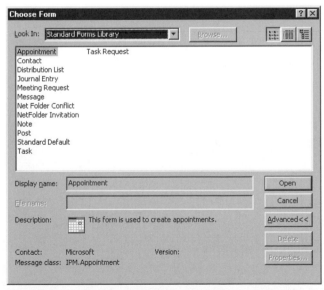

Figure 28-7. Specify the type of form to be used by the folder.

Configuring Properties for a Contacts Folder

When configuring properties for a contacts folder, you can set the following address book options on the Outlook Address Book tab:

- **Show This Folder As An E-Mail Address Book.** Select this option to have Outlook display contacts in a way that lets you select e-mail addresses from the Address Book dialog box.

- **Name Of The Address Book.** You can specify the address book name.

You can also specify options for the items linked to a contact in the Contacts folder by using the Activities tab of the folder's Properties dialog box (see Figure 28-8), as listed here:

- **Folder Groups.** You can select the group of folders that might contain activities related to contacts.

- **Copy, Modify, Reset, New buttons.** Click the appropriate button to add groups to or modify groups in the Folder Groups list.

- **Default Activities View.** You can select the default view that appears on the Activities tab of a contact form when you open a contact entry.

Figure 28-8. Use this tab to set the default view that appears on the Activities tab of a contact form in the folder.

Configuring AutoArchive Properties for a Folder

Outlook's AutoArchive feature automatically archives items after a specified period, which can help you avoid having folders cluttered with old messages, tasks, and so on. You configure archival properties on the AutoArchive tab of a folder's Properties dialog box. For details, see "Configuring the Automatic Archiving of Items," page 716.

Configuring Administration Properties for a Folder

Outlook provides options for setting administration properties for each folder. To change these properties for a public folder, you must have owner permissions for that folder. In addition, for all but the Initial View On Folder option, you must be running Outlook with Exchange Server. The following options are available on the Administration tab:

- **Initial View On Folder.** You can specify the view you see when you open a folder. Your choices are Normal, Group By Form, Group By Subject, Group By Conversation, and Unread By Conversation. The default view is Normal.

- **Drag/Drop Posting Is A.** This option lets you specify an item's format when you drag the item to a public folder.

- **Add Folder Address To.** You can choose to have Outlook add the folder address to your Personal Address Book. You can then send e-mail directly to the folder.

- **This Folder Available To.** You can specify the users who can access the folder. You can select all users who have access permissions, or you can limit access to the owner.

- **Folder Assistant.** While working online, you can modify processing rules for new items posted to the public folder.

- **Moderated Folder.** This option allows you to select moderators for this moderated folder.

- **Folder Path.** You can specify the location of the folder.

Configuring Form Properties for a Folder

Outlook items are based on forms, which standardize how information is distributed to other users and stored in Outlook. One example of a form is the contact form Outlook provides when you create a new contact entry.

> For more information on forms, see Chapter 3, "Working in and Configuring Outlook," and Chapter 40, "Designing and Using Forms."

On the Forms tab of the Properties dialog box, you can set or view the following form properties for a folder:

- **Forms Associated With This Folder.** This item shows a list of forms in the Folder Forms Library associated with the folder.

- **Manage.** You can specify a form that you want to move to the Folder Forms Library, thereby listing it in the Forms Associated With This Folder list. You also can click the Manage button to set up a new form in the Folder Forms Library.

Chapter 28

703

- **Descriptions.** Add a description of a form you select in the Forms Associated With This Folder list. You can change the description by clicking Manage, selecting Properties in the Forms Manager dialog box, and then changing the Comments box in the Form Properties dialog box. Click OK twice to save your changes.

- **Allow These Forms In This Folder.** You can specify the types of forms you allow in the folder. (The folder must be a public folder.) You can specify that only forms from this list be allowed in the folder; that only forms from this list as well as standard forms be allowed in the folder; or that any form be allowed in the folder. If you select the second option, forms such as messages, tasks, and even documents (for example, Microsoft Word files or Microsoft Excel worksheets) can be stored in the folder.

> **note** If you run Outlook with Exchange Server, your folders might have public folders set up by system administrators or others who have folder creation privileges. In that case, you can administer permissions properties for these folders using the Permissions tab. For information on folder permissions, see "Granting Access to Folders," page 687.

Using Web Views with Folders

The popularity of the Internet and its usefulness to businesses and individuals make it almost imperative that software include features for accessing the World Wide Web. Outlook offers such features, providing ways for users to access the Web without switching to a different program. This section describes how you can access the Web by specifying a Web page as a home page for a folder.

Why Use Web Views?

When you assign a Web page as a home page for a folder, you make it convenient and easy to access intranet or Internet resources. The primary reason to use a Web view in a folder is to access a Web site or intranet resource without leaving Outlook. As shown in Figure 28-9, you can open a folder that includes a Web page as a home page and then access another page from there. You no longer have to start a separate Web browser, such as Microsoft Internet Explorer, to open the Web page.

Figure 28-9. You can view a Web page without leaving Outlook.

Assigning a Web Page to a Folder

You can assign a Web page to any folder in your folder list.

To assign a Web page, follow these steps:

1 Right-click a folder and choose Properties.

2 Click the Home Page tab (see Figure 28-10 on the next page).

3 Set Web page view properties as necessary, using the following options:

- **Show Home Page By Default For This Folder.** Select this option if you want Outlook to display the Web page rather than the existing default folder view.

- **Address.** Specify the URL of a local or remote HTML page or another Internet resource, such as an FTP site.

- **Browse.** Click to browse for a URL.

- **Restore Defaults.** Click to restore the default settings (no Web page).

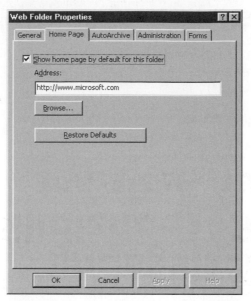

Figure 28-10. Specify a Web page view for a folder using this dialog box.

4 Type the URL (Internet or local address) for the Web page you want to display. You also can click Browse and select a Web page from the Find Web Files dialog box. Click OK after selecting a page to return to the Home Page tab.

5 Click OK.

> **note** Once you set a Web view for a folder, you cannot switch between the Web view and normal view (that is, a folder view without a Web page showing) unless you disable the Show Home Page By Default For This Folder option.

Removing a Web Page from a Folder

After a while, you might tire of using a Web view in a folder, or the Web page might become obsolete.

To remove a Web page from a folder, follow these steps:

1 Right-click the folder and choose Properties.

2 Click the Home Page tab.

3 Clear the Show Home Page By Default For This Folder check box.

4 Click OK.

Using a Folder's Web Page

Each time you open a folder with a Web page view, Outlook displays the specified Web page according to the Home Page options you selected. If the Web page includes hyperlinks, you can click them to navigate to other pages or sites. In addition, you can type a different URL in the Address box in Outlook and press Enter to display a new Web page inside the Outlook folder.

Using Multiple Personal Folders

Items you create and receive in Outlook are stored in personal folder (PST) files. These files are stored by default in the following locations, which vary according to your operating system:

- **Microsoft Windows 9x.** The default location is \Windows\Local Settings\Application Data\Microsoft\Outlook. On systems running Windows 9x that are configured to maintain unique user profiles (useful where multiple users share a single Windows 9x computer), the user profiles are stored in the \Profiles folder. On these systems, Outlook places the storage files by default in \Profiles\<*user*>\Local Settings\Application Data\Microsoft\Outlook.

- **Microsoft Windows NT.** The default location for systems running Windows NT is \%systemroot%\Profiles\<*user*>\Local Settings\Application Data\Microsoft\Outlook, where %systemroot% by default is \Winnt.

- **Microsoft Windows 2000.** The default location is \Documents And Settings\<*user*>\Local Settings\Application Data\Microsoft\Outlook. On systems running Windows 2000 that were upgraded from Windows NT, the user profiles still reside in the \Winnt\Profiles folder. On these systems therefore, Outlook places the storage files by default in \%systemroot%\Profiles\ <*user*>\Local Settings\Application Data\Microsoft\Outlook. As with Windows NT, %systemroot% defaults to \Winnt.

If you don't use Outlook with Exchange Server, you use personal folders for storing your Outlook information and data. (With Exchange Server, your messages, calendar, and other items are stored centrally on the server.)

You can create multiple personal folders to help you organize your data. For example, you can store e-mail messages associated with a project or a client in one folder and store other messages and items in a more general folder. Another useful way to set up multiple personal folders files is to use one for archiving. This can help you back up your data more consistently, and Outlook can prompt you at different intervals to ensure that your archive is up to date. Outlook even includes the Archive.pst file in which you can archive items.

> **note** As Outlook copies items to the archive file, it removes them from their original location.

You can also use a personal folders file to share information with other users on your network. The users must have read/write permissions to open the file.

After you create a personal folders file, you can add it to the Outlook Shortcuts group on the Outlook Bar just as you add any other folders. You then can access the personal folders file simply by clicking it.

> For information about adding a folder shortcut, see "Adding a Folder Shortcut to the Outlook Bar," page 696.

Adding a Personal Folder

A personal folder can have any name you give it. By default, the names take the form Personal Folder(1).pst, Personal Folder(2).pst, and so on. At the top of the folder list, you can see the name of the active personal folder, which by default appears as Personal Folders.

To add a personal folder, follow these steps:

1 Choose File, New, Outlook Data File to open the New Outlook Data File dialog box, shown in Figure 28-11.

2 Select Personal Folders File (.pst).

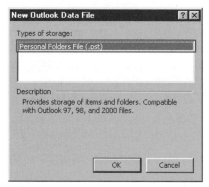

Figure 28-11. Click the Personal Folders File (.pst) option to create a personal folder.

3 Click OK. The Create Or Open Outlook Data File dialog box appears.

4 In the File Name box, type a name for the new personal folders file.

5 Click OK. The Create Microsoft Personal Folders dialog box appears.

6 In the Name box, type a name for the folder. This name appears in the folder list after you create the folder.

7 In the Encryption Settings area, select the type of encryption you want for this folder. When you encrypt your folder, you ensure that other programs can't read it. Select No Encryption if you don't want to encode your personal folder. Compressible Encryption, which is the default setting, encrypts the personal folder file so that the file can be compressed. Best Encryption sets up the personal folder so that it has the tightest encryption possible.

8 If you want to protect your personal folders file further, type a password in the Password box and retype it in the Verify Password box. Each time Outlook starts, you'll be prompted to enter this password to access your personal folders file. If you want, you can save the password in your password list so that Outlook can retrieve the password when it starts.

> **tip** If you want to limit who can access your personal folders file, you should not save your Outlook password in the password list.

9 Click OK.

10 The new personal folders item appears in the folder list.

> **note** After you remove items from a personal folders file, the file size of the personal folders file is not reduced. To reduce the size, you must use the Compact command. To do this, choose Files, Data File Management and select your personal folders file in the Outlook Data Files dialog box. Choose Settings and then choose Compact Now in the Personal Folders dialog box.

Removing a Personal Folder

If you no longer need a personal folders file, you can delete it. Before deleting, however, be sure to save any items you want to keep or to archive the data in another folders file.

When you are ready to delete a personal folders file, you cannot simply delete it from the folders list; instead, you must follow these steps:

1 Choose File, Data File Management to open the Outlook Data Files dialog box.

2 Select the personal folders file you want to remove.

3 Click Remove.

4 When prompted about removing the PST file, click Yes to remove it or No to discontinue the deletion process. The personal folders files is removed if you click Yes.

5 Click Close.

Chapter 28

709

Managing Data

As you use Outlook, you'll find that folders will become full of messages, appointments, and other items. One way to manage this data is to copy or move it between folders so that the data is organized according to how you work. In addition, you need to make sure your data is backed up and archived properly in case you accidentally delete data or a system failure occurs.

In this section, you'll learn how to copy and move data between folders, how to archive data automatically and manually, and how to restore data in case of a crash or a rein-stallation of Outlook.

Copying and Moving Data Between Folders

Occasionally, you might need to move or copy data from one location to another. For example, perhaps you've received an e-mail message from a client connected with a project you're managing. Instead of keeping that message in the Inbox folder, where it might get lost with all the other messages you receive every day, you can move it to a folder devoted to that particular project.

To move data to another folder, follow these steps:

1 Open the folder list and click the folder that includes the message or other item you want to move.

2 Right-click and choose Move To Folder to open the Move Items dialog box (see Figure 28-12).

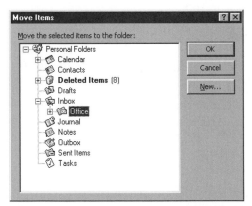

Figure 28-12. Use the Move Items dialog box to move data to a different location.

3 Select an existing folder and click OK, or click New to create a folder in which to store the moved data.

> **tip** Select the topmost folder in the list (such as Personal Folders) to move the data to the root of the folder store.

4 Click OK. The data is moved to the selected location.

> **tip** Choose Edit, Undo Move if you need to move the item back to its original location. This command is effective only immediately after you've performed the move and before you do anything else.

Another way to move data is to select it in the folder and drag it to a new location. Similarly, you can copy data by holding down the Ctrl key while you drag.

Archiving Your Data Automatically

Archiving your data is similar to storing old clothes or toys in your house's attic. You take the data out of folders and move it to another place for safekeeping. You might need to access that data at a later time, but right now it's just getting in the way (much like that old suit or hula hoop you don't use now).

The Outlook AutoArchive feature archives data automatically according to settings you configure for each folder or all your folders. You might want to archive every day if you receive new data that you don't want to take the chance of losing overnight. Or you might want to set AutoArchive to run once a week.

To set up AutoArchive, follow these steps:

1 Right-click a folder and choose Properties.

2 Click Archive Items In This Folder Using The Default Settings (see Figure 28-13 on the next page).

3 Click the Default Archive Settings button to open the AutoArchive dialog box.

4 Click Run AutoArchive Every 14 Days.

5 Click OK twice.

6 Repeat these steps for each folder you want to archive.

By default, Outlook starts AutoArchive every 14 days and archives your data in the selected folder to the Archive.pst personal folders file.

> For information about changing the AutoArchive settings, see "Configuring the Automatic Archiving of Items," page 716.

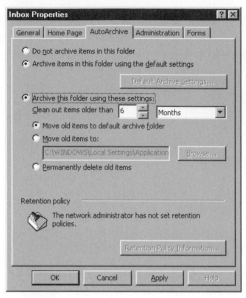

Figure 28-13. Use the AutoArchive feature to archive the data in your folders.

Archiving Your Data Manually

You can archive data not only automatically but also manually—for example, before leaving on vacation or when you need to move your files to a new machine.

To archive data manually, perform these steps:

1 Choose File, Archive.

2 Select one of the following options in the Archive dialog box (see Figure 28-14):

■ To archive all folders using preset AutoArchive settings, click Archive All Folders According To Their AutoArchive Settings. When you click this option, the remaining options in this dialog box become unavailable. Go to step 7.

■ To archive individual folders and their subfolders, click Archive This Folder And All Subfolders. Go to step 3.

3 Select the folder you want to archive. If the folder includes subfolders, those folders are archived as well.

4 In the Archive Items Older Than drop-down list, specify the latest date from which Outlook should start archiving data. For instance, if you want to archive data older than today's date, select that date. Otherwise, all your data in the selected folder will not be archived.

Figure 28-14. Select the way you want to archive data in all or selected folders.

5 If you have specified that a folder should not be archived automatically (see "Configuring the Automatic Archiving of Items," page 716, for more information on this setting), but you want to archive this folder now, select the check box labeled Include Items With "Do Not AutoArchive" Checked.

6 To change the personal folders file that will store your archive, click Browse and then choose the file and folder where the archive will be stored. You also can type the path and file name in the Archive File box if you know this information.

7 Click OK.

Outlook begins archiving your data. If the folder contains a large amount of data, archiving might take several minutes (or hours). You can watch the status of the archiving by looking at the right side of Outlook's status bar. When the process has finished, the folder will be empty and the Archive.pst file (or whichever archive file you specified in step 6) will contain the data you just archived.

Restoring Data After a Crash or a Reinstallation

Suppose you've worked on a project for six months and you've been diligent about archiving messages and other items from the project. You come into work one day and find that your system has crashed and Outlook has lost all your data. You need the archived data to get back all your lost information and continue working. How do you get it back?

Chapter 28

713

You can restore data from an archive file in two ways: drag items from a PST file to a folder, or import a PST file.

The following steps show you how to drag data from a PST file:

1 Choose File, Open, Outlook Data File to open the Open Outlook Data File dialog box (see Figure 28-15).

Figure 28-15. Select the PST file that contains the data you want to restore.

2 Select the file that contains the archived items you want to restore.

3 Click OK. The archive folder (named Archive Folders by default) now appears in your folder list.

4 Click the plus sign (+) next to Archive Folders (or the name you've given this folder) to expand the folder. Expand subsequent folders if necessary until your data is in the right pane.

5 Drag the folder or item to the original folder in which the data was stored.

6 Continue dragging items until they all are restored.

To restore items by importing a PST file, follow these steps:

1 Choose File, Import And Export to open the Import And Export Wizard.

2 Select Import From Another Program Or File and click Next.

3 Select Personal Folder File (.pst) and click Next.

4 On the Import Personal Folders wizard page (see Figure 28-16), type the name of the file you want to import in the File To Import box. Or click Browse to locate the file using the Open Personal Folders dialog box.

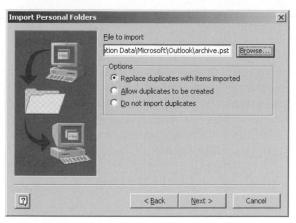

Figure 28-16. Specify the name of the file you want to import.

5 Select one of the following import options pertaining to duplicate data:

- To replace duplicate items that might be in your folders during import, select Replace Duplicates With Items Imported.

- To create duplicate items, select Allow Duplicates To Be Created.

- To prevent Outlook from creating duplicates or writing over existing data, select Do Not Import Duplicates.

6 Click Next.

7 Select the folder from which you want to import data.

8 If the archived folder includes subfolders you want to import as well, select the Include Subfolders option.

9 To filter data, click the Filter button. You can filter by using search strings, SQL (Structured Query Language), and other advanced querying methods. Click OK after filling out your filter information.

10 Select one of the following destination options:

- To import data to the current folder—that is, the folder currently selected—select Import Items Into The Current Folder.

- To import data so that the folder name is the same as one listed in the Select The Folder To Import From list, select Import Items Into The Same Folder In. Then, in the drop-down list under this last option, select the personal folders file name.

11 Click Finish.

Outlook displays a window showing you the progress of the import process. The archive folder appears in the folder list (if the folder list is open), but it is removed when the operation is completed.

Configuring the Automatic Archiving of Items

Outlook provides several ways to configure and manage your data-archiving settings. For example, suppose that you want Outlook to run AutoArchive every day, but you want to be prompted before it starts. You can configure AutoArchive to do just that. In addition, you might want to delete old items after a specific date (say, after a message sits in the Inbox for six months). This section shows you how to configure AutoArchive to handle many of your archiving needs.

To display AutoArchive properties, do the following:

1 Right-click a folder and choose Properties to open the Properties dialog box.

2 Click the AutoArchive tab.

3 Click Archive Items In This Folder Using The Default Settings or Archive This Folder Using These Settings.

The following sections use the AutoArchive tab as a starting point for changing archive settings.

Run AutoArchive Every *n* Days

Outlook allows you to run AutoArchive on a per-day cycle. For example, if you want to run it each day, set it to run every 1 day. To archive every other day, set AutoArchive to run every 2 days, and so on.

> **note** Outlook has different aging periods for different types of items. Calendar, Notes, Journal, Drafts, and Inbox folders have a default of 6 months. Outbox is 3 months, and Sent Items and Deleted Items are 2 months. Contacts folders do not have an AutoArchive option, so you must manually archive them.

To set the length of time between AutoArchive sessions, click the Default Archive Settings button to open the AutoArchive dialog box (see Figure 28-17). Set the Run AutoArchive Every *n* Days option to the number of days you want between archiving sessions. The number you enter must be between 1 and 60.

Chapter 28

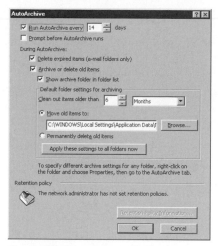

Figure 28-17. Set up Outlook to run AutoArchive at specified intervals.

Prompt Before AutoArchive Runs

You can have Outlook display a message before it starts an AutoArchive session. The message includes a Cancel button to let you cancel the AutoArchive for that day.

To activate this option, select Prompt Before AutoArchive Runs in the AutoArchive dialog box.

Delete Expired Items

In your message folders, AutoArchive can delete messages if they are older than a specified amount of time. To set this option, open the AutoArchive dialog box for a message folder and select the Delete Expired Items option. Also make sure that the Archive Or Delete Old Items option is selected.

In the Default Folder Settings For Archiving area, set the amount of time you want to pass before AutoArchive automatically deletes e-mail messages. The default is 6 months, but you can set this to as high as 60 months or as low as 1 day.

Archive Or Delete Old Items

If you want AutoArchive to archive or delete old Outlook items, select the Archive Or Delete Old Items option. Then set the amount of time that should elapse before old items are archived or deleted. Again, the default is 6 months, but you can set it to as high as 60 months or as low as 1 day.

Show Archive Folder In Folder List

If you want Outlook to display your archive folder in the folder list, select the Show Archive Folder In Folder List option. You might want to select this option if you think you'd like to be able to see which items have been archived. Also, you might find that some items are removed from your working folders (such as Inbox or Calendar) before you want them removed. By showing the archive folder in the folder list, you can quickly and easily move items back to a working folder.

Default Folder Settings For Archiving

In the Default Folder Settings For Archiving area, you can set the number of days that should pass before e-mail messages or other items are archived or deleted (see the previous two sections).

In addition, this area includes options for the way old items are handled. In the Move Old Items To option, you can specify a PST file to which Outlook should move archived items. Click the Browse button to identify a different location and the PST file in which you want to store archives.

On the other hand, if you want to delete archived items, select Permanently Delete Old Items and Outlook will delete items during the AutoArchive sessions. This option is probably not a good choice if you want to retain information for long periods of time.

Apply Settings To All Folders

If you want these AutoArchive settings to apply to all your folders, click Apply These Settings To All Folders Now. Any settings you establish for individual folders (see the next section) are not overridden by the default settings in the AutoArchive dialog box.

AutoArchive Settings For Individual Folders

When you configure AutoArchive settings, you can use the default settings just described, or you can specify options for individual folders.

To take the latter approach, click Archive This Folder Using These Settings on the AutoArchive tab in the folder's Properties dialog box and set the following options:

- **Do Not Archive Items In This Folder.** You can specify that the current folder should not be archived.

- **Clean Out Items Older Than** *n*. This option lets you specify the number of days, weeks, or months that should pass before AutoArchive removes items in the selected folder.

- **Move Old Items To Default Archive Folder.** You can have Outlook move old items to the folder specified for default AutoArchive settings. This folder varies by operating system. For instance, in Windows 98, this folder is the Archive.pst file in \Windows\Local Settings\Application Data\Microsoft\ Outlook. To change this, see "Default Folder Settings for Archiving," page 718.

- **Move Old Items To.** This option lets you specify a different folder in which to archive old items. Click Browse to locate a different folder or file.

- **Permanently Delete Old Items.** You can direct Outlook to delete items in this folder during archiving.

Setting Retention Policy

Your system administrator might enforce company retention policies for your mailbox. If you are running Outlook with Exchange Server, your administrator can set retention polices that you can't override with AutoArchive settings. For example, your company might require that all e-mail messages be saved and archived to backup tapes or disks and then retained for seven years. As much as you try, you can't change these settings without having the appropriate permissions. To view retention policy settings, click the Retention Policy Information button on the AutoArchive tab.

Chapter 28

Finding and Organizing Data

Although some people use Microsoft Outlook only for e-mail, the majority of people use all the personal information manager (PIM) features the program has to offer. Because a PIM is only as good as its ability to help you search for and organize data, Outlook offers a solid selection of features to help you do just that.

This chapter shows you how to perform simple and advanced searches to locate data. You'll learn how to search using the Find A Contact tool, the Find Bar, and the Advanced Find dialog box. The chapter also explores various ways you can organize your Outlook data, for example, by creating additional folders for storing specific types of messages.

Using the Find A Contact Tool to Search for Contacts

If you're like most Outlook users, your Contacts folder will grow to contain a lot of contact entries—typically, too many to allow you to browse through the folder when you need to quickly find a particular contact. You're also likely to encounter situations in which, for example, you need to locate contact information but can't remember the person's last name. Fortunately, Outlook makes it easy to locate contact data, providing the Find A Contact box for searching right on the Standard toolbar (see Figure 29-1 on the next page).

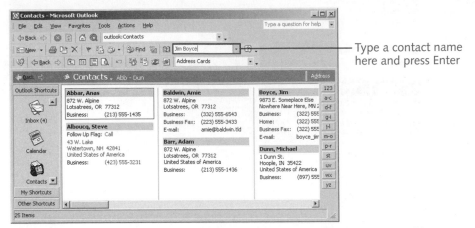

Type a contact name
here and press Enter

Figure 29-1. The Find A Contact box allows you to find a contact entry quickly.

To locate a contact, click the Find A Contact box on the Standard toolbar, type the search criteria (such as a first name, last name, or company), and press Enter. If Outlook finds only one contact that matches the search criteria, it opens the contact entry for that person. Otherwise, Outlook displays the Choose Contact dialog box (see Figure 29-2), from which you select the contact entry to open.

Figure 29-2. Select a contact when Outlook finds more than one that fits your search.

> **tip** Find A Contact is useful when you need to perform a quick search for a contact based on a limited amount of data. To locate contacts and other Outlook items based on multiple search conditions, see "Using Advanced Find," page 725.

Chapter 29

Using the Find Bar

The Find A Contact feature searches only the Contacts folder. When you're looking for messages or other Outlook items (including contacts), you can use the Find Bar (see Figure 29-3). The Find Bar lets you quickly search the current folder, all mail folders, the Inbox, and the Sent Items folder. It also provides a Choose Folder command you can use to select any other folder to include in the search. To display the Find Bar, choose Tools, Find.

> **tip** Choose Tools, Find to hide the Find Bar. You also can press Ctrl+E to show or hide the Find Bar.

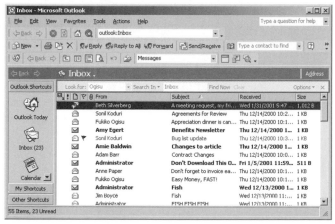

Figure 29-3. Use the Find Bar to perform simple searches of all Outlook items.

Using the Find Bar is easy. In the Look For box, type the data you want to find, such as a name, e-mail subject, or keyword contained in the item. Click Search In to specify where you want to search. The first item in the list is always the current folder. The other options are as follows:

- **All Mail Folders.** Search the Drafts, Inbox, Outbox, and Sent Items folders.

- **Mail I Received.** Search the Inbox.

- **Mail I Sent.** Search the Sent Items folder.

- **Choose Folders.** Display the Select Folder(s) dialog box, shown in Figure 29-4 on the next page, from which you can select multiple folders.

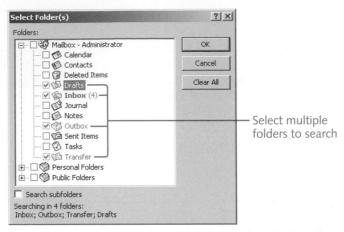

Select multiple folders to search

Figure 29-4. You can search multiple folders by selecting them in the Select Folder(s) dialog box.

After you specify the search data and location, you can click Options on the Find Bar to specify that you want to search all text in each message. Clear this option if you want to search only headers. When you're ready to start the search, click the Find Now button. Outlook organizes the current view to show the results of the search (see Figure 29-5). Click the Clear button to restore the previous view.

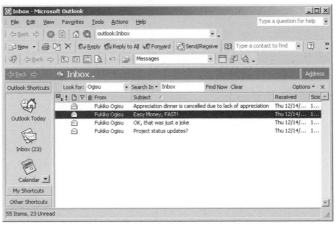

Figure 29-5. Outlook displays the results of the search so that you can select and view the items you need.

Chapter 29

Using Advanced Find

In addition to the Find A Contact tool and the Find Bar, Outlook provides an Advanced Find feature for performing advanced searches that require specifying multiple search conditions.

The Advanced Find Dialog Box

Choose Tools, Advanced Find or press Ctrl+Shift+F to open the Advanced Find dialog box (see Figure 29-6). You can use this dialog box to search for any type of Outlook item using multiple search conditions.

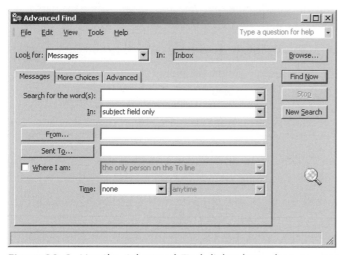

Figure 29-6. Use the Advanced Find dialog box when you need to search using multiple conditions.

The options provided by the Advanced Find dialog box change depending on the type of item you select in the Look For drop-down list. If you select Contacts, for example, the options change to provide specialized search criteria for contacts, such as restricting the search to a name, company, or address. Selecting Messages in the drop-down list changes the options so that you can search the subject field of messages, search the subject and message body, or specify other search criteria specific to messages.

> **note** When you select a different item type in the Look For drop-down list, Outlook clears the current search and starts a new one. Outlook does, however, prompt you to confirm that you want to clear the current search.

On the Messages tab of the Advanced Find dialog box (refer to Figure 29-6), you specify the primary search criteria. The following list summarizes all the available options (although not all options appear at all times):

- **Search For The Word(s).** Specify the word, words, or phrase for which you want to search. You can type words individually or include quotes around a phrase to search for the entire phrase. You also can select from a previous set of search words.

- **In.** Specify the location in the Outlook item where you want to search, such as only the subject of a message. The options available in this list vary according to the type of item you select in the Look For drop-down list.

- **From.** Specify the person who sent you the message. Type the name or click From to browse the address book for the name.

- **Organized By.** Specify the person who generated the meeting request.

- **Sent To.** For messages, specify the recipients to whom the message was sent.

- **Attendees.** Specify the people scheduled to attend a meeting.

- **E-Mail.** Browse the address book to search for contacts by their e-mail addresses.

- **Time.** Specify the creation or modification time, the start or end time, or other time properties specific to the type of item for which you are searching.

- **Named.** Specify the file name of the item for which you're searching. You can specify a single file name or use wildcards to match multiple items. The Named box appears if you select Files or Files (Outlook/Exchange) in the Look For drop-down list.

- **Of Type.** Choose the type of file for which to search when using the Files or Files (Outlook/Exchange) options.

- **Journal Entry Types.** Specify the journal entry type when searching the journal for items.

- **Contact.** Browse for a contact associated with an item for which you're searching.

- **Where I Am.** When searching for messages, specify that you are the only person on the To line, on the To line with others, or on the Cc line with others.

- **Status.** Search for tasks based on their status. You can select Doesn't Matter, Not Started, In Progress, or Completed.

Specifying Advanced Search Criteria

You use the More Choices tab of the Advanced Find dialog box (see Figure 29-7) to specify additional search conditions to refine the search.

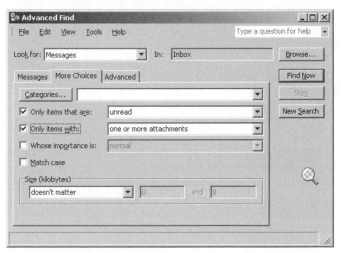

Figure 29-7. Use the More Choices tab to refine the search.

The options on the More Choices tab are the following:

- **Categories.** Specify the category or categories associated with the items for which you are searching. You can type the categories separated by commas or click Categories to open the Categories dialog box and select categories.

- **Only Items That Are.** Search for items by their read status (read or un-read).

- **Only Items With.** Search for items by their attachment status (one or more attachments or no attachments).

- **Whose Importance Is.** Specify the importance (High, Normal, or Low) of the items for which you are searching.

- **Match Case.** Direct Outlook to match the case of the text you entered as the search criteria with the case of matching text. Clear this option to make the search case-insensitive.

- **Size.** Specify the size criteria for the items in your search. You can select one of several options to define the size range in which the item must fall to match the search.

The More Choices tab is the same for all Outlook items except the Files search item. With Files selected in the Look For drop-down list, the More Choices tab is limited to Match Case, Size, and the additional option shown on the next page.

● **Match All Word Forms.** Outlook searches for all word forms of the text you specified for the search. For example, entering *play* would cause Outlook to search for *play*, *playing*, *played*, *plays*, and other word forms of *play*. Clear this option to search for only the words specified on the Files tab.

You can use the Advanced tab (see Figure 29-8) of the Advanced Find dialog box to create more complex searches. On this tab, select the fields to include in the search as well as the search conditions for each field. You can build a list of multiple fields.

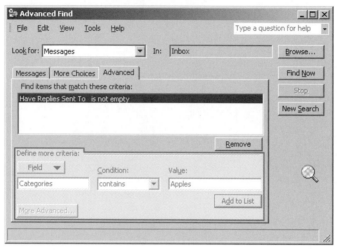

Figure 29-8. On the Advanced tab, select the fields to search and their search criteria.

Organizing Data

Searching for data and organizing data usually go hand in hand. One of the main motivations for organizing your data is that you want to be able to find it easily. Even with perfect organization, however, you'll still need to perform searches now and then because of the sheer amount of data that might be involved. Outlook provides several ways to organize your data. Whereas other chapters focus on specific ways to organize your Outlook items, this section provides an overview of ways you can organize certain types of items and points you to the appropriate chapters for additional information.

Organizing Your E-Mail

E-mail messages probably make up the bulk of your Outlook data. For that reason, organizing your messages can be a challenge. Outlook offers several features that will help you organize your messages so that you can find and work with them effectively and efficiently.

Using Folders

One of the best ways to organize your e-mail messages is to separate them in different folders. For example, if you deal with several projects, consider creating a folder for each project and moving each message to its respective folder. You can create the folders as subfolders of your Inbox or place them elsewhere, depending on your preferences. You might even create a folder outside the Inbox called Projects and create subfolders for each project under that folder.

For more information on creating and managing folders, see Chapter 28, "Managing Folders, Data, and Archiving."

Using Rules

Rules are one of the best tools you have in Outlook for organizing messages. You can apply rules to selectively process messages—moving, deleting, copying, and performing other actions on the messages based on the sender, the recipient, the account, and a host of other message properties. You can use rules in combination with folders to organize your e-mail messages. In the multiple projects example described in the previous section, for example, you might use rules to automatically move messages for specific projects to their respective folders. You can apply rules to messages when they arrive in the Inbox or any time you need to rearrange or organize.

For a detailed discussion of rules, see "Processing Messages Automatically," page 231.

Using Colors

Outlook uses color to help organize your e-mail messages. The headers for messages that you've flagged for action appear in red, for example. When you mark an item as completed, Outlook changes it back to the default color. In addition, if you create rules to apply certain colors to specified e-mail messages, the color can provide a visual indicator of the sender, the subject, the priority, or other properties of the message. In this way, you can see at a glance whether a particular message meets certain criteria.

Using Views

Views give you another important way to organize your Outlook data. The default views organize specific folders using the most common criteria. You can customize Outlook Today view using HTML to provide different or additional levels of organization. You can also create custom views to organize your data to suit your preferences.

For more information on customizing, see "Customizing Outlook Today View," page 623, and "Creating and Using Custom Views," page 631.

Using the Organizer Pane

You can organize your Inbox and other folders manually, or you can use the Ways to Organize area, or the organizer pane, which gives you quick access to the organizational features Outlook provides. Open a folder and choose Tools, Organize to view the organizer pane (see Figure 29-9). Using this feature to organize your e-mail folders is relatively easy.

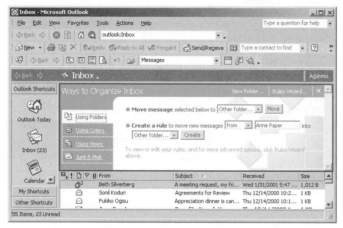

Figure 29-9. Use the organizer pane to create rules and organize your message folder in other ways.

The organizer pane gives you four options for organizing the current folder. Clicking the link for a particular option changes the options displayed in the organizer pane. The following list explains the types of actions you can perform with each option:

- **Using Folders.** Create rules to move messages to other folders based on the sender or recipient of the messages.

- **Using Colors.** Color messages sent to or from an individual. You can also specify that messages sent only to you are displayed in a specific color.

- **Using Views.** Select from several predefined views.

- **Junk E-Mail.** Create rules that apply a user-specified color to messages that fit the junk and adult content criteria defined in your Outlook rules.

> You'll find additional information on creating rules through the organizer pane in Chapter 8, "Filtering, Organizing, and Using Automatic Reponses."

Organizing Your Calendar

You can use the organizer pane in your Calendar folder (see Figure 29-10) to organize items in your calendar.

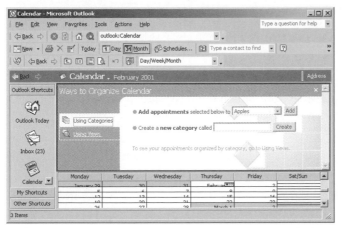

Figure 29-10. Use the organizer pane in the Calendar folder to apply categories to calendar items and select a view.

To assign categories to calendar items, click the Using Categories link. Select the items, and then select the category you want in the drop-down list. You can also use the organizer pane to create a category.

> For a detailed discussion of categories, including how to modify the Master Category List and how to share categories with others, see Chapter 4, "Using Categories and Types."

You can change the calendar view from the organizer pane, which allows you to switch to a view that organizes your data the way you want. To change your view, click the Using Views link in the organizer pane and then select an existing view from a list. (This provides the same functionality as choosing View, Current View, followed by the view you want to use.)

Within the Calendar folder, color labels offer another means of organizing your schedule data. You can assign any of ten different labels to items on your calendar to help you quickly identify them. Each label has its own color, so when you assign a label to an item it appears in that color on the calendar. Outlook provides a set of predefined labels (such as Birthday, Anniversary, and Phone Call), but you can modify the labels to suit your needs.

To assign a label to an item, right-click the item on the calendar, choose Label, and then select the label to assign. To specify your own text for each label color, right-click an item, choose Label, and then choose Edit Labels.

Organizing Contacts, Tasks, and Notes

Like your other Outlook folders, the Contacts, Tasks, and Notes folders have an organizer pane that you can use to organize your contacts, tasks, and notes. The organizer pane gives you three options for organizing contacts and tasks:

- **Using Folders.** Use this option to move selected items to another folder, which you can select from a drop-down list in the organizer pane (refer to Figure 29-9).

- **Using Categories.** Click this link to assign selected items to one or more categories and create new categories.

- **Using Views.** Click this link to select a view. This is the same as choosing View, Current View, followed by the view you want to use.

The Notes folder provides only the Using Folders and Using Views options and does not let you specify categories in its organizer pane. You can assign categories to a note, however, by right-clicking the note and choosing Categories.

Backing Up, Exporting, and Importing Information

If you use Microsoft Outlook on a daily basis to manage e-mail, appointments, and contacts, losing the information you've stored in Outlook could cause significant problems. Outlook data can be lost in a number of ways, from accidental deletion to file corruption to hard disk failure. In addition, a user who purchases a new computer might leave behind information when transferring data information to the new machine.

This chapter discusses two different but complementary processes: using the backup and restore process to protect your Outlook information store, and moving information from one place to another using the Import And Export Wizard. Both processes involve creating copies of your data, but the methods used to create these copies—and the way you use the copies—are quite different.

Backing Up and Restoring Data

An important part of working with a computer system is ensuring that you protect any critical data against loss. You protect your data by making a *backup*, a copy of the information that you can store on another disk or on a backup tape. In the event of a critical failure, you can then use this copy to replace or restore any lost information.

Outlook stores information in two primary ways: in a personal folder or within a shared database. Corporate networks often use the second option, in which a Microsoft Exchange Server

733

stores user information in mailboxes—space reserved for each user in the Exchange Server's database. When you open Outlook, the client machine contacts the Exchange Server and reads information, such as the contents of the Contacts folder or the Inbox, directly from the server. In this type of configuration, the message store is on the server, and no data is actually stored on your computer. The network administrator is generally responsible for backing up the server, and with it the Exchange Server database that contains all the users' information.

> For information about server-based backup procedures, see Chapter 39, "Backup Strategies and Virus Protection."

If your network does not use a centralized server, Outlook information is stored in a PST file, a set of personal folders containing the message store for your data. In this scenario, each user has his or her own PST file or even multiple personal folder files. PST files can be located either on the local hard disk of your computer or in a home directory on the server. Although server-based PST files and local PST files are identical from a functional standpoint, they aren't identical from a backup perspective. Generally, the network administrator regularly backs up server-based user home directories, so if the PST files are in your home directory, you shouldn't have to do backups on your own (although you can, of course).

With local message stores, however, normal network backup strategies do not apply. Most networks don't back up every hard disk on every machine. It simply isn't efficient. Similarly, if you're a home user, you don't have a server to which you can save data or a network administrator to watch over the server. In such cases, you need to take steps on your own to protect your data. Individual backup and restore scenarios apply to these kinds of cases.

> **note** Archive files are simply additional sets of personal folders. Users who archive their messages for later reference should also back up these archive files. For more information on archiving, see Chapter 28, "Managing Folders, Data, and Archiving."

Backing Up Your Outlook Data

Three primary options are available for backing up Outlook data:

- Exporting some or all information to a backup PST file
- Copying the PST file to another disk
- Using a backup program to save a copy of the PST file to tape (or another disk)

Table 30-1 lists the features available in each backup option.

Table 30-1. Backup options in Outlook

Feature	Export	Copy	Backup
Complete backup	Yes	Yes	Yes
Partial backup	Yes	No	No
Automated backup	No	Yes	Yes
Media-supported backup	Disk	Disk	Disk, tape

The process of exporting information is discussed later in the chapter. The following sections focus on the use of backup programs and PST copies.

Backing Up Your Entire Mailbox

Before you back up data stored in Outlook, you must first determine exactly what sort of message store is being used. To find this information, choose File, Data File Management. In the Outlook Data Files dialog box (see Figure 30-1), you'll see any message stores that are in use.

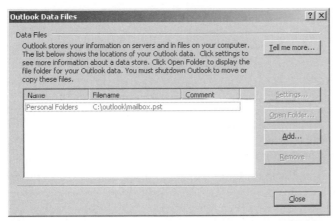

Figure 30-1. The Outlook Data Files dialog box lists message stores in use.

If no files are displayed in the Outlook Data Files dialog box, this generally means that your Outlook information is stored on an Exchange Server and that local backup isn't necessary. If you want backup copies, you must use the export process, described later in this chapter. If the dialog box lists one or more files, a file-based message store is in use for the profile, and it's stored in the path shown in the Filename column. If a personal folders file is listed in the dialog box, that file is usually where mail is stored. This is not always the case, though, because you could simply be using the file as an archive or an export location, leaving most information on an Exchange Server.

Clicking the Settings button in the Outlook Data Files dialog box opens the Personal Folders dialog box, shown in Figure 30-2, where you can rename the PST file, compress

735

it, or set a password for it. This dialog box also shows the path of the PST file, which you should check. If the location listed is a local drive (generally drive C), the PST file is being stored locally and needs to be backed up. If the computer is on a network, and the drive in the path is drive H, drive M, or another location that appears to be network-related, find out where the file is stored, and check with the network administrator to verify whether it is currently being backed up.

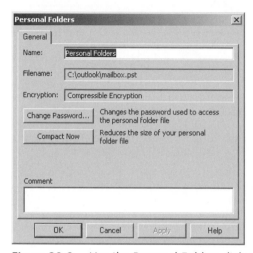

Figure 30-2. Use the Personal Folders dialog box to check the location of the personal folder file.

> **note** File backup is generally the domain of the computer tech or network administrator. The toughest lesson that people in those jobs learn is that most of the work is in planning, not in doing. By carefully determining the nature of the e-mail environment, you can avoid duplicating work that has already been done and ensure that your backup strategy is both effective and efficient.

After you have verified that the message store is not being backed up elsewhere and is stored in a PST file, you need to choose which kind of backup to do. Both of the following methods work well, and each has its advantages.

Backing Up Using File Copy

The first backup method is as old as computing itself. Back in the Stone Age (1990 or so), when I had a file I wanted to safeguard, I simply put a floppy in my Tandy and saved a copy of the file there. I could then put that floppy in a safe location for later use. The backup method discussed here is the same process, taken to the next level.

Personal folders or archive files can be extremely large—often hundreds of megabytes—so simply saving a PST file to a floppy disk isn't an option anymore. As files have grown, though, so have the methods available for moving them around. Any of the following options would be acceptable to use with a "floppy" backup method:

- Recordable (CD-R) or Rewritable (CD-RW) CD drive
- Zip drive or some other large-capacity storage disk (Jaz or SyQuest, for example)
- Network server drive
- A drive on another computer on the network
- A separate hard disk in the machine where the PST is stored

Not all options are created equal, however. Using a CD-R is an expensive option because you must burn another disk each time you run a backup. The CD-RW option works well, but the expense of buying the CD-RW drive can be prohibitive. Zip, Jaz, and SyQuest drives all work well but are also an expense. If your computer is on a network, the best option is to copy the PST to the network server. This serves two purposes. First, the file will be duplicated to another spot on the network. Second, the administrator is probably backing up the server drives, so the file will also be saved to a backup tape during the next backup.

InsideOut

Be certain to check with your network administrator about the recommended policy for backing up PST files in your organization. If, for example, PST files are not allowed on your network because of resource allocation, you'll want to know this and choose another backup method, rather than copying your PST file to the network only to find it deleted the next week. Remember that whatever the merits of a particular backup method, it's critical that your IT staff support it.

If you are saving to a CD-R or CD-RW, you can use the CD burner's interface to copy the file. If you're using a Zip drive, a SyQuest drive, or a network location, simply drag the file to your chosen backup location. Remember that sometimes the PST file cannot be copied if it is open. It's also a good idea to close Outlook before starting the backup copy process.

InsideOut

When copying, be careful not to accidentally *move* the PST file instead. If you move it, you'll find no message store when you reopen Outlook. Although this is not a critical problem—you simply need to copy the file back to the correct location—it doesn't inspire confidence in users. The best option here is to automate the copy, after checking with your administrator; see "Scheduling Automatic Backups," page 741.

Chapter 30

Backing Up Using Microsoft's Backup Utility

If you prefer to use a graphic backup option or if you have access to a tape backup unit, this second method is for you. Both Microsoft Windows 98 and Microsoft Windows 2000 (all versions) include a Backup application in System Tools. You can use this application to identify files for archiving, and it offers the following enhancements over a standard file copy:

● Allows simple setup of a backup plan by using wizards

● Has options for verifying the backup

● Has built-in restore and scheduling options

To use the Windows 2000 Professional backup tool, open Backup by choosing Start, Programs, Accessories, System Tools. In Figure 30-3, the Mailbox.pst file is selected for backup and will be saved in the Backup.bkf file. The location of the backup file is specified in the lower left portion of the window.

Figure 30-3. You can back up a file using the Backup tool in Windows.

> **caution** Although having the backup file in the same directory as the PST file is great for display purposes, it's a horrible backup strategy. If the drive becomes corrupted or the directory under which the PST file is saved is deleted, both the message store and its backup would be lost. Always save the BKF file to another drive or to tape.

To start the backup, click the Start Backup button. You'll need to specify a number of options, including whether to verify the backup. When the process is finished, a dialog box similar to the one shown in Figure 30-4 appears. From this dialog box, you can view a report that records any events—and, more important, any errors—that might have occurred during the backup process.

```
┌─────────────────────────────────────────────┐
│ Backup Progress                       [?][X] │
├─────────────────────────────────────────────┤
│  The backup is complete.              [ Close ] │
│                                                  │
│  To see a report with detailed information about │
│  the backup, click Report.            [ Report... ] │
│                                                  │
│  Media name:   │ Media created 2/20/2001 at 9:09 AM │
│                                                  │
│  Status:       │ Completed │                       │
│                                                  │
│                Elapsed:                          │
│  Time:         │          │                       │
│                                                  │
│                Processed:      Estimated:        │
│  Files:        │          1 │ │          1 │      │
│                                                  │
│  Bytes:        │     49,400 │ │     49,400 │      │
└─────────────────────────────────────────────┘
```

Figure 30-4. The backup process generates a summary report.

Restoring Your Data

Anyone who works with computers long enough will eventually experience a critical error. A drive will become corrupted, a virus will get through your virus software's protection, or you'll accidentally delete something you need. This is the point when all the time and trouble you've invested in backing up your data will pay dividends.

Depending on how you created your backup file, you will have one of two options: you can simply recopy your PST file from the CD or network drive where you stored it, or you can run the Backup utility and use the Restore tab to bring back the missing file or files. From there, you can select the backup file that contains the PST and then determine which files to restore and where to put them. In Figure 30-5, the backup file contains a copy of a mailbox.pst file originally stored in D:\outlook.

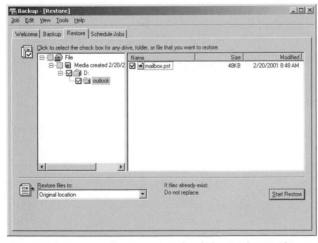

Figure 30-5. Use the Restore tab of the Backup utility to help restore a file.

Note that by default the Backup utility restores a file to its original location. This is generally the best choice, because if the PST file isn't restored to the proper location, Outlook won't be able to find it.

Whichever method you use, be certain to carefully check the drive for errors and viruses before you restore your data. You don't want to restore the file only to see it destroyed again a few hours later.

> **tip** It's important to be familiar with the restore process before a disaster-recovery process is underway. You should occasionally try restoring your backed-up PST file to another computer in order to verify that your backups work. This will help to ensure that the restore process will work and that you know how to perform the necessary tasks.

Troubleshooting

You're having problems with a restore operation.

Problems with a restore operation can come from several sources. One of the first things to check is whether you are in fact logged on as the correct account, especially if you're supporting another user. When you're connecting to the Exchange Server or bringing back information from an offline folder (OST) file, you'll need to provide the user's credentials or, preferably, be logged on as the user. When you restore a PST file, you'll also need access to the directory to which the file needs to be restored (such as the user's home directory).

Corrupted backups can present additional problems during a restore operation. What if the saved copies of your information are bad? In this situation, the best option is to go back and try to find a saved copy of the PST that is not corrupt. Most companies keep archived backup tapes for weeks or even months. You might lose some recent information if you have to do this, but losing a week of data is better than losing it all.

Another option for dealing with a corrupted backup is to run the Inbox Repair Tool (Scanpst.exe). This tool, which is included with Microsoft Office and Windows 9x, can be used to remove corruption from PST and OST files. The problem with the Inbox Repair Tool, however, is that it works by simply deleting any portions of the PST file that are corrupt. Thus, when you reopen the PST file, information will be missing.

If you have the choice of restoring from an older backup or using Scanpst.exe, it's probably preferable to choose the older backup. Both methods leave you with missing information, but at least with the older backup you know the period of time that's missing. Using Scanpst.exe puts you in the unpleasant situation of knowing that data is missing but not knowing exactly what has disappeared.

Scheduling Automatic Backups

The Microsoft Backup utility has built-in support for automating backups. If you're planning to automate the backup process, you'll almost certainly want to leverage the advantages of this tool. The Backup utility uses *jobs* to schedule tasks. A job is a set of commands and a schedule for executing those commands.

> **note** In Windows 2000 Professional, you must have appropriate rights to schedule backups. Groups that have this access are Administrators, Power Users, and Backup Operators.

To create a new backup job, open Backup and start the Backup Wizard. Select the files you want to back up and the backup file in which you want to place them. While in the wizard, you can click Advanced to see additional options, including Type Of Backup and When To Back Up.

With Outlook personal folders, selecting the type of backup—Normal, Copy, Incremental, Differential, or Daily—isn't critical. Although these types vary in terms of which files they back up, depending on when the files were modified, none of them allows you to back up only the changes to a particular file. If the file has changed at all, the entire file is backed up. Because a set of personal folders is held in a single file regardless of its size, you must back up the entire file or nothing. In most cases, if you're scheduling only the backup of the PST file, you can simply use the default type of backup (Normal).

The most important option for scheduling the job is specifying when to back up. You can choose to run the backup immediately or schedule it for later. If you select Later, you can enter a name for the backup job and click Set Schedule to open the Schedule Job dialog box, shown in Figure 30-6 on the next page.

You can schedule backups to occur as often as needed. Remember that frequent backups will allow you to recover more completely from a problem. If you back up the PST file weekly, you could lose up to seven days of data if the message store is lost. If you back up the PST nightly, you risk losing only one day.

After you complete the schedule, make sure that sufficient room is available for the backup. Change tapes or free up drive space as needed. Check occasionally to ensure that the scheduled task is running properly and that the backups are good.

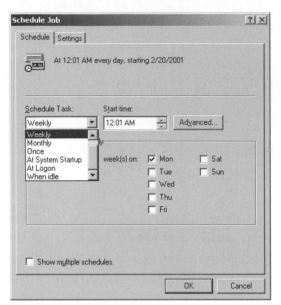

Figure 30-6. You can schedule backups to occur automatically.

Using the Offline Folders Option

If you're on a network and want to have a backup of your message store available locally, one possible option is to use offline folders. Offline folders allow you to access your message store when you're away from the office. To use offline folders, you must create an offline folder (OST) file, which is stored on the local drive of your computer.

In a sense, OST files provide backup in reverse: instead of saving data to a server to back it up, the offline process saves the information from the server to the workstation. Although offline folders don't offer a standard backup, an occasional synchronization to an offline store is an easy way to create a second copy of Outlook data. If the PST file or the Exchange Server mailbox is lost, you need only open Outlook and choose to work offline to access the lost data. At that point, the data must be exported to a PST file and then can be imported back, as explained in the following section.

> For more information on setting up and using offline folders, see "Using Offline Folders," page 861.

Exporting Data

The previous section discussed backup, which creates a duplicate copy of your message store for disaster-recovery purposes. You might also want to make copies of part or all of the message store for use in other applications. You can do this by using the export process, in which you save information to a different PST file or transform data for use in Microsoft Access, Microsoft Word, or other programs. (The reverse process, importing data, is covered in the next section.) Table 30-2 shows the file types and formats that are available for export or import with Outlook 2002.

Table 30-2. Supported export and import options

	File extension	Import	Export
Microsoft Schedule+ 1.0	CAL	Yes	No
Microsoft Schedule+ 7.x	SCD	Yes	No
Microsoft Schedule + Interchange	SC2	Yes	No
Microsoft personal folder file	PST	Yes	Yes
Microsoft Exchange Personal Address Book	PAB	Yes	Yes
Microsoft Internet Mail (Microsoft Internet Explorer 3.02)	PST	Yes	No
Microsoft Outlook Express		Yes	No
ACT! 2.0, 3.0, or 4.0 for Windows	DBF	Yes	No
ECCO 3.0, 3.01, 3.02, or 4.00	ECO	Yes	No
Eudora Light (1.54 or 3.0.1)		Yes	No
Eudora Pro 2.2, 3.0, or 3.0.1		Yes	No
Netscape Mail 2.02, 3.0, or 3.01		Yes	No
Netscape Messenger 4.0		Yes	No
Lotus Organizer 1.0, 1.1, 2.1, and 97	ORG, OR2, OR3	Yes	No
Comma-separated values (MS-DOS)	CSV	Yes	Yes
Comma-separated values (Windows)	CSV	Yes	Yes
Tab-separated values (MS-DOS)	TXT	Yes	Yes
Tab-separated values (Windows)	TXT	Yes	Yes
iCalendar	ICS	Yes	No
vCalendar	VCS	Yes	No
vCard	VCF	Yes	No
Microsoft Access	MDB	Yes	Yes
Microsoft Excel	XLS	Yes	Yes
Microsoft FoxPro	DBF	Yes	Yes
dBASE	DBF	Yes	Yes

Chapter 30

The export process in Outlook is extremely straightforward. It allows you to use a wizard to send copies of information from the Outlook message store. This section looks at three export options in some depth: exporting messages, exporting addresses, and exporting data to a file.

Exporting Messages

You can copy messages and other items into a new or existing set of personal folders. Unlike backing up, this option lets you choose which items you want to export and which you want to exclude. You can use the Import And Export Wizard to export messages to a file, although a nonwizard option is also available. You might already know how to use the AutoArchive feature to move messages out of your message store and into a long-term storage location in another PST file. Using the Import And Export Wizard to export messages works in a similar way; the major difference is that when messages in the store are exported, they aren't removed; instead, they are copied, as they are during backup.

For information about using AutoArchive, see "Archiving Your Data Automatically," page 711.

To export the contents of the Inbox to a folder, follow these steps:

1 Choose File, Import And Export to start the Import And Export Wizard, as shown in Figure 30-7. Only two export options are available: Export To A File and Export To The Timex Data Link Watch. It should be immediately obvious that one of these options has relatively limited usefulness (unless you have one of those snazzy watches).

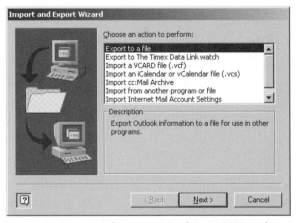

Figure 30-7. Use the Import And Export Wizard to export data to a file.

2 Select Export To A File and click Next.

3 The options available on the next page break down into four basic types: text files, databases, spreadsheets, and a personal folder file. Figure 30-8 shows most of the formats available for exporting. Although you can export your messages in any of these formats, you'll probably find PST files the most useful. For this example, select Personal Folder File (.pst) and click Next.

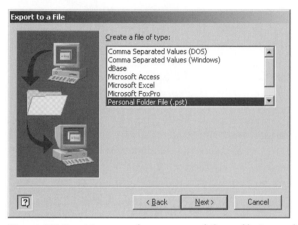

Figure 30-8. You can choose one of these file types for exporting.

4 On the Export Personal Folders page, select the folder you want to export and specify whether subfolders should be included.

> **note** Your options are somewhat limited in this selection. If you want to export the Inbox and the Sent Items folders, for instance, you must either export the top-level personal folders (with subfolders) or run the export twice: once for the Inbox and then again for Sent Items.

5 If you want to specify a filter, click the Filter button. Figure 30-9 on the next page shows the Filter dialog box. By using a filter, you can search a large message store so that only relevant messages are located and exported. This option could be useful, for instance, if you need to send all correspondence with representatives of BigCo, Inc., to a new sales representative who will be dealing with that firm. You could export the relevant messages to a PST file that you could send to the new rep, who could then import them. After you've specified any needed filters, click OK to close the Filter dialog box and return to the wizard page. Then click Next.

Chapter 30

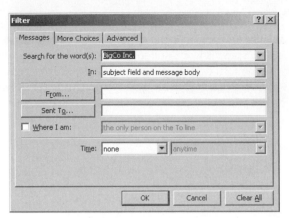

Figure 30-9. Use the Filter Dialog box to export only those messages that fit certain criteria.

6 On the final wizard page, specify the location where you want to save exported information and specify how duplicate items should be handled. If no export file exists, specify the path and name of the file to be created. If an export file does exist, browse to the file you want to use. When you click Finish, the wizard creates the personal folders file (if it is new), runs the export, and then closes the file.

Exporting Addresses

Like messages, address lists can be exported out of Outlook for use elsewhere. Exporting addresses is similar to exporting messages: you use the same Import And Export Wizard. The difference is that addresses are sometimes exported to a database or a spreadsheet to allow users easier access to phone numbers, addresses, and other information.

To export the address list to Access, for instance, simply start the Import And Export Wizard. Select Export To A File, and then select Microsoft Access. The wizard will prompt you to select the Contacts folder and to provide a name for the Access database that will be created for the exported addresses.

The primary difference between exporting to a personal folder file and exporting to a database lies in mapping out the fields for the database itself. From the wizard, you can click the Map Custom Fields button to open the Map Custom Fields dialog box, shown in Figure 30-10. In the figure, for example, only the business-related fields have been mapped for export. Choosing only needed fields reduces the size of the database and allows a quicker export.

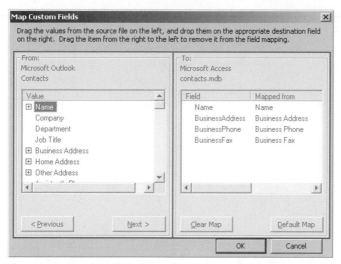

Figure 30-10. Use this dialog box to map fields for export into an Access database.

After you've finished the field mapping, click OK and then click Finish to create the new database file and export the contact information into it.

> **note** When you're exporting to a database, you don't have a filter option. Therefore, if you're exporting only certain records, you should create a subfolder. You can place all the contacts to be exported in that folder, which is then the target of the export.

Exporting Data to a File

Occasionally, data in PST format simply isn't usable for a particular task. In such cases, Outlook gives you a number of options for other export formats, such as Excel, Access, or various text file formats. For instance, if you need to export information from Outlook into a third-party software package, or if you want to use the information in any capacity for which a direct export path is not available, your best option might be to export the needed information to a basic text file, either tab-delimited or comma-delimited. Figure 30-11 on the next page shows how contacts are distilled into text fields during this sort of export.

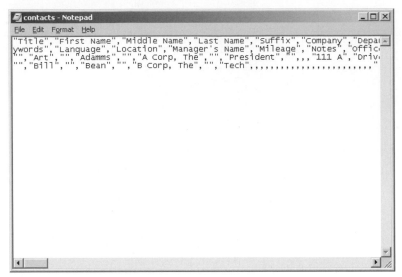

Figure 30-11. This contact information has been exported into a basic text file.

Importing Data

Data transfer is a two-way street, of course, and any discussion of how to take information out of Outlook would be incomplete without a discussion of how to bring information back in as well. As mentioned earlier, far more options are available for bringing information in than for sending information out.

Importing Data to Outlook

The process of importing data into your Outlook message store is the same regardless of whether you're importing information into a personal folder or an Exchange Server mailbox. You begin the process by identifying exactly what type of information you want to import and whether Outlook can properly access and import the data. Outlook supports numerous import sources, including the following:

- cc:Mail archives
- iCalendar or vCalendar files (VCS extensions)
- Microsoft Mail files (MMF extensions)
- Other e-mail applications such as Eudora, Netscape Mail/Messenger, Microsoft Internet Mail, and Outlook Express
- Personal Address Book files (PAB extensions)

- Personal folder files (PST extensions)

- Programs such as ACT!, dBase, ECCO, Lotus Organizer, Access, Excel, FoxPro, and Schedule+

- Text files

- vCard files (VCF extensions)

Because many of these applications use different structures for formatting data, depending on the product version, it's important to know which version created the file you're importing.

The next sections examine some examples of importing information into Outlook. To begin the import process for any of the examples discussed in these sections, use the Import And Export Wizard.

Importing Internet Mail Account Settings

When upgrading an e-mail system to Outlook, you can often save time and avoid configuration problems by importing the Internet mail settings from the previous system. This process does not bring over any messages or addresses; it simply transfers any existing Internet e-mail account information to the current Outlook profile. This option works only if the computer on which Outlook is installed had previously been using a different e-mail client, such as Outlook Express or Netscape Messenger.

The wizard itself is extremely straightforward, taking you through all the steps of verifying and reestablishing the account. Fields are prefilled with information taken from the detected settings; you can modify them as needed during the import process. After you have imported the information, the new service will often require you to exit, log off, and restart Outlook before it will be active. At that point, you should be able to receive and send Internet e-mail through Outlook.

> **newfeature!**
> **note** The migration to Outlook 2002 often also involves switching to an Exchange Server. In such cases, the Exchange Server then takes over Internet e-mail responsibilities, and the old settings are unnecessary.

Importing Internet Mail and Addresses

In addition to importing Internet e-mail configuration settings, as just discussed, the other step involved in migrating e-mail data to Outlook is to bring in any address lists or saved messages that were stored in the previous system. To properly import the information from your old system, Outlook must have a converter—software that understands the format of the existing messages or addresses. Converters for Eudora, Netscape's e-mail products, and earlier Microsoft e-mail systems are included with Outlook 2002. You can also import cc:Mail archives, and third-party vendors supply additional converters for less common e-mail systems.

To import an existing message store, follow these steps:

1 Choose File, Import And Export. When the wizard starts, select Import Internet Mail And Addresses.

2 Specify the program from which you are migrating the data. After you select the application, you must specify what to import: messages, addresses, or both.

> **note** No filters are available during this process. Rule exports are available only with Outlook Express.

3 If you are importing only e-mail messages, click Finish.

4 If you are importing address book entries as well as e-mail messages, click Next and select either the Contacts folder or the Personal Address Book as the destination. (In most cases, the Contacts folder is the preferred destination; it is the default.)

5 Specify how Outlook should handle duplicates. The default entry, Allow Duplicates To Be Created, can create a bit of cleanup work (deleting the duplicate entries that might be created for certain contacts), but it guards against accidental information loss from overwriting the wrong contact entry.

6 Click Next, and then click Finish. The wizard runs the import and then displays the Import Summary dialog box (see Figure 30-12). If the import has gone well, you'll see an indication that all the messages have been imported. If you see that only a portion of the total messages have been imported, you'll know that a problem occurred and not all the information was transferred.

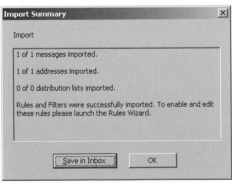

Figure 30-12. The Import Summary dialog box tells you how successful the import was.

Importing a vCard File

One of the handiest ways to share contact information is by using vCards. When you receive a vCard from someone, you can import the card into your Contacts folder for later use. Start the Import And Export Wizard, and select Import A vCard File (.vcf). Browse to the directory where you saved the VCF file, select the file, and click Open. The file will be imported as a new contact entry in your Contacts folder.

> For details about using vCards to share contact information, see "Sharing Contacts with vCards," page 415.

> **tip** If you receive the VCF file as an e-mail attachment, you can double-click the VCF file icon to import the card into your Contacts folder.

Importing an iCalendar or a vCalendar File

Numerous options, including iCalendar and vCalendar files, are available to users who want to share calendar information. Although they're used for much the same purpose, iCalendar and vCalendar work in different ways.

You use iCalendar (iCal) to send calendar information out across the Web to anyone using an iCal-compatible system. Users who receive an iCalendar meeting invitation simply accept or decline the meeting, and the information is automatically entered into their calendars. An import process is generally not necessary.

In contrast, you use vCalendar files much as you use vCards: they allow you to create a meeting and send it out as an attachment to other attendees. Attendees can then double-click the attachment or use the import process to bring this meeting into their schedules. If necessary, users can also import iCalendar meetings the same way.

> **note** The file name extension used for vCalendar files is VCS; iCalendar files use an ICS extension.

Importing from Another Program File

You've now seen most of the common import options. However, you'll also occasionally encounter situations in which you might need to import other types of information, such as third-party data, text files, and so on.

Perhaps the most important of these other possibilities is importing information from another PST file. This could involve bringing back information from an archive, restoring lost messages from a backup, or even completing the process in the example discussed earlier, in which you need to give a new sales rep the records of all messages sent to

Chapter 30

BigCo, Inc. If three or four other employees had all exported messages to PST files, the easiest option for the new rep would be to import them back into his or her own message store for easy access.

The following steps describe the process of importing from an existing PST file. Keep in mind that other file import options are similar, although the particular data and formatting of each file will, of course, dictate certain changes in the import process.

To import from an existing PST file, perform the following steps:

1 Start the Import And Export Wizard. Select Import From Another Program Or File and click Next.

2 In the list of file types, select Personal Folder File (.pst).

3 Browse to the PST file you want to import. If you want to import four PST files, you must import each one separately. Specify how to handle duplicates on the same page and click Next.

> **tip** As mentioned earlier, allowing Outlook to create duplicates minimizes the risk of overwriting data, but it does increase the size of the store. If you're importing a number of PST files that might have overlapping data (if many recipients were copied on the same messages, for example), it's often better to avoid importing duplicates.

4 On the wizard page shown in Figure 30-13, select the folders to import— either the entire store or only a particular folder or set of folders.

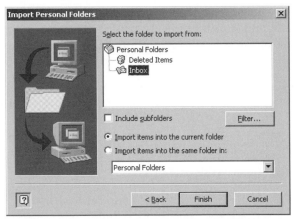

Figure 30-13. Select the folder on the Import Personal Folders page.

5 The wizard allows you to filter the data you're importing the same way you filter exported data. Click the Filter button to open the Filter dialog box and add any filters you need.

6 Specify the folder into which the data should be imported.

752

7   Click Finish to begin the import. Depending on the size of the data, the process can take a few minutes or more.

---

tip   **Use subfolders for importing and exporting**

Our fictional sales rep could create a subfolder called BigCo under the Inbox and then select that folder before starting the Import And Export Wizard. Note that by choosing to import only from the PST file's Inbox and selecting Import Items Into The Current Folder, the sales rep could bring all the messages from the PST file into his or her message store without having to flood the Inbox with old BigCo information. Creating subfolders for importing and exporting can be an extremely good way to keep track of where information is coming from and what you are sending out.

Chapter 30

Part 7

Using and Administering Outlook with Exchange Server

Chapter 31

Exchange Server Overview and Setup

Microsoft Exchange Server is an incredibly feature-rich and versatile collaboration and messaging server. Because it's so powerful, Exchange Server is also an extremely complex piece of software, especially when distributed across multiple locations. In this chapter, you'll find information on installing and configuring Exchange 2000 Server in a simple environment.

Because many more variables exist than can be covered here, this chapter doesn't include architectural considerations or "best practices." Extensive documentation is available from both Microsoft and other sources on proper design practices and on the installation and administration of Exchange Server in general.

> **note** Useful references for information on Exchange Server include *Microsoft Exchange 2000 Server Administrator's Companion*, by Walter J. Glenn and Bill English (Microsoft Press, 2000); and *Introducing Microsoft Exchange 2000 Server,* by JoAnne Woodcock (Microsoft Press, 2000).

Introduction to Exchange Server

At the most basic level, Exchange Server is a mail server. By implementing a number of flexible protocols—including IMAP, POP, SMTP, X.400, and LDAP—Exchange Server provides a full messaging and collaboration system. Almost all the features implemented in Microsoft Outlook and Exchange Server are transported over the same messaging infrastructure.

Although Exchange Server 2000 was released in 2000, Exchange Server 5.5 is still widely implemented in many organizations. Exchange Server 5.5 uses a transactional mailbox store and a separate directory store based on the Lightweight Directory Access Protocol (LDAP). Because the Exchange Server 5.5 directory isn't integrated with the Microsoft Windows user directory, mailboxes and user accounts are logically separate. This lack of integration with Active Directory and the separation between users and mailboxes adds administrative overhead, a disadvantage that is overcome by Exchange 2000 Server.

Unlike Exchange Server 5.5, which evolved from earlier versions of Exchange, much of Exchange 2000 Server has been completely redesigned. One of the main reasons for this redesign was to fully integrate Exchange with Active Directory. The Exchange Directory store has been completely removed, and Active Directory is used in its place. For this reason, you must install Exchange 2000 Server on an Active Directory server running Windows 2000 Service Pack 1 or later.

Installing Exchange Server

Unlike installing most software, installing Exchange Server isn't simply a matter of "Insert CD, click Next, click Next, click Finish." You must take many factors into account before you install Exchange Server. The following list includes only a few examples:

- Determine the number of users you need to support, in order to decide how many servers you need in your organization.

- For each server, decide how many administrative groups and how many message stores per server make sense, given performance and fault tolerance considerations.

- Decide whether you need to create a front-end–back-end server structure.

- Take a look at hardware requirements and ensure that all the hardware is in place and functioning properly.

- Make sure you've installed the latest service pack on each server.

InsideOut

As this section indicates, you have numerous issues to consider when planning for and deploying Exchange 2000 Server, particularly in a large enterprise that requires multiple servers. If you are installing Exchange 2000 Server on a single server or in a test environment to become familiar with it, however, installation is relatively easy, and you can forgo a lot of the planning and deployment issues involved in an enterprise roll-out. This chapter provides an overview of the Exchange 2000 Server installation process to help you get started in single-server and test environments.

Chapter 31: Exchange Server Overview and Setup

You can choose from several possible scenarios when installing Exchange Server. One scenario is installing Exchange Server 5.5 on Windows NT 4.0, but this chapter focuses on installing Exchange 2000 Server on Windows 2000 Server.

Before you begin installation, read the Release Notes included on the Exchange Server CD. The Release Notes list the system requirements, including the software and Service Packs you must install before you actually install Exchange Server. The installation process involves first installing the operating system, including all components required in the Release Notes, followed by any required Service Packs and other updates, and then finally Exchange Server itself.

Installing Windows 2000 Server

The first step in installing Exchange 2000 Server is to install Windows 2000 Server. The following Windows 2000 services must be present for Exchange 2000 Server to work: the World Wide Web, NNTP, and SMTP services within Internet Information Services. Keep in mind that the easiest time to install these is during the initial installation.

After you've installed Windows 2000 Server, you must install Active Directory, which configures the server as a domain controller. To install Active Directory, open the Configure Your Server Wizard (see Figure 31-1), located in the Administrative Tools folder.

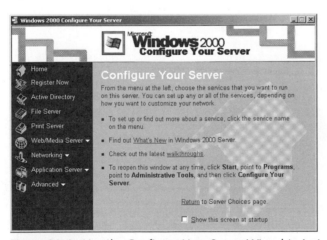

Figure 31-1. Use the Configure Your Server Wizard to install and configure many parts of Windows 2000 Server, including Active Directory.

To begin the installation of Active Directory, click Active Directory on the left side of the Configure Your Server Wizard page. The wizard will explain the steps on the right. Click Start to run the Active Directory Installation Wizard, which walks you through the process of configuring Active Directory.

The first step is to decide whether this server will join an existing domain or be a domain controller in a new domain. The example installation shown in this chapter's illustrations creates a new domain. Next, you must decide whether the new domain is a new domain tree or a child of an existing domain. A new domain tree would be development.tld, for example, while a child of that tree would be code.development.tld. The example installation creates a new domain tree.

The final decision you must make about domain structure is whether this is the first domain tree in a forest or a tree in an existing forest. A *forest* is a group of domain trees that don't share a *contiguous namespace.* (Domains in a tree must share a namespace.) The contiguous namespace refers to the domain suffix, such as development.tld. Domains in a forest share trust relationships and resource location information. The example installation creates a new forest.

The next step in the process is to specify the domain name of the new domain, as shown in Figure 31-2. This should be (but isn't required to be) a proper Domain Name Service (DNS) name. If you want this domain to be connected to the Internet, it's best to use a properly registered name.

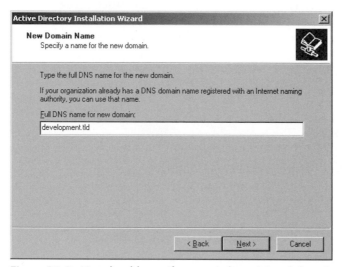

Figure 31-2. You should specify a properly registered domain name if your network is (or ever will be) connected to the Internet, but any name is OK for a private system.

Figure 31-3 shows the next page in the Active Directory Installation Wizard. By default, the prefix of the domain name you specified is used as the NetBIOS domain name. This name will be used by any systems that don't fully implement Active Directory

client functionality, such as Windows NT 4.0 and Windows 9*x*. You can choose anything for this name, but it should be a unique domain name on the network and
should be descriptive enough to tie it to the full domain name that Windows 2000
Server clients will use.

---

tip **Register the domain name now**

Even if you don't have an Internet connection for your local area network (LAN) now,
you should plan for one. Changing domain names down the road isn't possible—
instead, you'll have to remove Active Directory (demoting the domain controller) and
create a new domain with the correct name. Obviously, this can have consequences
across the enterprise. Register a public domain name now, and use it for your installation, even if you don't need a public domain at this time. A little foresight will save
considerable effort and aggravation later.

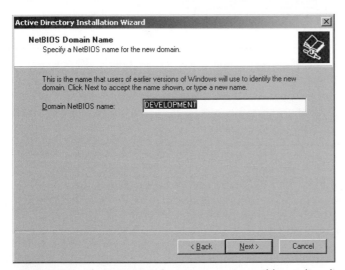

Figure 31-3. The NetBIOS domain name is used by earlier clients such as Windows NT 4
and Windows 9*x*.

You must now specify where the Active Directory database and logs are to be stored.
For the best performance, these directories should be on fast access devices, such as
Redundant Army of Inexpensive Disks (RAID) 0+1 arrays; and they should be on separate disks and separate disk controllers if possible. Figure 31-4 on the next page shows
the Active Directory Installation Wizard with these paths specified.

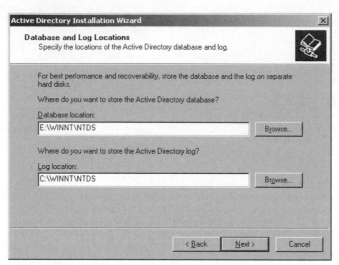

Figure 31-4. You must specify the paths for the Active Directory database and logs.

> **note** For a small implementation that has only a few hundred users, it's not essential to store the Active Directory database and logs on fast access devices or to use separate disks and disk controllers, because there are fewer changes and reads from the database. In such a situation, RAID isn't necessary for performance, although it can still be useful for redundancy and fault tolerance.

The next step is to specify the Sysvol folder. Domain controllers share this folder for replication purposes. If the DNS Server service isn't installed, the wizard will ask whether you want to install it. Unless you already have DNS servers in place and don't need an additional DNS server, or unless you want to install DNS yourself manually, allow the wizard to install DNS.

Figure 31-5 shows the next page in the Active Directory Installation Wizard. You must decide how the permissions for user and group objects should be structured. The default is to allow anonymous access to domain information (Permissions Compatible With Pre-Windows 2000 Servers).

> **caution** If you select the option Permissions Compatible Only With Windows 2000 Servers, any server applications running on non-Windows 2000 servers that are part of a pre-Windows 2000 domain won't be able to access the information they require from the domain controllers.

Chapter 31: Exchange Server Overview and Setup

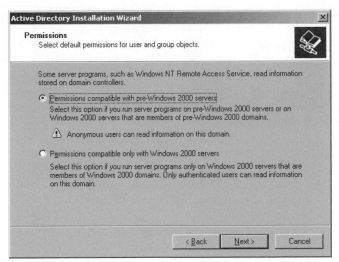

Figure 31-5. You must specify the configuration of permissions for domain objects. The second option is more secure but isn't backward compatible with older servers or older domains.

You must set a password for the Administrator account when starting the computer in Directory Services Restore Mode. This mode is used to repair or restore files in the event of damage or corruption of the directory. Finally, you'll see a summary of the options you set during the configuration process; clicking Next will begin the installation of Active Directory. From this point, the Active Directory installation is completely automated; an installation status window displays each step as it progresses.

The configuration process installs Active Directory (and DNS if it isn't installed already), sets the configuration you specified, and sets file, directory, and Active Directory object permissions to secure the server. When the installation is completed, you must reboot the server.

---

tip   **Demoting domain controllers**

After you complete the domain controller installation, you might decide that you want to remove Active Directory and restore the computer's status to a member or stand-alone server. To accomplish this, you can run DCPROMO to demote the domain controller. Click Start, Run and type **DCPROMO** in the Run dialog box. This starts the Active Directory Installation Wizard, which you can use to demote the domain controller.

Installing Windows 2000 Service Pack 1

After you have installed Active Directory, you must install Windows 2000 Service Pack 1 or later. An important note about this Service Pack is that every time you perform an installation that requires the Windows 2000 Server distribution CD (for example, when you install new services), you must reinstall the Service Pack to ensure that you have the latest version of the installed files. For that reason, it's a good idea to first install everything you require before installing the Service Pack.

The simplest way to install the Windows 2000 Service Pack is by using Windows Update. Open Microsoft Internet Explorer and enter the URL *http://windowsupdate.microsoft. com.* Click the Product Updates button on the left, and the Windows Update site automatically detects any updates that your system requires. Figure 31-6 shows an example of the Windows Update page with the Windows 2000 Service Pack 1 selected. A few items on the Windows Update page must be selected and installed individually, including Service Pack 1 and Internet Explorer 5.0 and 5.5. If you want to install other updates, you must come back to this page after these are installed. When you select the update, click the Download button to begin installation.

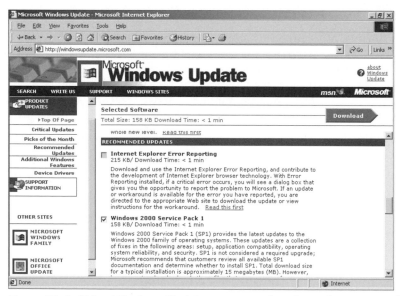

Figure 31-6. Using Windows Update, you can select the updates to install, and they're automatically downloaded and installed.

Figure 31-7 shows the Service Pack setup dialog box. You must accept the license agreement by selecting the first check box. Selecting the second check box causes the Service Pack installer to make backup copies of all files that it overwrites so that you can uninstall it later. When you click the Install button, the Service Pack installer determines what is installed on your system and downloads and installs any updates to those services. It won't install any files related to services that aren't installed.

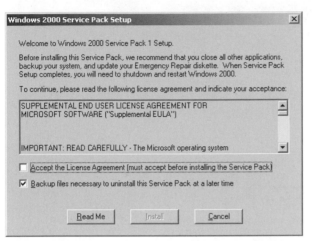

Figure 31-7. You must accept the license agreement and choose whether to make backup copies of the files being updated.

You should select and install any available Critical Updates, which are critical security and functionality fixes. You'll also find it useful to install any Compatibility Updates, Driver Updates, and the High Encryption Pack to keep your system as up-to-date as possible.

> **note** If you've already installed a Service Pack that has made changes to your system and has copied files from the Windows 2000 distribution media, you'll need to click the Show Installed Updates button at the top of the list of updates. This will display all updates, including those that have been installed. You can select the Service Pack to reinstall and update any changed files.

Installing Exchange 2000 Server

When you have a functional Windows 2000 Server installation and you've installed Service Pack 1 or later, you can begin to install Exchange 2000 Server. When you insert the Exchange 2000 Server CD, the screen shown in Figure 31-8 on the next page appears. If CD Autorun is disabled, run Launch.exe from the CD. Click Exchange Server Setup to open the Microsoft Exchange 2000 Installation Wizard.

Part 7: Using and Administering Outlook with Exchange Server

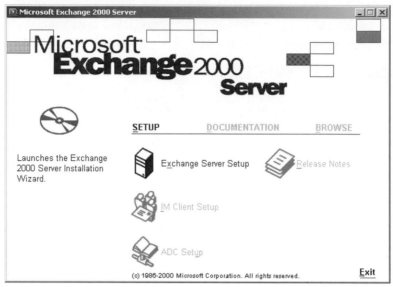

Figure 31-8. This is the starting point for installing Exchange 2000 Server.

You begin by accepting the license agreement and entering your CD key. When your CD key is accepted, you see the wizard page shown in Figure 31-9, where you can choose which components to install and specify a location for the files. (Figure 31-9 shows the default Typical installation.) The listed connectors are required only if you're running an additional mail server and want mail connectivity with Exchange Server.

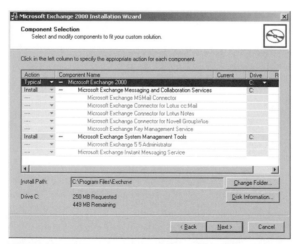

Figure 31-9. You must select the individual components to install and the location in which to install them.

The next step is to decide whether to create a new Exchange Server organization or to join or upgrade an existing Exchange Server 5.5 organization. This chapter's example installation assumes that this will be the first Exchange Server in the network and therefore creates a new organization. On the next wizard page, you must assign a name to the organization. The Exchange Server organization contains everything that will be interconnected on your network. Exchange Server systems in separate organizations can't communicate, except through SMTP. Finally, you must accept the license agreement again, as Exchange 2000 Server supports only per-seat licensing. The last page of the wizard is a summary of the options you just chose. Click Next to install Exchange 2000 Server.

During the installation of Exchange 2000 Server, you'll notice one of the insecurities caused by installing Active Directory using the Permissions Compatible With Pre-Windows 2000 Servers option, as shown in Figure 31-10: members of the built-in "Pre-Windows 2000 Compatible Access" group are able to see the members of hidden distribution groups.

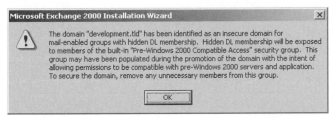

Figure 31-10. The wizard warns you that hidden distribution groups will be exposed to certain members if you selected the Permissions Compatible With Pre-Windows 2000 Servers option during the Active Directory installation.

On its final page, the wizard displays the status of the installation. The installer performs a number of actions, including installing files and modifying the Active Directory schema to integrate the features of Exchange.

Installing Exchange Server 5.5

Installing Exchange Server 5.5 is similar to installing Exchange 2000 Server, except that the requirements are Windows NT 4 with Service Pack 3 or later (although Service Pack 4 or later is recommended). If you want to install Outlook Web Access, you must install Internet Information Server 4. While Exchange 2000 Server relies on many features that are integrated into Windows 2000 Server, Exchange Server 5.5 is a more comprehensive package and therefore has simpler requirements and installation.

Upgrading to Exchange 2000 Server from Exchange Server 5.5

Upgrading from Exchange Server 5.5 to Exchange 2000 Server can be complicated, and each deployment is a little different. For that reason, this section covers only an overview of the required steps.

In the most basic example of such an upgrade, you might have a single Windows NT 4.0 Server running Exchange Server 5.5 that you want to upgrade to Exchange 2000 Server.

For that scenario, the basic steps to follow are these:

1 Ensure that the Exchange Server 5.5 has Service Pack 3 for Exchange or later installed.

2 Upgrade the server from Windows NT 4.0 to Windows 2000 Server and install Windows 2000 Service Pack 1 or later.

3 Install the Active Directory Connector (ADC) from the Exchange 2000 Server CD. This step is required in order to copy the data from the Exchange Server 5.5 directory into Active Directory so that Exchange 2000 Server will have access to it.

> **note** You can't use the Active Directory Connector included with Windows 2000 Server. Instead, you must use the ADC that comes with Exchange 2000 Server.

4 After you install the connector, the directory data should be replicated into Active Directory, and you can upgrade your Exchange Server 5.5 installation to Exchange 2000 Server.

> **note** Microsoft's Exchange 2000 Server Upgrade series covers upgrading to Exchange 2000 in detail and is available at *http://www.microsoft.com/technet/exchange/guide/default.asp*. The Guide to Upgrading from Exchange 5.5 Server to Exchange 2000 Server is available at *http://www.microsoft.com/technet/exchange/e2kguide.asp*.

Adding Mailboxes

You add mailboxes in Windows 2000 with Exchange 2000 Server at the same time that you add the user account (they are essentially the same object in Active Directory) from the Active Directory Users And Computers tool.

To add a mailbox, follow these steps:

1 Navigate to the Users container in the tree on the left of the Active Directory Users And Computers tool, right-click the Users container, and then choose New, User.

2 Enter the user's name information and logon name, as shown in Figure 31-11. The logon name for pre-Windows 2000 systems is generated automatically, but you can change it.

Figure 31-11. Specify the user's name and logon name.

3 Next, specify an initial password for the user, and select password options. Figure 31-12 on the next page shows this step.

---

tip If Account Is Disabled is selected, the mailbox will still be functional, but the user won't be able to log on to the domain using the account.

Part 7: Using and Administering Outlook with Exchange Server

Figure 31-12. Set an initial password and password options.

4 Next create the Exchange Server mailbox. Choose the server and mailbox
   store where the mailbox will reside, and then set the mailbox alias, as shown
   in Figure 31-13.

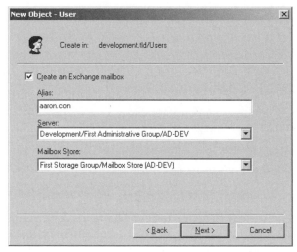

Figure 31-13. When Exchange Server is installed, you can create a mailbox.

5 You'll see a summary of the selections you have made. Click Finish to create
   the account and the mailbox.

As you can see, setting up a mailbox during the user creation process is optional. If a
user doesn't have a mailbox, however, the Exchange tabs will be missing from the user's
Properties dialog box.

Chapter 31: Exchange Server Overview and Setup

You can also create a mailbox by right-clicking the user and choosing Exchange Tasks to start the Exchange Task Wizard. On the Available Tasks page, choose Create Mailbox and click Next. Specify the mailbox alias, and choose the server and mailbox store where the mailbox will reside (see Figure 31-14).

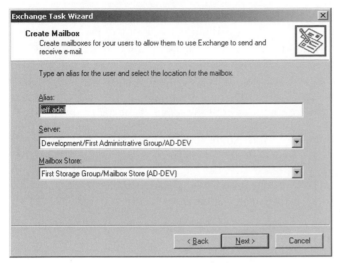

Figure 31-14. Specify the user's alias and a location for the mailbox.

The mailbox is created after you specify its configuration. Figure 31-15 shows the Task Summary page, which displays the results of the mailbox creation task.

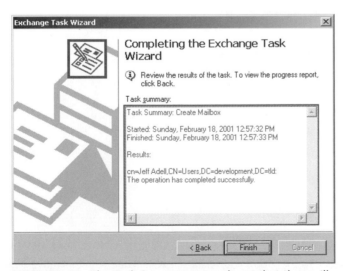

Figure 31-15. The Task Summary page shows that the mailbox was created.

Creating Distribution Groups

You create distribution lists in Exchange 2000 Server by assigning e-mail addresses to security groups or by creating special groups called distribution groups that aren't used for security purposes.

The easiest way to establish e-mail distribution to a group of users is to assign an e-mail address to a security group. It's preferable to assign the e-mail address to a universal group because the address will then be effective across the entire organization; global and local groups, in contrast, are limited in scope. It is possible, however, to assign addresses to global and local groups, and this might even be advantageous if you have only one domain or if you want to limit the scope of the distribution list.

To create a distribution list by assigning an e-mail address to a security group, follow these steps:

1 Open the Active Directory Users And Computers tool and locate the group to which you want to assign an address.

2 Right-click the group and choose Exchange Tasks to start the Exchange Task Wizard.

3 On the Available Tasks page (see Figure 31-16), select Establish An E-Mail Address and click Next.

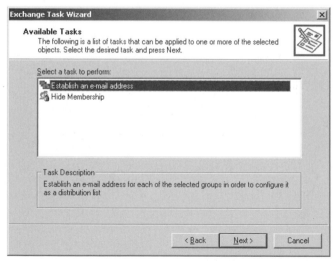

Figure 31-16. Select from the list of available Exchange Tasks.

4 Assign an alias to the group and select the Associated Administrative Group in which the group will reside, as shown in Figure 31-17.

Chapter 31: Exchange Server Overview and Setup

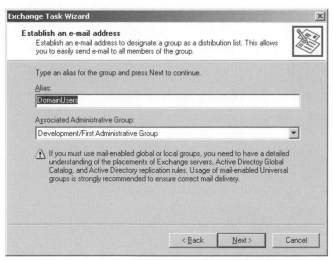

Figure 31-17. You must assign an alias to the group.

5 Click Next. The last page in the wizard displays a task summary showing the results of the operation. The distribution group should now appear in the Global Address List, and you should be able to send mail to it.

Troubleshooting

You can't create universal security groups.

When you install Windows 2000 Server, one of the decisions you must make is whether domain controllers need to support Windows NT servers and domain controllers. If you do have Windows NT servers and domains that access applications within the Windows 2000 domain, your Windows 2000 domains must operate in *mixed mode*.

You can't create universal security groups in a mixed mode domain, however. Instead, you must change your domains to *native mode*, which supports only Windows 2000 domain authentication. This means you must upgrade your existing Windows NT domains to Windows 2000 and Active Directory.

The second method of configuring mail distribution is through a distribution group. A distribution group is advantageous because you can assign an owner to the group who has the ability to control group membership.

To create a new distribution group, follow these steps:

1 Navigate to the Users container in the left pane of the Active Directory Users And Computers tool, right-click the Users container, and then choose New, Group.

Part 7: Using and Administering Outlook with Exchange Server

2 Specify the group name and select Distribution in the Group Type box (see
Figure 31-18). You can set the Group Scope option to Local, Global, or
Universal, but universal distribution groups are preferable because they're
more tolerant of the architecture of large Active Directory implantations. You
can have problems with mail delivery if you use local or global groups and
the Active Directory infrastructure isn't distributed properly.

Figure 31-18. You must specify the new group's name, scope, and type.

3 Specify the group's Exchange alias and the Administrative Group where it will
reside, as shown in Figure 31-19.

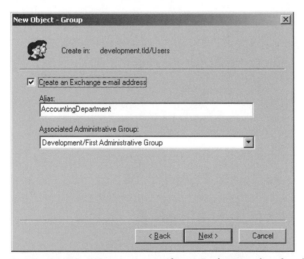

Figure 31-19. You must specify an Exchange alias for the new group.

4 A summary window displays the configuration options you have chosen. Click Finish to create the group. The group should now appear in the Global Address List and be able to accept e-mail.

Next it's time to populate the group with users. You can delegate the authority for populating a group and controlling group membership to a user. This eases the strain on administrators because they don't have to add and remove users every time a change occurs.

To populate a group with users, follow these steps:

1 Open the Active Directory Users And Computers tool and locate the distribution group.

2 Right-click the group, choose Properties, and then click the Managed By tab.

3 Click the Change button, and then select the user who will manage the group and click OK. Click OK again to close the Properties dialog box. The user assigned as the manager can now open Outlook and the Address Book.

4 Right-click the distribution group and choose Properties. The Properties dialog box shows the members of the group.

5 Click the Modify Members button. In the Distribution List Membership dialog box, you can change the group membership (see Figure 31-20). From this dialog box, you can add members, remove members, and view their properties.

Figure 31-20. Use this dialog box to change the membership of the group.

Creating Public Folders

Public folders are useful for sharing information and collaboration in Exchange Server and Outlook. They provide a central place to store information, such as tasks for an entire group. You can use the Exchange System Manager to create public folders, but they're easier to create using Outlook. An administrator must create public folders, unless the permissions on the Public Folders container in Exchange System Manager have been changed.

Follow these steps to create a public folder:

1 Open the folder list in Outlook.

2 Navigate to Public Folders, All Public Folders.

3 Right-click All Public Folders and choose New Folder.

4 Give the new folder a name and assign it a type, as shown in Figure 31-21.

5 Click OK to create the new folder.

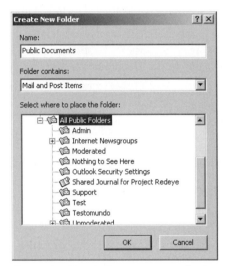

Figure 31-21. Assign a name and a type to a new public folder.

The new folder should now be accessible to everyone. By default, everyone is assigned Author permission. If you want to restrict access, you can change the permissions for the folder. To do so, right-click the newly created folder, choose Properties, and then click the Permissions tab. You can assign permissions to the users who require them, but if you assign owner permission to users, they will be able to delete the folder and change its permissions.

For detailed information about creating and managing public folders, see "Setting Up Public Folders," page 810.

Chapter 32

Configuring the Exchange Server Client

Although you can use Microsoft Outlook with other types of mail servers, you derive the greatest benefit when you use Outlook with Microsoft Exchange Server. Added benefits include the Out Of Office Assistant, the ability to recall messages, the ability to delegate functions to an assistant, and the use of server-side message rules.

You can connect to an Exchange Server using any of several protocols, including POP3, NNTP, IMAP, and even HTTP. This means two things: you can connect to an Exchange Server using e-mail clients other than Outlook (Outlook Express or Eudora, for example), and you can use a service provider other than the Exchange Server client within Outlook to connect to the server. To get all the benefits afforded by the combination of Outlook and Exchange Server, however, you must use the Exchange Server client provided with Outlook.

This chapter explains how to add the Exchange Server client to an Outlook profile and configure its settings.

For detailed information on adding other service providers to an Outlook profile, see Chapter 2, "Advanced Setup Tasks." You'll find additional information on setting up Internet e-mail accounts in Chapter 6, "Using Internet Mail."

Outlook as an Exchange Server Client

The Microsoft Exchange Server service in Outlook allows you to use Outlook as a client for Exchange Server. Of all the services supported by Outlook, Exchange Server offers the broadest range of functionality, providing excellent support for collaboration, information sharing, group scheduling, and more.

> The remaining chapters in Part 7, "Using and Administering Outlook with Exchange Server," cover a broad range of topics to help you use Outlook effectively as an Exchange Server client.

Setting up an Exchange Server account in Outlook isn't difficult but does require several steps, as follows:

1 In the Outlook 2002 Startup Wizard, move to the Server Type page. To reach the Server Type page if your profile already includes a mail account, right-click the Outlook icon on the desktop and choose Properties. Then click E-Mail Accounts, click Add A New E-Mail Account, and click Next.

2 Select Microsoft Exchange Server and then click Next.

3 On the Exchange Server Settings page, specify the following information:

■ **Microsoft Exchange Server.** Specify the NetBIOS or Domain Name Service (DNS) name of your Exchange Server or its IP address. You don't have to include a double backslash (\\) before the server name.

■ **User Name.** Specify the name of your mailbox on the server. You can specify your logon account name or mailbox name. For example, my logon account is *jboyce* and my mailbox is *Jim Boyce*.

■ **Check Name.** After you enter your logon or mailbox name, click Check Name to check the specified account information against the information on the server. If you specify your logon name, clicking Check Name automatically changes the user name to your mailbox name. Outlook indicates a successful check by underlining the user name.

4 Click More Settings to open the Microsoft Exchange Server dialog box (see Figure 32-1).

5 Configure the options in the dialog box according to the information in the following sections.

Chapter 32: Configuring the Exchange Server Client

Figure 32-1.   Use the Microsoft Exchange Server dialog box to configure additional options.

Troubleshooting

You're having problems logging on.

If your local logon credentials are different from the account credentials on your Exchange Server, you'll receive an error message stating that you don't have permission to open the folders for your mailbox unless you change the authentication scheme. Click More Settings, click Advanced, and then select None in the Logon Network Security drop-down list. This allows you to specify the appropriate account credentials for the Exchange Server.

If your local logon credentials match your Exchange Server account credentials, you can use the Password Authentication option and bypass the need to enter your account name and password. Or simply change your local logon account and password to match the Exchange Server account, if possible.

Configuring General Properties

You use the General tab of the Microsoft Exchange Server dialog box (refer back to Figure 32-1) to configure the account name, the connection state, and other general settings, as follows:

- **Exchange Account.** Specify the name under which the account appears in your Outlook configuration. This name has no bearing on the Exchange Server name or your account name. For example, you might name the account *Office E-Mail*, *Work Account*, or *Microsoft Exchange Server*.

- **Automatically Detect Connection State.** Direct Outlook to detect the connection state (offline or online) at startup and choose the appropriate state. Use this option if your computer is connected to the network all the time. Use this option also if you're setting up an Exchange Server account on a notebook computer under a profile you use when the notebook is connected to the network.

- **Manually Control Connection State.** Control the connection state at startup. Use this option if you're setting up an Exchange Server account on a computer that is sometimes disconnected from the network (a notebook computer, for example) or that always accesses the Exchange Server remotely. See the following three options for more information.

- **Choose The Connection Type When Starting.** Choose which method Outlook uses to connect to the Exchange Server at startup. If this option is selected, Outlook prompts you each time it starts, asking whether you want to connect to the network or work offline. Clear this option if you want Outlook to make that determination.

- **Connect With The Network.** Connect to your Exchange Server through the network rather than initiating a dial-up connection. Use this option if your computer is hardwired to the network or always online, such as with a DSL, cable modem, or other persistent remote connection.

- **Work Offline And Use Dial-Up Networking.** Use Dial-Up Networking to connect to the Exchange Server. Specify the connection options on the Connection tab.

For information about setting connection options, see "Configuring Connection Properties," page 783.

- **Seconds Until Server Connection Timeout.** Specify the timeout for connection attempts to the Exchange Server. If you are working remotely over a slow connection, increase this value to give Outlook more time to establish the connection to the server.

Increase TCP Timeout for Shared Connections

If you use Internet Connection Sharing (ICS) or demand-dial router connections, you've no doubt had your client computer time out while waiting for the ICS or demand-dial router to establish a connection. This can cause a remote connection to the Exchange Server to fail.

TCP sets a retransmission timer when it attempts the first data transmission for a connection, with an initial retransmission timeout value of 3 seconds. TCP doubles the retransmission timeout value for each subsequent connection attempt, and by default attempts retransmission two times. The first attempt is made at 3 seconds, the second at 3 + 6 seconds, and the third at 3 + 6 + 12 seconds, for a maximum timeout of 21 seconds. Increasing the initial retransmission timer to 5 seconds results in a total maximum timeout of 5 + 10 + 20, or 35 seconds.

For Microsoft Windows 2000 and Windows NT 4.0 clients, the initial TCP retransmission timeout is defined by the registry value HKEY_LOCAL_MACHINE\System\CurrentControlSet\Services\Tcpip\Parameters\InitialRtt. The InitialRtt value is a REG_DWORD with a valid range from 0 to 65535 and specifies the timeout in milliseconds.

The number of connection attempts is defined by the registry setting HKEY_LOCAL_MACHINE\System\CurrentControlSet\Services\Tcpip\Parameters\TcpMaxDataRetransmissions. The TcpMaxDataRetransmissions value is also a REG_DWORD with a valid range of 0 to 65535.

Configuring Advanced Properties

You use the Advanced tab of the Microsoft Exchange Server dialog box (see Figure 32-2 on the next page) to configure additional mailboxes to open as well as security and offline processing settings. Why use additional mailboxes? You might own two mailboxes on the server and need access to both of them. For example, if you are the system administrator, you probably have your own account and need to manage it as well as the Administrator account. Or perhaps you've been delegated as an assistant for a set of mailboxes and need to access them to manage someone's schedule. The Advanced tab is where you add additional mailboxes that you own or for which you've been granted delegate access.

Figure 32-2. Use the Advanced tab to configure additional mailboxes and security settings.

The options on the Advanced tab follow:

- **Open These Additional Mailboxes.** Define the set of mailboxes you want Outlook to open. These can be mailboxes that you own or for which you've been granted delegate access.

- **Encrypt Information.** Determine whether Outlook uses encryption to secure transmission between your system and the server. Select When Using The Network to encrypt data when you're connected to the server through a network connection. Select When Using Dial-Up Networking to encrypt data while you're connected by a dial-up connection. You can select both.

- **Logon Network Security.** Specify the type of authentication to use when connecting to the Exchange Server. The Password Authentication option causes Exchange Server to use NTLM (NT LAN Manager) challenge/ response to authenticate on the server using your current logon account credentials. This is the standard authentication mechanism in NT domains. Distributed Password Authentication (DPA) is a challenge/response authentication protocol that uses passwords and a trusted authentication server to authenticate logons. DPA maps a generic user name in the domain to a set of users maintained in a database. Select DPA if your server uses Microsoft Membership Directory Services for authentication. Selecting None causes Outlook to prompt you for the account and password.

- **Offline Folder File Settings.** Set up an offline folder (OST) file to use as your data cache while working offline. You need to use an OST file only if the account is configured to store your data in your Exchange Server mailbox. If your primary data file is a personal folders (PST) file, or if you don't work offline, you don't need an OST file.

782

To learn how to configure personal folder files and offline storage using OST files, see "Controlling Where Outlook Stores Exchange Server Messages and Data," page 785.

Troubleshooting

You have different passwords locally and on the domain, and you can't open your mailbox.

Outlook prompts you to specify the logon credentials and domain if your current logon credentials differ from the account credentials on the server or in its domain (see Figure 32-3). For example, assume that you use the name *jimb* for your local logon, but your domain account is *jboyce,* and each has its own password. In that case, you must set up Outlook to use None as the authentication scheme, which causes it to prompt you as shown in Figure 32-3.

Figure 32-3. Outlook prompts for logon credentials if your current credentials differ from those on the server or its domain.

If your user account is the same locally and on the Exchange Server but the passwords are different, however, you'll receive an error message indicating that Outlook can't open the mailbox. This occurs because Outlook is trying to use your local logon password, not the password from the server. You can fix this in one of two ways. Either change your local password to match your password on the server (use the Passwords icon in Control Panel), or configure the properties for the account to use None as the authentication method. This will cause Outlook to prompt you for the credentials for the server. Specify the account and password on the server, not your local password.

Configuring Connection Properties

The Connection tab of the Microsoft Exchange Server dialog box (see Figure 32-4 on the next page) allows you to specify how your computer connects to the Exchange Server. You can connect through the local area network (LAN), through Dial-Up Networking, or through a third-party dialer such as the one included with Microsoft Internet Explorer. The LAN connection option applies if you're connecting over a hardwired connection—for example, when your computer is connected to the same network as the server. You should also use the LAN option if you connect to the server over a shared dial-up connection hosted by another computer.

Figure 32-4. Use the Connection tab to specify how Outlook connects to the Exchange Server.

Click Connect Using My Phone Line to use an existing Dial-Up Networking connection or to create a new dial-up connection. Select the desired connection from the drop-down list, and then click Properties if you need to modify the dial-up connection. Click Add if you need to add a dial-up connection.

If you need help configuring and using dial-up connections, see "Configuring Dial-Up Networking Options," page 147.

If you want to connect to the Internet or your remote network using the dialer included with Internet Explorer or a dialer included with a third-party dial-up client, click Connect Using Internet Explorer's Or A 3rd Party Dialer.

Configuring Remote Mail Properties

You can use the Remote Mail tab of the Microsoft Exchange Server dialog box (see Figure 32-5) to configure how Outlook processes messages for your Exchange Server account through remote mail.

With remote mail you can download message headers without downloading the message body or attachments, which allows you to review messages without downloading them. This is particularly useful if you have a message with a very large attachment waiting for download and you have a slow connection to the server. Being able to preview messages through remote mail and optionally delete messages without downloading them is also useful when you have a corrupted message in your message store that is preventing you from downloading your messages normally.

The following list explains the options on the Remote Mail tab:

- **Process Marked Items.** Retrieve items you have marked for download.

- **Retrieve Items That Meet The Following Conditions.** Retrieve only items that meet the conditions defined by the specified filter (see following item.)

- **Filter.** Click to open the Filter dialog box in which you specify conditions the message must meet for Outlook to download it from the server.

- **Disconnect After Connection is Finished.** Disconnect from the server after Outlook finishes updating headers and transferring items.

For detailed information about remote mail, see Chapter 13, "Processing Messages Selectively."

Figure 32-5. Use the Remote Mail tab to configure how Outlook processes messages through remote mail.

Controlling Where Outlook Stores Exchange Server Messages and Data

When you create an Exchange Server account, Outlook defaults to storing your data in your Exchange Server mailbox. However, you can add a PST file to store your data, including Calendar, Contacts, e-mail folders, and other folders. This capability is different from using an OST file as an offline cache. You should understand the ramifications of changing your storage location before doing so.

For information about the default folder location where Outlook creates store files under each operating system, see "Where Storage Files Are Located," page 15.

If you maintain your data on the Exchange Server, chances are good that the Exchange Server system administrator backs up your data on a regular basis. Your local system, however, might not be backed up as frequently, if at all, unless you perform the backup yourself or your workstation is included in a regular network backup strategy. Therefore, if you use a PST file to store your data and that file becomes corrupted or lost, you could lose all your e-mail, contacts, and other information unless you have a backup.

> **note** If you add an Exchange Server account to a profile that already contains a POP3 account, Outlook uses the current store location defined by the profile for Exchange Server. This means your data is stored in the local PST file rather than in your Exchange Server mailbox. Therefore, you should check and perhaps change the location after adding the Exchange Server account.

The best solution is to use your Exchange Server mailbox as the primary storage location and use the OST file for offline storage. This strategy not only allows your data to be backed up easily by the Exchange Server system administrator but also gives you the ability to work offline. Plus, your offline data store can act as a backup for your online store. Perhaps most important, however, is that other users will be able to access your calendar, contacts, and other information more easily (subject to the permissions you set) than if your store were located on your local computer or in a network share.

> **tip** If you use other accounts in the same profile as Exchange Server, you might want to reconfigure the location where messages from your other accounts are stored. Also, you might want to use message rules to automatically move messages between folders and stores. For detailed help on setting up and using rules, see "Using Rules to Move Messages Between Accounts," page 247.

If you decide that you want to change the location where Outlook stores your data—either to point it to a local file or to restore your Exchange Server mailbox as the location—you can do so by changing the properties for your account.

Follow these steps to configure the storage location for your data:

1 If Outlook is open, choose Tools, E-Mail Accounts to open the E-Mail Accounts Wizard. If Outlook is not open, right-click the Outlook icon on the desktop and choose Properties, and then click E-Mail Accounts.

2 Select View Or Change Existing E-Mail Accounts and click Next.

3 If you don't need to create the other PST file (it already exists), go to step 7. Otherwise, click New Outlook Data File.

4 Click Add, select the type of store file to create, and click OK.

Chapter 32: Configuring the Exchange Server Client

5 Specify the name and location for the file and click OK.

6 In the Create Microsoft Personal Folders dialog box (see Figure 32-6), specify properties based on the following list:

- **Name.** Specify the name under which you want the folders to appear in Outlook. This is not the file name for the store file, but you can use the same name for both if you want.

- **Encryption Setting.** Specify the encryption level for the folder file. Click No Encryption if you don't want Outlook to encrypt your PST file. Click Compressible Encryption if you want Outlook to encrypt the file with a format that allows compression to conserve space. Note, however, that Outlook does not compress the file. Instead, you must use the compression capabilities offered by your operating system (such as NTFS compression) or by a third-party application. Choose Best Encryption for highest security. PST files formatted using Best Encryption can be compressed but not as efficiently as those that use Compressible Encryption.

- **Password.** Specify an optional password to protect your PST file from access by others.

- **Save This Password In Your Password List.** Save the password for your PST file in your local password cache, eliminating the need for you to enter the password each time you open the PST file. Clear this option if you want Outlook to prompt you each time (which provides greater security).

Figure 32-6. Specify settings for the PST file.

> **tip** It's possible for others to gain access to your PST file and bypass the optional password, even if your data file is configured to use compression. For best security, keep your sensitive data on the Exchange Server rather than in a PST file. Or use NTFS permissions to secure the folder where your PST file is located, granting applicable permissions only to users who need access to that folder or your PST file.

7 Click OK to create the file.

8 Click Close to close the Outlook Data Files dialog box.

9 In the Deliver New E-Mail To The Following Location drop-down list, select the location where you want your data stored. Your Exchange Server mailbox appears in the list as Mailbox—*<name>*, where *<name>* is the name of your mailbox on the Exchange Server.

10 Click Finish to complete the change. Outlook informs you that you've changed the default location for mail delivery as well as the storage location for your other standard Outlook folders.

11 Click OK and restart Outlook for the change to take effect.

12 When Outlook prompts you (see Figure 32-7) to allow it to re-create the shortcuts on the Outlook Bar, click Yes to rebuild the Outlook Bar or No to leave it as is. (When you change the default storage location for your data, the shortcuts on the Outlook Bar become obsolete.)

> **note** If you have custom shortcuts on the Outlook Bar, those shortcuts are deleted when Outlook rebuilds the Outlook Bar, but you can re-create them afterward. If you don't want to have to re-create them, you can click No when prompted about rebuilding the Outlook Bar. However, you'll have to manually re-create the shortcuts to the default Outlook items, which is generally more trouble than manually re-creating your custom shortcuts.

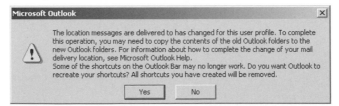

Figure 32-7. Unless you need to maintain existing custom shortcuts, allow Outlook to re-create your Outlook Bar.

Chapter 33

Messaging with Exchange Server

Messaging with Microsoft Exchange Server is a highly complex process. Mail routing decisions, for example, are based on a large number of factors. When an e-mail message is sent in Exchange 2000 Server, it is placed in the message store and queued for routing. Then the message is routed to a queue for local delivery or for remote delivery, depending on whether or not the recipient is on the same mailbox store as the sender. The message is delivered by SMTP to Internet mail systems or other Exchange 2000 Servers, by Exchange Connector to any system that is connected by one, or by X.400 or Remote Procedure Calls (RPC) to an Exchange Server 5.5.

This chapter focuses on some common messaging topics that are related specifically to Exchange Server, such as recalling sent messages, setting messages to expire, and working with the Global Address List. This chapter also covers voting, which is another feature that relies on Exchange Server. The discussion assumes that you're using Microsoft Outlook for messaging with Exchange Server. Other chapters cover many topics that are more specifically applicable to Outlook's messaging capabilities. For example, see Chapter 7, "Sending and Receiving Messages," to learn about message composition, replies, and using send/receive groups to synchronize your Exchange Server mailbox.

> **note** To learn more about message routing in Exchange Server, you can read the white paper "Understanding Message Routing in Microsoft Exchange 2000 Server," at *http://www.microsoft.com/Exhange/techinfo/Routing.htm*.

Storing Messages

Exchange Server stores e-mail messages (as well as other objects such as tasks and calendar items) in the mailbox store. Exchange 2000 Server allows multiple mailbox stores on a single server, which provides a number of advantages, especially in larger sites. Several single stores are more manageable than one large store, making backups and restores faster. In addition, the failure of one store affects only the users on that store.

The mailbox store is a fully transactional database (like Microsoft SQL Server) based on the Microsoft JET database engine. Because it is a transactional database, it uses both a database and *transaction logs,* which store each transaction before it is committed to the database.

You can use transaction logs to roll back or recommit the database if a problem arises. If the last database backup was 8 hours ago, for example, a full restore of the database after a crash would lose 8 hours of information. But if the transaction logs were stored on a separate physical device and were not lost during the crash, they could be applied to the restored database to recover the data written to the database since the backup. Transaction logs are normally removed when a good backup is completed.

> To learn how to create accounts and designate the location for incoming messages, see "Configuring Accounts and Services," page 40.

Although you can also store e-mail messages locally in an Outlook personal folders (PST) file, this method is not recommended because the data is backed up only when the user's workstation is backed up.

> For detailed information on configuring the storage location for an Exchange Server account, see "Controlling Where Outlook Stores Exchange Server Messages and Data," page 785.

Sending Messages

When you send messages in Outlook while connected to an Exchange Server, you have more options than you do when you use a regular Internet mail account—for example, you have the ability to recall messages, and you have access to a Global Address List.

To send a new message, you have three choices:

- In the Inbox or another message folder, click the New toolbar button.
- Choose File, New, Mail Message.
- Click the arrow beside the New toolbar button and choose Mail Message.

Whichever method you use, a new message form opens, as shown in Figure 33-1.

Set your message options
within the message form

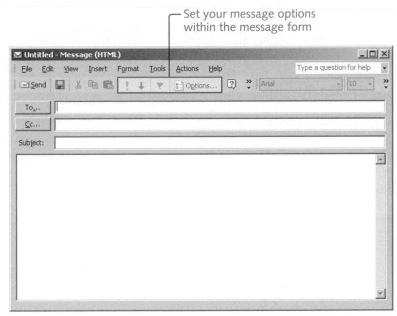

Figure 33-1. Write a message and choose the options for this message using the standard message form.

Addressing Messages

You can designate the recipients of your message in two ways. The first method is to click the To or Cc button to open the Select Names dialog box (see Figure 33-2). By default, the Global Address List is displayed.

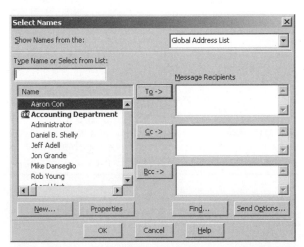

Figure 33-2. The Select Names dialog box displays the available address books.

The Global Address List (GAL) contains all users in the entire organization, except those who are explicitly hidden. You can define other address lists in the Exchange 2000 Server System Manager to filter addresses by any criteria, such as location.

To add a message recipient, select the recipient from the list on the left and then click the To, Cc, or Bcc button. Clicking the Properties button will display the recipient's properties so that you can verify his or her contact information.

One of the most useful features of the Select Names dialog box is the Find feature. Click the Find button to open the Find dialog box, shown in Figure 33-3. You can search the address book by any of the criteria shown, such as Title, Company, or Department. The ability to search the address book is most useful when you have a large organization and no address lists are defined.

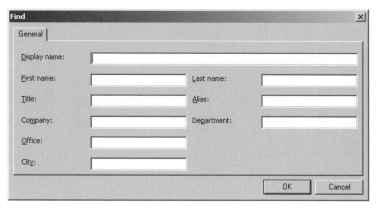

Figure 33-3. You can search the address list for recipients matching specific criteria.

The second way to add recipients to a message is the simplest: type the recipient's name or alias in the To or Cc box on the message form. An Exchange alias is another way of referring to an account. In most cases, an alias is the same as a user's Windows user name.

---

tip   **Cut your typing time**

You don't have to type the complete name or alias in the To or Cc box, as long as the part of the name you type is unique. For example, if only one name in the address book matches *Bob*, you can type **Bob** as the recipient, even if the recipient's name is Bob Smith and the alias is *bob.smith*. If the recipient's name is Robert Smith and the alias is *bob.smith*, you can type either **Rob** or **bob**—both will resolve to Robert Smith.

Checking Names

As soon as you finish typing a recipient's name and move the cursor out of the box, Outlook checks the name. If the name is not unique or can't be found, it is underlined in red. When this occurs, you'll need to manually check the name.

You can also check a recipient's name by clicking Check Names on the message toolbar or by pressing Ctrl+K. When a problem arises, a dialog box opens and indicates whether the name is not unique or not found. When the name is not unique, all matches are displayed so that you can make a selection.

> **tip** If the name you typed is causing a problem, check the spelling of the name. This sounds simple enough, but a small mistake can prevent the name from being resolved. You might need to use the Global Address List or another address list to find the correct name.

Setting Message Importance and Sensitivity

When you set the level of importance for a message, an icon indicating the level is displayed by default in the mailbox folder of the message recipients (although they can remove the Importance field from the display). By default, messages are sent with normal importance and display no icon. Messages designated with a High importance level have a red exclamation mark, and messages with Low importance are displayed with a blue down arrow.

You can set the importance level (or priority level) of a message in two ways. You can click either the red exclamation mark or the blue down arrow on the message toolbar (refer to Figure 33-1 on page 791). If you click either button again, the message returns to normal importance. Or, if Word is not your e-mail editor, in the message you can choose View, Options or click the Options button to open the Message Options dialog box (see Figure 33-4 on the next page). Then make your selection in the Importance drop-down list.

InsideOut

Changing the importance level of a message does more than simply change the way the message is displayed to the recipient. Many types of mail transports such as X.400 use the message importance level as a metric for determining the routing of messages. Messages with High importance are given a higher priority in the queue and are sent before Low importance messages. (Actually, the process is more complex than that, but the intricacies of mail routing are beyond the scope of this book.) It is poor etiquette to send all your messages with High priority set, however; if you overuse the setting, recipients will start to ignore the importance settings completely.

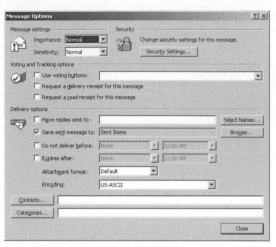

Figure 33-4. Set the importance and sensitivity in the Message Settings area of the Message Options dialog box.

Message sensitivity, like message importance, appears as a flag on the message that the recipient sees. By default, message sensitivity is not shown in Outlook's message folder views. (You can add it to the view, of course, by choosing View, Current View, Customize Current View and using the Show Fields dialog box.) However, if the message sensitivity is not set to Normal (the default), Outlook does display the sensitivity level when the message is opened or viewed in the preview pane. You can set one of four levels of sensitivity—Normal, Personal, Private, or Confidential—in the Sensitivity drop-down list in the Message Options dialog box (see Figure 33-4).

Redirecting Replies

If for some reason you don't want to receive the reply to your message, you can have the reply sent to someone else.

To redirect a reply, follow these steps:

1 Choose View, Options or click the Options button on the message toolbar to open the Message Options dialog box.

2 Select the Have Replies Sent To check box, and your name (the sender) is added as a recipient in the text box.

3 Delete your name from the box and either type each recipient's name (separated by semicolons) or click the Select Names button to select the names from the address book. Select each name in the list, click Reply To, and then click OK to have Outlook add those names to the Have Replies Sent To box. Click Close to save these options.

Each recipient listed in the Have Replies Sent To box receives any replies to the selected message. Figure 33-5 shows the Message Options dialog box with redirected replies.

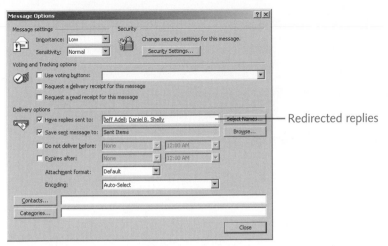

Figure 33-5. Replies to your message will now be sent not to you but to the listed recipients.

Using Delivery and Read Receipts

Delivery and read receipts are useful tracking features. The delivery receipt is sent to you when the message is delivered. The read receipt is sent when the message's status changes from unread to read. (This status can change automatically in the preview pane, when the recipient opens the message, or when the recipient right-clicks the message and chooses Mark As Read.) Delivery and read receipts are not supported on all mail clients. Most mail clients that do support them allow the user (that is, the recipient) to choose not to send receipts, so you can't always rely on these receipts to confirm what you need to know. Figure 33-6 shows an example of a delivery receipt.

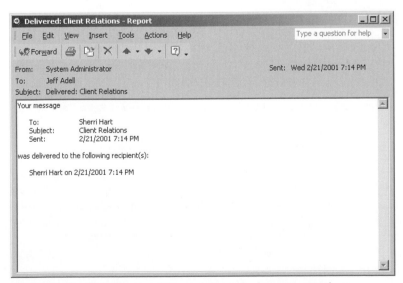

Figure 33-6. Delivery receipts are returned when requested.

795

To set a delivery receipt, a read receipt, or both for a message, follow these steps:

1 In the message form, choose View, Options or click the Options toolbar button to open the Message Options dialog box (see Figure 33-7).

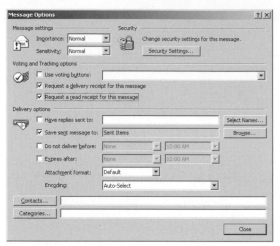

Figure 33-7. You can request receipts in the Message Options dialog box.

2 Select the Request A Delivery Receipt For This Message option, the Request A Read Receipt For This Message option, or both.

3 Click the Close button.

You can set up your mail to request delivery and read receipts by default for each message you send out.

To do so, follow these steps:

1 Choose Tools, Options to open the Options dialog box.

2 On the Preferences tab, click E-Mail Options. Then click the Tracking Options button to open the Tracking Options dialog box.

3 In the For All Messages I Send, Request option, select Read Receipt, Delivery Receipt, or both.

4 Click OK three times to close the three dialog boxes.

---

tip In the Tracking Options dialog box, you can prevent Outlook from sending out read receipts to the senders of messages you receive. You can also direct Outlook to move any receipts to a specified folder.

Saving Messages

By default, Outlook saves messages you send by placing copies of the messages in the Sent Items folder. New outgoing messages are also saved to the Drafts folder every three minutes. You can change the defaults for both of these behaviors. You can also, of course, override these defaults for a specific message when necessary.

To change these default message behaviors for saving drafts and saving sent items, follow these steps:

1 Create your message.

2 Choose View, Options or click the Options toolbar button to open the Message Options dialog box.

3 To change the folder where the sent message is saved, click the Browse button and select the folder. Or, if you don't want to save the sent message, clear the Save Sent Message To check box.

4 Click OK to close the Message Options dialog box.

To specify how new unsent messages should be automatically saved, follow these steps:

1 Choose Tools, Options.

2 On the Preferences tab, click E-Mail Options, and then click Advanced E-Mail Options.

3 Select the folder in which unsent items should be saved, turn AutoSave on or off, and set the AutoSave interval.

4 Click OK to close each of the dialog boxes.

Controlling When Messages Are Delivered

When a message is sent, it is delivered immediately by default. You can, however, delay message delivery until a specified time. To do so, choose View, Options or click the Options toolbar button to open the Message Options dialog box. Select the Do Not Deliver Before check box and then set the date and time using the drop-down lists. Because delayed sending is a feature of Exchange Server, you can close Outlook as soon as you click the Send button.

Setting Messages to Expire

Just as you can delay the delivery of a message, you can also set a message to expire. The message expires and is removed from the recipient's mailbox after a specified period of time whether or not it has been read. You might want to have a message expire if its contents become stale after a certain amount of time or if you want to ensure that the message is deleted. To set this option, open the Message Options dialog box, select Expires After, and then set a date and time. The message will no longer be available to the recipient after that time.

Linking a Contact Item to a Message

When sending an e-mail to a friend or colleague, it's sometimes useful to link contact information to provide a reference to the message as well as a way to sort and filter the message. For example, sales representatives who share information about client relations might want to provide a way of sorting this information. To link a contact item to a message, open the Message Options dialog box and click the Contacts button. Select the contact to link and then click OK. The recipient can now view the contact information in the Message Options dialog box for the received message or in a message view if that view displays the contacts field.

Assigning a Category to a Message

You assign a category to a message by clicking the Categories button in the Message Options dialog box. You can use the Master Category List to assign any relevant categories to the message. These categories can be used for sorting, grouping, and filtering messages.

> For complete information about assigning and working with categories, see Chapter 4, "Using Categories and Types."

Recalling a Sent Message Before It's Read

There are many reasons why you might want to recall a message. For example, perhaps the message contains a mistake or is now obsolete. You can recall a message you have sent as long as the recipient has not read it and the message is still stored on an Exchange Server. Messages sent to recipients using other mail servers cannot be recalled.

To recall a sent message, double-click the message in the Sent Items folder to open it. Choose Action, Recall This Message to open the dialog box shown in Figure 33-8. Select whether you want to simply delete all unread copies of the message or delete them and replace them with another message. You can also receive a response reporting the success or failure of each recall attempt.

> **caution**   For a number of reasons, sometimes unread messages cannot be recalled.

Figure 33-8. This dialog box is displayed when you attempt to recall a message.

Copying Global Addresses to Your Contacts Folder

You can easily copy addresses from the Global Address List to your Contacts folder by following these steps:

1 Choose Tools, Address Book.

2 Click the address you want to add to your Contacts folder.

3 Choose File, Add To Personal Address Book or click the Add To Personal Address Book toolbar button. The entry from the GAL opens in a contact form.

4 Make any necessary changes.

5 Click Save And Close. The contact information is now in your Contacts folder.

Adding External Addresses to the Global Address List

All *mail-enabled* users and groups—those who have a mailbox and have been assigned an address—are placed in the Global Address List. If you want to add others, such as those outside the organization, to the GAL, you must make them mail-enabled contacts. (Mail-enabled contacts are the equivalent of Custom Recipients in Exchange Server 5.5.)

To create a mail-enabled contact, follow these steps:

1 In the Active Directory Users And Computers snap-in, right-click the container to which the contact should be added (usually the Users container), and then choose New, Contact.

2 Enter the contact name information and click Next.

3 On the wizard page shown in Figure 33-9, click the Modify button to add an e-mail address associated with the contact.

Figure 33-9. If you add an Exchange Server e-mail address for a contact external to the organization, that contact appears in the GAL.

4 Select the address type, which is usually SMTP unless other Exchange 2000 Server connectors are installed, and specify the address. Click OK.

5 Click Next and then click Finish to create the mail-enabled contact. After a few moments, the new mail-enabled contact appears in the GAL.

Restricting Access to the Global Address List

If you're an administrator, you can set access to the Global Address List. You might want to do this if you provide specific address lists for groups of users and want to restrict them from seeing users in the entire organization.

To restrict access to the GAL, follow these steps:

1 Open Exchange System Manager and navigate to Recipients, All Global Address Lists.

2 Right-click Default Global Address List and choose Properties.

3 Click the Security tab. The security settings for the various users and groups are listed in this tab.

4 By default, the Authenticated Users group has List Contents permission. Click to remove this permission, thus removing access to the GAL for all users except those for whom access is explicitly granted.

Voting in Outlook

Another feature in Outlook that takes advantage of Exchange Server is voting. Outlook's voting feature is useful when you want to solicit input from a group of message recipients. Perhaps you are looking for approval on a proposal, holding an informal election in your organization, or just want to get the group's input on an issue.

With the voting feature, you solicit and tally votes from the group. Outlook provides predefined voting responses, but you can also create your own. In this section, you'll learn how to include voting buttons on messages, tally returned votes, and configure voting options.

Here's how voting works in general: You create a message containing the question or document on which the group will be voting. Next, you add voting buttons to the message. Then you send the message. Recipients cast their vote by clicking the appropriate button. Outlook prompts them to confirm the vote and then sends the reply message back to you.

Sending a Message for a Vote

Sending a message for a vote is simple. In fact, as long as you want to use one of Outlook's default set of voting options, the process takes only a few clicks.

Using the Default Voting Responses

Use the following steps to create a message and add voting buttons to it:

1 Open Outlook and start a new message or open an existing message from your Drafts folder.

2 Click the Options toolbar button to open the Message Options dialog box.

3 In the Voting And Tracking Options area, select Use Voting Buttons. In the drop-down list, select the group of voting buttons you want to include (see Figure 33-10 on the next page).

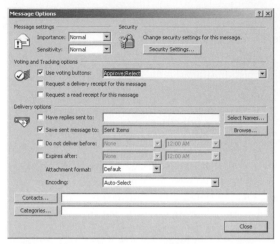

Figure 33-10. You select voting buttons in the Message Options dialog box.

4 Click Close.

5 Make any final changes to the message, including adding an attachment or
configuring message options such as importance level.

6 Click Send to send the message.

Using Custom Responses

Outlook doesn't limit you to the default sets of voting options (such as Accept/Reject).
You can create your own set that includes the responses you need for any situation. For
example, suppose you're planning a company appreciation banquet and need to final-
ize the menu. You want to give everyone a choice of entree and collect those responses
for the caterer. What better way to do it than electronically through Outlook?

Here's how:

1 Compose your message.

2 Click Options to open the Message Options dialog box.

3 Select Use Voting Buttons.

4 Click the text portion of the Use Voting Buttons drop-down list, making sure
to highlight the existing text. Type your custom vote options separated by
semicolons, as shown in Figure 33-11.

Chapter 33

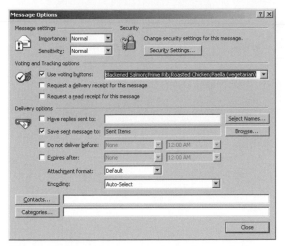

Figure 33-11.   You can create custom vote responses.

5 Click Close.

6 Make any final adjustments to the message as needed.

7 Click Send.

Casting Your Vote

When you receive a message that includes voting buttons, the response buttons appear
on the message form between the header and the toolbar (see Figure 33-12). In addition, Outlook displays a message in the preview pane, if it's open, to prompt you to
vote (see Figure 33-13 on the next page).

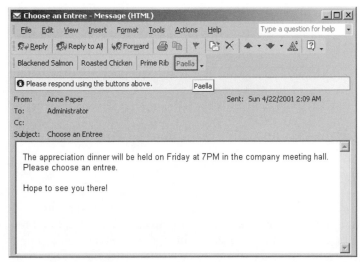

Figure 33-12.   Click a button on the message form to vote.

Chapter 33

803

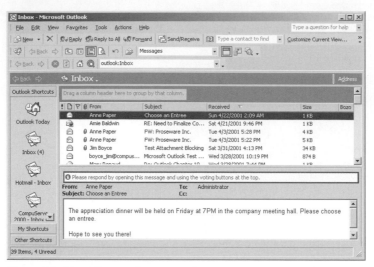

Figure 33-13. The preview pane shows a message prompting you to vote.

> **tip** Want to vote without opening the message? Simply right-click the message header and choose your vote response from the shortcut menu.

Voting is easy: just click a button to cast your vote. Outlook displays a simple dialog box asking whether you want to send the vote now or edit your response. To send the message without modification, select Send The Response Now. To cast your vote and open the message as a reply so that you can include text in your response, select Edit The Response Before Sending.

> **tip** Outlook doesn't automatically close the message window when you cast a vote, which makes it easy to accidentally vote more than once. You must close the message window manually.

When you cast a vote, Outlook changes the subject of the message to include your vote. For example, if the original subject is Choose An Entree and you click the Blackened Salmon button, the subject of the reply returned to the sender is Blackened Salmon: Choose An Entree.

Viewing and Sorting Votes

Votes come back to you in the form of messages. You can view the vote summary in a few ways. If the preview pane is displayed, you can click the message and then click the summary message in the InfoBar, as shown in Figure 33-14. Or you can open the Sent Items folder, open the original message, and click the Tracking tab. Either method displays the Tracking tab, shown in Figure 33-15.

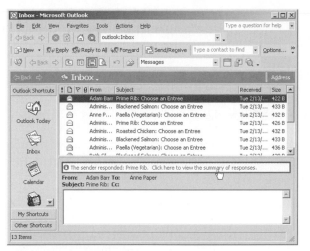

Figure 33-14. Click the summary message in the InfoBar to display the Tracking tab.

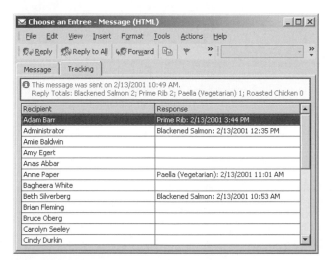

Figure 33-15. Open the message from the Sent Items folder as an alternative way to access the Tracking tab.

InsideOut

Don't rely on Outlook as a voting tool for crucial questions. It is an acceptable tool, however, for such issues as choosing entrees and polling for parking problems. Also understand that although you can vote more than once, only your first vote is recorded. This can be confusing if you aren't expecting that behavior; also, note that the voting buttons are not removed after you vote.

The Tracking tab summarizes the votes, with individual responses displayed one per line. The responses are also totaled in the InfoBar. If you want a printout of the vote responses, print the messages with the Tracking tab open.

Unfortunately, Outlook doesn't give you a way to sort the vote tally. You can, however, copy the data to Microsoft Excel to sort it.

To copy voting data to Excel, follow these steps:

1 Select the rows you want to copy. (Select a row and hold down the Shift key to select contiguous responses, or hold down the Ctrl key to select noncontiguous ones.)

2 Press Ctrl+C to copy the data to the clipboard.

3 Open Excel.

4 Select a cell in Excel and then press Ctrl+V to paste the data.

5 Choose Data, Sort to open the Sort dialog box and then click OK to accept the default settings and sort the spreadsheet.

Setting Options for Voting

You can configure a handful of options in Outlook to configure how Outlook handles voting.

To configure these settings, follow these steps:

1 Open Outlook and choose Tools, Options.

2 On the Preferences tab, click E-Mail Options.

3 Click Tracking Options to open the Tracking Options dialog box (see Figure 33-16). The Tracking Options dialog box has the following options that relate to voting:

■ **Process Requests And Responses On Arrival.** Outlook processes and tallies responses when they arrive. If you clear this option, you must open each response to have Outlook tally it.

■ **Delete Blank Voting And Meeting Responses After Processing.** Outlook deletes voting responses that have no additional comments added to them.

4 Select the options you want to use and click OK to close the Tracking Options dialog box. Then click OK twice more to close the E-Mail Options dialog box and the Options dialog box.

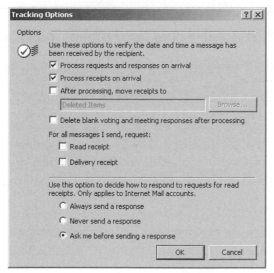

Figure 33-16. Use the Tracking Options dialog box to configure voting options.

Troubleshooting

Votes aren't being automatically tallied.

Outlook's ability to automatically tally votes without the user having to open each message might not be apparent at first. It can take several minutes even on a completely idle system for Outlook to process the messages. If you need to process them more quickly, select all the responses, right-click the selection, and choose Open Selected Items to open them all at once. Keep in mind, however, that you'll end up with an open message form for each response, which you'll then have to close.

Chapter 34

Sharing Information with Others

Microsoft Outlook has several features that allow you to share data with other users. You can share personal folder files, allow other users to access folders in your Exchange Server mailbox, use public folders to post messages and shared files, and use the Network News Transport Protocol (NNTP) service in Microsoft Exchange Server to set up a news server for sharing information.

This chapter examines many of these features and explains how to configure and use them to share information with others. The chapter also looks at security features that help you share your data but still protect it, ensuring that other users can access only the data you want them to see.

Sharing Overview

You have several options for sharing data in Outlook. The first is to configure delegate access for a folder, which gives another user—whom you designate as your delegate—access to that folder. When you assign a delegate for a folder, you specify the level of permission the delegate has in the folder, which determines the actions he or she can take with the folder and its items. For example, you might let a delegate view your existing calendar items and create new ones but prevent the delegate from viewing items marked as private. In addition, you can grant the delegate not only access to the folder but also send-on-behalf-of privileges for that folder, which means the delegated user can send messages on your behalf—for example, the delegate could send meeting request messages under your name.

> For a detailed explanation of delegation, see Chapter 27, "Delegating Responsibilities to an Assistant."

Another option for sharing data is your ability to grant permissions for a private folder, allowing other users to access the folder contents and perform other actions in the folder. This is similar to assigning delegate access for a folder, except that it does not give the other users send-on-behalf-of privileges for the folder. Depending on the permissions you assign, users can, for example, view items, create new items, or create subfolders.

> For information about granting permissions for a folder, see "Granting Access to Folders," page 687.

The third data-sharing option is to use public folders, which are stored on your Exchange Server. As you can with private folders, you can configure permissions for public folders that you create, controlling the actions others can take in the folders. You might use public folders to share documents or other files, post messages for review or comment by your coworkers, share contacts, or share other types of data. You can create public folders by using Outlook, or the Exchange Server administrator can create public folders by using the Exchange System Manager.

This chapter focuses on using public folders to share data. The following section explains how to create and configure public folders through Outlook. Later sections of the chapter explain how to use public folders, create a message board, manage public folders, and use the NNTP service to configure a news server.

Setting Up Public Folders

Public folders reside on the Exchange Server, where other users can access them. The primary function of public folders is to allow you to share messages, contacts, documents, and other items. Exchange Server also uses public folders to provide the folder structure for newsgroups, in which you can read and post messages. Although you can't set up a news server through Outlook, you can create public folders that function much the way a news server does and that even allow you to moderate the discussion.

When you view the folder list in Outlook, you'll probably see two subfolders listed under the Public Folders branch: Favorites and All Public Folders, shown in Figure 34-1. The Favorites folder, discussed later in this chapter, gives you quick access to public folders you use often. The All Public Folders branch shows the folders available on the server. All Public Folders by default includes only the Internet Newsgroups folder, but other folders will also appear if other users have created them by using Outlook or if the Exchange Server administrator has created them by using the Exchange System Manager.

Figure 34-1. Public folders appear in Outlook under the Public Folders branch.

Creating a Public Folder

If you have the necessary permissions on the server, you can use Outlook to create public folders. The Exchange Server administrator configures permissions on the server to allow or deny individuals or groups the ability to create public folders. This section assumes that you've been given the appropriate permissions to create folders.

> To learn how to configure permissions on Exchange Server to control users' ability to create public folders in a message store, see "Controlling the Ability to Create Public Folders in Exchange Server 5.5," page 829, or "Controlling the Ability to Create Public Folders in Exchange 2000 Server," page 840.

Follow these steps to create a public folder:

1 Open Outlook. If the folder list is not currently displayed, choose View, Folder List or click the folder drop-down menu and click the push pin to keep the list open.

2 Expand the Public Folders branch, right-click the folder in which you want to create the new public folder, and choose New Folder to open the Create New Folder dialog box, shown in Figure 34-2 on the next page.

Figure 34-2. You can specify a different location for the new folder in the Create New Folder dialog box.

3 Type a name for the folder in the Name box, and then select the folder type in the Folder Contains drop-down list.

The folder type determines the type of items that you can create in the folder. For example, to create a folder for sharing messages, select Mail And Post Items, or select Contact Items to create a shared folder for contacts.

4 To change the location where the folder will be created, select a new parent folder in the Select Where To Place The Folder list. Then click OK to create the folder.

Configuring Folder Properties

After you create a folder, you'll want to configure its properties, including the permissions to control access. To configure a public folder's properties, right-click the folder and choose Properties. The following section explains the options you can set on each tab of the folder's Properties dialog box.

Setting General Properties

Use the General tab (see Figure 34-3) to specify the folder's name, add a description, specify the default form for posting to the folder, configure Exchange views, and view the size of the folder.

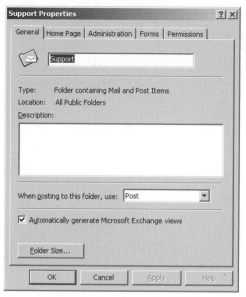

Figure 34-3. Use the General tab to configure basic folder properties.

The General tab includes the following properties:

- **Name.** Use the text box at the top of the General tab to specify the name for the public folder. (To rename the folder later on, right-click it in the folder list and choose Rename.)

- **Description.** Enter an optional description for the folder in this text box. This description does not appear in Outlook when users browse the public folder list; it does appear if the user opens the Properties dialog box for the folder.

- **When Posting To This Folder, Use.** Use this drop-down list to select the form to use for adding new items to the folder. Outlook by default uses a specific form based on the folder type. If you want to use a different form, select Forms in the drop-down list to display the Choose Form dialog box (see Figure 34-4 on the next page), where you can select the form.

- **Automatically Generate Microsoft Exchange Views.** Select this check box if Microsoft Exchange client users also connect to the server and need access to the public folder. You can clear this check box if only Outlook clients connect to the server or require access to the public folder.

- **Folder Size.** Click this button to view the current size of the folder (the amount of space used by the folder's contents).

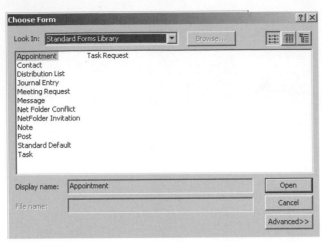

Figure 34-4. Use the Choose Form dialog box to select the form for posting new items to the public folder.

Defining a Folder Home Page

Use the Home Page tab of the folder's Properties dialog box to assign a Web page to the folder. Enter the URL for the page in the Address box, and then select the option Show Home Page By Default For This Folder. When the user opens the folder, the specified page will open in the folder window.

InsideOut

In Outlook 2002, the only way to view the Web page associated with a folder is to set it as the default view on the Home Page tab. In previous versions, you could open a folder to view it normally and then select the Web page from the View menu. The new behavior forces you to either use a Web page for the folder or use the standard view. This can be inconvenient as you can't switch between the two views without changing the properties for the folder, and it can limit the usefulness of assigning a Web page to a folder.

Configuring Administration Properties

The Administration tab (see Figure 34-5) provides several options that let you determine how the folder displays information, specify which users have access to the folder, and affect many other behaviors.

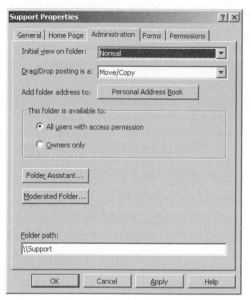

Figure 34-5. Use the Administration tab to control a wide range of options for the folder.

The Administration tab includes the following options:

- **Initial View On Folder.** Use this drop-down list to define the way the folder's contents are displayed to the user by default. When the folder is open, the user can change the view by using the View menu.

- **Drag/Drop Posting Is A.** This option determines how Outlook handles items that users drag to the folder. If you select Move/Copy, the item takes on the same properties as the original item. A message, for example, appears to be from the person who sent it or created it originally, and the subject remains unchanged. If you select Forward, Outlook modifies the item to indicate that it has been forwarded, and the item's sender is changed to indicate the person who placed the item in the folder.

- **Add Folder Address To.** Click this button to add the folder to your Personal Address Book. Then you can easily post messages to the folder by selecting it from the address book.

- **This Folder Is Available To.** This group allows you to control which users have access to the folder. Select All Users With Access Permissions to allow all users who have the appropriate permissions for the folder to access the folder. Select Owners Only to limit access to only those users who are designated as the folder owners. Select Owners Only whenever you need to make changes to the folder and want to prevent users from posting items to the folder while you're working on it. Those who are not owners receive a message indicating that the folder is currently unavailable if they attempt to access it when the Owners Only option is in effect.

- **Folder Assistant.** Click this button to open the Folder Assistant, which allows you to apply rules to the folder. For details, see "Applying Rules To Folders," page 819.

- **Moderated Folder.** Click this button to set up a moderated folder. For details, see "Setting Up a Moderated Message Board," page 822.

- **Folder Path.** This box specifies the path to the folder. You can change the folder location by entering a different path.

Setting Up Forms

The Forms tab of the folder's Properties dialog box allows you to specify the forms that people can use when posting items to the folder. You might want to limit posting to a specific form. For example, suppose that you're using a public folder to solicit survey responses and you've created a form for the survey. You would probably want to limit postings to only those responders who used the correct survey form.

The following three options on the Forms tab control which forms can be used:

- **Only Forms Listed Above.** Select this option to allow only the forms explicitly associated with the folder to be used for posting. These forms are listed in the Forms Associated With This Folder list.

- **Forms Listed Above And The Standard Forms.** Select this option to allow the use of Outlook standard forms in addition to the forms in the associated list.

- **Any Form.** Select this option to allow the use of any form to post items to the folder.

You can add other forms and associate them with a folder when necessary. For example, perhaps you've created a special form to use to obtain survey responses. On the Forms tab, click Manage to open the Forms Manager dialog box, shown in Figure 34-6. You use the Forms Manager to select a forms library, install forms, configure their properties, copy forms between libraries, and associate forms with the folder.

> For a complete discussion of creating custom forms, see Chapter 40, "Designing and Using Forms."

Chapter 34: Sharing Information with Others

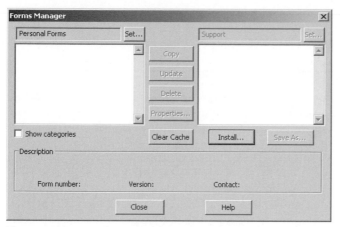

Figure 34-6. Use the Forms Manager to associate forms with a public folder.

Setting Permissions on Public Folders

You can control which users have access to public folders by setting permissions for the folders. You do so on the Permissions tab of the folder's Properties dialog box, shown in Figure 34-7.

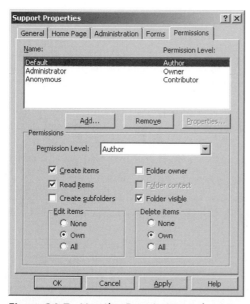

Figure 34-7. Use the Permissions tab to control the actions users can perform in a public folder.

> **note** A Summary tab replaces the Permissions tab if another user created the folder. The Summary tab allows you to view permissions for the folder but doesn't let you change them.

Each folder includes three permission groups by default: Default, Anonymous, and *<owner>*, where *owner* is the person who created the folder. The Default permission group applies to all authenticated users for whom an explicit permission has not been defined. Default is assigned Author permission initially, letting authenticated users create new items, read existing items, view the folder, and edit and delete items that they own.

The Anonymous permission group controls access by users who connect to the server anonymously—for example, through a Web browser (including through Outlook Web Access, or OWA). Anonymous users by default have only the ability to create new items in the folder; they cannot view it or make other modifications. For users to access a public folder anonymously, the Exchange Server administrator must configure permissions on the server to allow anonymous access. The Anonymous permission group lets you specify the types of access that anonymous users have in public folders that you create.

> To learn how to configure anonymous access, see "Controlling Anonymous Access to Public Folders in Exchange Server 5.5," page 830; and "Controlling Anonymous Access to Public Folders in Exchange 2000 Server," page 834.

The third permission group, which appears by default, is for the person who created the folder (typically, you). The owner has full permissions in the folder and can create items, view items, create subfolders, and edit and delete items, including items owned by other users. You can give other users full control of a folder by granting them Owner permissions.

You can assign permissions to individual users or to distribution groups. When you click Add on the Permissions tab, Outlook displays the Add Users dialog box, shown in Figure 34-8. The Name list includes users from the Global Address List as well as mail-enabled security and distribution groups.

> **tip** **Use security groups for messaging in Exchange 2000 Server**
>
> In Exchange Server 5.5, you can use only distribution groups for messaging; security groups, therefore, do not appear in the Add Users dialog box. In Exchange 2000 Server, however, you can also use mail-enabled security groups to send and receive messages. This means that mail-enabled security groups do show up in the Add Users dialog box when you configure properties for public folders on an Exchange 2000 server. Security groups that are not mail-enabled don't appear in the list. Outlook shows mail-enabled groups regardless of their type (domain local, global, or universal). For a discussion of creating distribution groups in Exchange Server, see "Creating Distribution Groups," page 772.

Chapter 34: Sharing Information with Others

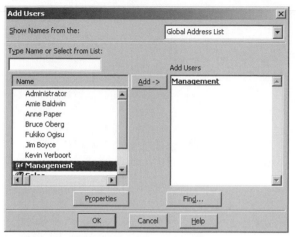

Figure 34-8. Use the Add Users dialog box to add permissions for users and groups.

You configure and add permissions for public folders the same way you configure permissions for private folders. To learn about setting permissions, see "Configuring Access Permissions," page 687.

Applying Rules to Folders

Another aspect of setting up a public folder is creating rules that apply to items when they arrive in the folder. Rules help you perform actions automatically in the folder. For example, perhaps you want all messages posted to a public folder to be forwarded to a specific e-mail address. Or maybe you want to delete messages that come from specific senders or that have certain text in the subject field. Maybe you want messages with attachments to be moved to a different folder. Whatever the case, you can use rules to perform the action automatically, the same way you can use rules to automatically process messages that come into your Inbox.

> For a complete discussion of creating and using rules to process the Inbox and other private folders, see "Processing Messages Automatically," page 231.

You configure rules for a public folder by using the Properties dialog box for the folder. Click the Administration tab, and then click Folder Assistant to open the Folder Assistant dialog box, shown in Figure 34-9 on the next page.

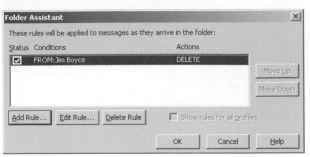

Figure 34-9. The Folder Assistant dialog box lists rules currently assigned to the folder.

In addition to listing currently assigned rules, the Folder Assistant dialog box lets you modify, delete, and add rules. Click Add Rule to display the Edit Rule dialog box when you want to add a rule (see Figure 34-10). The options available are similar to the options for creating a rule by using the Rules Wizard. You can click Advanced to set additional advanced conditions for the rule, as shown in Figure 34-11.

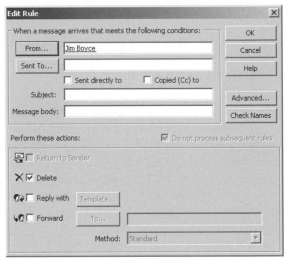

Figure 34-10. Use the Edit Rule dialog box to define conditions and actions for the folder rule.

This chapter does not cover creating folder rules in depth because the process is similar to creating message rules with the Rules Wizard, discussed in detail in an earlier chapter. If you need help building folder rules, review Chapter 8, "Filtering, Organizing, and Using Automatic Responses."

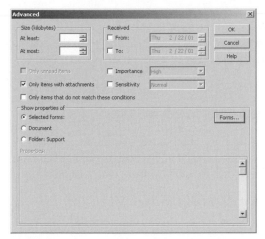

Figure 34-11. Use the Advanced dialog box to set additional conditions for the rule.

Setting Up a Message Board

You can use public folders to set up a message board that allows others to post and re-ply to messages. This is similar to using a news server, although the end result is slightly different. You use Outlook or OWA to follow a conversation thread, rather than using a newsreader such as Microsoft Outlook Express. In addition, the message board looks and functions like a mail folder; it doesn't organize messages by conversation thread by default, as a newsreader does. However, you can change the folder's view to organize the messages by conversation thread (see Figure 34-12), which gives you much the same effect. The advantage over a news server is that the message board does not require an administrator for setup or maintenance.

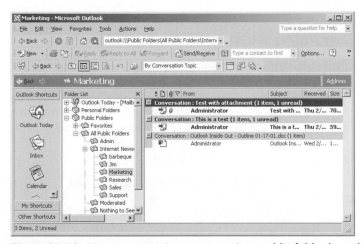

Figure 34-12. You can organize messages in a public folder by subject.

Chapter 34

A message board can be either *moderated* or *unmoderated*. In an unmoderated board, any user can post a message directly to the board, depending on his or her permissions in the public folder. No one controls what messages are posted to the board. With a moderated message board, messages are sent to a designated moderator, who decides whether to post the messages.

Setting Up an Unmoderated Message Board

An unmoderated message board is pretty much a free-for-all. As mentioned, anyone with access to the folder can post any message. However, you can control access to the folder through the folder's permissions, thereby limiting who can post messages.

Follow these steps to create an unmoderated message board:

1 Open Outlook, and expand the Public Folders branch.

2 Right-click the folder where you want to create the new folder and choose New Folder.

3 In the Create New Folder dialog box, specify the name and folder type, change the location if needed, and click OK.

4 Right-click the newly created folder and choose Properties. Click the Permissions tab.

5 On the Permissions tab, set the permissions for Default and Anonymous to control the actions users can perform with messages in the folder.

6 Use the Permissions section to configure the folder permission. If you don't want participants to be able to edit or delete the messages they post, select Create Items, Read Items, and Folder Visible; set Edit Items and Delete Items to None; and then click OK.

Setting Up a Moderated Message Board

One additional step is required when setting up a moderated message board—you must specify the moderator.

Follow the steps outlined in the previous section for creating an unmoderated message board, and then follow these additional steps to configure the board as moderated:

1 In Outlook, right-click the public folder and choose Properties.

2 Click the Administration tab, and then click Moderated Folder to display the Moderated Folder dialog box, shown in Figure 34-13.

Chapter 34: Sharing Information with Others

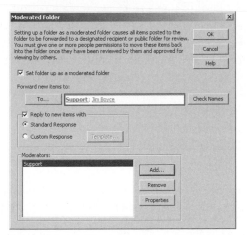

Figure 34-13. You can add multiple moderators to a folder.

3 Select the Set Folder Up As A Moderated Folder check box to configure the folder as a moderated folder. (Clear this option to make the folder unmoderated.)

4 Configure additional options, using the following list as a guide:

- **Forward New Items To.** Specify the addresses of the moderator (or moderators) who will receive new messages for posting consideration. You also can specify the name of another public folder where the moderators will place the messages for review.

- **Reply To New Items With.** Select this check box to have a reply sent automatically to participants when they post a message. Clear this option if you don't want a reply sent.

- **Standard Response.** Use this option to have a standard reply sent to participants when they post a message.

- **Custom Response.** Select this option to create your own message template, which is used to reply to participants when they post messages.

- **Moderators.** Use the options in this group to specify which users are designated as moderators. You must list the moderators here even if you've already entered their names in the Forward New Items To box (which specifies only that copies be sent to the designated addresses).

> **tip** You can have copies of posted messages sent to people who are not moderators. Just add their addresses in the Forward New Items To box, but don't add them to the Moderators list.

Chapter 34

Acting as a Moderator

If you've been designated as a moderator, you can review messages before you post them to the folder. Depending on how the folder is configured, the messages are either placed in a holding folder or sent to your Inbox. To review the messages, open the folder where they're located (or your Inbox) and read them. If you find them acceptable for posting, open the folder list and simply drag the message to the appropriate posting folder.

---

tip   **Configure drag-and-drop posting**

The setting Drag/Drop Posting on the Administration tab of the folder's Properties dialog box determines what happens when you drag messages to the folder. Select Move/Copy if you want the message to retain its existing subject and sender. Select Forward if you want the message to appear to be forwarded from you. The former option is probably the one you want to use for moderated public folders.

Working with Public Folders

Working with public folders isn't as difficult as you might think. This section of the chapter will bring you up to speed on navigating, posting in, and using public folders after they are set up.

Navigating Public Folders

As mentioned, Public Folders by default includes an All Public Folders branch. This branch serves as the root for all public folders on the server. Navigating public folders is just like navigating your private folders. Expand All Public Folders, and then select the folder you want to view. The folder's contents appear in the folder pane.

Posting Information

You post information to a public folder in much the same way you add items to a private folder. Open the folders list and navigate to the public folder you want to use. Click New on the toolbar to use the default form for the folder. You can also click the drop-down arrow beside New to create a different type of item. Outlook opens the specified form, and you fill it out just as you would for a private folder. Figure 34-14 shows the default form for posting messages to a public folder.

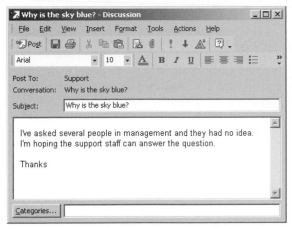

Figure 34-14. Outlook provides a simple form for posting messages to a public folder.

After you enter the information on the form, you can post your message in the following ways:

- To save the item to the folder without closing the form, choose File, Save or click the Save button on the toolbar.

- To post the message and close the form, click the Post button on the toolbar, choose File, Post, or press Ctrl+Enter. The message then appears in the public folder, and the form closes.

Troubleshooting

The Post toolbar button is missing.

You might think that Outlook's developers forgot to include a Post button on the toolbar—the button that allows you to post the message and close the form without using the menu. Actually, it's there, although it's sometimes hidden because both toolbars by default appear on one line. You can show the Post button by dragging the form's border to make it wider. Or you can click the small down arrow at the right edge of one of the toolbars and choose Show Buttons On Two Rows. The Post button will then appear at the left edge of the Standard toolbar.

Replying to Posts in a Public Folder

When viewing messages posted to a public folder, you have three options for responding to the post: you can reply to the folder, reply to the sender, or forward the message.

Replying to the Folder

Replying to the folder is just like replying to an e-mail message except the reply is simply posted to the public folder. To reply, right-click the message and choose Post Reply To Folder. Outlook opens the message form shown in Figure 34-15. This form is similar to one you would use to reply to an e-mail message. Add your comments and click Post to post your reply to the folder.

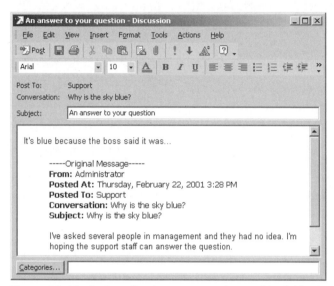

Figure 34-15. Post replies to a message in a public folder by using a form much like an e-mail message form.

Replying to the Sender

When you post a reply to the folder, the reply is placed directly in the folder rather than being sent to the person who originated the message you're replying to. If you prefer, you can send your reply to the originator rather than posting it in the folder. The message then goes out as a regular e-mail reply to the originator's e-mail address. To reply to a post in this way, right-click the message and choose Reply or click the Reply button on the toolbar.

Forwarding Messages

In addition to replying directly to a message's originator or posting replies to the folder, you can also forward the message to others. This works exactly the same way as forwarding a message from your Inbox or from another folder. Right-click the message and choose Forward, or click the Forward button on the toolbar.

Using the Favorites Folder

The Favorites folder under the Public Folders branch is not the same as the Favorites folder in your operating system. The latter contains shortcuts to frequently used Web sites, allowing you to access those sites quickly and easily. The Favorites folder under the Public Folders branch allows you to create shortcuts to public folders that you use frequently. This isn't an important feature if you deal with only a handful of public folders, but it can be a real time-saver if you work with Internet newsgroups on your server through Outlook or if your server contains numerous folders. Don't struggle to find the one folder you want among many in the folder list; simply place the folder in your Favorites folder and access it from there.

Adding folders to Favorites is easy—just drag the folder to the Favorites folder, and Outlook creates a shortcut to the folder. When you want to use the folder, open it from the Favorites folder rather than from Public Folders

Sharing Documents and Other Files Through Public Folders

You can use public folders to share files, messages, and other Outlook items. For example, you might place common documents such as policies, procedures, contracts, and databases in a public folder to allow coworkers to use them.

You have two main options for sharing files through public folders: using attachments or placing the files directly in the folder. The method you choose depends completely on how you want others to access the files and whether you want to attach a message to a particular file. For example, you might use an attachment when you need to include instructions or other information about using the file. When added information isn't necessary, simply place the file in the folder.

To use an attachment, create a new post as you would without an attachment. With the form still open, click the paper clip icon on the toolbar, select the file to attach, and then click Post. To place a file directly in a public folder, open Outlook and then open the public folder in which you want to place the file. Locate the file in Microsoft Windows Explorer, and simply drag the file to the folder.

> **tip** **Send a file from an application**
>
> You can send a document from an Office application to a public folder. Open the application and choose File, Send To, Exchange Folder. The application displays a Send To Exchange Folder dialog box where you select the folder in which you want to place the file. You must have Outlook configured as the default application for e-mail to allow the application to send the document to the folder.

Chapter 34

Using Public Folders Offline

One of Outlook's strengths is that it gives you the ability to work offline. For example, you can work from home or use a portable computer while on the road, connecting to the server only when you need to synchronize folders. In addition to working with your Outlook folders offline, you can work with public folders offline.

newfeature!

In previous versions of Outlook, you configured public folders for offline use by setting the properties for the folder. In Outlook 2002, you configure a folder for offline use by using the Send/Receive Groups dialog box (discussed shortly). You can have the folders synchronize each time you perform a send/receive operation through your primary send/receive group, or you can create a group specifically for synchronizing your public folders and synchronize them separately from your mailbox folders.

> **note** You need to set up an offline store before you can use any Exchange Server folders offline. For details on configuring an offline store, see "Working Offline with Exchange Server," page 859.

Follow these steps to set up a send/receive group to synchronize public folders:

1 Open Outlook and choose Tools, Send/Receive Settings, Define Send/Receive Groups.

2 In the Send/Receive Groups dialog box, select the existing group you want to use to synchronize public folders or create a new group specifically for synchronization.

3 Click Edit. In the Send/Receive Settings dialog box, select Include Account In This Send/Receive Group and then scroll through the Check Folders list and expand the Public Folders branch.

4 Expand Favorites and select the folders you want Outlook to make available offline.

5 Click OK, and then click Close to return to Outlook.

6 Perform a send/receive operation with the send/receive group to synchronize the public folders with your offline store.

Troubleshooting

Your public folders aren't available offline.

If you've configured a send/receive group to synchronize your public folders for offline use, but the folders aren't accessible when you're working offline, make sure you've synchronized the folders at least once with the server. As is the case with your other Outlook folders, you can't work offline until you synchronize the folders at least once.

Managing Public Folders

As you learned earlier in this chapter, you can create public folders on an Exchange Server through Outlook, depending on your permissions on the server. You also can modify the properties of folders for which you have owner permission. In addition, administrators can manage public folders through Exchange Server. This section explores some of the most common administration tasks you might need to perform as an administrator of public folders in Exchange Server.

> **note** This section is not intended to cover all aspects of either Exchange Server management or public folders. Instead, it focuses on some of the most common administrative issues you'll face with public folders. In addition, the chapter itself focuses primarily on Exchange 2000 Server rather than Exchange Server 5.5. For a complete discussion of Exchange 2000 Server management, refer to *Microsoft Exchange 2000 Server Administrator's Companion,* by Walter J. Glenn and Bill English (Microsoft Press, 2000).

Managing Public Folders in Exchange Server 5.5

Most management tasks for public folders in Exchange Server 5.5 are most easily accomplished through Outlook, as explained in previous sections. You can create public folders, view their contents, add and modify items, and perform other actions, depending on the permissions you've been assigned for a particular folder. One action you'll likely want to perform with the Exchange Administrator is to configure the ability to create public folders.

Controlling the Ability to Create Public Folders in Exchange Server 5.5

By default, Exchange Server 5.5 allows all users to create top-level public folders. In most cases, you'll probably want to impose some restrictions to narrow the list of users who can create folders.

Follow these steps to restrict who can create public folders:

1 Open the Exchange Administrator, expand the Site, and select the Configuration container.

2 In the right pane, double-click Information Store Site Configuration to display its Properties dialog box and then click the Top Level Folder Creation tab, shown in Figure 34-16 on the next page.

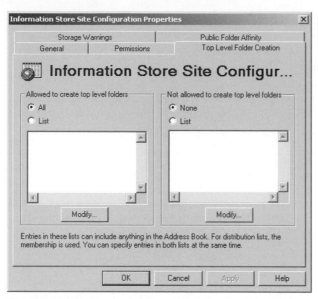

Figure 34-16. Use the Top Level Folder Creation tab to control users' ability to create public folders in the store.

3 If you want to specify explicitly which users and groups can create public folders, click List in the Allowed To Create Top Level Folders group and then click Modify to specify the users or groups who can create public folders. Click OK when you're satisfied with the list.

4 If you want to specify explicitly which users cannot create public folders, thereby allowing all others to do so, click List in the Not Allowed To Create Top Level Folders group, and then click Modify. Build the list and click OK.

5 Click OK to close the Information Store Site Configuration Properties dialog box.

Controlling Anonymous Access to Public Folders in Exchange Server 5.5

You can control anonymous access to public folders in Exchange Server 5.5 either at the server level or at the organizational level. Each server uses the defaults defined at the organizational level unless you specify otherwise. You need to configure anonymous access—either allowing or preventing it—through the HTTP, IMAP, and NNTP protocols.

> **note** The procedure described here takes you through all the configuration changes that affect anonymous access through various protocols. You might not want to make all these changes, however, depending on your network's configuration, the types of data you need to make available, and how your users need to access that data. Take some time to examine these issues to determine how anonymous access fits—or does not fit—into your enterprise.

Follow these steps to configure anonymous access default settings at the organizational level:

1 Open the Exchange Administrator.

2 Expand the Configuration container and click the Protocols object.

3 Double-click HTTP in the right pane to open the HTTP (Web) Site Settings Properties dialog box.

4 On the General tab (see Figure 34-17), select or clear the Allow Anonymous Users To Access The Anonymous Public Folders check box. This allows or denies anonymous access through the Web to public folders published by the server on the Internet.

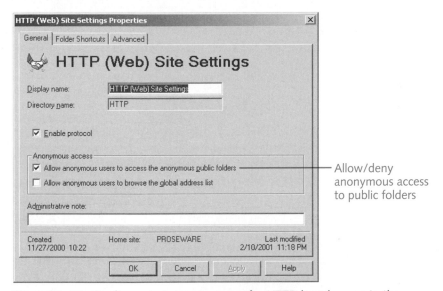

Allow/deny
anonymous access
to public folders

Figure 34-17. Configure anonymous access for HTTP-based access in the HTTP protocol's Properties dialog box.

5 Click OK, and then double-click IMAP to open the IMAP (Mail) Site Defaults Properties dialog box.

6 On the General tab (see Figure 34-18 on the next page), clear the Include All Public Folders When A Folder List Is Requested check box if you want to prevent anonymous access. This prevents public folders from being included in response to a client's request to list folders on the server.

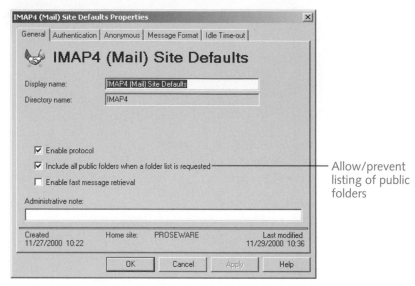

Allow/prevent listing of public folders

Figure 34-18. Configure anonymous access through IMAP in the IMAP protocol's Properties dialog box.

7 Click the Anonymous tab in the Properties dialog box and clear the Allow Anonymous Access check box if you want to prevent anonymous access to the folders. If you want to allow anonymous access, select this check box and specify the anonymous account name in the IMAP4 Anonymous Account box.

8 Click OK. Then double-click NNTP to open the NNTP (News) Site Defaults Properties dialog box.

9 Click the Anonymous tab (see Figure 34-19), and select the Allow Anonymous Access check box to allow anonymous access. Clear the check box to prevent anonymous access.

10 Click OK.

You can also configure anonymous access at the server level rather than at the organizational level. For example, you might want to allow anonymous access on one server for public use but prevent anonymous access on all others where confidential information is stored. In the Exchange Administrator, expand the Configuration container, and then expand the Servers container. Expand the server you want to configure and click the Protocols object. In the right pane, double-click IMAP4 or NNTP to configure the properties for those two protocols. The options are the same as those you configure at the organizational level.

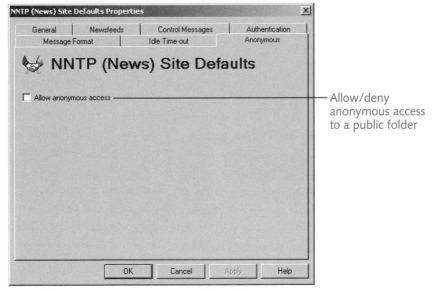

Figure 34-19. Use the Anonymous tab to allow or prevent anonymous access.

Setting Client Permissions in Exchange Server 5.5

In addition to configuring protocols, you might also want to configure permissions for anonymous users on specific folders.

Follow these steps to configure public folder permissions under Exchange Server 5.5:

1 Open the Exchange Administrator, and expand the Folders\Public Folders branch.

2 Select the public folder whose properties you want to configure. Choose File, Properties or press Alt+Enter to open the folder's Properties dialog box.

3 On the General tab, click Client Permissions to display the Client Permissions dialog box (see Figure 34-20 on the next page).

Chapter 34

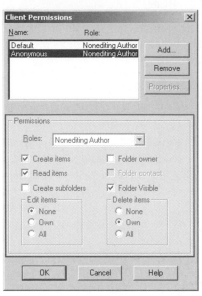

Figure 34-20. Use the Client Permissions dialog box to control the actions anonymous users can take in a public folder.

4 Select Anonymous in the Name list, and then use the Roles drop-down list and other options in the dialog box to specify the actions that anonymous users can perform in the folder.

5 Click OK to close the Client Permissions dialog box, and then click OK to close the folder's Properties dialog box. Repeat the process for other folders as needed.

Managing Public Folders in Exchange 2000 Server

While you can manage some aspects of public folders through Outlook, you have much broader control through the Exchange System Manager with Exchange 2000 Server. For example, you can apply storage limits, decide how the folder should appear in the address list, and configure many other properties not available from Outlook. The following sections discuss some of the most common administrative tasks you might want to perform on public folders in Exchange 2000 Server.

Controlling Anonymous Access to Public Folders in Exchange 2000 Server

One of the administrative tasks you might want to perform in Exchange 2000 Server is to control anonymous access to public folders through various protocols such as HTTP, IMAP, and NNTP.

> **note** The procedure described here takes you through all the configuration changes that affect anonymous access using various protocols. Which of these changes you make depends on how your users need to access data, your network's configuration, and the types of data you need to make available. Examine these issues in detail to determine what changes you need to make to control anonymous access.

Follow these steps to configure anonymous access in Exchange 2000 Server:

1 Open the Exchange System Manager, and expand the Administrative Group where the server in question is located. Expand the Protocols container under the server.

2 Expand the HTTP container, and expand the Exchange Virtual Server container under it. Right-click the Public virtual directory and choose Properties.

3 In the Public Properties dialog box, click the Access tab and click Authentication to open the Authentication Methods dialog box (see Figure 34-21).

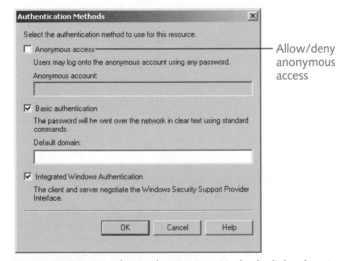

Allow/deny anonymous access

Figure 34-21. Use the Authentication Methods dialog box to allow or prevent anonymous access through HTTP.

4 If you want to allow anonymous access to public folders through HTTP (clients access the folders through a Web browser), select Anonymous Access and then click in the Anonymous Account box and type the account name to use for anonymous access. Typically, the account name is IUSR_<*computer*>, where *computer* is the server name.

5 Click OK to close the Authentication Methods dialog box. Then click OK again to close the Public Properties dialog box.

Chapter 34

835

Part 7: Using and Administering Outlook with Exchange Server

6 Expand the IMAP4 container, right-click the virtual server, and choose Properties to open the IMAP4 Properties dialog box for the server. On the General
tab (see Figure 34-22), select or clear Include All Public Folders When A
Folder List Is Requested to either list or not list public folders for IMAP clients.

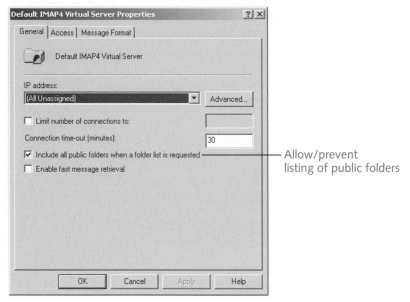

Figure 34-22. Use the General tab of the IMAP protocol's Properties dialog
box to control listing of public folders for IMAP clients.

7 Click OK and expand the NNTP container. Right-click the NNTP virtual server
and choose Properties.

8 Click the Access tab and click Authentication to open the Authentication
Methods dialog box (see Figure 34-23).

9 Select or clear the Allow Anonymous check box to allow or deny anonymous
access to the folders through NNTP. If you allow anonymous access, click
Anonymous and choose the user account to be used to gain access to resources when an anonymous connection is made. Then click OK.

10 Click OK to close the Authentication Methods dialog box. Then click OK to
close the virtual server's Properties dialog box.

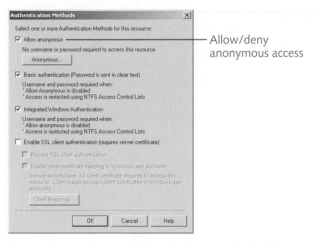

Figure 34-23. Use the Authentication Methods dialog box to allow or deny anonymous access.

Changing Address List Display Properties in Exchange 2000 Server

You can configure public folders to appear in the Global Address List (and in other address lists you create and make available on the server), which allows users to select a folder as the destination when sending or posting a message. By default, Exchange 2000 Server hides public folders from the address lists. If you want a folder to appear in the address lists, you must configure one of the folder's properties accordingly.

Follow these steps to properly configure a folder's properties:

1 Open the Exchange System Manager and configure it to display Administrative Groups (if it doesn't already).

> **tip** To display Administrative Groups in the Exchange System Manager, right-click Organization and choose Properties. Select Display Administrative Groups and click OK.

2 Right-click the folder and choose Properties. Click the Exchange Advanced tab, shown in Figure 34-24 on the next page.

Chapter 34

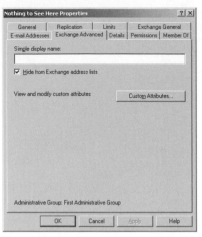

Figure 34-24. Use the Exchange Advanced tab to configure address book behavior for public folders.

3 In the Simple Display Name box, enter the alias name you want Exchange Server to use for the folder in address lists. For example, you might specify an alias of Support Tools for a public folder named support.tools.common.

4 If you want to hide the folder from the address lists, select Hide From Exchange Address Lists. Clear this option to have the folder appear in address lists.

5 Click OK to close the Properties dialog box.

Setting Folder Limits in Exchange 2000 Server

You can configure limits on a public folder to control the size of the folder and its contents. The folder can use the store's default limits (this is the default setting), or you can specify limits specifically for the folder. Four settings control folder limits. To view them, right-click the folder in the Exchange System Manager, choose Properties, and then click the Limits tab, shown in Figure 34-25.

The following settings control public folder limits:

● **Use Public Store Defaults.** Select this option to use the limit settings assigned at the store level. Clear this option to set individual limits for the folder.

● **Issue Warning At (KB).** Use this option to specify the size, in kilobytes, that the folder should reach before Exchange Server issues a warning to the administrator. You can specify a value from 0 to 2,097,151.

- **Prohibit Post At (KB).** When the folder reaches the size that you specify
with this option, users can no longer post items to the folder.

- **Maximum Item Size (KB).** This option lets you specify a maximum size
for each posted item.

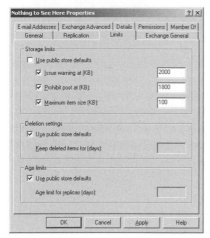

Figure 34-25. Use the Limits tab to configure storage limits for the folder.

> **tip** If you allow public folders to use the public store defaults, a single folder can use all
> available disk space within a store. It's a good idea to assign individual limits to
> "space-hogging" folders.

You also can use the options in the Deletion Settings group to set the amount of time
that deleted items remain in the folder before they are permanently deleted. You can
configure the folder to use the store's default or specify an individual setting for the
folder. Another option you can configure is the length of time that replicated items can
remain in the folder before they are deleted.

Setting Client Permissions in Exchange 2000 Server

Outlook lets you configure folder permissions to control the actions that users can perform in a folder. You can also configure those options through the Exchange System
Manager. Right-click the folder, choose Properties, and then click the Permissions tab.
Click Client Permissions to display the Client Permissions dialog box, shown in Figure
34-26 on the next page. This dialog box is essentially identical to the one offered by
Outlook for setting client permissions. For details on configuring these permissions,
see "Setting Permissions on Public Folders," page 817.

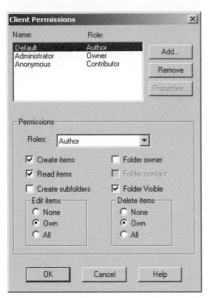

Figure 34-26. You can configure client access permissions through the Exchange
System Manager.

Controlling the Ability to Create Public Folders in Exchange 2000 Server

Although, as an administrator, you can configure the ability to create public folders
through Outlook, you might prefer to do so through Exchange instead. For example,
you might need to refine the permissions to allow or deny other actions as well, which
is not possible through Outlook.

Follow these steps to configure the ability to create public folders and set other
permissions:

1 Open the Exchange System Manager, display Administrative Groups, right-
click the Public Folders branch, and choose Properties.

2 Click the Security tab, shown in Figure 34-27.

3 Select the Everyone group and configure Create Public Folder and Create Top
Level Public Folder permissions. Generally, you'll want to remove these permissions from the Everyone group and assign the permissions through other
security groups as needed, unless you want all users to be able to create
public folders.

4 Click Advanced and review the security settings for the Everyone group,
adjusting as needed to suit your security requirements.

5 Click OK to close the Advanced Control Settings For Public Folders dialog
box. Then click OK again to close Public Folders Properties dialog box.

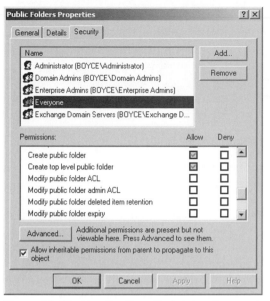

Figure 34-27. Use the Security tab to allow or deny the ability to create public folders.

Managing a Newsgroup Server

You can use Exchange Server 5.5 and Exchange 2000 Server to host Internet newsgroups, allowing users to participate in public discussions, to access files and support data, and to communicate with others across the Internet. The ability to host newsgroups is integrated into both Exchange Server 5.5 and Exchange 2000 Server. This section focuses primarily on configuring newsgroups in Exchange 2000 Server. The process is similar to that of Exchange Server 5.5.

You can use Exchange 2000 Server to create a news server to host your own newsgroups, or you can configure it to pull a news feed from a public news server to provide a complete set or a subset of the public Internet newsgroups, depending on your needs. For example, suppose that you want to set up a news server to provide technical support information exchange with your customers. By using Exchange 2000 Server as the server, you allow your customers to access messages through the Internet using a newsreader; your in-house staff can access messages through Outlook.

If you want, you can also create newsgroups in the NNTP service and not associate them with Exchange Server public folders. As a result, local users won't have access to the newsgroups through Outlook, but they can view the newsgroups using an NNTP newsreader such as Outlook Express, depending on their permissions on the virtual server. Because this book focuses on Outlook, however, this chapter assumes that you want to integrate the two.

Chapter 34

> **note** This chapter focuses on configuring a news server to host your own newsgroups. For
> a discussion of configuring a news server to pull public news feeds, see *Running
> Microsoft Internet Information Server,* by Leonid Braginski and Matt Powell
> (Microsoft Press, 1998). Most of the process is the same, with the exception that you
> must also set up a news feed from a public news server.

NNTP + Outlook = Internet Newsgroups

If you've browsed your folder list in Outlook, you've no doubt come across the Public
Folders/Internet Newsgroups branch. Exchange 2000 Server uses this public folder to
expose newsgroups to Outlook users, giving users the ability to read and post messages,
and, depending on their permissions, to create additional newsgroups. Public folders
do not by themselves provide for a news server, however. Exchange 2000 Server uses the
NNTP service included with Microsoft Windows 2000 Server to provide the back-end
functionality. Local Outlook users can connect to the server and view the newsgroups
through the Public Folders/Internet Newsgroups branch; remote users can connect to
the server using Outlook Express or another newsreader to read and post messages.

When you install Exchange 2000 Server, Setup adds the NNTP service and configures a
default NNTP virtual server, configuring it to respond on all unassigned IP addresses.
Setup also creates a default virtual directory that points to the Public Folders/Internet
Newsgroups public folder. The result is that new newsgroups and messages are stored
in the Public Folders/Internet Newsgroups folder, including those added by remote
users through the NNTP service. A user browsing the Public Folders/Internet Newsgroups branch through Outlook sees a given set of folders, as shown in Figure 34-28.
When a remote user connects to the server through a newsreader such as Outlook
Express, that user sees that same set of newsgroups, as shown in Figure 34-29. By
pointing the default virtual directory for the NNTP server to the Public Folders/Inter-
net Newsgroups public folder, Exchange 2000 Server provides two different views of
the same data, each applicable to a particular type of user.

Troubleshooting

You can't get newsgroup access through Outlook.

Many users complain that Outlook doesn't include a dedicated newsreader, but instead requires that you use an external newsreader such as Outlook Express to work
with newsgroups. Although you can't use Outlook to connect to an external news
server (unless it's an Exchange Server), you can use it to read public newsgroups if
they are hosted on your Exchange Server. Network administrators can address these
users' complaints by configuring a local Exchange 2000 Server to pull a news feed
from a public news server. As a result, users have access to public newsgroups through
Outlook. An added bonus is that the administrator can control the newsgroups that are
pulled from the remote server, restricting the groups that appear on the local server.

Figure 34-28. Newsgroups appear under the Public Folders/Internet Newsgroups branch in Outlook.

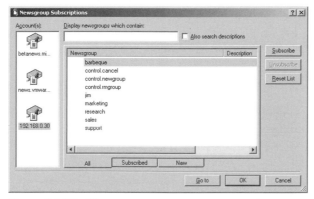

Figure 34-29. The same newsgroups appear when a user connects through a newsreader such as Outlook Express.

Configuring NNTP Server Properties

Because Setup automatically creates a default NNTP virtual server when you install Exchange 2000 Server and points the default virtual directory to the Public Folders/ Internet Newsgroups branch, this folder is the root for newsgroups on the server.

You'll probably want to adjust a few properties if you're setting up your own news server. The following sections explain many common setting adjustments.

> **note** The following sections don't cover all the NNTP service properties, although the procedures included here give you access to all the properties.

Configuring Server IP Address, Ports, and Connection Limits

The NNTP virtual server by default is configured to respond on all unassigned IP addresses on the server. This means that the server responds to NNTP requests that come in for IP addresses for which no other NNTP virtual server is explicitly configured on the server. If multiple IP addresses are bound to your server, you might prefer to assign a specific IP address to the server to simplify administration or DNS configuration. You also might want to configure connection limits and timeouts for the server, limiting the number of users who can connect concurrently and setting a timeout period that, when reached, will disconnect idle users.

You configure these properties on the General tab of the Properties dialog box for the virtual server, as follows:

1 Open the Exchange System Manager, open the Administrative Group in which the server resides, and then expand the server's Protocols/NNTP branch.

2 Right-click the Default NNTP Virtual Server branch and choose Properties to open the General tab, shown in Figure 34-30.

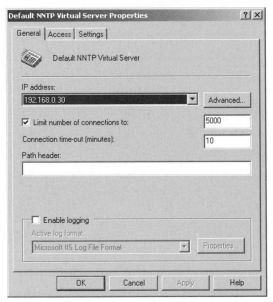

Figure 34-30. Configure address, connection limits, and timeouts on the General tab.

3 In the IP Address drop-down list, select the IP address on which you want the virtual NNTP server to respond.

4 Select the Limit Number Of Connections To check box if you want to impose a limit on the number of concurrent users, and then enter a value in the associated text box. The default is 5000 users.

5 Use the Connection Time-Out box to specify the number of minutes after which idle users are disconnected. Click OK to close the Properties dialog box.

The NNTP server uses the standard TCP port 119 and SSL port 563 by default, but you can change those port settings if you have a special deployment topology that requires it. With the General tab open, click Advanced to edit the port assignments.

Preventing Anonymous Access

The NNTP service by default allows anonymous connections to the news server. This might not be a problem for you if you're setting up a news server for public access. You'll probably want to prevent anonymous access for a private news server, however.

Follow these steps to prevent anonymous access for a private server:

1 Open the Exchange System Manager and open the server's Protocols/ NNTP branch.

2 Right-click the Default NNTP Virtual Server branch and choose Properties. Then click the Access tab.

3 Click Authentication to display the Authentication Methods dialog box, shown in Figure 34-31.

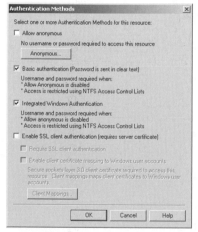

Figure 34-31. Control anonymous access and other authentication options in the Authentication Methods dialog box.

4 Clear the Allow Anonymous check box, configure other authentication options as needed, and click OK. Close the server's Properties dialog box.

> **tip** Use the Settings tab to impose limits on posting size, to allow feed posting from other servers, and to configure additional options for the virtual server.

Chapter 34

Creating Newsgroups

You can create newsgroups in two locations on the server: in the Public Folders/Internet Newsgroups folder or under the NNTP virtual server. The server treats the Public Folders/Internet Newsgroups folder as the root for the newsgroup list because it associates the default virtual directory for the server with that folder. When you add other folders under that folder, they appear as newsgroups to users connecting through either Outlook or an NNTP newsreader. In addition, newsgroups you add directly under the NNTP service appear under the root of the news server. Figure 34-32 illustrates an example. Users see the same unified hierarchy regardless of whether they browse the news server using Outlook or using an NNTP newsreader.

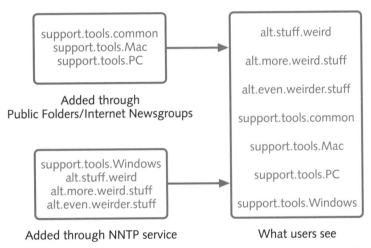

Figure 34-32. Exchange combines the two newsgroup structures into a single hierarchy for users.

You can create newsgroup folders in the Public Folders/Internet Newsgroups folder just as you can in any other public folder.

Follow these steps to create newsgroups through the NNTP service:

1 Open the Exchange System Manager, expand the server's Protocols/NNTP branch, and expand the Default NNTP Virtual Server branch.

2 Click the Newsgroups node to view the existing newsgroups. Right-click Virtual Directories and choose New, Newsgroup to start the New Newsgroup Wizard.

3 On the wizard page, type the name for the newsgroup using dotted format, such as support.tools.common, and then click Next.

4 Enter an optional description and pretty name for the newsgroup and click Finish.

> **tip** **Use pretty names**
>
> Some news clients can use a *list prettynames* command to view the newsgroup list using the assigned pretty name rather than the default name. The pretty name is another alias for the newsgroup that can be displayed by clients. For example, you might use Common Support Tools as the pretty name for support.tools.common. You can leave these fields blank if you prefer.

Setting Up Moderated Newsgroups

New newsgroups that you add to a virtual server are unmoderated by default. You can easily configure a newsgroup to be moderated, however, which causes all new posts to be sent to a designated moderator for review before posting in the newsgroup.

Follow these steps to set up a moderated newsgroup:

1 Open the Exchange System Manager, expand the server's Protocols/NNTP branch, right-click the Default NNTP Virtual Server branch, and choose Properties.

2 In the Properties dialog box, click the Settings tab, shown in Figure 34-33.

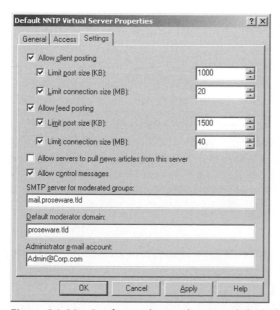

Figure 34-33. Configure the moderator's default domain and SMTP server on the Settings tab.

3 In the SMTP Server For Moderated Groups box, type the SMTP server to which posts should be sent for review by the moderator.

4 In the Default Moderator Domain box, specify the domain in which the moderator's account resides. You can leave this box blank if you specify the full e-mail address for the moderator in step 7.

5 Click OK to close the Properties dialog box, and then click the Newsgroups node.

6 Create the newsgroup or open the Properties dialog box for an existing newsgroup and select the Moderated check box, as shown in Figure 34-34.

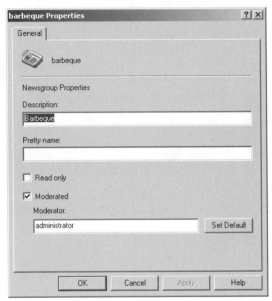

Figure 34-34. Designate the newsgroup as moderated and identify the moderator.

7 In the Moderator box, enter the e-mail address of the moderator. If you prefer, you can specify only the user name, and Exchange Server will combine it with the domain specified in step 4 to determine where to direct messages for review.

8 Click OK to close the Properties dialog box.

Chapter 35

Working Offline and Remotely

Microsoft Outlook provides several features that allow you to work offline (while you are not connected to your mail server) as well as from a remote location. Using the offline feature and Outlook's offline storage, which contains copies of all the folders and items in your Microsoft Exchange Server mailbox, you can work with contacts, messages, and other items stored in your mailbox without being connected to the server (except to perform periodic synchronizations). You can create and delete items, add folders, and make other changes while offline; Outlook synchronizes those changes the next time you connect to the server and perform a send/receive operation.

The primary feature in Outlook that supports remote use is remote mail, which lets you process message headers without downloading the message bodies. You can preview message headers, delete messages from the server without downloading them, and perform other selective processing. You can perform similar tasks with POP3, IMAP, and HTTP accounts, but only Exchange Server accounts can take advantage of the filters and other options provided through send/receive groups.

> **note** This chapter focuses on the offline and remote features in Outlook used in conjunction with Exchange Server. If you are looking for ways to work offline and remotely using other types of e-mail servers and accounts, see Chapter 13, "Processing Messages Selectively."

Offline vs. Remote

Offline use and remote use are two separate issues in Outlook. When you work offline, your computer is not connected to the Exchange Server. This usually means you're working on a computer that uses a dial-up connection to the server or on a portable computer that you connect to the server through a docking station on the local area network (LAN). You can be working offline even while your computer is connected to the LAN when the Exchange Server is down for maintenance.

You can perform most of the same functions offline that you perform when you're connected to the server. You can create messages, contacts, and other Outlook items, schedule meetings, and carry out other common Outlook tasks. The items you create and the changes you make to your folders and their contents, however, are made to the offline store, rather than to your Exchange Server mailbox store. When you reconnect to the server, Outlook synchronizes the offline store with the mailbox store. Any items that arrived in the mailbox while you were working offline are added to your offline store when Outlook performs the synchronization.

In contrast, working remotely generally means working with Outlook from a location other than the LAN on which the Exchange Server is located. For example, you might dial in to your LAN with a modem, connect to it through the Internet, or even connect through a demand-dial connection between two offices. Whatever your location, you can be working either offline or online when you work remotely. The only consideration is whether or not you are connected to the server. If you are not connected to the server, you are working offline and remotely. If you are connected to the server, you are simply working remotely.

With Outlook's remote mail feature, you can read message headers without downloading the message itself. Remote mail is useful when you receive a very large message in your mailbox and don't want to download it, when your mailbox contains a corrupted message that is preventing you from downloading other messages, or when your mailbox contains a message infected by a worm or virus. You can connect with remote mail, delete the message without reading or downloading it, and continue processing the other messages normally.

Establishing a Remote LAN Connection

To work remotely, you need to establish a remote connection to the server. How you accomplish this depends on the connection options available on your LAN and how the network administrator configured the LAN. Following are the most common methods for establishing a remote LAN connection:

- **Dial up to a Remote Access Services server on the LAN.** In this scenario, the LAN includes a Remote Access Services (RAS) server that allows clients to dial in to the network using a modem or other device (such as an ISDN connection). The RAS server could be the Exchange Server or another server on the network, depending on the size of the organization and the load on the Exchange Server. Depending on the configuration of the RAS server, dial-up clients might have access to the network or only to the Exchange Server.

- **Connect through a virtual private network connection from the Internet.** If your Exchange Server is connected to the Internet and your LAN includes a virtual private network (VPN) server, one of the best options for retrieving e-mail messages is to create a VPN connection to the LAN and then connect to the Exchange Server. A VPN server allows clients to establish secure connections to the network through a public network such as the Internet.

- **Connect through the Internet.** You can connect to an Exchange Server across the Internet without establishing a secure connection through a VPN. Without the security provided by a VPN, however, your e-mail messages and authentication data will be subject to interception and compromise. If this doesn't pose an unacceptable security risk for you, this can be the least expensive option if your LAN already includes an Internet connection.

- **Use a demand-dial connection between two networks.** If you have two or more offices, those offices might connect using a demand-dial connection. The connection might take place over a standard dial-up line or use ISDN or another communication method. The demand-dial interface allows the two routers that connect the offices to establish the connection when a client requests it, such as when you connect to synchronize your Outlook data.

Using Dial-Up and VPN Servers

If your network includes a dial-up server, you need to create a dial-up connection to the server to access your Exchange Server mailbox remotely. The process of setting up a dial-up connection is much the same regardless of the operating system you use on your client computer, although some minor differences do exist. Creating a connection to a network dial-up server is much the same as creating a connection to the Internet.

> For details on setting up a dial-up connection, see "Configuring Dial-Up Networking Options," page 147.

You can use Microsoft Windows NT Server or Microsoft Windows 2000 Server to provide dial-up access to the LAN as well as VPN connectivity. Both platforms include RAS and VPN server features and support multiple concurrent connections. You can also use Windows NT Workstation or Windows 2000 Professional as your dial-up server, but they support only one connection at a time. Windows 95 and 98 both include dial-up server capability, but they allow you to connect only to the dial-up computer and do not provide the pass-through access to the network that Windows NT and

Windows 2000 provide. For example, you can't dial in to a Windows 9*x* dial-up server
and through that connection gain access to servers or other computers on the dial-up
computer's LAN. You can access resources only on the Windows 9*x* dial-up computer.

---

tip **Don't compromise your network's security**

If your network doesn't currently include a RAS server, but your workstation includes
a modem and your computer is running Windows NT Workstation or Windows 2000
Professional, you might be considering setting up your computer as a RAS server to
provide access to your LAN and Exchange Server. Although this is possible, you should
avoid doing so, particularly if you are not the network administrator. Adding a dial-up
server—even one that accepts only one incoming connection at a time—poses security risks for your computer and the network. It also raises several configuration issues
that can be answered only in the context of the entire network, not just your single
computer (such as how the server will assign an IP address to clients).

Because this book focuses specifically on Outlook and its integration with Exchange
Server, all the details of how to set up a RAS or VPN server aren't covered. You are,
however, pointed in the right direction for more information.

Windows NT RRAS

In Windows NT, Routing and Remote Access Service (RRAS) lets you set up a dial-up
server and a VPN server. Note that RRAS is not the same as Remote Access Service
(RAS), which is included with Windows NT Server.

If you don't have RRAS installed on your computer, you can download it from
Microsoft's Web site at *http://www.microsoft.com/NTServer/nts/downloads/winfeatures/
rras/rrasdown.asp*. The file for Intel-based systems is Mpri386.exe. To install RRAS, you
need Windows NT Server with Service Pack 3 or later. If the RAS service included with
Windows NT is currently installed, remove it and restart the server. Then double-click
the Mpri386.exe file to start the installation process.

---

tip If you are running Windows NT Server on an Alpha platform, use the Alpha version of
RRAS, available at Microsoft's Web site.

If you intend to set up a VPN server, you first need to add the Point-to-Point Tunneling
Protocol (PPTP) to the server. To do so, right-click Network Neighborhood and choose
Properties. Click the Protocols tab and click Add. Select Point-to-Point Tunneling Pro-
tocol, and click OK to add the PPTP protocol.

Then, whether you're setting up the server for remote access or VPN, you must configure the properties for the server on the Services tab of the Network dialog box. Select Routing and Remote Access Service and click Properties to start the configuration process. RRAS adds a management tool to the Administrative Tools folder so that you can manage RRAS.

You also need to configure the properties for each user to allow or deny dial-up access. By default, all users are denied dial-up access. Open User Manager from the Administrative Tools folder on the Start menu, open the user's account, and click the Dialin button to configure the dial-in permission for the user. Repeat the process for any other users to whom you want to grant dial-in access.

Windows 2000 RRAS

When you install Windows 2000, Setup installs the Routing and Remote Access Service automatically, so you don't need to add it. However, you do need to enable and configure the service.

To do so, follow these steps:

1 Choose Start, Programs, Administrative Tools, Routing And Remote Access to open the RRAS console.

2 In the console, expand the branch in the left pane to locate the server, right-click the server, and choose Configure And Enable Routing And Remote Access to start the Routing And Remote Access Server Setup Wizard.

3 On the wizard page, specify the type of RRAS server you want to configure, either Remote Access Server or Virtual Private Network (see Figure 35-1).

Figure 35-1. Select the type of RRAS server you want to configure.

4   Click Next and follow the wizard's prompts to configure the server. The wizard prompts you for the following information:

   ▪ **Protocols.** Specify the protocols to be supported, which must already be installed on the RRAS server. All installed protocols are enabled for RRAS by default, but you can disable specific protocols after the wizard finishes.

   ▪ **Network interface.** The wizard prompts for the network interface to assign to remote clients, which determines where the addresses and other access properties come from. If addresses will be allocated through DHCP (Dynamic Host Configuration Protocol) in a multi-homed server (one with multiple network interfaces), select the network interface where the DHCP server is located.

   ▪ **IP address assignment.** You can assign addresses through DHCP (see the preceding option) or from a static address pool. If you choose a static pool, the wizard prompts you for the range of addresses to use.

   ▪ **RADIUS (Remote Authentication Dial-In User Service).** You can configure the RRAS server to use RADIUS for authentication and accounting. You specify the IP address or host name for the primary and alternate RADIUS servers, along with the RADIUS shared secret, which is essentially a password the RRAS server uses to authenticate its right to access the RADIUS servers. Windows 2000 includes a RADIUS server called Internet Authentication Service (IAS) that you can use for RRAS and other applications requiring RADIUS authentication. You can also use any other RADIUS server.

5   Click Finish to initiate the configuration process.

---

tip   **Configure RRAS for multiple functions**

Although the wizard prompts you to select one type of RRAS server, you can configure the server to perform one or more of the listed functions (such as remote access and VPN). Configure the server using the wizard, and then configure the other properties through the RRAS console. For example, you might configure the server for remote access and then add VPN ports to allow the server to function as a remote access and a VPN server.

After you configure RRAS and start the service, you can manage it through the RRAS console, shown in Figure 35-2. Initially, you should focus on three areas of the console. The Ports node lets you configure dial-up ports, including adding additional VPN ports and modems. Use the Remote Access Clients node to view connected clients and, if needed, disconnect clients. Use the Remote Access Policies branch to create the remote access policies that you want to apply for your dial-up users.

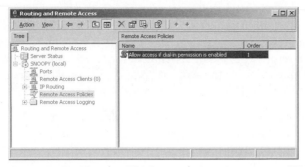

Figure 35-2. Use the RRAS console to manage your RRAS server.

At a minimum, you need to modify the Allow Access If Dial-In Permission Is Enabled policy so that users with dial-in permission in their accounts or in their group policy can connect. The policy is configured to deny access by default. To change the policy, double-click it to open its Properties dialog box (see Figure 35-3). Click Grant Remote Access Permission and click OK.

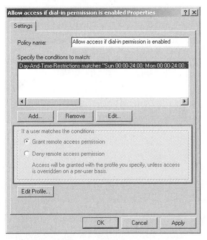

Figure 35-3. Configure the default remote access policy to allow access or create additional policies as needed.

Connecting Through the Internet

You can connect your client computer to the Exchange Server through the Internet. To do so, you must create on the client a Dial-Up Networking connection to your ISP, or your computer must be connected to the Internet through a dedicated connection (a cable modem or DSL, for example). In addition, the server must have a dedicated connection to the Internet.

> For an explanation of how to create dial-up connections for all Windows platforms, see Chapter 6, "Using Internet Mail."

When you configure your Microsoft Exchange Server service in Outlook, you must specify the Exchange Server for the account. You can enter a DNS (Domain Name System) name, an IP address, or the server's NetBIOS name. If you enter a DNS name or an IP address, Outlook resolves the NetBIOS name of the server and uses that for the connection. The next time you view the account's properties, you'll find that the NetBIOS name has replaced the IP address or DNS name you entered previously.

In some cases, Outlook can't resolve the address of the server. For example, suppose that you're configuring Outlook on a home computer that you use to connect to your Exchange Server on your office LAN, but you are not currently dialed in to the Internet. Because you are not connected directly to the LAN and there is no WINS server to provide NetBIOS name-to-address resolution, your computer will be unable to resolve the IP address of the server from its name. Connect to the Internet first and then set up the account or modify the computer's Lmhosts file (explained in the next section).

Modifying the Lmhosts File

You can include an entry in the Lmhosts file that maps the IP address of the server to the NetBIOS name. Lmhosts is located in the %systemroot%\System32\Drivers\Etc folder on systems running Windows NT and Windows 2000 and in the \Windows folder of systems running Windows 9*x* and Windows Me. The folder also contains a sample file, Lmhosts.sam, that provides examples of how to add entries to the Lmhosts file. If you do not have an Lmhosts file, save the Lmhosts.sam file as Lmhosts (no extension) and modify it as needed. Generally, all you need to do is open the file in Notepad, scroll to the end of the file, and add a line that includes the IP address of the server, a tab, and the NetBIOS name of the server.

> **tip**   **Speed up name resolution**
>
> Although Outlook can connect to Exchange Server without changes to the Lmhosts file (provided it was able to resolve the name from the IP address or DNS name when you first configured the account), modifying Lmhosts to include an entry for the server will make Outlook connect to the server more quickly in subsequent sessions.

Joining the Domain in Windows 2000

If you use Windows 2000 as your client operating system, placing your computer in the same domain as the server has the same results as modifying the Lmhosts file. For example, if your remote LAN domain is microsoft.com, you could place your workstation in the microsoft.com domain as well.

Windows 2000 by default appends the workstation's domain suffix to unresolved hosts before resolving them. Therefore, when your computer attempts to resolve the server's host name to an address, it appends the domain suffix and resolves the Fully Qualified Domain Name (FQDN) of the server. For example, if your server's host name is bart and your domain is microsoft.com, Windows 2000 appends the suffix and attempts to resolve bart.microsoft.com.

For resolution by server name to work, your server must have a host record in the DNS zone for the server. The zone encompasses the host and other DNS records for the domain. The host record specifies the IP address of the server and allows clients to resolve the host's IP address from its FQDN. You also must configure your workstation's domain suffix and DNS properties accordingly.

Follow these steps:

1 Right-click My Computer and choose Properties.

2 Click the Network Identification tab and then click Properties.

3 Click More, click in the Primary DNS Suffix Of This Computer box, and then type the domain suffix for the remote domain of your Exchange Server (see Figure 35-4).

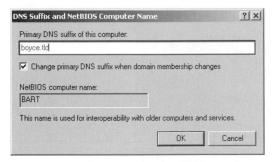

Figure 35-4. Configure the workstation's domain in the DNS Suffix And NetBIOS Computer Name dialog box.

4 Click OK twice.

5 When Windows prompts you to restart the computer, do so.

6 Open the Network And Dial-Up Connections folder.

7 Right-click your connection to the Internet and choose Properties. If this is a dial-up connection, click the Networking tab. Select the TCP/IP protocol and then click Properties.

8 Click Advanced and then click the DNS tab.

9 Click the Append Primary And Connection Specific DNS Suffixes option and then click OK.

10 Close the remaining dialog boxes by clicking OK in each.

Configuring the Internet Connection

In addition to configuring your computer to allow Outlook to resolve the server's address, you also need to tell Outlook how to connect to the Internet in order to connect to the server.

You do so through the account settings, as follows:

1 Right-click the Outlook icon on the desktop and choose Properties (or double-click the Mail icon in Control Panel).

2 If you don't use multiple profiles, skip to step 3. If you use multiple profiles, click Show Profiles. Select the profile you want to change and then click Properties.

3 Click E-Mail Accounts, select View Or Change Existing E-Mail Accounts, and then click Next.

4 Select the Exchange Server account and click Change.

5 Click More Settings and then click the Connection tab (see Figure 35-5).

Figure 35-5. Use the Connection tab to configure your computer's connection to the server.

6 Select one of the following:

■ **Connect Using My Local Area Network (LAN).** Select this option if your computer is connected to a LAN with a direct connection to the Internet. Use this option also if your computer connects to the Internet through a shared dial-up connection hosted by another computer on the network (such as ICS in Windows 98 or Windows 2000).

■ **Connect Using My Phone Line.** Select this option if you connect to the Internet through a dial-up connection. Also select the dial-up connection in the Use The Following Dial-Up Networking Connection drop-down list.

■ **Connect Using Internet Explorer's Or A 3rd Party Dialer.** Select this option if you use a third-party dialer or the Internet Explorer dialer to connect to the Internet.

7 Click OK, and then close the dialog box for the account and the profile.

---

tip You can select the LAN option even if you use a dial-up connection. However, you'll have to dial the connection before launching Outlook or configure your system to use autodial when a client requests a connection that isn't available.

Working Offline with Outlook and Exchange Server

There are a few specific issues and settings you need to consider when working with Outlook offline. This section explains how to configure Outlook's startup mode and offline folders and how to use an offline address book.

Configuring Startup Options

When you start Outlook, it attempts by default to determine the online/offline status of the server. If the server is unavailable, Outlook starts in offline mode and uses the offline folder specified in your profile for displaying existing items and storing new items (such as e-mail messages) before synchronizing with Exchange Server. If you've configured autodial in your operating system, Outlook dials the connection to the ISP or RAS server. However, you might want to exercise more control over Outlook's startup mode and when it connects. For example, you might prefer to have Outlook start in offline mode so that you can compose messages or perform other tasks before you connect and synchronize with the server.

You configure startup options by setting the properties for the Exchange Server account in your profile, as outlined here:

1 Right-click the Outlook icon on the desktop and choose Properties (or double-click the Mail icon in Control Panel).

2 If you don't use multiple profiles, skip to step 3. If you use multiple profiles, click Show Profiles. Select the profile you want to change and then click Properties.

3 Click E-Mail Accounts, select View Or Change Existing E-Mail Accounts, and then click Next.

4 Select the Exchange Server account and then click Change.

5 Click More Settings and then click the General tab (see Figure 35-6.)

Figure 35-6. Use the General tab to configure startup options for Outlook.

6 Configure the following settings:

- **Automatically Detect Connection State.** Outlook detects the connection state at startup and enters online or offline mode accordingly.

- **Manually Control Connection State.** You control the connection state when Outlook starts. The following three options work in combination with this option.

- **Choose The Connection Type When Starting.** Outlook prompts you to select the connection state when it starts. This allows you to select between online and offline states.

- **Connect With The Network.** Connect through your local LAN to Exchange Server. You can use this option if you connect to the Internet through a dedicated connection such as a cable modem or a DSL connection.

- **Work Offline And Use Dial-Up Networking.** Start in an offline state and use Dial-Up Networking to connect to Exchange Server. On the Connection tab, specify the dial-up connection you want to use.

- **Seconds Until Server Connection Timeout.** Specify the timeout, in seconds, for the server. Outlook attempts a connection for the specified amount of time; if Outlook is unable to establish a connection in the specified period, it times out. You might want to increase this setting if you connect to the Internet through a shared dial-up connection hosted by another computer on your LAN.

> **tip** **Increase TCP/IP timeout**
>
> You might want to change your TCP/IP timeout values if you change the Seconds Until Server Connection Timeout option in Outlook. Increasing the TCP/IP timeout increases the length of time that your computer waits for TCP/IP connections to succeed before timing out. See the sidebar "Increase TCP Timeout for Shared Connections," page 78, for details on configuring the TCP/IP timeout.

Using Offline Folders

Although you don't have to use offline folders when you work with Exchange Server over a remote connection, you do need a set of offline folders to work offline. If you haven't set up offline folders and can't connect to the remote server, Outlook can't start. One of your first tasks after you create your dial-up connection and configure your Exchange Server account should be to configure a set of offline folders.

> **note** The offline folder (OST) file does not appear as a separate set of folders in Outlook. In effect, Outlook uses it transparently when your computer is offline.

You can associate one set of offline folders with the Exchange Server account in your profile. The offline file has an OST file extension and stores a copy of all the folders and items in your Exchange Server mailbox. Outlook synchronizes the data between the two. For example, suppose that you create an e-mail message and a new contact item while working offline. The message goes in the Outbox folder of the offline store, and the new contact item goes in the Contacts folder of the offline store. When you next connect to the server and perform a synchronization, Outlook moves the message in the local Outbox to the Outbox folder on your Exchange Server, and the message then gets delivered. Outlook also copies the new contact item in your local Contacts folder to the Contacts folder stored on the Exchange Server. Any additional changes, including those at the server (such as new e-mail messages waiting to be delivered), are copied to your local offline folders.

An OST file, like a personal folders (PST) file, contains Outlook folders and items. One difference, however, is that you can have only one OST file, while you can have multiple PST files. Also, Outlook synchronizes the offline store with your Exchange Server automatically but does not provide automatic synchronization for PST files.

For more information on adding PST files to a profile, see "Adding Other Data Stores," page 50.

Follow these steps to configure offline storage with an OST file:

1   If Outlook is running, choose Tools, E-Mail Accounts. Otherwise, right-click the Outlook icon on the desktop, choose Properties, and then click E-Mail Settings.

2   Select View Or Change Existing E-Mail Accounts and click Next.

3   Select the Exchange Server account and click Change.

4   Click More Settings and then click the Advanced tab.

5   Click Offline Folder File Settings to open the dialog box shown in Figure 35-7.

Figure 35-7. Specify the file name and other settings for the OST file.

6   In the File box, specify a path and name for the OST file.

7   Select the necessary encryption setting and click OK.

8   On the Advanced tab, verify that the Enable Offline Use option is selected and click OK.

9   Click Next and then click Finish.

Synchronizing with the Exchange Server Mailbox

After you add an OST file to your profile, you need to synchronize the file with your Exchange Server mailbox at least once before you can work offline.

Follow these steps to synchronize your offline folders:

1   Connect to the remote network where your Exchange Server is located using the Internet, a dial-up connection to a remote access server on the remote LAN, or other means (such as ISDN, cable modem, or DSL).

2 Open Outlook.

3 Choose Tools, Send/Receive, Microsoft Exchange Server. Outlook then synchronizes with the Exchange Server.

> **note** If you specified a name for the account other than the default Microsoft Exchange Server, select that account name on the Send/Receive menu. You'll find the account name on the General tab of the account's Properties dialog box.

Synchronizing with Send/Receive Groups

The preceding section explained how to synchronize your offline folders and your Exchange Server mailbox. Sometimes, though, you might not want to synchronize all folders each time you perform a send/receive operation. You can use send/receive groups to define the actions that Outlook takes when sending and receiving. For example, you might want to create a send/receive group that sends only mail waiting in your local Outbox and doesn't retrieve waiting messages from the server.

> For a detailed discussion of send/receive groups, see "Controlling Synchronization and Send/Receive Times," page 190.

Using an Offline Address Book

Whether you're composing messages offline or creating tasks to assign to others, chances are good that you want access to your Exchange Server address book so that you can address messages to other users in your organization. If the Global Address List (GAL) doesn't change very often on the server (employee turnover at your company is low), you can get by with downloading the offline address book infrequently. Otherwise, you'll need to update the offline address book more often.

> **tip** Download additional address lists
>
> You can download additional address lists from the server if the Exchange Server administrator has created additional address books and given you the necessary permissions to access them. Additional address books give you quick access to addresses that are sorted using different criteria than the GAL uses or access to other addresses not shown in the GAL (such as external contacts).

To download the address book manually whenever you want an update, follow these steps:

1 Choose Tools, Send/Receive, Download Address Book to open the Offline Address Book dialog box (see Figure 35-8).

Figure 35-8. Use the Offline Address Book dialog box to specify options for downloading the offline address book.

2 Select options as needed from the following:

- **Download Changes Since Last Send/Receive.** Download only changes made since the last time you performed a send/receive operation. Clear this option to download the entire address list.

- **Full Details.** Download all address information, including phone, fax, and office location. You must select this option if you want to send encrypted messages, because you need the users' digital signatures.

- **No Details.** Download only e-mail addresses and no additional address book details.

- **Choose Address Book.** Select the address book you want to download.

3 Click OK to download the address book.

In addition to performing manual offline address book updates, you also can configure a send/receive group to download the address book.

Follow these steps to do so:

1 In Outlook, choose Tools, Send/Receive Settings, Define Send/Receive Groups.

2 Select the send/receive group in which you want to configure the address book download, and then click Edit.

Chapter 35: Working Offline and Remotely

3 On the Accounts bar, select your Exchange Server account (see Figure 35-9).

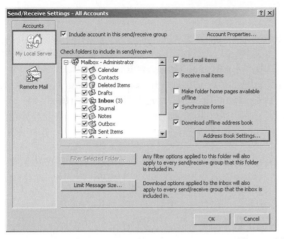

Figure 35-9. You can configure automatic offline address book synchronization.

4 Select the Download Offline Address Book check box, and then click Address Book Settings to open the Offline Address Book dialog box.

5 Configure settings as necessary in the Offline Address Book dialog box (discussed in the preceding set of steps) and then click OK.

6 Click OK to close the Send/Receive Settings dialog box.

Each time you synchronize folders using the send/receive group, Outlook downloads the offline address book according to the settings you specified. You probably won't want to configure this option for the default All Accounts send/receive group unless you have a fast connection to the server and your offline address book changes frequently. One option is to create a send/receive group that downloads only the offline address book and does not process any other folders. However, this is essentially the same as choosing Tools, Send/Receive, Download Address Book. Consider how often you need to download the address book and work that task into your send/receive groups as you see fit.

Using Remote Mail

Outlook's remote mail feature lets you manage your messages without downloading them from the server. With remote mail, you connect to the e-mail server, download the headers for new messages, and disconnect. You can take your time reviewing the message headers to decide which ones you want to download, which ones you want to delete without reading, and which ones can remain on the server for later. Then you can connect again and download the messages you've marked to retrieve, leaving the others on the server or deleting them, depending on how you marked the message headers.

To learn how to work with headers using remote mail, see "Working with Message Headers," page 368.

Remote mail is useful when you have a message with a very large attachment waiting on the server, and you want to retrieve only your most critical messages without spending the time or connect charges to download the attachment. You can connect with remote mail and select the messages for downloading, leaving the one with the large attachment on the server for when you have more time or are back in the office and can download it across the network or through a broadband Internet connection.

Remote mail is also useful when a corrupt message in your mailbox might prevent Outlook from downloading your messages. You can connect with remote mail, delete the problem message without attempting to download it, and then continue working normally.

The remote mail feature, strictly defined, works only with Exchange Server accounts; but Outlook also provides features similar to remote mail for POP3, IMAP, and HTTP accounts. For details on performing selective processing for other types of accounts, see "Understanding Remote Mail Options," page 366.

Remote Mail vs. Offline Folders

Remote mail and offline folders fulfill two different functions. Offline folders let you synchronize your local offline folders with your Exchange Server mailbox, allowing you to work offline. Remote mail lets you manage headers remotely without downloading their associated messages. You'll probably use both at one time or another. In fact, to use remote mail, you must either use an offline folder or configure your mail for delivery to a set of personal folders.

note You can achieve much the same effect with send/receive groups that you can with remote mail. For example, you can configure a send/receive group to download only message headers and not message bodies and then perform a send/receive operation on that group to retrieve the message headers.

Configuring Your System for Remote Mail

You must configure your Exchange Server account for offline use and add an offline folder file to your configuration. Or you must add a PST file to the configuration and configure it as the delivery store for mail. In most cases, you probably don't want to use a PST file to store your Exchange Server messages, preferring to leave them on the Exchange Server. For Exchange Server accounts, therefore, an offline file is the way to go.

Follow these steps to configure your Exchange Server account for offline use:

1 If Outlook is running, choose Tools, E-Mail Accounts. Otherwise, right-click the Outlook icon on the desktop, choose Properties, and then click E-Mail Accounts.

2 Select View Or Change Existing E-Mail Accounts and click Next.

3 Select the Exchange Server account and click Change.

4 Click More Settings and then click the Advanced tab.

5 Click Offline Folder File Settings to open the Offline Folder File Settings dialog box (shown earlier in Figure 35-7 on page 862).

6 Accept the default file path and name, type a new one, or click Browse to locate and select a file.

7 Select one of the following options and then click OK:

- **No Encryption.** Slightly faster performance but less security.

- **Compressible Encryption.** Moderate performance and increased security with the ability to compress the data file for storage efficiency.

- **Best Encryption.** Trades performance for optimum security. The OST file cannot be compressed, but you gain better encryption for increased security.

8 If you did not specify an existing OST file, Outlook prompts you to create one. Click Yes to create the file.

9 Make sure the Enable Offline Use option is selected, and then click OK to close the Microsoft Exchange Server dialog box.

10 Click Next and then click Finish.

Before you can work offline, you must first synchronize the offline folder file with your Exchange Server mailbox. Generally, you can do so by simply connecting to Exchange Server and performing a full send/receive operation.

Downloading Message Headers

When processing messages selectively, you first download the message headers and then decide what actions you want to perform with each message, based on its header.

Downloading message headers for an account is easy:

1 In Outlook, choose Tools, Send/Receive, Work With Headers, Download Headers.

Chapter 35

2   Select one of the following (the options vary depending on the number of accounts on your system):

- **This Folder.** Download message headers for the currently selected folder.

- **All Accounts.** Download message headers for all accounts. (Outlook downloads only headers in the account's Inbox folder.)

- *<Account Name>.* Select a specific account whose headers you want to download.

Outlook then performs a send/receive operation but downloads only headers from the specified account or accounts. If you want to save on connect charges, you can disconnect from the server to review your messages to decide what action to take on each.

The icon for a message header whose associated message has not been downloaded is the standard envelope icon, just as it is for downloaded but unread messages. However, Outlook also includes an icon in the Header Status column of the Inbox to indicate that the message has not yet been downloaded.

Controlling Remote Mail Through Send/Receive Groups

Rather than working with message headers manually, as explained in Chapter 13, "Processing Messages Selectively," you might prefer to process them automatically by configuring remote mail options in a send/receive group. This section explains how.

Remote mail provides options that you can use to control how it handles the downloading of items, among other processes. Although you can add remote mail to any send/receive group, it's good practice to set up a separate send/receive group just for remote mail. That way, you can process messages through remote mail by simply synchronizing folders with that particular send/receive group.

To configure the remote mail options, follow these steps:

1   Choose Tools, Send/Receive Settings, Define Send/Receive Groups to open the Send/Receive Groups dialog box (see Figure 35-10).

For more information on controlling message processing with send/receive groups, see "Controlling Synchronization and Send/Receive Times," page 190.

2   Click New.

Chapter 35: Working Offline and Remotely

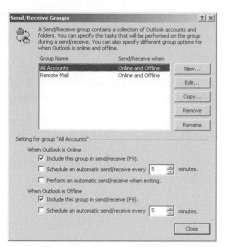

Figure 35-10. Use the Send/Receive Groups dialog box to configure how
Outlook processes your accounts.

3 Specify Remote Mail as the name of the new send/receive group. Outlook
opens the Send/Receive Settings dialog box for the group (see Figure 35-11).

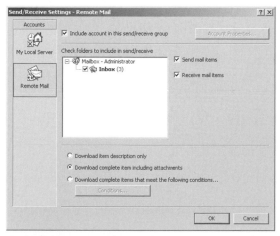

Figure 35-11. Use the Send/Receive Settings dialog box to configure options
for Remote Mail.

4 On the Accounts bar, select Remote Mail.

5 Select Include Account In This Send/Receive Group to activate the options in
the dialog box for the account. The Remote Mail account is the only account
that should be active for this send/receive group. If others are active, select
them on the Accounts bar and clear the Include Account In This Send/Re-
ceive Group check box. Inactive accounts have a red X on their icons.

6 Configure the following settings:

■ **Send Mail Items.** Outlook sends outgoing messages when you process this send/receive group.

■ **Receive Mail Items.** Outlook retrieves messages when processing this send/receive group. See the following settings for information on how to restrict what Outlook retrieves.

■ **Download Item Description Only.** Download message headers only.

■ **Download Complete Item Including Attachments.** Download headers, message bodies, and attachments (a standard receive operation).

■ **Download Complete Items That Meet The Following Conditions.** Selectively process messages using filters, as explained next, in step 7.

7 If you selected the last option, click Conditions to open the Filter dialog box (see Figure 35-12), which allows you to set up conditions that messages must meet to be processed. Click Advanced to open the Advanced dialog box (see Figure 35-13). Using both dialog boxes, you can define filters that download messages based on size, sender, recipient, attachments, importance, and many other conditions. Configure the options as needed and close the dialog boxes.

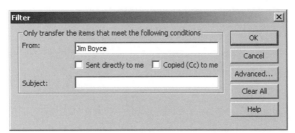

Figure 35-12. You can specify simple filters to control the downloading of messages.

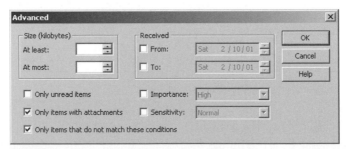

Figure 35-13. You can also create more advanced, complex filters for downloading messages.

8 Click OK to close the Send/Receive Settings dialog box, and click Close to close the Send/Receive Groups dialog box.

Accessing Messages Through a Web Browser

Microsoft introduced Outlook Web Access (OWA) in Microsoft Exchange Server 5.0 so that clients could access their Exchange Server mailboxes through a Web browser. OWA is also included in Microsoft Exchange Server 5.5. In addition, Microsoft has made significant improvements in OWA in Exchange 2000 Server to provide support for a larger number of users, better performance, and improved functionality for clients.

This chapter explores OWA and explains how to configure it under both Exchange Server 5.5 and Exchange 2000 Server. In addition to learning how to configure OWA, you'll also learn why OWA can be an important feature to implement and how best to put it to work for you.

The chapter doesn't provide an exhaustive look at OWA's technology or deployment, but rather serves to explain common configuration and management tasks associated with OWA. Although you'll find information about Exchange Server 5.5 and OWA, the discussion focuses primarily on Exchange 2000 Server because of the added benefits it offers.

Overview of Outlook Web Access

With OWA and a Web browser, users can send and receive messages, view and modify their calendars, and perform most of the other tasks available through Outlook or an Exchange Server client. Exchange 2000 Server provides some additional features not included in Exchange Server 5.5. OWA itself added some of these features; others are available in combination with Microsoft Internet Explorer 5.0 or later.

Outlook provides full access to an Exchange Server mailbox. Although OWA isn't intended as a replacement for Outlook, it is useful for roaming users who want to access the most common mailbox features when they don't have access to their personal Outlook installation. Linux, UNIX, and Macintosh users can also benefit from OWA by accessing Exchange Server mailboxes and participating in workgroup messaging and scheduling. In addition, OWA can save the administrative overhead, support, and licensing costs associated with deploying Outlook to users who don't need all that Outlook has to offer. These users can use a free Web browser to access many functions provided by Exchange Server.

OWA Features

Because e-mail is the primary function of Exchange Server and Outlook, OWA supports e-mail access. Users can view message headers and read messages (see Figure 36-1) as well as send, reply to, forward, and delete messages. This last capability—deleting messages—might seem commonplace but is a useful feature. If your mailbox contains a very large attachment or a corrupted message that is preventing you from viewing your messages in Outlook, you can use OWA to delete the message without downloading or reading it. Just open your mailbox in your Web browser, select the message header, and delete the message.

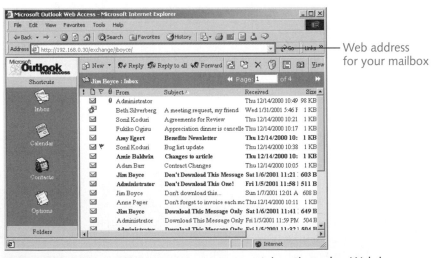

Web address for your mailbox

Figure 36-1. Using OWA, you can access your Inbox through a Web browser.

Chapter 36: Accessing Messages Through a Web Browser

---

tip   **Use remote mail for selective download**

You can use the Outlook remote mail feature to download only message headers and not message bodies. For details on using remote mail with Exchange Server, see "Using Remote Mail," page 865. For details on using remote mail with other types of e-mail servers, see "Understanding Remote Mail Options," page 366.

Exchange 2000 Server offers a few new features for messaging with OWA. For example, while the current and previous versions support rich-text messages, OWA 2000 now supports HTML-based messages as well. You also can access embedded objects in messages, another feature not supported by Exchange Server 5.*x*.

As mentioned earlier, you're not limited to just messaging—you can also access your Calendar folder through OWA. You can view and modify existing items and create appointments (see Figure 36-2). You can't perform all of the same scheduling tasks through OWA that you can with Outlook, but the ability to view your schedule and add appointments is useful, particularly when you're working from a remote location or a system without Outlook installed.

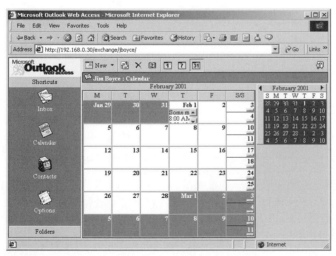

Figure 36-2.   Use OWA to manage your schedule as well as your e-mail messages.

Contacts are another type of item you can manage through OWA. You can view and modify existing contact items and add new ones (see Figure 36-3 on the next page). Other new features in OWA 2000 include support for ActiveX objects, named URLs for objects rather than GUIDs (globally unique identifiers), multimedia messages, and public folders containing contact and calendar items.

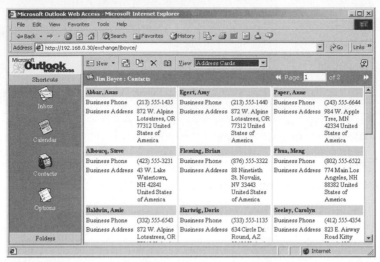

Figure 36-3. You can also work with your Contacts folder through OWA.

For all its usefulness, OWA has some limitations. For example, you can access your Tasks folder, but you can't create tasks. Likewise, you can view the Journal folder, but you can't add journal entries. You can't use your mailbox offline through OWA as you can through Outlook and an offline folder (OST) file. Unlike Outlook, OWA doesn't support timed delivery and expiration for messages, a spelling checker, reminders, or Outlook rules for processing messages.

Web Browser Options

To access your mailbox through OWA, you can use any Web browser that supports JavaScript and HTML version 3.2 or later, including Internet Explorer 4.0 or later and Netscape 4.0 or later. Some features, however, rely on Internet Explorer 5.*x*, including drag-and-drop editing, shortcut menus, and native Kerberos authentication. In addition, browsers that support DHTML (Dynamic HTML) and XML (Extensible Markup Language) offer a richer set of features than those that do not. For example, Internet Explorer 5.*x* offers an interface for OWA that is much closer to the native Outlook client, including a folder tree for navigating and managing folders as well as a preview pane.

> **note** Kerberos authentication allows users to access multiple resources across the enterprise with a single set of user credentials, a capability Microsoft refers to as *single sign-on*.

OWA Architecture

Active Server Pages (ASP) provide communication between the client and Exchange Server 5.*x*. Thus, when you access a mailbox on the Exchange Server through OWA, your target URL is an ASP page on the server. The server then uses MAPI (Messaging Application Programming Interface) to handle messaging requests generated through that page. Because the primary components of OWA are the ASP files that allow the client to generate messaging requests through the Web, OWA functions primarily as a Web site hosted under IIS (Internet Information Services, the Web service included with Microsoft Windows NT and Microsoft Windows 2000). The site uses ASP to process client requests and then uses HTTP to communicate with the Exchange Server. The server uses MAPI to manipulate the message store. The combination of ASP and MAPI imposes a performance overhead that limits OWA's capabilities in Exchange Server 5.*x* and reduces the number of users a server can support through OWA.

Exchange 2000 Server uses a different architecture that improves performance and thereby increases the number of users a server can support. OWA in Exchange 2000 Server relies on HTML and DHTML rather than ASP. The user's browser still uses HTTP to connect to the site, but IIS simply passes the request to the Exchange Server and transmits replies back to the client. Therefore, although OWA requires some IIS configuration, it's now integrated in Exchange 2000 Server as part of the WebStore.

The WebStore provides a single store for multiple data elements, including e-mail messages, documents, and Web pages, and supports important features such as offline and remote client access. It supports multiple protocols, including HTTP, WebDAV, and XML, giving developers several options for building applications that integrate with the WebStore. The WebStore doesn't exist exclusively for OWA's benefit. Instead, it offers a richer set of features and capabilities for storing and accessing data through means other than just Outlook.

Authentication Options

OWA provides three options for authentication:

- **Basic.** Use clear text and simple challenge/response to authenticate access. This option offers the broadest client support but also offers the least security because passwords are transmitted as clear text.

- **Integrated Windows.** Use the native Windows authentication method for the client's operating system. On systems running Windows 2000, for example, Internet Explorer uses Kerberos to authenticate on the server. Other Windows platforms, including Windows 9x, Windows NT, and Windows Me, use NTLM challenge/response rather than Kerberos. Integrated Windows authentication provides better security than basic authentication because passwords are encrypted. The client doesn't need to enter authentication credentials because the browser uses the client's Windows logon credentials to authenticate on the OWA server.

> **note** Windows NT LAN Manager (NTLM) challenge/response authentication is the default authentication mechanism in Windows platforms earlier than Windows 2000.

- **Anonymous.** Use anonymous access for public folders in the Exchange Server store. This option can simplify administration.

In addition to these authentication methods, OWA supports the use of Secure Sockets Layer (SSL) to provide additional security for remote connections.

Topology Considerations for Deploying OWA

If you host only one Exchange 2000 Server computer, you have few considerations for deploying the server. If you have multiple servers, however, you need to think about how you will structure your Exchange Server environment. You should use a front-end–back-end server scheme if possible when you provide access to your Exchange Servers through HTTP (OWA), IMAP, or POP3 to users on the Internet. The front-end server sits on the Internet, either outside the firewall or inside a perimeter firewall, and accepts requests from clients on the Internet. The front-end server uses Lightweight Directory Access Protocol (LDAP) to query the Active Directory (AD) on the domain controller for the location of the requested resource (a mailbox, for example) and passes the request to the appropriate back-end server.

A front-end server is a specially configured Exchange 2000 Server. A back-end server is a normal Exchange 2000 Server that handles requests from the front-end server just as it does from other clients. Any server not configured as a front-end server acts by default as a back-end server. Figure 36-4 illustrates a sample front-end–back-end configuration.

Chapter 36: Accessing Messages Through a Web Browser

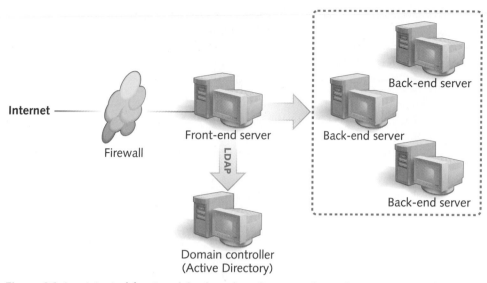

Figure 36-4. A typical front-end–back-end configuration for Exchange Server and OWA.

An advantage to using a front-end–back-end topology is that you expose only one namespace to the Internet. Because the front-end server functions as the point of entry for your back-end Exchange Servers, clients don't need to know that other servers exist. Without a front-end server, each user must know the name of the server hosting his or her mailbox and enter the appropriate URL, such as *http://mail2.proseware.tld*. You make it much easier to expand and rearrange the back-end server configuration without affecting your users by providing a front-end server as the entry point to the Exchange Server network. Users can simply connect to *http://mail.proseware.tld* and gain access to their accounts, regardless of where the accounts reside on the network. You can set up multiple front-end servers when you have a high volume of traffic through the front-end server.

Front-end servers also offer a performance advantage when you need to use SSL to provide additional security between the client and the server. The front-end server can be configured for SSL and perform the associated encryption and decryption, removing that load from the back-end servers. This frees up additional processor time for the back-end servers to process messaging requests from clients.

Another important reason to use a front-end server is that it gives you the ability to place the back-end servers behind a firewall. The front-end server doesn't expose the mail system to intrusion because it hosts no mailboxes. You can considerably reduce the risk of denial-of-service attacks on your back-end servers by configuring the front-end server to perform authentication before relaying requests to the back-end servers.

When a request comes in to a front-end server, the server uses LDAP to query the Active Directory to determine the location of the requested data. The front-end server then passes the request to the appropriate back-end server using HTTP port 80. SSL and encryption are never used between the front-end and back-end servers because the front-end server always uses port 80. This is true even when clients are using SSL for their connection with the front-end server. This also means that back-end servers must listen on port 80 and can't use a nonstandard port. Clients must connect directly to servers with nonstandard ports, specifying the appropriate port number in the URL.

The front-end server acts as a proxy between the client and the back-end servers. The back-end servers handle the traffic from the front-end server just as they handle any other HTTP traffic, sending responses to the front-end server, which forwards them to the clients. Clients never know that the server processing their requests is different from the one they specified in the URL.

A front-end–back-end topology offers two options for authentication. The client can authenticate on the front-end server, which provides implicit authentication on the back-end server. Or the client can use explicit logon at the back-end server. In the former, clients specify the URL of the front-end server but don't include their account name in the URL (such as *http://mail.proseware.tld*). In the latter, clients add their account name, such as *http://mail.proseware.tld/jboyce*.

Explicit logon is useful when you need to access a mailbox you don't own but for which you have access permissions. When you use explicit logon, the front-end server extracts the user portion of the URL and combines it with the SMTP domain name to construct a fully qualified STMP address. The front-end server looks up the address in the Active Directory and forwards the request to the back-end server for the user based on the information it finds in the AD.

As you begin planning how you will deploy and manage your Exchange Servers in light of OWA, keep the front-end–back-end topology requirements in mind. Decide which strategy—including the placement of front-end servers in relationship to firewalls—makes the most sense for your organization.

Configuring OWA in Exchange Server 5.5

By default, OWA is not installed when you install Exchange Server 5.5. Instead, you must select it during installation. If you've already installed Exchange Server but didn't install OWA, perform a backup of your Exchange Server system (just for good measure), and then run Setup again to add OWA. Installation is simply a matter of selecting OWA in the components list.

note Before you install OWA for Exchange Server 5.5, make sure you've installed IIS 4.0 or later. OWA for Exchange 2000 Server requires IIS 5.0.

Setup adds OWA to the default Web site as a virtual directory named Exchange when you install OWA in Exchange Server 5.5. You configure many of the properties for OWA through the IIS console, but others are configured through the Exchange Administrator. The following sections explain how to configure various properties for OWA in Exchange Server 5.5. They are intended to provide a primer to the most common configuration tasks rather than complete coverage of OWA administration.

Enabling and Disabling OWA Globally in Exchange Server 5.5

By default, Setup enables OWA. If you want to prevent Exchange Server from responding to HTTP requests, however, you can disable the HTTP protocol.

Follow these steps to enable or disable the HTTP protocol in Exchange Server:

1 Open the Exchange Administrator, and then expand the site in which you want to configure OWA.

2 Click the Protocols branch.

3 In the right pane, double-click HTTP (Web) Site Settings to open the dialog box shown in Figure 36-5.

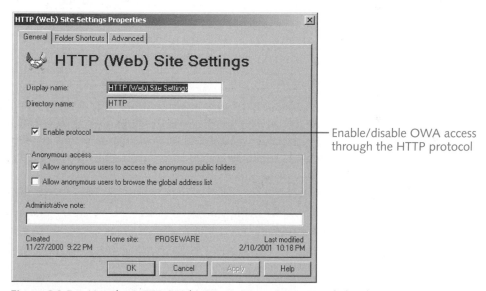

Figure 36-5. Use the HTTP (Web) Site Settings Properties dialog box to enable or disable HTTP.

4 Select the Enable Protocol option to enable OWA, or clear the option to disable it.

5 Click OK.

Enabling and Disabling OWA for Individual Users in Exchange Server 5.5

You can enable or disable OWA not only at the site level but also for specific mailboxes.

You do this by enabling or disabling the HTTP protocol for the mailbox, as described here:

1 Open the Exchange Administrator, and then open the Recipients container.

2 Double-click the mailbox for which you want to configure OWA, to open the mailbox's Properties dialog box.

3 Click the Protocols tab (see Figure 36-6).

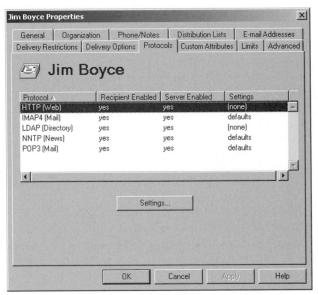

Figure 36-6. You can configure protocols for individual mailboxes to control the types of access the user has to the mailbox.

4 Select HTTP and then click Settings.

5 Select Enable HTTP For This Recipient to enable OWA for the user, or clear the option to disable OWA.

6 Click OK, and then close the mailbox's Properties dialog box.

Controlling Anonymous Access to Public Folders in Exchange Server 5.5

You can configure Exchange Server to allow anonymous access to public folders, which is useful if you post public messages or data to the folders. You might want to deny anonymous access, however, if the data in the public folders is for internal use only.

Follow these steps to allow or deny anonymous access to public folders:

1 Open the Exchange Administrator, open the site, and click the Protocols branch at the site level.

2 In the right pane, double-click HTTP.

3 Select the option Allow Anonymous Users To Access The Anonymous Public Folders to allow access, or clear the option to deny access.

4 Click OK to close the dialog box.

Publishing Public Folders in Exchange Server 5.5

You can publish Exchange Server public folders for anonymous access by users who connect to the Exchange Server through a Web browser.

You do this by creating folder shortcuts through the Exchange Administrator:

1 Open the Exchange Administrator, open the site, and click the Protocols object at the site level.

2 In the right pane, double-click HTTP.

3 Click the Folder Shortcuts tab (see Figure 36-7).

Figure 36-7. Use the Folder Shortcuts tab to publish public folders.

4 Click New, select the folder for which you want to create the shortcut, and then click OK.

5 Click OK to close the HTTP (Web) Site Settings Properties dialog box.

Configuring the Global Address List in Exchange Server 5.5

You can configure the Global Address List to allow or deny anonymous access and also configure the number of addresses that the Global Address List returns.

Follow these steps to configure the address list:

1 Open the Exchange Administrator, open the site, and click the Protocols object at the site level.

2 In the right pane, double-click HTTP.

3 Click the General tab.

4 Select the option Allow Anonymous Users To Browse The Global Address List to allow anonymous access, or clear the option to prevent it.

5 Click the Advanced tab (see Figure 36-8).

6 Specify a maximum number of entries to be returned or select No Limit, and click OK.

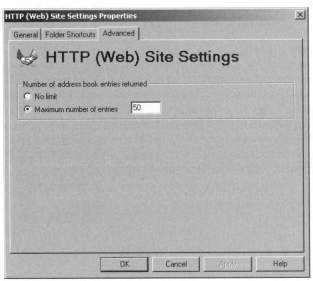

Figure 36-8. Use the Advanced tab to specify options for the address list.

Configuring OWA in Exchange 2000 Server

You configure OWA in Exchange 2000 Server using the Exchange System Manager console and the Active Directory Users And Computers console. Although you can also configure certain aspects of OWA through the Internet Services Manager console, these changes are overwritten by changes you make through the Exchange System Manager. You should work with Active Directory Users And Computers and the Exchange System Manager for most configuration tasks, using the IIS console only for tasks not available elsewhere. Typical configuration tasks include specifying which users can access their mailboxes through OWA, which authentication methods to allow, and which public folders are exposed to clients.

Enabling and Disabling OWA Globally in Exchange 2000 Server

Unlike the situation in Exchange Server 5.5, OWA is enabled or disabled for a given virtual server through the properties of that server in IIS. You have two primary means for disabling OWA on a global basis: remove the Exchange virtual directories or configure security for them to prevent access by all or by most, depending on your needs. For example, you might deny access to a virtual directory to all but a specific range of IP addresses.

InsideOut

I don't recommend removing the virtual directories because getting them back again and functioning can be difficult. Instead, simply deny access to the virtual directories for all IP addresses. This has the same result as removing the virtual directories—no one can get to them, and therefore no one can use OWA on the virtual server. If you decide later to implement OWA, all you need to do is change the restrictions and possibly tweak authentication.

Follow these steps to configure security for the Exchange virtual directories:

1 From the Administrative folder, open the Internet Services Manager console.

2 Expand the Default Web Site entry, right-click the Exchange virtual directory, and choose Properties.

3 Click the Directory Security tab (see Figure 36-9 on the next page).

Chapter 36

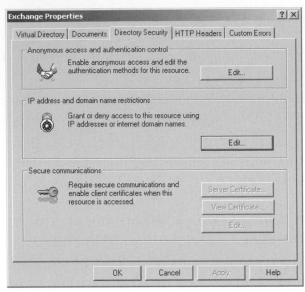

Figure 36-9. You control security and access for the virtual directory on the Directory Security tab.

4 In the IP Address And Domain Name Restrictions group, click Edit to display the IP Address And Domain Name Restrictions dialog box (see Figure 36-10).

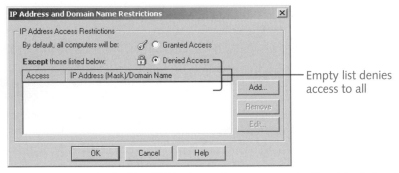

Empty list denies access to all

Figure 36-10. To disable OWA, deny all users access to the virtual directory.

5 Click the Denied Access option to deny access to all, effectively disabling OWA. Alternatively, if you want to allow access by specific addresses or domains, click Add to display the Grant Access On dialog box (see Figure 36-11). You can grant access based on the individual IP address, the subnet (group of computers), or the client's domain name.

6 Close all dialog boxes and return to the IIS console.

7 Repeat these steps on the Public and Exadmin virtual directories if you need to restrict access to those as well.

Chapter 36: Accessing Messages Through a Web Browser

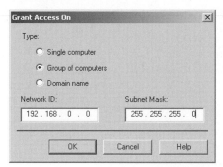

Figure 36-11. You can grant selective access to the virtual directory.

InsideOut

Granting or denying access based on domain name requires a reverse Domain Name System (DNS) lookup for each client, which can impose a lot of overhead on the server and generate a ton of network traffic. It also requires that you configure host records in DNS for each host. Although this is made simpler by the ability of Windows 2000 to automatically register host names in DNS, it can still be difficult to set up and administer, particularly when you must support non–Windows 2000 clients (such as Windows NT and Windows 9x). I recommend that you use this method only if your server can handle the load.

Enabling and Disabling OWA for Individual Users in Exchange 2000 Server

OWA is enabled for all users by default when Setup installs Exchange 2000 Server. You might want to limit the users who can use OWA, however, for security, performance, or other reasons.

You configure OWA access through the Active Directory Users And Computers console:

1 Open the console and choose View, Advanced Features.

2 Expand the Users branch and double-click the user for whom you want to deny access.

3 Click the Exchange Advanced tab (see Figure 36-12 on the next page).

4 Click Protocol Settings to open the Protocols dialog box.

5 Select HTTP and then click Settings.

6 Clear the Enable For Mailbox option and click OK.

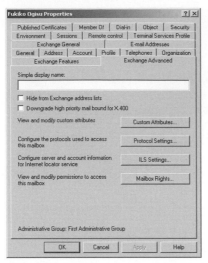

Figure 36-12. Configure protocols for individual accounts on the Exchange Advanced tab.

7 Click OK to close the Protocols dialog box, and then configure any other settings as needed for the user.

8 Close the user's Properties dialog box.

Troubleshooting

Public, Exchange, and Exadmin virtual directories display the Stop icon.

If the Public, Exchange, and Exadmin virtual directories show a Stop icon in the IIS console (indicating an error), try stopping and then restarting the Default Web Site. This problem seems to occur when IIS can't find the paths referenced by the virtual directories, which results from the Exchange services not being fully started before the site starts up. This could point to a server that needs tuning or simply to a lack of sufficient hardware to handle the job.

Controlling Anonymous Access to Public Folders in Exchange 2000 Server

Exchange 2000 Server creates a virtual directory named Public under the Default Web Site to provide access to public folders through the Web. You can configure the properties for the Public virtual directory to control whether users have anonymous or authenticated access to the folders. Providing anonymous access through the virtual directory's security settings, however, doesn't necessarily grant anonymous access to the folder. You can configure properties for the folder through the Exchange System Manager to further refine access.

> **tip** To access public folders through the Web, point your browser to *http://<server>/public*, where <server> is the DNS name or IP address of the server hosting the virtual directory.

Follow these steps to allow or deny anonymous access to public folders:

1 From the Administrative Tools folder, open the IIS console.

2 Expand the Default Web Site entry, right-click the Public virtual directory, and choose Properties.

3 Click the Directory Security tab.

4 In the Anonymous Access And Authentication group, click Edit to display the Authentication Methods dialog box (see Figure 36-13).

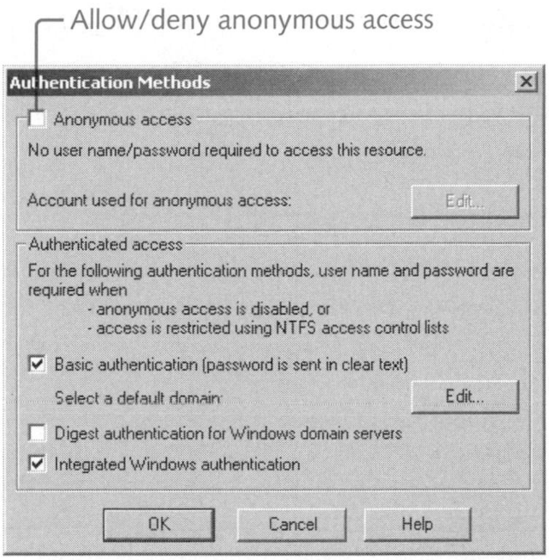

Figure 36-13. Use the Authentication Methods dialog box to allow or deny anonymous access.

5 Select the Anonymous Access check box to allow anonymous access to the virtual directory, or clear this check box to deny anonymous access.

6 Click OK and then close the dialog box for the virtual directory.

As mentioned, you can further control access to public folders by configuring their security settings in the Exchange System Manager.

Here's how to configure these settings:

1 Open the Exchange System Manager and then open the Administrative Group containing the public folder or folders you want to configure.

2 Right-click the folder branch or a specific folder (depending on the level at which you want to set security) and choose Properties.

3 Click the Security tab.

4 Configure security for individuals and groups as needed, and then click OK.

5 Repeat the process for other public folders as needed.

Publishing Public Folders in Exchange 2000 Server

After you create additional public folders by using the Exchange System Manager, you can make them available through the Web by adding virtual directories for them under a virtual server (which doesn't have to be the same server on which the folders are hosted). You don't need to go through this process if you added the public folders through the existing Public Folders root, which is already accessible through the Public virtual directory. The folders appear automatically through the Web after you add them.

> For detailed information on creating and managing public folders, see "Creating Public Folders," page 775.

Follow these steps to add the virtual directory after you create the public folders through the Exchange System Manager:

1 From the Administrative Tools folder, open the IIS console.

2 Expand the Default Web Site entry, right-click the Public virtual directory, and choose New, Virtual Directory to start the Virtual Directory Creation Wizard.

3 Specify the following information when prompted by the wizard:

■ **Alias.** Specify the folder name you want users to see.

■ **Directory.** Browse the Exchange virtual volume and select the folder to be added (see Figure 36-14).

Figure 36-14. Select a folder from the Exchange virtual volume.

■ **Permissions.** Set the permissions for the virtual directory to control the actions users can perform. These can be overridden by properties you configure with the Exchange System Manager.

4 Right-click the newly created virtual directory in the IIS console and choose Properties.

5 Configure additional properties, such as access restrictions, as needed.

6 Click OK to close the virtual directory's Properties dialog box.

Public folders that you make accessible in this way do not show up by default when users browse the public folder store through *http://<server>/public*. They behave like FTP virtual folders in that a user must specify the path to them explicitly in the URL. Therefore, if you added a public folder under the Public virtual directory and gave it the alias *support*, users would connect to the URL *http://<server>/public/support* to use the folder. Or you could add a DNS alias to point to the virtual directory so that clients could connect to the directory using a simpler URL.

Troubleshooting

You get an HTTP Error 403 when trying to access public folders.

Suppose that you create a public folder in the Exchange System Manager and then add it as a new virtual directory under the Public virtual directory. When you try to browse to the folder by specifying its URL, you receive HTTP Error 403-Forbidden and a message stating that you are not authorized to view the page. The problem is that you have not allowed directory browsing. To correct this, open the properties for the virtual directory, click the Virtual Directory tab, select the Directory Browsing option, and then click OK.

Configuring a Front-End Server in Exchange 2000 Server

If you're using a front-end–back-end topology to configure the front-end server, you need to change one setting, as explained here:

1 Open the Exchange System Manager and locate the server in the Servers branch under the server's Administrative Group.

2 Right-click the server and choose Properties.

3 Click the General tab.

4 Select the option This Is A Front-End Server and then click OK.

5 To have the change take effect, restart the Exchange and IIS services or restart the server.

Chapter 36

Back-end servers handle requests from the front-end server just as they handle any other request, so you do not need to configure the back-end server.

When you designate an Exchange Server as a front-end server, you are directing the server to forward all HTTP, POP3, and IMAP4 traffic to the back-end servers. The front-end server can still host an information store and user mailboxes, but these mailboxes are accessible only through MAPI. You can't access the front-end server's store with any of these protocols because the server forwards all HTTP, POP3, and IMAP4 traffic.

Using OWA

After you install and configure OWA on the server, users can begin accessing their mailboxes through their Web browsers rather than (or in conjunction with) Outlook. This section explains how to connect to the Exchange Server and use OWA to access your mailbox.

Connecting to the Server

Typically, you connect to the Exchange Server through the URL *http://<server>/exchange*, where <server> is the DNS name, IP address, or NetBIOS name of the server. (The NetBIOS option is applicable only on an intranet or when you use WINS or Lmhosts to map the NetBIOS name to the server's IP address.) This URL isn't set in stone. The system administrator might have changed the virtual directory name for security purposes. Or the proper URL might be in the form *http://<mail.domain.tld>*, where <mail> is a host name on the network and <domain.tld> is your server's domain name. Check with the system administrator if you're not sure what URL to use to connect to the Exchange Server.

> **note** WINS (Windows Internet Name Service) maps NetBIOS names (computer names) to IP addresses, performing a service similar to that provided by DNS (although DNS maps host names, not NetBIOS names). You can use an Lmhosts file to perform NetBIOS name-to-address mapping without a WINS server, just as you can use a Hosts file to perform host name-to-address mapping without a DNS server.

Depending on the server's authentication settings, you might be prompted to log on. Enter your user name and password for the Exchange Server account. If the account resides in a different domain from the one in which the server resides, enter the account name in the form *<domain>\<account>*, where *<domain>* is the logon domain and *<account>* is the user account.

When you connect to your mailbox, you should see a page similar to the one shown in Figure 36-15 for Exchange 2000 Server or Figure 36-16 for Exchange Server 5.5. OWA opens your Inbox by default, but you can switch to other folders as needed. The left pane functions much as the Outlook Bar does, and you can select folders from it.

Chapter 36: Accessing Messages Through a Web Browser

(Throughout this chapter, I'll refer to the left pane as the Outlook Bar for simplicity.)
The right pane changes to show the folder's contents.

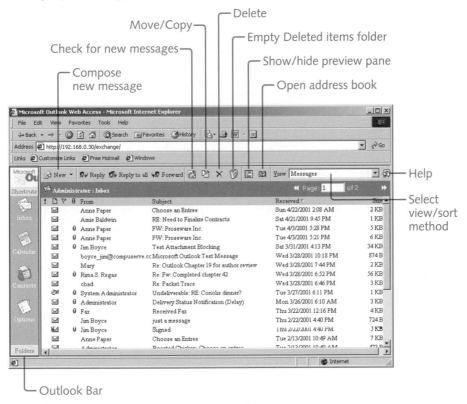

Figure 36-15. This is a typical look at a mailbox in OWA 2000.

Figure 36-16. This is a typical look at a mailbox in OWA 5.5.

> **note** The interface for OWA changed slightly between versions 5.5 and 2000. The follow-
> ing sections assume that you're using OWA to access an Exchange 2000 Server, but
> the procedures are similar for OWA 5.5. Also note that some features are not available
> with OWA 5.5 or with versions of Internet Explorer earlier than 5.0.

Sending and Receiving Messages

OWA automatically shows your current messages when you connect. To read a message, double-click its header to display a window similar to the one shown in Figure 36-17.

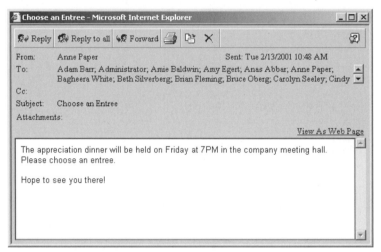

Figure 36-17. OWA displays messages in a separate window.

> **tip** Each message in OWA 5.5 acts like a hyperlink. You can click once on a message to
> open it. Select the check box beside a message to select the message without
> opening it.

As in Outlook, you can reply to or forward e-mail messages. Simply click the Reply or Reply To All button to reply to a message, or click the Forward button to forward a message. OWA opens the form shown in Figure 36-18. Add additional addresses as needed and type your text. If you want to add an attachment, click the Add Attachment toolbar button. OWA opens the window shown in Figure 36-19 so that you can add one or more attachments to the message.

Click to add an attachment

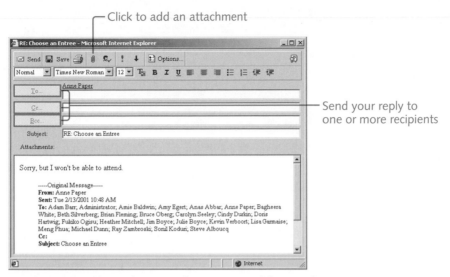

Figure 36-18. This is the OWA form generated for a reply.

Send your reply to
one or more recipients

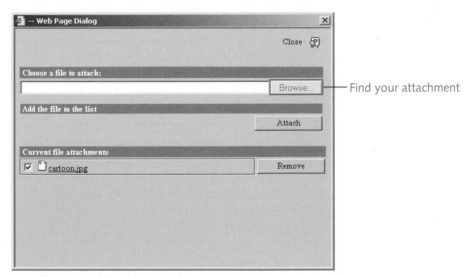

Find your attachment

Figure 36-19. OWA allows you to add attachments to e-mail messages.

You can set a handful of options for the message by clicking the Options toolbar button.
These correspond to options you have in Outlook (see Figure 36-20 on the next page).

Chapter 36

Figure 36-20. Configure message options, such as importance.

---

tip **Page through the Inbox**

If you maintain a lot of messages in your Inbox, they probably won't all fit on one page. OWA displays the number of pages in your Inbox at the top of the window to the right of the toolbar. You can type a page number or use the arrow buttons to page through the Inbox.

When you want to create a message, click the New toolbar button (refer to Figure 36-15). OWA opens a form similar to the one shown previously in Figure 36-17. You can specify addresses, attachments, body text, and other message properties.

---

tip To check for new messages, click the Check For New Messages toolbar button.

Sorting Messages

OWA by default displays messages sorted by date and time received. You can sort the messages by other properties as well. To do so, select an option from the View drop-down list on the OWA toolbar (refer to Figure 36-15). You can display only unread messages; sort by sender, subject, sent to, or conversation thread; or view only unread messages by conversation thread.

Copying and Moving Messages

The combination of Internet Explorer 5.x and Exchange 2000 Server allows you to copy and move messages by dragging in OWA. Open the folder containing the messages you want to copy or move. Click the Folders button in the left pane to open the folder list (as shown in Figure 36-21). To move messages, drag them from the right pane to the destination folder in the folder list. If you want to copy the messages rather than moving them, hold down the Ctrl key while dragging.

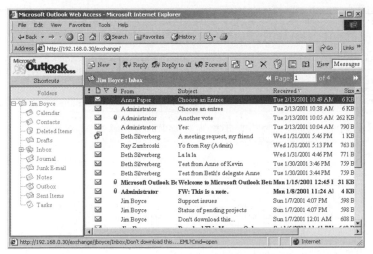

Figure 36-21. Drag messages to the folder list to copy or move them.

> **tip** You can click the Move/Copy toolbar button to copy or move selected messages.

Deleting Messages

Deleting messages in OWA is a good way to clean out your mailbox when you don't
have Outlook handy. It's also particularly useful for deleting large or corrupted messages
that would otherwise prevent Outlook from downloading your messages normally.

To delete messages in OWA, just select the messages and click the Delete toolbar button. OWA moves the messages to the Deleted Items folder.

> **tip** To delete in OWA 5.5, place a check mark beside the messages you want to delete
> and click the Delete Marked Items toolbar button. OWA deletes the messages and
> refreshes the page.

Working with Other Folders

As mentioned, OWA does not limit you to working only with your Inbox. You can
work with your Calendar, Contacts, and other Outlook folders as well as with other
message folders. In short, all folders stored in your mailbox, as well as public folders,
are available.

Chapter 36

Selecting a Different Folder

When you select a different folder on the Outlook Bar, OWA displays the contents of the selected folder in the right pane. Click the Folders button on the Outlook Bar to display the folder list, which you can use to select folders other than those shown in the Shortcuts group.

---

tip   In OWA 5.5, you can select folders from the folder list that appears between the left and right panes for all folders except the Calendar folder. Click the Up One Folder icon above the folder name to move to the parent folder in Calendar.

Creating New Folders

You can create new folders in OWA, subject to your permissions on the server, by following these steps:

1   Click the arrow beside the New toolbar button.

2   Choose Folder to open the Create New Folder dialog box (see Figure 36-22).

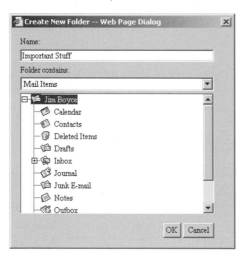

Figure 36-22.   Use the Create New Folder dialog box to create a folder in OWA.

3   In the Name box, specify a name for the folder.

4   In the Folder Contains drop-down list, select the type of folder.

5   Select the parent folder in the folder list.

6   Click OK to create the folder.

> **note** OWA 5.5 limits you to creating seven public folders for messages.

Copying, Moving, Renaming, and Deleting Folders

While in OWA, you can copy, move, and delete folders in your Exchange Server mailbox. To perform either of the first two actions, display the folder on the Outlook Bar, right-click it, and choose either Copy or Move. OWA displays a dialog box containing a folder list in which you can select the destination folder.

To rename a folder, right-click the folder on the Outlook Bar and choose Rename. If you want to delete the folder, right-click it and choose Delete.

Working with Calendar, Contacts, and Other Items

In addition to working with the Inbox or other message folders, you can also manage your schedule, contacts list, and other items and folders on the Exchange Server.

Calendar Folder

To manage your schedule, click the Calendar icon on the Outlook Bar. OWA updates the right pane to display your Calendar folder. Click the toolbar buttons to choose between Day, Week, or Month view. The page also includes a Date Navigator similar to the one in Outlook, which you can use to select dates (see Figure 36-23).

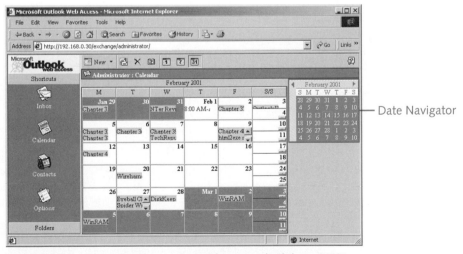

Date Navigator

Figure 36-23.   You can view and modify your schedule in OWA.

Click the New toolbar button or click the arrow beside New and choose Appointment to display an appointment form similar to the one in Outlook. Use the appointment form to specify the title, the time, and other properties for an appointment, just as you would in Outlook.

Contacts Folder

You can also view and manage contacts in OWA. Click the Contacts icon on the Outlook Bar to display the Contacts folder (see Figure 36-24). The default view is Address Cards, similar to the default view in Outlook. You can choose a different view in the View drop-down list.

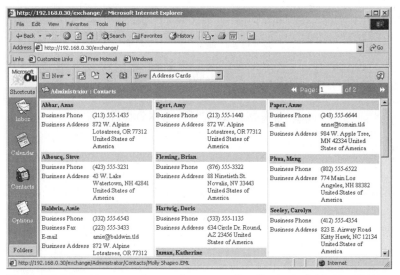

Figure 36-24. You can view and manage the Contacts folder in OWA.

Simply double-click a contact entry in the list to open a form that contains detailed information for that contact. Click New on the toolbar to open the form shown in Figure 36-25, which you can use to create new contact entries. Click Save And Close to save a new contact entry or to save changes to an existing contact entry.

Other Folders

In OWA, as in Outlook, you can work with the Journal, Notes, and other folders in your Exchange Server mailbox. OWA, however, allows you to create only messages, contact items, and appointments. You can view but not create items in the other folders.

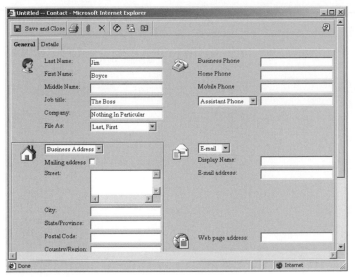

Figure 36-25. The form for creating contact entries in OWA is similar to the contact form in Outlook.

Configuring the Out Of Office Assistant in OWA

The Out Of Office Assistant automatically responds to messages when you are out of the office. The Out Of Office Assistant functions essentially as a server-side rule, replying to messages as they arrive in your Inbox. Although you usually configure the Out Of Office Assistant in Outlook, you can also configure it in OWA.

For details on using the Out Of Office Assistant, see "Using the Out Of Office Assistant,"
page 254.

To configure the Out Of Office Assistant in OWA, connect to the server by using your Web browser and open the Shortcuts group on the Outlook Bar. Click the Options icon to view the Options page (see Figure 36-26 on the next page), where the Out Of Office Assistant properties appear. To turn on the Out Of Office Assistant, click I'm Currently Out Of The Office. In the AutoReply box, type the message that you want the Exchange Server to send as a reply to messages that arrive in your Inbox. Click Save to save the changes. When you want to turn off the Out Of Office Assistant, open the Options page again and click I'm Currently In The Office.

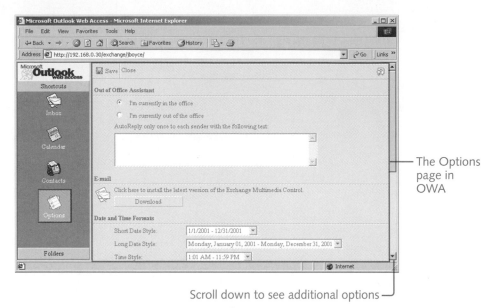

The Options page in OWA

Scroll down to see additional options

Figure 36-26. Configure the Out Of Office Assistant on the Options page.

Configuring Time and Calendar Options for OWA

You can also use the OWA Options page (see Figure 36-27) to set a few other options for OWA (in addition to the Out Of Office Assistant, as just discussed). You can configure date and time options, calendar options, and contact options as well as change your password. You can also download the Exchange Multimedia Control, an ActiveX control that provides support for multimedia messages.

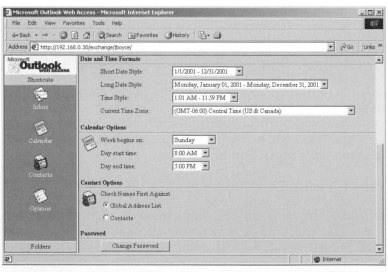

Figure 36-27. Use the Options page to configure additional OWA options.

Network, Platform, and Deployment Considerations

A number of network configuration and architecture factors come into play when you set up client and server computers running Microsoft Outlook and Microsoft Exchange Server. While it's true that you can get Outlook and Exchange Server to work in almost any environment, taking the time to understand the vast number of architectural considerations will make setup and deployment a lot easier. This chapter outlines some of these best practices; more information is available in the Exchange-related and Outlook-related white papers on Microsoft's MSDN Web site, *http://msdn.microsoft.com*.

Workgroup and Domain Setup

You must deploy Exchange 2000 Server in a Microsoft Windows NT or Microsoft Windows 2000 domain. (As described in Chapter 31, Exchange 2000 Server runs only on a Windows 2000 Server with Active Directory and Service Pack 1 or later.) When you use Exchange Server 5.5 on a Windows NT 4.0 Server, the Exchange directory is separate from the Windows user directory—the two do not interact. When you want to create distribution lists, you add Exchange Server mailboxes to those lists. In contrast to the disparate nature of Windows NT 4.0 and Exchange Server 5.5, Windows 2000 Server and Exchange 2000 Server have full integration between the Exchange directory and the Windows Active Directory. Active Directory contains a type of group known as a distribution group. You cannot use a distribution group for security purposes—you can use it only for sending e-mail. A distribution group is much like a distribution list in Exchange Server 5.5, except that it consists of a group of users rather than a group of mailboxes.

You can also add e-mail addresses to Windows 2000 security groups in Exchange 2000 Server. Right-click the group in Active Directory Users And Computers, choose Properties, and add an e-mail address on the General tab. Because distribution lists often mirror security groups, this feature eases the administrative burden of assigning mailboxes to distribution lists.

Using Roaming Profiles

Using a roaming profile gives your desktop a consistent look and feel, no matter which workstation you're using. Normally, your user profile contains cookies, Favorites, and History from Microsoft Internet Explorer; the Application Data directory; files stored in personal folders; and the Send To and Start menu contents. In addition, when you use Outlook without Exchange Server, the personal folders (PST) file containing Outlook data is stored in the Application Data directory. If you configure a roaming profile, all this data follows you to each computer you use.

> **note**   Don't confuse the term *roaming profile* with an Outlook profile. The two are not synonymous. The former stores your working environment in Windows NT or Windows 2000, and the latter stores your Outlook settings.

The process of configuring a roaming profile is similar in Windows NT and Windows 2000. You must store the roaming profile in a network share (such as \\<server>\profiles), and it should appear in directories named after the user name.

If you have an existing profile, you can configure a roaming profile by following these steps:

1 In Control Panel, double-click the System icon, and then click the User Profiles tab, shown in Figure 37-1.

2 Select the profile you want to use as a roaming profile, and then click the Copy To button.

3 In the Copy Profile To box, enter the directory to which the profile should be copied, such as \\<server>\profiles\username, and click OK to copy. The profile should now be stored in that directory.

4 To assign the roaming profile to a user in Windows 2000 Server, open Active Directory Users And Computers and select the user. Then right-click and choose Properties. Or, for Windows NT, open the User Manager For Domains tool, select the user, and choose User, Properties.

Chapter 37: Network, Platform, and Deployment Considerations

Figure 37-1. You can use the User Profiles tab to copy a local user profile to a shared network location, where you can use it as a roaming profile.

5 In Windows 2000 Server, click the Profile tab, and enter the profile location in the Profile Path box. This path should be **\\<*server*>\profiles\%username%**, which will automatically use the user name as the directory name. Click OK. Or, for Windows NT, click the Profile button and enter the path to the profile, such as **\\<*server*>\profiles\%username%**, in the User Profile Path box.

If you copied an existing profile to the specified directory (as described here), that profile is used the next time the user logs on; otherwise, a new default profile is created based on the default user profile maintained by Windows. Figure 37-2 shows the Profile tab with a user profile path assigned.

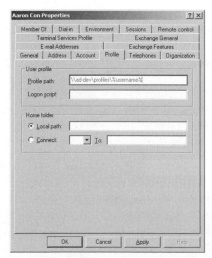

Figure 37-2. Use the Profile tab to assign a path to a roaming profile.

Troubleshooting

Logon is slow after you set up a roaming profile.

You should notice very little difference in logon time with a newly created roaming profile, as compared to the time required to log on without a roaming profile. As you work
with a profile over time, however, logon time invariably starts to increase. The reason
for this is the size of the profile—Windows must copy your profile folders and their
data from the server to the workstation each time you log on. As the number of cookies, cached Web pages, and items in your Outlook PST file (if you use one) increases,
logon time increases because more and more data must be copied from the server.

You can reduce logon time by preventing certain folders from being copied with the
profile. For example, you might not need to include your Temporary Internet Files
folder, Cookies folder, or Favorites folder in the roaming profile. To exclude folders,
open the Registry Editor and open HKEY_CURRENT_USER/Software/Microsoft/
Windows NT/CurrentVersion/Winlogon. Set the value of ExcludeProfileDirs to include
the directories you want to exclude from the profile; use a semicolon to separate multiple folders, such as **Favorites;Temporary Internet Files;Cookies**. Add other folders as
needed to prevent them from being copied across the network during logon. Note,
however, that certain functions won't be available if you exclude folders. For example,
you won't see your favorites when you browse the Internet from a remote computer.

Configuring Folders and Permissions

One primary reason for providing users with a data-storage location on the network is
to reduce the amount of data transferred with a roaming profile. Rather than including
a user's PST file in a roaming profile and having it copied across the network each time
the user logs on, you can place that PST on a network share where the user can access it
from any location on the local area network.

In most cases, you can have two types of shared storage: a private directory that only
the user can access (a *home directory*) and a public directory that everyone can access.
The public directory can contain software for distribution along with other files that
users want to share.

How you set up a home directory depends on the server's operating system and the
operating system used by each client. You have some additional flexibility in assigning
home folders if your users have Windows 2000 workstations rather than Windows 9*x*,
Windows Me, or Windows NT. This additional flexibility comes from the way in which
Windows 2000 handles Universal Naming Convention (UNC) paths. Other Windows
platforms support UNC paths in the form \\<*server*>\<*share*>, where <*server*> is
the name of the server and <*share*> is the name of the folder share point. On systems
that are not running Windows 2000, you can't specify a UNC path in the form

Chapter 37: Network, Platform, and Deployment Considerations

\\<*server*>\<*share*>\<*folder1*>\<*folder2*>, where <*folder1*> is a subfolder of <*share*> and <*folder2*> is a subfolder of <*folder1*>. Non–Windows 2000 platforms support paths only in the form \\<*server*>\<*share*>.

In Windows 2000, however, you can specify these longer UNC paths. For this reason, you can share a folder as the parent folder for all user home folders and use that folder as the share name when assigning a home folder, rather than sharing each user's home folder separately. For example, suppose that you create a folder on server srv1 named Users and share that as \\srv1\Users. When you specify the user's home folder in the user account properties, you can specify \\SRV1\Users\<*userfolder*>, where <*userfolder*> is the user's home folder under the Users share point. You do not have to share <*userfolder*> separately. This is a major administrative improvement over Windows NT. You don't even have to create the folder yourself—Windows 2000 creates it automatically, as you'll learn in the next section.

> **note**   From an administrative perspective, it isn't practical to host user folders on a FAT volume. You really need to use NTFS (NT file system) to ensure adequate security for each user's folder. This section assumes that you're setting up your user folders on an NTFS volume.

Before you begin creating user folders, determine which operating systems your users are running. If they all use Windows 2000, you can use the procedure explained in the following section. If you need to support Windows NT, Windows 9*x*, or Windows Me clients, however, you'll need to make one change: rather than assigning the path \\<*server*>\Users\<*username*> for the home folder, you must create individual shares, one per user, and specify that share name for the user's home folder. For example, if you need to assign a home directory to the user *jboyce*, create a folder named jboyce under the Users folder and share that as *jboyce*. Then specify \\<*server*>\jboyce as the user's home directory. (For the complete procedure, see "Setting Up a Home Folder in Windows NT Server," page 907.)

Share Permissions vs. NTFS Permissions

Share permissions, which you set on the Sharing tab of the folder's Properties dialog box when you share a folder, control who can access the share from the network. NTFS permissions, which you set on the Security tab, control who can access the folder itself, both locally and from the network. (NTFS permissions also require NTFS as the file system rather than FAT.) Users who have no share permissions for a folder can't see the share in Network Neighborhood. Users who have share permissions but no NTFS permissions can see the shared folder but receive an access-denied error message if they try to open the folder. Share permissions, then, act as the first line of defense against unauthorized access, and NTFS permissions allow you to apply a more granular level of security.

Setting Up a Home Folder in Windows 2000 Server

If all your client computers run Windows 2000, follow these steps in Windows 2000 Server to assign a home folder to a user:

1 Decide the server and path where the user's folder will reside and create the folder. I recommend creating a folder named \Users.

2 Right-click the folder and choose Sharing to open the Sharing tab of the folder's Properties dialog box. Select Share This Folder and enter Users as the share name.

3 Click OK to share the folder.

4 Right-click the Users folder and choose Properties. Then click the Security tab.

5 Clear the Allow Inheritable Permissions From Parent To Propagate To This Object check box. Click Remove when prompted.

6 Click Add. Locate and select Administrators in the Select Users, Computers Or Groups dialog box, and click Add. Then click OK.

7 Read & Execute, List Folder Contents, and Read permissions are now assigned to the Administrators group. Select Full Control and click OK to apply the permission changes (see Figure 37-3).

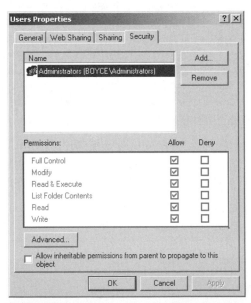

Figure 37-3. Use the Security tab to configure folder permissions.

8 Open the Active Directory Users And Computers console, right-click a user account, and choose Properties. Then click the Profile tab.

9 On the Profile tab (see Figure 37-4), select the Connect option and then select a drive letter in the drop-down list. Windows 2000 Server assigns this drive letter to the user's home folder when the user logs on.

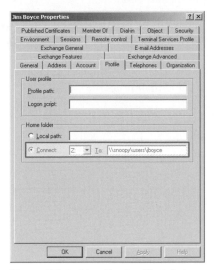

Figure 37-4. Use the Profile tab to specify the user's home directory.

10 In the To box, enter **\\\<server>\Users\\<username>**, where *<server>* is the name of the server where you created and shared the Users folder and *<username>* is the user's logon name.

11 Click OK to close the Properties dialog box. Windows 2000 Server creates the user's home folder in the specified location and grants the user full control.

tip If you can't remember the user's logon name, enter \\\<server>\Users\%username% for the home folder. Windows 2000 Server converts the %username% variable to the user's logon name and creates the appropriate folder.

Setting Up a Home Folder in Windows NT Server

Windows NT Server requires a slightly different procedure than Windows 2000 Server because of the differences in how the two systems apply security. The following procedure assumes that your client computers run Windows NT and must have the home folder specified in the form \\\<server>\\<username>, where *<username>* is the name of the user's home folder share point. If you have Windows 2000 clients that authenticate in the Windows NT Server domain, you can specify the home folder for these users in the form \\\<server>\\<sharepoint>\\<folder>, where *<folder>* is the user's home directory folder under the *<sharepoint>* shared folder. (See the previous section for details on using these extended UNC paths for Windows 2000 clients.)

Troubleshooting

Creating home folders for multiple users is time-consuming.

The process described in this section doesn't take very long when you're creating home folders for only a few users. But if you're facing the task for several dozen—or even several hundred—it can seem quite daunting. Unfortunately, Windows 2000 Server doesn't let you specify the profile for multiple users at one time (although you can select multiple users at one time and set certain properties across all selected users). One way to speed up the process slightly, if you don't have too many users to configure, is to simply highlight the path to the profile using the %username% variable (\\<server>\Users\%username%) and press Ctrl+C to copy the text to the clipboard. Open the next user's Profile tab, click in the To box, and press Ctrl+V to paste the path string from the clipboard.

Follow these steps to assign home folders in Windows NT Server:

1 Decide where user folders will be stored, log on as Administrator, and create the parent folder (such as \Users). You do not need to share this folder.

2 Right-click the folder you just created and choose Properties. Click the Security tab, and click Permissions to open the Directory Permissions dialog box (see Figure 37-5).

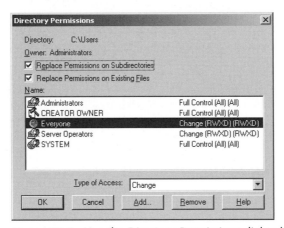

Figure 37-5. Use the Directory Permissions dialog box to configure access.

note If you specify a home folder in the form \\<server>\<sharepoint>\<folder> for a Windows NT, Windows 9x, or Windows Me user, that user will receive the folder \\<server>\<sharepoint> as a home folder rather than the correct one.

3 Verify that the Administrators group has full control, and select the Everyone group. Click Remove and then click OK.

4 Create folders in the \Users folder, one per user, giving each a name that matches the user's logon name.

5 Right-click the folder and choose Properties. Then grant the user's account full control.

6 Share the user's folder using a share name that matches the user's account name. Repeat for the other users' folders.

7 In Windows NT Server, open User Manager For Domains and select the user. Choose User, Properties and then click Profile to open the User Environment Profile dialog box. Alternatively, you can double-click the user and then click Profile.

8 Select Connect (see Figure 37-6), select a drive letter (the default is Z), and enter the path to the home directory. Enter a path in the form \\\<server>\<share>, where <server> is the computer sharing the folder and <share> is the user's home directory share name. You can use %username% in place of the actual folder name and let Windows NT Server replace it with the user name, if you prefer.

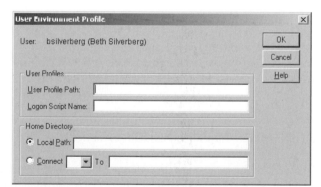

Figure 37-6. Use the User Environment Profile dialog box to specify the home directory path.

9 Click OK to close the User Environment Profile dialog box and then close the user's Properties dialog box.

Troubleshooting

Home directories don't work for Windows 9*x* clients.

You might have realized by trial and error that you can't assign home directories for Windows 9*x* and Windows Me clients the same way you assign them for Windows NT or Windows 2000 users. Windows 9*x* and Windows Me will not recognize drive mapping on the Profile tab of the user's Properties dialog box. Instead, you must perform the mapping by using the user's logon script. The following sample script will map drive Z to the share \\srv1\jboyce:

```
NET USE Z: \\SRV1\JBOYCE
```

Providing Network Access

Depending on the configuration of your network and your requirements, you have several issues to consider when providing remote network access: whether to provide outgoing access to the Internet or incoming access to your private network—or both.

Providing Shared Internet Connections

Innumerable methods are available for providing access to the Internet for your internal network. When you have only one computer, Internet access is simple: use a modem and configure Dial-Up Networking, or use a cable modem or ADSL modem and an Ethernet card. When you have more than one system on your network, however, providing remote access is more complex.

The first method of providing Internet access is to use a network device such as a router or firewall capable of Network Address Translation (NAT). If you use ISDN, ADSL, a cable modem, or any other kind of dedicated link, the provider can often issue a number of IP addresses and configure a device for that access. By connecting the customer premise equipment (CPE) such as the router or modem and the workstations to a hub or switch, and assigning the IP addresses given to you by the service provider, all the systems should have access to the Internet.

If you have a network connection with only one IP address, you can share the connection in several ways. You can use a device capable of packet forwarding and NAT, such as a firewall, Windows 2000 Server, or even Microsoft Proxy Server. The client computers and one interface of the device that will be doing NAT must all be connected to a hub or switch. The other interface of the NAT device must be connected to the CPE. You must then configure the device to perform NAT and assign the computers on the network addresses from the NAT pool (usually private IP addresses). When that configuration is in place, all systems should have access to the Internet. If you're using Microsoft Proxy Server, however, each client system must have its proxy server address set.

You configure NAT for a Windows 2000 Server from the Routing And Remote Access console found on the Administrative Tools menu. Right-click the server in the left pane and select Configure And Enable Routing And Remote Access to start the Routing And Remote Access Server Setup Wizard. In this wizard, you must specify that this is an Internet Connection Server and then specify that it will be using NAT. Select which network adapter is connected to the Internet, and NAT will start automatically.

The second way to provide Internet access is with Windows Internet Connection Sharing (ICS), which is essentially NAT included with Windows 2000. The only types of connection supported with ICS are dial-up and virtual private network (VPN) connections. To allow sharing, open the Properties dialog box for an existing connection in the Network And Dial-up Connections window and click the Sharing tab. Select the Enable Internet Connection Sharing For This Connection check box. After you click OK to save the changes to the connection properties, the IP address assigned to the network adapter of the computer changes to a static address assigned by ICS. All computers on the network that will use this shared connection must have their network adapters configured to automatically obtain IP address information. The ICS system assigns those addresses.

Providing Remote Network Access

You have a few ways to configure access into your network from the outside. You might want to provide this access for users at home or for a server or users at a branch office, for example. Windows operating systems provide dial-up remote access and remote access with VPNs. Both are configured similarly. As mentioned, the Routing And Remote Access console is located on the Administrative Tools menu in Windows 2000 Server. If no other Routing and Remote Access Services (RRAS) are configured on this system, right-click the server name and click Configure And Enable Routing And Remote Access to launch the Routing And Remote Access Server Setup Wizard. Select either Remote Access Server for a dial-up server or VPN server. Then enter configuration information for the VPN or dial-up clients.

A number of third-party products are also available for providing access to your network, including dedicated dial-up and VPN servers, as well as a number of routers and firewalls that provide VPN access into a network. As always, what works best in your network will be a function of the layout and architecture of that network.

When Multiple Users Share One Computer

Windows 2000 and Windows NT 4.0 are both full multiuser network operating systems, so local profiles are handled automatically. Users receive a profile directory the first time they log on to a system, and their settings are stored in that directory. Any number of users can log in and have profiles, and they will each see their own desktop when they are on that system. Windows 98 is not a full-fledged network operating system and doesn't provide this feature automatically. To enable Windows 98 user profiles, first open Control Panel, Passwords. Click the User Profiles tab and select Users Can Customize Their Preferences And Desktop Settings. For each profile, you have two options for User Profile Settings: Include Desktop Icons And Network Neighborhood Contents In User Settings and Start Menu And Program Groups In User Settings. Figure 37-7 shows the User Profiles tab with User Profiles enabled.

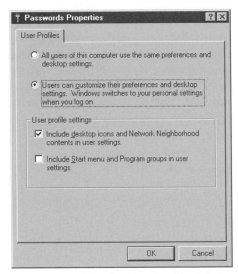

Figure 37-7. Use the User Profiles tab to enable user profiles so that users can have customized settings when they log in to a Windows 98 computer.

Data security is an important factor to consider when multiple users use a computer. When using a workstation (Windows 2000 or Windows NT) with a hard disk formatted with NTFS, you can set permissions for files so that other users who log in to that computer cannot access those files. By default, only the user and the Administrators group can access the user's profile directory on the local computer (where most documents and settings are saved). You might, however, want to add a folder to store other data on the hard disk and set security for that folder. To configure security for a folder, right-click it, choose Properties, and then click the Security tab, which displays who has access to the folder. By default, the folder will inherit the permissions of the folder in which it was created. In most cases, this is full access for everyone. You can add and remove users from the list and set their access level. In Windows 2000 Server, you must clear the Allow Inheritable Permissions From The Parent To Propagate To This Object check box, and then click Remove when prompted to remove any inherited permissions.

Group Policy Considerations for Outlook and Office

In Windows 2000 Server with Active Directory, group policies allow you to configure settings at the site, domain, Organizational Unit (OU), or local workstation level. Group policies are similar to system policies created with the System Policy Editor in Windows NT 4.0, although group policies provide much more power and flexibility. Only a few group policies apply to Outlook. In addition, you can apply group policies to Windows 2000 clients only. Windows 9x, Windows Me, and Windows NT do not support group policies (although they do support system policies).

> **note** This section is not intended as complete coverage of group policies or how to manage them. Rather, it points you to a few policies you might need to apply for Outlook users.

Follow these steps to view and edit group policies:

1 Open the Active Directory Users And Computers console.

2 Right-click the domain or OU for which you want to set policies and select Properties.

3 In the Properties dialog box, click the Group Policy tab.

4 Select the policy to edit (the default policy in this case) and click Edit. This opens the Group Policy console, from which you can change the policies.

> **note** For more information on setting and creating group policies, take a look at *Microsoft Windows 2000 Resource Kit* (Microsoft Press, 2000) or go to *mspress.microsoft.com* for other books with more in-depth information on this topic.

While it's beyond the scope of this book to discuss creating and applying new group policies, the following sections explain some of the policy settings you might want to modify for your Outlook users.

> **note** The following discussion assumes that you want to apply group policies at the domain or OU level. Use the Active Directory Sites And Services console to apply group policy at the site level, or use the Local Security Policy console to apply policies to the local computer.

Setting Default Programs Through Policy

The Programs policy, which is the first policy that applies to Outlook, defines the default programs for e-mail, contacts, and scheduling.

To change default programs, follow these steps:

1 Open User Configuration/Windows Settings/Internet Explorer Maintenance in the Group Policy console. Double-click the Programs policy in the right pane.

2 When you're prompted to import the current settings of Internet Explorer to this system, click Import The Current Program Settings.

3 Click the Modify Settings button. In the resulting dialog box, you can change the default applications for e-mail, newsgroups, contacts, and calendar. Make any changes you want.

4 Click OK and then click OK again to apply the policy. The settings you just configured will now be the default for all users in the selected domain or OU.

Redirecting Folders Through Policies

Another change you might want to make is to apply group policies to redirect folders. These policies allow you to specify where to store folders that are normally stored in the profile directory, such as My Documents and the desktop. You can configure these folders so that applications have a consistent look and feel for all users or to lock down certain features. You can also redirect the My Documents folder to a network location so that it can be backed up more easily and so that it's always available, no matter where the user is logged in.

To configure folder redirection through group policies, open the Active Directory Users And Computers console, right-click the OU or domain, and choose Properties. Click the Group Policy tab, select the policy you want to edit, and click Edit. You'll find the folder redirection policies under the User Configuration/Windows Settings/Folder Redirection branch (see Figure 37-8). Right-click the folder you want to redirect and choose Properties to open the Properties dialog box for the folder. Figure 37-9 shows the Properties dialog box for the desktop folder.

Chapter 37: Network, Platform, and Deployment Considerations

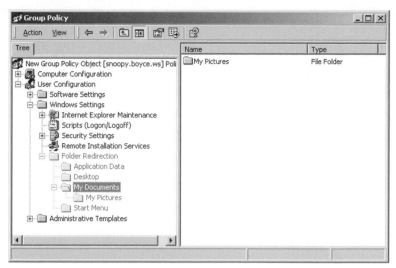

Figure 37-8. Folder redirection policies are located under the User Configuration/
Windows Settings/Folder Redirection branch.

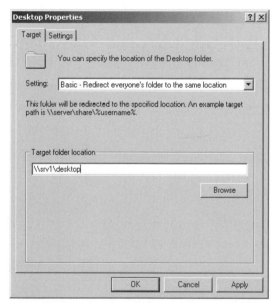

Figure 37-9. Use the folder's Properties dialog box to define its redirection policy.

In the Setting drop-down list on the Target tab, select the type of policy you want to
apply:

- **No Administrative Policy Specified.** Folders will not be redirected through
  policy at this level, but they could be redirected by group policy at higher
  levels (such as at the domain or site level).

- **Basic – Redirect Everyone's Folder To The Same Location.** Folders for all
  users will be redirected to the same location.

- **Advanced – Specify Locations For Various User Groups.** Folders will be
  redirected on a per-group basis.

If you select Basic, you then specify the path in the Target Folder Location box. If you
select Advanced, the Security Group Membership list appears on the Target tab, and
you can click Add to add groups and specify their folder redirection path.

On the Settings tab (see Figure 37-10), you can specify additional options that determine how the folder is redirected and how users access it. The following list summarizes these options:

- **Grant The User Exclusive Rights To** *<folder>*. The user has exclusive
  rights to the folder and all other users, including administrators, have no
  rights in the folder.

- **Move The Contents Of** *<folder>* **To The New Location.** Windows 2000
  copies the contents of the user's current folder to the redirected folder.

- **Leave The Folder In The New Location When Policy Is Removed.** The
  folder remains redirected even if the policy is later removed.

- **Redirect The Folder Back To The Local Userprofile Location When Policy
  Is Removed.** The folder is moved back to its original location as defined by
  the user's profile.

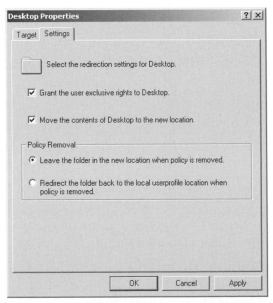

Figure 37-10. Use the Settings tab to set other redirection properties.

Supporting Outlook Under Exchange Server

By itself, Microsoft Outlook is an excellent information manager and e-mail client. When you use Outlook as a client for Microsoft Exchange Server, several features become available to you that make Outlook even better. Outlook is the client of choice for Exchange Server because of its integration with Exchange.

One of the greatest advantages of using Outlook with Exchange Server is data integrity. Instead of being stored on a local computer in a file, data is stored on the server in a fully transactional database. Transactions are logged before being committed to the database so that, in the event of a system failure, you can re-create any lost transactions from the logs. You can back up the database to retain the data of all users, ensuring that it is safe despite either workstation or server failures.

Another major advantage of using Outlook with Exchange Server is single-instance storage. Single-instance storage is used by Exchange Server when it receives a large file destined for multiple users. The file is stored in the database only once and referenced in each message to which it is attached. This reduces disk storage requirements for the database, which can be a significant savings if you have a large user base.

This chapter offers a look at some of the most common management tasks you're likely to perform in support of Outlook users under both Exchange Server 5.5 and Exchange 2000 Server. In addition to learning about client options for Exchange Server, you'll also learn about mailbox management tasks, such as creating mailboxes, setting delivery options, and setting storage limits. The chapter also covers several other management topics, including configuring alternate recipients for a mailbox, forwarding messages automatically, archiving messages, and enabling Instant Messaging. In addition, it also examines group scheduling, a feature in Outlook and Exchange Server that simplifies collaboration among users.

Understanding Client Options for Exchange Server

You have several options when it comes to client applications for Exchange Server, including Outlook, Outlook Web Access, Outlook Express, and any other client that supports the SMTP and POP3 protocols. This section presents a quick overview of these client applications.

Outlook

Outlook is optimized for use with Exchange Server. No other client can provide the functionality that Outlook does. Outlook is designed to fully integrate with Exchange Server, and it supports all of Exchange Server's collaboration features, including advanced meeting requests with automatic resource booking and sharing of free/busy times. Another advantage of using Outlook with Exchange Server is that instead of downloading mail from the server, as a POP3 client would, Exchange Server pushes the mail to the client as soon as the mail is received.

Troubleshooting

You can't connect Outlook to an Exchange Server.

If you're unable to connect Outlook to an Exchange Server, check your firewall settings. It's possible to open ports on your firewall if your server is Exchange Server 5.5 (see Microsoft Knowledge Base article Q176466 for details), but Exchange 2000 Server requires a large number of open ports—so many, in fact, that this solution is not feasible. Using a virtual private network (VPN) is a far better solution than opening firewall ports, because data is sent encrypted and eavesdropping is much more difficult.

Outlook Web Access

Using Internet Information Services, Outlook Web Access (OWA) lets users access Exchange Server mailboxes from anywhere on the Internet (if the server is publicly accessible) via a Web browser. Microsoft Internet Explorer 5 or later is recommended for use with OWA, as it fully supports DHTML (Dynamic HTML) and XML (Extensible Markup Language). Other supported browsers include Internet Explorer 5 for

Macintosh, Internet Explorer 4, and Netscape Navigator 4, although the functionality of these browsers is more limited. OWA provides the most functionality of all client options except Outlook, offering scheduling, meeting, and collaboration capabilities.

> For detailed information on Outlook Web Access, see Chapter 36, "Accessing Messages Through a Web Browser."

Outlook Express

Outlook Express is essentially an SMTP/POP3 mail client and therefore provides only e-mail services. Outlook Express downloads mail from the Exchange Server to the local system using POP3 and sends mail using Exchange Server or SMTP. Outlook Express can download meeting requests, but it displays the meeting request information as text in the body of the message; you can't respond to the request as you can in Outlook.

Other Mail Clients

Other mail clients, such as Netscape Messenger and Eudora, also work with Exchange Server. You must configure these mail clients to use the Exchange Server for POP3, SMTP, and IMAP. Some packages can even interact with the calendar and contact features of Exchange Server by using the iCalendar and vCalendar formats for calendar items and the vCard format for contact items.

Managing User Mailboxes

One of the major differences between Exchange 2000 Server and Exchange Server 5.5 is administration. Because Exchange 2000 Server is fully integrated with Active Directory, most user administration is performed from the Active Directory Users And Computers console. With Exchange Server 5.5, the Exchange Administrator is used for administration.

Managing Mailboxes in Exchange 2000 Server

When you use Exchange 2000 Server with Windows 2000 Server and Active Directory, you add user mailboxes at the same time that you add the user accounts. Exchange 2000 Server is fully integrated with Active Directory; there is no distinction between the user account and the mailbox (as there is in Exchange Server 5.5).

To manage user mailboxes in Exchange 2000 Server, open the Active Directory Users And Computers console from the Administrative Tools menu. If you're the system administrator, you'll want to have all options available to you, so be sure to select the Advanced Features on the View menu. Figure 38-1 on the next page shows the Active Directory Users And Computers console.

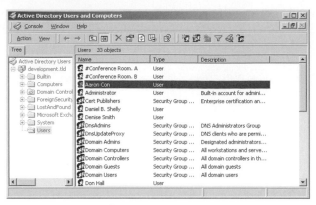

Figure 38-1. Use the Active Directory Users And Computers console to configure mailbox settings for Exchange 2000 Server.

To configure a user's mailbox, right-click the user, choose Properties, and click the Exchange General tab in the Properties dialog box (see Figure 38-2). This tab contains the basic configuration options for the mailbox, described in the following discussion.

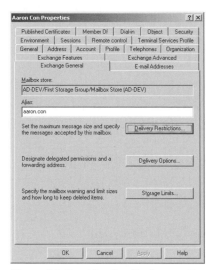

Figure 38-2. Use the Exchange General tab to view and set general configuration options for the mailbox.

The Mailbox Store box displays the database where the user data is kept (in LDAP, or Lightweight Directory Access Protocol, form). In the Alias box, you can set the user's mailbox alias and e-mail address. The mailbox alias is usually set to the user name by default. Under most conditions, the SMTP address of a mailbox is *<alias>@<server>*. The alias is also another way of referring to the mailbox in Outlook.

Click the Delivery Restrictions button on the Exchange General tab to open the Delivery Restrictions dialog box (see Figure 38-3), where you can specify restrictions on incoming and outgoing messages.

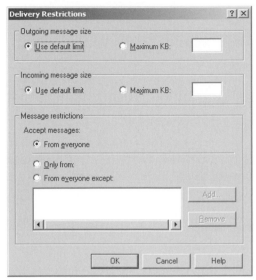

Figure 38-3. Use the Delivery Restrictions dialog box to set restrictions on incoming and outgoing messages.

The Outgoing Message Size and Incoming Message Size settings control the maximum allowed size (in KB) of outgoing and incoming messages. By default, the limits apply to all users in the Exchange System Manager. The Accept Messages settings control who can send messages to this mailbox. You can choose to accept messages only from specified users (a deny-all-except method) or to accept messages from all users except those specified, which is useful for blocking mail from nuisance users. By default, all messages are accepted.

Clicking the Delivery Options button on the Exchange General tab opens the Delivery Options dialog box (see Figure 38-4 on the next page), where you can configure mail delivery to and from this mailbox.

The Send On Behalf option lets you specify other users who will be able to send messages on behalf of the user whose mailbox you're configuring. Add those specified users to the Grant This Permission To box. (A message sent on behalf of another user will indicate who sent it and on whose behalf.) Use the Recipient Limits option to set the maximum number of recipients to whom a message can be sent. Exchange 2000 Server by default uses the global limits set in the Exchange System Manager (as explained later in this section).

Figure 38-4. Use the Delivery Options dialog box to configure mail delivery to and from the mailbox.

For information about mail forwarding options, see "Configuring Alternate Recipients," page 930.

Clicking the Storage Limits button on the Exchange General tab opens the Storage Limits dialog box, which lets you control the mailbox storage space limits (see Figure 38-5).

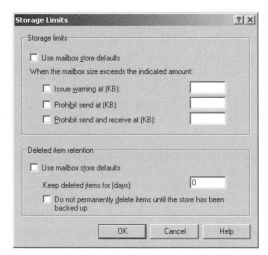

Figure 38-5. Use the Storage Limits dialog box to set the size limits and deleted item retention options for the mailbox.

The Storage Limits options define the amount of storage space (in KB) that a mailbox can use. If the mailbox exceeds the limit specified in Issue Warning At (KB), the user receives a notification that the mailbox has reached its size limit. If the mailbox exceeds the Prohibit Send At (KB) limit, the user can't send messages until the size of the mailbox is reduced. If the Prohibit Send And Receive At (KB) limit is exceeded, the user can't send or receive messages.

> **caution** Use the Prohibit Send And Receive limit only as a last resort, because it causes incoming mail to bounce.

The Deleted Item Retention options in the Storage Limits dialog box let you choose how to handle deleted items. Exchange Server allows you to retain deleted items even after you empty the Deleted Items folder. In the Keep Deleted Items For (Days) box, you can specify the number of days that deleted items are kept. Selecting the Do Not Permanently Delete Items Until The Store Has Been Backed Up check box retains deleted items until the next backup of the mailbox store. This way, you can recover deleted items from backups without keeping them on the server any longer than necessary. By default, both sets of Storage Limit options are set to the global limits configured in the Exchange System Manager (as explained later in this section).

Next, return to the Properties dialog box and click the E-Mail Addresses tab. This tab displays the e-mail addresses associated with the mailbox, as shown in Figure 38-6.

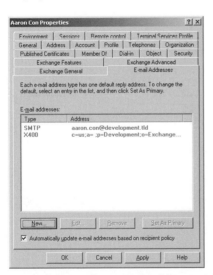

Figure 38-6. The E-Mail Addresses tab displays the existing addresses for the mailbox and lets you add, remove, and edit addresses.

The addresses currently assigned to the mailbox include an SMTP address and an X400 address, which are automatically generated when you create the mailbox. From this tab, you can add new addresses or change existing addresses for the mailbox—for example, you might want to add SMTP aliases. To add an address, click New. Exchange Server displays a list of the address types you can add. In this case, you should add only SMTP or X400 addresses because the connectors for other mail system types (such as Microsoft Mail) are not installed. Select the address type, click OK, and then specify the address. Click OK to add the new address to the mailbox.

If you select Automatically Update E-Mail Addresses Based On Recipient Policy on the E-Mail Addresses tab, the addresses for this mailbox will change when the recipient policy changes. The recipient policy controls how the e-mail addresses are formatted when you create them. In the example shown in Figure 38-6 on the previous page, the format is *<firstname>.<lastname>@<domain>* for SMTP addresses. This check box is selected by default, thereby simplifying the task of globally changing the format of e-mail addresses, which was nearly impossible with earlier versions of Exchange Server.

Also in the Properties dialog box, the Exchange Advanced tab (see Figure 38-7) is used to configure advanced options, which are necessary only in specific cases.

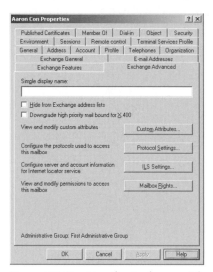

Figure 38-7. Use the Exchange Advanced tab to set special options.

In the Simple Display Name box on the Exchange Advanced tab, you can specify a display name that will be used in case a system is not capable of displaying the default display name. For example, if the normal display name uses Chinese characters, the simple display name might be in English characters.

When selected, the Hide From Exchange Address Lists check box prevents the user from being displayed in any Exchange Server address lists. Selecting the Downgrade

High Priority Mail Bound For X.400 check box removes the High priority flag from a message if it is traversing an X.400 connection. This feature causes messages to conform to the original 1984 X.400 standard. Clicking the Custom Attributes button on this tab allows you to set values for any of Exchange Server's 15 custom attributes. Custom attributes are extra fields you can use for virtually any purpose. Custom applications that use Outlook and Exchange Server can also use custom attributes.

Clicking the Protocol Settings button on the Exchange Advanced tab opens the Protocols dialog box, which displays the protocols you can use to access the mailbox. By selecting a protocol and then clicking the Settings button, you can configure the protocol as well as enable or disable it for the mailbox. (HTTP has no configuration settings; you can only enable or disable it.) You can set the message encoding type and options as well as the character set for the protocol. By default, these settings are configured globally (for all mailboxes) from the Exchange System Manager and can be changed by the Exchange Administrator.

Clicking the ILS Settings button on the Exchange Advanced tab allows you to configure an Internet Locator Service (ILS) server and account for the mailbox. An ILS server is essentially a server that stores address information about Internet users.

Clicking the Mailbox Rights button opens a Permissions dialog box for the mailbox, which lets you (as an administrator) assign rights to the mailbox to other users. Normally the mailbox owner assigns these rights by using delegates in Outlook, but an administrator can force mailbox rights by using this dialog box. This is necessary only when you're assigning the rights to a resource mailbox to the resource administrator.

You can also use the Exchange System Manager to manage user mailboxes. Figure 38-8 shows the default Exchange System Manager window.

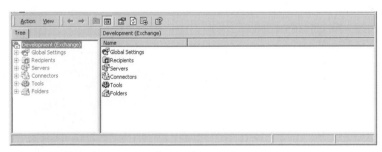

Figure 38-8. You can use the Exchange System Manager to manage user mailboxes.

Chapter 38

You can use the Exchange System Manager to set the default message size limits and the maximum number of recipients. Double-click Global Settings in the left pane, right-click Message Delivery, and choose Properties. Click the Defaults tab to set the default size limits and maximum number of recipients for messages. These defaults apply to all users unless they have been overridden, as previously discussed.

To use the Exchange System Manager to manage mailbox size and deleted item retention defaults, follow these steps:

1 Double-click the organization in which the server resides to expand the tree if needed.

2 Double-click Servers in the left pane, and then double-click the server for which you want to set defaults.

3 Double-click the storage group that contains the mailbox store you want to configure.

4 Right-click the mailbox store and choose Properties.

5 Click the Limits tab and set the default mailbox size limits and deleted item retention options, as discussed earlier. These settings apply to all users in the selected mailbox store.

Managing Mailboxes in Exchange Server 5.5

User mailboxes are created at the same time as user accounts in Exchange Server 5.5 and Microsoft Windows NT Server 4.0, unless the administrator chooses otherwise. Mailboxes and user accounts in these systems are logically separate entities, however. You use the Microsoft Exchange Administrator, shown in Figure 38-9, to manage these mailboxes.

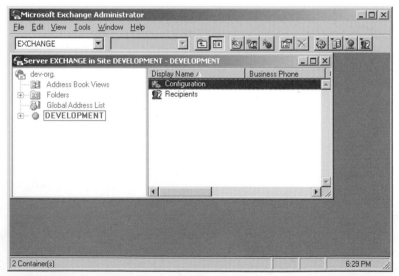

Figure 38-9. Use the Microsoft Exchange Administrator to manage user mailboxes.

Chapter 38: Supporting Outlook Under Exchange Server

To begin managing user mailboxes on a system running Exchange Server 5.5, follow
these steps:

1 Choose Start, Programs, Microsoft Exchange, Microsoft Exchange Administrator. The Exchange Server organization name (dev-org. in this example) appears at the root of the tree in the left pane.

2 Double-click the site (Development in this example), double-click Configuration, and then double-click Servers.

3 Double-click the server name (Exchange in this example) and click Server Recipients. All recipients on the selected server are displayed in the right pane.

4 Double-click a user to display that user's Properties dialog box.

Figure 38-10 shows the General tab of the Properties dialog box. Use this tab to set
general information such as the user's name, address, and organizational information. In
the Name group, the Display option controls how the mailbox appears in address lists.
The alias is another way to reference the mailbox. The Primary Windows NT Account
button and the accompanying text box are the most important part of the General tab.
They let you specify the user account that owns the mailbox. Unless other permissions
are set for the mailbox, only the specified account and the service account under which
Exchange Server runs can log in to the mailbox.

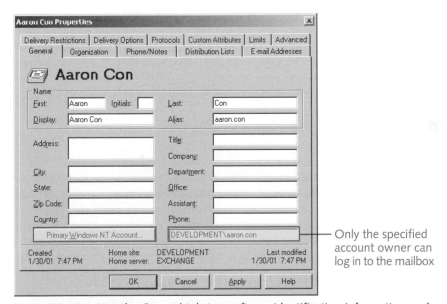

Only the specified
account owner can
log in to the mailbox

Figure 38-10. Use the General tab to configure identification information and specify
the mailbox owner.

Use the Organization tab of the Properties dialog box to specify which users report directly to the current user or to set the user's manager. Setting the user's manager causes the user to show up as a direct report; specifying another user as a direct report causes the current user to show up as that user's manager. Use the Phone/Notes tab to specify the user's phone numbers and to add any relevant notes. On the Distribution Lists tab, you can add the user to distribution lists; it also lists the mailbox's membership. To add the user to distribution lists, click the Modify button and select the lists. The E-Mail Addresses tab functions in exactly the same manner as it does in Exchange 2000 Server (described in the previous section).

Figure 38-11 shows the Delivery Restrictions tab. Delivery restrictions in Exchange Server 5.5 work similarly to those in Exchange 2000 Server, but they don't work on a deny-all-except or accept-all-except list; instead, two separate lists are used to obtain the same result.

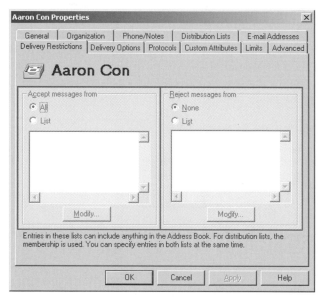

Figure 38-11. Use the Delivery Restrictions tab to set limits on who can send messages to the mailbox.

You can use the Delivery Options tab for two purposes: to configure alternate recipients (discussed in the following section) and to grant send-on-behalf-of privileges to other users. The Protocols tab functions the same way it does in Exchange 2000 Server: the protocol settings you specify override the global protocol defaults.

The Custom Attributes tab is also used the same way it's used in Exchange 2000 Server, except that 10 custom attributes are available instead of 15. Figure 38-12 shows the Limits tab of the Properties dialog box for a user in Exchange Server 5.5. Once again, the features found on the Limits tab are functionally identical to corresponding features found in Exchange 2000 Server.

Chapter 38: Supporting Outlook Under Exchange Server

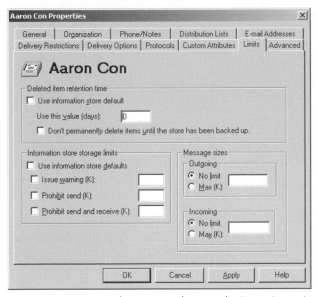

Figure 38-12. Use the Limits tab to set limits on incoming and outgoing message size and to configure deleted item retention and mailbox size.

Figure 38-13 shows the Advanced tab of the Properties dialog box. On this tab, you can specify the options listed on the next page.

Figure 38-13. Use the Advanced tab to set advanced miscellaneous settings for the mailbox.

- **Simple Display Name.** Sets a name that will be used when a client system is not capable of displaying the default display name. For example, if the normal display name uses Chinese characters, the simple display name might be in English characters.

- **Directory Name.** Displays the mailbox name used for mail routing.

- **Trust Level.** Controls the replication of mailbox information during directory synchronization with other systems. If the mailbox trust level is greater than the container trust level, mailbox information is not replicated.

- **ILS Server** and **ILS Account.** Specifies an Internet Locator Service server and account for the mailbox. The ILS server is used to publicly store information about the mailbox.

- **Home Server.** Specifies the server whose information store will hold the mailbox. This is a useful feature for organizations that have multiple servers in a site, since having the mailbox on a local server will decrease access time.

- **Hide From Address Book.** Prevents the mailbox from appearing in any address lists.

- **Outlook Web Access Server Name.** Specifies which server running OWA should be used with this mailbox if it is different from the default Web access server.

- **Downgrade High Priority X.400 Mail.** Sends High priority X.400 messages with Normal priority for compatibility reasons.

- **Container Name.** Displays the name of the container that stores the mailbox in the Exchange directory store.

- **Administrative Note.** Provides a descriptive note that can be viewed only with the Exchange Administrator.

Configuring Alternate Recipients

Alternate recipients are recipients who receive all mail sent to a mailbox, either instead of or in addition to the mailbox user.

Specifying Recipients in Exchange 2000 Server

To specify alternate recipients in Exchange 2000 Server, follow these steps:

1 Open Active Directory Users And Computers and select the Users container under your domain. Right-click the user and choose Properties.

2 Click the Exchange General tab, and then click the Delivery Options button.

3 In the Delivery Options dialog box, click Forward To. Click the Modify button to specify the user to whom the messages will be forwarded, and then click OK.

4 If you want the messages to go to both the original and alternate recipients, select the Deliver Messages To Both Forwarding Address And Mailbox check box. Click OK.

Figure 38-14 shows an example of the Delivery Options dialog box with an alternate recipient configured.

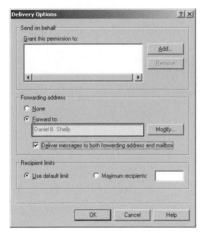

Figure 38-14. You can specify alternate recipients in the Delivery Options dialog box.

Specifying Recipients in Exchange Server 5.5

To specify an alternate recipient in Exchange Server 5.5, follow these steps:

1 Open the Exchange Administrator.

2 Double-click the site, double-click Configuration, double-click Servers, double-click the server name, and then click Server Recipients.

3 Double-click a user to open that user's Properties dialog box. Click the Delivery Options tab.

4 Click Alternate Recipient, and then click the Modify button to select a user. Select the user from the address book and click OK.

5 If you want the messages to go to both the original and alternate recipients, select the Deliver Messages To Both Recipient And Alternate Recipient check box. Click OK.

Forwarding Messages to Users' Internet Mail Accounts

Forwarding mail to Internet mail accounts is similar to configuring an alternate recipient, except that the alternate recipient in this case must have an Internet mail address. A problem arises, however, because you cannot specify an Internet mail address as the alternate recipient—you must specify an Exchange Server mail recipient. To solve this problem, you can create *mail-enabled contacts* in Exchange 2000 Server and *custom recipients* in Exchange Server 5.5.

Creating Mail-Enabled Contacts in Exchange 2000 Server

To create a mail-enabled contact in Exchange 2000 Server, follow these steps:

1 Open Active Directory Users And Computers.

2 In the left pane, right-click the container to which you want to add the contact, and choose New, Contact.

3 Enter the contact's name information, as shown in Figure 38-15. This information should be unique to the user. If this is a user's home account, specify it as such. Click Next.

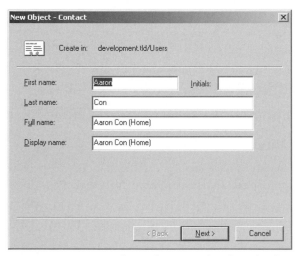

Figure 38-15. Specifying the name details is the first step in creating a mail-enabled contact.

4 Specify the e-mail address of the contact to make the contact mail-enabled. (First ensure that the alias is unique.) You can click the Modify button to specify an address. Select the address type from the list and click OK. Then enter the address and click OK.

5 Click Next to continue. A summary page of the contact information is displayed. Click Finish to create the contact.

To add the contact as an alternate recipient, follow these steps:

1 Open the user's Properties dialog box in the Active Directory Users And Computers console.

2 On the Exchange General tab, click the Delivery Options button.

3 Click Forward To, and then click the Modify button to add the new contact.

4 When you've added the contact, click OK twice to close the Delivery Options and the Properties dialog boxes. Messages to that mailbox will now be forwarded to the contact.

Creating Custom Recipients in Exchange Server 5.5

The process for forwarding messages to an Internet mail account in Exchange Server 5.5 is similar to the process in Exchange 2000 Server, except that you create a custom recipient instead of a mail-enabled contact.

To create a custom recipient in Exchange Server 5.5, follow these steps:

1 Open the Exchange Administrator, select the site in the left pane, and click Recipients.

2 Choose File, New Custom Recipient. Select an e-mail address type, as shown in Figure 38-16.

Figure 38-16. When creating a custom recipient, you must first specify the mail address type.

3 Enter the e-mail address and click OK. The Properties dialog box for a custom recipient appears. The tabs available are a subset of those available for a regular mailbox. Enter a name for the custom recipient and ensure that the display name and alias are unique. Click OK to save the custom recipient.

4 To set the forwarding, open the Properties dialog box for the mailbox and click the Delivery Restrictions tab.

5 Click the List button and click Modify to add the recipient. Choose the newly created custom recipient from the address book and click OK.

6 Click OK (or Apply) to close the Properties dialog box. All messages to the mailbox will now be forwarded to the custom recipient.

Archiving (Journaling) All Messages

Message archiving (known as *journaling* in Exchange Server 5.5) is the retention of all incoming and outgoing messages. In Exchange Server 5.5, message journaling is available only for mail that passes through the Mail Transfer Agent (MTA), whereas message archiving in Exchange 2000 Server is more granular: messages to or from a specific message store are archived. Some organizations use message journaling to enforce employee terms of service or to discover malicious activity.

> **note** Before you begin archiving and reading the mail of employees in your organization, you would do well to consult your corporate lawyer. Many administrators go so far as to have management put in writing the order to read users' mail, in order to ensure that they cannot be blamed if an employee files suit against the company.

Archiving in Exchange 2000 Server

In Exchange 2000 Server, message archiving is done on a per-mailbox-store basis.

To archive messages for a particular store, follow these steps:

1 Open the Exchange System Manager. In the left pane, navigate to the mailbox store whose messages you want to archive (see Figure 38-17).

2 Right-click the mailbox store and choose Properties.

3 On the General tab of the store's Properties dialog box, select the Archive All Messages Sent Or Received By Mailboxes On This Store check box to enable message archiving.

4 Click the Browse button to select a mailbox or distribution list from the address list. This mailbox (or list) will receive all the archived messages.

It's useful to create a mailbox specifically for message archiving. You could also use the Administrator mailbox—the Administrator account shouldn't be in use in a secure Windows network—because that mailbox receives a relatively high volume of mail, especially if you have a large user base. If you use a separate mailbox, it's useful to grant access to all users who need access so that they can open the mailbox in Outlook while logged on as themselves. Figure 38-18 shows the General tab of the store's Properties dialog box with message archiving enabled.

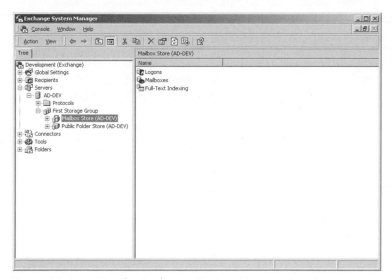

Figure 38-17. Use the Exchange System Manager to set up message archiving for specific mailbox stores.

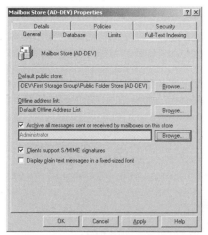

Figure 38-18. In this example, the Administrator mailbox will receive the archived mail.

Journaling in Exchange Server 5.5

Message journaling in Exchange Server 5.5 is performed for every message that is transferred over the MTA. It's much more complex to implement than archiving in Exchange 2000 Server. Each server must be running at least Exchange Server 5.5 Service Pack 1 or later. To implement message journaling in Exchange Server 5.5, follow these steps:

1 Determine the distinguished name of the recipient who will receive the journaled mail. A distinguished name uniquely identifies an object and its location. The recipient might be a mailbox, a custom recipient, or a public folder. To determine the distinguished name, you must run the Exchange Administrator in raw mode.

---

caution Running the Exchange Administrator in raw mode is dangerous because this mode exposes all the directory schema attributes that make up individual objects. Never change any settings unless directed to do so by a Microsoft support engineer.

---

1 To open the Exchange Administrator in raw mode, open a command prompt and type *<x>*:\exchsrvr\bin\admin /r, where *<x>* is the drive on which Exchange Server is installed.

2 Locate the recipient who will receive journaled messages, select that recipient, and choose File, Raw Properties.

3 Select Obj-Dist-Name in the Object Attributes list. The distinguished name of an object will be displayed in the Attribute Value box, as shown in Figure 38-19. Make a note of the distinguished name.

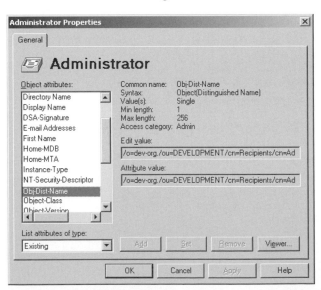

Figure 38-19. View the distinguished name in the Attribute Value box.

4 In the registry, specify this distinguished name as the recipient for journaled messages. Open the Registry Editor and locate the key HKEY_LOCAL_ MACHINE\SYSTEM\CurrentControlSet\Services\MSExchangeMTA\Parameters. Add the string value *Journal Recipient Name* to that key, and set the value to the distinguished name noted in step 4.

5 By default, message journaling is performed at the organization level. To change message journaling to the site or server level, set a DWORD value named *Per-Site Journal Required* to HKEY_LOCAL_MACHINE\SYSTEM\ CurrentControlSet\Services\MSExchangeMTA\Parameters. A value of 0 specifies organization-level message journaling, a value of 1 specifies site-level message journaling, and a value of 2 specifies server-level message journaling.

6 Ensure that all private information store messages are routed through the Exchange Server MTA—they are normally delivered without the MTA if the sender and receiver are on the same information store. Also ensure that Internet Mail Service (IMS) messages are routed through the private information store. This must be done on any server on which you are performing message journaling—for example, each server in the site if you are journaling on a per-site basis, or only on an individual server if you are journaling on a per-server basis.

7 To route all private information store messages through the MTA, set a DWORD value of 1 named *No Local Delivery* in HKEY_LOCAL_MACHINE\ SYSTEM\CurrentControlSet\Services\MSExchangeIS\ParametersSystem. To route all Internet Mail Service mail through the private information store, set a DWORD value of 1 named *RerouteViaStore* in HKEY_LOCAL_MACHINE\ SYSTEM\CurrentControlSet\Services\MSExchangeIMC\Parameters. This must be done on each server running the IMS if there is more than one. (A site often has more than one IMS for redundancy.)

Message journaling should now be enabled and all messages routed through the MTA should be sent to the specified recipient.

Configuring and Enabling Instant Messaging

Exchange 2000 Server provides an Instant Messaging feature that is essentially a private version of the MSN Messenger Service. This feature must be enabled on both a global basis and a per-user basis.

To enable Instant Messaging, follow these steps:

1 Ensure that the Microsoft Exchange Instant Messaging Service is installed. Instant Messaging is optional when you install Exchange. You can install it later, as shown in Figure 38-20, but the Exchange services will be stopped during the installation process.

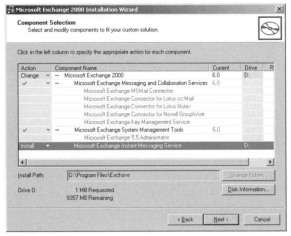

Figure 38-20. Instant Messaging is an option when Exchange Server is initially installed; you can add it later from the Exchange Server CD.

2 Open the Exchange System Manager. Double-click Servers in the left pane, and then select the server on which you want to create the Instant Messaging virtual server. Click Protocols, and then click Instant Messaging (RVP).

3 Right-click in the right pane and choose New, Instant Messaging Virtual Server to start the New Instant Messaging Virtual Server Wizard. Click Next.

4 Specify the required display name for the new virtual server. Click Next.

5 Specify an existing IIS Web site to enable for Instant Messaging and click Next. You can use the default Web site, but each Instant Messaging virtual server you create in the future must have a unique site. Click Next.

6 Specify the required DNS name for the virtual server. By default, the server name is specified, but you can set it to anything you choose. Click Next.

7 Select the Allow This Server To Host User Accounts check box, shown in Figure 38-21, to make the new virtual server a home server. Click Next.

8 Click Finish to close the wizard.

Chapter 38: Supporting Outlook Under Exchange Server

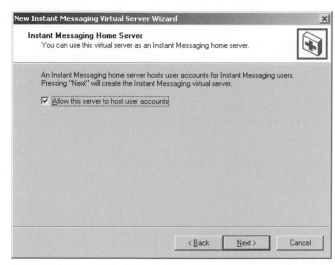

Figure 38-21. Only Instant Messaging home servers can host users.

Figure 38-22 shows the new Instant Messaging virtual server in the Exchange System
Manager.

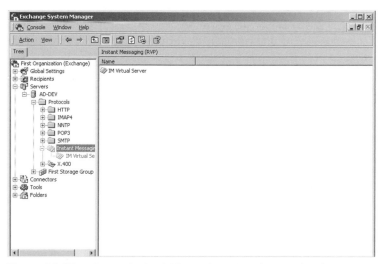

Figure 38-22. A new Instant Messaging virtual server has been created.

To enable the Instant Messaging feature for specific users, follow these steps:

1 Open the Active Directory Users And Computers console.

2 Right-click the user for whom you want to enable Instant Messaging, and choose Properties. Click the Exchange Features tab.

3 Click Instant Messaging, and then click the Enable button. You must specify the Instant Messaging home server and domain name, as shown in Figure 38-23.

Figure 38-23. When enabling Instant Messaging, you must specify the home server and domain name.

4 Select the domain name you assigned to the newly created Instant Messaging virtual server—this is the default in most cases—and click the Browse button to select an Instant Messaging home server, as shown in Figure 38-24.

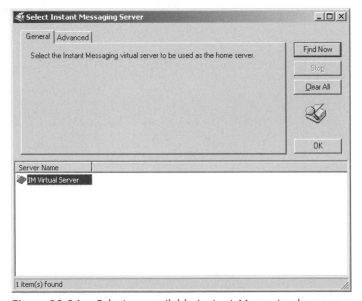

Figure 38-24. Select an available Instant Messaging home server.

5 Select the newly created Instant Messaging virtual server from the list and
click OK. Click OK to close the Enable Instant Messaging window.

Figure 38-25 shows the user's Properties dialog box with Instant Messaging enabled.

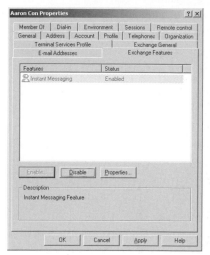

Figure 38-25. Instant Messaging has been enabled for this user.

To enable Instant Messaging for a group of users, follow these steps:

1 Select all users for whom you want to enable Instant Messaging. Right-click
the selection and choose Exchange Tasks.

2 Click Next. Select Enable Instant Messaging from the list of tasks, and then
click Next.

3 Specify the home server and domain name, and click Next. The next page of
the wizard shows the progress of the task, and then a summary page displays
the results.

4 Click Finish to close the summary.

Managing Group Scheduling
with Exchange Server

E-mail is certainly not the only function provided by Exchange Server, and managing
mailboxes is just one of the management tasks you'll need to perform in Exchange
Server to support Outlook users. Group scheduling is another very useful and important

feature made possible by Outlook and Exchange Server. This section offers an overview of group scheduling to help you implement and manage it in your organization.

Chapters 18 and 19 explained how to use Outlook to set up appointments and meetings and to allocate resources. If you are using Outlook with Exchange Server, however, you have an additional tool for scheduling meetings: the group scheduling feature. Because Exchange Server stores all user information in a single database, managers and resource allocators in an organization can have easy access to schedule and contact information for all members of the organization. Managers can get an overview of what their teams are doing by viewing the team members' joint schedules. A receptionist who needs to locate employees can check the database for Outlook schedules, which can serve as an in/out board. Anyone who needs to plan a meeting can create and save a list of invitees to streamline the process. And scheduling is simplified because you can view free/busy information for all invitees in a single place.

As this section explains, you can use the group scheduling feature in two ways: by using your organization's internal Exchange Server database, or by using the Microsoft Office Internet Free/Busy Service.

Creating a Group Schedule

To see how the group scheduling feature can work in your organization, open Outlook's Calendar folder. Choose Actions, View Group Schedules to display the Group Schedules dialog box, shown in Figure 38-26.

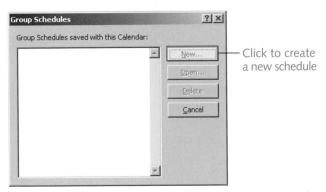

Figure 38-26. As you create custom group schedules, they're listed here.

To create a new schedule, click New. In the Create New Group Schedule dialog box, shown in Figure 38-27, type a name for the new group schedule.

Use a name that is descriptive and easily identifiable. In Figure 38-27, for instance, the user is creating a group schedule for the company's engineers. After you've entered a name, click OK. The group scheduling window is displayed for the new group, as shown in Figure 38-28.

Chapter 38

Figure 38-27. When naming schedules, use simple but descriptive names.

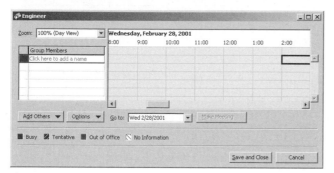

Figure 38-28. The group scheduling window is displayed for the Engineers group.

Adding Members to the Group

Next you must create a list of group members. In the group scheduling window, click
Add Others. You can either add members from an address book or from a public folder.
When you click Add From Address Book, Outlook opens the Select Members dialog
box, shown in Figure 38-29.

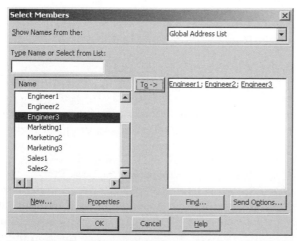

Figure 38-29. Use this dialog box to add users to the group schedule.

943

This dialog box lists users who can be added to the group schedule list. Select each member in the Name list and click To to add that person to the list. You can use the Exchange Server Global Address List or other address lists to which you have scheduling information access. (Additionally, any resources that need to be monitored can be added to this list.) After you've added all the people who need to be included in this group, click OK to close the dialog box.

For information about how to schedule a resource, see "Scheduling Resources," page 530.

Viewing a Group Schedule

In the group scheduling window, you'll now see a list of the group members you selected, with each individual's schedule information displayed to the right, as shown in Figure 38-30. Note the legend in the lower left that indicates what the color coding represents.

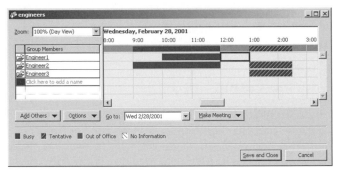

Figure 38-30. Scheduling information for each user in the group schedule is shown on a different line.

Each schedule shows blocks of time that are designated as follows:

- **Busy.** The member is not available. You cannot schedule over this block of time. These appointments are shown in solid blue.

- **Tentative.** The block of time is tentatively scheduled—perhaps an appointment for that time has not yet been confirmed, or a meeting at that time is not a priority for the member. If you schedule over a tentative appointment, the member will need to decide which appointment to attend. Tentative appointments are colored with diagonal blue and white stripes.

- **Out Of Office.** The member is on vacation, at a conference, or otherwise unavailable. These times are shown in purple.

- **Open.** Open time is indicated by gray areas. The member has no appointments or meetings on the calendar, and this block of time can be scheduled.

● **No Information.** Exchange Server has no information about the member's schedule. Such blocks of time are shown as white areas with diagonal black lines (not included in Figure 38-30). This might indicate that the member does not use Outlook, that the account is new, or that the account has problems.

If you have been given the appropriate permissions, you can view specific listings of meetings and appointments on a group member's schedule, rather than seeing only color-coded blocks of time. Thus a manager or a receptionist could know not only that someone is out of the office but also where that person has gone.

For privacy reasons, only users who are specifically given permission can view the details of other people's calendar entries. For information about giving other users permission to view your Calendar folder, see "Sharing Your Calendar," page 509.

In Figure 38-30, the three engineers in the group have schedules that keep them busy at different times. The top bar of the group schedule is a composite of the three individual schedules and allows you to see at a glance which times are open for all group members. By scrolling left or right, you can check on previous or future times. You can also change views by using the Zoom drop-down list.

Setting Up a Meeting or Sending E-Mail

You can use group schedules as a starting point for setting up a meeting or sending an e-mail message. Figure 38-31 shows some of the available options. When you choose one of these options, Outlook opens a new meeting request form or a message form, and you can create the meeting request or the message just as you normally would in Outlook.

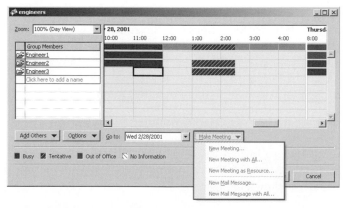

Figure 38-31. You can take a variety of actions based on the group schedule information.

Adding Group Members from Outside the Organization

If you need to schedule a meeting that includes Outlook users who do not have accounts on your local Exchange Server, you'll find it a bit more difficult to view their schedule information. They can, however, allow you to access their information by using the Microsoft Office Internet Free/Busy Service. This free service, based on Microsoft Passport, lets Outlook users make their schedule information available on the Web, allowing other Passport holders to see their schedule information even if the users are not on the same system.

To set up Outlook to share free/busy information, choose Tools, Options and click the Calendar Options button. Near the bottom of the Calendar Options dialog box, click Free/Busy Options to open the dialog box shown in Figure 38-32.

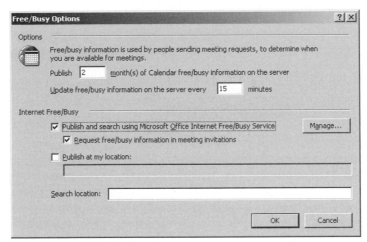

Figure 38-32. These are your options for configuring free/busy information.

At the top of the dialog box are two options that determine how much of your schedule information will be posted to the server and how often Outlook updates the information to the network. If your schedule changes often during the day, you might want to update more regularly than every 15 minutes. If your organization plans many months in advance, you might want to publish more than two months of data.

Below these options are the Internet Free/Busy settings. Select the two check boxes titled Publish And Search Using Microsoft Office Internet Free/Busy Service and Request Free/Busy Information In Meeting Invitations. To complete this setup, each group member will also need to visit the Microsoft Office Internet Free/Busy Web site and grant access to his or her schedule, as shown in Figure 38-33.

Chapter 38: Supporting Outlook Under Exchange Server

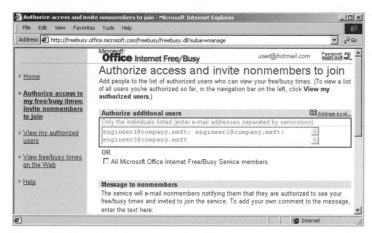

Figure 38-33. Use the Microsoft Office Internet Free/Busy Web site to manage who has access to your free/busy information.

Microsoft's Internet Free/Busy site offers three basic options:

- **Authorize Access To My Free/Busy Times; Invite Nonmembers To Join.** This option allows you to specify which users have access to your schedule. If users who need to view your schedule are not Microsoft Passport holders, you can invite them to join from here as well.

- **View My Authorized Users.** Here you can see the list of users who can access your schedule, and you can remove authorization as needed.

- **View Free/Busy Times On The Web.** Use this option to view the free/busy information of other users, if you have the proper authorization.

For more information, see "Publishing Your Schedule," page 513.

Chapter 39

Backup Strategies and Virus Protection

Microsoft Outlook gives users the ability to archive messages, providing a layer of protection against workstation crashes, and the ability to periodically clean out user folders, removing old messages. When it's used with Microsoft Exchange Server, Outlook typically stores messages on the server. For that reason, it's important to develop and implement a backup strategy for Exchange Server that insures against lost messages, corrupt message stores, or even a completely irretrievable Exchange message store.

Protecting your clients against hardware or software failures is only one aspect of providing fault tolerance and redundancy. Protecting against viruses and worms is equally important. A single worm spread by e-mail can do billions of dollars in damage across the globe, but a thoughtful and carefully implemented virus protection strategy can save you from those losses.

This chapter examines backup and virus protection strategies and offers tips on how to protect your servers and your client workstations from lost data, lost productivity, and, most important, the financial consequences that come with each. In addition, this chapter examines some changes you can make to the way your Exchange Servers host their message stores to improve fault tolerance and speed up the recovery process if it becomes necessary.

Implementing a Backup Strategy

Every system administrator has at least one horror story to tell about a critical server that failed and took out important data. Those administrators who implemented a thoughtfully planned and carefully executed backup strategy can end their stories on a high note—the server was rebuilt and restored from a backup copy. Those who didn't implement a backup strategy have no pleasant end to their tales. (Some are probably working elsewhere.)

Assume, for example, that your company maintains all of its accounting data on a particular server. The data includes customer billing records, payroll records, tax returns, and all other accounting data for the business. You feel secure because the server implements a RAID 5 array for all of its volumes, and you know that if a drive fails the spare will take over and you can simply hot-swap a new one. The server never misses a beat or loses a single bit of data.

Unfortunately, your server isn't adequately grounded. Over time, static builds up and causes the RAID controller to lose its configuration for one of the RAID channels. Suddenly, the volume with all the accounting data is no longer accessible.

"No problem," you say to yourself. You just have to reenter the array configuration, and the volume will come back with its data intact. You faithfully recorded the drive order and other parameters for the array when you set up the volume. You rebuild the configuration and reboot, and….

The data is corrupted. You reboot and let the operating system rebuild the drive, but each successive repair makes the data less and less consistent. Finally you realize that you will have to reformat the volume and start from scratch. Does this sound like a plausible scenario? It is, because it happened to me.

Where would you be at this point if you had no up-to-date backup? Your company's entire financial history is gone. You can't bill customers, generate any revenue, or report that revenue to the shareholders or the IRS. Forget the fact that you can't run payroll, because you don't have any revenue coming in to pay your employees, anyway. Your company is going to either spend the next several months rebuilding its financial data from paper records or simply close its doors. Neither prospect is very appealing, especially if you're the person who was supposed to ensure that a recoverable backup was available for every contingency.

Having a backup strategy in place and faithfully following through with that strategy on a daily basis can mean the difference between your company being in business or going belly-up. It can also mean the difference between a paycheck and unemployment for the administrator who is charged with overseeing that backup strategy. Think about the consequences of a server disaster, and you'll quickly realize how important an effective backup strategy can be to your company and also to you personally.

You should also consider a scenario in which your server experiences a failure but you do have a backup on hand. Is that backup current? What if a simple error or oversight results in the data being a week old? What would it cost the company to restore just one week's worth of work? You must take into account the feasibility of the restore process in relation to your work flow. Can you afford to have an entire department on hold while you restore a server? These are questions you need to ask yourself as you begin to develop a backup strategy.

You Can Back Up, But Can You Restore?

Backing up your data—whether it's on an Exchange Server or a client workstation—is only half the battle of securing the data. Many administrators overlook a few key issues. Can you restore the data from the backup set? Is there anything in the backup set? Don't just back up and forget about it. Test the backups to ensure that they contain data and that you can restore them. Faulty backup media, a bad head on a tape drive, or another unforeseen problem could render your backups useless.

After each backup, restore at least one file from the set to a new location to verify that the data resides in the backup set and can be restored. Restoring to a new location allows you to perform the restore operation without replacing the existing copy of the file. You can then remove the restored copy once you're sure the backup set is valid.

Developing the Strategy

Developing and implementing a backup strategy means more than simply buying a backup program and scheduling regular backups. You must also consider disaster prevention as well as recovery, hardware requirements, and the time needed to restore a backup set and rebuild a server, as well as the human factors—who is going to perform and verify the backups, who will serve as an assistant if the administrator isn't available, and how much time can each department afford to lose? This section examines these issues in the context of working with Exchange Server and Outlook.

Hardware Considerations

Before you reach the point of choosing backup hardware, take the time to evaluate your server (or servers). A RAID (redundant array of independent disks) disk subsystem is a crucial component of any server that needs to enjoy maximum uptime. Various levels of RAID implementation offer different levels of fault tolerance and redundancy. At a minimum, each server volume should implement RAID 5, which provides data striping for improved performance and parity for fault tolerance. Ideally, the drives in each RAID array should be hot-swappable, and you should include a spare drive in each array to allow the array to fail over to the spare drive without losing any data. You can then pull the failed drive and insert another to replace the hot spare that is now functioning as a data drive. Your users need never know that a drive failed.

> **note** *Fault tolerance* refers to the ability of a system to suffer a fault, such as a failed drive, and continue to function normally or with minimal disruption. RAID 5 arrays provide fault tolerance by automatically recovering from a failed drive; they bring a spare drive on line to repair the volume set (assuming that they have been configured with a spare). *Redundancy* refers to the elements of a system that provide backup components that can take over in the event a similar component fails, or that share the work load and minimize the effects of a failure by continuing to offer their services.

In mission-critical situations, consider implementing RAID 50, which combines RAID 5 with mirroring. Each volume comprises a RAID 5 array, and each array (or at least the most important) is mirrored to other RAID 5 arrays. If one array fails, the other takes over, keeping the data online while you repair the damaged array. Keep in mind that this solution requires a combination of hardware and software to implement and can be very expensive; check with your server vendor for solutions that will fit your budget and technical requirements.

Another point to consider is the type of backup hardware you should include in your backup strategy. A common approach has been to use tape to back up servers, and tape is still a viable solution, particularly when long-term backup storage is required. Many administrators find, however, that restoring from tape can take too long. It can take several hours to restore and verify a 10-GB volume, and during that time you might have one or more departments offline, waiting for the server to come back up. The resulting lost business or lost productivity can have a huge financial impact on your company.

You should therefore consider implementing backup hardware that allows you to quickly restore data when needed, in addition to tape or other media. One solution is to add another server and use it to back up your critical data. Another solution is to add a storage area network (SAN) device, such as a Quantum Snap Server, that allows you to add storage space to the network with little effort. These devices consist of drive arrays and embedded CPUs that allow the unit to function as a file server without the addition of any software. Typically, setting up a SAN device involves little more than plugging it in and configuring a few settings—a job that takes minutes, compared to the hours required to install a server.

> **note** You'll find more information on the Quantum Snap Server at *http://www.quantum.com/products/snap+appliances/default.htm*. Check with your hardware supplier for other SAN options.

Backup hardware platforms   You can choose from among several types of backup hardware when you begin planning your backup strategy. Each type has advantages and disadvantages in terms of performance and cost. The following list summarizes the most common options:

Chapter 39: Backup Strategies and Virus Protection

AIT (Advanced Intelligent Tape)   These drives—manufactured by Sony—are fast and efficient. Sony also builds special tape library versions of these drives. Each AIT-1 cartridge can hold up to 35 GB uncompressed or up to 90 GB using built-in hardware compression. AIT-2 can compress to 130-GB capacity. AIT drives can transfer data at 4 MB/second or 10 MB/second using the same hardware compression.

CD-R/CD-RW (Compact Disc–Recordable/Rewritable)   CD-R and CD-RW drives use specially formatted compact discs. CD-R media is writable once, and CD-RW is writable multiple times. If you need a backup medium for a small number of files (generally no more than 1 GB) and relatively slow backup speed, CD-R and CD-RW are good choices. CD-R/RW storage media can store from 640 to 700 MB (more with software compression) on each disc. The speed of CD-R and CD-RW drives varies and can range from 5 to 50 MB/minute. New technologies from Sony are breaking the bounds of traditional CD-R media with a 1.4-GB disk. Also, a conglomerate of other makers, including Toshiba, is working on "Grayscale" technologies that measure 6 shades rather than simple 1s and 0s, theoretically increasing storage space five times over, to roughly 3.5 GB.

DAT (Digital Audio Tape)   Originally designed as an audio media storage format, DAT finally stumbled into a market that wanted it: backup. Though faster and more efficient than consumer platforms, DAT is still behind in other areas, making it less attractive for large enterprise uses. DAT cartridges contain 4 mm wide tape and a helically scanning rotating head assembly very similar to VCR technology (which is, in fact, what DAT technology was derived from) and can hold anywhere from 2 to 96 GB of media depending on compression. Transfer speeds are effectively 1.1 MB/second.

DLT (Digital Linear Tape)   These high-end tape drives are known for their large capacities and fast transfer rates. They feature built-in hardware-based compression and can, depending on maker and configuration, store anywhere from 10 to 220 GB of data. Transfer rates tend to be in the range of 5 MB/second to 20 MB/second but can go as low as 1.5 MB/second and as high as 80 MB/second (with Ultra Fast Wide SCSI III).

DVD-RAM (Digital Versatile Disc Random Access Memory)   DVD-RAM might be the newest kid on the block, but it's also the largest. A single DVD-RAM disc, which is nearly indistinguishable from a CD, can hold 2.6 GB on each side, for a total of 5.2 GB. Transfer rates vary radically between drives that are first, second, and third generation, but none are fast enough to store large of amounts of data quickly. DVD-RAM drives generally write to disk at 1,400 KB/second, which is equivalent to a 1x CD-ROM drive.

MO (Magneto-Optical)   MO drives are stable, quite sturdy, and nearly impossible to alter, despite being rewritable in an MO drive. The drives utilize both lasers and a magnetic head. The laser heats up a point on the disc surface to 200 degrees, and the magnet changes the polarity of the location. This can be done thousands of times per disc. MO drives can use 1.3-GB 3.5-inch discs or 5.2-GB 5.25-inch discs. Transfer rates range from 60 MB/minute to 120 MB/minute.

Travan/QIC   These drives are relatively fast but are held back by conversely low storage capacities. One tape can hold from 4 to 50 GB, and read/write speeds range from 30 MB/minute to 120 MB/minute. Prices, however, are low, which makes them perfect for low-end requirements such as a home office or workgroup environment.

Other cartridge-based devices   Zip, Jaz, SuperDisk, and HiFD drives are generally used only at the desktop level and do not have capacities that exceed the 2 GB maximum of the Jaz drive from Iomega. They are, however, great for personal use, workstation backup, and big file SneakerNet. Capacities range from 100 MB for the original Zip to 2 GB for the Jaz. The SuperDisk and HiFD drives can hold 120 MB and 200 MB, respectively, with the added bonus of 3.5-inch floppy backward compatibility. Transfer rates range from 30 MB/minute to 480 MB/minute.

Media libraries   Storing 220 GB on an AIT cartridge is great, unless your workplace manages a terabyte or two. That's where media libraries come in handy. These systems, developed for essentially any available media platform, can load and unload media as needed while sophisticated systems monitor and manage the data flow in and out. If you need to back up more data than can comfortably fit on a given storage medium, consider a media library as a solution. Check with your hardware vendor for solutions that fit your technical requirements and budget.

Hardware Connection Options

All backup platforms are limited to either a single or a few connection options. Most consumer-grade platforms use parallel, serial, USB, or FireWire (IEEE-1394, high-speed serial), and enterprise products on the low end can connect the same way. But performance problems exist with these connection options. Two formats lead the way in robustness and speed: SCSI and Fiber Channel. Quickly gaining market share, however, is the growing use of Ultra ATA 66/100 (a very fast ATAPI, or IDE, implementation).

Most consumer-grade and small business systems use either ATAPI or SCSI, with a smaller selection of products using USB and even fewer using FireWire. Most products for small to medium office systems are also available in ATAPI and SCSI interface formats. Enterprise-grade systems typically do not utilize USB or FireWire—much less serial or parallel solutions—but generally use SCSI or Fiber Channel.

Here are a few important considerations for choosing a connectivity option for your backup hardware:

- Speed and reliability are the most important factors. Consider the time it takes to perform a backup with a given technology, but, more important, consider the time required to restore from the backup. It usually doesn't matter if a full server backup takes ten hours to complete, but waiting ten hours while the server is rebuilt is often impractical.

- It's not wise (or cheap) to replace an existing bus installation. If your backplane is Fiber Channel, it would be a costly waste of time to replace it with SCSI RAID arrays. Likewise, if you already have SCSI in place, consider SCSI backup solutions first.

- Keep local area network (LAN) backups close to the source. Moving data over large distances to get to a backup facility is costly, time-consuming, and eats up bandwidth like gangbusters. Several smaller installations are better and faster than one big one.

- Try to keep cable lengths short. You must of course keep them within specification limits, but it behooves you to keep cables as short as possible for reduced interference and improved speed.

Software Considerations

Server and Storage Area Network (SAN) backup options require a backup program that not only supports your applications (more on this later) but also supports backup to devices other than tape. Retrospect is one company that offers several backup options supporting backup to tape, removable media (Zip and Jaz drives, for example), CD-R and CD-RW, and server volumes (hard disks.) Several others offer the same capability, as do certain shareware applications.

If you're backing up exclusively to tape, most backup applications can at least offer basic backup and restore features, although many support only SCSI tape devices. Exchange Server introduces an additional consideration, however. Unless it's specifically designed to work with Exchange Server, a backup application will fail to back up the message store and other database files in recoverable form. For example, the Backup application included with Microsoft Windows NT Server and Microsoft Windows 2000 Server do not support backup of Exchange Server.

Backup applications that support Exchange Server typically do so through an add-on Exchange Server agent. Two examples are Backup Exec from Veritas (*http://www.veritas. com*) and Retrospect from Dantz (*http://www.dantz.com*). Veritas charges for its Exchange Server agent; Dantz offers its agent for free. The Exchange Server agents make use of the Exchange Server Application Programming Interface (API) to access the store's database file, which is otherwise locked and unavailable to other applications.

As you begin to evaluate backup solutions for Exchange Server, keep in mind that the backup application must specifically support Exchange Server. Also look at other special backup requirements, such as backing up SQL databases. Many backup application developers offer SQL agents in addition to Exchange Server agents.

Structuring Exchange Server for Recoverability

Selecting the right backup hardware and software solutions for Exchange Server is only one aspect of developing and implementing a backup strategy. You should also consider how you can structure Exchange Server storage to improve recoverability in the event of a hardware failure or a corrupted message store. This section examines these issues and provides tips on how to fine-tune Exchange Server's data storage.

Allocating Storage in Exchange Server

Structuring the way Exchange Server stores its data can be very important, and it involves both software and hardware issues. Consider implementing multiple volumes and separating your key Exchange Server files across those volumes, rather than hosting them all on one volume. That way, if a volume fails, you need to restore only one set of files rather than all your files. This could mean a restore operation of several minutes rather than several hours.

> **note** Performance is another important reason to segregate your Exchange Server files on different drives. In the case of SCSI subsystems, each volume can be reading or writing concurrently with others, which can have a significant positive impact on performance.

Storage allocation in Exchange Server 5.5 The Exchange Performance Optimizer in Exchange Server 5.5 allows you to specify where the log files, data store, and other Exchange files will go.

Follow these steps to start the process:

1 Choose Start, Programs, Microsoft Exchange, Microsoft Exchange Performance Optimizer.

2 Click Next in the Microsoft Exchange Performance Optimizer Wizard. The wizard stops the Exchange services.

3 Use the next page of the wizard (see Figure 39-1) to supply information about how you use your server. Then click Next.

4 The wizard then analyzes the server's hard disks to determine the optimum location to store the Exchange Server database and log files. When the analysis is complete, click Next to see the wizard's recommendations for locating the files (see Figure 39-2).

5 Review the wizard's recommendations and adjust as needed by changing the path specified in each box. Make your decisions based on the amount of available space on each volume and the relative speed of each volume compared to the others. Ideally, you'll want to separate the log files from the store files, with both on fast volumes. The store files generally require the most available space.

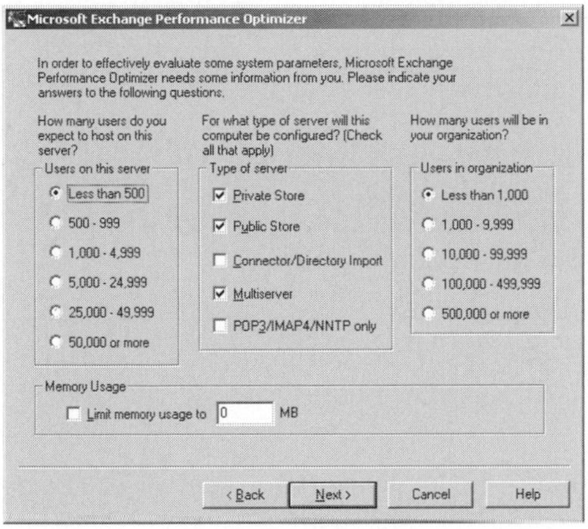

Chapter 39: Backup Strategies and Virus Protection

Figure 39-1. Specify the number of users, the types of stores, and other information about the server.

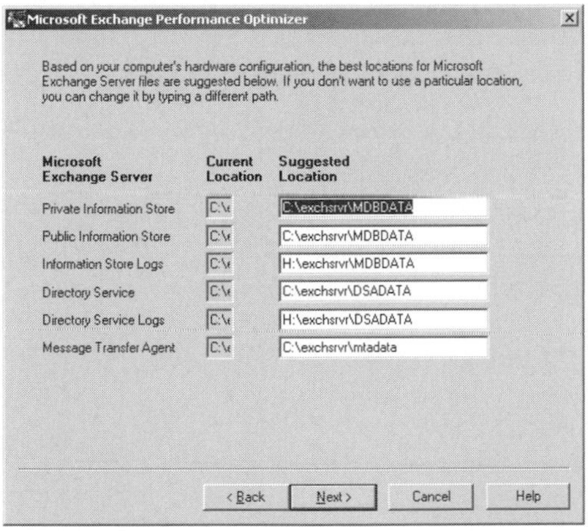

Figure 39-2. The Microsoft Exchange Performance Optimizer Wizard recommends storage locations based on your system's configuration and performance.

6 Click Next to execute the changes or click Cancel to cancel the process and close the Exchange Performance Optimizer.

> **note** If you choose to cancel the process, you must manually restart the Exchange services.

7 Follow the wizard's prompts to complete the optimization process.

Storage allocation in Exchange 2000 Server   Exchange 2000 Server doesn't provide an optimization wizard that automatically moves your message store database or log files, but it does provide a way for you to move the files manually. The process isn't as difficult as you might think and requires only a few actions in the Exchange System Manager.

957

Start by determining where you want to locate the Exchange Server database and logs files, based on available disk capacity and speed considerations. You'll need to first configure the log file location and then handle the database files in a separate procedure.

Follow these steps to configure the log file location:

1 Open the Exchange System Manager and configure it to show Administrative Groups if you have not already done so.

> **tip** To display Administrative Groups, right-click the organization and choose Properties. On the General tab, select Display Administrative Groups and click OK.

2 Expand the Administrative Group where the store is located, expand the Servers branch, and expand the server where the store is located. Right-click the storage group and choose Properties to display the First Storage Group Properties dialog box (see Figure 39-3).

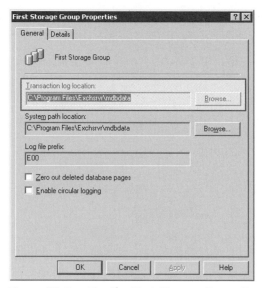

Figure 39-3. Use the First Storage Group Properties dialog box to configure the log file location.

3 Click Browse beside the Transaction Log Location box to open the Transaction Log dialog box, in which you can select the new location for the transaction logs.

4 Select the folder in which you want to relocate the log files and click OK to return to the First Storage Group Properties dialog box.

5 Click OK or Apply. The Exchange System Manager prompts you to verify the change. Click Yes to continue with the change or click No to cancel. If you click Yes, the Exchange System Manager dismounts the store, moves the files, and remounts the store. While this operation is taking place, users are unable to access the store.

6 After the store comes back online, perform a full backup of the store. Moving the log files invalidates existing full and differential backups. (If you plan to also move the database files, move them before performing the backup.)

---

tip **Change the location of temporary and recovered files**

The System Path Location box on the General tab of the First Storage Group Properties dialog box specifies the location where Exchange 2000 Server stores temporary and recovered files. You can click Browse beside this box to change the location, if needed. The default location is \Program Files\Exchsrvr\mdbdata.

Depending on your server's configuration, you might also want to move the two database files for the store. The Priv*(n)* .edb file, where *(n)* is a number, is used to store the Exchange Rich Text Format database. Exchange Server stores messages sent by MAPI clients in this database. The Priv*(n)* .stm file is the streaming database file, which stores messages sent using Multipurpose Internet Mail Extensions (MIME). You can co-locate the EDB and STM files in the same folder or store them in separate folders, depending on your server's available disk capacity and the performance considerations discussed earlier.

---

note The Exchange Rich Text Format database is not the same as Rich Text Format (RTF), which is used by many word processing applications as a common file format.

When you've determined the best location for the database files, follow these steps to move the files:

1 Perform a complete backup of your Exchange Server data store (or stores), as a precaution in the event of a problem during the move operation.

2 Open the Exchange System Manager and expand the Administrative Group where the store is located. (If necessary, refer to the previous procedure for instructions on how to display Administrative Groups.)

3 Expand the Servers branch, and then expand the server and storage group where the store is located.

4 Right-click the mailbox store and choose Properties.

5 In the Mailbox Store Properties dialog box, click the Database tab (see Figure 39-4 on the next page).

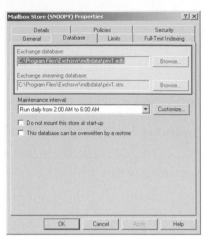

Figure 39-4.   Use the Database tab to view the location of the store and
(optionally) move it.

6   Click Browse beside the Exchange Database box to pick a new location for
the EDB file. Select the folder and click OK to return to the Database tab.

7   Click Browse beside the Exchange Streaming Database box to pick a new
location for the STM file. Select the folder and click OK to return to the
Database tab.

8   Click OK or Apply. The Exchange System Manager prompts you to confirm
the move. Click Yes to continue or No to cancel. (While the move is taking
place, users cannot access the store.)

In addition to moving the transaction logs and the private store database, you might also
decide to move the public store database (containing public folders), particularly if the
public folders contain a large amount of data.

The process is similar to moving the mailbox store:

1   Open the Exchange System Manager and expand the Administrative Group
where the store is located.

2   Expand the storage group, right-click the Public Folder Store branch, and
choose Properties to open the Properties dialog box for the store.

3   Click the Database tab and then click Browse beside the Exchange Database
box to select a new location for the EDB file. Then click OK.

4 Back on the Database tab, click Browse beside the Exchange Streaming Database box to select a new location for the STM file. Then click OK.

5 Click OK or Apply to move the store. Exchange Server takes the store offline during the move, making it unavailable to users during that time.

Using Multiple Message Stores in Exchange 2000 Server

Another structural change you might make to your Exchange Servers is to use multiple message stores rather than hosting all mailboxes in a single store. For example, suppose that you have a sales department of 100 people, who rely heavily on Exchange Server to process orders. If all those users are contained in a single store and the store becomes corrupted, all 100 will be unable to work while you restore the message store. If you break up the storage into four separate message stores, a maximum of 25 employees will be affected by a store going offline. In addition, restoring a given message store will take less time because it will contain less data.

A *storage group* in Exchange 2000 Server is a set of Exchange database files that share a single transaction log and are managed as a single unit for administration, archiving, and restoration. Each storage group can contain up to six databases, and a single server can use up to four storage groups, for a total of 24 databases per server. Each database in a storage group functions independently of the others and can be either mounted or dismounted (started or stopped). If a database becomes corrupted, Exchange 2000 Server won't mount it, but the corrupted database will not affect the other databases in the storage group. This arrangement improves reliability in situations where you need to limit downtime as much as possible. You can repair the affected database and remount it without taking down the others. Plus, the failure of a single database doesn't affect the information store (Store.exe) process—it can continue to manage the other databases.

---

tip **Reserve one database for recovery**

Although you can create six databases in a storage group, you should limit yourself to only five for recoverability reasons. The Information Store Integrity Checker (Isinteg.exe) requires a temporary database for analyzing a store database. If you create six databases in a storage group, you'll have to dismount one additional database to run Isinteg. Rather than taking down a group of users, limit the number of databases you create in a storage group to five, leaving one available for Isinteg.

Setting up storage groups is not a difficult task. The general process is as follows:

1 Create an additional storage group, if necessary.

2 Create an additional mailbox store (or stores).

3 Distribute users from existing store to new stores.

Hosting Multiple Organizations with Storage Groups

The ability to separate users into multiple databases in a storage group, or even into multiple storage groups, has implications not only for organizations that host only their own users but also for organizations that host users in different companies. You could host multiple companies on a single Exchange Server 5.x server, but doing so isn't practical from an administration perspective. Plus, having all the businesses in a single database means that when the database goes down, all your customers are affected.

With Exchange 2000 Server storage groups, you might host each company in a different database or even host each in its own storage group, depending on the number of users in each company and other factors. Thus a single database or storage group going down means that only one business is affected, not all of them. When a problem does occur, you can repair the affected database without affecting the others, limiting downtime to a single company or even a single department within a company.

Storage groups also give you greater flexibility for administration when you host multiple companies. For example, companies might have different archival requirements. One company might need weekly backups, while another might need backups daily or even more frequently. By separating the companies into different databases, you can back up their databases separately and with different frequency as needed.

note The following procedure assumes that you want to create an additional storage group for the new mailbox store. If you prefer, you can create a new mailbox store in the existing storage group; if that's the case, you can skip to step 4 of the procedure. Also, because this procedure assumes that you have some experience managing Exchange 2000 Server, it does not delve into all configuration aspects in detail.

Follow these steps to create the storage group and the mailbox store:

1 Open the Exchange System Manager, and then open the Administrative Group in which the existing store is located.

2 Expand the Servers branch in the Administrative Group, right-click the server, and choose New, Storage Group to display the Properties dialog box shown in Figure 39-5.

Chapter 39: Backup Strategies and Virus Protection

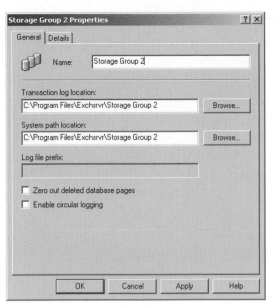

Figure 39-5.   Enter the storage group name, transaction log location, and other properties.

3   Set options on the General tab using the following list as a guide:

- **Name.** Specify the name by which the new storage group should be displayed in the Exchange System Manager.

- **Transaction Log Location.** Specify the path used for storing the transaction log. The default is \Program Files\Exchsrvr\<name>, where <name> is the storage group name specified in the Name box.

- **System Path Location.** Specify the location for storing temporary and recovered files. The default is the same as the default transaction log location.

- **Log File Prefix.** This box displays the log file prefix assigned to the transaction logs. It is blank when you create a new storage group but displays the prefix when you view the properties for an existing storage group.

- **Zero Out Deleted Database Pages.** Select this option to have Exchange Server remove deleted database pages from the hard disk. Removing the pages provides better security because deleted data is actually deleted from the disk, but deleting the pages imposes additional overhead that affects performance.

- **Enable Circular Logging.** Select this option to allow Exchange Server to perform circular logging on the storage group, replacing log files that have a time stamp older than the checkpoint file.

4 Right-click the storage group and choose New, Mailbox Store.

5 Set options on the General tab (see Figure 39-6) using the following list as a guide:

- **Name.** Specify the name for the mailbox store. Exchange Server uses the same name by default for the store file names.

- **Default Public Store.** Specify the location for the public store file. When creating a new store, you can accept the default or click Browse to select an existing store.

- **Offline Address List.** Specify the offline address list, which is downloaded by users and used for addressing when working offline. When creating a new store, you can accept the default address list or click Browse to select an existing one.

Figure 39-6. Configure properties for the new mailbox store on the General tab.

- **Archive All Messages Sent Or Received By Mailboxes On This Store.** Select this option to archive to a mailbox all messages sent and received by users with mailboxes in the store. It's a good idea to create a mailbox specifically for archiving messages. You can select any recipient in the directory. If you want to archive to a mailbox within the new store, be sure that this option is cleared. Then create the store, create the mailbox to use for archiving, open the Properties dialog box for the store, and select this option, specifying the mailbox. Note that archiving to a different store provides an additional level of redundancy—if the archive mailbox resides in a different store, you can still retain the archived messages even if the originating store is lost and unrecoverable.

- **Clients Support S/MIME Signatures.** Select this option if you want the mailboxes in the new store to support S/MIME for digital signatures and encryption. Outlook versions 98 and later support S/MIME.

- **Display Plain Text Messages In A Fixed-Sized Font.** Select this option to have Exchange Server use a fixed-size font (10-point Courier) to retain formatting for diagrams, columns, and so on in plain-text messages.

6 Click the Database tab and specify the location for the EDB and STM files. Then click OK to create the new store.

After you create the store (or during the creation process), you can use the additional tabs in the mailbox store's Properties dialog box to configure storage limits, indexing, recipient policies, and other options.

> **note** Details about configuring the additional properties of the store fall outside the scope of this book. For more information, see the *Microsoft Exchange 2000 Server Administrator's Companion*, by Walter J. Glenn and Bill English (Microsoft Press, 2000).

With the new store created, you can begin moving mailboxes from their existing store (or stores) to the new one. You perform the move operation from the Active Directory Users And Computers console, not from the Exchange System Manager.

The following steps explain how:

1 Open the Active Directory Users And Computers console, and locate the user whose mailbox you want to move.

2 Right-click the user and choose Exchange Tasks.

3 Click Next when the Exchange Tasks Wizard appears.

4 Select Move Mailbox and click Next.

5 Select the target server in the Server drop-down list.

6 Select the target store in the Mailbox Store drop-down list, and then click Next.

7 Click Finish when the wizard indicates that the move is complete.

Backing Up User Data

Perhaps your company doesn't use Exchange Server. Or perhaps your users frequently use personal folders to store much of their data outside their Exchange Server mailboxes. Whatever the case, you'll probably want to provide a backup mechanism that protects individual users from hardware failures and lost data.

Although you can use the built-in Backup application included with all versions of Microsoft Windows to back up a user's local data, this application is not the most efficient or flexible backup solution. It doesn't support compression and, until Windows 2000, supported only backing up to tape. It also lacks all but the most rudimentary scheduling capability, making it a poor choice for automated backups.

You can take one of two approaches to backing up your users' Outlook data (and other files): initiate the backups on each workstation or use a backup agent to back up the files to a server. In the former approach, the backup software runs on the user's computer and can back up either to local media or to a network server, depending on the capabilities of the backup application. In the latter, a server-based backup application combines with a client-side agent to back up the client's workstation from the server. This option is often the most reliable and gives the administrator the ability to control and monitor the backup operation.

A large number of backup applications are on the market today, many of which provide server-side backup of clients through backup agents—for example, Backup Exec from Veritas and Retrospect from Dantz. After you evaluate and identify the backup solution that's right for your organization, take the time to map out a backup strategy for your network to ensure successful and reliable client backup.

Here are some important points to consider:

- Will the solution provide for automatic backups of client data? A product that offers scheduled local backups is one solution, but a server-side solution that can back up client files to a server offers more control.

- How easy is it to recover specific files? If you spend hours trying to recover a single file (such as a personal folders file) for a user, look for a more effective solution.

- Will (or should) users be able to initiate the recovery? If you want users to initiate a recovery themselves, you should implement a solution that offers that capability. This saves the administrator from having to handle the recovery process.

Providing Virus Protection

Hardware and software failures are by no means the only source of anguish for the average administrator. Viruses and worms have become major problems for system administrators. For example, estimates have identified losses of greater than a billion dollars as a result of outages and interruptions caused by the Melissa and ILOVEYOU viruses. Companies ground to a halt, systems shut down, systems administrators turned off mail servers, and general chaos ensued.

Viruses and worms can be quite damaging in many ways. Here's what the Melissa virus is capable of doing:

- Replicating itself to any shared resource to which it can connect

- Gathering and sending passwords for software and services to an Internet mailbox

- Sending itself to all addresses in the infected system's Outlook Address Book

The effects of a particularly virulent virus or worm can be devastating for a company. It can bring your mail servers to a quick halt because of the load it imposes on them with the sheer amount of traffic it generates. Bandwidth, both local and across WAN (wide area network) links, is affected as multiple copies of infected messages flood the network. Files can become infected, rendering them unusable and subjecting users to reinfection. This means you must recover the files from backups, making an adequate backup strategy even more important than usual.

One often overlooked effect that viruses have on a company is the public relations nightmare they can create. How would your customers react if they received a flood of infected messages from your users that brought their mail servers to a screeching halt and damaged their production files? Forget for a moment the ire of your customers' system administrators. Could your company survive the ill will generated by such a catastrophe?

My guess is that it would not. Therefore, developing and implementing an effective virus protection strategy is as important—perhaps more so—than developing a backup strategy. When you examine your antivirus needs, approach the problem from two angles: protecting against outside infection and preventing an outgoing flood of infected messages. You can approach the former through either client-side or server-side solutions, but the latter typically requires a server-side solution.

Implementing Server-Side Solutions

Whether or not your organization uses Exchange Server, your first line of defense against viruses and worms should reside between your LAN and the Internet. Many antivirus solution vendors offer server-side products that monitor traffic coming from the Internet and detect and block viruses in real time. One such product is WebShield from Network Associates (*http://www.nai.com*). WebShield is part of NAI's Total Virus Defense product, which also includes client antivirus software and GroupShield Exchange, an antivirus solution for Exchange Server. Another solution that filters viruses before they get to your network is Panda Software's Panda Antivirus for Firewalls, which works in conjunction with any firewall that supports Content Vectoring Protocol (CVP) to allow the firewall and the antivirus product to interact. You should also consider Symantec's Norton AntiVirus for Firewalls, which supports firewalls from several vendors.

Stopping viruses before they get into your LAN is a great goal, but even the best products sometimes miss. If your organization uses Exchange Server, you should also consider installing an Exchange-based antivirus solution. Network Associates offers GroupShield Exchange, and Panda Software offers Panda Antivirus for MS Exchange Server. A third solution is Norton AntiVirus for Microsoft Exchange. Each of these applications works at the API level with Exchange Server to provide real-time virus detection and removal/ quarantine. Other companies also offer antivirus solutions for Exchange Server.

In addition to scrubbing network and Exchange Server traffic for viruses, you also should implement a solution that provides real-time virus detection for your network's file servers. These solutions scan the server for infected files as files are added or modified. For example, a remote user might upload a file containing a virus to your FTP server. If local users open the file, their systems become infected and the virus begins to spread across your LAN. Catching and removing the virus as soon as the file is uploaded to the FTP server is the ideal solution.

Consider all these points as you evaluate server-side antivirus products. Some might be more important to you than others, so prioritize them and then choose an antivirus suite that best suits your needs and priorities.

Implementing Client-Side Solutions

In addition to blocking viruses and worms at the server, you should also provide antivirus protection at each workstation, particularly if your server-side virus detection is limited. Even if you do provide a full suite of detection service at the server, client-side protection is a vital piece of any antivirus strategy. For example, suppose that your server provides Web-based virus filtering, scanning all network traffic coming from the Internet. Because of traffic load, the server misses a virus in a downloaded file. A user opens the file, infects his or her system, and the virus begins replicating across the LAN. If the user has a client-side antivirus solution in place, the virus is blocked before it can do any damage.

Use the following criteria to evaluate client-side antivirus solutions:

- **Are frequent updates available?** In a given day, several new viruses appear. Your antivirus solution is only as good as your virus definition files are current. Choose a solution that offers daily or (at most) weekly virus definition updates.

- **Can updates be scheduled for automatic execution?** The average user doesn't back up documents on a regular basis, much less worry about whether antivirus definition files are up-to-date. For that reason, it's important that the client-side antivirus solution you choose provide automatic, scheduled updates.

- **Does the product scan a variety of file types?** Make sure the product you choose can scan not only executables and other application files but also Microsoft Office documents for macro viruses.

> For details on setting options in Outlook that can prevent infection through macro-borne viruses, see "Setting Macro Security," page 661; and "Protecting Against Office Macro Viruses," page 364.

You'll find several client-side antivirus products on the market. Some popular ones include Symantec's Norton AntiVirus (*http://www.symantec.com*), Network Associates' VirusScan (*http://www.nai.com*), and Panda's Antivirus for Servers and Desktops. Many other products are available that offer comparable features.

newfeature!
Configuring Blocked Attachments

Attachment blocking is an important new feature in Outlook 2002. Outlook can now block certain types of attachments, preventing users from opening attached files that could infect their systems—for example, a JavaScript file, which could execute malicious code on a user's system to damage or steal data. Outlook blocks other types of files as well. Chapter 12 provides a complete discussion of Outlook's attachment blocking feature from the user's perspective; see "Protecting Against Viruses in Attachments," page 360. This chapter, in contrast, focuses on how to configure attachment blocking at both the server and the client.

Outlook and Exchange Server provide two levels of attachment blocking. Level 1 attachments (see Table 39-1 on the next page) cannot be opened by the user. You can view the message itself, but Outlook disables the elements in the interface that would otherwise allow you to open or save the attachment to disk. Chapter 12 offers a couple of ways to work around this restriction. Figure 39-7 shows how Outlook handles a Level 1 blocked attachment.

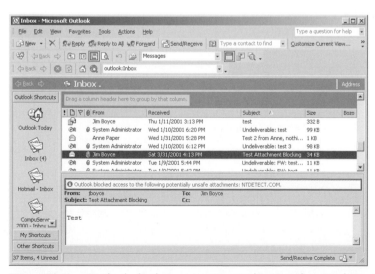

Figure 39-7. Outlook displays a message indicating the attachment is blocked and cannot be opened.

Chapter 39

For information about how to work around the restrictions on Level 1 attachments, see "Level 1 Attachments," page 360.

Although you cannot open Level 2 attachments directly in Outlook, you can save them to disk and open them outside Outlook. You can configure Level 2 attachments only at the Exchange Server level, making them applicable only to Exchange Server accounts and not to external POP3, IMAP, or HTTP-based accounts. However, you can make modifications to the client's registry to change the Level 1 list (explained later in this chapter), and these modifications do affect non–Exchange Server accounts. This means you can completely unblock Level 1 attachments for non–Exchange Server accounts to allow these attachments to be opened in Outlook, but you can't have them treated as Level 2 attachments (which forces the user to save them to disk before opening them).

Table 39-1. Level 1 attachments

File Extension	Description
ADE	Microsoft Access project extension
ADP	Microsoft Access project
BAS	Microsoft Visual Basic class module
BAT	Batch file
CHM	Compiled HTML Help file
CMD	Microsoft Windows NT/Windows 2000 command script
COM	Microsoft MS-DOS program
CPL	Control Panel extension
CRT	Security certificate
EXE	Program
HLP	Help file
HTA	HTML program
INF	Setup Information File
INS	Internet Naming Service
ISP	Internet Communication settings
JS	Microsoft JScript file

Table 39-1. *(continued)*

File Extension	Description
JSE	Microsoft JScript Encoded Script file
LNK	Shortcut
MDA	Microsoft Access add-in program
MDB	Microsoft Access program
MDE	Microsoft Access MDE database
MDZ	Microsoft Access wizard program
MSC	Microsoft Common Console document
MSI	Microsoft Windows Installer package
MSP	Microsoft Windows Installer patch
MST	Microsoft Visual Test source files
PCD	Photo CD image or Microsoft Visual Test compiled script
PIF	Shortcut to MS-DOS program
REG	Registration entries
SCR	Screen saver
SCT	Microsoft Windows Script Component
SHS	Shell Scrap Object
URL	Internet shortcut
VB	Microsoft VBScript file
VBE	Microsoft VBScript Encoded script file
VBS	Microsoft VBScript file
WSC	Microsoft Windows Script Component
WSF	Microsoft Windows Script file
WSH	Windows Script Host settings file

note The Level 2 attachment list is empty by default.

InsideOut

Apparently the theory for Level 2 attachments is that the user has a client-side antivirus solution in place that will scan the file automatically as soon as the user saves the file to disk. Or perhaps the theory is that you can rely on the user to manually perform a virus-check on the file. Neither of these scenarios is a sure bet by any means. Even if the user has antivirus software installed, it might be disabled or have an outdated virus definition file. That's why it's important to provide virus protection at the network and server levels to prevent viruses from reaching the user at all.

It's also important to educate users about the potential damage that can be caused by viruses and worms. Too often these infect systems through user ignorance—users receive an attachment from a known recipient, assume that it's safe (if they even consider that the file could be infected), and open the file. The result is an infected system and potentially an infected network.

Configuring Attachments in Exchange Server

You can configure attachment blocking in two locations: at the Exchange Server or at the user's workstation. Configuring attachment blocking at the server is the most effective and efficient; and it gives you, as an administrator, control over attachment security. It also allows you to tailor security by groups within your Windows NT or Windows 2000 domains.

Before you can configure attachment security in Exchange Server, you must install the Outlook Security Features Administrative Package (AdminPak), which is included on the Microsoft Office XP CD.

> **note** You must use a computer running Windows 2000 Server or Windows 2000 Professional to customize the security settings on an Exchange Server. This computer need not be the server but can be a workstation.

The first task is to extract the files from the installation file:

1 On a system running Windows 2000, insert the Office XP CD.

2 Create a folder on the local computer to contain the files. (The steps outlined here assume that you're creating a folder named AdminPak for the files.)

3 Open the folder \Ork\Files\PFiles\OrkTools\Ork10\Tools\AdmPack.

4 Double-click the file Admpack.exe and extract it to the folder created in step 2.

The following sections continue the process.

Installing the Trusted Code Control

After you extract the files to the server, the next step is to install the Trusted Code control so that Exchange Server will allow the security template you use to set security options to function without conflicting with the security features embedded in Exchange Server.

Follow these steps to install the Trusted Code control:

1 Log on as Administrator to the Windows 2000 computer you're going to use to manage Exchange Server attachment security.

2 Copy the file Hashctl.dll from the AdminPak folder to the %systemroot%\System32 folder (typically \Winnt\System32).

3 Choose Start, Run and enter the following command in the Run dialog box:

   regsvr32 hashctl.dll

4 Click OK or press Enter. Then click OK in the resulting informational dialog box.

5 Copy the file Comdlg32.ocx from the AdminPak folder to the %systemroot%\System32 folder. Click Yes when prompted to replace the existing file.

6 Choose Start, Run and enter the following command in the Run dialog box:

   regsvr32 comdlg32.ocx

7 Click OK or press Enter. Then click OK in the resulting informational dialog box.

Creating a Public Folder to Contain Custom Security Settings

Before you can customize security settings for Exchange Server, you must create a public folder to contain the custom settings. Set the folder's access control lists (ACLs) so that all users who need custom security settings have read access to the folder. Only users who will have administrative permission to change security settings on a global basis should be given Write, Edit, or Delete permissions for the folder.

note The following procedure assumes that you're creating the public folder in Exchange 2000 Server. The procedure is similar for Exchange Server 5.5.

Follow these steps to create and configure the public folder:

1 Open the Exchange System Manager and expand the Administrative Group. Then expand the Folders\Public Folders branch.

Part 7: Using and Administering Outlook with Exchange Server

2 Right-click Public Folders and choose New, Public Folder to open the Properties dialog box shown in Figure 39-8.

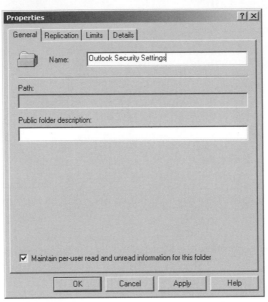

Figure 39-8. Use this Properties dialog box to specify the properties for the new public folder.

3 In the Name box on the General page, type **Outlook Security Settings**. Alternatively, you can type **Outlook 10 Security Settings** for the name, if you prefer, but you must use one of these two.

4 If needed, enter a description for the folder in the Public Folder Description box.

5 Click OK to create the folder.

6 Right-click the folder you just created and choose Properties. Click the Permissions tab.

7 Click Client Permissions to open the Client Permissions dialog box, shown in Figure 39-9.

8 Select Default, clear the Create Items option, and verify that Read Items and Folder Visible are selected.

9 Select Anonymous and select None in the Roles drop-down list.

10 If you want to grant other users or groups the ability to modify security settings, click Add and select a user or group. Click OK and then configure that user's or group's permissions as Owner by selecting Owner in the Roles drop-down list.

11 Click OK to close the Client Permissions dialog box, and then click OK to close the Properties dialog box for the folder.

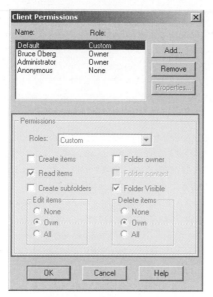

Figure 39-9. Configure ACLs for the folder in the Client Permissions dialog box.

Outlook stores the settings in the public folder when you create custom security settings (explained in the following section). When a user opens Outlook, the program checks the public folder for custom security settings and looks for settings that apply to that user. If it finds such settings, Outlook uses those settings for the current session.

Creating Custom Security Settings

After you set up the public folder, you can create custom security settings if you've been given the necessary permissions for that folder (see the previous section). You create security settings using the SecuritySettings.oft template supplied with the AdminPak.

Here's how to open the template:

1 Open Outlook and click the arrow beside the New button on the Standard toolbar. Select Choose Form to open the Choose Form dialog box.

2 In the Look In drop-down list, select User Templates In File System.

3 Click Browse and open the AdminPak folder. Click OK.

4 Select OutlookSecurity in the template list and click OK.

5 When Outlook prompts you to select a folder, select the Outlook Security Settings public folder.

6 Outlook then displays the Default Security Settings form, shown in Figure 39-10 on the next page.

7 Choose Tools, Forms, Publish Forms.

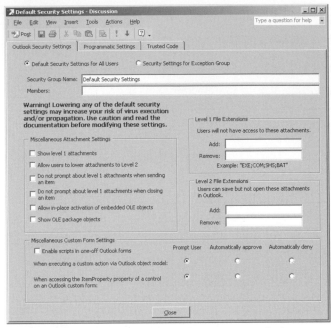

Figure 39-10. Create custom settings on the Default Security Settings form.

8 In the Publish Form As dialog box, select the Outlook Security Settings public folder.

9 Type **Outlook Security Form** in the Display Name and Form Name boxes and click Publish.

10 Scroll to the bottom of the form and click Close to close the Default Security Settings form. When you're prompted to save changes, click No.

> **note** If the Close toolbar button is not operational on your system (an apparent bug in the form), click the Close button (X) in the upper right corner of the form.

Next create a set of security settings to use as the default for all users who do not have their own custom settings. In most cases, you should leave the security settings at their defaults, making only minor modifications as needed, and then create custom forms for specific users or groups.

Follow these steps to create the default settings:

1 In Outlook, click the arrow beside the New button on the Standard toolbar and select Choose Form.

2 In the Choose Form dialog box, open the Outlook Security Settings public folder. Choose the security template and then click Open.

3 On the Outlook Security Settings tab (refer to Figure 39-10), verify that Default Security Settings For All Users is selected, make modifications to settings as needed (explained later), scroll to the bottom of the form, and click Close.

4 Click Yes when prompted to save changes.

Now that you have a set of default security settings, you can begin creating custom settings for individuals and groups. From the Outlook Security Forms public folder, open the security form you just saved. On the Outlook Security Settings tab, select Security Settings For Exception Group. Then configure settings on the form using the following list as a guide:

- **Security Group Name.** Specify a name for this group of settings. For example, you might use the name Unrestricted Level 1 Access for a group of settings that allows full access to Level 1 attachments.

- **Members.** Type member names separated by semicolons. In Exchange 2000 Server, you can enter the name of a distribution list or a security group rather than individual names. If a user is added to more than one security group, the most recently created group takes precedence. Press Ctrl+K to resolve typed names to valid addresses. If any name remains without an underline, check it for spelling errors.

> **note** You cannot use Exchange Server 5.5 distribution lists to specify security members.

> **tip** **Add member names more easily**
>
> The security form doesn't include a button that lets you browse the Global Address List and select members for the group. If you need to add several members, open a message form as if you were composing a new e-mail message and click the button beside the To box. Select users from the address list as needed, and close the Select Names dialog box. Highlight all the names in the To box, press Ctrl+C to copy them to the clipboard, and then click in the Members box on the security form and press Ctrl+V to paste the list in the box.

- **Show Level 1 Attachments.** Select this option to allow the group to open Level 1 attachments.

- **Allow Users To Lower Attachments To Level 2.** Select this option to allow the group to demote Level 1 attachments to Level 2, which lets a user save the attachments to disk and then open them.

- **Do Not Prompt About Level 1 Attachments When Sending An Item.** This option disables the warning that normally appears when a user tries to send a Level 1 attachment. The warning explains that the attachment could cause a virus infection and that the recipient might not receive the attachment (because of attachment blocking on the recipient's server). To disable this message for users who are posting Level 1 attachments to a public folder, you must also select the following option.

- **Do Not Prompt About Level 1 Attachments When Closing An Item.** This option disables the warning that normally appears when the user closes a message, appointment, or other item that contains a Level 1 attachment. See the previous option regarding posting to a public folder.

- **Allow In-Place Activation Of Embedded OLE Objects.** Select this option to allow the group to open embedded OLE objects (such as Excel spreadsheets, Access databases, and other documents) by double-clicking the object's icon.

> **note** Users can always open embedded OLE objects if Microsoft Word is their e-mail editor, regardless of how this option is set.

- **Show OLE Package Objects.** Select this option to show embedded OLE objects in e-mail messages. Hiding the objects prevents the user from opening them.

- **Level 1 File Extensions.** Use this group of controls to modify the Level 1 attachment list. Type the file extensions of the attachments (without the period) and separate multiple file types with semicolons. Use the Add field to add to the list and the Remove field to remove from the list.

- **Level 2 File Extensions.** Use this group of controls to modify the Level 2 attachment list. Type the file extensions of the attachments, separated by semicolons. Use the Add box to add to the list and the Remove box to remove from the list.

- **Enable Scripts In One-Off Outlook Forms.** This option allows scripts to be executed if the script and the form layout are contained in the message.

- **When Executing A Custom Action Via Outlook Object Model.** This setting determines the action Outlook takes if a program attempts to execute a task using the Outlook object model. For example, a virus could incorporate a script that uses the Outlook object model to reply to a message and attach itself to that message, bypassing Outlook's security safeguards. Select Prompt User to have Outlook prompt the user to allow or deny the action. Select Automatically Approve to allow the program to execute the task without prompting the user. Select Automatically Deny to prevent the program from executing the task without prompting the user.

- **When Accessing the ItemProperty Property Of A Control On An Outlook Custom Form.** This setting determines the action Outlook takes if a user adds a control to a custom Outlook form and binds that control to any ad-

dress information fields (To or From, for example). Select Prompt User to
have Outlook ask the user to allow or deny access to the address fields when
the message is received. Select Automatically Approve to allow access without
prompting the user. Select Automatically Deny to deny access without
prompting the user.

Troubleshooting

You added an alias to a security form, but the settings are not applied to that user.

If you open an existing security form and add a member to the group without changing any other settings, the change might not be applied properly for that user. To
ensure that the setting takes effect, make at least one other change to the form. If
you don't want any permanent changes applied to the form, simply modify a setting
and then set it back to its original state. For example, select a check box and then
clear it. Then close the form and click Yes to save changes.

After you configure the settings as needed, close the form and save changes. Exchange
Server then prompts you twice to supply authentication information. Enter account credentials that have Administrative permissions for the public folder. Outlook then saves
the item in the folder using the name you specified on the form as the subject of the
posted message (see Figure 39-11).

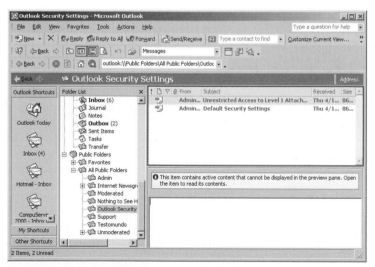

Figure 39-11. Outlook stores security settings as messages in the Outlook Security
Settings public folder.

Troubleshooting

A group of security settings don't work.

When you save a group of security settings, Exchange Server prompts you for authentication credentials with the permissions necessary to create the security settings. If you enter incorrect credentials, such as the wrong user name or password, Exchange Server creates the form, but the security settings will not work. You can't simply edit the form and repair the problem. Instead, you must delete the form and create a new one, this time using the correct authentication credentials.

Modifying Security Settings

You can easily modify security settings after you create a group. Open Outlook with an account that has the permissions necessary to make changes in the folder, and then open the Outlook Security Settings public folder. Double-click the form to open it. Make changes as needed, close the form, and click Yes to save the changes.

Configuring Clients for Custom Security

Simply creating security settings doesn't mean that they will automatically be in effect for users. You must configure Outlook on each user's computer to look to the Exchange Server for custom security settings. You do so by modifying settings in the user's registry. Although you can make these changes on a case-by-case basis, doing so isn't usually practical, particularly if you need to change the registries of several hundred (or more) users.

note If you deploy Outlook using system policies, the Outlk10.adm file administrative template automatically passes customized security settings to users when they log on. Otherwise, you must modify users' registries using the methods described in this section. The Microsoft Office XP Resource Kit offers a detailed explanation of how to deploy Office with system policies.

You enable custom security settings on a user's computer by adding a value to the user's registry and setting it according to your public folder configuration and security requirements. You can create this value manually, either at the user's computer or by remotely editing the registry. However, it's much more practical to customize the registry through the user's logon script or by placing a registry script on a server and having the user double-click the script to incorporate the registry change.

First you need to create the registry script, as described here:

1 On a system where Outlook 2002 is installed, choose Start, Run and type **regedit** in the Run dialog box to open the Registry Editor.

2 Open the registry key HKEY_CURRENT_USER\Software\Policies\Microsoft\
Security. If the key does not exist, create it.

3 Create a new DWORD value in the key and name it *CheckAdminSettings*.

4 Set the value of *CheckAdminSettings* to one of the following:

> **note** If this key is not present on the user's system, Outlook uses the default security settings.

- **0**   Use the default security settings.

- **1**   Search for applicable security settings in the Outlook Security Settings public folder.

- **2**   Search for applicable security settings in the Outlook 10 Security
  Settings public folder.

- **Any other value**   Use the default security settings.

5 Choose Registry, Export Registry File to open the Export Registry File dialog
box. Enter a name for the REG file, specify a path, and click Save.

> **note** If you plan to distribute the registry file via e-mail or across the LAN, place the REG
> file in a share on a network server that is accessible to the users. Create separate fold-
> ers under the root of the share, and use NTFS permissions to control access to the
> folders if you need to distribute different REG files to different users.

6 Notify your users of the availability of the custom security settings. Instruct
them to add the registry settings by using the REG file, or apply the change
for them automatically by using logon scripts.

If you choose not to incorporate the registry change through the users' logon scripts, you
can place the REG file on a network server or send the users a shortcut to the file on the
server. They can then follow the shortcut in the message to open the REG file and apply it. The registry settings are applied automatically when a user opens the REG file.

Troubleshooting

Users don't receive the REG file in e-mail.

In order to broadcast the REG file to users through e-mail, you must insert a link to
the REG file, not the REG file itself. REG files are included in the default Level 1 attachment list and are therefore blocked by Outlook. So you must save the REG file to
a shared folder on a network server, compose a message to the users, and enter the
UNC path to the REG file in the body of the message. As an alternative, you could
place the REG file in a public folder and insert a shortcut to the file in the message.

Chapter 39

Configuring Attachment Blocking Directly in Outlook

The previous sections explained how to configure attachment blocking for Exchange Server users. Non–Exchange Server users can also control attachment blocking, although the method for modifying the attachment list is different. So if you use Outlook in a workgroup or on a stand-alone computer without Exchange Server, you can still control which attachments Outlook prevents you from opening. You simply have fewer options for controlling and applying security settings.

To change the Level 1 attachment list, you must modify a registry setting on your local computer. You can remove file types from the list, but you cannot add them. To apply the changes across multiple computers, distribute a registry script file. You can distribute this file through a logon script, place it on a network share for users to access, or send users a message containing a shortcut to the file.

InsideOut

The ability to remove file types from the Level 1 attachment list is a welcomed feature, but one addition that would be great to see in a future release is the ability to add file types to the attachment list as well.

Follow these steps to create the necessary registry settings and optionally export them as a REG file for other users:

1 On a system with Outlook 2002 installed, choose Start, Run and type **regedit** in the Run dialog box.

2 In the Registry Editor, open the key HKEY_CURRENT_USER\Software\ Microsoft\Office\10.0\Outlook\Security.

3 In that key, add a string value named *Level1Remove*.

4 Set the value of *Level1Remove* to include the file extensions of those files you want removed from the Level 1 attachment list, separated by semicolons. The following example removes Microsoft Installer (MSI) files and Help (HLP) files from the list:

msi;hlp

5 If you want to share the customized registry with other users, choose Registry, Export Registry File. Then select a location for the REG file and click Save. Distribute the REG file to the other users as described previously.

Chapter 40

Designing and Using Forms

Even without any custom programming, Microsoft Outlook provides an excellent set of features. In fact, many organizations don't need anything beyond what Outlook offers right out of the box. Others, however, sometimes have special needs that are not addressed adequately by Outlook—perhaps because of the way these organizations do business or because of specific requirements in their particular industries. In such cases, you have ample opportunity to extend the functionality of Outlook through custom design and programming.

For example, you might need to add some additional fields to your message forms or your meeting request forms. Perhaps you need an easier way for users to perform mail merge operations with Microsoft Word and Outlook contacts lists. Or maybe you simply want to fine-tune your forms to add your company logo or special instructions or warnings for users.

Whatever your situation, you can easily make changes to the existing Outlook forms, or you can even design new ones. The changes you make can be simple or complex: you might add one or two fields to the standard contact form, or you might add a considerable amount of program code to allow Outlook to perform custom tasks or interact with other Microsoft Office applications. This chapter starts you on the right path by explaining how Outlook uses forms and how you can customize them to suit your needs.

Forms are such a normal part of everything we do on computers that we sometimes take them for granted. It's still true, however, that a lot of programs used all over the world can be accessed only via screens that provide monochrome text and puzzling menus with strange codes and submission sequences. With their versatility and ease of use, forms offer a revolutionary approach—and you can unlock their power with several mouse clicks and some solid planning. This chapter discusses the rationale for using Outlook forms as part of a software solution for individual computing needs. It also examines the types of forms you can modify and create and how the forms are created, published, and stored.

With Outlook, you can employ two basic strategies for form development. The first is to use or modify a standard form. The second is to create your own form from scratch. With either strategy, it's important to remember that you're programming events that are specifically associated with the item involved, not with the Outlook application generally. In other words, when you put code behind your form, you're dealing with events related to the item that's represented by the form. For example, if you were to design a form to create a custom e-mail message, you'd probably program a common event named *Item_Send,* which occurs when the item (the message) is sent. You couldn't program the form to respond to an event that fires (that is, occurs or executes) when the item is specifically shipped from the Outbox to another user's Inbox or when the user's view changes from one folder to another. This is because in form development you can access only the events associated with the item in question.

Overview of Standard Forms, Item Types, and Message Classes

Outlook uses a combination of forms, item types, and message classes as its fundamental components. Although you don't need to understand much about any of these three components to use Outlook, a developer must understand them reasonably well—and, obviously, the more you know, the more powerful your Outlook-based solution will be.

Outlook Forms

Outlook provides numerous predefined forms that you can use as the foundation of your form-based solution. These standard forms include the following:

- Appointment form
- Contact form
- Journal entry form
- Meeting request form
- Message form
- Post form
- Task form
- Task request form

As this list of Outlook forms indicates, the basic item types available in a typical Outlook/Microsoft Exchange application are each represented by a corresponding form.

Each of these forms comes with built-in user interface elements and corresponding functionality. For example, the appointment form, shown in Figure 40-1, has interface elements and functions that relate to setting appointments, such as generating reminders and controlling the calendar display. The contact form, in contrast, is designed to permit the addition or modification of contact information.

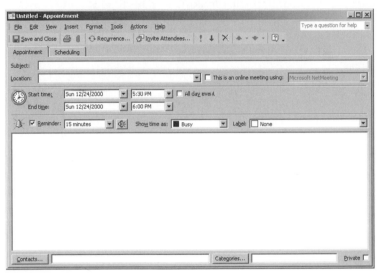

Figure 40-1. The appointment form is one of the numerous forms that Outlook provides.

Outlook Item Types

Several basic item types are part of an Outlook installation. These item types include the following:

- MailItem
- ContactItem
- TaskItem
- AppointmentItem
- PostItem
- NoteItem

> **note** Two other item types are also built into Outlook: *JournalItem* and *DistributionListItem*. This book does not cover these two types, but you can find information about them by consulting the Microsoft MSDN Web site at *http://msdn.microsoft.com/library/ default.asp?URL=/library/officedev/vbaol10/olmscOutlookItemObjects.htm*.

These item types represent built-in functionality. If you have ever used Outlook to create an e-mail message or to add an appointment to your calendar, you have benefited from this functionality. And, of particular importance, this functionality is accessible to you as you develop custom solutions with Outlook. Outlook provides corresponding forms for each of these item types, and these standard forms are designed with behaviors that directly relate to the item types they represent. You can extend the behaviors of these forms and leverage all the functions and properties of the item types, some of which are not exposed in the standard forms. In addition, you can reach beyond Outlook to incorporate the functionality of other Microsoft Office applications such as Microsoft Word, Microsoft Excel, Microsoft PowerPoint, Microsoft Project, Microsoft Visio, and any application or control that exposes a programmatic COM interface.

> **note** For a good overview of COM and COM+, take a look at *Understanding COM+* by David S. Platt (Microsoft Press, 1999).

Outlook Message Classes

Although forms and item types are the basic elements you need to understand to create a custom Outlook solution, it's helpful to know what a message class is and how it relates to Outlook form development. A message class represents to Outlook internally what an item type represents to a user or developer externally. In other words, when a user opens an e-mail message from the Inbox, that message is a *MailItem*. Internally, however, Outlook calls it by a different name, *IPM.Note*. IPM (interpersonal message) is a holdover from previous generations of Microsoft's messaging legacy. All messages in Outlook are representations of an IPM of some sort. A calendar item, for example, is an *IPM.Appointment*. The list of default message classes includes the following:

- IPM.Note
- IPM.Contact
- IPM.Appointment
- IPM.Task
- IPM.Post

Again, unless you're developing a fairly sophisticated collaborative solution, these message classes won't surface often. But understanding what they mean to Outlook will help as you progress in your use of the program and in developing Outlook solutions.

Creating Custom Forms from Standard Forms

A standard form is a great point of departure for developing a custom solution. For example, have you ever sent an e-mail message with an attached document to someone and forgotten to include the attachment? In a large company, this rather common error could amount to hundreds, if not thousands, of extra e-mail messages being sent each day as users send follow-up messages containing the omitted attachments. By adding a small script to the standard mail message form, you can avoid this problem. You can programmatically assess whether an attachment has actually been added to the e-mail message and prompt the user to add one if needed.

To begin working with the standard forms, choose Tools, Forms. Then select Design A Form to display the Design Form dialog box, shown in Figure 40-2. You can simply select one of the standard forms listed in this dialog box and begin working with the form in design mode. Later sections in the chapter will discuss how to save and publish the forms you modify or create.

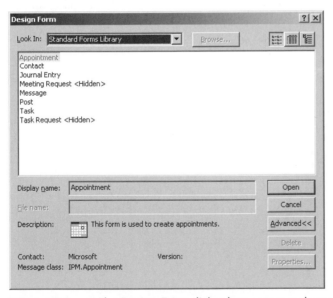

Figure 40-2. In the Design Form dialog box, you can choose the type of form you want to create.

What if you want to work with an item type not found in the list Outlook provides? Furthermore, what if you want to then create a form that relates to that custom item type? This functionality, which makes Outlook and Office development more powerful than ever, is possible with the Web Storage System in Microsoft Exchange 2000 Server; see "The Web Storage System," page 1008.

Chapter 40

> **tip** **Avoid scripts when opening forms for design**
>
> When you choose to redesign an existing form, that form might have a script with event handlers that will fire when you open the form in design mode. Usually, however, you don't want to have code firing when you're trying to design a form. To keep this from happening, hold down the Shift key as you click the form to open it for design. The code will still be present and will run when you debug the form. But it will not run while you open, design, and save the form.

Compose vs. Read

Obviously, one of the most basic processes in Outlook is sending and receiving messages and documents. Although this is a fairly simple process, it requires a close look. In nearly all cases, the form a sender employs to compose an e-mail message is not the exact form that the receiver of that message uses to read the message. For example, although a user can edit the Subject field when composing a message, the recipient can't, under normal circumstances, edit the subject. This is because the standard forms have Compose and Read areas.

Figure 40-3 shows a message being composed; Figure 40-4 shows the same message after it has been received.

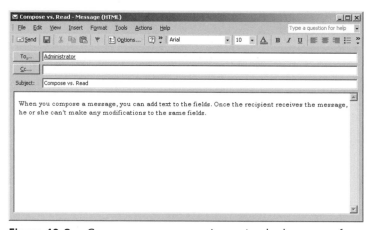

Figure 40-3. Compose a message using a standard message form.

Notice that some of the fields, such as Subject and To, can't be modified by the recipient in the Read version. It is, however, entirely possible to configure a form with identical Compose and Read areas. Whether this makes sense for your Outlook solution is up to you.

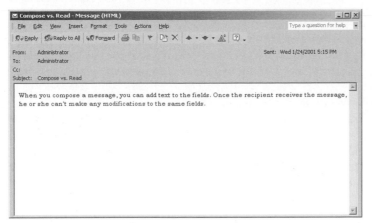

Figure 40-4. Here is the same message, shown in Figure 40-3, after it has been re-ceived. Notice that some fields can no longer be modified.

When you're working with a standard form in design mode, you can switch between the Compose and Read pages by clicking the Edit Compose Page and Edit Read page buttons on the Form Design toolbar. In Figure 40-5, the Compose page of the standard message form is ready for editing. When you click Edit Read Page, the Read area of the form appears for editing, as shown in Figure 40-6 on the next page.

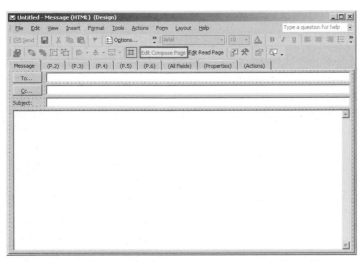

Figure 40-5. This standard Compose area is ready for editing.

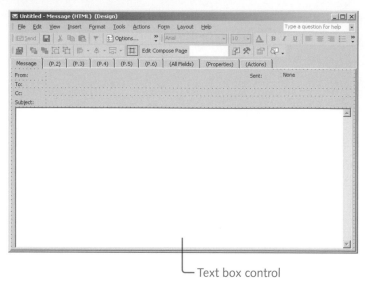

Text box control

Figure 40-6. The Read area for a message item looks similar to the Compose area.

Because this is a standard form, a number of controls are already on the form. For example, the text box control for the body of the message is the largest element on the form. This control is bound to an Outlook field. The following section examines fields and what they mean to an Outlook solution; working with controls is discussed later in the chapter.

Outlook Fields

An Outlook field represents a discrete unit of information that is intelligible to Outlook, such as the Bcc and To fields in an e-mail message. You don't need to tell Outlook that e-mail messages have these fields—they are already included in the standard form. Outlook provides a number of fields that you can use, and you can also add new fields. In theory, an unlimited number of fields are available, but the most common practice is to use a generous number of the built-in fields and a judicious number of new, user-defined properties. For now, the discussion focuses on the fields already available to you.

Because it provides so many built-in fields, Outlook groups them to make it easier to find the ones you need. For example, some fields, such as To, From, Subject, Importance, Expires, Due By, Created, Size, and Attachment, are particular to e-mail messages. Other fields, such as City, Children, and Birthday, are associated with Outlook contacts. You can, however, use fields from different logical areas to suit your needs on any form you're designing—for example, Outlook doesn't prevent you from adding a Birthday field to an e-mail form.

> **note** You can also find more information on user-defined fields at Microsoft's support site at *http://support.microsoft.com*. See article ID number Q290656.

When you work with a form, you can view the available fields in the Field Chooser dialog box, shown in Figure 40-7. To display this dialog box, click the button to the right of the Edit Read Page toolbar button; clicking this button shows or hides the Field Chooser. In the Field Chooser, the fields are organized by categories and displayed in a list. You can choose a category in the drop-down list and then search in the body of the Field Chooser for the fields you need.

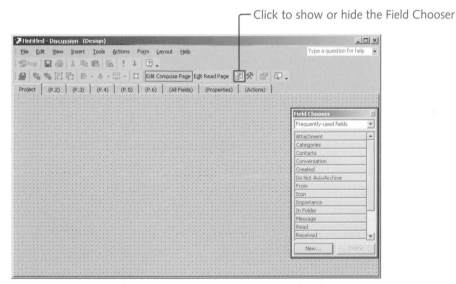

Figure 40-7. The Field Chooser dialog box allows you to view and choose the fields available for use.

Item Types and Fields

The scrollable list of fields shown in the Field Chooser in Figure 40-7 contains all the fields available for a form published in a certain folder. The standard item types come with a number of fields already defined. For example, a mail message comes with To, Subject, Body, and Sent fields already defined. Although you have the full battery of fields available as you modify or create a form, you can speed your development time and decrease your effort by carefully selecting the standard form that most closely corresponds to the solution you're developing. This way, you can leverage as many built-in fields as possible. Later in the chapter, you'll learn how to represent these fields on your form via controls; see "Adding and Arranging Controls," page 995.

Creating Custom Forms from Scratch

Working with standard forms is great if you want to build a solution that is directly related to one of the Outlook item types. However, you might need an Outlook form that isn't based on an item type at all. For example, you might want to create a form that allows users to report their work hours or initiate a purchase order. Although you could base these examples on a standard form, they could just as easily require a completely new form, which you need to create.

The good news is that creating a completely new form sounds like more work than it actually is. In fact, Outlook doesn't really permit you to create forms completely from scratch, although you can certainly achieve the same effect. You have two ways to create a form that doesn't contain any built-in form elements:

- Modify a standard form by deleting all built-in interface elements from the form and adding your own.

- Modify a standard form by hiding the page that contains built-in interface elements and showing a new page that contains elements that you add.

You'll learn how to add pages to forms in the next section. First let's look at how to break down a standard form to a blank form by removing built-in interface controls.

The following steps show how to turn a standard post form into a blank form:

1 Choose Tools, Forms.

2 Select Design A Form.

3 Select the post form and click Open. The form opens in design mode with the Message page selected.

4 Click each control (TextBox, Label, Button, and so on) on the Message page and delete it.

5 With the Message page still selected, choose Form, Rename Page.

6 Type a new name in the dialog box, and click OK.

The form now looks like the form shown earlier in Figure 40-7. The figure shows a modified Compose area for this form, but you can also modify the Read area. Of course, you'll also want to make these pages do something, but for now you at least have a blank form to work with.

Creating Multipage Forms

A multipage form allows you to fit a great deal of information on one form while also reducing confusion for the user. For example, you could create a form on which employees could both report their time for the week and report any expenses for which they need reimbursement. By using two pages, one form can serve both needs.

Any form can be a multipage form; all possible pages are already on the form you create or modify. However, these pages are not automatically visible. If you look closely at the names on the page tabs shown previously in Figure 40-7, you'll see that, except for the first name in the list, the name of each page is enclosed in parentheses, indicating that the page is not visible. To change the *Visible* property of a page, click its tab and then choose Form, Display This Page.

> **tip** You can make all pages visible, but you cannot make all pages invisible. If you try to do so, Outlook tells you that at least one page must be visible on the form.

The first (default) page of a form, which is initially visible, has Compose and Read capabilities already available, as mentioned earlier. The additional pages on a form, which are initially invisible, don't have these capabilities until you add them. To do so, select one of these pages and choose Form, Separate Read Layout, which activates the Edit Compose Page and Edit Read Page command bar buttons.

Adding and Arranging Controls

The real power of forms comes from the controls you place on them. To construct a truly robust Outlook forms solution, you need to carefully plan what the form is supposed to do; what pieces of information it will display, modify, save, or send; which controls will display these information units; and how the controls will be laid out. You can put two types of controls on a form: a control bound to an Outlook field and a control that is not bound. This section looks first at field-bound controls.

As mentioned earlier, Outlook fields represent units of information. They are also bound to specific control types, such as drop-down lists, text boxes, command buttons, labels, or check boxes.

To represent a field on your form, follow these steps:

1 Display the Field Chooser and select a field category in the drop-down list.

2 From the scrollable list in the Field Chooser, drag a field onto the form.

3 Format the control as needed.

> **tip** **Work with the users of the form**
>
> You can place any number of controls on a form, but it's a good idea to plan your form with an eye toward its usability. Work closely with those individuals who will be using the form to ensure that it corresponds to their real needs. Find out how the users want the forms to be laid out, and listen to their suggestions about how the information should flow. No matter how much work you put into your solution, it won't be useful unless the users embrace it.

You can resize, move, or rename a control, and you can change a number of its properties. To resize the control, select the control (by clicking it) and place your pointer over one of the control handles, which are represented by small boxes. When a small arrow appears, you can drag the handle in the appropriate direction to resize the control.

To move a control to a new location, simply drag it. Notice that the form canvas is covered with a grid. Each point on the grid is a possible location for a corner or other relevant point on a control. You can define the distances between the points on this grid. This is important, because the greater the scale of the grid (the greater the distance between points on the grid), the fewer places you can locate a control on your form. Conversely, the smaller the scale, the more you can refine the positioning of your controls.

To change the grid, follow these steps:

1 Choose Form, Set Grid Size.

2 Type a number for the height and width spacing.

3 Click OK.

The smaller the number you use for spacing, the smaller the scale. This means that more points on the grid will appear, and you can have more control over where your objects fit on the grid. The default is 8, but 3 is a good number to choose for greater positioning control.

InsideOut

When you're using controls on forms, you can be tempted to make one form do too much. Although there's no precise limit for the number of controls that can be included on one form, the recommendation is using fewer than 300. However, experience with custom forms development suggests that even 200 is excessive. You should try to keep the number of controls down to a few dozen or so when possible. Forms that try to do too much usually become confusing to users, and they often do not perform as well. Keeping your forms focused and giving them a crisp design make them easier to code and debug, too. If you find that your form is overloaded, consider creating a COM add-in to allow a broader application context.

Properties

Controls have a number of properties that you can view and modify. To find out what these properties are, right-click a control and choose Properties from the shortcut menu to display the Properties dialog box. Figure 40-8 shows a Properties dialog box for a text box control.

Figure 40-8. You can use the Properties dialog box to modify the properties of a control.

Display

The Display tab of a control's Properties dialog box (refer to Figure 40-8, for example) shows the most commonly used properties of the particular control. Changing the setting of a property in this dialog box enables the Apply button; clicking Apply or OK sets the value of that property for the selected control.

> **tip** If you're unsure about the purpose of a property shown in the Properties dialog box, click the question mark button at the top of the dialog box, and then click the property to display a brief description of it.

The default names of controls are rather generic, such as *TextBox1* or *CheckBox1*. You'll want to change these to names that are more descriptive for your solution, such as *txtFirstName* or *chkHasVacation*.

> **note** You can learn more about naming conventions for controls by visiting Microsoft's MSDN Web site at *http://msdn.microsoft.com/library/default.asp?URL=/library/devprods/vs6/vbasic/vbcon98/vbconcodingconventionsoverview.htm*.

Chapter 40

Value

The Value tab of the Properties dialog box contains a number of settings that relate to the field value that the control represents. As mentioned, each control in the Field Chooser list is bound to an Outlook field. When you modify the properties of a control, you can change the field to which that control is bound.

To change the bound-field property, click the Choose Field button and select the field to which you want to bind the control from the drop-down list. Make sure that the field value is bound to the correct property of your control. Normally, the field value is tied to the control's *Value* property; this is rarely changed. However, you can change this setting so that, for example, the value of a field is tied to your control's *Enabled* property. In this case, if the value of the field is True, the control is enabled; if the value is False, the control is not enabled.

You can also set the initial value of your control to display a default value. Select the Initial Value check box, and then type an initial value in the text box. This value doesn't have to be a predetermined one—you can have it correspond to a dynamic value, such as the current day or the concatenation of Subject field and the current date. To make the initial value more dynamic, click the Edit button to open the dialog box shown in Figure 40-9.

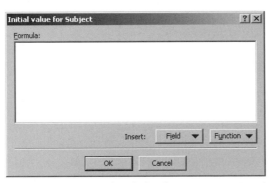

Figure 40-9. Use this dialog box to customize the initial value for a control.

In this dialog box, you establish a formula for the initial value of your control. For example, you can simply insert a built-in function, such as *Date( )*, for the formula.

To insert a built-in function—the *Date( )* function, in this example—follow these steps:

1 Click the Function button.

2 Choose Data/Time, Date( ).

3 Verify that this function appears in the Formula text box.

4 Click OK, and then click OK to close the Properties dialog box.

When the form is run, the text box control you created will contain the current date as its value. This does not mean, however, that you can't change the value of the text box.

Validation

The Validation tab of the Properties dialog box allows you to set certain properties that relate to how (or whether) the value of the control is validated. For example, if you create a form for a purchase order, you might want to ensure that users indicate the quantity of parts they want to order. The order-processing department will send you many thanks for requiring certain values before the purchase order gets to them, as it reduces the amount of information traffic and busy work needed to process an order.

Suppose that you've added a control to your form that requires a value for a text box, and that value is required to be less than or equal to 10 characters. If the user fails to enter a valid value, Outlook will display a message that prompts the user to enter a correct value.

To set the properties on the Validation tab that will be necessary for this example, follow these steps:

1 Display the Properties dialog box, and click the Validation tab.

2 Select the A Value Is Required For This Field check box.

3 Select the Validate This Field Before Closing The Form check box.

4 Click the Edit button (to the right of the Validation Formula text box).

5 Click the Function button.

6 Choose Text, Len(string) and confirm that the formula text box contains the *Len(string)* function.

7 After the text of this function, type **<=10** in the Formula text box.

8 Click OK.

9 In the Display This Message If The Validation Fails box, type the following text (including the quotation marks):

"Please enter a value between 1 and 10 characters."

10 Click OK to close the Properties dialog box.

When a user works with your form, the text box for which this validation has been defined must contain a value, and the value must be less than or equal to 10 characters. If the value the user enters is 11 characters or more, Outlook will display a message box containing the validation text you provided when the user tries to send the form. The user can then make the appropriate changes to the text box value and attempt to resend the form.

Standard Controls

This chapter has thus far concentrated on controls that are bound to Outlook fields and that appear in the Field Chooser. However, these aren't the only controls you can add to a form. In fact, you can use a virtually unlimited number of controls. A thorough discussion of the nature of these controls is beyond the scope of this book, but this section takes a brief look at some of the standard controls as well as a control that comes as part of installing Office on your computer.

Controls appear on a Controls Toolbox, which is a small, resizable window made visible when you click the button just to the right of the Field Chooser toolbar button on the form. Figure 40-10 shows the Toolbox.

Figure 40-10. The Controls Toolbox allows you to add controls to your form.

As the pointer hovers over the control icons in the Toolbox, the name of each control appears. To add one of these controls to your form, simply drag the control icon onto the form. You can then resize and reposition the control or set its properties, as discussed earlier.

> **note** Refer to *Programming Microsoft Outlook and Microsoft Exchange (Second Edition)*, by Thomas Rizzo (Microsoft Press, 2000), to learn more about the properties, methods, events, and possible uses of the standard controls.

These standard controls are useful but limited. As your skills in developing Outlook-based solutions progress, you'll find that you need functionality that transcends the abilities of the standard controls provided in the Toolbox. Fortunately, other controls are available and also accessible via the Toolbox window. For example, you can add an Excel PivotTable control to a form.

Follow these steps to add the PivotTable control to the Toolbox:

1 Right-click an empty area of the Toolbox window.

2 Choose Custom Controls.

3 Scroll down the Available Controls list and click the box next to the Microsoft Office PivotTable 10.

4 Click OK.

You can now add this control to a form and work with its specific properties and behaviors just as you did for the standard controls.

Custom controls can make your Outlook solution extremely robust and powerful. However, be aware that the control you're using might not exist on the computer of the person receiving the message. In other words, while you might have the PivotTable control on your computer, the person who uses your form to compose a message or who receives a message composed on your form might not have the PivotTable control installed. For your solution to work well, you need to make sure that the custom controls you use are properly distributed and installed on other users' computers.

note Methods of distributing custom controls can vary widely. Some controls come without an installing package, many use Microsoft Installer, and others use a third-party installation mechanism. You should read the documentation that accompanies your custom control or consult the manufacturer to determine the best method for distributing your control.

After creating your form, you can test it to see what it looks like when it is run. With the new form open, choose Form, Run This Form. This won't cause the form to close or disappear. Instead, Outlook produces a new form based on the form you've just created. The newly created form is an actual running form that you can send and read.

Adding Graphics to Forms

Although developing solutions in Outlook can require much thought and effort, users might not necessarily share your enthusiasm and excitement about the forms you've created. One way to increase acceptance and usability is to add some pleasing graphics to the forms. These graphics can come in a variety of formats, such as JPG, GIF, WMF, EMF, and ICO.

One way to add a graphic to your form is to use the image control from the Control Toolbox. Initially, the control will appear as a gray square. You can resize it, just as you can resize any of the standard controls, although it's a good idea to place the picture in the control before you resize it. Set the picture source for the image control by using a property in the Advanced Properties dialog box, shown in Figure 40-11 on the next page.

Chapter 40

Figure 40-11. Use the Advanced Properties dialog box to select a picture to insert into the image control.

Follow these steps to insert a picture in your control:

1 Right-click the image control.

2 Choose Advanced Properties.

3 In the list of properties, scroll down to the *Picture* property.

4 To the far right of the Apply button, click the small button that displays ellipses points (…).

5 Use the Load Picture dialog box to navigate to the picture you want to appear in the image control, and then click Open.

6 Close the Advanced Properties dialog box and verify that the control now contains the picture you chose.

---

tip **Change the source of your images at runtime**

As is the case with all the controls you use on a custom form, you can change the values of many of their properties when the form is running. For example, you can create a form with an image that changes based on certain criteria. You can add code to your form that alters the setting of the control's *Picture* property and thus loads an image into the control that is different from the image you specified at design time.

Another way to make your forms more attractive and usable is to add an icon to buttons on the forms. You can configure the command button available in the Toolbox to display both a text caption and a graphic. For example, if your button sends a custom message to a recipient when clicked, you could add an envelope image to the button to convey the notion of sending a message. To have the button display an image, set the *Picture* property for the button just as you would for an image control. You can also set the *Picture* property for other controls, such as text boxes and labels.

In addition, you can display a custom icon in the form's title bar. Outlook always displays a default icon in the upper left corner of a form, indicating whether it is a task form, an appointment form, and so on. You can change this icon by clicking the Properties tab of your form when you're working in design mode. Click the Change Large Icon button or the Change Small Icon button and navigate to the ICO file you want to use. The Large Icon setting tells Outlook which image to display when a user displays the properties of the form. The Small Icon setting specifies the title bar image and the image that is shown when the form is displayed in an Outlook folder.

Using Office Documents to Create Outlook Forms

If you have installed Outlook, you probably also have Word, Excel, and PowerPoint installed. These other programs provide an even more powerful Outlook form solution: you can use documents, spreadsheets, and slide presentations as the form of a message. For example, suppose that you created a form that required a user to enter a lot of values and send the form to someone else. The recipient then has to type those values into an Excel spreadsheet. Wouldn't it make more sense to have the first user type the values directly into the spreadsheet at the outset? If your company already uses an Excel spreadsheet for expense reimbursements, you can leverage this by letting employees use the spreadsheet as they always have—the only difference is that each employee will now set a recipient or a public folder as the spreadsheet's destination.

While you could have the users open the document, make changes, and then choose File, Send To, Mail Recipient to mail the document, you might prefer to incorporate the document into a standard form. For example, perhaps you want to broadcast an Excel spreadsheet to a group of users to show sales status or other data. You can create a standard message form but in place of (or in addition to) the message body, add an Excel custom control that pulls the spreadsheet data from a server, updating the data when the user opens the form from his Inbox.

Covering this type of form development falls outside the scope of this chapter, but you might only need a nudge in the right direction to begin adding these custom controls to your own forms.

Here's how:

1 In Outlook, choose Tools, Forms, Design A Form to open the Design Form dialog box.

2 Select Message in the Standard Forms Library and click Open.

3 Resize the message body control to make room for the spreadsheet control.

4 Right-click the Controls Toolbox and choose Custom Controls to open the Additional Controls dialog box.

Chapter 40

1003

5 Scroll through the Available Controls list to locate and select the Microsoft Office Spreadsheet 10 control. Then click OK to add it to the Controls Toolbox.

6 Click the Spreadsheet control in the Controls Toolbox and drag it to your form. Figure 40-12 shows a Spreadsheet control added to a message form.

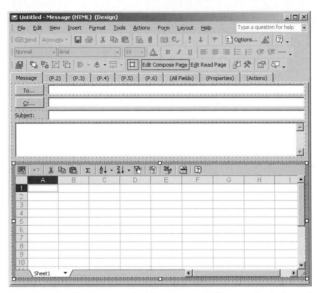

Figure 40-12 You can add custom Office controls to a form to publish or accept data input.

7 Resize the Spreadsheet control to fit the form as needed, then right-click the toolbar portion of the control and choose Advanced Properties.

8 Use the properties on the control's Properties dialog box to specify the data location and other properties to define the data.

9 Make other design changes as needed to the form and then save or publish the form.

If you browse through the Additional Controls dialog box you'll find a wide range of additional controls you can add to your forms. You can add charts, PivotTables, database forms, and many other controls to create powerful and useful forms.

Publishing and Sharing Forms

After you create your form and define its behaviors, properties, and settings, you'll want to make it available to users. First, however, you'll need to preserve your form, in one of these two ways:

● Publish the form to a folder or other location

● Save the form as a file

Publishing Forms

Believe it or not, you don't need to explicitly save a form to retain it, allow it to be used, and make it available for later modification. This is contrary to the lesson you've learned from having to rewrite so many unsaved documents that you lost after power outages. However, publishing a form is a lot like saving the form. When you finish your form, you can publish it to a specific folder location. You can publish it to your Inbox or another folder in your mailbox, a public folder, or your Personal Forms Library.

Follow these steps to publish a form to a folder or forms library:

1 Choose Tools, Forms, Publish Form to open the Publish Form As dialog box.

2 In the Look In drop-down list, choose the folder or forms library where you want to publish the form.

3 Specify the display name and the form name.

4 Click Publish to close the dialog box.

---

tip **Create a staging area for your forms**

When you're creating a form, it's a good idea to keep the production version of the form separate from the development version. Create a special production folder where you publish the forms you're working on. When you complete a form design, publish the form in this staging folder at least occasionally, so you don't lose the modifications you've made to the form. Restrict your staging folder access to those who are designing forms for your organization.

After you publish a form, the folder in which you publish it contains the form itself and all the underlying information that another person's instance of Outlook needs to understand the form.

---

note If you are using a version of Exchange Server earlier than Exchange 2000 Server, you can usually publish your form to the Organizational Forms Library. For information on this, see *http://msdn.microsoft.com/library/officedev/off2000/ rehowSaveFormIntoFormsLibraryPublishFormAs.htm*. You can also visit the link *http://www.microsoft.com/Exchange/en/55/help/default.asp?url=/Exchange/en/55/ help/documents/server/XGS06010.HTM*. For information about using this forms library with Exchange 2000 Server, see Knowledge Base article ID Q271816.

Publishing Forms Programmatically

You can also publish a form by using code. This technique can be helpful if you're creating custom forms with code and want to publish them to either a public folder or a personal folders file. The following code shows how to create a custom form and publish it when a user clicks a button on an Outlook form:

```
Dim objNS
Dim objFolder
Dim objItem
Dim objNewForm

Sub cmdCreateNewTaskForm_Click()
  Set objNS = Item.Application.GetNamespace("MAPI")
  Set objFolder = objNS.GetDefaultFolder(13)   'Publishes to Tasks
  Set objItem = Application.CreateItem(3)       'Creates a TaskItem
  Set objNewForm = objItem.FormDescription      'Get the task form
  objNewForm.Name = "Our New Form"              'Customize the
                                                'form name
  objNewForm.DisplayName = "New Form Display"   'Customize display

  objNewForm.PublishForm 4, objFolder           'Publish the form

End Sub
```

In the last line of this sample code, the constant *4* causes the form to be published to the organizational forms library. If you don't have an organizational forms library, you will receive an error when the code executes. You can use a different value to change the location to which the form is published. For example, a value of *0* publishes the form to the default location. Refer to *http://support.microsoft.com/support/kb/articles/q285/2/02.asp* for more information on other constants you can use to specify the location for publishing the form.

Sharing Forms in Public Folders

The best way to make your form available to others is to publish it in a public folder (assuming that Outlook is being used with Exchange Server). When you do this, users who connect to that public folder will have access to your form and will be able to use it just as if they had created and saved it on their own computers. Outlook takes care of all the underlying work with form definitions, so you won't need to do anything special to make sure that another user's instance of Outlook can understand the definitions.

For detailed information on using public folders in Exchange Server, see Chapter 34, "Sharing Information with Others."

If you aren't sure whether the intended users of your form will have access to the form definition where it's published, you'll want to save the form definition and make it available to these target users. Saving a form means saving the definition of the form as a file in a file system directory. Thus, while publishing a form doesn't allow a user to use the file system search tools to search for the form, saving the form does make this possible. Forms saved to a local disk have an OFT extension. There is nothing terribly mysterious about this file—it's just another file that is comprehensible to Outlook, just as a DOC file is intelligible to Word. You can even send your form definition to others as a mail attachment, and they'll able to open the form and use it as if it were published.

Saving a form definition does make the form harder to maintain, however. If you save the form as a file with an OFT extension, distribute it to a large number of users, and then make a change to the form, all users of the form need to receive the updated file. Publishing the form to a public folder prevents this confusion. In that case, after you modify the form, you republish the form in the folder. The next time a user opens the form, he or she will be the beneficiary of the latest modifications.

Troubleshooting

Users can't access your custom form.

After you've completed and published your custom form, you might hear from a user who reports receiving this message when trying to access the form: *The custom form could not be opened, and Outlook will use an Outlook form instead. The object could not be found.* You should first make sure that your form is properly published. If the form is not published so that Outlook can find it, or if an OFT file is not available, Outlook won't be able to open the file.

Sometimes, however, Outlook reports this error even when the form is available. The cause might be corruption in a file named Frmcache.dat. The Frmcache.dat file contains information that Outlook uses to prevent multiple instances of the same form from being loaded. Outlook checks the cache to see whether a form using the same message class name is in the cache before attempting to display a form. Outlook copies the form definition to the cache if it does not exist, or it loads the definition already in the cache, and then displays the form. In addition, if a change has been made to a form, Outlook copies the new form definition to the cache. The file is located at Documents And Settings*profile name*\\Local Settings\\Application Data\\Microsoft\\FORMS on a computer running Windows 2000 or at Windows\\Forms on computers running earlier versions of Windows.

If this file is indeed corrupted, reinstalling Outlook can solve the problem. But there is a simpler way. You could try closing Outlook and deleting the Frmcache.dat. Or, you can locate an instance of Outlook that does display the form properly and copy that profile's instance of Frmcache.dat to the profile of the offending instance, thus overwriting the file.

Publishing to local folders or to the Personal Forms Library is perfectly acceptable, but you might find that many of your solutions are destined for a wider audience, which, in an Exchange Server environment, can be reached only through public folders. You'll also find that you can develop much more powerful solutions by learning to leverage Exchange 2000 Server's innovative Web Storage System technology, described in the following section.

newfeature!
The Web Storage System

The way solutions are developed in Outlook is changing. Developers are being asked to create Outlook forms for tasks that cannot always be accommodated in traditional ways. For example, users want to access Outlook data in custom forms as well as in HTML forms. They sometimes want their Outlook data to be Web-addressable in a browser, and they want to host Web pages in Outlook that integrate HTML views of their data with traditional Outlook forms and views.

Perhaps the most significant recent change to the world of Outlook development has been the introduction of the Web Storage System with the release of Exchange 2000 Server. Although Outlook does not require Exchange 2000 Server and the Web Storage System, you'll find some distinct advantages inherent in using them as the foundation for an Outlook custom solution.

These advantages include the ability to create custom data repositories for information accessed through Outlook, to create workflow solutions used by Outlook applications, and to more seamlessly integrate Web data with Outlook. The purpose of this section is to introduce the Web Storage System and show how it can enhance what Outlook can display and how Outlook items are organized.

> **note** Even if you do not yet have Exchange 2000 Server or SharePoint Portal Server, you can begin learning about Web Storage System technologies. Download the Web Storage System SDK from the Microsoft MSDN download center, found at the following location: *http://msdn.microsoft.com/downloads/default.asp?URL=/code/sample.asp?url=/MSDN-FILES/027/001/556/msdncompositedoc.xml*. You can also download the Web Storage System Developer Tools found in the MSDN download center at the following location: *http://msdn.microsoft.com/downloads/default.asp?URL=/code/sample.asp?url=/MSDN-FILES/027/001/557/msdncompositedoc.xml*. These tools include the Web Storage System Explorer, a tool used to browse the Web Storage System in a hierarchical fashion.

The Web Storage System is a data-storage technology that you can use to store data-rich objects in a hierarchical fashion and to make the objects directly addressable via a URL. The Web Storage System underlies Exchange 2000 Server, and a version of it underlies SharePoint Portal Server, the new product Microsoft has introduced for enterprise collaboration and knowledge management.

The Web Storage System takes its name partly from its inherent ability to store items that can be accessed through a Web browser. Using this system, you can access items stored in Exchange Server using a Web browser, by typing the URL for an item. For example, users are accustomed to seeing their messages in Outlook's Inbox, but they can see the same messages rendered in HTML by using browsers to navigate to the address of a message, such as *http://myserver/exchange/user1/inbox/newmessage.eml*. Messages and other standard Outlook item types are stored with an EML extension in the Web Storage System; other item types with other extensions can also be stored and remain addressable via a URL.

Think of the Web Storage System as a hierarchical database, just as a file system and the Microsoft Windows registry are hierarchical databases. When you navigate a local disk using Windows Explorer, you see the hierarchy of directories and files located on the disk. In contrast to previous versions of Exchange Server, in which you could not easily view the raw database, the Web Storage System allows you to view the complete messaging store with Windows Explorer, because it appears in Windows as just another disk with directories and files. In fact, the Web Storage System is essentially a custom file system.

Compared to previous databases in which Outlook items and data were stored, the Web Storage System is more easily extended and customized. Most people couldn't access the underlying database storage before. Now the architecture of the Web Storage System allows administrators, developers, and users alike to view and modify the Exchange Server database in increasingly sophisticated ways. With more direct control over the underlying data storage mechanism for Outlook, you can use Outlook in innovative and more powerful ways.

Creating Custom Databases for Outlook Data

Previously, making significant modifications to the underlying storage structure for your Outlook data was a major undertaking when you were using Outlook and Exchange Server. For example, in earlier versions of Exchange Server, you could create custom message classes with special properties, but it was difficult to organize these message classes into a broader hierarchical schema. If you assume, for instance, that your organization has contacts, it probably also has different contact types. You might want to have a global contact type, with each additional contact type being an extension of the global contact type. Your hierarchy might look something like the one shown in Figure 40-13.

As Figure 40-13 on the next page shows, each category of contacts is specialized, but each is still a subset of the more general contact type. Properties such as first name, last name, phone number, and e-mail address characterize the global contact type. Instead of creating these properties for each subtype, you'll find it easier to have the subtypes simply inherit the properties of the global type. As a result, you will have defined explicit relationships between the types for your organization. Typically, your business needs you to continue defining types with properties, subtypes, and so forth for other data requirements in your organization. Combining all these relationships into one context constitutes a *schema* in the Web Storage System. The types of items that you have defined are called *content classes*. Content classes represent types of items you want to store in Exchange Server and access through your Outlook application.

Figure 40-13. A sample hierarchy of contacts for an organization might look like this.

In summary, the Web Storage System makes it possible to define schema information for the items in your organization. This schema information can be used by schema-aware applications to carry out searching, indexing, and many other operations that allow developers to create rather sophisticated applications. It's important to remember that schemas in the Web Storage System define only the characteristics of an item type; they don't specify how an item type looks or how it behaves inside Outlook. The actual representation of content classes is a different matter.

Figure 40-14 shows a view of an item stored in the Web Storage System. As you look at the properties, you'll notice that each property is defined by a certain data type, such as *String* or *Int*, and each has an associated value.

Figure 40-14. This is a view of an item stored in the Web Storage System.

One reason the Web Storage System is so powerful is that you can extend properties such as those listed in Figure 40-14. Additionally, you can access the database through ActiveX Data Objects (ADO) just as you would access a SQL or Microsoft Access database. You can then query and modify the database by using common methods for database manipulation. Thus, you could create an Outlook application that uses a SQL statement to access certain data items and then displays or modifies the fields returned in a recordset. The Web Storage System makes working with Outlook data in Exchange Server essentially equivalent to working with data on other common database platforms.

Connecting Item Types to Forms

You have learned that the Web Storage System stores items and that each item is defined by its type or content class, characterized by certain relationships and properties, all within the context of an organized schema. However, the schema does not specify directly how to present the items. In the Web Storage System, each item is a collection of properties and their corresponding values, and you can view these properties in a variety of ways.

For instance, you can view a contact item within an Outlook form. However, the actual form used for displaying the information could be of any design. Initially, the form might show only a few properties of the item type, such as first name and last name. You could later update the form to include other properties defined for that item type or content class in the Web Storage System. Accordingly, the way the data is stored is distinct from the way it is displayed. This is not new to the Web Storage System. However, the ability to easily display the items in Web-friendly ways is new. You can view an item in Exchange 2000 Server in a custom Outlook form, or you can associate the item with custom HTML forms and address it via a simple browser URL.

You can exploit this technique to combine browser views of Outlook data with the traditional Outlook views of the same data. For example, because Outlook folders are items in the Web Storage System, they are defined by a specific content class. By using a mechanism called the Forms Registry and leveraging the tight coupling between Internet Information Server (IIS) and Exchange 2000 Server, you can configure Exchange Server to produce a custom Web page that displays Exchange items every time someone accesses the folder. Thus, instead of using the traditional Outlook view, the page can look like the one shown in Figure 40-15.

Figure 40-15, taken from the Microsoft Fabrikam solution example, shows the contents of an Exchange Server public folder, but the contents are shown in a Web page rather than in an Outlook view. You can configure this same page as the default view for a folder by configuring the Home Page option for public folders. You can develop subsequent pages to display the properties for the items listed on this page, or you can choose to use a custom Outlook form to display the items instead.

For information about setting up a Web page as the default view for a public folder, see "Defining a Folder Home Page," page 814.

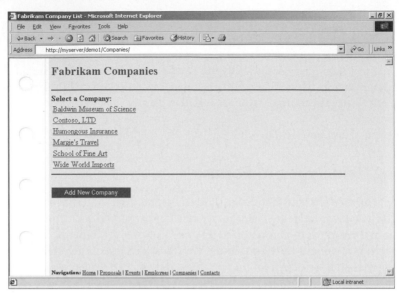

Figure 40-15. You can view the contents of an Exchange public folder as a Web page.

> **note** The Microsoft Fabrikam solution samples showcase the power of Microsoft Office XP with dashboard technologies, workflow, the Web Storage System, and other leading Microsoft technologies. The samples are available on the Microsoft Office XP evaluation CD.

Workflow Solutions for Outlook

Because the Web Storage System allows developers to extend the properties of items stored in Exchange Server, you can define properties in many ways. Workflow solutions for Exchange Server make it possible to create a workflow process for an Outlook folder. You create solutions using the Microsoft Office Developer tools, such as the tools for laying out and coding workflow processes. The workflow process is an organized path your Outlook items travel from creation to deletion. For example, you can create a workflow solution that allows for the approval of reimbursement requests. You can create the request item by using a custom Outlook form. When you store the item in Exchange Server, the workflow engine associates the item with a workflow process and adds special workflow properties to the item in the Web Storage System. These properties allow the engine to know the stage in the process where an item is currently located.

Although the steps involved in properly creating and implementing workflow solutions for Exchange Server are beyond the scope of this book, it is useful to know that Exchange 2000 Server and the Web Storage System can enhance the way users interact with Outlook by adding workflow processes. Most organizations have workflow processes in place for many of their employees' daily tasks. Moreover, many users do the bulk of their work inside Outlook. The Web Storage System and Exchange 2000 make it possible to connect what users are doing to a structured workflow process.

Chapter 41

Programming Forms with VBScript

You can often develop a reasonably powerful custom solution in Microsoft Outlook simply by creating and using Outlook forms with standard and custom controls. However, this approach has limits. For example, what if you want a new task to be created every time a user sends your custom form? What if you want to send a meeting request when your form is submitted? What if you want to connect to a database and fill in a drop-down list on your form with values from a specific database table?

Although it isn't practical to explain how to code for all these problems in this introductory chapter, the preceding list offers good examples of some of the tasks that are difficult, if not impossible, to accomplish using only custom forms that have no underlying custom program code. This chapter looks at developing custom form solutions with computer code and custom fields. You'll strengthen your understanding of programming basics and learn how you can begin to apply this understanding to developing a custom Outlook solution.

To create a solution that involves working with dynamic data, launching new items, and animating other programs, you could search for a control that already has these behaviors built in. But don't spend too much time looking, because you're unlikely to find a control with functionality so specifically tailored to your needs. The way to create powerful forms is by writing code.

For some people, writing code in an Outlook solution simply means learning the syntax of Microsoft Visual Basic, Scripting Edition (VBScript) and some of the properties, methods, and events of Outlook and Outlook forms. For other people, writing code might seem much more daunting. No matter what your level of programming experience is, this chapter will provide some basic knowledge you need to begin programming Outlook forms.

Understanding Scripting

Programming languages such as C++, Microsoft Visual Basic, VBScript, and C# (pronounced "C sharp") provide access to computer resources at different levels. The basic rule is that the "lower" you go, the more you need to know. Think of it as similar to programming a microwave: when you enter a combination of settings to defrost a chicken that weighs 1.3 pounds, you're programming the oven to do certain things. At a lower level, a program inside the microwave takes the settings you provide and translates them into a cooking plan that the machine can execute. Most often, lower-level programming languages, which are usually designed for speed and scalability, are used to create sophisticated, complex applications. However, the learning curve for these languages can be prohibitive for someone who wants to simply use some controls to create a form that sends an e-mail message. This is where a higher-level language such as VBScript steps in, giving the power of programming to users who don't have extensive backgrounds in computer science.

As the name implies, VBScript is a *scripting language*. A scripting language can create an unlimited number of programmatic solutions relatively quickly. Always remember, however, that you are trading true power and performance for simplicity and speed of development. Unlike a compiled programming language, a scripted language is interpreted—that is, the statements of instruction are reduced to a simple sequence of statements that are then executed by what is called a *command interpreter*. For each scripting language, a corresponding scripting engine provides this interpreter, along with other basic services to execute the script. When you program Outlook forms, you don't need to do anything to install this engine or ensure that your scripts will actually be executed. Outlook has with this engine built in; all you need to do is open up the Script Editor and begin writing code.

Because Outlook uses VBScript as the language for form development, you need to know the syntax of VBScript. You also need to know which interfaces are available for you to manipulate with lines of code. The next section provides this information.

A Brief Overview of VBScript

VBScript is a subset of the Microsoft Visual Basic programming language. The VBScript engine is portable, which means the engine can be embedded in or used by a lot of different programs, such as Microsoft Internet Explorer or Outlook. As mentioned earlier, VBScript is already embedded in Outlook. You can begin writing form-based code, and those who use your forms will benefit from the code behind the forms without having to install anything special to make the forms work. Because the VBScript engine is a true subset of the complete Visual Basic language, it is less complex and therefore easier to learn.

Understanding Objects and Properties

Object is probably one of the most overused words in the world of computer programming. Over time, the word has come to represent many different things to people in the IT field. Because the focus of this book is not hard-core computer science, this chapter will remain relatively introductory and cover only what you need to get your Outlook solution moving along. In this context, the following section discusses the notion of an object and what it means to your Outlook solution.

Objects

At the simplest level, an object in your Outlook development environment represents Outlook, the program itself, and other elements in Outlook (such as a text box) that expose properties, methods, or events with which you can interact programmatically. Outside the world of computing, the definition of an object is widely understood. For example, you know that a book is an object. It has certain properties such as height, weight, color, number of pages, title, author, and so on. You can also perform certain actions with a book: you can open it, close it, turn pages one at a time, flip to the end, return to the beginning, and fold the corners to mark your location.

A significant aspect of programming a custom solution using VBScript or Visual Basic for Applications (VBA) is manipulating Outlook items. For example, you add a text box to a form and then add or change the text it displays by setting a property of that text box object. You display or close a form by using a *Show* or *Hide* method on the form, treating the form as a complete object rather than showing or hiding the individual controls on the form. When a user clicks a button on a form, that button object generates a *Click* event. You add the code you want Outlook to execute when the button is clicked.

Thinking of Outlook items as programmable objects will help you begin to understand how you can create custom solutions with VBScript and VBA. Don't think of your custom program as pages and pages of program code. Instead, think of it as a collection of forms, controls, and other objects whose properties you can set, either at design time or through program code when the form runs, to make it perform the tasks you intend.

Properties

Properties are attributes of an object, describing some aspect of how an object behaves. To return to an earlier analogy, an object in Outlook can have some of the same properties as a book. For example, a form has height, width, and other basic properties that describe appearance. A command button has properties such as height, width, position, caption, name, and color. The more you know about the properties of the objects you use, the more you can do with those objects.

To set the property of an object, you must reference the object and follow it with a period and then the name of the property. The following code sample shows how to set the property of an object:

```
cmdAddAppointment.Caption = "Add Appt."
```

In this example, assume that your form contains a command button named *cmdAddAppointment*. You manipulate the *Caption* property of that button by setting it to some new value. How do you know that the button has this property? For any given object, you must read documentation to know the available properties and other behaviors for that object. For example, a text box does not have a *Caption* property, but a label does; both these controls have a *Font* property.

Notice that in the preceding example the *Caption* property required a string of characters between quotes. This is because the *Caption* property is predefined to accept characters strung together and not numbers, bitmaps, or other kinds of data. When you work with properties, you need to learn which types of data each property accepts to accurately apply property settings for your objects.

Understanding Events and Methods

Events and *methods* are two other powerful behaviors of a form or other object in Outlook. To continue with the previous analogy, you can do a number of things with a book: you can open it, close it, and so on. Put another way, the book possesses a number of methods such as *OpenBook*, *CloseBook*, *TurnPage*, *GoToEnd*, *GoToBeginning*, and *AddBookMark*. These method names are intuitive. The creators of any object model usually give intuitive names to the methods that their object exposes.

You can also associate certain events with a book. For example, when you finish reading the book, you might have to return it to the library. When you open the book for the first time, you might have to remove the book's dust jacket. To return to the microwave analogy, when the microwave completes the cooking plan you've provided, this event causes an alarm to sound. In other words, the microwave has a *CookingPlanCompleted* event that fires when the time runs out. When this event occurs, the alarm sounds.

In the world of Outlook development, you'll interact with many objects, some of which will expose certain events. Arguably, the most common event to fire is some kind of *Click* event, which fires when a user clicks a command button or other control. Notice the terminology: an event *fires* when something else happens. This is important to remember, because it is easy to get methods and events confused. Just remember that methods are actions you can take with an object, while events fire in response to an action—perhaps in response to a method or the changing of a property setting.

Creating Scripts and Using the Editor

Now that you have a little background information about the properties, methods, and events of the objects you can include in your solution, you're ready to begin writing code. Where do you write it? Theoretically, you can write the code in any program you want—in Microsoft Word, Notepad, or any other text editor. However, where you write the code is not as important as where it must reside to be able to run. Outlook has a window, or code editor, where all code must be placed before it can run. To access this code editor in Outlook, choose Form, View Code when your form is open. You can also click the View Code button to the right of the Control Toolbox button. In either case, the window shown in Figure 41-1 will appear. Any code that you want to run for your Outlook form must be contained in this window.

Figure 41-1. You can write and run the code for your form in the Script Editor window.

InsideOut

The Outlook Script Editor provides roughly the same level of functionality as Notepad or another basic text editor. However, the menu bar of this editor does contain the Outlook Object Library Help, shown in Figure 41-2 on the next page. The Object Library will come in handy as you develop your programming skills in Outlook. To access this help, choose Help, Microsoft Outlook Object Library Help from the editor's command bar. It's helpful to take some time to understand the Outlook object model.

Chapter 41

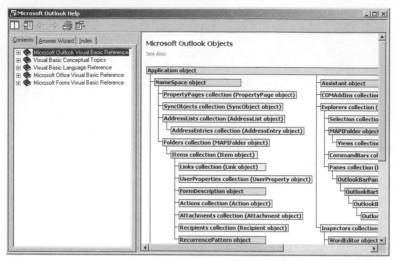

Figure 41-2. Use Outlook Object Library Help when writing code for Outlook.

The other features of the Script Editor—an Event Handler window and an Object Browser window—are of marginal benefit. Both windows, which are accessible from the Script menu, open simple dialog boxes that allow you to insert small bits of text into the Script Editor window. The problem is that the text excerpts provided in these windows are not displayed in any contextual way, so unless you already know the full object model, the textual excisions don't make much sense.

When you've finished writing your code sample, all you need to do is close the Script Editor window. Choose File, Close or close the window by clicking the X in the upper right corner. You don't need to do anything special to save the script; it is automatically stored with the form when you publish or save the form.

For information about publishing and saving forms, see "Publishing and Sharing Forms," page 1004.

Referencing Controls

One of the most common problems faced by Outlook forms programmers is trying to access the properties and methods of controls. This is because Outlook requires you to perform an extra step before you can acquire a reference to a control on a form. In other languages, such as Visual Basic or VBA, you can begin to use methods for a control as soon as you place that control on a form, simply by using its name. For example, if you draw a combo list box control on a form in Visual Basic and name it *cboEmployees*, you can use the following code to add items to the list in the control:

```
cboEmployees.AddItem "Employee One"
```

> **note** The name of the combo box object in this example is prefixed with *cbo* to indicate that it is a combo box. This helps you identify the type and function of a control when you're browsing or editing your script code.

In Outlook's VBScript environment, it is not possible to add items to the list the way you do in Visual Basic (for reasons that are beyond the scope of this book). To begin adding items to *cboEmployees* with VBScript, you first need to declare a variable and set *cboEmployees* equal to that new variable. You then use the new variable to execute methods and set properties.

The following code sample illustrates how to get a reference to a control named *cboEmployees* on a form and then add an item to that control programmatically:

```
Dim cboEmployeesRef
Set cboEmployeesRef = Item.GetInspector._
  ModifiedFormPages("P.2").Controls("cboEmployees")
cboEmployeesRef.AddItem "Employee One"
```

Notice the new variable in play here, *cboEmployeesRef*. This is actually just an empty container that you use to fill with a pointer to the real combo box control, *cboEmployees*. Figure 41-3 shows the form.

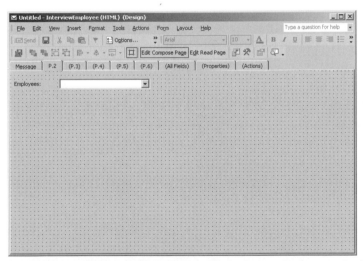

Figure 41-3. This example places a combo box control on an Outlook form.

The control is on the second page of the form; the caption for this page is *P.2*. You use this name in your code to find out which page the control was placed on. Then you sift through the collection of controls on this page of the form to find the one that interests you—in this case, *cboEmployees*. You next set your variable equal to the control you've found on this form page. With the variable now acting on behalf of the real control, you can use the properties and methods of that control by referencing the variable, in this case, *cboEmployeesRef*.

1019

InsideOut

Although you need the special reference to the control to be able to work with properties and methods on an Outlook form, you don't use the special reference name when dealing with events. In other words, while you must write *cboEmployeesRef.AddItem* to add an item, the events associated with *cboEmployees* are listed under that name and not under the name *cboEmployeesRef*. Confused? Don't worry—you aren't the first to find it a little befuddling. After you work with forms for a short while, you'll find it a little more comprehensible.

Using Methods

Methods are invoked by referencing the programmable object followed by a period and the method name. Let's go back to the form with *cboEmployees*. Suppose that you want to execute the *AddItem* method of the *cboEmployees* combo box. First you must build and use a form on which you can place the combo box.

Follow these steps to create the form:

1 While in Outlook, open a new standard message form in design mode.

2 Leave the Message form page alone for now. Make the second page visible by clicking its tab and choosing Form, Display This Page.

3 Add a label control to the form and position it in the upper left corner of the form.

For details on adding controls such as labels to a form, see "Adding and Arranging Controls," page 995.

4 Add a combo box control to the form and position it just to the right of the label control.

5 Right-click the label, choose Properties from the shortcut menu, and set the label's caption equal to *Employees:*.

6 Right-click the combo box, choose Properties from the shortcut menu, and set its name to *cboEmployees*.

7 Verify that your form now looks like the one shown previously in Figure 41-3.

Now you must prepopulate this combo box with a few values so that when the user opens the form, the combo box provides a list of employees. To do this, you need to write code in an event handler for the item itself. To simplify things for this example, assume that you'll place explicit values in the control's list. (In the real world, you'd use a few more lines of code to dynamically populate the control with an available list of employees or e-mail addresses from a database.) This code goes in the *Item_Open* event, which fires when a user opens the form. (Event handling is discussed in the following section.) For now, place the following code in the Script Editor:

```
Private cboEmployeesRef

Sub Item_Open()
  Set cboEmployeesRef = Item.GetInspector._
    ModifiedFormPages("P.2").Controls("cboEmployees")
  cboEmployeesRef.AddItem "Employee One"
  cboEmployeesRef.AddItem "Employee Two"
  cboEmployeesRef.AddItem "Employee Three"
  cboEmployeesRef.AddItem "Administrator"
  cboEmployeesRef.ListIndex = 0
End Sub
```

If this seems confusing, it's because of the assumption that you know what you're supposed to type after the *AddItem* method is invoked. The only way you could know this is by reading documentation to learn how the combo box in this example works. Reading code others have written can also help you learn the properties, methods, and events of the objects you use. If you fail to type the correct syntax or you try to execute a method that doesn't exist, Outlook presents an error message. As you fix problems in your code, pay careful attention to the messages you receive.

Event Handling

In the code sample used in the preceding section, you wrote code for adding employees to the combo box between the following lines:

```
Sub Item_Open()

End Sub
```

These lines bracket what is known as a *procedure*. Think of a procedure as a small program that runs inside your form. In this example, the procedure runs in correspondence with a specific event. The code between *Sub Item_Open( )* and *End Sub* will run whenever the form is opened. Because this procedure is tied to an event, it is called an *event handler*. You place the code to populate the combo box in this event handler because you want the combo box to be filled every time the form is opened.

Other common event handlers are *Item_Close*, *Item_Send*, and *CommandButton_Click*.

Using Variables

You'll find variables useful when you develop an Outlook form solution; they are useful in other programming environments as well. If you ever took algebra, the notion of a variable will be familiar to you. If you've never heard of or used variables before, don't worry; they're easily understood. This section takes a look at an example of variables outside the computing world and also discusses scope.

Scope

In VBScript (as in any programming language), there exists the notion of scope. *Scope* refers to the context in which a variable is active. Say that you're going to the movies with friends. Two friends stand in line for you while you park the car. While one friend (Friend1) waits for you at one movie theater, another friend (Friend2) waits for you at a different movie theater. Friend1's scope is the line where she is waiting. The same is true of Friend2. Just because Friend1 is first in line at one theater doesn't mean that your place is first in line at the other theater. The scopes are separate.

Pay attention to where you declare variables and to the words you use to declare them, because these factors determine the scope of your variable. The words, or *statements*, for declaring a variable in VBScript are *Dim*, *Public*, or *Private*. Use *Dim* only when you declare a variable within a procedure or function. *Public* and *Private* are used to declare variables at the beginning of a code module. *Private* is the most commonly used statement; use it when coding Outlook forms. You use *Public* to make variables or procedures in the module available to other code modules. Because this isn't possible in Outlook form development, you don't need to worry about the *Public* statement.

Variables

Think of a *variable* as a temporary container for something else. In the movie example, you asked two friends to wait in line for you while you parked the car. Your friends were actually the variables—they represented you. In computing terms, a variable is a named place in computer memory. You can give a variable just about any name you want. This variable will hold a place in memory and store some other data, such as a number or a string of characters. Whatever is contained in the variable is the *value* of that variable, and you can set, change, and read the value when needed.

Declaration

Before you can start using a variable, you should declare that variable. In VBScript, you aren't actually obligated to declare variables, but doing so is always a good idea. It's also a good idea to add comments to variable declarations that are obscure or less easily understood, thereby allowing readers of your code to understand what the variable represents. When you *declare* a variable, you're telling the scripting engine that you have a variable of a specific name and that any time this name is used, the variable is being used. Again, declare variables by using a *Dim* or *Private* statement.

In the code sample on page 1021, you used the *Private* statement to declare a variable called *cboEmployeesRef*. This variable held a pointer, or reference, to the actual combo box control. The scope of this variable is global because you made the declaration at the beginning of the module and not in a specific procedure or function. As you become more comfortable with programming, you'll find that you might make many declarations, both within and outside procedures. The following code sample is taken from a rather sophisticated form:

```
Private mobjSession          ' CDO Session
Private mobjNS               ' Namespace
Private mstrCurrentUserName  ' Name of current form user form user
Private mstrCustomerID       ' CustomerID retrieved from database

Sub cmdModifyCustomer_Click()
  On Frror Resume Next

  Dim objMessage       ' Temporary message holder
  Dim objRecipient     ' Recipient object that will receive message
  Dim strEmployeeID    ' The assigned Customer Agent's ID

    ⋮
End Sub
```

Notice how the variables were declared and commented. Notice also that the sub-procedure contains its own variable declarations. These are usually made at the beginning of a procedure and not throughout, making the code more readable. Remember that other people will inevitably need to read, understand, and support your code, so it is more than just a professional courtesy to write, organize, format, and comment your code carefully.

Using Constants

Like variables, *constants* are containers for data. You can place a text string in a variable or in a constant and then reference and use both in much the same way. The essential difference between variables and constants is this: after you set the values of constants at design time, the program can read these values only at run time. Variables, however, allow the program to change their value when appropriate. Given this difference, constants are declared and used to hold information that you don't want to change while the program is being executed. For example, suppose that your code contains some procedures that all need to use the following string: "Region: 2330n; Section: 4; District: 5." Typing this in over and over in each procedure would be tedious. In addition, what if the company reorganized Section 4 into Sections 4A and 4B and also renamed the region? You would then have to go into your code and replace the string in each procedure. The risk for error and the amount of effort required (even with the magic of Copy/ Paste) is higher than if you were simply to declare a constant in one part of your code and use that constant in all the procedures. Your constant declaration would look like the code shown on the next page.

```
Const AGENT_LOCATION
= "Region: 2330n; Section: 4; District: 5."
Const PO_AUTHCENTER
= &HA02D001E ' Hex value for PO authorization
```

This code contains another constant (*PO_AUTHCENTER*) that illustrates an especially useful aspect of constants: they can make esoteric values readable. The code contains a hexadecimal value that corresponds to an authorization number for purchase orders. The hexadecimal value won't make much sense to other people who have to read the code. Furthermore, if your code contains several of these cryptic values, you'll probably become confused as well. Using constants allows you to assign this enigmatic value a user-friendly name that will make sense.

Declare constants at the beginning of your code module, and use the *Const* keyword, followed by the name of the constant in uppercase characters. Using all uppercase letters is a common practice that allows readers of your code to easily determine whether the name they are about to use is a variable or a constant. Make sure your constant name is user-friendly and comprehensible within the context of your business solution. Using names that are too short or known only to you will diminish some of the advantages that constants provide. After you provide a name for your constant, type an equal sign followed by the value of the constant.

Retrieving and Setting Field Values

Outlook has a number of item types that form the basis of practically any collaborative Outlook solution. Each item type has a number of fields or properties that you can set and read in your code. You can easily set these fields or properties by referencing the *Item* object and the property in question.

The following code sets the Subject field of a *MailItem*:

```
Item.Subject = cboEmployeesRef.List(cboEmployeesRef.ListIndex)
```

This code sets the *Subject* property of the *Item* object to the text value of the currently selected item in the combo box.

The value of the *Subject* property is also accessible for reading purposes. For example, you might want to put code in the *Item_Send* event to first check to see whether the Subject field is blank. If it is blank, set the value equal to the text shown in the combo box; otherwise, leave the value as the user typed it. The code would look like this:

```
If Len(Item.Subject) = 0 Then
  Item.Subject = cboEmployeesRef.List(cboEmployeesRef.ListIndex)
End If
```

The preceding code checks the length of the *Subject* property. If the length of that property is 0, you know that the user has not typed any text into the Subject field. You can then let the code do a little work for the user by automatically adding a value to the field.

Chapter 41

Retrieving User-Defined and Other Properties

You can create your own custom properties. These are properties that your solution requires but that are not provided by the item types available to you. For example, if you deal with employees, you might want to have a property that refers to an ID for the division in which an employee works. None of the item types that Outlook provides has a *DivisionID* property. The good news is that you can add a new property for this data. These user-defined properties, sometimes called user-defined fields, can also be bound to controls. In Chapter 40, "Designing and Using Forms," you learned to bind controls to item properties; see "Value," page 998. You can bind these same controls to a user-defined property the same way you bind them to a regular, built-in property.

The sample form in this chapter contains a list of employees. A senior manager selects an employee and sends the message to someone who is supposed to interview the employee. When the user receives the message and opens it, she or he is given the opportunity to click a button and automatically add a task to a private task list. This task will already contain the name of the person to be interviewed in the subject line.

This form will be defined with two pages, both with Compose and Read areas. On the Compose area of the second page is a combo box that will be populated with employee names. The Read area of the second page will contain a couple of labels, one of which will be bound to a user-defined property. This page should look like the one shown in Figure 41-4. To get to this stage, you need to create a new property for the form, named *EmployeeToInterview*.

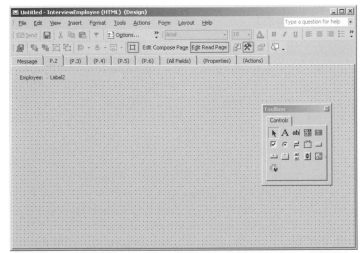

Figure 41-4. The Read area of the second form page contains two label controls.

Chapter 41

Follow these steps to create the new user-defined property:

1 Activate the separate Read and Compose areas by choosing Form, Separate Read Layout.

2 With the form selected, choose the All Fields tab in design mode. You should see the pane shown in Figure 41-5.

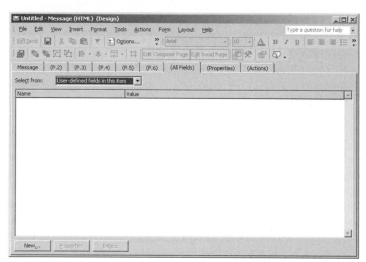

Figure 41-5. Use the All Fields tab to create a new user-defined property.

3 Click New and type the name of the new property (*EmployeeToInterview*). Click OK. Optionally, you can type in a default value for this user-defined property in the Value column.

Notice that this user-defined property stores text. When you create a user-defined property, you can decide what type of data the property will hold. You can also prescribe the format of the data the property holds. For example, if you define a new property called *AmountSaved* and choose the *Currency* data type, you could choose how to display the currency values—for example, you might want to omit decimal values and keep the figures at the dollar level only.

When you create user-defined properties, you can bind controls to them. In this case, you bind the second label (*lblEmployee*) on the Read area of the second page to the user-defined property *EmployeeToInterview*. You also add code so that when the user sends the form, the value of the new property is set equal to the value shown in the combo box. Without this additional code, the value shown in the label bound to the user-defined property would not be the dynamic value the user has chosen in the combo box. In other words, you have created a user-defined property for this item. When the user chooses an employee from the combo box and sends the message, the value of the combo box is stored in the user-defined property. When the recipient reads the message, the label on the second page is already populated with the value of the user-defined property. The following code is necessary to make the form function properly:

```
Private cboEmployeesRef

Sub Item_Open()
  If Item.Size = 0 Then
    Item.To = "Administrator"
    Set cboEmployeesRef = Item.GetInspector._
        ModifiedFormPages("P.2").Controls("cboEmployees")
      cboEmployeesRef.AddItem "Employee One"
      cboEmployeesRef.AddItem "Employee Two"
      cboEmployeesRef.AddItem "Employee Three"
      cboEmployeesRef.AddItem "Administrator"
      cboEmployeesRef.ListIndex = 0
  End If
End Sub

Sub Item_Send()
  If Len(Item.Subject) = 0 Then
    Item.Subject = cboEmployeesRef.List(cboEmployeesRef.ListIndex)
    End If
  Item.UserProperties.Item("EmployeeToInterview").Value = _
    cboEmployeesRef.List(cboEmployeesRef.ListIndex)
End Sub
```

In this simple example, you both set and retrieve the values of the user-defined property. However, there's a little more to be said about user-defined properties. After you create a user-defined property, how can you be sure that recipients and users of your form will have access to it? What do you need to be able to manage these properties and ensure their integration in a solution? The short answer to these questions is that user-defined properties exist in the place where you publish your form.

For information on publishing forms, see "Publishing and Sharing Forms," page 1004.

For example, assume that you create a form to specify travel preferences, such as airplane seating choice and meal types. You create new user-defined properties for each piece of information and publish the form to your Inbox. Those properties are now available in your Inbox; you'll find them listed when you use the Field Chooser dialog box. As it happens, your form is so successful that you need to make it available to others, and you choose to publish the form in a public folder called Travel Planning. When you do this, the user-defined properties you created become available to anyone who opens your posts in that folder.

For information on using the Field Chooser, see "Outlook Fields," page 992.

Custom Formula and Combination Fields

Formula fields and combination fields allow you to join together multiple fields and manipulate their data. In some cases, the piece of information you want users to view in a list of sent items will be a field value that has been altered by a function, such as one that makes all characters in a field expressed in uppercase. In another example, think of an instance in which two fields contain important values for your solution, but users are accustomed to seeing the two values placed together, such as a given name and a surname. Rather than forcing users to enter three fields—one for the given name, one for the last name, and one for the union of the two—you can create a combination field that automatically displays the combination of the two other fields. Both formula and combination fields are constructed in much the same way as the other user-defined properties you've learned to create. However, instead of choosing a data type such as *Text* or *Number*, you choose *Formula* or *Combination*.

To create a combination field, follow these steps:

1 Open the form you're modifying in design mode.

2 Select the All Fields tab and click New.

3 Type a field name and select Combination for the type.

4 Click Edit.

5 Select the first option in the Combine Field Values By frame.

6 Click the Field button to add a field. Repeat this step for as many fields as you want to insert.

7 Click OK twice to complete the field addition.

Before you click OK, your NewField dialog box should look like Figure 41-6.

Figure 41-6. Create a combination field to simplify the way users view information.

In step 5, you chose the first option. The two options have to do with how empty field values are displayed. For example, in the case of combination fields, one or more of the fields might be empty, whereas others will contain complete values. You can have Outlook display all the complete fields by selecting the first option. On the other hand, if you combine two or more field values and you want only the first nonempty field to display, choose the second option. For example, you might choose this option when you want to use either a person's first name (if it has a value) or the person's nickname (if it has a value), but not both. In this case, you would include both fields in the combination but select the second option. Only the first field with a value is shown.

You create a formula field in much the same way you create a combination field, except that you choose the Formula type instead of the Combination type. When you click the Edit button, you see a Field button and a Function button in the dialog box, allowing you to insert functions as well as field names. The Function button greatly enhances the power of the field you have created by making available a large number of functions related to time, date, financial formulas, textual operations, and mathematical formulas.

The ability to employ user-defined properties expands what you can do with an Outlook solution. User-defined properties allow you to extend Outlook forms and item types to include information tailored to your organization and operations. Creating user-defined properties is a common task for building customized form-based solutions, and the properties should correspond to data elements in the environment where they will be used.

For More Information on VBScript and Outlook

This chapter has presented a brief introduction to programming Outlook solutions. Because the skills you acquire as you learn to use and extend Outlook will pay off for a long time, you'll undoubtedly want to deepen your understanding. There are numerous additional sources you can consult to do so.

Microsoft supplies a copious amount of documentation about Outlook and about building collaborative solutions around Outlook. The online documentation for Outlook and the Microsoft Office Developer Documentation are probably the best in the industry for any product. Although the MSDN Web site (*http://msdn.microsoft.com*) has an overwhelming but well-organized body of documentation, you might want to consider purchasing Microsoft Office Developer (MOD) as well. MOD not only offers more documentation than MSDN but also contains extremely useful code samples and other materials.

Some terrific magazines target developers of Outlook and Microsoft Office. DevX (*http://www.devx.com*) puts out a monthly periodical called *Exchange & Outlook* that covers a wide variety of topics for both the neophyte and the enterprise developer. Advisor (*http://www.advisor.com*) provides the *Microsoft Exchange* Outlook Advisor Zone. Informant Communications Group publishes the *Microsoft OfficePRO* magazine (*http://www.msofficepro.com*), which is designed for the Office developer but features articles of great use to the Outlook developer. Informant also sponsors the Microsoft

Office Deployment and Development Conference each year, a great place to meet other like-minded developers and gain in-depth exposure to the most significant technologies to emerge in the Office development arena.

The *Microsoft Office XP Resource Kit* and a wide selection of Microsoft Press books can aid you in learning about VBScript, Microsoft Office, and Microsoft Exchange development. Visit the Microsoft Press Web site (*http://mspress.microsoft.com*) to find the latest releases that discuss the most current technologies.

Using VBA in Outlook

Microsoft Visual Basic for Applications (VBA) is derived from the full Microsoft Visual Basic language and is featured in a number of products. Most notably, it is the primary programming language for all Microsoft Office applications as well as other products such as Visio and Great Plains software.

In this chapter, you'll be introduced to the VBA environment and some of the important concepts required to work with VBA. After this, you'll see some examples of simple ways to use VBA within Outlook to automate common tasks. It will help if you're familiar with a programming language, but you'll be able to run the samples simply by following the instructions.

on the CD   **note**   You'll find the code used to create the VBA applications in this chapter in the Author Extras section of the companion CD.

note   There are a lot of great books on VBA—whether you're a beginner or a more advanced user. Check out the mspress. microsoft.com site and your favorite bookstore for a title to fit your needs.

A Quick Look at Object Models

VBA was designed to be integrated into other applications. It allows a user to easily work with the functionality of its parent application, Visual Basic, as well as to access external functions and applications. To understand how to get the most out of VBA, it's important to understand the concept of an object model.

The term *object model* refers to the exposed functions of an application (the functions belonging to an application that you can access from within code). These functions are exposed as a set of objects, where each object has properties, methods, and events. The object model contains a set of definitions, or *classes,* that you can use to create objects.

You might think of a class as a design. Consider an architect's house plans. These define what the house should look like and what functions it should perform, but until the builder builds the house, the plan doesn't do anything except describe the house. When the builder builds the house, he or she is creating an *instance* of the architect's design. Although the builder might make many instances of the design when building a housing development, after a house (an instance) is created, it stands separate from any other house in the development.

The way you use the object model in VBA is similar to the way the plan is used to build a house. Select the set of functions you require, and then create an instance of the class that defines them. To accomplish this, you use VBA keywords and syntax.

Referencing Objects

To use objects in VBA, you must add a reference to them. This tells VBA that a specific group of objects exists and what classes are defined for these objects. To add a reference, start the VBA Editor and choose Tools, References. A list of objects is displayed. To add a reference to an object definition, just select the box next to the appropriate item in the list.

By looking at the Help file you can usually find out which references you need to set to perform certain operations. Some of the major ones for the examples in this chapter and the next are references to the object models of other Office applications. These appear in the list with the following names:

> Excel—*Microsoft Excel 10.0 Object Library*

> Word—*Microsoft Word 10.0 Object Library*

To access Outlook functionality from another application, you set a reference to the Outlook object model:

> Outlook—*Microsoft Outlook 10.0 Object Library*

For data access, it is useful to use ADO (ActiveX Data Objects):

> Data access—*Microsoft ActiveX Data Objects 2.6 Library*

A number of object models for ADO are available; the most recent is ADO 2.6.

Declaring and Instantiating an Object

To create an instance of an object, you first declare the object using the *Dim* statement. This statement dimensions a variable of that object type. The following statement, for example, declares a new variable of the *Word.Application* type:

```
Dim objWord as Word.Application
```

After you declare an object, you use the Set and New keywords to create an instance of the object. The variable you declared previously is assigned to this instance, after which you can start using the instance:

```
Set objWord = New Word.Application
```

You can now access all the functions and properties of the *Word.Application* object through the newly defined instance.

InsideOut

Whenever you create an instance of an object, especially an external application object, remember to dispose of it once you've finished working with it. You dispose of it by setting the object variable to Nothing:

```
Set objWord = Nothing
```

VBA is supposed to clean up all object references and dispose of them automatically when they fall out of scope, but often this does not happen. You are then left with objects that have no associations but are using memory. This situation can be especially harmful if the object you created is a large application like Microsoft Word that uses a significant amount of memory.

Properties, Methods, and Events

A *property* is a value associated with an object. An example of a property is the name of the object. Properties can be read-only or read-write. You usually use properties to tell an object how to represent itself or how to act.

A *method* is equivalent to a function in code, but it belongs to a specific object and can be accessed only through that object rather than being generally available. You can call the method of an object to perform a task and perhaps return a result. Methods can take parameters.

Chapter 42

An *event* is used by the object you have instantiated to tell your application that something is happening outside normal program flow. A great deal of the Microsoft Windows architecture is based on the availability of events (referred to as messages in relation to Windows).

Understanding VBA in Relation to VBS

Before Outlook 2000, the only option you had for developing code applications in Outlook was to use Microsoft Visual Basic, Scripting Edition (VBScript, or VBS). Although this allowed some customization, the introduction of VBA (Visual Basic for Applications) in Outlook 2000 allowed developers a far greater level of control throughout the entire product as well as easier integration with other members of the Office family. VBA differs from VBScript in a number of key ways. Most noticeably, VBA is a much friendlier environment to work in. This is a result of the editor supplied with the VBA engine and also because VBA is closer than VBS to a fully featured programming language such as Visual Basic.

An important difference between VBA and VBScript in Outlook is related to where you use the two languages. VBA allows you far greater control over Outlook than VBScript, which permits you to work only behind a particular custom form. In VBA, you can work at an application level, where you can control many interactions between different areas of Outlook as well as automate almost every interface action.

Overview of the VBA Development Environment

If you have programmed in one of the many VBA-enabled applications, you'll be familiar with the VBA environment in Outlook. It is the same environment used in all Office products as well as in a number of third-party applications.

The VBA environment is hosted as a window separate from the main Outlook application environment. To open the VBA Editor window from Outlook, choose Tools, Macro, Visual Basic Editor.

The environment consists of a number of windows and toolbars, some of which are displayed in Figure 42-1. The Project, Properties, and Debugging windows are integral to the VBA environment and can be docked on the edges of the environment. The Code and Form editors operate as MDI (multiple-document interface) windows, similar to the way multiple documents are displayed in Word or Excel. They all appear within the shell, and you can easily switch between them using the Window menu. To view or hide any of these windows, use the View menu.

Project window

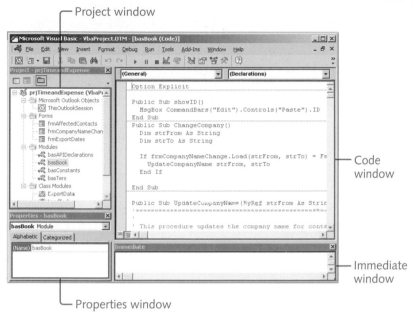

Code window

Immediate window

Properties window

Figure 42-1. The VBA environment contains a number of windows and toolbars.

The Project Window

The Project window displays the projects and files you work on. The files that make up a project are arranged as a tree under the Project entry in the Project window.

> **note** Unless you have the Microsoft Office Developer edition, you'll be able to work with only one project, the project associated with Outlook. Office Developer allows you to use the VBA environment to develop applications for use outside the current instance of Outlook. It also gives you a number of other development options that are useful to anyone looking to develop large applications using Outlook and other members of the Office family.

Following are descriptions of the different sections of the project tree:

Microsoft Outlook Objects This branch of the tree always exists and always contains at least one object called *ThisOutlookSession*. This is where you place code that works at the application level of Outlook. It represents the current instance of Outlook and gives you access to the application so that you can add code for some of the events that occur in Outlook. For example, if you want a task to occur when Outlook starts up, you place code in the *ApplicationStartup* event.

Forms   This branch of the tree holds an entry for any forms you have built. These are VB forms, which are not the same as Outlook forms. You would add VB forms to your application to allow a user to perform tasks that were not related to any of the custom areas of Outlook. For example, to perform a particular task, you might need to collect information from the user. You could build a custom VB form that is displayed when the user performs a specific task and that asks the user to provide some information.

> For a demonstration of using a custom VB form in this way, see "Adding a Form," page 1051.

Modules   Under this branch of the tree, you find all the code modules that contain general code. This is a sensible place to put common code that must be available to many areas of the application. It is also a good place to store macro code used by buttons to launch various parts of your Outlook application. Later in this chapter, when you discover how to implement custom toolbar buttons, you'll see that the code used for this purpose is placed in a module. You can have many modules in your project; it's standard practice to divide your code into logical functional areas and to then implement each functional area as a different module. For example, you might have some functions that perform operations on contact information, some that perform operations with calendar items, some that relate to the handling of errors, and some that are simply general code functions that can be used by any of the functional areas. In such a case, you should implement four modules called basContacts, basCalendar, basErrorHandling, and basGeneral. (The bas prefix is historical, referring to the fact that these are files containing BASIC code.)

Class Modules   In this area, you can build class modules to utilize throughout your code. Although they permit you to build functions, class modules, unlike ordinary modules, require that in order to use the functions you must create an instance of the class rather than simply calling the function name. Class modules are used to encapsulate similar functionality in a single area that can be utilized like any other objects in Outlook.

> **note**   The discussion of how and why to use class modules to develop applications in an object-oriented way is too complex to be covered here. I suggest that you consult books on developing object-oriented applications to get an understanding of the techniques and then apply these techniques in your Outlook applications by using classes. One useful book on this subject is *Programming Microsoft Visual Basic 6.0*, by Francesco Balena (Microsoft Press, 1999).

Follow these steps to add a new file to your VBA project:

1 Right-click the main area of the Properties window and choose Insert.

2 Choose one of the three file types (UserForm, Module, Class Module). Under the appropriate branch of the project tree, a new file is displayed with a generic name.

3 Rename the file using the Properties window.

For instructions on renaming, see "The Properties Window," below.

Although the files in the Project window are displayed and listed as separate items, they are stored not as individual files but as placeholders to their storage in Outlook. You can, however, import and export them as individual files to allow their use in other applications.

Follow these steps to export a file:

1 In the Project window, select the file you want to export.

2 Choose File, Export File or right-click and choose Export File.

3 Select the directory to which you want to export the file.

4 Name the file.

You also can import any VB or VBA module or class file into an Outlook project.

Follow these steps to import a file:

1 Right-click anywhere in the Project window or choose File, Import File.

2 Locate the file to import and select it in the dialog box. The imported file appears under the appropriate branch of the project tree.

All VBA code that you develop is saved in the VBAProject.OTM file. If you want to distribute an application, you need to send the VBAProject.OTM file and have people replace their existing VBAProject.OTM files with your new one. By default, the OTM file is located in C:\Documents And Settings\<*username*>\Application Data\Microsoft\Outlook.

The Properties Window

The Properties window is where you review and alter any configurable properties of the selected object. For any file selected in the Project window, a *Name* property appears in the Properties window, where you can change the name of the file. This window gets quite a workout when you're building a VB form because the form and every control you place on it are each associated with many properties.

For example, after adding the Module type file to the project, follow these steps to change the *Name* property of the file:

1 In the Project window, select the project file to rename. The Project window changes to display information about the selected file—in this case, the name.

2 Select the *Name* property and change it to something meaningful, such as *basCommonFunctions*.

3 Click away from the *Name* property, anywhere else in the VBA environment. The name of the file in the Project window changes to reflect the altered property.

To demonstrate a more complex set of properties, add a UserForm type file to the project. Notice that the Properties window is now full of customizable properties (see Figure 42-2).

Figure 42-2. Forms and controls have multiple properties that you can change in the Properties window.

The Debugging Windows

A number of debugging tools are available for debugging your VBA applications. You use these tools to investigate and alter the states of the objects in your code while the code is executing. These tools appear with information in different debugging windows that are displayed at the base of the screen. You can open the debugging windows by choosing View and then selecting the appropriate tools. Before you can use debugging tools, the code must be in break mode. To get into break mode while code is executing, press Ctrl+Break or set a breakpoint by selecting a line of code you're interested in and pressing F9. When the executing code reaches the breakpoint, the environment will go into break mode, and you can use the debugging tools.

Debugging tools include the following:

- **Immediate window.** View values and execute statements while in break mode.

- **Watches window.** View watches you have set up in VBA. A *watch* is an expression that evaluates as a program executes. This facility allows you to watch the value change without having to reexecute it manually, as you do in the Immediate window.

- **Locals window.** View the values of all local variables and objects.

> For a view of the Immediate window, see Figure 42-1, page 1035. The Immediate window is displayed at the bottom of the VBA environment.

> **note** For an in-depth discussion of how to use the debugging tools, consult *Microsoft Office 2000/Visual Basic for Applications Fundamentals,* by David Boctor (Microsoft Press, 1999).

The Code Window

When you double-click a file in the Project window, a new window opens in the main area of the screen. If you selected Module, ClassModule, or ThisOutlookSession, the Code window is displayed. You use this window to add code to Outlook.

The Object Window

If you double-click a form in the Project window, the Object window opens, displaying a graphical view of the form. To display the code for that form, do one of the following:

- Double-click the form or a control on it
- Right-click the form entry in the Project window and choose View Code
- Choose View, Code

VBA Toolbars

You can use three special toolbars when building VBA applications. Most of the functions available by clicking toolbar buttons are also available on a menu and are usually accessible through a shortcut key combination as well.

- The Debug toolbar gives you easy access to the debugging tools.
- The Edit toolbar contains the tools that make you more productive when writing code.
- The UserForm toolbar aids in building VB forms.

For a list of the specific tools on these toolbars, see Table 42-1 on the next page.

Table 42-1. VBA toolbar buttons and corresponding commands

Toolbar Button	Command	Description
	Run, Run	Executes the currently selected code or form
	Run, Reset	Stops the currently executing code and resets the project
	Run, Break	Breaks into the code execution at the current point
	Edit, List Properties/Methods	Opens a list in the Code window that contains the properties and methods available for the object
	Edit, List Constants	Opens a list in the Code window that contains the valid constants for the property you typed
	Edit, Quick Info	Provides the syntax for a variable, function, statement, method, or procedure selected in the Code window
	Edit, Parameter Info	Displays a pop-up window in the Code window containing information about the parameters of the function or statement
	Comment Block	Turns the selected block of code into comments; not available on a menu
	Uncomment Block	Removes the comment character from the selected block of code; not available on a menu
	Format, Align	Aligns all the selected controls on the form in the specified way

Toolbar Button	Command	Description
	Format, Center Horizontally	Centers all the selected controls in relation to each other; uses a drop-down menu to allow you to access different options
	Vertically	
	Format, Make Same Size, Width	Makes all the selected controls the same size; uses a drop-down menu to allow you to access different options
	Height	
	Both	

Understanding the Outlook Object Model

Once you're comfortable with the VBA environment, it's time to have a look around Outlook's object model. If you're familiar with object models in other Office applications, you'll notice that the Outlook object model is slightly different. This is a result, for the most part, of the relatively late inclusion of VBA and the different role that Outlook as an application plays. Whereas other Office applications such as Word and Excel are frameworks within which other objects (documents, workbooks, and sheets) are hosted and manipulated, Outlook is very much an application in its own right.

An entire book could be written about the more than 30 objects and collections in the Outlook object model. This section gives only an introduction to the key objects and collections that are required to start developing applications. Use the Microsoft Visual Basic Help, accessed from within the VBA Editor by pressing F1, to find out about the other objects in the Outlook object model.

Here is a brief look at some key objects:

- **Items.** The basic units of information in Outlook. An e-mail message, an appointment on your calendar, and a contact entry are all examples of items.

- **Folders.** The basic storage units. Folders contain items. Outlook has many folders, such as the Inbox, Sent Items, and Tasks folders.

- **Explorers.** The visual representation of the items in a folder. Outlook uses Explorers to display items. Examples of Explorers are the e-mail pane associated with the Inbox and the daily calendar view you see when you select the Calendar folder. Any one folder can be associated with a number of Explorers. For example, the Calendar folder has several Explorers so that you can display calendar items in different ways.

- **Inspectors.** The Outlook forms used to display an item. Inspectors are to items what Explorers are to folders: that is, the graphical Outlook representation of the information.

These objects are explained more fully in the next section. Before looking at these important Outlook objects in more detail, however, it's important to understand what is meant by the term *collection*. Some pieces of the object model are flagged as an object only, and others are flagged as an object and a collection. A *collection* is a group of objects that have the same type. For example, your Inbox contains a number of e-mail messages. Each message is a mail item object, and the Inbox folder contains a collection of these mail items. You can get at a particular member of a collection by using the *Item* method of the collection and giving it an index that is an integer value or a value that matches the default property of an object in the collection. For example, the following code returns the second e-mail message in the Inbox:

```
Set emlSecond = fdrInbox.Items.Item(2)
```

Alternatively, you can use a name that refers to the object. This example returns the e-mail folder called Outlook Book in the Folders collection:

```
Set fdrOutlookBook = myFolders.Item("Outlook Book")
```

To make the code that displays the second e-mail message work correctly, do the following:

1 Start Outlook and choose Tools, Macro, Visual Basic Editor (or press Alt+F11) to open the VBA Editor.

2 In the Project window, select Project1 and expand the tree until you see ThisOutlookSession.

3 Select ThisOutlookSession and press F7 to open the Code window.

4 Enter the following in the Code window:

```
Sub GetEmailItem()
    Dim emlSecond As MailItem
    Dim nsMyNameSpace As NameSpace
    Dim fdrInbox As MAPIFolder
```

```
    Set nsMyNameSpace = Application.GetNamespace("MAPI")
    Set fdrInbox = _
      nsMyNameSpace.GetDefaultFolder(olFolderInbox)

    Set emlSecond = fdrInbox.Items.Item(2)

    MsgBox "Second e-mail : " & vbCrLf & vbCrLf & _
           emlSecond.Subject & vbCrLf & emlSecond.Body
  End Sub
```

5 Go back to the main Outlook window and choose Tools, Macro, Macros.

6 Select ThisOutlookSession.GetEmailItem and click the Run button. A dialog box opens, containing the e-mail message.

Application, Namespaces, and Folders

At the core of the Outlook object model is the *Application* object, referred to as the *root object* because the rest of the hierarchy grows from it. The *Application* object provides access to all other Outlook objects. If you're accessing the Outlook object hierarchy from an external application, you must create an instance of the *Application* object before you can access any other objects. If you're working in Outlook, an instance of the *Application* object is always in existence; to access it, you use the Application keyword.

Although the *Application* object gives you access to many fundamental building block objects in Outlook, you must create an instance of the *Namespace* object if you want to access Outlook data. The *Namespace* object is an abstract root for Outlook data sources, which means that although you don't use it directly, it provides access to the objects below it in the object tree. Currently, the only data source supported is MAPI, which allows access to all Outlook data stored in the user's mail files. To get at the *Namespace* object of the Outlook application, use the *GetNameSpace* method of the *Application* object:

```
Application.GetNamespace("MAPI")
```

As you know, information in Outlook is maintained in folders. Some folders, such as Inbox, Outbox, and Sent Items, contain mail items; other folders contain other types of items. After obtaining an instance of the *Namespace* object, you can easily connect to any folders in Outlook. The *Namespace* object has a *GetDefaultFolder* method that takes a parameter of type *olDefaultFolders*. Type *olDefaultFolders* represents one of the default Outlook folders and can be any of the following constants:

olFolderCalendar	Returns a folder containing all calendar items
olFolderContacts	Returns a folder containing all contact items
olFolderDeletedItems	Returns a folder containing all deleted mail items
olFolderDrafts	Returns a folder containing all draft mail items
olFolderInbox	Returns a folder containing all Inbox mail items

olFolderJournal	Returns a folder containing all journal items
olFolderNotes	Returns a folder containing all note items
olFolderOutbox	Returns a folder containing all Outbox mail items
olFolderSentMail	Returns a folder containing all sent mail items
olFolderTasks	Returns a folder containing all task items
olPublicFoldersAllPublicFolders	Returns a folder containing all public folder items

For example, you can use the following code to create an object that represents all contact items:

```
Dim fdrContacts As Outlook.MAPIFolder
Set fdrContacts = _
  Application.GetNamespace("MAPI") _
    .GetDefaultFolder(olFolderContacts)
```

The *fdrContacts* variable has been declared as a MAPIFolder and assigned the Contacts folder. You could instead declare an *Application* object and a *Namespace* object as well, but unless you're going to use them repeatedly, it's just as efficient to use the defined *Application* property and the *GetNamespace* method call.

Efficient Use of the *Application* and *Namespace* Objects

If you want to retrieve a number of folders to work with, the following code is efficient because it retrieves an *Application* object and a *Namespace* object once and then uses them repeatedly:

```
Dim objApplication As Outlook.Application
Dim objNameSpace As Outlook.NameSpace
Dim fdrContacts As Outlook.MAPIFolder
Dim fdrNotes as Outlook.MAPIFolder

Set objApplication = Application
Set objNameSpace = objApplication.GetNamespace("MAPI")
Set fdrContacts = objNameSpace.GetDefaultFolder(olFolderContacts)
Set fdrNotes = objNameSpace.GetDefaultFolder(olFolderNotes)

'<Insert code here to work with the Contacts and Notes folders>

Set objApplication = Nothing
Set objNameSpace = Nothing
Set fdrContacts = Nothing
Set fdrNotes = Nothing
```

The following steps guide you through the process of creating code that sets up objects for the Notes and Calendar folders and then allows you to display contents from within each folder:

1 Start Outlook and choose Tools, Macro, Visual Basic Editor (or press Alt+F11) to open the VBA Editor.

2 In the Project window, select Project1 and expand the tree until you see the heading ThisOutlookSession.

3 Select ThisOutlookSession and press F7 to open the Code window.

4 Enter the following code in the Code window:

```
Sub ContactsAndNotes()
   Dim objApplication As Outlook.Application
   Dim objNameSpace As Outlook.NameSpace
   Dim fdrContacts As Outlook.MAPIFolder
   Dim fdrNotes As Outlook.MAPIFolder

   Set objApplication = Application
   Set objNameSpace = objApplication.GetNamespace("MAPI")
   Set fdrContacts = _
      objNameSpace.GetDefaultFolder(olFolderContacts)

   Set fdrNotes = _
      objNameSpace.GetDefaultFolder(olFolderNotes)

   MsgBox fdrNotes.Name & " (" & fdrNotes.Parent & ")"
   MsgBox fdrContacts.Name & " (" & fdrContacts.Parent & ")"

   Set objApplication = Nothing
   Set objNameSpace = Nothing
   Set fdrContacts = Nothing
   Set fdrNotes = Nothing
End Sub
```

5 Go back to the main Outlook window and choose Tools, Macro, Macros.

6 Select ThisOutlookSession.ContactsAndNotes and click the Run button. Two dialog boxes are displayed. The first contains the name of the Notes folder followed by the name of its parent folder; the second contains the name of the Contacts folder followed by the name of its parent folder.

Explorers, Inspectors, and Items

So far, you have been introduced to the Outlook objects required to access data in Outlook. An item is one piece of Outlook data. For example, an appointment on your calendar is stored in Outlook as an appointment item. When you use Outlook to look at items in folders, you're actually using an *Explorer* object for that particular item type.

Outlook provides different Explorers for the different types of items. If you use the Outlook interface to look at your calendar, contacts, notes, and journal items, you can see how markedly different the Explorers for the various items are.

The *Application* object contains a collection of Explorers that represent all the different Explorers available in Outlook. A number of methods are available for retrieving a specific *Explorer* object from Outlook:

- Use the *Item* method of the Explorers collection

- Use the *ActiveExplorer* method, which returns the currently Active Explorer in Outlook, if there is one:

  ```
  Dim expActive As Outlook.Explorer
  Set expActive = Application.ActiveExplorer()
  ```

- For a specific folder, use the *GetExplorer* method to return an instance of the Explorer for that folder:

  ```
  Dim expContacts as Outlook.Explorer
  Set expContacts = fdrContacts.GetExplorer
  ```

After you have an *Explorer* object, you can display that Explorer by calling the *Activate* method:

```
expContacts.Activate
```

Whereas the *Explorer* object is used to display a collection of items, an Inspector is used to display a specific item. You can think of an Inspector as the form you see when you look at a particular type of item. The ability to access Inspectors in code is useful if you want to create your own item and then allow your user to customize it. As with the Explorers, a collection of Inspectors is associated with the *Application* object. You can retrieve a specific Inspector in a number of ways:

- If an Inspector is open, a call to the *ActiveInspector* method returns that Inspector. You can access details of the item displayed in the Inspector by using the *CurrentItem* method:

  ```
  Dim insActive As Outlook.Inspector
  Dim itmCurrent As Object

  Set insActive = Application.ActiveInspector
  Set itmCurrent = insActive.CurrentItem
  ```

- You can access the Inspector associated with an item by using the *GetInspector* method:

  ```
  Dim insAppointments As Outlook.Inspector
  Dim itmAppointment As Outlook.AppointmentItem
  Set insAppointments = itmAppointment.GetInspector
  ```

After you have an *Inspector* object, you can display it and its associated item by calling the *Activate* method:

```
insAppointments.Activate
```

An alternative to creating an *Inspector* object is to create a new item and then call the item's *Display* method to display the item and thus the item's Inspector:

```
Dim fdrCalendar As Outlook.MAPIFolder
Dim itmAppointment As Outlook.AppointmentItem

Set fdrCalendar = _
  Application.GetNamespace("MAPI").GetDefaultFolder(olFolderCalendar)

Set itmAppointment = fdrCalendar.Items.Add

With itmAppointment
  .Subject = "Custom Appointment generated from Code"
  .Body = "Created in code and then displayed for you to edit"

  .Display
End With
```

To make the code that displays Explorers and Inspectors work, follow these steps:

1 Start Outlook and choose Tools, Macro, Visual Basic Editor (or press Alt+F11) to open the VBA Editor.

2 In the Project window, select Project1 and expand the tree until you see ThisOutlookSession.

3 Select ThisOutlookSession and press F7 to open the Code window.

4 Enter the following code in the Code window:

```
Sub ShowExplorers()
   Dim objApplication As Outlook.Application
   Dim objNameSpace As Outlook.NameSpace
   Dim fdrContacts As Outlook.MAPIFolder

   Dim expContacts As Outlook.Explorer

   Set objApplication = Application
   Set objNameSpace = objApplication.GetNamespace("MAPI")
   Set fdrContacts = _
      objNameSpace.GetDefaultFolder(olFolderContacts)
   Set expContacts = fdrContacts.GetExplorer

   expContacts.Activate

   Set objApplication = Nothing
   Set objNameSpace = Nothing
```

(continued)

Chapter 42

```
    Set fdrContacts = Nothing
    Set expContacts = Nothing

End Sub

Sub ShowContactsInspector()
    Dim itmContact As Outlook.ContactItem
    Dim insContact As Outlook.Inspector
    Dim fdrContacts As Outlook.MAPIFolder

    Set fdrContacts = _
      GetNamespace("MAPI").GetDefaultFolder(olFolderContacts)
    Set itmContact = fdrContacts.Items.Add

    With itmContact
      .FirstName = "Auto"
      .LastName = "Created"
      .Body = _
        "Created using the GetInspector method of an item"

    End With

    Set insContact = itmContact.GetInspector

    insContact.Activate

    Set itmContact = Nothing
    Set insContact = Nothing
    Set fdrContacts = Nothing

End Sub

Sub ShowAppointmentInspector()
    Dim fdrCalendar As Outlook.MAPIFolder
    Dim itmAppointment As Outlook.AppointmentItem

    Set fdrCalendar = _
      GetNamespace("MAPI").GetDefaultFolder(olFolderCalendar)

    Set itmAppointment = fdrCalendar.Items.Add

    With itmAppointment
      .Subject = "Custom Appointment generated from Code"
      .Body = _
        "Displayed by using the Display method of the item"

      .Display
    End With
```

```
        Set fdrCalendar = Nothing
        Set itmAppointment = Nothing

    End Sub
```

5 Go back to the main Outlook window and choose Tools, Macro, Macros.

6 Select one of the three new functions you have just built
(ThisOutlookSession.ShowExplorers, or ThisOutlookSession.ShowContactsInspector,
or ThisOutlookSession.ShowAppointmentInspector) and click the Run button.
ShowExplorers displays the Contacts Explorer; ShowContactsInspector displays the
Contacts Inspector, which allows you to add a new contact; and
ShowAppointmentInspector displays the Appointment Inspector, which allows you to
enter a new calendar appointment.

Troubleshooting

Your macro doesn't show up.

If you've written a macro in VBA, and it doesn't appear when you open the Macro
dialog box (press Alt+F8 from the main Outlook window), you can perform a number
of checks:

● Only Sub procedures appear in the Macro dialog box. Make sure that the procedures you've written begin with *Sub <name>* rather than *Function <name>*.

● The Sub procedures must be public. If your procedure is declared as *Private
  Sub <name>*, it will not appear.

● Only Sub procedures declared in either the *ThisOutlookSession* module or a
  code module can be seen in the Macro dialog box. Even public Sub procedures declared in classes cannot be seen, as you must instantiate the class in
  order to use them. The same is true of Sub procedures declared in forms.

Creating an Outlook Application with VBA

Now that you have seen how the VBA Editor works and how the Outlook object model
allows you to interact with Outlook, it's time to discuss how you can use this knowledge to build an application in Outlook. You can enhance Outlook in many ways by
developing a custom Outlook application. One way is to use the features of Outlook to
perform tasks that are not specifically Outlook tasks but can be implemented in an
Outlook interface. For example, you might enhance the Outlook calendar system so
that users could record information—in your company's time-entry system—about

Chapter 42

the work they perform. If users already record their appointments for the day using the calendar, you could add custom application code that examines this information and exports it as data for your time-entry system, which means that users wouldn't have to enter the information twice.

Another way to benefit from building custom Outlook applications is to automate tasks in Outlook that would otherwise require users to perform a significant amount of work. For example, users often have hundreds of contacts stored in their copy of Outlook. If they deal with large companies, they might have many contacts for a single company. If that company rebrands itself with a new name, all the contacts for the company would need to be updated.

The rest of this chapter looks at adding custom Outlook functionality to automate the process involved in the example just mentioned. The application consists of a number of elements:

- Outlook data-access functions to manipulate contact details
- Two custom forms for entering information and reviewing details
- A custom toolbar and button to give the user access to the functionality
- A printing function so that users can review the information

Accessing Outlook Data

One of the main reasons for adding custom VBA code to Outlook is to allow access to some of the data stored in Outlook. Using the objects described earlier, you can easily access data stored in Outlook and then utilize it in another form. In this example, you need to update the company name of all contacts from a specific company because the company has rebranded itself.

The following code has two strings that represent the original company name and its new name. For each item where the company name matches the *strFrom* variable, change the name to the string contained in *strTo* and call the *Save* method of the item:

```
Public Sub UpdateCompanyName(ByRef strFrom As String, ByRef strTo As
                             String)

   Dim fdrContacts As Outlook.MAPIFolder
   Dim objContactItem as Outlook.ContactItem

   'Create an instance of the Contacts folder.
   Set fdrContacts = _
     Application.GetNamespace("MAPI") _
       .GetDefaultFolder(olFolderContacts)

   'Loop through all contact items checking the CompanyName and
   'changing it if necessary.
```

```
    For Each objContactItem In fdrContacts.Items
      If objContactItem.CompanyName = strFrom Then
        objContactItem.CompanyName = strTo
        objContactItem.Save
      End If
    Next

End Sub
```

The preceding method looks at every contact item individually. This is not very efficient, however, especially if you have a large number of contacts. To improve efficiency, try using the following code in place of the *For…Each* loop. Rather than checking every item, this code uses the *Restrict* method of the *Items* collection of the folder object, which lets you apply a filter to the items before working with them. In this case, you should include only items in which the *CompanyName* property is equal to the value of the *strFrom* variable passed to the procedure. For a contacts list of 400 items, this reduces the processing time from 4 seconds to 1 second:

```
'Loop through the appropriate Contact items changing the Company
'Name.
For Each objContactItem In _
   fdrContacts.Items.Restrict("[CompanyName] = '" & strFrom & "'")
   objContactItem.CompanyName = strTo
   objContactItem.Save
Next
```

Adding a Form

The procedure in the preceding section converts one string value to another. One way to find out what these values are is to ask the user by adding a custom form to the application. To add a form to the project, right-click in the Project window and choose Insert, UserForm. The new form is displayed along with its properties and the Toolbox of controls. Add controls to the form until it looks like the form shown in Figure 42-3.

> For information about adding controls to a form, see "Adding and Arranging Controls," page 995.

Figure 42-3. Use this VBA form to tell the program the original and changed name of the company.

Chapter 42

8: Developing Custom
Forms and Applications

Add the following code to the form's Code window. It calls the *Load* function to instantiate the form and passes the *strFrom* and *strTo* variables to the *UpdateCompanyName* procedure:

```
Dim bContinue as Boolean

Public Function Load(strFrom As String, strTo As String) As Boolean
    'Initialize the cancel boolean.
    bContinue = True

    BuildComboList

    'Show the form.
    frmCompanyNameChange.Show

    If bContinue Then
        strFrom = cmbFrom
        strTo = txtTo
    End If

    Load = bContinue
End Function
```

This code maintains a *bContinue* Boolean value that stores information about whether to continue processing code when the form exits. It is also responsible for calling a function to fill the combo box with current company names and for displaying the form. The code to build the combo box list of existing companies follows:

```
Private Sub BuildComboList()
    Dim fdrContacts As Outlook.MAPIFolder
    Dim objContact As Outlook.ContactItem
    Dim strCompanyName As String

    'Create an instance of the Contacts folder.
    Set fdrContacts = _
        Application.GetNamespace("MAPI") _
        .GetDefaultFolder(olFolderContacts)

    fdrContacts.Items.Sort "[CompanyName]", False

    'Loop through the contact items extracting unique company names.
    For Each objContact In fdrContacts.Items
        If Trim(objContact.CompanyName) <> Trim(strCompanyName) Then
            cmbFrom.AddItem objContact.CompanyName
            strCompanyName = objContact.CompanyName
        End If

    Next
End Sub
```

This code uses the *Sort* method of the folder's *Items* collection to arrange the company names in order. This permits the function to loop through everything and discard duplicate values.

Finally, to allow you to execute the function you've just created from within Outlook, add the following procedure, which is associated with the toolbar button. This procedure calls the *Load* method of the *CompanyNameChange* form and then calls the *UpdateCompanyName* procedure to change the company name:

```
Public Sub ChangeCompany()
  Dim strFrom As String
  Dim strTo As String

  If frmCompanyNameChange.Load(strFrom, strTo) Then
    UpdateCompanyName strFrom, strTo
  End If

End Sub
```

Creating Custom Toolbar Buttons

Now that you've written some code, you need a way to let users access the functions. Some of this can be accomplished automatically by events that occur within Outlook, but often you need to add elements to the main Outlook interface to allow users to execute a piece of the code. A great way to do this is to add command bars and toolbar buttons to the Outlook application.

Two options are available for customizing command bars. The first is to add and change the command bars from the Outlook interface, as demonstrated in Chapter 23. This is a good technique if the changes you're making are to your own copy of Outlook and are permanent.

For information about modifying commands bars from the Outlook interface, see "Creating Custom Command Bars," page 614.

The second technique is to add the command bars using VBA. This gives you greater control over when the toolbars are added and removed and is particularly useful if you want a command bar or toolbar buttons to appear only at specific times. To add a command bar to the Outlook interface, you can use the following code:

```
Dim tlbCustomBar As CommandBar

Set tlbCustomBar = Application.ActiveExplorer.CommandBars _
  .Add(Name:="Custom Applications", Position:=msoBarTop, _
  Temporary:=True)

tlbCustomBar.Visible = True
```

This code declares an object of type *CommandBar* that will be used locally to perform commands on the command bar. To create a new command bar, you use the *Add* method of the *CommandBars* collection; this is a property of an Explorer object. To customize the new command bar, you can pass a number of parameters to the *Add* method. *Temporary:=True* tells the command bar to exist only as long as Outlook is open. If you were to close Outlook and reopen it again without rerunning this procedure, the command bar would no longer exist.

After you've added a command bar to the environment, you also need to add buttons. Follow three basic steps when adding buttons to a command bar:

1 Add the button to the command bar.

2 Associate the button with a function.

3 Format the button.

To add a button to the command bar, use the following code:

```
Dim btnNew As CommandBarButton
Set btnNew = tlbCustomBar.Controls.Add(Type:=msoControlButton)
```

You can associate a button with either the operation of any other button or menu in Outlook or with a custom function you've written in VBA. To associate the button with a built-in function, you must pass another parameter to the *Add* method:

```
Set btnNew = tlbCustomBar.Controls.Add(Type:=msoControlButton, _
    Id:=Application.CommandBars("Edit").Controls("Paste").ID)
```

This example adds a button to the custom toolbar that will perform the *Paste* function. The *ID* property takes an integer value, which in this case is retrieved from an existing control; you can achieve the same result by using *id:=22*.

If you want to allow the toolbar button to call a custom VBA procedure, you must set the *OnAction* property. Ensure that your function is declared as public and then enter the following code after creating the button to associate it with the named function:

```
Set btnNewCustom = _
    tlbCustomBar.Controls.Add(Type:=msoControlButton)
btnNewCustom.OnAction = "ChangeCompany"
```

This code associates the new button with a procedure called *ChangeCompany*.

Finally, when adding a button, you can format it by setting its style, giving it a caption, and perhaps giving it an icon. Buttons can have many styles that determine how they are displayed. To change the style, use the *Style* property:

```
btnNewCustom.Style = msoButtonIconAndCaption
```

To add a caption, use the *Caption* property. The *Caption* property specifies the text that is displayed on the button (if the chosen button style has a caption):

```
btnNewCustom.Caption = "Change Company Name"
```

Printing

As a final enhancement to the process of changing the company name for all contacts of that company, you can implement some print functionality. This will allow the users to view all the contacts that will be affected before the operation takes place and will give them the option to print a list of names, an individual contact detail, or all the contact details.

When using code to print information from Outlook, remember that all print methods use the default printer of the machine on which they are being performed. If there is no default printer or if the printer is unavailable, an error occurs. For this example, you can create the VBA form shown in Figure 42-4.

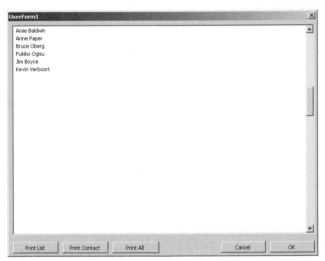

Figure 42-4. This form allows users to see and print details of all the contacts affected by the company name change.

The list box contains a list of the contact names affected by the company name change. The buttons allow the user to print the list (by printing the form), to print contact details for one contact, or to print all contacts. To print the form, you use the form's *PrintForm* method. Place the following code in the button click event handler. *Me* refers to the current form:

```
Me.PrintForm
```

Chapter 42

The following function prints contact information. This code takes a contact name as a string and then uses the *Find* method of the Contacts folder to return a *ContactItem* object. The *PrintOut* method of the item is used to print the object:

```
Private Sub PrintContact(strContactFullName As String)
  Dim fdrContacts As Outlook.MAPIFolder
  Dim objContactItem As Outlook.ContactItem
  Dim strFullName As String

  'Create an instance of the Contacts folder.
  Set fdrContacts = _
    Application.GetNamespace("MAPI") _
    .GetDefaultFolder(olFolderContacts)

  Set objContactItem = _
    fdrContacts.Items.Find _
    ("[FullName] = '" & strContactFullName & "'")

  objContactItem.PrintOut
End Sub
```

To complete this form, use the following code to fill the list box with relevant items:

```
Public Sub LoadList(strCompany As String)
  Dim fdrContacts As Outlook.MAPIFolder
  Dim objContactItem As Object

  Dim i As Integer
  Dim arrContacts() As String

  'Create an instance of the Contacts folder
  Set fdrContacts = _
    Application.GetNamespace("MAPI") _
      .GetDefaultFolder(olFolderContacts)

  For Each objContactItem In fdrContacts.Items _
    .Restrict("[CompanyName] = '" & strCompany & "'")
    If TypeOf objContactItem Is Outlook.ContactItem Then
      i = i + 1
      ReDim Preserve arrContacts(2, i)

    End If
    arrContacts(0, i - 1) = objContactItem.FullName
  Next

  lstAffectedContacts.Column = arrContacts
End Function
```

This function again creates a folder using the *Restrict* method, but this time it loops through the returned contacts and builds an array of contact names that can be used as the list for the list box.

Chapter 42

To add code that changes the names of contacts for a company, follow these steps:

1 Start Outlook and choose Tools, Macro, Visual Basic Editor (or press Alt+F11) to open the VBA Editor.

2 In the Projects window, select Project1.

3 Choose Insert, Module to add a custom module to the project.

4 Select the new module in the Project window, and then go to the Properties window. (Press F4 to show the window if it is not visible.)

5 Change the module name to *basChangeCompanyName*.

6 Press F7 to open the Code window for the module.

7 Enter the following code in the Code window:

```
Public Sub UpdateCompanyName(ByRef strFrom As String, ByRef
                             strTo As String)

   Dim fdrContacts As Outlook.MAPIFolder
   Dim objContactItem As Outlook.ContactItem

   'Create an instance of the Contacts folder
   Set fdrContacts = _
     Application.GetNamespace("MAPI") _
       .GetDefaultFolder(olFolderContacts)

   'Loop through the appropriate Contact items changing the
   'Company Name
   For Each objContactItem In _
     fdrContacts.Items.Restrict("[CompanyName] = '" & _
       strFrom & "'")
     objContactItem.CompanyName = strTo
     objContactItem.Save
   Next

End Sub

Public Function ChangeCompany()
   Dim strFrom As String
   Dim strTo As String

   If frmCompanyNameChange.Load(strFrom, strTo) Then
     UpdateCompanyName strFrom, strTo
   End If

End Function

Sub AddToolbar()
   Dim tlbCustomBar As CommandBar
```

(continued)

1057

```
Dim btnNew As CommandBarButton
Dim btnNewCustom As CommandBarButton

Set tlbCustomBar = Application.ActiveExplorer _
    .CommandBars _
    .Add(Name:="Custom Applications", _
    Position:=msoBarTop, Temporary:=True)

tlbCustomBar.Visible = True

Set btnNew = _
    tlbCustomBar.Controls.Add(Type:=msoControlButton)

Set btnNew = _
    tlbCustomBar.Controls.Add(Type:=msoControlButton, _
        ID:=ActiveExplorer.CommandBars("Edit") _
        .Controls("Paste").ID)

Set btnNewCustom = _
    tlbCustomBar.Controls.Add(Type:=msoControlButton)

btnNewCustom.OnAction = "ChangeCompany"
btnNewCustom.Style = msoButtonIconAndCaption
btnNewCustom.Caption = "Change Company Name"

End Sub
```

8 Add a custom form to the project by choosing Insert, UserForm.

9 Drag four label controls, a combo box control, a text box control, and two buttons to this form. Refer back to Figure 42-3 to see how to arrange them and change the captions for these controls as appropriate. Name them as follows:

  ■ Name the combo box control *cmbFrom*.

  ■ Name the text box control *txtTo*.

  ■ Name the OK button *cmdOK*.

  ■ Name the Cancel button *cmdCancel*.

10 Name the form *frmCompanyNameChange*.

11 Press F7 to switch from Form view to Code view, and then enter the following code in the Code window:

```
Dim bContinue As Boolean
Public Function Load(strFrom As String,
                        strTo As String) As Boolean
    'Initialize the cancel boolean.
    bContinue = True
```

```vba
   BuildComboList

   'Show the form
   frmCompanyNameChange.Show

   If bContinue Then
     strFrom = cmbFrom
     strTo = txtTo
   End If

   Load = bContinue
End Function

Private Sub BuildComboList()
   Dim fdrContacts As Outlook.MAPIFolder
   Dim objContact As Outlook.Object
   Dim strCompanyName As String

   'Create an instance of the Contacts folder.
   Set fdrContacts = _
     Application.GetNamespace("MAPI") _
       .GetDefaultFolder(olFolderContacts)

   fdrContacts.Items.Sort "[CompanyName]", False

   'Loop through the contact items extracting unique company
   'names
   For Each objContact In fdrContacts.Items
     If TypeOf objContact Is Outlook.ContactItem Then
       If Trim(objContact.CompanyName) <> Trim(strCompanyName) _
       Then
         cmbFrom.AddItem objContact.CompanyName
         strCompanyName = objContact.CompanyName
       End If
     End If

   Next
End Sub

Private Sub cmdCancel_Click()
   bContinue = False
   Unload Me
End Sub

Private Sub cmdOK_Click()
   bContinue = True
   Unload Me
End Sub
```

12 Add a second custom form to the project by choosing Insert, UserForm.

13 Drag a list box control and five buttons to this form. Arrange them and change their captions so that they look like the form shown in Figure 42-4. Name them as follows:

- Name the list box control *lstAffectedContacts*.

- Name the Print List button *cmdPrintList*.

- Name the Print Contact button *cmdPrintContact*

- Name the Print All button *cmdPrintAll*.

- Name the Cancel button *cmdCancel*.

- Name the OK button *cmdOK*.

14 Name the form *frmPrintContacts*.

15 Press F7 to switch from Form view to Code view, and then enter the following code in the Code window:

```
Private Sub cmdCancel_Click()
   Unload Me
End Sub

Private Sub cmdOK_Click()
   Unload Me
End Sub

Private Sub cmdPrintAll_Click()
   Dim i As Integer

   For i = 0 To lstAffectedContacts.ListCount - 1
      PrintContact lstAffectedContacts.List(i)

   Next i

End Sub

Private Sub cmdPrintContact_Click()
   PrintContact lstAffectedContacts
End Sub

Private Sub cmdPrintList_Click()
   Me.PrintForm
End Sub

Private Sub PrintContact(strContactFullName As String)
   Dim fdrContacts As Outlook.MAPIFolder
   Dim objContactItem As Outlook.ContactItem
   Dim strFullName As String
```

```
   'Create an instance of the Contacts folder.
   Set fdrContacts = _
     Application.GetNamespace("MAPI") _
       .GetDefaultFolder(olFolderContacts)

   Set objContactItem = _
     fdrContacts.Items.Find("[FullName] = '" & _
       strContactFullName & "'")

   objContactItem.PrintOut

   Set objContactItem = Nothing

End Sub

Public Sub LoadList(strCompany As String)
   Dim fdrContacts As Outlook.MAPIFolder
   Dim objContactItem As Outlook.ContactItem

   Dim i As Integer
   Dim arrContacts() As String

   'Create an instance of the Contacts folder
   Set fdrContacts = _
     Application.GetNamespace("MAPI") _
       .GetDefaultFolder(olFolderContacts)

   For Each objContactItem In fdrContacts.Items _
     .Restrict("[CompanyName] = '" & strCompany & "'")
     If TypeOf objContactItem Is Outlook.ContactItem Then
       i = i + 1
       ReDim Preserve arrContacts(2, i)

       arrContacts(0, i - 1) = objContactItem.FullName
     End If
   Next

   lstAffectedContacts.Column = arrContacts
End Sub

Public Function Load(strCompany As String)

   LoadList strCompany

   'Show the form.
   frmPrintContacts.Show

End Function
```

16 Add another button to the *frmCompanyNameChange* form with the caption *View Contacts* and the name *cmdViewContacts*. You use this button to open the second form.

17 Double-click the View Contents button to open the Code window, and enter the following code:

```
Private Sub cmdViewContacts_Click()
   frmPrintContacts.Load cmbFrom
End Sub
```

18 Go back to the main Outlook window and choose Tools, Macro, Macros. Select AddToolbar from the list and click the Run button. Two new toolbar buttons should now be visible in Outlook. One has a Paste icon and the other is labeled Change Company Name.

19 Click the second button, and your first form is displayed.

20 Select a company in the box, type the new company name in the text box, and then click OK. The company names of all contacts are changed.

Chapter 43

Integrating Outlook and Other Applications with VBA

Every application in both the immediate suite of Microsoft Office tools and the extended family of Office applications uses Microsoft Visual Basic for Applications (VBA) as its macro and programming language. This greatly simplifies the task of writing code to manipulate more than one Office application. After you understand the object models of the individual applications, you can write code to automate any of them from your application of choice.

> **note** The extended Office family includes products such as Microsoft Visio, Microsoft Project, and Microsoft MapPoint 2001. They are all VBA-enabled applications, which makes them ideal for integrating into Office solutions.

This chapter picks up where Chapter 42 left off. That chapter, "Using Visual Basic for Applications (VBA) in Outlook," introduced you to VBA, its essential components, and some simple procedures. Now this chapter looks at some basic ways you can use VBA to make Office applications interact. After you understand these fundamentals, you can extend your knowledge by learning each application's object model and finding new ways to make the products work in harmony.

> **on the CD**   **note** You'll find the code used to create the VBA applications in this chapter in the Author Extras section of the companion CD.

8: Developing Custom
Forms and Applications

Starting Other Office Applications

Although Microsoft Outlook might be your primary Office application, you probably need to use a variety of Office programs. For example, you might work with tasks in Outlook and then review the task information in a Microsoft Word document or a Microsoft Excel spreadsheet. To do this easily, you need to be able to launch these other programs from Outlook.

The task of opening another Office application is simple because the applications share a common language and the Office object model. To make the process easier, you tell the VBA environment about the application you intend to use by adding a reference to that application. Outlook then gathers information about all the possible operations of the application you referenced and can then display the possible operations as you work in the environment, as if this were part of the native Outlook object model. This process is known as *early binding*.

To add a reference to Excel, for example, follow these steps:

1 Start Outlook and choose Tools, Macro, Visual Basic Editor (or press Alt+F11) to open the VBA Editor.

2 In the VBA Editor, choose Tools, References to open the References dialog box (see Figure 43-1).

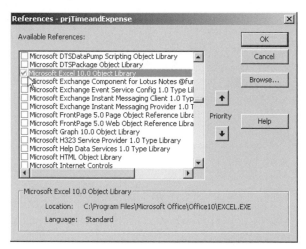

Figure 43-1. In this dialog box, you can add a reference to the Excel Object Library.

3 Click the entry for Microsoft Excel 10.0 Object Library.

4 Click OK.

Now that you've added a reference to the Excel object model, you can open an instance of Excel and any specific worksheet in it. The following code opens a specific Excel file:

```
Dim objExpenseEntry As Excel.Application

Set objExpenseEntry = New Excel.Application

objExpenseEntry.Visible = False
objExpenseEntry.Workbooks.Open "c:\temp\OutlookBook.xls"
objExpenseEntry.Visible = True
```

Because you added a reference to Excel, you can declare and instantiate the *Excel.Application* object just as you can any other object in Outlook. After you have an instance of Excel, you use the *Visible* and *Open* methods to open an Excel spreadsheet and display the Excel application.

You can use the same approach to open any other Office application. In general, do the following for the application you want to use:

1 Add a reference to the application.

2 Create an instance of the application in your code.

3 Manipulate the application using its standard object model.

4 Use the *Visible* property of the object to make the application visible.

Instantiation vs. Assignment

Instantiating refers to the process of creating an instance of an object. When you click the Word icon on your desktop, for example, you are instantiating a copy of Word that you can then use. The same is true when you use the following code from VBA:

```
Dim objX as Word.Application
```

This code says that at some time you'll use a *Word.Application* object and *objX* will be the placeholder for it. In the next line, you instantiate that object (create a new instance of Word):

```
Set objX = New Word.Application
```

This process is different from an *assignment*. For objects, an assignment takes a new variable you've created and points it at an already existing instance of an object rather than creating a completely new instance. The following code declares a placeholder for an Outlook folder type object:

```
Dim objY as Outlook.MAPIFolder
```

The next line indicates that you have a placeholder for a folder type object and want it to point to the Tasks folder:

```
Set objY = Application.GetNamespace("MAPI").GetDefaultFolder(olFolderTasks)
```

Everything you do with this folder now affects the Tasks folder in Outlook.

To add code that opens Excel from within Outlook, follow these steps:

1 Start Outlook and choose Tools, Macro, Visual Basic Editor (or press Alt+F11) to open the VBA Editor.

2 In the Project window, select Project1.

3 Expand the tree until you see the heading ThisOutlookSession and then select it.

4 Press F7 to open the Code window.

5 Choose Tools, References to open the References dialog box.

6 Scroll through the list in the dialog box until you find an entry for Microsoft Excel 10.0 Object Library and select it. Close the dialog box.

7 Enter the following code in the Code window:

```
Public Sub OpenExcel()
   Dim objExcel As Excel.Application
   Set objExcel = New Excel.Application
   With objExcel
     .Visible = False
     .Workbooks.Open "c:\temp\OutlookBook.xls"
     .Visible = True
   End With
End Sub
```

8 Create an Excel file named OutlookBook.xls and place it in the C:\Temp directory.

9 Return to the main Outlook window and choose Tools, Macro, Macros.

10 Select ThisOutlookSession.OpenExcel and click Run. The new Excel spreadsheet that you created opens in Excel.

InsideOut

To find out what you can do with an object for which you've created a reference, you can use a tool called the Object Browser, which can be opened from the View menu or by pressing F2 in the VBA Editor. With this tool, you can view either all the referenced libraries or a specific one. You can also look at all the declared properties, methods, events, and constants that are available for use. You can search on a keyword to see whether a property or function with that name is supported and to see how it's defined. For more information on using the Object Browser, consult the Help files.

Exchanging Data with Excel

Now that Excel is open, along with the workbook OutlookBook.xls, it's easy to exchange data with the workbook. For example, in Chapter 42, you created an application that changed the company name for all contacts in a specific company (see "Creating an Outlook Application with VBA," page 1049). Here, you can add a routine that saves the contact details as an Excel spreadsheet that you can then distribute to others in the company. The following procedure performs this routine:

```
Public Sub ExportContacts(strCompany As String)
  Dim fdrContacts As Outlook.MAPIFolder
  Dim fdrContactsByCompany As Outlook.Items
  Dim objExcel As Excel.Application
  Dim objWorkbook As Excel.Workbook
  Dim objWorksheet As Excel.Worksheet

  Dim itmContacts As Outlook.ContactItem
  Dim iCol As Integer
  Dim iRow As Integer

  Set fdrContacts = _
    Application.GetNamespace("MAPI") _
    .GetDefaultFolder(olFolderContacts)

  Set fdrContactsByCompany = _
    fdrContacts.Items.Restrict("[CompanyName] = '" & _
    strCompany & "'")

  Set objExcel = New Excel.Application
  Set objWorkbook = objExcel.Workbooks.Add
  Set objWorksheet = objWorkbook.Worksheets.Add
  objWorksheet.Name = "Contacts for " & strCompany

  Set itmContacts = fdrContactsByCompany.GetFirst

  If itmContacts Is Nothing Then
    MsgBox "There are no contacts for that company. " & _
          "Please enter a different company name."
    Exit Sub
  End If

  iRow = 1
  For iCol = 0 To itmContacts.ItemProperties.Count - 1
    objWorksheet.Cells(iRow, iCol + 1) = _
    itmContacts.ItemProperties(iCol).Name
  Next iCol

  iRow = iRow + 1
```

(continued)

```
For Each itmContacts In fdrContacts.Items _
  .Restrict("[CompanyName] = '" & strCompany & "'")

  For iCol = 0 To itmContacts.ItemProperties.Count - 1
    Debug.Print itmContacts.ItemProperties(iCol).Name
    If itmContacts.ItemProperties(iCol).Type = olText Then
      objWorksheet.Cells(iRow, iCol + 1) = _
        itmContacts.ItemProperties(iCol).Value
    End If
  Next iCol
  iRow = iRow + 1
Next

objExcel.Visible = True

End Sub
```

You should be familiar with a large portion of this code from Chapter 42. Here's the part of the code that opens a new copy of Excel, adds a workbook and worksheet, and names the worksheet after the company name used as the filter:

```
Set objExcel = New Excel.Application
Set objWorkbook = objExcel.Workbooks.Add
Set objWorksheet = objWorkbook.Worksheets.Add
objWorksheet.Name = "Contacts for " & strCompany
```

After an *Excel* object is available, it's time to start adding data to it. Begin by adding a row that will be the header for the columns of data. To do this, you use a collection associated with a contact item that holds all the different properties associated with that item. Each of these properties has a name, so it's a simple task to loop through them, writing the name value to cells in the first row of the Excel worksheet using the worksheet object's *Cells* method. This method allows you to specify a row and column location for the cell to access:

```
iRow = 1
For iCol = 0 To itmContacts.ItemProperties.Count - 1
  objWorksheet.Cells(iRow, iCol + 1) = _
    itmContacts.ItemProperties(iCol).Name
Next iCol
```

After all the headings have been added, it's time to add data to the worksheet. You do this using two nested loops. The outside loop steps through each contact item that matches the company name value. The inner loop then steps through each property of the specific item; if it's a text type property, it's saved in the appropriate cell in the worksheet:

```
iRow = iRow + 1
For Each itmContacts In fdrContacts.Items _
  .Restrict("[CompanyName] = '" & strCompany & "'")
```

```
    For iCol = 0 To itmContacts.ItemProperties.Count - 1
      If itmContacts.ItemProperties(iCol).Type = olText Then
        objWorksheet.Cells(iRow, iCol + 1) = _
          itmContacts.ItemProperties(iCol).Value
      End If
    Next iCol
    iRow = iRow + 1
  Next
```

The *If itmContacts.ItemProperties(iCol).Type = olText Then* test is performed to ensure that any data an Excel cell can't store, such as data of type object, is not written to Excel. To guard against errors, check each property before writing it to Excel to make sure it's a valid type. Another way to handle this issue would be to specify exactly which properties you want to write to Excel and then, rather than looping through every property of the item object, just write lines of code to export each selected property.

To add code that opens Excel and exports contacts from Outlook into an Excel workbook, follow these steps:

1 Start Outlook and choose Tools, Macro, Visual Basic Editor (or press Alt+F11) to open the VBA Editor.

2 In the Project window, select Project1.

3 Expand the tree to one level, expand the Modules branch, and then select the *basChangeCompanyName* module (which you built in Chapter 42).

4 Press F7 to open the Code window.

5 Enter the following code in the Code window:

```
Public Sub ExportContacts(strCompany As String)
  Dim fdrContacts As Outlook.MAPIFolder
  Dim fdrContactsByCompany As Outlook.Items
  Dim objExcel As Excel.Application
  Dim objWorkbook As Excel.Workbook
  Dim objWorksheet As Excel.Worksheet

  Dim itmContacts As Outlook.ContactItem
  Dim iCol As Integer
  Dim iRow As Integer

  Set fdrContacts = _
    GetNamespace("MAPI").GetDefaultFolder(olFolderContacts)

  Set fdrContactsByCompany = _
    fdrContacts.Items.Restrict("[CompanyName] = '" & _
    strCompany & "'")
```

(continued)

```
Set objExcel = New Excel.Application
Set objWorkbook = objExcel.Workbooks.Add
Set objWorksheet = objWorkbook.Worksheets.Add
objWorksheet.Name = "Contacts for " & strCompany

Set itmContacts = fdrContactsByCompany.GetFirst

If itmContacts Is Nothing Then
   MsgBox "There are no contacts for that company. " & _
          "Please enter a different company name."
   Exit Sub
End If

iRow = 1
For iCol = 0 To itmContacts.ItemProperties.Count - 1
   objWorksheet.Cells(iRow, iCol + 1) = _
     itmContacts.ItemProperties(iCol).Name
Next iCol

iRow = iRow + 1
For Each itmContacts In _
   fdrContacts.Items.Restrict("[CompanyName] = '" & _
   strCompany & "'")

   For iCol = 0 To itmContacts.ItemProperties.Count - 1
      Debug.Print itmContacts.ItemProperties(iCol).Name

      If itmContacts.ItemProperties(iCol).Type = olText Then
         objWorksheet.Cells(iRow, iCol + 1) = _
            itmContacts.ItemProperties(iCol).Value
      End If
   Next iCol
   iRow = iRow + 1
Next

objExcel.Visible = True

End Sub
```

6 Open the *frmCompanyNameChange* form (which you created in Chapter 42) and add a button to it. Give the button the caption *Excel* and the name *cmdExcel*.

7 Press F7 to open the Code window and enter this code:

```
Private Sub cmdExcel_Click()
   ExportContacts cmbFrom
End Sub
```

8 Return to Outlook and choose Tools, Macro, Macros. Select AddToolbar from the list and click Run. Click the Change Company Name button (which you created in Chapter 42). The form appears with the new Excel button.

9 Select a company in the combo box and click the Excel button. Excel opens, displaying a list of all the contacts for the selected company.

Exchanging Data with Word

A great way to use Outlook, Word, and VBA is to send a letter to a contact while viewing that contact's information. You can accomplish this by using some VBA code to automate Word.

Before you start, add a reference to the Word object model the same way you did for Excel on page 1064, except that this time you select Microsoft Word 10.0 Object Library in the list. This gives you access to all the objects in Word that are available using VBA.

The following procedure uses Word to create a letter document for each of the currently selected contacts:

```
Private Sub SendLetterToContact()
  Dim itmContact As Outlook.ContactItem
  Dim selContacts As Selection
  Dim objWord As Word.Application
  Dim objLetter As Word.Document
  Dim secNewArea As Word.Section

  Set selContacts = Application.ActiveExplorer.Selection

  If selContacts.Count > 0 Then
    Set objWord = New Word.Application

    For Each itmContact In selContacts
      Set objLetter = objWord.Documents.Add

      objLetter.Select

      objWord.Selection.InsertAfter itmContact.FullName
      objLetter.Paragraphs.Add

      If itmContact.CompanyName <> "" Then
        objWord.Selection.InsertAfter itmContact.CompanyName
        objLetter.Paragraphs.Add
      End If

      objWord.Selection.InsertAfter itmContact.BusinessAddress
```

(continued)

```
objWord.Selection.Paragraphs.Alignment = wdAlignParagraphRight

With objLetter
  .Paragraphs.Add
  .Paragraphs.Add
End With

With objWord.Selection
  .Collapse wdCollapseEnd
  .InsertAfter "Dear " & itmContact.FullName
  .Paragraphs.Alignment = wdAlignParagraphLeft
End With

Set secNewArea = objLetter.Sections.Add(Start:=wdSectionContinuous)

With secNewArea.Range
  .Paragraphs.Add
  .Paragraphs.Add
  .InsertAfter "<Insert text of letter here>"
  .Paragraphs.Add
  .Paragraphs.Add
End With

Set secNewArea = objLetter.Sections.Add(Start:=wdSectionContinuous)

With secNewArea.Range
  .Paragraphs.Add
  .InsertAfter "Regards"
  .Paragraphs.Add
  .Paragraphs.Add
  .InsertAfter Application.GetNamespace("MAPI").CurrentUser
End With

    Next
    objWord.Visible = True

  End If
End Sub
```

The first section of code declares all the variables and objects you'll use. Notice the use of both Outlook and Word objects:

```
Dim itmContact As Outlook.ContactItem
Dim selContacts As Selection
Dim objWord As Word.Application
Dim objLetter As Word.Document
Dim secNewArea As Word.Section
```

The second section investigates Outlook to access the selected items. The program creates a *Selection* object from the currently selected items; as long as at least one item is selected, an instance of Word is created using the *New Word.Application* call. The program then loops through each item in the *Selection* collection and displays Word by setting the *Word.Application* object's *Visible* property to True:

```
Set selContacts = Application.ActiveExplorer.Selection

If selContacts.Count > 0 Then
  Set objWord = New Word.Application

  For Each itmContact In selContacts
  'Construct Letter Here
  ⋮
  Next
  objWord.Visible = True
End If
```

The heart of the letter construction is performed in the loop, where the documents are created and populated. The program starts by creating a new document in Word using the *Add* method of the document's collection:

```
    Set objLetter = objWord.Documents.Add
```

After this, you can start inserting data into the newly created document. You use the *InsertAfter* method of the *Word.Selection* object, which adds lines of text, and the *Add* method of the *Paragraphs* object, which adds new paragraphs (blank lines) to the document:

```
    objLetter.Select
    objWord.Selection.InsertAfter itmContact.FullName
    objLetter.Paragraphs.Add

    If itmContact.CompanyName <> "" Then
      objWord.Selection.InsertAfter itmContact.CompanyName
      objLetter.Paragraphs.Add
    End If

    objWord.Selection.InsertAfter itmContact.BusinessAddress
    objWord.Selection.Paragraphs.Alignment = wdAlignParagraphRight

    With objLetter
      .Paragraphs.Add
      .Paragraphs.Add
    End With

    With objWord.Selection
      .Collapse wdCollapseEnd
      .InsertAfter "Dear " & itmContact.FullName
      .Paragraphs.Alignment = wdAlignParagraphLeft
    End With
```

(continued)

```
Set secNewArea = objLetter.Sections.Add(Start:=wdSectionContinuous)

With secNewArea.Range
  .Paragraphs.Add
  .Paragraphs.Add
  .InsertAfter "<Insert text of letter here>"
  .Paragraphs.Add
  .Paragraphs.Add
End With

Set secNewArea = objLetter.Sections.Add(Start:=wdSectionContinuous)
```

To finish the letter, you need to add a signoff. The program extracts the name of the current user of Outlook and inserts this in the letter:

```
With secNewArea.Range
  .Paragraphs.Add
  .InsertAfter "Regards"
  .Paragraphs.Add
  .Paragraphs.Add
  .InsertAfter Application.GetNamespace("MAPI").CurrentUser
End With
```

When you've finished, the final letter looks similar to the one shown in Figure 43-2.

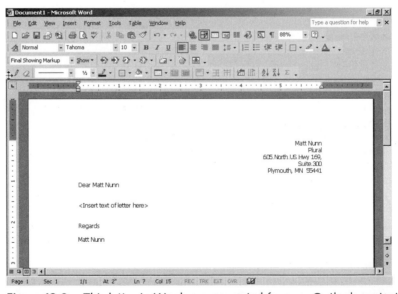

Figure 43-2. This letter in Word was generated from an Outlook contact item.

This solution leaves Word visible for the user to work with. It would be simple to completely automate the letter production by inserting any text for the body of the letter at this time and then saving it automatically:

```
objLetter.SaveAs "c:\temp\" & itmContact.FullName & ".doc"
objLetter.Close
```

To add code that prepares a set of letters for selected contacts, follow these steps:

1 Start Outlook and choose Tools, Macro, Visual Basic Editor (or press Alt+F11) to open the VBA Editor.

2 In the Project window, select Project1.

3 Choose Insert, Module to add a custom module to the project.

4 In the Project window, select the new module.

5 Go to the Properties window (press F4 to display the window if it's not visible) and change the module name to *basExternalApps*.

6 Press F7 to open the Code window for the module.

7 Choose Tools, References to open a dialog box displaying a list of items.

8 Scroll through this list until you find the entry for Microsoft Word 10.0 Object Library and then select it. Close the dialog box.

9 Enter the following code in the Code window:

```
Sub AddToolbar2()
  Dim tlbCustomBar As CommandBar
  Dim btnNewCustom As CommandBarButton

  Set tlbCustomBar = Application.ActiveExplorer.CommandBars _
    .Add(Name:="Custom External Applications", _
        Position:=msoBarTop, Temporary:=True)
  tlbCustomBar.Visible = True

  Set btnNewCustom = _
    tlbCustomBar.Controls.Add(Type:=msoControlButton)

  btnNewCustom.OnAction = "SendLetterToContact"
  btnNewCustom.Style = msoButtonIconAndCaption
  btnNewCustom.Caption = "Send Letter to Contact"

End Sub

Public Function SendLetterToContact()
  Dim itmContact As Outlook.ContactItem
  Dim selContacts As Selection
  Dim objWord As Word.Application
  Dim objLetter As Word.Document
  Dim secNewArea As Word.Section
```

(continued)

1075

```
Set selContacts = Application.ActiveExplorer.Selection

If selContacts.Count > 0 Then
  Set objWord = New Word.Application

  For Each itmContact In selContacts
    Set objLetter = objWord.Documents.Add

    objLetter.Select

    objWord.Selection.InsertAfter itmContact.FullName
    objLetter.Paragraphs.Add

    If itmContact.CompanyName <> "" Then
      objWord.Selection.InsertAfter itmContact.CompanyName
      objLetter.Paragraphs.Add
    End If

    objWord.Selection.InsertAfter itmContact.BusinessAddress

    objWord.Selection.Paragraphs.Alignment = _
      wdAlignParagraphRight

    With objLetter
      .Paragraphs.Add
      .Paragraphs.Add
    End With

    With objWord.Selection
      .Collapse wdCollapseEnd
      .InsertAfter "Dear " & itmContact.FullName
      .Paragraphs.Alignment = wdAlignParagraphLeft
    End With

    Set secNewArea = _
      objLetter.Sections.Add(Start:=wdSectionContinuous)

    With secNewArea.Range
      .Paragraphs.Add
      .Paragraphs.Add
      .InsertAfter "<Insert text of letter here>"
      .Paragraphs.Add
      .Paragraphs.Add
    End With

    Set secNewArea = _
      objLetter.Sections.Add(Start:=wdSectionContinuous)
```

```
      With secNewArea.Range
        .Paragraphs.Add
        .InsertAfter "Regards"
        .Paragraphs.Add
        .Paragraphs.Add
        .InsertAfter Application.GetNamespace("MAPI").CurrentUser
      End With

    Next
    objWord.Visible = True

  End If
End Function
```

10 Go back to the main Outlook window and choose Tools, Macro, Macros.

11 Select AddToolbar2 in the list, and then click the Run button. A new custom button with the name Send Letter To Contact is added to the toolbar.

12 Switch to the Contacts folder in Outlook and select one or more contacts.

13 Click the button labeled Send Letter To Contact to display one Word document for each selected contact.

---

tip **Press F1 if you need help**

If you get stuck while programming in VBA, your first course of action should be to press the F1 key to launch the context-sensitive Help feature. The Help window will provide information about whatever you're currently working with, be it a keyword, an object property, or a window in the environment.

Exchanging Data with Access

Now that you've seen how to manipulate Word and Excel from Outlook using instances of the *Word.Application* or *Excel.Application* object, it's time to look at how you can bring data into Outlook from Microsoft Access. Suppose that you have an Access application that holds details of projects and associated tasks and that you need to import the task data from Access and turn it into Outlook tasks. To accomplish this, you could use the following code:

```
Public Sub ImportTasksFromAccess()

  Dim fdrTasks As Outlook.MAPIFolder
  Dim itmTask As Outlook.TaskItem
```

(continued)

```
Dim rsTasks As ADODB.Recordset
Dim conTasks As ADODB.Connection
Dim strConnectionString As String

'Set the connection string and open the connection
Set conTasks = New ADODB.Connection
strConnectionString = "Provider=Microsoft.Jet.OLEDB.4.0;" & _
                      "Data Source=C:\Temp\OutlookBook.mdb;" & _
                      "Persist Security Info=False"
conTasks.Open strConnectionString

'Attempt to retrieve task records from the database for the given job
Set rsTasks = New ADODB.Recordset
rsTasks.Open "select * from Tasks" , _
  conTasks, adOpenStatic, adLockReadOnly

Set fdrTasks = _
  Application.GetNamespace("MAPI").GetDefaultFolder(olFolderTasks)

'Add tasks
Do While Not rsTasks.EOF
  Set itmTask = fdrTasks.Items.Add

  With itmTask
    'Add custom properties to the task item
    .UserProperties.Add "TaskID", olText

    'Populate the task properties
    .UserProperties("TaskID") = rsTasks.Fields("TaskID")
    .Subject = rsTasks.Fields("Name")
    .Body = IIf(IsNull(rsTasks.Fields("Description")), "", _
                rsTasks.Fields("Description"))
    .PercentComplete = rsTasks.Fields("PercentComplete")
    .Save

  End With

  rsTasks.MoveNext
  Loop
End Sub
```

This procedure uses ADO (ActiveX Data Objects), which provides a simple way to read
data in a Microsoft data store such as Access or SQL Server. The code reads the Access
database and then stores all retrieved task records as Outlook tasks. ADO is an efficient
way to extract data from either an Access database or a more complex database system
such as SQL Server. To change this procedure to work with SQL Server or a different
Access database, you need to alter only the *Connection* string.

For every record in the ADO recordset, the *Items.Add* method creates a new task item in the Tasks folder. The basic properties of each task are then assigned values from the record.

In this example, you add a *UserProperty* to the *Task* object for storing the ID value of the Task record. You use a *UserProperty* to access a custom field. To add a *UserProperty* to an item, you use the *Add* method of the *UserProperties* collection associated with the item, giving the property a name and a type:

```
.UserProperties.Add "TaskID", olText
```

You can then assign data to it by referencing the specific property as you would any other collection item:

```
.UserProperties("TaskID") = rsTasks.Fields("TaskID")
```

To add code that opens Access and imports information, follow these steps:

1 Copy the OutlookBook.mdb file (from the CD accompanying this book) to C:\Temp.

2 Start Outlook and choose Tools, Macro, Visual Basic Editor (or press Alt+F11) to open the VBA Editor.

3 In the Project window, select Project1.

4 Select the *basExternalApps* module, which you created in the preceding section.

5 Press F7 to open the Code window for the module.

6 Choose Tools, References to open the References dialog box.

7 Scroll through the list until you find Microsoft ActiveX Data Objects 2.6 and then select it. (If 2.6 is not available, select the largest number in the list.) Close the dialog box.

8 Enter the following code in the Code window:

```
Public Sub ImportTasksFromAccess()

    Dim fdrTasks As Outlook.MAPIFolder
    Dim itmTask As Outlook.TaskItem

    Dim rsTasks As ADODB.Recordset
    Dim conTasks As ADODB.Connection
    Dim strConnectionString As String
```

(continued)

1079

```
'Set the connection string and open the connection
Set conTasks = New ADODB.Connection
strConnectionString = "Provider=Microsoft.Jet.OLEDB.4.0;" & _
                      "Data Source=C:\Temp\OutlookBook.mdb;" & _
                      "Persist Security Info=False"
conTasks.Open strConnectionString

'Attempt to retrieve task records from the database
'for the given job
Set rsTasks = New ADODB.Recordset
rsTasks.Open "select * from Tasks" , _
  conTasks, adOpenStatic, adLockReadOnly

Set fdrTasks = _
  GetNamespace("MAPI").GetDefaultFolder(olFolderTasks)

'Add tasks
Do While Not rsTasks.EOF
  Set itmTask = fdrTasks.Items.Add

  With itmTask
    'Add custom properties to the task item
    .UserProperties.Add "TaskID", olText

    'Populate the task properties
    .UserProperties("TaskID") = rsTasks.Fields("TaskID")
    .Subject = rsTasks.Fields("Name")
    .Body = IIf(IsNull(rsTasks.Fields("Description")), "", _
                rsTasks.Fields("Description"))
    .PercentComplete = rsTasks.Fields("PercentComplete")
    .Save

  End With

  rsTasks.MoveNext
  Loop
End Sub
```

9 Locate the *AddToolbar2* procedure and add the following code to the end of it:

```
Set btnNewCustom = _
  tlbCustomBar.Controls.Add(Type:=msoControlButton)

btnNewCustom.OnAction = "ImportTasksFromAccess"
btnNewCustom.Style = msoButtonIconAndCaption
btnNewCustom.Caption = "Import Tasks From Access"
```

10   Go back to the main Outlook window and choose Tools, Macro, Macros.

11   In the list, select AddToolbar2, and then click the Run button. A new custom menu button with the name Import Tasks From Access is added to the toolbar.

12   Switch to the Tasks folder in Outlook and click the Import Tasks From Access button. Tasks are created within Outlook that represent the tasks stored in the OutlookBook.mdb database.

InsideOut

When you use ADO, it's important to ensure that all users have the same version of ADO installed on their computers. If the versions differ, you could get unpredictable results from any code written using ADO.

To check the ADO version from code, you can use the *Version* property of the ADO *Connection* object. Declare an ADO *Connection* object, as shown here:

```
Dim ado as New ADODB.Connection
```

and then investigate the *Version* property:

```
ado.Version
```

You can now display a message asking users to update if they're running a different version.

Automating Outlook from Other Applications

You've seen how to integrate other applications by writing code in Outlook to manipulate them. It's just as easy to add code to other VBA-enabled applications to automate Outlook functionality. A common task in an external application is to use Outlook to send an e-mail message. In the following example, Outlook is automated from Excel to send an e-mail message that includes the current workbook:

```
Sub SendCurrentWorkbook(streMail As String)

    Dim objOutlook As Outlook.Application
    Dim itmNewEMail As Outlook.MailItem
    Dim itmNewTask As Outlook.TaskItem

    Set objOutlook = New Outlook.Application

    Set itmNewEMail = objOutlook.CreateItem(olMailItem)
```

(continued)

1081

```
With itmNewEMail
  .To = streMail
  If ActiveWorkbook.Path = "" Then
    ActiveWorkbook.Save
  End If
  .Attachments.Add ActiveWorkbook.Path & "\" & ActiveWorkbook.Name
  .send
End With

End Sub
```

This function shows how to automate Outlook to send e-mail messages by creating an instance of Outlook, as you did with Word and Excel, using the *Outlook.Application* object. After this object exists, you work just as if you were inside Outlook, creating a mail item and adding an attachment to it. To send the current workbook for review, use the *SendForReview* method:

```
ActiveWorkbook.SendForReview stremail, , False, True
```

Troubleshooting

When an external application tries to access Outlook, access is blocked.

When an external application tries to automate e-mail within Outlook, the new security features of Outlook step in to block the access. You'll receive a message asking you whether you want to allow the external application to access your e-mails. This blocking is intended to stop viruses such as the Melissa virus from replicating by automatically sending themselves in e-mails from Outlook. Currently, there is no workaround for this issue, as any possible fix would allow viruses to bypass the security. You can choose to allow access, but you should do this only when you're certain that the application making the request is under your control.

Because you've sent an e-mail for someone to review, it would be useful to add a task to remind you to follow up that review in a specified number of days. To do this, add the following block of code to the example procedure:

```
Set itmNewTask = objOutlook.CreateItem(olTaskItem)

With itmNewTask
  .Subject = "Excel Workbook sent to - " & streMail
  .Body = "Follow up on details"
  .DueDate = Date + 3
  .Attachments.Add ActiveWorkbook.Path & "\" & ActiveWorkbook.Name
  .Save
End With
```

This code creates a new task item with a due date three days from today and attaches the Excel workbook so that you'll have a record of what is being reviewed. You can send this task and the Excel file to someone by adding the following code:

```
.Recipients.Add streMail
.Assign
.send
```

Here, another recipient is added to the list, and then the *Assign* method of the task item is called. This method allows a task to be assigned (delegated) to another user and must be used to alter the task item before it can be sent to any other user. The item is then sent using Outlook. If you go into Outlook and look in the Sent Items folder, you can see all the items that have been created and sent by this procedure.

To add code that sends an Excel workbook, follow these steps:

1 Start Excel with a new worksheet.

2 Choose Tools, Macro, Visual Basic Editor (or press Alt+F11) to open the VBA Editor in Excel.

3 Select the project in the Project window, and then choose Insert, Module.

4 Name the module *basSendExcelWorkBk* and press F7 to open the Code window for the module.

5 Choose Tools, References to open the References dialog box.

6 Scroll through the list until you find Microsoft Outlook 10.0 Object Library and then select it. Close the dialog box.

7 Enter the following code in the Code window:

```
Option Explicit

Sub EMailWorkbook()
    SendCurrentWorkbook "nunnm@plural.com"

End Sub

Sub SendCurrentWorkbook(streMail As String)

    Dim objOutlook As Outlook.Application
    Dim itmNewEMail As Outlook.MailItem
    Dim itmNewTask As Outlook.TaskItem

    Set objOutlook = New Outlook.Application

    Set itmNewEMail = objOutlook.CreateItem(olMailItem)
```

(continued)

```
With itmNewEMail
  .To = streMail

  If ActiveWorkbook.Path = "" Then
    ActiveWorkbook.Save
  End If
  .Attachments.Add ActiveWorkbook.Path & "\" & _
              ActiveWorkbook.Name
  .Send
End With

Set itmNewTask = objOutlook.CreateItem(olTaskItem)

With itmNewTask
  .Subject = "Excel Workbook sent to - " & streMail
  .Body = "Follow up on details"
  .DueDate = Date + 3
  .Attachments.Add ActiveWorkbook.Path & "\" & _
              ActiveWorkbook.Name
  .Save
  .Assign
  .Recipients.Add streMail
  .Send
End With

End Sub
```

8 Replace the e-mail address *nunnm@plural.com* with an e-mail address you can use.

9 With the cursor still in the function, press F5 to run the code. An e-mail is sent to the selected address with the Excel workbook as an attachment, and a task is placed in the Outlook Tasks folder.

Outlook and XML

XML (Extensible Markup Language) is the new standard format for data exchange throughout the IT industry. In Office XP, Excel and Access have native support for XML as a data transfer method. Outlook can join in by using a little bit of VBA code to automate the building of XML.

You can use the following procedure to save the contents of a folder as XML:

```
Sub SaveAsXML()

  Dim fdrActive As Outlook.MAPIFolder
  Dim rsXML As ADODB.Recordset
```

```
      Set fdrActive = ActiveExplorer.CurrentFolder
      Set rsXML = New ADODB.Recordset

      Dim itmType As Object
      Dim iCol As Integer

      On Error Resume Next
      rsXML.AddNew
      For Each itmType In fdrActive.Items
        For iCol = 0 To itmType.ItemProperties.Count - 1
          If itmType.ItemProperties.Item(iCol).Type = olText Then
            rsXML.Fields.Append _
                itmType.ItemProperties.Item(iCol).Name, adVarChar, 5000
          End If
        Next iCol
      Next

      If rsXML.State = adStateClosed Then
        rsXML.Open
      End If

  On Error GoTo NextItem

      For Each itmType In fdrActive.Items
        rsXML.AddNew

        For iCol = 0 To itmType.ItemProperties.Count - 1
          If itmType.ItemProperties.Item(iCol).Type = olText Then
            rsXML.Fields(itmType.ItemProperties.Item(iCol).Name).Value = _
              IIf(IsNull(itmType.ItemProperties.Item(iCol).Value), "", _
                itmType.ItemProperties.Item(iCol).Value)
          End If
        Next iCol
        rsXML.Update

  NextItem:
    Next

      On Error GoTo 0
      rsXML.Save "c:\temp\" & fdrActive.Name & ".xml", adPersistXML

  End Sub
```

This procedure has two key pieces of code. The first uses ADO to create a new recordset in memory and adds all the possible fields for the types of items that are being processed. This is accomplished by looping through the *ItemProperties* collection, much as you did when writing data to Excel, and appending fields with the same names as the properties to the recordset object:

```
For iCol = 0 To itmType.ItemProperties.Count - 1
  If itmType.ItemProperties.Item(iCol).Type = olText Then
    rsXML.Fields.Append _
          itmType.ItemProperties.Item(iCol).Name, adVarChar, 5000
  End If
Next iCol
```

The second core piece of code is the one that writes the data into the recordset and then saves that data as an XML file. For every item in the folder, the code adds a new record to the ADO recordset and fills each of its fields with the corresponding Outlook item value:

```
For Each itmType In fdrActive.Items
  rsXML.AddNew
  For iCol = 0 To itmType.ItemProperties.Count - 1
    If itmType.ItemProperties.Item(iCol).Type = olText Then
      rsXML.Fields(itmType.ItemProperties.Item(iCol).Name).Value = _
        IIf(IsNull(itmType.ItemProperties.Item(iCol).Value), "", _
            itmType.ItemProperties.Item(iCol).Value)
    End If
  Next iCol
  rsXML.Update
Next
```

To save the data as XML, simply call the *Save* method of the ADO recordset object and save it as an XML type file:

```
rsXML.Save "c:\temp\" & fdrActive.Name & ".xml", adPersistXML
```

This exports a file using the ADO *Persist* method, which stores the ADO recordset data as XML-Data Reduced (XDR) format. You could just as easily have reimported the data into an ADO recordset by using the *Open* method of an ADO recordset object and opening a file:

```
rsData.Open mstrXMLPath & "TimeTasks.xml", , , , adCmdFile
```

The procedure shown here for exporting XML data is generic and will fail if the folder you're exporting contains multiple different item types or if some of the items have custom parameters and some don't. To solve these problems, you might want to take a more customized route, in which you make a decision about exactly what to export instead of looping through all the properties. The preceding method exports everything, including a number of ID values that are not required outside Outlook.

To add code that exports a folder as an XML file, do the following:

1 Start Outlook and choose Tools, Macro, Visual Basic Editor (or press Alt+F11) to open the VBA Editor.

2 In the Project window, select Project1.

3 Select the *basExternalApps* module, which you created previously.

4 Press F7 to open the Code window for the module.

5 Enter the following code in the Code window:

```
Sub SaveAsXML()

  Dim fdrActive As Outlook.MAPIFolder
  Dim rsXML As ADODB.Recordset

  Set fdrActive = ActiveExplorer.CurrentFolder
  Set rsXML = New ADODB.Recordset

  Dim itmType As Object
  Dim iCol As Integer

  On Error Resume Next
  rsXML.AddNew
  For Each itmType In fdrActive.Items
    For iCol = 0 To itmType.ItemProperties.Count - 1
      If itmType.ItemProperties.Item(iCol).Type = olText Then
        rsXML.Fields.Append _
              itmType.ItemProperties.Item(iCol).Name, adVarChar, 5000
      End If
    Next iCol
  Next

  If rsXML.State = adStateClosed Then
    rsXML.Open
  End If
On Error GoTo NextItem

  For Each itmType In fdrActive.Items
    rsXML.AddNew

    For iCol = 0 To itmType.ItemProperties.Count - 1
      If itmType.ItemProperties.Item(iCol).Type = olText Then
        rsXML.Fields(itmType.ItemProperties.Item(iCol).Name).Value = _
          IIf(IsNull(itmType.ItemProperties.Item(iCol).Value), "", _
              itmType.ItemProperties.Item(iCol).Value)
      End If
    Next iCol
    rsXML.Update

NextItem:
  Next

  On Error GoTo 0
  rsXML.Save "c:\temp\" & fdrActive.Name & ".xml", adPersistXML

End Sub
```

6 Locate the *AddToolbar2* procedure and add the following code to the end of it:

```
Set btnNewCustom = _
    tlbCustomBar.Controls.Add(Type:=msoControlButton)

btnNewCustom.OnAction = "SaveAsXML"
btnNewCustom.Style = msoButtonIconAndCaption
btnNewCustom.Caption = "Save Current Folder As XML"
```

7 Go back to the main Outlook window and choose Tools, Macro, Macros.

8 In the list, select AddToolbar2 and then click the Run button. A new custom menu button with the name Save Current Folder As XML is added to the toolbar.

9 Select a folder in Outlook and click the Save Current Folder As XML button. An XML file containing the contents of that folder is created and placed in C:\Temp.

Part 9

Appendixes

Appendix A
Installing and Updating Outlook

You install Microsoft Outlook 2002 either locally from a CD-ROM or network share or remotely through a number of methods. You also can install Outlook from either the Microsoft Office XP CD-ROM or the Outlook 2002 CD-ROM. The process for installing from either CD-ROM is similar, except that fewer options are available for products to install.

Installing Locally

To install Outlook locally, locate and run Setup.exe from the install medium. If the CD-ROM is used and AutoRun is enabled, setup should start automatically. The first step in installing an Office application is to enter your User Name, Organization, Initials, and Product Key and then click Next, as shown in Figure A-1. Accept the license agreement and then click Next to continue.

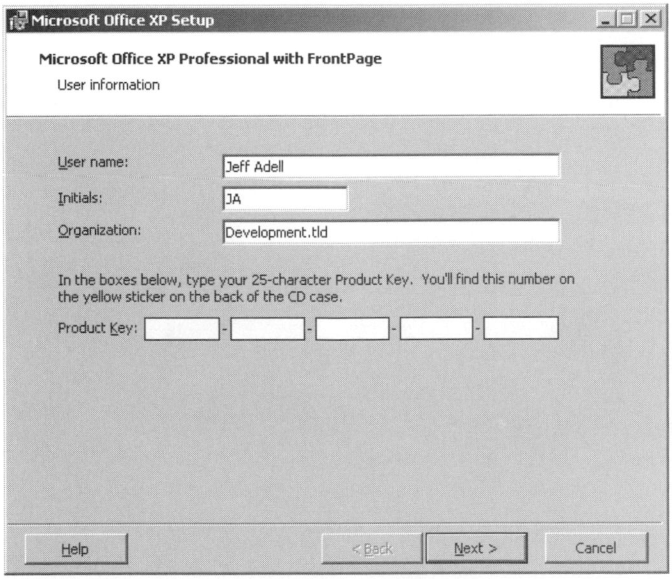

Figure A-1. You'll find the 25-character product key on the CD-ROM case.

Figure A-2 (on the next page) shows the third window in the installation process. To install Outlook (or Office) with the default options in the directory shown, select Install Now. You can also select Complete to install all available options or select Custom to install only the options you want. Click Next to continue.

The window in Figure A-3 is shown only when installing Office, not Outlook. Choosing the applications you want to install and clicking Next installs those applications with the typical options. You can also choose the options to install for each application by selecting Choose Detailed Installation Options For Each Application and clicking Next to continue.

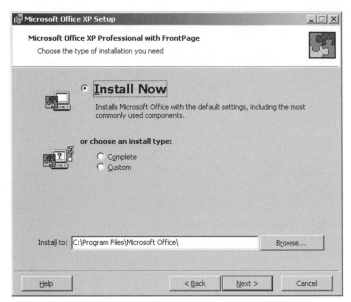

Figure A-2. You can choose the type of installation you want (Complete or Custom) or select a target directory.

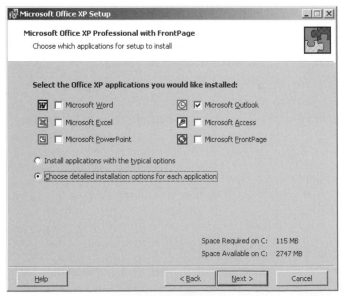

Figure A-3. If you selected Custom in the previous window (shown in Figure A-2), you must now select the applications you would like to install.

Appendix A: Installing and Updating Outlook

Figure A-4 shows the window displayed when you select Choose Detailed Installation Options For Each Application. You can expand any of the selections and select or clear specific options. For most options, there are a number of installation choices. Choosing Run From My Computer installs the option locally. If you choose Not Available, the option will not be installed. If you choose Installed On First Use, the option will be installed the first time it is used. The installation media (network or CD-ROM) must be available at that time.

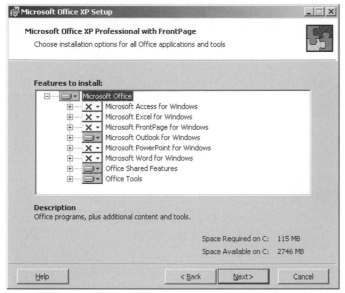

Figure A-4. If you selected the detailed installation option in the last window, this window is displayed. You can choose the options and whether they will be installed now, installed on first use, or not available.

Figure A-5 on the next page shows the summary of the options selected through the installation process. Clicking the Install button installs the applications shown in the summary.

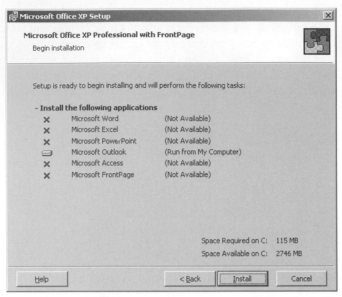

Figure A-5. This screen presents a summary of the selected installation options; clicking Install begins the installation process.

Setup Command-Line Options

You can choose from many options when running the Office Setup.exe file from the command line. A detailed outline of these options can be found in the *Microsoft Office XP Resource Kit* toolbox in a file called Setupref.doc. Only a summary of the available commands is provided here:

- Select **/i** *<msifile>* to run setup using the specified MSI file. Select **/a** *<msifile>* to create an administrative installation point using the specified MSI file. Select **/f{option}** *<msifile>* to repair the installation of Office on the system. The available options are listed in the Setupref.doc file. You must run **/j{option}** *<msifile>* from an administrative installation point, and it will advertise Office on the system. Office components are installed the first time they're run. Select **/x** *<msifile>* to remove Office, but the specified MSI file must be the same as the MSI file used to install Office. For all these options, the MSI file must be in the same directory as the Setup.exe file.

- Select /q{option} to set the user interface level for the install. The default when the /q switch is omitted in the option is *f* for full interaction. The other available options are *r* for reduced where no input is required but full status and progress indicators are shown, *b* for basic where only basic progress indicators are shown, and *n* for none, in which no interface is shown. Specifying /q with no option defaults to none. Adding a plus sign (+) to the *n* or *b* option displays a message when the install is complete (for example, /qn+).

- Select /l{options} logfile to log the installation to the specified file. See the Setupref.doc file for a complete list of available options. Select /**settings** filename to specify the customized INI file that setup will use. Select /**wait** to keep the Setup.exe process running while the installer finishes. Normally, the Setup.exe process calls the installer and terminates.

The last options that can be specified from the command line are public properties. Values for public properties are specified on the command line in the form *property=value*.

Automated Installations

You can provide users with an automatic installation of Office. Use the following steps:

1 Create an administrative installation point for Office by running Setup.exe /a <*msifile*>. The <*msifile*> must be the MSI file you want to install.

2 At the prompt, type your organization name, the location for the administrative installation point, and the product key. Click Next to continue.

3 Accept the license agreement, and click Install. Office will then be installed to the specified location.

The next step is to run the installation. The automated installation method does not install Office to the local computer; it simply advertises the applications that are installed on their first use from the administrative installation point. You can also apply transforms (MST files) created with the Custom Installation Wizard included with the *Microsoft Office XP Resource Kit* to customize the installation.

To advertise the Office applications, run Setup.exe /jm *<msifile>* /t *<mstfile>* /qn to advertise to all users on the local computer. You can substitute /ju for /jm if you want to advertise only to the current user, and the transform (/t *<mstfile>*) is optional. Because /qn is specified, no user interface is shown. /qb is also an acceptable option, and only basic progress and status information will be shown. With the /j option, you can also add /settings *<inifile>* to use an INI file created by the Setup INI Customization Wizard included with the Office XP Resource Kit. Both the Custom Installation Wizard and the Setup INI Customization Wizard are covered in more detail in Appendix B, "Office XP Resource Kit."

One advantage to using an automated installation is that it can be done from a login script so that every user receives the advertised applications. This leads us to the next section on remote installation.

Remote and Push Installation Options

As was specified in the last section, remote installation can be performed from a login script by using the Setup.exe /j option to advertise the Office applications. Transforms and setup INI files can be specified to customize the installation. A section could be added to the login script that checks to see whether the process has already been done (by checking for the existence of a file or directory) and if not, runs the setup program with no user interaction.

The login script method of remote installation is not the most elegant solution. Without careful testing and supervision, the process can fail. A better method of installing Office (and many other applications) remotely is by using Microsoft Systems Management Server (SMS) or IntelliMirror with Microsoft Windows 2000. Both these systems provide similar services for the remote installation of software. IntelliMirror is meant to advertise software to the client machines, and the software is installed when users select it from their Add/Remove Programs Control Panel. SMS takes a different approach and builds software packages that are installed on the client systems regardless of user intervention. Another advantage to SMS is that it is meant to be highly scalable to very large networks and provides many more management features than remote software installation.

Appendix A: Installing and Updating Outlook

Updating Outlook and Office

You update Outlook and Office from the Office Update Web site at *http:// officeupdate.microsoft.com* (see Figure A-6).

Figure A-6. Visit the Office Update Web site to download and install updates and fixes for Office applications.

Click the Auto Update button to continue updating Office. When you select Auto Update, the Office Update site determines which updates you require. You can then choose which ones you want to download and install. The updates are grouped based on their importance. Critical updates are first, followed by recommended updates. Critical updates encompass issues such as security fixes, and recommended updates are small bug fixes and feature additions.

Appendix B

Office XP Resource Kit

The Microsoft Office XP Resource Kit (ORK) offers tools and some documentation that you can use to make complex tasks easier. Most of the tools provided are geared toward custom installation and maintenance, which helps administrators with large user bases who want to avoid unnecessary deskside visits.

Resource Kit Tools

You can use most of the tools provided with the Resource Kit to create customized versions of Office for delivery over the network. You can both customize the initial install and modify the client installation.

Answer Wizard Builder

Use the ORK Answer Wizard Builder to build custom help files for Office applications. Creating custom answer files is useful for companies that want to add information to Office help. For example, a corporation might have custom applications based on Microsoft Outlook or use Microsoft Word or Microsoft Excel in a certain way. That corporation might want to develop custom answer files to include in those applications, with instructions on how to use its custom applications.

CMW File Viewer

Use the CMW File Viewer to view the files created by the Custom Maintenance Wizard, which creates update files to change the default installation of Office. The CMW File Viewer changes the binary format CMW files to human-readable text and opens them in Notepad. Using the CMW File Viewer, you can review the changes that the CMW file will make to the organization, features, registry, files, and so forth.

Corporate Error Reporting

Office crash events are sent directly to Microsoft's crash-reporting servers. Crash events are captured when Office crashes for any reason. Use Corporate Error Reporting to forward your Office crash reports to a server on your network. Then you can review the reports of the crashes, determine what is occurring, and take preventive action. You can also forward crash information to the Microsoft crash-reporting servers in batches. You can choose which crash information to send and which to discard. Corporate Error Reporting is configured by setting a registry value on the client systems, which specifies the location for the crash-reporting application included with Office to dump crash information.

Custom Installation Wizard

Use the Custom Installation Wizard to create Microsoft Windows Installer transform files (MST files) to customize the installation of Office from a network share to the client computers. You must first specify the MSI file (the default Windows Installer file) and then the name and location of the MST file. The customization begins with the specification of the target install directory for the client systems and the organization name. You must then specify the behavior of the installer with regard to previous versions of Office; which Office features to install; an OPS file created with the Profile Wizard (if any); user settings and preferences; and files, shortcuts, or registry entries to add to or remove from the client system. You must also specify additional servers to store the distribution files, Office security settings, additional packages to add during the install, Outlook profile settings, Outlook default settings, and miscellaneous setup configuration values. The settings are then saved to the MST file. To install using the MST file, you run Office Setup from the command line and specify the transform file as instructed in the summary page of the Custom Installation Wizard.

Custom Maintenance Wizard

Use the Custom Maintenance Wizard to create a CMW file that is used to modify the installation of Office on a client system. Using the wizard to create the file based on an existing MSI file, you can modify the organization name, which Office features are installed, settings and preferences for every Office application, other files on the client computer, registry entries on the client, server distribution points, Office security settings, Outlook profile defaults, and Outlook default settings. To apply the settings to a client system, you copy the Custom Maintenance Wizard to the server share where Office is located and run it in apply mode from the command line.

MST File Viewer

Use the MST File Viewer to view files created with the Custom Installation Wizard. The MST files created by the Custom Installation Wizard are essentially modified MSI files that control the installation of Office on client computers. The MST file viewer converts the binary MST file to a text file and opens it in Notepad. From there, you can review the installation details, such as the organization name, Office features to install, and settings and preferences.

OPS File Viewer

Use the OPS File Viewer to view files created by the Profile Wizard. The viewer converts the binary format OPS file to a text format and displays it using Notepad, where you can review the settings.

Package Definition Files

The Package Definition Files folder contains the package definition files for Microsoft SMS for the distribution of Office using SMS. These files can be used to do a "hands-off" installation of Office to client systems. Even when you use the Custom Installation Wizard, minimal attention is needed at the desktop. A properly implemented SMS architecture allows you to force the distribution of software from a central server—a useful feature for organizations with multiple distributed sites.

Profile Wizard

The Profile Wizard is used to configure an OPS file that contains user settings and preferences. The Profile Wizard saves the current settings on the local machine to a file for restore later or for distribution to client systems. To create an OPS file, you must configure the settings and preferences in each Office application you want to include in the file and close all Office applications. Next start the Profile Wizard, and specify the location for the OPS file and for which applications you want to save settings. After the profile has been saved to a file, it can be restored using the Profile Wizard, either from the graphical interface or from the command line as instructed in the summary page of the Wizard.

Removal Wizard

Use the Removal Wizard to clean up any installations of previous versions of Office on the local computer. The Removal Wizard provides three options. Use the first option to remove all unused Office related files that might have been left by previous versions of Office. The Removal Wizard displays a list of these unused files and allows you to choose which to remove. Use the second option to choose which applications to remove. You can select from a list of the installed applications and choose which to keep and which to remove. Use the third option to remove all previous versions of Office. This removes all files related to the earlier versions.

Setup INI Customization Wizard

Use the Setup INI Customization Wizard to configure the Setup.ini file that is used for a network installation of Office. Using this tool, you can change the level of logging used during setup and also can specify which MSI files are installed when setup is run. This makes it possible to install more than one application with a single instance of the setup program. You can choose the order in which the software specified by the MSI files is installed. In the window where the order of the installation is configured, you can choose to apply any transform files created with the Custom Installation Wizard to customize the installation. Finally the wizard will display a summary of the options, and you can create the new INI file.

System Policy Editor

The System Policy Editor included with the Office Resource Kit is similar to that which comes with Microsoft Windows NT 4.0. You can use it to create system policies for both Windows NT 4.0 and Windows 2000. I recommend that you use group policies for Windows 2000 instead of system policies, but system policies will still function. System policies created in either Windows NT 4.0 or Windows 2000 will work on computers running both Windows NT 4.0 and Windows 2000. Policies created in either Windows 95 or Windows 98 will also work on both 95 and 98. System policies control many aspects of the client computer, including the display in the Start menu and Control Panel.

Resource Kit Documentation

Documentation included with the Resource Kit includes the International folder, the Office folder, and the Custom Alerts folder. The International folder contains information about configuring international language support for Microsoft Office.

The Office folder provides documents related to the inner workings of Microsoft Office. One of the files, Filelist.xls, contains a list of the files in Office and a description of the relevant Office feature. Formats.doc provides a list of the OLE database formats supported by Office. IE5feats.xls contains a list of the Office features that are dependent on Internet Explorer 5. Regkey.xls provides a list of the registry keys used with Office.

The Custom Alerts folder contains a pair of XLS files that explain how to create redirections to Web sites when certain errors occur. These files can be useful to redirect users to Web sites developed by your in-house support personnel and provide detailed explanations for tasks such as adding printers.

Appendix C
Update and Troubleshooting Resources

Resources are available both on the Internet and offline for updating, troubleshooting, and supporting Microsoft Outlook 2002. You can easily update Outlook and Microsoft Windows by using the Windows Update and Microsoft Office Update Web sites. In addition, many troubleshooting and support resources are available from Microsoft and from third parties in the form of Web sites, mailing lists, and books. This appendix presents some of the most useful and most comprehensive resources.

Update Resources

There are two main update resources available for Office and Windows: Office Update and Windows Update. These provide software updates, including security, bug fixes, and additional features.

Office Update. You can find this site at *http://office.microsoft.com*. Office Update is the main site used to download and install updates to Office. You can click the Auto Update link to determine which updates are available for your version of Office. You can select from the available updates, and they will download and install automatically. The updates include Service Releases, security updates, and bug fixes. The Office Update site also includes add-ins and extras for Office, including help and tutorials, clip art, and templates.

Windows Update. You can find this site at *http://windowsupdate.microsoft.com*. Windows Update is the central site for updating Windows NT, Windows 2000, Windows 95, Windows 98, and Windows Me. You click Product Updates to determine which updates are available for your system. The Update catalog is displayed, categorized by five types of updates. Listed are Critical Updates that address security problems and issues that affect the function of Windows; Picks of the Month, which are additional features that can be added; Recommended Updates, which are software fixes that are not critical to the system; Additional Windows Features, which are Windows software that adds specific functions required by only a few users; and Device Driver updates.

Troubleshooting and Support Resources

There are a number of troubleshooting and support resources available for Outlook and Microsoft Exchange Server. The following are Microsoft Support Resources, third-party Web-based resources for Outlook and Exchange, and a pair of excellent Exchange Server books.

Microsoft Knowledge Base. You can find this site at *http://support.microsoft.com*. Knowledge Base is the main site for support on all Microsoft products. You can select a product and then enter a query to view the Knowledge Base–related articles, which cover many of the problems you might encounter in the administration of Outlook and Exchange.

Microsoft TechNet. You can find this site at *http://microsoft.com/technet/*. TechNet is a subscription-based product. When you purchase TechNet, you receive a package of CD-ROMs and a binder to hold them. Monthly, you receive the CD-ROMs that have been updated. The TechNet CD-ROMs contain almost everything available on the Microsoft support Web sites. For example, the entire Knowledge Base is on one CD-ROM, another contains Service Packs, and so on.

Microsoft Press Web. You can find this site, which lists all books published by Microsoft Press, at *http://mspress.microsoft.com*. You can browse the titles and even buy online.

Microsoft Product Support Services (PSS). PSS is usually the last resort for problems, primarily because it costs money. A support call is placed to (800) 936-4900, and you are put in touch with a support engineer—usually immediately, although sometimes it takes a couple of hours for a callback. The engineer will work through your problem with you and find an answer. One of the greatest advantages of using PSS is that the engineers are able to escalate problems to high-level personnel to help solve your problem. If your problem is the result of a software bug and there is a hot fix available for that issue, you will not be charged for the call.

Third-Party Resources

Outlook

Slipstick. You can find this site at *http://www.slipstick.com*. Slipstick is a collection of resources including files and articles on Outlook and Exchange. It's one of the most extensive sites of its type and contains links to many third-party Outlook add-ins, links to important patches, and Knowledge Base articles. The articles explain how to do many complex tasks with Outlook and offer troubleshooting tips.

CDO Live. You can find this site at *http://www.cdolive.com/*. CDO Live is a great resource for Collaborative Data Objects (CDO) code resources. There are articles and tips on CDO programming as well as code samples. CDO Live also has links to third-party Outlook add-ins written with CDO.

Helen Feddema. You can find this site at *http://www.helenfeddema.com/*. This home page offers resources for CDO programming with Office. There are many code samples, most of which deal with OLE and controlling Office applications from other applications.

Exchange

Simpler-Webb Inc. Exchange Resources. You can find this site at *http://www.swinc.com/resource/exchange.htm*. This site offers important resources for supporting Exchange, the first of which are the Exchange 5.5 FAQ and the Exchange 2000 FAQ. These documents are the result of the most common questions asked on the Exchange mailing list, a must-read for anyone supporting Exchange. They cover many issues that come up in the day-to-day operation of Exchange servers that aren't covered anywhere else, including methods of moving servers and disaster recovery. The SMTP instructions are a comprehensive resource that walks you through the steps of connecting your Exchange server over a nondedicated link. In this scenario, your ISP queues your mail on its server; retrieving it is a complex operation made easier with this document.

FAQ. You can find this site at *http://www.exchangefaq.org*. This is another extensive FAQ site for Exchange. Often these FAQ sites are an excellent resource for problem solving because they cover issues not addressed in other documentation, such as troubleshooting common problems.

Swynk.com. You can find this site at *http://www.swynk.com*. This site is an extensive resource for Microsoft BackOffice information. There are many articles dealing with both Exchange and Windows 2000 and an excellent Exchange mailing list. From *http://ls.swynk.com/scripts/lyris.pl*, you can choose Exchange Discussions and join the list. This is a very heavy-traffic list, but it is populated by people who know Exchange very well. Make sure you check the FAQ and the archives before posting your question.

The Exchange Code. You can find this site at *http://www.exchangecode.com*. Exchange Code is another resource with CDO applications for Outlook and Exchange. It provides many code samples, and is also the home of the AutoAccept scripts. These scripts are difficult to implement, but when they are in place they provide Exchange 5.5 with an excellent method of accepting resource bookings automatically.

Microsoft Exchange 2000 Server Administrator's Companion. This is a comprehensive book from Microsoft Press on Microsoft Exchange 2000. It contains information on planning, implementation, and administration, including security, ongoing maintenance, and troubleshooting. It also contains a section that explains the basic working of Exchange 2000 to give you an introduction to the architecture of the server.

Deploying Microsoft Exchange Server 5.5 (Notes from the Field). This book, also from Microsoft Press, is a collection of real-world experience put together by Microsoft Consulting Services employees, based on their many implementations of Microsoft Exchange 5.5. This book walks you through the design of a proper Exchange 5.5 architecture, including server sizing, migration planning, upgrading from previous versions of Exchange, and multiple-site replication and synchronization.

Appendix D
Outlook Files and Registry Keys

To help you further customize Microsoft Outlook, this appendix includes the following: a list of Outlook configuration files, a list of the different file name extensions used by Outlook, and a list of the Outlook registry keys.

Table D-1 lists configuration files used by Outlook.

Table D-1. Outlook configuration files

File Name	Description
Adult Content Senders.txt	Contains additional rules for the Adult Content Senders
Exception List.txt	Contains exceptions to the Junk Senders rule
Extend.dat	Contains a list of Outlook extensions and add-ins
Frmcache.dat	Includes the forms cache
<Outlook profile name>.fav	Includes Outlook Bar shortcuts
<Outlook profile name>.nick	Contains nNames of the Automatic Name Check feature
Outcmd.dat	Includes customizations to menus and toolbars
VbaProject.otm	Includes macro and VBA code
Views.dat	Contains some of the information on custom views
Outlbar.inf	Contains the Setup file for Outlook Bar structure

Appendix D

Table D-2 lists the various file name extensions used by Outlook.

Table D-2. File name extensions supported by Outlook

File Name Extension	Description
CAL	Microsoft Schedule+ 1.0 files
CFG	Form setup files
CSV	Comma-separated values files for Microsoft Windows
DBF	ACT!, FoxPro, and dBASE database files
DLL	Dynamic-link libraries
DOC	Microsoft Word or WordPad files
ECF	Extension configuration files
ECO	ECCO files
EXE	Executable files
FDM	Form message files
HTM, HTML	Hypertext Markup Language files
INF	Initialization files
MDB	Microsoft Access database files
MSG	Outlook message file format
OCX	Microsoft ActiveX control files
OFT	Outlook template files
ORG, OR2	Lotus Organizer files
OSS	Files created when saving searches
OST	Files created when saving messages for offline storage

Appendix D: Outlook Files and Registry Keys

File Name Extension	Description
PAB	Outlook Personal Address Book files
PST	Outlook Personal folder and AutoArchive files
RTF	Rich Text formatted files
SC2	Microsoft Schedule+ interchange files
SCD	Microsoft Schedule+ 7x files
TXT	ASCII text files, tab-separated values files, and comma-separated files for DOS
VCF	vCard files
VCS	vCalendar files
WAB	Windows Address Book files
XLS	Microsoft Excel workbook files

Outlook uses the preceding files as well as the registry to store configuration and customization information. The registry is a centralized database of system and application settings that is managed by Windows. To see the contents of the registry, you use the Registry Editor. With the Registry Editor you can view, edit, print, and export your registry settings.

The Registry Editor actually combines a couple of files to create a single view of your registry settings. These files are stored on your computer in DAT files. When you open the Registry Editor, these files are displayed in a hierarchical format to make viewing and editing them easy.

> **caution** The Registry Editor does not have an undo command with which to return your settings back to the ones you had before you started editing. As you work with the registry, do not make any changes unless you know they are the right ones. Making the wrong edit can cause Outlook, other programs, and even Windows to stop working correctly.

Table D-3 on the next page lists registry files used by Microsoft Outlook.

Table D-3. Outlook registry keys

Registry Key	Description
HKEY_CURRENT_USER\Software\Microsoft\Office\10.0\Outlook\	General Outlook configuration key
HKEY_CURRENT_USER\Software\Microsoft\Office\10.0\Outlook\Appointment	Appointment settings
HKEY_CURRENT_USER\Software\Microsoft\Office\10.0\Outlook\AppointmentRequest	Appointment request settings
HKEY_CURRENT_USER\Software\Microsoft\Office\10.0\Outlook\AutoConfiguration	Autoconfiguration settings
HKEY_CURRENT_USER\Software\Microsoft\Office\10.0\Outlook\Contact	Contacts folders settings
HKEY_CURRENT_USER\Software\Microsoft\Office\10.0\Outlook\CustomizableAlerts	Alerts settings
HKEY_CURRENT_USER\Software\Microsoft\Office\10.0\Outlook\DataViz	Output data settings
HKEY_CURRENT_USER\Software\Microsoft\Office\10.0\Outlook\DistList	Distribution list settings
HKEY_CURRENT_USER\Software\Microsoft\Office\10.0\Outlook\Forms	Forms settings
HKEY_CURRENT_USER\Software\Microsoft\Office\10.0\Outlook\IM	Instant Messenger settings
HKEY_CURRENT_USER\Software\Microsoft\Office\10.0\Outlook\Journal	Journals folder
HKEY_CURRENT_USER\Software\Microsoft\Office\10.0\Outlook\JournalEntry	Journal entries settings
HKEY_CURRENT_USER\Software\Microsoft\Office\10.0\Outlook\Message	Message data
HKEY_CURRENT_USER\Software\Microsoft\Office\10.0\Outlook\Note	Notes folder
HKEY_CURRENT_USER\Software\Microsoft\Office\10.0\Outlook\OfficeExplorer	Office Binder settings
HKEY_CURRENT_USER\Software\Microsoft\Office\10.0\Outlook\OfficeFinder	Office Find Fast settings
HKEY_CURRENT_USER\Software\Microsoft\Office\10.0\Outlook\OLFax	WinFax settings
HKEY_CURRENT_USER\Software\Microsoft\Office\10.0\Outlook\Options	Option settings
HKEY_CURRENT_USER\Software\Microsoft\Office\10.0\Outlook\OST	Offline storage file settings

Appendix D: Outlook Files and Registry Keys

Registry Key	Description
HKEY_CURRENT_USER\Software\Microsoft\Office\10.0\Outlook\Preferences	Outlook user preferences settings
HKEY_CURRENT_USER\Software\Microsoft\Office\10.0\Outlook\Printing	Outlook print settings
HKEY_CURRENT_USER\Software\Microsoft\Office\10.0\Outlook\Report	Outlook report settings
HKEY_CURRENT_USER\Software\Microsoft\Office\10.0\Outlook\Scripting	Outlook script settings
HKEY_CURRENT_USER\Software\Microsoft\Office\10.0\Outlook\Security	Outlook secure folder settings
HKEY_CURRENT_USER\Software\Microsoft\Office\10.0\Outlook\Setup	Outlook setup information
HKEY_CURRENT_USER\Software\Microsoft\Office\10.0\Outlook\Signatures	Message signature settings
HKEY_CURRENT_USER\Software\Microsoft\Office\10.0\Outlook\Task	Task folder settings
HKEY_CURRENT_USER\Software\Microsoft\Office\10.0\Outlook\Today	Outlook Today settings
HKEY_CURRENT_USER\Software\Microsoft\Office\10.0\Outlook\UserInfo	Outlook user information
HKEY_CURRENT_USER\Software\Microsoft\Office\10.0\Outlook\WAB	Windows Address Book information
HKEY_CURRENT_USER\Software\Microsoft\Office\Outlook\AddIns	Outlook add-ins information
HKEY_CURRENT_USER\Software\Microsoft\Office\10.0\Outlook\OMIAccountManager	Account information
HKEY_CURRENT_USER\Software\Microsoft\Shared Tools\Journaling	Outlook Journal settings
HKEY_CURRENT_USER\Software\Microsoft\WAB	Windows Address Book information
HKEY_CURRENT_USER\Software\Microsoft\Windows Messaging Subsystem\Profiles\Outlook	Outlook Personal Folders files information
HKEY_CURRENT_USER\Software\Microsoft\Mail	Microsoft Project workgroup mail settings

Appendix E
Outlook Add-Ins

One of the many benefits of Microsoft Outlook is that it is extensible. Many third parties have written programs that integrate with Outlook to add features, automate repetitive tasks, or enable Outlook to work with other products or services. This software can be a COM add-in, a Microsoft Visual Basic for Applications (VBA) macro, a template or message form, or a helper file used by Outlook. This chapter explores a few of the many add-ins available and tells you where to get them. This is only a small subset of the many add-ins available for Outlook. For additional add-ins, look on *http:// office.microsoft.com* or search the Web. Another great site for Outlook information is *http://www.slipstick.com*, which has a comprehensive list of add-ins and services for Outlook. Keep an eye on these Web sites for updated information about Outlook 2002.

Some of the security features in Outlook 2002 might result in dialogs prompting you when an add-in tries to access address information on items in your mailbox or send mail on your behalf. This action protects you so that viruses can't replicate using Outlook. If you're using Outlook with a Microsoft Exchange Server, your Exchange administrator might allow approved add-ins to avoid these prompts. Speak to your administrator if you have any questions.

Most of these add-ins come with installers, but some of them require you to manually copy or import files into Outlook. All the add-ins without setup programs have instructions on their Web page; if you don't know how to install the add-in, read the author's site for more information. Some of these add-ins are free, but others are shareware or require you to pay before you download. Many of them have trial versions on their Web sites, however, so if you find one that interests you, check out its site and see whether you can try out an evaluation version.

Most COM add-ins are loaded when Outlook starts. If the add-in causes problems, such as hangs when you start Outlook, Outlook will notice this and automatically disable the add-in on successive starts. To re-enable the add-in, choose Tools, Options, Other, Advanced Options, COM Add-Ins.

> **Note** The add-ins discussed in this appendix were written for previous versions of Outlook, and not all of them have been tested with Outlook 2002 at the time of printing. The authors of these add-ins might be releasing updates for Outlook 2002; check with the software vendor if you have problems running the add-ins in Outlook 2002.

Add-Ins in the Box

Save My Settings Wizard   Save My Settings was available for Microsoft Office 2000 from *http://office.microsoft.com* but it now comes in the Office XP box and is included in the typical installation of Office XP. Choose Start, Programs, Microsoft Office Tools. This add-in allows you to save and restore the custom configuration you've done on all the Office XP applications. You can save settings to your local hard disk or upload them to *http://office.microsoft.com*. The add-in makes a backup of registry settings and related files used by Office. Here are some of the Outlook settings that are backed up:

- Configuration information you set by choosing Tools, Options (such as your preferred editor, message format, send/receive group settings, and many more)
- Custom views
- Nicknames
- Favorites
- COM add-ins, Exchange Client Extensions, and VBA projects
- Signatures
- Stationery

newfeature!

Smart Tags   Smart tags is a new feature in Office XP. Each Office application has certain tags that it recognizes. For example, if you're composing an HTML e-mail message using Word, and you type **Lisa Garmaise** in the message box, a dotted underline will appear under the name. When you hover the cursor over the name, a small icon will appear; click on it, and you can choose to add Lisa to your list of contacts, send her a message or a meeting request, and a few other options. If Lisa is already one of your contacts, you can choose at this point to insert her address into the message (see Figure E-1).

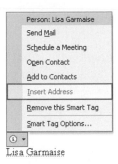

Figure E-1. Add an address from an Outlook contact into a WordMail message.

Several other smart tags are included in the box, such as company information and re-cent company news from MSN. These smart tags are extensible; Office XP has a Smart Tag Software Development Kit (SDK) that can be used to develop additional smart tags.

Recover Deleted Items If you use Outlook with an Exchange Server, your adminis-trator might have configured your server to retain deleted items for a certain number of days. If your server is configured this way, you can use the Recover Deleted Items add-in from Outlook to access items you emptied from your server-side Deleted Items folder. To access this add-in, select your Deleted Items folder and choose Tools, Recover Deleted Items. You can turn this menu option off by choosing Tools, Options, Other, Advanced Options, Add-In Manager, and clearing Deleted Items Recovery.

Calendar and Contact Add-Ins

eBay Reminder: *http://www.schmidks.de/ebayrem.htm* eBay Reminder is a VBA macro that lets you easily add appointments to your calendar for the auctions that in-terest you. Just open Microsoft Internet Explorer to the auction and run the macro from Outlook. eBay Reminder creates a calendar item with the start and end times set to the end of the auction and a reminder for several hours in advance. To install the eBay Reminder, you copy files to your local machine and then import them into Outlook. Instructions are on the Web site.

Aladdin Envelopes and Labels: *http://www.software-solutions.co.nz/ aladdins_el/alelabout.htm* Aladdin allows you to select a contact and print an en-velope or label with the appropriate name and address. You can even add graphics to your printouts. Aladdin supports many Avery and Zweckform label styles. Go from contact to printed envelope in only three mouse clicks.

DialRight for Outlook: *http://www.dialright.com/download/outlook/*   If you live in North America and have a lot of contacts with outdated area codes in their phone numbers, download DialRight to update your contacts' area codes to the new ones. This add-in is free for fewer than 2,500 contacts.

Productivity Enhancements

Glance: *http://www.cwilliware.com/glance/*   Glance runs in your system tray and gives you one-click access to common functions, such as creating a new appointment or message, or opening a specific folder. It runs Outlook in the background so that your taskbar isn't cluttered, but you still will receive reminders.

Actioneer: *http://www.actioneer.com*   With Actioneer, you can type a natural language query, such as **T.P.S. Report due Tuesday**, and it will create and save a task in Outlook with the appropriate subject and a due date of the following Tuesday, with no further interaction required from you. Actioneer can also tie in to Web services, such as Amazon.com, with a query such as **find book** <*author*>. There are dozens of Web services supported. Your client can search only the ones you're interested in; just configure the client at the Actioneer Web site. You can even suggest additional Web services using a form on Actioneer's Web site in case you would like it to work with a service that isn't in its catalog.

80-20 Retriever: *http://www.80-20.com/products/retriever/index.htm*   80-20 Retriever is a search portal that provides speedy full-text searching of all messages, including attachments. 80-20 indexes the data in your mailbox and allows you to perform quick searches through a folder home page, either on Outlook Today or in a separate folder.

Custom Outlook Buttons: *http://www.freevbcode.com/ ShowCode.Asp?ID=1892*   This add-in makes it easy to add buttons to the toolbar and specify a program, file, or URL to open when the button is clicked. This add-in is provided with source code, so you can see exactly what it's doing. You don't need to compile it yourself to install it; however, you just need to copy a couple of files to the Office installation directory on your computer (usually something like C:\Program Files\Microsoft Office\Office10). The instructions page says to "register" the DLL; this means that you should open a command prompt to the directory where you placed the file and type **regsvr32** <**nameofdll.dll**>.

CyberSecretary: *http://www.ivitar.com/cybersecretary/*   CyberSecretary puts a friendly face on Outlook. Interview and hire one of several secretaries who can help you throughout the day. Want the *Wall Street Journal* or *New York Times* on your computer every morning? No problem—your secretary can take care of that, show you the day's *Dilbert,* or remind you to hang out at the watercooler or coffee bar. CyberSecretary can keep you updated on stocks you're interested in, remind you for events due in Outlook, search the Internet for you, add expenses to your journal (and create an expense report), and even play games with you. Tell your secretary to take a break, and he or she will retire to the system tray until needed.

Mail Management

Spam Deputy: *http://members.home.net/spamdeputy/*   If you receive a piece of unwanted mass e-mail, you can send it to SpamCop.Net. SpamCop is an organization that will send complaints to the administrators responsible for the spammer's Internet access. Spam Deputy simplifies this process of reporting spammers from Outlook. Select a message, click Spam Deputy, fill in a few fields, and the complaint is sent. It's still up to the administrator to respond to the complaint, but this is the first step in stopping unwanted mass e-mail.

GazNet Anti-Spam: *http://Website.lineone.net/~garyjb/Spam/*   GazNet Anti-Spam is a list of known spammers, over 14,000 at time of printing. Keeping a current list of junk e-mailers helps you reduce the amount of spam in your mailbox. To turn on the junk e-mail feature in Outlook, click on Organize on the Tools menu, select the Junk E-Mail option, and click Turn On. To add a sender to the list, right click on the message in Outlook, and choose Junk E-mail, Add to Junk Senders List. This will create a file on your computer named Junk Senders.txt (the file will not exist until you add a sender to it). To install the GazNet Anti-Spam list, copy the file from the above Web site over the existing Junk Senders.txt. If you want to save the junk senders you had previously added, make sure to add them to the GazNet list on your computer. After the file is copied to your computer, Outlook will flag messages from any of the senders in the list as junk mail. GazNet's list is regularly updated, so check the Web site periodically to maintain an up-to-date list.

CaSaveAtt: *http://www.ornic.com/actions/casaveatt.shtml*   CaSaveAtt is a custom action for Outlook's Rules Wizard that allows you to save attachments on messages to your local hard disk. You can configure it to delete the attachment from the message after the save is complete and tell CaSaveAtt to run a program on the attachment after it's saved to your computer.

MailAlert: *http://www.diamondridge.com/software/mailalert/index.htm*   Do you want to be notified of incoming e-mail but don't want to keep Outlook open all day? Install MailAlert, which adds an icon to your system tray that can check many types of accounts (MAPI/Exchange, IMAP, POP3) at the same time. Do you *not* want to be notified of messages from mailing lists, but *do* want a pop-up window when your boss sends you mail? No problem. Configure MailAlert to notify you in a particular way, based on the message author, subject, or body.

MailListKing: *http://www.xequte.com/listking/index.html*   Manage mailing lists with MailListKing. Set it up to periodically scan your folders for messages with sub-scription and cancel-subscription requests, and automatically add and remove addresses from a list database. MailListKing supports bulk operations, such as canceling a user's subscription from all mailing lists. It also can be configured to remove addresses from the database if messages to that address bounce a certain number of times.

ReplyMate: *http://www.redearthsoftware.com/*   If you find yourself sending the same text in e-mail to different people, take a look at ReplyMate. Enter the text once in ReplyMate, and the next time you compose an e-mail, a couple of clicks will insert the data into the message. Use ReplyMate to respond to frequently asked questions or paste in often-used URLs.

Email Templates: *www.emailtemplates.com*   This add-in is a collection of templates that automate repetitive tasks. It functions similarly to ReplyMate, but it's more extensible. Included in the initial download are some default templates: Announce New Employee, Follow Up To Our Call, We've Moved!, and Link To Frequently Asked Questions.

You can create your own templates or edit the sample templates. With the Rules Wizard, you can set up Outlook to autorespond to incoming e-mail with a specific message. If you tend to answer the same questions in e-mail repeatedly, such as requests for information on your company's products or services, create a template with advertising information for your products. Then have Outlook reply to any messages with "product request" in the subject using your template. E-mail templates are also scriptable using TCL (Tool Command Language).

ZipOut 2000: *http://www.microeye.com/zipout/index.html*   ZipOut is a flexible program that helps manage the size of your mailbox and messages you send. When you send mail, ZipOut can automatically compress the attachments into a ZIP or a self-extracting EXE file, saving on network bandwidth and on disk space on the client or server. It also allows you to compress or delete attachments to items in your mailbox so that they take up less disk space. You can schedule the compression to happen at regular intervals and notify you of the results.

eCleaner: *http://www.techsoup.org/sub_downdetails.cfm?downloadid=29* eCleaner is a free utility that removes HTML tags, hard returns, special characters (such as >>), and other formatting you might not like that can add up and clutter long threads. It's easy to use: copy the contents of an unreadable message into eCleaner and click a button.

CloudEight Stationery: *http://thundercloud.net/stationery/*   CloudEight has a variety of attractive stationery available free on its Web site. With stationery you can easily create messages with attractive backgrounds, borders, graphics, fonts, and colors. Install the stationery, and then from Outlook choose Actions, New Mail Message Using, More Stationery to browse the installed selections. CloudEight offers stationery for cat lovers, Disney fans, and for special occasions such as birthdays and holidays.

ExLife: *http://www.ornic.com/add-ins/exlife.shtml*   ExLife is a replacement for Outlook's Rules Wizard that offers some extra options, such as automatically saving attachments or redirecting (bouncing) messages without changing the original headers.

General Add-Ins

Outback: *http://www.silverlaketech.com/outback.html*   Outback simplifies the process of backing up your Outlook settings and data files. The base version of the product can back up your personal folder files and remind you regularly about performing backups. Outback Plus, an expanded version of the product, adds more backup capability, such as backing up your signature, stationery, views, address books, and rules, and archiving your Internet Explorer Favorites and cookies.

When you have a backup, you can easily restore your data—either to the same machine or to another—after a failure.

MSHelp Request Form: *http://slipstick.com/dev/olforms/mshelp.htm*
Microsoft MSHelp is an automated service that allows users to send messages requesting product information or specific Knowledge Base articles, and get responses via e-mail. This form allows you to request either an index of available articles or five specific articles. The form validates the format of your request and sends the message to *mshelp@microsoft.com*.

Microsoft Add-Ins: *http://office.microsoft.com/Downloads*   Microsoft has many add-ins for Outlook available on the Office Download Center. From the site you can access service releases, updates and patches, stationery, services, and other freebies to improve your Outlook eXPerience. Keep a bookmark on this site to look for add-ins in the future.

Write Your Own Add-In

After trying some of these add-ins, you might be wondering how you can write an add-in yourself. COM add-ins are compiled programs written in programming languages such as Visual Basic or C++. Macros are easier to write. Add them to Outlook via the Visual Basic Editor (VBE) by choosing Tools, Macro, Visual Basic Editor. You also can hook into the rest of the Office XP products to create even more powerful add-ins.

A good starting place for learning how to write add-ins to Outlook can be found at *http://support.microsoft.com/support/kb/articles/q230/2/25.asp* or in *Programming Microsoft Outlook and Microsoft Exchange, Second Edition*, by Thomas Rizzo (Microsoft Press, 2000).

Appendix F
Outlook Symbols

Microsoft Outlook 2002 uses a number of icons and graphic symbols to help you identify items and the status of items quickly. If, for example, you see an exclamation point next to an e-mail message, you know that this message has an importance level of High. Some of the symbols are used in more than one Outlook tool. For example, you will see a paper clip icon next to any e-mail message that includes a file attachment. The same icon appears next to calendar, task, journal, and contact items that have attachments.

The following sections show each Outlook symbol and include a brief explanation of each icon.

Outlook Message Symbols

Symbols found in Outlook Message appear in Table F-1.

Table F-1. Outlook Message symbols

Symbol	Description
	An unopened message
	An open message
	A message you have forwarded
	A message you have replied to
	A message with high importance
	A message with low importance
	A message with a file attachment
	A message flagged for a follow-up
	A message with follow-up completed
	An undeliverable e-mail message
	Important information about a message
	A message sent from a project manager using Microsoft Project
	A message saved or unsent (such as in the Drafts folder)
	An encrypted message

(continued)

Table F-1. *(continued)*

Symbol	Description
	A meeting request
	A meeting request that has been tentatively accepted
	A meeting request that has been accepted
	A meeting request that has been rejected
	A meeting that has been canceled
	A message with a digital signature
	A requested task
	A task that is accepted
	A task that is declined

Outlook Contacts Symbols

Symbols found in Outlook Contacts appear in Table F-2.

Table F-2. Outlook Contacts symbols

Symbol	Description
	An individual contact
	A distribution list
	A contact with an attachment
	A contact flagged for a follow-up
	A contact with follow-up completed
	A contact whose activities have been recorded in Outlook Journal

Outlook Calendar Symbols

Symbols found in Outlook Calendar appear in Table F-3.

Table F-3. Outlook Calendar symbols

Symbol	Description
	A nonrecurring appointment
	A recurring appointment
	A nonrecurring meeting
	A recurring meeting
	An item with a file attachment
	A meeting or appointment item with an alarm set
	A recurring meeting or appointment
	A meeting request
	A private meeting or appointment
	The start time of a meeting or appointment
	The end time of a meeting or appointment

Outlook Tasks Symbols

Symbols found in Outlook Tasks appear in Table F-4.

Table F-4. Outlook Tasks symbols

Symbol	Description
	A task
	A recurring task
	A task with a file attachment
	An uncompleted task
	A completed task
	A task with high importance

(continued)

Table F-4. (continued)

Symbol	Description
↓	A task with low importance
	A task assigned to you
	A task assigned to another person
	An accepted task
	A rejected task

Outlook Journal Symbols

Symbols found in Outlook Journal appear in Table F-5.

Table F-5. Outlook Journal symbols

Symbol	Description
	A conversation
	A document
	A fax
	A letter
	A meeting
	A meeting cancellation
	A meeting request
	A meeting response
	A new call
	A note
	A remote session
	A task
	A task request
	A task response
	A Microsoft Word file

Appendix F: Outlook Symbols

Symbol	Description
	A Microsoft Excel file
	A Microsoft PowerPoint file
	A Microsoft Access file
	A Microsoft Project file
	An appointment
	Meeting or appointment requests and responses

Appendix G
Outlook Shortcuts

This appendix lists Outlook keyboard shortcuts you can use instead of using the mouse and menu or toolbar commands. Keyboard shortcuts are useful for those tasks you perform many times a day. They're quicker than using the mouse, and they allow you to keep your fingers on the keyboard at all times.

Working with Outlook

Use these shortcuts when you want to navigate Outlook or perform Outlook tasks using the keyboard.

Navigating Outlook

The following shortcuts are helpful for navigating Outlook.

Action	Keyboard Shortcut
Go to next item when an item is open	Ctrl+, (comma)
Go to previous item when an item is open	Ctrl+. (period)
Switch between Folder List and main Outlook window	F6 or Ctrl+Shift+Tab
Go to different folder	Ctrl+Y
Expand or collapse a group when a group is selected	+ (plus) or - (minus) on numeric keypad

Creating Items or Files

Use the following shortcuts when creating Outlook items or files.

Action	Keyboard Shortcut
Create appointment	Ctrl+Shift+A
Create contact	Ctrl+Shift+C
Create distribution list	Ctrl+Shift+L
Create folder	Ctrl+Shift+E
Create journal entry	Ctrl+Shift+J

(continued)

(continued)

Action	Keyboard Shortcut
Create meeting request	Ctrl+Shift+Q
Create new message	Ctrl+Shift+M
Create note	Ctrl+Shift+N
Create Office document	Ctrl+Shift+H
Create post in folder	Ctrl+Shift+S
Create task	Ctrl+Shift+K
Create task request	Ctrl+Shift+U
Show ScreenTip for active element	Shift+F1
Save file to default Outlook folder	Ctrl+S or Shift+F12
Send	Alt+S
Save as	F12
Undo last action	Ctrl+Z or Alt+Backspace
Delete	Ctrl+D
Print	Ctrl+P
Move item	Ctrl+Shift+V
Copy item	Ctrl+Shift+Y
Check names using Outlook or Word e-mail editor	Ctrl+K or Alt+K
Run spelling checker	F7
Flag item for follow-up	Ctrl+Shift+G
Forward message	Ctrl+F
Send, post, or invite all using Outlook e-mail editor	Ctrl+Enter
Find items	F3 or Ctrl+E
Search for text in specified items	F4
Find next occurrence of text during search	Shift+F4
Run Advanced Find	Ctrl+Shift+F
Activate editing in a field (does not work in icon view)	F2

Formatting Shortcuts

Use the following shortcuts when formatting.

Action	Keyboard Shortcut
Display Format menu	Alt+O
Format text as italics	Ctrl+I
Format text as bold	Ctrl+B
Format text with underline	Ctrl+U
Insert bullets	Ctrl+Shift+L
Switch case of selected text	Shift+F3
Increase indent	Ctrl+T
Decrease indent	Ctrl+Shift+T
Left-align text	Ctrl+L
Center-align text	Ctrl+E
Increase font size	Ctrl+] (right bracket)
Decrease font size	Ctrl+[(left bracket)
Cut selected text or image	Ctrl+X or Shift+Delete
Copy selected text or image	Ctrl+C or Ctrl+Insert
Paste item from clipboard	Ctrl+V or Shift+Insert
Undo all formatting	Ctrl+Shift+Z or Ctrl+Spacebar

Printing Shortcuts

The following shortcuts can be used when printing.

Action	Keyboard Shortcut
Open print preview	Ctrl+F2
Zoom during print preview	Alt+Z
Print preview page setup	Alt+S or Alt+U
Print print preview	Alt+P
Close print preview	Alt+C

E-Mailing

Use the following shortcuts in Outlook E-Mail.

Action	Keyboard Shortcut
Switch to Inbox	Ctrl+Shift+I
Check for new mail	Ctrl+M or F5
Switch to Outbox	Ctrl+Shift+O
Reply to message	Ctrl+R
Reply to all	Ctrl+Shift+R
Create new message	Ctrl+N
Display Address Book	Ctrl+Shift+B
Switch to Outbox folder	Ctrl+Shift+O
Mark message as read	Ctrl+Q

Using Calendar

The following shortcuts can be used in Outlook Calendar.

Action	Keyboard Shortcut
Accept task from TaskAssign message	Alt+C
Decline task from TaskAssign message	Alt+D
View from 1 to 9 days	Alt+ number of days
View 10 days	Alt+0 (zero)
Switch to weeks	Alt+- (hyphen)
Switch to months	Alt+= (equal sign)
Switch between Calendar, TaskPad, and Folder List	Ctrl+Tab or F6
Select previous appointment	Shift+Tab
Go to previous day	Left Arrow key
Go to next day	Right Arrow key
Go to same day in following week	Alt+Down Arrow key
Go to same day in previous week	Alt+Up Arrow key

Appendix G: Outlook Shortcuts

Action	Keyboard Shortcut
In Day view, select time that begins work day	Home
In Day view, select time that ends work day	End
In Day view, select previous block of time	Up Arrow key
In Day view, select next block of time	Down Arrow key
In Day view, select block of time at top of screen	Page Up
In Day view, select block of time at bottom of screen	Page Down
In Day view, extend or reduce selected time	Shift+Up Arrow key or Down Arrow key
In Day view, move appointment when cursor is in the appointment	Alt+Up Arrow key or Down Arrow key
In Day view, change appointment start or end time when cursor is in the appointment	Alt+Shift+Up Arrow key or Down Arrow key
In Week or Month views, go to first day of week	Home
In Week or Month views, go to last day of week	End
In Week view, go to same day of week in previous week	Page Up
In Month view, go to same day 5 weeks previous	Page Up
In Week view, go to same day of week in following week	Page Down
In Month view, go to same day 5 weeks in the future	Page Down
In Week or Month views, move appointment up	Alt+Up Arrow key
In Week or Month views, move appointment down	Alt+Down Arrow key
Modify length of time in selected block	Shift+Left, Right, Up, or Down Arrow key; or Shift+Home or End
In Date Navigator, go to first day of current week	Alt+Home

(continued)

(continued)

Action	Keyboard Shortcut
In Date Navigator, go to last day of current week	Alt+End
In Date Navigator, go to same day in previous week	Alt+Up Arrow key
In Date Navigator, go to same day in next week	Alt+Down Arrow key
In Date Navigator, go to first day of month	Alt+Page Up
In Date Navigator, go to last day of month	Alt+Page Down

Using Contacts

The following shortcuts can be used in Outlook Contacts.

Action	Keyboard Shortcut
Dial selected contact	Ctrl+Shift+D
Enter name in Find A Contact box	F11
Select specific card	Type one or more letters of a contact's name until that contact is selected (Outlook searches on the beginning of the first or last name depending on which comes first on the Contact card)
Select first card in list	Home
Select next card	Down Arrow key
Select previous card	Up Arrow key
Select last card in list	End
Select first card on current page	Page Up
Select first card on following page	Page Down
Select closest card in next column	Right Arrow key
Select closest card in previous column	Left Arrow key
Select or cancel active card	Ctrl+Spacebar
Extend selection to previous card and cancel cards after starting point	Shift+Up Arrow key
Extend selection to next card and cancel cards before starting point	Shift+Down Arrow key

Appendix G: Outlook Shortcuts

Action	Keyboard Shortcut
Extend selection to next card	Ctrl+Shift+Down Arrow key
Extend selection to previous card	Ctrl+Shift+Up Arrow key
Extend selection to last card in list	Shift+End
Extend selection to first card in list	Shift+Home
Extend selection to first card on previous page	Shift+Page Up
Extend selection to last card on last page	Shift+Page Down
When a card is selected, move to next card	Ctrl+Down Arrow key
When a card is selected, move to previous card	Ctrl+Up Arrow key
When a card is selected, move to first card in list	Ctrl+Home
When a card is selected, move to last card in list	Ctrl+End
When a card is selected, move to first card on previous page	Ctrl+Page Up
When a card is selected, move to first card on next page	Ctrl+Page Down
When a card is selected, move to closest card in previous column	Ctrl+Left Arrow key
When a card is selected, move to closest card in next column	Ctrl+Right Arrow key
When a card is selected, move to a field in active card	F2
When a card is selected, move to next field	Tab
When a card is selected, move from last field of a card to first field in next card	Tab
When a card is selected, move to previous field	Shift+Tab
When a card is selected, move from first field of a card to last field in previous card	Shift+Tab
When a card is selected, move to next field	Enter
When a card is selected, add a line to a multiline field	Enter

(continued)

(continued)

Action	Keyboard Shortcut
When a card is selected, move to previous field without leaving active card	Shift+Enter
When a card is selected, display insertion point in active field	F2
When a field in a card is selected, add a line in a multiline field	Enter
When a field in a card is selected, move to beginning of a line	Home
When a field in a card is selected, move to end of a line	End
When a field in a card is selected, move to beginning of a multiline field	Page Up
When a field in a card is selected, move to end of a multiline field	Page Down
When a field in a card is selected, move to previous line in a multiline field	Up Arrow key
When a field in a card is selected, move to next line in a multiline field	Down Arrow key
When a field in a card is selected, move to previous character in a field	Left Arrow key
When a field in a card is selected, move to next character in a field	Right Arrow key

Using Tasks

The following shortcuts can be used in Outlook Tasks.

Action	Keyboard Shortcut
Accept a task	Alt+C
Decline a task	Alt+D

Using Journal and Tasks

Use the following shortcuts in Outlook Journal and Outlook Tasks.

Action	Keyboard Shortcut
Select previous item	Left Arrow key (for Journal), Up Arrow key (for Tasks)
Select next item	Right Arrow key (for Journal), Down Arrow key (for Tasks)
Select several adjacent items	Shift+Left Arrow key or Shift+Right Arrow key
Select several nonadjacent items	Ctrl+Left Arrow key+Spacebar or Ctrl+Right Arrow key+Spacebar
Open selected items	Enter
Display items one screen above on-screen items	Page Up
Display items one screen below on-screen items	Page Down
Select first ungrouped item on timeline or first item in group	Home
Select last ungrouped item on timeline or last item in group	End
Display first ungrouped item on timeline or first item in group	Ctrl+Home
Display last ungrouped item on timeline or last item in group	Ctrl+End
Expand selected group	Enter or Right Arrow key
Collapse selected group	Enter or Left Arrow key
Select first group on timeline	Home
Select previous group	Up Arrow key
Select next group	Down Arrow key
Select last group on timeline	End

(continued)

1135

(continued)

Action	Keyboard Shortcut
Select first on-screen item in expanded group or first offscreen item to right	Right Arrow key
Move back in increments of time same as increments shown on time scale	Left Arrow key
Move forward in increments of time same as increments shown on time scale	Right Arrow key
Select upper time scale when lower time scale is selected	Shift+Tab
Select lower time scale when upper time scale is selected	Tab
Select first on-screen item or on-screen group when lower time scale is selected	Tab

Adding Web Information

Use the following shortcuts when you want to add Web information to items.

Action	Keyboard Shortcut
Edit URL in body of item	Ctrl+left mouse button
Specify Web browser	Shift+left mouse button
Insert hyperlink when Word is e-mail editor	Ctrl+K

Working with Help

Use these keyboard shortcuts when you want to work with Outlook Help, the Microsoft Office Assistant, and the Ask a Question box.

Action	Keyboard Shortcut
Turn on Office Assistant	Press Alt+H+O
Display Assistant balloon	F1
Close message or tip in Assistant	Esc
Select item in Assistant balloon list	Alt+number
Display additional Help topics in Assistant balloon list	Alt+Down Arrow key

Appendix G: Outlook Shortcuts

Action	Keyboard Shortcut
Display previous Help topics in Assistant balloon list	Alt+Up Arrow key
Move to Help button in some wizards	Tab
Show Assistant in some wizards or dialog boxes	Spacebar
Use Help window and turn off Assistant	F1, Alt+O, Alt+U, Enter; F1 to display Help window
If Assistant is off, open Help window	F1
If Assistant is off, switch between Help topic and Contents, Answer Wizard, Index pane	F6
If Assistant is off, select Show All or Hide All at top of topic	Tab
If Assistant is off, select previous hidden text, hyperlink, Show All, or Hide All	Shift+Tab
If Assistant is off, perform action of selected Show All, Hide All, hidden text, or hyperlink	Enter
If Assistant is off, open Options menu	Alt+O
Hide Show Contents, Answer Wizard, and Index tabs	Alt+O, T
Display previously viewed topic	Alt+O, B
Display next previously viewed topic	Alt+O, F
Return to specified home page	Alt+O, H
Stop from opening a Help topic	Alt+O, S
Open Internet Explorer Options dialog box	Alt+O, I
Refresh a topic	Alt+O, R
Print all book topics or a selected topic	Alt+O, P
Close Help window	Alt+F4
Switch to next Help tab	Ctrl+Tab
Switch to Contents tab	Alt+C
Switch to Answer Wizard tab	Alt+A
Switch to Index tab	Alt+I

(continued)

(continued)

Action	Keyboard Shortcut
Open selected book or Help topic	Enter
Display next book or Help topic	Down Arrow key
Select previous book or Help topic	Up Arrow key
Display shortcut menu	Shift+F10
Go to next Help topic	Alt+Right Arrow key
Go to previous Help topic	Alt+Left Arrow key
Select previous hidden text or hyperlink	Shift+Tab
Scroll toward beginning or end of Help topic	Up Arrow key or Down Arrow key
Scroll toward beginning or end of Help topic in large increments	Page Up or Page Down
Go to beginning or end of Help topic	Home or End
Print current Help topic	Ctrl+P
Select entire Help topic	Ctrl+A
Copy selected items to clipboard (selected items must be in right pane)	Ctrl+C
Use Ask A Question box	F10 or Alt, and then Tab to question box
Move cursor to bottom of screen	Page Down
Go to item at top of screen	Page Up
Extend or reduce selected items	Shift+Up Arrow key or Shift+Down Arrow key
Go to next or previous item, but do not extend selection	Ctrl+Up Arrow key or Ctrl+Down Arrow key
Select or cancel active item	Ctrl+Spacebar
Move every item in selection to top in list order (in-cell editing must be turned off)	Ctrl+Home
Move every item in selection to bottom in list order (in-cell editing must be turned off)	Ctrl+End
Expand a group	Enter or Right Arrow key
Collapse a group	Enter or Left Arrow key

Appendix G: Outlook Shortcuts

Action	Keyboard Shortcut
Select previous group	Up Arrow key
Select next group	Down Arrow key
Select first group	Home
Select last group (or move to first group and then last group if display set to Categories)	End
Select first item on-screen in an expanded group or first item offscreen to right (in Contacts, if display set to Categories, press Down Arrow key to select first record of expanded group)	Right Arrow key

Appendix H
Outlook Fields and Properties

The following table lists the fields and the associated field properties available in
Microsoft Outlook 2002.

Field Name in Outlook Field Chooser	Equivalent Outlook Object Model Property	DataType	Write
% Complete	PercentComplete	Number	N
Account	Account	Text	Y
Actual Work	ActualWork	Duration	Y
Address Selected	N/A	Reserved	N
Address Selector	N/A	Reserved	N
All Day Event	AllDayEvent	Yes/No	Y
Anniversary	Anniversary	Date/Time	Y
Assigned	DelegationState	Number	N
Assistant's Name	AssistantName	Text	Y
Assistant's Phone	AssistantTelephoneNumber	Text	Y
Attachment	Attachments	Yes/No	N
Bcc	BCC	Text	Y
Billing Information	BillingInformation	Text	Y
Birthday	Birthday	Date/Time	Y
Business Address	BusinessAddress	Text	N
Business Address City	BusinessAddressCity	Text	Y
Business Address Country	BusinessAddressCountry	Text	Y
Business Address PO Box	BusinessAddressPostOfficeBox	Text	Y
Business Address Postal Code	BusinessAddressPostalCode	Text	Y
Business Address State	BusinessAddressState	Text	Y
Business Address Street	BusinessAddressStreet	Text	Y
Business Fax	BusinessFaxNumber	Text	Y
Business Home Page	BusinessHomePage	Text	Y

(continued)

Appendix H

(continued)

Field Name in Outlook Field Chooser	Equivalent Outlook Object Model Property	DataType	Write
Business Phone	BusinessTelephoneNumber	Text	Y
Business Phone 2	Business2TelephoneNumber	Text	Y
Callback	CallbackTelephoneNumber	Text	Y
Car Phone	CarTelephoneNumber	Text	Y
Categories	Categories	Text	Y
Cc	CC	Text	Y
Changed By	N/A	Text	N
Children	Children	Text	Y
City	HomeAddressCity	Text	Y
Color	Color	Number	Y
Comments	Comments	Text	N
Company	Companies	Text	Y
Company Main Phone	CompanyMainTelephoneNumber	Text	Y
Company Name	CompanyName	Text	Y
Complete	Complete	Yes/No	Y
Computer Network Name	ComputerNetworkName	Text	Y
Contact	FormDescription.ContactName	Text	Y
Contacts	Links	Text	Y
Content	Body	Text	Y
Conversation	ConversationTopic	Text	N
Country	HomeAddressCountry	Text	Y
Created	CreationTime	Date/Time	N
Customer ID	CustomerID	Text	Y
Date Completed	DateCompleted	Date/Time	Y
Defer Until	DeferredDeliveryTime	Date/Time	Y
Department	Department	Text	Y
Distribution List Name	DLName	Text	N
Do Not AutoArchive	NoAging	Yes/No	N

Appendix H: Outlook Fields and Properties

Field Name in Outlook Field Chooser	Equivalent Outlook Object Model Property	DataType	Write
Download State	N/A	Text	N
Due By	FlagDueBy	Date/Time	Y
Due Date	DueDate	Date/Time	Y
Duration	Duration	Text	N
E-Mail	Email1Address	Text	Y
E-Mail 2	Email2Address	Text	Y
E-Mail 3	Email3Address	Text	Y
E-Mail Selected	N/A	Text	Y
E-Mail Selector	N/A	Text	Y
End	End	Date/Time	Y
Entry Type	Type	Text	N
Expires	ExpiryTime	Date/Time	Y
File As	FileAs	Text	N
First Name	FirstName	Text	Y
Flag Status	FlagStatus	Number	N
Follow-Up Flag	FlagRequest	Yes/No	N
From	SentOnBehalfOfName	Text	N
FTP Site	FTPSite	Text	Y
Full Name	FullName	Text	Y
Gender	Gender	Text	Y
Government ID Number	GovernmentIDNumber	Text	Y
Have Replies Sent To	ReplyRecipientNames	Text	N
Hobbies	Hobby	Text	Y
Home Address	HomeAddress	Text	N
Home Address City	HomeAddressCity	Text	Y
Home Address Country	HomeAddressCountry	Text	Y
Home Address PO Box	HomeAddressPostOfficeBox	Text	Y

(continued)

Appendix H

(continued)

Field Name in Outlook Field Chooser	Equivalent Outlook Object Model Property	DataType	Write
Home Address Postal Code	HomeAddressPostalCode	Text	Y
Home Address State	HomeAddressState	Text	Y
Home Address Street	HomeAddressStreet	Text	Y
Home Fax	HomeFaxNumber	Text	Y
Home Phone	HomeTelephoneNumber	Text	Y
Home Phone 2	Home2TelephoneNumber	Text	Y
Icon	FormDescription.Icon	Object	N
Importance	Importance	Number	Y
In Folder	Parent	Text	N
Initials	Initials	Text	Y
Internet Free Busy Address	InternetFreeBusyAddress	Text	Y
ISDN	ISDNNumber	Text	Y
Job Title	JobTitle	Text	Y
Journal	Journal	Yes/No	Y
Junk E-Mail Type	N/A	Text	N
Language	Language	Text	Y
Last Name	LastName	Text	Y
Last Saved Time	N/A	Date/Time	N
Location	Location	Text	Y
Mailing Address	MailingAddress	Text	N
Mailing Address Indicator	N/A	Text	N
Manager's Name	ManagerName	Text	Y
Meeting Status	MeetingStatus	Number	N
Message	Body	Text	Y
Message Class	MessageClass	Text	N
Message Flag	FlagStatus	Text	Y
Middle Name	MiddleName	Text	Y
Mileage	Mileage	Text	Y

Field Name in Outlook Field Chooser	Equivalent Outlook Object Model Property	DataType	Write
Mobile Phone	MobileTelephoneNumber	Text	Y
Modified	LastModificationTime	Date/Time	N
Nickname	NickName	Text	Y
Notes	Body	Text	Y
Office Location	OfficeLocation	Text	Y
Optional Attendees	OptionalAttendees	Text	Y
Organizational ID Number	OrganizationalIDNumber	Text	Y
Organizer	Organizer	Text	Y
Other Address	OtherAddress	Text	N
Other Address City	OtherAddressCity	Text	Y
Other Address Country	OtherAddressCountry	Text	Y
Other Address PO Box	OtherAddressPostOfficeBox	Text	Y
Other Address Postal Code	OtherAddressPostalCode	Text	Y
Other Address State	OtherAddressState	Text	Y
Other Address Street	OtherAddressStreet	Text	Y
Other Fax	OtherFaxNumber	Text	Y
Other Phone	OtherTelephoneNumber	Text	Y
Outlook Internal Version	OutlookInternalVersion	Text	N
Outlook Version	OutlookVersion	Text	N
Owner	Owner	Text	N
Pager	PagerNumber	Text	Y
Personal Home Page	PersonalHomePage	Text	Y
Phone *n* Selected	N/A	Text	Y
Phone *n* Selector	N/A	Text	Y
PO Box	HomeAddressPostOfficeBox	Text	Y
Primary Phone	PrimaryTelephoneNumber	Text	Y
Priority	Importance	Number	N

(continued)

(continued)

Field Name in Outlook Field Chooser	Equivalent Outlook Object Model Property	DataType	Write
Private	Sensitivity	Number	N
Profession	Profession	Text	Y
Radio Phone	RadioTelephoneNumber	Text	Y
Read	UnRead	Yes/No	N
Received	ReceivedTime	Date/Time	N
Recurrence	RecurrencePattern.RecurrenceType	Number	N
Recurrence Pattern	N/A	Text	N
Recurrence Range End	RecurrencePattern.PatternEndDate	Date/Time	N
Recurrence Range Start	RecurrencePattern.PatternStartDate	Date/Time	N
Recurring	IsRecurring	Yes/No	N
Referred By	ReferredBy	Text	Y
Remind Beforehand	ReminderMinutesBeforeStart	Number	Y
Reminder	ReminderSet	Yes/No	N
Reminder Override Default	ReminderOverrideDefault	Yes/No	N
Reminder Sound	ReminderPlaySound	Yes/No	N
Reminder Time	ReminderTime	Date/Time	N
Reminder Topic	N/A	Text	N
Remote Status	RemoteStatus	Number	N
Request Status	N/A	Number	N
Requested By	N/A	Text	Y
Required Attendees	RequiredAttendees	Text	Y
Resources	Resources	Text	N
Response Requested	ResponseRequested	Yes/No	N
Retrieval Time	N/A	Number	N
Role	Role	Text	Y
Schedule+ Priority	SchedulePlusPriority	Text	N
Send Plain Text Only	N/A	Yes/No	N
Sensitivity	Sensitivity	Number	N

Appendix H: Outlook Fields and Properties

Field Name in Outlook Field Chooser	Equivalent Outlook Object Model Property	DataType	Write
Sent	SentOn	Date/Time	N
Show Time As	BusyStatus	Number	N
Size	Size	Number	N
Spouse	Spouse	Text	Y
Start	Start	Date/Time	Y
Start Date	StartDate	Date/Time	Y
State	HomeAddressState	Text	Y
Status	Status	Number	N
Street Address	HomeAddressStreet	Text	Y
Subject	Subject	Text	Y
Suffix	Suffix	Text	Y
Team Task	TeamTask	Yes/No	N
Telex	TelexNumber	Text	Y
Title	Title	Text	Y
To	To	Text	Y
Total Work	TotalWork	Number	Y
Tracking Status	TrackingStatus	Number	N
TTY/TDD Phone	TTYTDDTelephoneNumber	Text	Y
User Field 1	User1	Text	Y
User Field 2	User2	Text	Y
User Field 3	User3	Text	Y
User Field 4	User4	Text	Y
Web Page	WebPage	Text	Y
ZIP/Postal Code	HomeAddressPostalCode	Text	Y

Index to Troubleshooting Topics

Index

Note: Italicized page references indicate figures, tables, or code listings.

About the Author

Jim Boyce has been an engineering technician, a production planner, and a systems administrator for a UNIX-based CAD system. He spent seven years as a senior instructor for Texas State Technical College, where he taught electromechanical design, basic drafting, CAD, and programming. During that time, Jim began writing for CAD publications such as *Cadence Magazine* and *CADalyst Magazine*. He has also written for *PC Magazine* and *InfoWorld* on a variety of topics.

Jim has authored or coauthored more than 45 books on computer-related topics. He specializes in operating systems and business productivity applications and has written extensively about Office, Windows 9*x*, Windows NT, and Windows 2000. He is a former contributing editor of *Windows Magazine* and frequent contributor to several publications and Web sites, including techrepublic.com. Jim currently writes the Windows 2000 Professional TechMail Tips for techrepublic.com and frequently writes features for the site.

Jim was a founding partner of Prairie Communications, Inc., an ISP and computer services and development firm that now specializes in Web development under the name Minnesota WebWorks (*http://www.mnww.com*). Today Jim is vice president of WebWorks.

A native of Texas, Jim now lives in Minnesota with his wife, Julie. They are the biological parents of one daughter and over the last three years have adopted five siblings from Russia—four boys and a girl—now ages 4 through 12. They are also the proud grandparents of a wonderful grandson. Jim is a licensed private pilot and certified golf addict.

The manuscript for this book was prepared and galleyed using Microsoft Word 2000. Pages were composed by Microsoft Press using Adobe PageMaker 6.52 for Windows, with text in Minion and display type in Syntax. Composed pages were delivered to the printer as electronic prepress files.

coverdesigner
GIRVIN/Strategic Branding & Design

coverillustration
Daman Studio

interiorgraphicdesigner and interiorartist
James D. Kramer

principalcompositor
Barbara Levy

principalcopyeditor
Patricia Masserman

indexer
Shane-Armstrong Information Systems

for ProImage

projectmanager
Jimmie Young

leadcopyeditor
Mary Renaud

copyeditors
Susan Pink and Nancy Albright

technicaleditors
Michelle Roudebush and Allen L. Wyatt

Work smarter
as you experience
Office XP
inside out!

You know your way around the Office suite. Now dig into Microsoft Office XP applications and *really* put your PC to work! These supremely organized references pack hundreds of timesaving solutions, trouble-shooting tips and tricks, and handy workarounds in concise, fast-answer format. All of this comprehensive information goes deep into the nooks and crannies of each Office application and accessory. Discover the best and fastest ways to perform everyday tasks, and challenge yourself to new levels of Office mastery with INSIDE OUT titles!

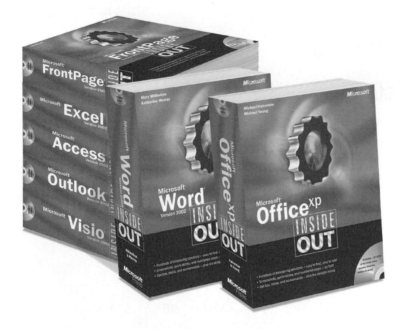

- **MICROSOFT® OFFICE XP INSIDE OUT**
- **MICROSOFT WORD VERSION 2002 INSIDE OUT**
- **MICROSOFT EXCEL VERSION 2002 INSIDE OUT**
- **MICROSOFT OUTLOOK® VERSION 2002 INSIDE OUT**
- **MICROSOFT ACCESS VERSION 2002 INSIDE OUT**
- **MICROSOFT FRONTPAGE® VERSION 2002 INSIDE OUT**
- **MICROSOFT VISIO® VERSION 2002 INSIDE OUT**

Get a **Free**
e-mail newsletter, updates,
special offers, links to related books,
and more when you

register on line!

Register your Microsoft Press® title on our Web site and you'll get
a FREE subscription to our e-mail newsletter, *Microsoft Press
Book Connections.* You'll find out about newly released and upcoming
books and learning tools, online events, software downloads, special
offers and coupons for Microsoft Press customers, and information
about major Microsoft® product releases. You can also read useful
additional information about all the titles we publish, such as detailed book descriptions, tables of contents and indexes, sample
chapters, links to related books and book series, author biographies,
and reviews by other customers.

Registration is easy. Just visit this Web page and fill in your information:

http://mspress.microsoft.com/register

Microsoft®

Proof of Purchase

Use this page as proof of purchase if participating in a promotion or rebate offer on
this title. Proof of purchase must be used in conjunction with other proof(s) of
payment such as your dated sales receipt—see offer details.

Microsoft® Outlook® Version 2002 Inside Out
0-7356-1282-X

CUSTOMER NAME

Microsoft Press, PO Box 97017, Redmond, WA 98073-9830

MICROSOFT LICENSE AGREEMENT

Book Companion CD

IMPORTANT—READ CAREFULLY: This Microsoft End-User License Agreement ("EULA") is a legal agreement between you (either an individual or an entity) and Microsoft Corporation for the Microsoft product identified above, which includes computer software and may include associated media, printed materials, and "online" or electronic documentation ("SOFTWARE PRODUCT"). Any component included within the SOFTWARE PRODUCT that is accompanied by a separate End-User License Agreement shall be governed by such agreement and not the terms set forth below. By installing, copying, or otherwise using the SOFTWARE PRODUCT, you agree to be bound by the terms of this EULA. If you do not agree to the terms of this EULA, you are not authorized to install, copy, or otherwise use the SOFTWARE PRODUCT; you may, however, return the SOFTWARE PRODUCT, along with all printed materials and other items that form a part of the Microsoft product that includes the SOFTWARE PRODUCT, to the place you obtained them for a full refund.

SOFTWARE PRODUCT LICENSE

The SOFTWARE PRODUCT is protected by United States copyright laws and international copyright treaties, as well as other intellectual property laws and treaties. The SOFTWARE PRODUCT is licensed, not sold.

1. **GRANT OF LICENSE.** This EULA grants you the following rights:

   a. **Software Product.** You may install and use one copy of the SOFTWARE PRODUCT on a single computer. The primary user of the computer on which the SOFTWARE PRODUCT is installed may make a second copy for his or her exclusive use on a portable computer.

   b. **Storage/Network Use.** You may also store or install a copy of the SOFTWARE PRODUCT on a storage device, such as a network server, used only to install or run the SOFTWARE PRODUCT on your other computers over an internal network; however, you must acquire and dedicate a license for each separate computer on which the SOFTWARE PRODUCT is installed or run from the storage device. A license for the SOFTWARE PRODUCT may not be shared or used concurrently on different computers.

   c. **License Pak.** If you have acquired this EULA in a Microsoft License Pak, you may make the number of additional copies of the computer software portion of the SOFTWARE PRODUCT authorized on the printed copy of this EULA, and you may use each copy in the manner specified above. You are also entitled to make a corresponding number of secondary copies for portable computer use as specified above.

   d. **Sample Code.** Solely with respect to portions, if any, of the SOFTWARE PRODUCT that are identified within the SOFTWARE PRODUCT as sample code (the "SAMPLE CODE"):

      i. **Use and Modification.** Microsoft grants you the right to use and modify the source code version of the SAMPLE CODE, *provided* you comply with subsection (d)(iii) below. You may not distribute the SAMPLE CODE, or any modified version of the SAMPLE CODE, in source code form.

      ii. **Redistributable Files.** Provided you comply with subsection (d)(iii) below, Microsoft grants you a nonexclusive, royalty-free right to reproduce and distribute the object code version of the SAMPLE CODE and of any modified SAMPLE CODE, other than SAMPLE CODE, or any modified version thereof, designated as not redistributable in the Readme file that forms a part of the SOFTWARE PRODUCT (the "Non-Redistributable Sample Code"). All SAMPLE CODE other than the Non-Redistributable Sample Code is collectively referred to as the "REDISTRIBUTABLES."

      iii. **Redistribution Requirements.** If you redistribute the REDISTRIBUTABLES, you agree to: (i) distribute the REDISTRIBUTABLES in object code form only in conjunction with and as a part of your software application product; (ii) not use Microsoft's name, logo, or trademarks to market your software application product; (iii) include a valid copyright notice on your software application product; (iv) indemnify, hold harmless, and defend Microsoft from and against any claims or lawsuits, including attorney's fees, that arise or result from the use or distribution of your software application product; and (v) not permit further distribution of the REDISTRIBUTABLES by your end user. Contact Microsoft for the applicable royalties due and other licensing terms for all other uses and/or distribution of the REDISTRIBUTABLES.

2. **DESCRIPTION OF OTHER RIGHTS AND LIMITATIONS.**

   - **Limitations on Reverse Engineering, Decompilation, and Disassembly.** You may not reverse engineer, decompile, or disassemble the SOFTWARE PRODUCT, except and only to the extent that such activity is expressly permitted by applicable law notwithstanding this limitation.

   - **Separation of Components.** The SOFTWARE PRODUCT is licensed as a single product. Its component parts may not be separated for use on more than one computer.

   - **Rental.** You may not rent, lease, or lend the SOFTWARE PRODUCT.

   - **Support Services.** Microsoft may, but is not obligated to, provide you with support services related to the SOFTWARE PRODUCT ("Support Services"). Use of Support Services is governed by the Microsoft policies and programs described in the user manual, in "online" documentation, and/or in other Microsoft-provided materials. Any supplemental software code provided to you as part of the Support Services shall be considered part of the SOFTWARE PRODUCT and subject to the terms and conditions of this EULA. With respect to technical information you provide to Microsoft as part of the Support Services, Microsoft may use such information for its business purposes, including for product support and development. Microsoft will not utilize such technical information in a form that personally identifies you.

- **EULA Rights Transfer.** You may permanently transfer all of your rights under this EULA, provided you retain no copies, you transfer all of the SOFTWARE PRODUCT (including all component parts, the media and printed materials, any upgrades, this EULA, and, if applicable, the Certificate of Authenticity), **and** the recipient agrees to the terms of this EULA.

- **Termination.** Without prejudice to any other rights, Microsoft may terminate this EULA if you fail to comply with the terms and conditions of this EULA. In such event, you must destroy all copies of the SOFTWARE PRODUCT and all of its component parts.

3. **COPYRIGHT.** All title and copyrights in and to the SOFTWARE PRODUCT (including but not limited to any images, photographs, animations, video, audio, music, text, SAMPLE CODE, REDISTRIBUTABLES, and "applets" incorporated into the SOFTWARE PRODUCT) and any copies of the SOFTWARE PRODUCT are owned by Microsoft or its suppliers. The SOFTWARE PRODUCT is protected by copyright laws and international treaty provisions. Therefore, you must treat the SOFTWARE PRODUCT like any other copyrighted material **except** that you may install the SOFTWARE PRODUCT on a single computer provided you keep the original solely for backup or archival purposes. You may not copy the printed materials accompanying the SOFTWARE PRODUCT.

4. **U.S. GOVERNMENT RESTRICTED RIGHTS.** The SOFTWARE PRODUCT and documentation are provided with RESTRICTED RIGHTS. Use, duplication, or disclosure by the Government is subject to restrictions as set forth in subparagraph (c)(1)(ii) of the Rights in Technical Data and Computer Software clause at DFARS 252.227-7013 or subparagraphs (c)(1) and (2) of the Commercial Computer Software—Restricted Rights at 48 CFR 52.227-19, as applicable. Manufacturer is Microsoft Corporation/One Microsoft Way/Redmond, WA 98052-6399.

5. **EXPORT RESTRICTIONS.** You agree that you will not export or re-export the SOFTWARE PRODUCT, any part thereof, or any process or service that is the direct product of the SOFTWARE PRODUCT (the foregoing collectively referred to as the "Restricted Components"), to any country, person, entity, or end user subject to U.S. export restrictions. You specifically agree not to export or re-export any of the Restricted Components (i) to any country to which the U.S. has embargoed or restricted the export of goods or services, which currently include, but are not necessarily limited to, Cuba, Iran, Iraq, Libya, North Korea, Sudan, and Syria, or to any national of any such country, wherever located, who intends to transmit or transport the Restricted Components back to such country; (ii) to any end user who you know or have reason to know will utilize the Restricted Components in the design, development, or production of nuclear, chemical, or biological weapons; or (iii) to any end user who has been prohibited from participating in U.S. export transactions by any federal agency of the U.S. government. You warrant and represent that neither the BXA nor any other U.S. federal agency has suspended, revoked, or denied your export privileges.

DISCLAIMER OF WARRANTY

NO WARRANTIES OR CONDITIONS. MICROSOFT EXPRESSLY DISCLAIMS ANY WARRANTY OR CONDITION FOR THE SOFTWARE PRODUCT. THE SOFTWARE PRODUCT AND ANY RELATED DOCUMENTATION ARE PROVIDED "AS IS" WITHOUT WARRANTY OR CONDITION OF ANY KIND, EITHER EXPRESS OR IMPLIED, INCLUDING, WITHOUT LIMITATION, THE IMPLIED WARRANTIES OF MERCHANTABILITY, FITNESS FOR A PARTICULAR PURPOSE, OR NONINFRINGEMENT. THE ENTIRE RISK ARISING OUT OF USE OR PERFORMANCE OF THE SOFTWARE PRODUCT REMAINS WITH YOU.

LIMITATION OF LIABILITY. TO THE MAXIMUM EXTENT PERMITTED BY APPLICABLE LAW, IN NO EVENT SHALL MICROSOFT OR ITS SUPPLIERS BE LIABLE FOR ANY SPECIAL, INCIDENTAL, INDIRECT, OR CONSEQUENTIAL DAMAGES WHATSOEVER (INCLUDING, WITHOUT LIMITATION, DAMAGES FOR LOSS OF BUSINESS PROFITS, BUSINESS INTERRUPTION, LOSS OF BUSINESS INFORMATION, OR ANY OTHER PECUNIARY LOSS) ARISING OUT OF THE USE OF OR INABILITY TO USE THE SOFTWARE PRODUCT OR THE PROVISION OF OR FAILURE TO PROVIDE SUPPORT SERVICES, EVEN IF MICROSOFT HAS BEEN ADVISED OF THE POSSIBILITY OF SUCH DAMAGES. IN ANY CASE, MICROSOFT'S ENTIRE LIABILITY UNDER ANY PROVISION OF THIS EULA SHALL BE LIMITED TO THE GREATER OF THE AMOUNT ACTUALLY PAID BY YOU FOR THE SOFTWARE PRODUCT OR US$5.00; PROVIDED, HOWEVER, IF YOU HAVE ENTERED INTO A MICROSOFT SUPPORT SERVICES AGREEMENT, MICROSOFT'S ENTIRE LIABILITY REGARDING SUPPORT SERVICES SHALL BE GOVERNED BY THE TERMS OF THAT AGREEMENT. BECAUSE SOME STATES AND JURISDICTIONS DO NOT ALLOW THE EXCLUSION OR LIMITATION OF LIABILITY, THE ABOVE LIMITATION MAY NOT APPLY TO YOU.

MISCELLANEOUS

This EULA is governed by the laws of the State of Washington USA, except and only to the extent that applicable law mandates governing law of a different jurisdiction.

Should you have any questions concerning this EULA, or if you desire to contact Microsoft for any reason, please contact the Microsoft subsidiary serving your country, or write: Microsoft Sales Information Center/One Microsoft Way/Redmond, WA 98052-6399.